THE FORMS OF THE OLD TESTAMENT LITERATURE

Editors

ROLF P. KNIERIM • GENE M. TUCKER • MARVIN A. SWEENEY

*Published

D1117835

HOSEA

EHUD BEN ZVI

The Forms of the Old Testament Literature

VOLUME XXIA/1

WILLIAM B. EERDMANS PUBLISHING COMPANY
GRAND RAPIDS, MICHIGAN / CAMBRIDGE, U.K.

© 2005 Wm. B. Eerdmans Publishing Co.

Wm. B. Eerdmans Publishing Co.
255 Jefferson Ave. S.E., Grand Rapids, Michigan 49503 /
P.O. Box 163, Cambridge CB3 9PU U.K.

Printed in the United States of America

10 09 08 07 06 05   7 6 5 4 3 2 1

Library of Congress Cataloging-in-Publication Data

Ben Zvi, Ehud, 1951-
Hosea / Ehud Ben Zvi.
p.   cm.   — (Forms of the Old Testament Literature; v. 21A/1)
Includes bibliographical references.
ISBN-10: 0-8028-0795-X (pbk.: alk. paper)
ISBN-13: 978-0-8028-0795-3
1. Bible. O.T. Hosea — Commentaries. 2. Bible. O.T. Hosea — Criticism, Form.
I. Title. II. Series.

BS1565.53.B46   2005
224′.607 — dc22
2005052107

www.eerdmans.com

CONTENTS

Abbreviations and Symbols

I. Miscellaneous Abbreviations and Symbols

b.	Babylonian Talmud
BCE	before the Common Era
ca.	*circa* (about)
cf.	compare
ch(s).	chapters
ct.	contrast
diss.	dissertation
dtr.	Deuteronomistic
ed.	editor(s); edited by; edition
e.g.	for example
ET	English translation
et al.	*et alii* (and others)
fem.	feminine
FS	*Festschrift*
HB	Hebrew Bible
Heb.	Hebrew
IH	Israelian Hebrew
Intro.	Introduction
K	Ketib
lit.	literally
LXX	Septuagint
m.	Mishnah
Mak.	*Makkot* (talmudic tractate)
masc.	Masculine
MT	Masoretic Text
Mur	Murabbaʿat Text
n.	note
NF	new series
OT	Old Testament

Pesh.	Peshitta
pl.	plural
Q	Qere
repr.	reprint(ed)
rev. ed.	revised edition
sg.	singular
Sukk.	*Sukkot* (talmudic tractate)
Tg.	Targum
tr.	translator(s); translated by
v(v).	verse(s)
vol.	volume
Vg.	Vulgate
→	cross reference to another section of the commentary
//	parallel
(§)§	section(s)

II. Publications

AB	Anchor Bible
ACEBTSup	Amsterdamse cahiers voor exegese en bijbelse theologie — Supplement
AOAT	Alter Orient und Altes Testament
ATD	Alte Testament Deutsch
ATSAT	Arbeiten zu Text und Sprache im Alten Testament
AusBR	*Australian Biblical Review*
BASOR	Bulletin of the American Schools of Oriental Research
BEATJ	Beiträge zur Erforschung des Alten Testament und des antiken Judentum
BeO	*Bibbia e oriente*
BHS	*Biblia Hebraica Stuttgartensia*
Bib	*Biblica*
BibInt	*Biblical Interpretation*
BibOr	Biblica et orientalia
BJRL	*Bulletin of the John Rylands Library*
BN	*Biblische Notizen*
BR	*Biblical Research*
BVB	Brem- und Verdische Bibliothek
BWANT	Beiträge zur Wissenschaft vom Alten and Neuen Testament
ByF	*Byzantinische Forschungen*
BZ	*Biblische Zeitschrift*
BZAW	Beihefte zur Zeitscrift für die alttestamentliche Wissenschaft
CAD	*Assyrian Dictionary of the Oriental Institute of the University of Chicago*
CANE	*Civilizations of the Ancient Near East,* ed. Jack M. Sasson et al. (New York: Scribner, 1995)

CB	Coniectanea biblica
CBQ	*Catholic Biblical Quarterly*
CBET	Contributions to Biblical Exegesis and Theology
DJD	Discoveries of the Judean Desert
DMOA	Documenta et monumenta orientis antiqui
Enc. Judaica	*Encyclopaedica Judaica*
EstBib	*Estudios bíblicos*
ETL	*Ephemerides theologicae lovanienses*
FOTL	Forms of the Old Testmant Literature
GKC	*Gesenius' Hebrew Grammar,* ed. Kautsch, trans. Cowley
HAR	*Hebrew Annual Review*
HBT	*Horizons in Biblical Theology*
HTR	*Harvard Theological Review*
HUCA	*Hebrew Union College Annual*
ICC	International Critical Commentary
Int	*Interpretation*
JAB	*Journal for the Aramaic Bible*
JANES	*Journal of the Ancient Near Eastern Society*
JBL	*Journal of Biblical Literature*
JCS	*Journal of Cuneiform Studies*
JFSR	*Journal of Feminist Studies in Religion*
JM	P. Joüon and T. Muraoka, *A Grammar of Biblical Hebrew* (Subsidia biblica 14/I-II; Rome: Pontifical Biblical Institute, 1991)
JNES	*Journal of Near Eastern Studies*
JNSL	*Journal of Northwest Semitic Languages*
JPS	Jewish Publication Society
JQR	*Jewish Quarterly Review*
JSJ	*Journal for the Study of Judaism*
JSOT	*Journal for the Study of the Old Testament*
JSOTSupS	Journal for the Study of the Old Testament Supplement Series
JSPSupS	Journal for the Study of the Pseudepigraphy Supplement Series
JSS	*Journal of Semitic Studies*
JTS	*Journal of Theological Studies*
KAT	Kommentar zum Alten Testament
KJV	King James (Authorized) Version
LHBOTS	Library of Hebrew Bible/Old Testament Supplement
MAL	Middle Assyrian Laws
NAB	New American Bible
NAC	New American Commentary
NASB	New American Standard Bible
NCB	New Century Bible
NEB	New English Bible
NIBC	New International Biblical Commentary
NIV	New International Version

NJB	New Jerusalem Bible
NJPSV	New Jewish Publication Society Version
NRSV	New Revised Standard Version
NRT	*La nouvelle revue théologique*
NTT	*Nieuw theologisch Tijdschrift*
OBO	Orbis biblicus et orientalis
Or	*Orientalia*
OTE	*Old Testament Essays*
OTL	*Old Testament Library*
OtSt	Old Testament Studies
OTWSA	*Oud Testamentiese Werkgemeenschap in Suid-Afrika*
OudSt	*Oudtestamentische Studiën*
PEQ	*Palestine Exploration Quarterly*
RB	*Revue biblique*
ResQ	*Restoration Quarterly*
RevExp	*Review and Exposition*
RevQ	*Revue de Qumran*
RevScRel	*Revue des sciences religieuse*
RSV	Revised Standard Version
SAA	State Archives of Assyria
SAAS	State Archives of Assyria Studies
SBL	Society of Biblical Literature
SBLDS	Society of Biblical Literature Dissertation Series
SBLMS	Society of Biblical Literature Monograph Series
SBLSP	*Society of Biblical Literature Seminar Papers*
SBS	Stuttgarter Bibelstudien
SEÅ	*Svensk exegetisk årsbok*
SHANE	Studies in the History of the Ancient Near East
SIL	Studies in Linguistics
SJOT	*Scandinavian Journal of the Old Testament*
SLA	Studien der Luther-Akademie
STAR	Studies in Theology and Religion
TA	*Tel Aviv*
TAD	B. Porten and A. Yardeni, *Textbook of Aramaic Documents* (Jerusalem: Hebrew University, Dept. of the History of the Jewish People; Winona Lake, IN: Eisenbrauns, 1986-89)
UBL	Ugaritisch-biblische Literatur
UF	*Ugarit Forschungen*
VT	*Vetus Testamentum*
VTSup	*Vetus Testamentum* Supplements
WMANT	Wissenschaftliche Monographien zum Alten und Neuen Testament
ZAH	*Zeitschrift für Althebraistik*
ZAW	*Zeitschrift für die alttestamentliche Wissenschaft*

Editors' Foreword

This volume is the seventeenth published in the series Forms of the Old Testament Literature (FOTL). The following foreword complements the forewords to volumes published thus far.

The reader will realize a difference between the chronological sequence in which the individual volumes appear and their positions in the order of the commentary. That is because the publication of the volumes depends on the working schedules of the individual contributors, which are also influenced by their participation in the ever-widening range of research. The order of the volumes in the commentary follows the sequential order of the books in the Protestant Churches, even where on occasion more than one biblical book is treated in the same volume or where two volumes are used for one biblical book. Excepted from this order are the books of Job, Proverbs, Ruth, Song of Songs, Ecclesiastes/Qoheleth, and Esther, whose combined treatment under *"Wisdom Literature"* is already published in volume XIII. The commentary on Lamentations likewise appears in volume XV on *Psalms, Part 2*.

An international, inter-confessional, and eventually inter-religious team of scholars contributes to the project, originally launched by Knierim and Tucker almost four decades ago. Its membership has changed and expanded over the years. After many years as Co-Editor together with Knierim, Tucker relinquished his position after his retirement from the Candler School of Theology. Sweeney, since 1994 Professor at the Claremont School of Theology and Claremont Graduate University, has succeeded Tucker as Co-Editor of the series.

During the early stages of deliberations, it had become clear that the project should not be a handbook about the results of the work of form-criticism, including method and exemplification. Nor should it be an encyclopedia of the identified genres and their settings in their typical societal traditions. These aspects are already on record through the results of the history of the discipline originally — and appropriately — called form-*history* (Form *Geschichte*) rather than form-*criticism*. The expression "form criticism" is retained in this commentary only with the conscious implication that form criticism involves the study of the genres and settings of the societal traditions of the texts. Instead of the two above-mentioned options for conceiving, organizing, and publishing the project, the Co-Editors determined that it should be a commentary, in which all texts throughout all books of the Hebrew Bible are form-critically interpreted. This goal is the result of both programmatic and didactic considerations.

The Co-Editors recognized programmatically that form-critical work must include all of what only in part had been done in the past, and what originally had been considered to be outside the task of biblical form-criticism in its search for the oral traditions behind the written texts: The form-critical interpretation of all literary texts and works themselves of the Bible, including the extant texts of the biblical books. The reality of the Bible as — not oral but — written literature exists in its own right, with its own societal genres and settings and traditions. This fact also applies to the specific texts of our extant Bibles.

The Co-Editors also recognized that the original form-critical method was inadequately conceived since the search for societal traditions or conditions behind the texts was conducted without form-critical study of the social and literary conditions in which these texts were produced and in which they function. As long as the societal identity of our texts themselves was not first established independently, the inherited method could not demonstrate how the societal conditions behind the text, which were claimed to be discovered by investigators, would indeed be the matrices of the texts' own societal identity. More than once could it be said or thought that the structure of a genre claimed to be found in a text indeed fails to explain that text.

The inclusion in form-critical study of the written, and especially the texts which are before us as readers, has meant that this study begins with the form-critical interpretation of the unique expression of the texts, because it encounters them in their individuality in the first place. In whatever way they reflect or represent typical traditions, they exist in their individuality. The unique character of texts consists of diverse elements and aspects; but these elements are subservient to the texts conceived in their entireties. These texts are formed in conceptually structured units, which represent the order of the texts. The study of this sort of structure reveals the aspects by which the text is governed or controlled as an entirety. And its results lead to the investigation of whether or not such structure reflects the tradition of a particular genre and its setting(s), or forms of expression outside the traditional societal conventions.

Thus, while the commentary is based on the basic aspects in the contribution of form-criticism's legacy to biblical interpretation, preeminently of genre and setting, it is the presentation and interpretation of the structure of each identified text before everything else, from the large to the small units, that represents the essential addition to the form-critical method in this commentary. For a discussion of this current state in the form-critical study of the Hebrew Bible, see *The Changing Face of Form Criticism for the Twenty-First Century* (ed. Marvin A. Sweeney and Ehud Ben Zvi; Grand Rapids, Michigan, and Cambridge, UK: Eerdmans, 2003).

Didactically speaking, by beginning the interpretation of a text with the presentation and discussion of its own structure, the method established in this commentary should offer all readers the opportunity to be guided into the study of a biblical text — into their involvement in understanding its presented structure, from which they may then be led to the subsequent discussion of the traditions of genre, setting, and intention/function/meaning. Indeed, the study of the texts' structures can be carried out independently, and by all. It is also important for any kind of biblical exegesis, and for the study of any text as well, not just as the first step of form-critical work.

The use of the present commentary is by and large self-explanatory, and in line with the policy of this series. It is to be used alongside the Hebrew text and/or a translation of the text. Major literary corpora are introduced by general bibliographies covering wider information, while form-critical bibliographies relevant for the discussion of the individual units are placed at the end of such units. The system of the sigla used for the presentation of the texts' structure indicates the relationship of the parts, including the super- and/or subordination of the parts within the unity of a text. The traditional chapter and verse divisions of the Hebrew/Aramaic text, and where necessary also the versification of the New Revised Standard Version, are supplied in the right-hand margin of the structure diagrams.

The present volume includes a glossary of the genres discussed in the commentary. The definitions of the genres were provided by Professor Ben Zvi. They will be included in the volumes containing the glossary of genres and the indices, which are planned for the eventual conclusion of the series.

The Co-Editors acknowledge with profound appreciation the contribution of numerous persons and institutions to the work of the project. All of the individual contributors have received significant financial, secretarial, and student assistance from their respective institutions. In particular, the editors have received extensive support from their universities. Without it, the work hardly would have gone on. At Claremont, the Institute for Antiquity and Christianity has from its own inception provided tangible support that stimulates not only individual but also team research. Emory University and its Candler School of Theology have likewise provided tangible support and encouragement. The editors are particularly indebted to Gene M. Tucker for — still — having undertaken the task of editing this volume by his former student.

ROLF P. KNIERIM
MARVIN A. SWEENEY

Author's Preface

Several people and institutions made the writing of this commentary not only possible, but also an enjoyable experience. It is a pleasant duty to mention some of them. I was honored and delighted when Rolf P. Knierim and Gene M. Tucker invited me to write a commentary on the book of Hosea. I wish to express my thanks to Rolf and Gene, the editors of this series at that time. I would also like to express my thanks to Marvin A. Sweeney, who is now one of the editors, for his support and for our interesting conversations about prophetic literature.

I have learned and continue to learn much from my teacher and good friend, Gene Tucker. He has provided me with support, encouragement, and much insight since the first day we met. As editor of the series, he has carefully read and improved the manuscript of this commentary. Of course, any errors that remain are my responsibility.

I presented papers on matters that directly relate to this commentary or that strongly influenced my thinking on the book of Hosea at different professional meetings during the last years. I owe a particular debt of gratitude to my colleagues for their feedback at these meetings. Likewise I wish to express my gratitude to the many colleagues who commented, both publicly and in private, on the basic methodological approach I took in my commentary on the book of Micah in this series, and which governs this commentary as well. Their comments have helped me to refine this approach.

I am also indebted to my students at the University of Alberta who have been most precious companions of mine in the learning journey that led to this commentary, to their enthusiasm and insight. This commentary would have never been completed without the incredible dedication of the people at interlibrary loan at the University of Alberta, and the University's support of this service.

Most of all, my thanks are due to Perla, my wife, for her love, friendship, and unfailing support. I would like to dedicate this volume to her and to all my children.

Chapter 1

Introduction to the Book of Hosea, A Particular Instance of YHWH'S Word

R. Abma, *Bonds of Love: Methodic Studies of Prophetic Texts with Marriage Imagery* (Studia Semitica Neerlandica; Assen: Van Gorcum, 1999); E. Achtemeier, *Minor Prophets I* (NIBC; Peabody: Hendrickson, 1996); L. Alonso Schökel and J. L. Sicre Diaz, *Profetas, II* (Madrid: Cristiandad, 1980); F. I. Andersen and D. N. Freedman, *Hosea* (AB 24; New York: Doubleday, 1980); D. Barthélemy et al., *Critique Textuelle de l'Ancient Testament, III* (OBO 50/3; Fribourg: Éditions Universitaires, 1992); G. V. Blakenbaker, *The Language of Hosea 1–3* (PhD dissertation; Claremont Graduate School, 1976); C. Bucher, *The Origin and Meaning of ZNH Terminology in the Book of Hosea* (PhD dissertation; Claremont Graduate School, 1988); M. J. Buss, *The Prophetic Word of Hosea* (BZAW 111; Berlin: A. Töpelmann, 1969); J. Calvin, *Commentary on Hosea*, pp. 34-530 in J. Calvin, *Commentaries on the Twelve Minor Prophets*, vol. 2 (transl. J. Owen; Grand Rapids: Baker, n.d.); H. Cohen, *The Commentary of Rabbi David Kimhi on Hosea* (Columbia University Oriental Studies, vol. XX; New York: AMS Press, 1966; orig. pub., Columbia Univ. Press, 1929); D. R. Daniels, *Hosea and Salvation History* (BZAW 191; Berlin: de Gruyter, 1990); G. I. Davies, *Hosea* (NCB; Grand Rapids, MI: Eerdmans, 1992); G. Eidewall, *Grapes in the Desert. Metaphors, Models, and Themes in Hosea 4–14* (CB Old Testament Series 43; Stockholm: Almqvist & Wiksell, 1996); G. I. Emmerson, *Hosea: An Israelite Prophet in Judean Perspective* (JSOTSupS 28; Sheffield: JSOT Press, 1984); P. A. Franklyn, *Prophetic Cursing of Apostasy: The Text, Forms and Traditions of Hosea 13* (PhD dissertation; Vanderbilt University, 1986); R. E. Fuller, "The Twelve," E. Ulrich et al., *Qumran Cave 4. X. The Prophets* (DJD XV; Oxford: Clarendon Press, 1997) 221-317; D. A. Garret, *Hosea, Joel* (NAC 19a; Nashville: Broadman and

Holman Publishers, 1997); A. Gelston, *The Peshiṭta of the Twelve Prophets* (Oxford: Clarendon Press, 1987); H. L. Ginsberg, "Hosea," *Enc. Judaica,* vol. 8, cols. 1010-1024; W. R. Harper, *Amos and Hosea* (ICC; Edinburgh: T&T Clark, orig. ed. 1905; 1979 printing); E. K. Holt, *Prophesying the Past. The Use of Israel's History in the Book of Hosea* (JSOTSupS 194; Sheffield: Sheffield Univ. Press, 1995); D. A. Hubbard, *Hosea* (Tyndale Commentary; Downers Grove, IL: InterVarsity Press, 1989); M. J. Hynniewta, *The Integrity of Hosea's Future Hope: A Study of the Oracles of Hope in the Book of Hosea* (PhD dissertation; Union Theological Seminary, Richmond, VA, 2002); J. Jeremias, *Der Prophet Hosea* (ATD; Göttingen: Vandenhoeck & Ruprecht, 1983); Y. Kaufmann, *Toldot HaEmunah HaYisraelit,* vol. 3 (Tel Aviv: Bialik-Dvir, 1955-56) 93-146 [in Hebrew]; Alice A. Keefe, *Woman's Body and the Social Body in Hosea* (JSOTSupS 338; Sheffield: Sheffield Academic Press, 2001); D. Kidner, *The Message of Hosea* (Downers Grove, IL: InterVarsity Press, 1981); P. J. King, *Amos, Hosea, Micah — An Archaeological Commentary* (Philadelphia: Westminster, 1988); W. Kuhnigk, *Nordwestsemitische Studien zum Hoseabuch* (Biblica et Orientalia 27; Rome: Biblical Institute Press, 1974); F. Landy, *Hosea* (Readings; Sheffield: Sheffield Academic Press, 1995); J. Limburg, *Hosea-Micah* (Interpretation; Atlanta: John Knox, 1988); A. Lipshitz, *Ibn Ezra Commentary on Hosea* (New York: Sepher-Hermon Press, 1988); M. Luther, *Lectures on Hosea,* ed. H. C. Oswald, *Luther's Works,* vol. 18 (St. Louis: Concordia Publishing House, 1975) 1-76; A. A. Macintosh, *Hosea* (ICC; Edinburgh: T&T Clark, 1997); J. Mauchline, "The Book of Hosea," *The Interpreter's Bible* (New York: Abingdon/Cokesbury Press, 1951-57), vol. 6 (1956) 552-725; J. L. Mays, *Hosea* (OTL; Philadelphia: Westminster, 1975); W. E. Mills, *Hosea-Joel* (Bibliographies for Biblical Research. Old Testament Series, 21a; Lewiston, NY: Mellen Biblical Press, 2002); G. Morris, *Prophecy, Poetry and Hosea* (JSOTSupS 219; Sheffield: Sheffield Academic Press, 1996); Th. Naumann, *Hoseas Erben: Strukturen der Nachinterpretation im Buch Hosea* (BWANT 131; Stuttgart: Kohlhammer, 1991); H.-D. Neef, *Die Heilstraditionen Israels in der Verkündigung des Propheten Hosea* (BZAW 169; Berlin: de Gruyter, 1987); M. Nissinen, *Prophetie, Redaktion und Fortschreibung im Hoseabuch: Studien zum Werdegang eines Prophetenbuches im Lichte von Hos 4 und 11* (AOAT 231; Kevelaer: Butzon & Bercker, 1991); J. D. Nogalski, *Literary Precursors to the Book of The Twelve* (BZAW 217; Berlin: de Gruyter, 1993); idem, *Redactional Processes in the Book of the Twelve* (BZAW 218; Berlin: de Gruyter, 1993); E. Nwaoru, *Imagery in the Prophecy of Hosea* (Ægypten und Altes Testament 14; Wiesbaden: Harrassowitz, 1999); B. Oestreich, *Metaphors and Similes for Yahweh in Hosea 14:2-9 (1-8): A Study of Hoseanic Pictorial Language* (Frankfurt am Main: P. Lang, 1998); E. J. Pentiuc, *Long-Suffering Love. A Commentary on Hosea with Patristic Annotations* (Brookline, MA: Holy Cross Orthodox Press, 2002); D. N. Premnath, *The Process of Latifundation Mirrored in the Oracles Pertaining to the 8th Century B.C.E. in the Books of Amos, Hosea, Isaiah and Micah* (PhD dissertation; Graduate Theological Union, 1984); Y. Qyl, *Hosea* in Y. Qyl et al., *The Twelve,* vol. 1, *Hosea-Jonah* (Daʿat HaMiqra; Jerusalem: Mosad HaRav Kuk, 1973) 3-48+יקׁג [in Hebrew]; Radak (see *Miqraot Gedolot*); Rashi (see

Miqraot Gedolot); W. Richter, *Biblia Hebraica transcripta. Kleine Propheten* (ATSAT 33.10; St. Ottilien: Eos Verlag, 1993); M. Roberts and J. Elias, Trei Asar — *The Twelve Prophets, vol. 1* (Brooklyn, NY: Mesorah Publications, 1995); W. Rudolph, *Hosea* (KAT 13/1; Gütersloh: Gütersloher Verlaghaus Gerd Mohn, 1966); A. Schart, *Die Entstehung des Zwölfprophetenbuchs* (BZAW 260; Berlin: de Gruyter, 1998); L. Alonso Schökel and J. L. Sicre, *Profetas* (2 vols.; Nueva Biblia Española — Comentario; Madrid: Ediciones Cristiandad, 1987); Y. Sherwood, *The Prostitute and the Prophet. Hosea's Marriage in Literary-Theoretical Perspective* (JSOTSupS 212; Sheffield: Sheffield Academic Press, 1996); H. Shy, *Tanhum Ha-Yerushalmi's Commentary on the Minor Prophets* (Jerusalem: Magnes, 1991); H. Simian-Yofre, *El desierto de los dioses. Teología e Historia en el libro de Oseas* (Córdoba, Spain: El Almendro, 1993); U. Simon, *Abraham Ibn Ezra's Two Commentaries on the Minor Prophets. An Annotated Critical Edition*, vol. 1, *Hosea-Joel-Amos* (Ramat Gan: Bar Ilan University, 1989; in Hebrew); N. Snaith, *Mercy and Sacrifice. A Study of the Book of Hosea* (London: SCM Press, 1953); idem, *Amos, Hosea and Micah* (London: Epworth Press, 1956); D. Stuart, *Hosea-Jonah* (Waco: Word, 1987); M. A. Sweeney, *The Twelve Prophets, vol. 1: Hosea, Joel, Amos, Obadiah, Jonah* (Brit Olam; Collegeville, MN: Glazier/Liturgical Press, 2000); idem, *King Josiah of Judah. The Lost Messiah of Israel* (Oxford: Oxford University Press, 2001); G. A. Tooze, *Framing the Book of the Twelve: Connections Between Hosea and Malachi* (PhD dissertation; Iliff School of Theology and University of Denver, 2002); R. Törnkvist, *The Use and Abuse of Female Sexual Imagery in the Book of Hosea, A Feminist-Critical Approach to Hos 1–3* (Acta Universitatis Upsaliensis — Uppsala Women's Studies A. Women in Religion 7; Uppsala: Uppsala Univ. Library, 1998); J. M. Trotter, *Reading Hosea in Achaemenid Yehud* (JSOTSupS 328; Sheffield: Sheffield Academic Press, 2001); H. Utzschneider, *Hosea, Prophet vor dem Ende: Zum Verhältniss von Geschichte und Institution in der alttestamentlichen Prophetie* (OBO 31; Freiburg, Schweiz/Göttingen: Universitätverlag/Vandenhoeck & Ruprecht, 1980); J. M. Ward, *Hosea. A Theological Commentary* (New York: Harper & Row, 1966); A. Weiser, *Die Propheten Hosea, Joel, Amos, Obadja, Jona, Micha* (ATD 24; Göttingen: Vandenhoeck and Ruprecht, 1985); J. Wellhausen, *Skizzen und Vorarbeiten Fünftes Heft. Die kleinen Propheten übersetzt, mit Noten* (Berlin: Georg Reimer, 1892); I. Willi-Plein, *Vorformen der Schriftexegese innerhalb des Alten Testaments: Untersuchungen zum literarischen Werden der auf Amos, Hosea und Micah zurückgehenden Bücher im hebräischen Zwölfprophetenbuch* (BZAW 123; Berlin: de Gruyter, 1971); H. W. Wolff, *Hosea. A Commentary on the Book of the Prophet Hosea* (Hermeneia; Philadelphia: Fortress, 1974; original German, 1965); G. A. Yee, *Composition and Tradition in the Book of Hosea. A Redactional Critical Investigation* (SBLDS 102; Atlanta: Scholars Press, 1987); Y. J. Yoo, *Israelian Hebrew in the Book of Hosea* (PhD dissertation; Cornell University, 1999); M. D. Zulick, *Rhetorical Polyphony in the Book of the Prophet Hosea* (PhD dissertation; Northwestern University, 1994).

Structure

*Note: References to verses point always at the Hebrew text and its versification in this commentary, unless explicitly stated.

The book of Hosea is a written text that shows a great deal of literary sophistication. It may rightly be called a BOOK — though the term does not appear in the text — because of its written character and because it is a self-contained literary unit with a clear beginning and conclusion that shows a significant degree of textual coherence and distinctiveness. The book of Hosea is not merely a "book," but a PROPHETIC BOOK. On these issues see Genre below, and for a more extensive discussion, see Ben Zvi, "The Prophetic Book: A Key Form of Prophetic Literature" (cf. Ben Zvi, *Micah,* 4).

It is the book that claims to be, and was composed to be treated as, an authoritative writing for its readership — that is, as "scripture." The book is explicitly characterized by its title as *YHWH's word* (Hos 1:1). The book claims that it provides the readers who are competent to read it with knowledge that originated in the divine (i.e., YHWH's word) and valid knowledge about the divine (i.e., an authentic representation of YHWH's positions, actions, plans, and indirectly YHWH's character). To be sure, if the community of readers at which the book was aimed accepted such claims, they would find the book worthy of reading and rereading, of copying and recopying, and as a result, the book would be transmitted from one generation of readers to the next. The fact that this was the case leads one to assume that at least the ancient literati accepted the authority of the book.

As per its title, the present is a form-critical, historical study of the *Book of Hosea*, not of any unverifiable text of a forerunner of this book, nor any hypothetical source that is construed by bringing together different sections of the book, and omitting others, and thus creating a new whole (see below). Moreover, the focus here is on the book as it was read, reread, meditated upon (cf. Josh 1:8; Hos 14:10; and see Sir 38:34–39:3) by the literati, among whom and for whom the book in its present form was composed. These literati were the only social group that held the level of literacy required to read, reread, and understand the book directly (cf. Hos 14:10).

It is worth stressing at this point that I am *not* advancing any theological or ideological claim about the priority of the understanding of the ancient readership on which this study focuses over that of any other group of readers located at any other point in time and within any other kind of social environment. The point is that (a) actual reading and rereading of a text implies concrete readers and (b) the social identity, the world of knowledge, the theology and ideology of these readers, all influence the process of reading and rereading carried out by these readers. It is worth stressing that the ancient reading and rereading of the book of Hosea was an interpersonal rather than personal affair and thus involved a community of readers or, better, rereaders. Therefore, a commentary on the book and the message that it carries within a readership has to be explicit about the identity of the readership to which it is referring. The emphasis on the book as it stands derives also from the conviction that the meaning of the different READINGS that compose the book (see below) is constantly influenced by their being part and parcel of the book. For instance, Hos 1:1 serves as a constant reminder of the world in which the book is set. There are also numerous cross-references among the different READINGS in the book. All these cross-references serve well texts meant to be read and reread. They create signposts for the readers that remind them of particular issues dealt with in the book as a whole. They contribute to the creation of networks of various readings continuously informing each other, and, to some extent, shaping the meaning of each other in various ways. Thus, the cross-references create multiple potential meanings, as expected in texts to be read and reread. In other words, READINGS do not stand by themselves as separate units; rather, they stand and gain particular significance within a context of the entire book.

To be sure, it is most likely that written sources underlie the present book. It is also likely that the present book is the end result of some redactional processes. This being said, the book of Hosea — that is, this particular instance of YHWH's word — is a book that is presented to its intended readers as a unit, and that asks them to approach it as such and carries particular meanings as such (see above). There is no indication that the intended readership of the book was asked to divide it into potential sources, read each of them separately and then reconstruct the possible redactional processes that led to the book in its present form. There is also no reason to assume that any historical (ancient) community read the book in such a manner. Accordingly, a historical commentary on the BOOK of Hosea (to be distinguished from studies about the historical prophet Hosea or any possible, though hypothetical, forerunner or preexisting tradition) has to deal with the book as a whole and, of course, as a written document to be read and reread, again and again. (On the importance of being meant for reading and rereading see Ben Zvi, *Signs of Jonah: Reading and Rereading in Ancient Yehud; Micah; Obadiah;* "Introduction: Writings, Speeches, and the Prophetic Books — Setting an Agenda.")

To be sure, it is still possible for historians to try to study, in a similar manner, texts other than the present book of Hosea, such as its hypothetical forerunners. But such attempts face serious systemic hurdles. To begin with, such a study must start with the reconstruction of the text of the forerunner — that is, the object of the study. But scholarly reconstructed texts cannot but be hypothetical and unverifiable, and rarely command any consensus. It is worth stressing also that redactional and authorial processes may not only bring new material into a source text but also may exclude and completely reshape material as the way in which the Chronicler worked with the books of Samuel and Kings clearly shows. But how can a scholar reconstruct an omitted text? Can a scholar reconstruct the Bathsheba narrative in Samuel out of Chronicles?

Furthermore, this is not a study of the life of a historical prophet. First, the readers of the book are not asked to listen to the words of a contemporary prophet, but to read and reread a book about an ancient prophet, YHWH, and Israel. They have access to the book, and through the book they construe their image of the prophet of old. The Hosea of the book is a literary and ideological character that lives within the world of the book. This character is, of course, integrated in one way or another into the general constructions of Israel's past that are agreed upon among the literati who constitute the target readership of the book, as well as the social location of its authorship. Significantly, there are numerous markers that show that the readers are supposed to understand their particular readings within their *Sitz im Buch* rather than within any precise historical context associated with the life of the historical prophet or even that of the literary prophetic character portrayed in the book. The book of Hosea is not about mimesis or historicity, but about learning about YHWH, Israel's past and future, and the relations between the two. It is a book meant to be read and reread by a target readership that is supposed to identify with the main ideological characters (YHWH, Israel), even if it lives far removed from the circumstances in which the book is set.

In accordance with the general guidelines of the series, this commentary explores neither matters of textual criticism nor, and above all, the study of the *books* of Hosea that existed in ancient languages other than Hebrew (e.g., LXX, Peshiṭta, Vulgate, Targum). Occasional brief references and minimal bibliography are included, however. The same holds true for Qumranic versions (4QXIIc, d, g) and interpretations of Hosea (4Q166; 4Q167). At points at which this commentary is grounded on an understanding of an expression or verse that is substantially at odds with that reflected in influential English translations, the understanding assumed here will be explicitly mentioned.

Turning to the STRUCTURE mentioned above, it is easy to notice that it makes no reference to the Book of the Twelve. Of course, the book of Hosea is now in a collection of twelve prophetic books. But the book of Hosea, just as the other prophetic books included in the collection, shows a strong textually inscribed request to its primary readership to understand it as distinct from the others, and as a unit in itself. These textually inscribed markers include the presence of a clear beginning that includes an explicit title, a clear conclusion, the ubiquitous presence of a particular language (see Setting) and its explicit association with a single and unique prophetic character. These markers set each book apart from the others in the collection (see Ben Zvi, "Twelve Prophetic Books"). For this reason the book of Hosea is studied here as a unit in itself, rather than as a subunit of a "Book of the Twelve." (For studies of the book of Hosea, or sections thereof, as an integral part of the Book of the Twelve, see among others, Nogalski, *Literary Precursors;* Schart, *Entstehung des Zwölfprophetenbuchs;* Jeremias, "Die Anfänge des Dodekapropheton"; Tooze, *Framing the Book of the Twelve;* and the recent contributions gathered in Redditt and Schart, eds., *Thematic Threads in the Book of The Twelve,* which include a qualified version of this type of approach, see Albertz, "Exile as Purification.")

Hosea shows the basic structure that characterizes all prophetic books, whether they be within the collection of "The Twelve" or not, as for instance, the book of Isaiah. This structure consists of (a) an introduction, (b) a conclusion, and (c) the body of the book that consists of a series of PROPHETIC READINGS. The introduction of Hosea characterizes it as such, provides a title for the book, identifies it as a separate book, associates it with a particular prophetic figure from the past, and serves to set the world of the book in a particular time within the construction of their own past held by the intended and primary readers and rereaders. The conclusion of Hosea not only sets the boundary of the book, but as most conclusions of prophetic books do, it also provides an interpretative key for the book as a whole, and conveys a sense of uniqueness to the entire work (see Ben Zvi, "Prophetic Book"). Unlike other prophetic books, however, the conclusion of the book of Hosea reflects on the book as such, and on its role in society. As a result, the concluding high note of the third SET of READINGS (Hos 14:2-9) serves a role comparable to other thematic conclusions in prophetic books (e.g., Joel 4:18-21; Mic 7:18-20; Am 9:13-15; Obad 17-21; Mic 7:18-20), in addition to its role in its particular SET of READINGS. As such it may be considered the conclusion of the body of the book.

The third and main element in all prophetic books consists of PROPHETIC READINGS. A book, that is, a written document or product, cannot contain anything but "writings" or, better, "readings," that is, "writings meant to be read." These are, of course, PROPHETIC READINGS: literary units within a prophetic book that show textually inscribed, discursive markers that were likely to suggest to its intended and primary readership that they were supposed — or at least invited — to read and reread these sections as cohesive subunits within the frame of the prophetic book as a whole (see Ben Zvi, *Micah,* 188; idem, "Prophetic Book"). These READINGS are, of course, DIDACTIC READINGS. The readership is supposed to learn through the continuous reading, rereading, and studying of the book, and others to whom the book or portions thereof were read are also supposed to learn by listening to particular instances of YHWH's word, that is, prophetic books. Given the success of these books, there is strong likelihood that the primary readership or a significant portion of it resembled in many ways the intended readership of the book and approached it in a similar manner (see Ben Zvi, "Prophetic Book"; cf. D. C. Kraemer, "Intended Reader"). The PROPHETIC READINGS in the book of Hosea are organized in three SETS OF READINGS. Each SET begins with references to judgment in the past of the community of readers, and concludes with a note of hope for the same community. Whereas the judgment looks at and interprets the past, the hope looks at the (distant) future of the community of readers.

To be sure, although all these units are DIDACTIC PROPHETIC READINGS, they are not all the same. *Each reading* may evoke images of different social interactions and situations — a point that will be discussed further in the commentary. Given the literary character of the book and its readings, images of such social interactions and situations may easily defamiliarize and lead to constructions that do not occur in the "real" world. Further, since the book and each of its readings were meant to be read and reread, the READINGS are likely to convey a multiplicity of meanings and of associations; moreover, the intended rereaders approached them in a way that is informed to some extent by other READINGS in the book (see Ben Zvi, *Micah,* 4-8 and passim, and idem, "Prophetic Book").

The basic conceptual "structure" governing the book is found in a very common metanarrative in postmonarchic Israel (on the date of the present book of Hosea see Setting). This metanarrative can be summarized as follows: (a) YHWH chose Israel long ago and became its patron; (b) Israel — the client — broke its obligations towards its patron, or, in theological terms, Israel sinned against YHWH; (c) YHWH punished Israel (a stage associated with the fall of the monarchic polities and socio-cultic systems), but since YHWH still "loves" Israel, the deity will not exterminate Israel nor abrogate its patronship, which ideologically is tantamount to the former; and (d) since YHWH did not abrogate its patronship, at an undefined but certain future time, YHWH will bring this relationship to its proper (ideal) form. Stage (a) in this metanarrative may be addressed through different images of asymmetrical relationships common within the ideological discourses of the time, including, among others, father/son, husband/wife, king/subject, farmer/heifer. It may also be addressed through references to memories agreed upon within society — or at least its literati — about past Israel. These include references to the Exodus, to Jacob, to the meeting between YHWH and Israel in the desert. (It should be stressed that social memories do not have to be historically accurate or inaccurate; rather they have to be included among the facts about the past agreed upon by a certain community.) Such references interact with a set of available, agreed-upon social memories and legitimize and strengthen the persuasive appeal of the manifestation of the metanarrative that occurs in a particular READING within the book. Stage (b) in the metanarrative is manifested in numerous references to Israel's sins. To be sure, the sins should be such that justify, or more than justify, the terrible divine punishment inflicted on Israel. For obvious reasons, the reported sinful activities are associated, in the main at least, with the period in which the world portrayed in the book is set. This being said, the text may refer to previous periods and even to a period that closely follows the beginning of the YHWH-Israel relationship. In these cases, the communicative message is that the sins associated with the later period are not a temporal "aberration" but a manifestation of long-held attributes of Israel. In addition, one may note that there is a certain repertoire of general images that are often used to characterize Israel as sinful. These involve cultic wrongful behavior, wrongful powerful elites, trusting foreign mighty kings or deities other than YHWH, and the like. For obvious reasons, in prophetic books stage (c) of this metanarrative is manifested as divine announcements of horrifying punishment/judgment. These announcements may be general, may refer to the fall of the monarchic polities, and may include metaphorical images of the deity such as a devouring lion — and in the case of Hos 5:12, as moth and rottenness. It goes without saying that from the perspective of the postmonarchic rereadership of the book these announcements were fulfilled, but as their very existence as a community reading and rereading these books shows, YHWH has not obliterated Israel, nor will the deity do so. On the contrary, the very fact that they have access to a reliable rendition of YHWH's word in the form of books such as the book of Hosea and the hope this divine word conveys for the future show that YHWH has not removed YHWH's patronship over Israel. Stage (d) finds its manifestation in divine announcements of future bliss in which images of that which the authorship and target readership considered to be idyllic come to the forefront.

Neither the book of Hosea nor other prophetic books (except Jonah) are narratives. The book as a whole does not develop any explicit narrative plot. Yet, the mentioned metanarrative is continually activated and reinforced among the target readership of the book as they read, reread, and study it. This conceptual metanarrative provides building blocks, as it were, for the construction of the READINGS in the book. The latter often contain some of these conceptual units, but rarely all. More importantly, as the book is taken as a whole, different stages in this metanarrative are revisited again and again, each time from a different perspective, and through various images, each of which provides a slightly different insight. The matter is not one of redundancy at all, but of constructing a more sophisticated multilayered approach to these matters through an interwoven tapestry of the individual (and partial) threads represented by constructions, and images that appear in particular READINGS or sections of READINGS. Although this conceptual metanarrative is at work in a number of prophetic books in which the world of the book is set in monarchic times, unlike the case in most other prophetic books, the particular manifestations of this metanarrative in Hosea focus on northern Israel's past (as opposed to Judah's past). This feature is consistent with the world portrayed in the book, and it allows the readership to evoke images usually associated, in the social memories agreed upon by the literati, with northern Israel's sin/s (e.g., worship of the calves, idolatry, northern sanctuaries and esp. Beth-el, non-Davidic kings, worship of "baal," and the like), and with northern history (e.g., its relations with Assyria, Egypt). Yet the book consistently reminds its readers that northern Israel did not stand alone, but rather its story is relevant because it is a manifestation of transtemporal Israel, as is monarchic Judah, and the readership of the book as well. All these matters are addressed in detail (and as relevant to the unit under discussion in the following chapters).

9

It may be noted that "transtemporal" is a far more precise description of the character of this Israel than "atemporal." Within the relevant discourses, Israel was never conceived as existing outside time, but rather as a closely-knit continuum existing *across* time; in fact, across all time since the moment YHWH "selected" Israel into being. The same holds true for the foundational relationship between YHWH and Israel.

Turning to the formal (as opposed to "conceptual") STRUCTURE that is advanced at the beginning of this chapter, we will discuss this STRUCTURE at length under STRUCTURE in the following chapters.

An editorial comment: Although the terms "reader" and "readership" may be used for any rereader and rereadership, their use here might mislead some of the readers of this commentary if these terms do not remind them that most of the reading of the book of Hosea, and other biblical books, was in fact rereading. Yet a constant use of terms such as "rereader" and "rereadership" — or "(re-)reader" and "(re-)readership" — may be fastidious for some readers of this commentary. Thus the policy adopted here — except in this introductory unit — is to refer to them as "reader," "readership" and the like for the most part. However, as a signpost to the importance of the issue at stake, the terms "rereader" and "rereadership" will appear more than a few times in the commentary.

Genre

A few considerations on Genre are in order before addressing the question of the genre of the book of Hosea. Genres are not "platonic models," but constructs that exist in particular communities of readers (or listeners in some cases). These communities live in particular historical circumstances. Genre is an attribute assigned to a work that evolves out of the interaction between a particular readership and text. It concerns textually inscribed markers, but also involves the attribution by the readership of intentions to the implied author of the work. The latter, unlike the actual author, is a construction of the readership and changes according to different social and historical settings (cf. E. Ben Zvi, *Signs of Jonah,* 129-54). Genre has to do with the expectations of a particular readership. Since the latter change from readership to readership, because they are socially and historically dependent, so may the readers' construction of genre change.

Although each book is unique and is likely to play to some or even a large degree with socially shared expectations within the particular group for which the book was targeted, each assumes a readership that is well aware of possible genres and their main features. Moreover, genres do not exist by themselves, but as a part of a "universe" of possible genres that exists within the discourse/s of the target readership, which in turn would assign — implicitly or explicitly — particular works to one or another of the existing genres in their repertoire. As they do so, they shape a most important interpretative key for their understanding of the work.

Genre has much to do with interpretation and, therefore, much to do with power and authoritativeness too. A writer writing a work meant to be recognized by the target readership as YHWH's word, as a prophetic book, is claiming power and authority. In a comparable manner, a primary readership consisting of very few bearers of high literacy within a largely illiterate society cannot but claim power and authority when they maintain that the books they hold, and they alone can and do read for themselves and that they alone can read to, and interpret for others are YHWH's word. All these considerations emphasize that genres are not transtemporal but clearly associated with particular groups and their social, historical, ideological, and discursive circumstances.

The genre of the book of Hosea can be described as "Prophetic Book," or to be more precise, "Authoritative, Ancient Israelite Prophetic Book." Of course, this genre is a subset of (ancient Israelite) authoritative "book." Such an ancient "book" may be defined as a self-contained written text that was produced within ancient Israel, is characterized by a clear beginning and conclusion, has a substantial level of textual coherence and of textually inscribed distinctiveness vis-à-vis other books, and that, accordingly, leads its intended and primary readers (and rereaders) to approach it in a manner that takes into account this distinctiveness. An "authoritative book" is one that communicates an explicit or implicit claim for social and theological/ideological authoritativeness, and was likely accepted as such by at least some substantial sector of the ancient (re)readership. It is to be stressed that this definition applies to books that were included eventually in the Hebrew Bible, and to many that were not (e.g., book of Jubilees, Enoch, Temple Scroll, etc.). The basic difference between the two groups is not to be found in the presence or absence of claims to authoritativeness or any formal or genre marker, but on the level and range of the acceptance of the textually inscribed claims by different communities within Israel and through time. The question of whether plainly nonauthoritative books were copied and passed from generation to generation in the *early* Second Temple period remains opens, but, significantly, none of them is extant. Limited resources and the social location of the literati's writing — see below — may have been less than conducive to the "success" and "reproduction" of such highly literate texts that carry no claim for social authority.

An "Authoritative, Ancient Israelite Prophetic Book" is by definition a subset within the genre of "Authoritative Ancient Israelite Book." It is an authoritative text written to be read and reread that presents itself as YHWH's word and is associated with a prophetic personage. It must share substantial features with other prophetic books (e.g., Isaiah, Micah, Zephaniah) and be presented to its target readership as unlike authoritative books such as Genesis, Deuteronomy, Kings, Proverbs, or Psalms. It is worth stressing that such a subset was already recognized in antiquity. It consisted of books that claim an association with a prophetic personage of the past (e.g., Isaiah, Jeremiah, Amos, Micah) and that are presented to their intended and primary readership as YHWH's word and, accordingly, as books that claim to convey legitimate and authoritative knowledge about YHWH. Each prophetic book is associated with a prophetic personage, and *no* prophetic book is associated with more than one prophetic personage.

Since the book was considered to provide legitimate knowledge about YHWH and YHWH's ways, and as such was included in the accepted repertoire of prophetic books, the communicator must have been construed as "authoritative." Had this not been the case, there would have been no reason to continue studying, copying, reading, and reading to others this text. But the authoritative communicator was certainly not the actual historical author of the book (or a composite figure of authors and editors). The authoritative communicator was the implied author that the readers construed through their readings and rereadings of the text (see below). Readings were (and are, in general) by necessity socially and historically dependent. These ancient readers approached a text with a particular world of knowledge. The latter included, in addition to the obvious linguistic abilities to decode the words of the text, ideological or theological viewpoints, a construction of the past, an understanding of the present, hopes and fears for the future, a literary/theological awareness that set their book within the frame of the general cultural repertoire, as well as literary sensibilities. Thus the nature of the communicator with whom the actual ancient readers and rereaders of the book of Hosea interacted was dependent on their particular worldview and world of knowledge. (I have expanded on these matters elsewhere. See Ben Zvi, *Jonah;* idem, "The Prophetic Book.").

On the question of the possible genre of the subunits of an AUTHORITATIVE, ANCIENT ISRAELITE PROPHETIC BOOK see STRUCTURE, above, and Ben Zvi, "The Prophetic Book."

Setting

The social setting in which the book of Hosea — as a whole — was produced is characterized by an authorship and readership able to produce, read, and reread this text. The following studies on the particular READINGS demonstrate that both the authorship and readership are to be found among literati who were the few bearers of high literacy in their society. The latter are usually associated with urban centers and with social and political circumstances that allow for the training and maintenance of cadres of literati, and for the production, reading, and rereading of their works.

It goes without saying that the production, copying, reading, and rereading of these texts require the channeling of social resources for that purpose and the instruction and maintenance of bearers of high literacy. (See Ben Zvi, "Introduction: Writings, Speeches, and the Prophetic Books — Setting an Agenda," and bibliography mentioned there; see also E. Ben Zvi, *Micah.*)

Each of these READINGS also reflects the world of these literati, and in particular their worldviews, central features of which may be referred to as "the spirit of the time" or the general "mindset" of the period within this particular group in society. READINGS tend to assume, express, reflect on, and, in general, reinforce these general worldviews. Moreover, the text associates these worldviews with the godly voices that populate the world of the text. In particular, YHWH is characterized as the speaker who voices them. As a result, the readers of the book are asked to identify with a deity that is authoritatively imagined as sharing their *Weltanschauung*. Much of the studies under Settings in this commentary discuss how particular READINGS contribute to our knowledge of the intellectual and ideological setting of the primary and intended readership, which for the most part is presented to the readers as that of YHWH and godly human characters in the world portrayed by the book.

Of course, this intellectual setting did not include abstract ideas existing outside any discursive patterns. The mentioned intellectual setting or atmosphere includes networks of images, metaphors, expressions, puns on words, word pairs, and shared social memories of the past — whether they point at historical events in the present sense of the term or not. It is to be stressed that comparisons made in this commentary between any of the above as they appear in the book of Hosea with their occurrences in other books should not be construed as attempts to reconstruct lines of copying among authors (or editors), but as reflections of the largely shared sea of expressions and ideas from which prophetic books were composed and through which they were read.

As mentioned above, the book was composed by literati and for literati, but when did these literati live? Certainly, it makes a difference if they were northern Israelites in the 9th or early 8th century, Judahites during the Hezekianic or Josianic period, Judahites living in the neo-Babylonian province of Judah, or Yehudites in Persian, Jerusalem-centered Yehud. The vast majority of scholars on Hosea have assigned some sections, redactions, additions, or the like to either late monarchic Judah or postmonarchic times. Needless to say, by logical necessity, the present book of Hosea cannot pre-date any of the above; in fact, it cannot pre-date the so-called "final edition" of the book. In other words, there is a widespread agreement that the literati who composed, and for whom the present book was composed, lived either in late monarchic Judah or postmonarchic times (concerning the former, see, among others, Emmerson, *Hosea;* Yoo, *Israelian Hebrew;* Sweeney, *Twelve Prophets;* concerning the latter, see, among others, Yee, *Composition and Tradition;* Mays, *Hosea;* Vermeylen, "Osée"; Wolff, *Hosea*). Even Ginsberg, who proposed that there were two clearly separate Hoseas, each with his own style and message, namely, Hosea A who lived in the early 860s BCE and to whom Hosea 1–3 is to be attributed, and a Hosea B who lived in the middle to late 740s BCE and to whom Hosea 4–14 is to be attributed, maintained that there are a number of Judahite additions he associated with Hezekianic times and with the collection of literary works in his times. (See Ginsberg, "Hosea"; for the division of the book into two separate works written by separate Hoseas, see also Kaufmann, *Toldot*).

The reasons for the widespread agreement mentioned above are clear. Even scholars who tend to accept *a priori* the historical circumstances mentioned in the superscription over any other possible historical settings for both the location of the historical prophet and the production of the prophetic texts — a position I have strongly criticized elsewhere, see Ben Zvi, "History and Prophetic Texts," and which, in my opinion, should be rejected — recognize the presence of clear tensions between (a) the world in which the book of Hosea seems to be set (monarchic, northern Israel) and which they identify with the original setting of the book or of many of its prophetic texts, and (b) many of the explicit, textually inscribed claims of the book. For instance, even the superscription that to a large extent serves as their historical key does not fit well with a Hoseanic, northern Israelite, late monarchic period. As a result, proposals for a redactional history of the superscription must be advanced, so a kernel that is consistent with their assumption about the original setting of the book may be construed (see Hos 1:1 STRUCTURE). Another example: Numerous references to Judah (and one explicit reference to David) reveal a perspective that is not consistent with an actual historical (as opposed to literary) northern Israelite setting. Thus either Judah is transformed into Israel, so as to construct a text that can be associated with a northern Israelite setting, or some of these texts are assigned to later redactional levels or additions.

But which setting is more likely, late monarchic Judah or postmonarchic times? Since there is no *a priori* reason to prefer one to the other, the historical-critical question is *not* whether one is somehow able to make sense of a prophetic text within the historical setting mentioned as the earliest possible date (here, late monarchic Judah). Instead the question should be phrased in terms of which setting provides the most reasonable historical background for such a text. In other words, the setting that involves the least unproven premises requires acceptance as the preferable option. Moreover, one has to take into account that the world of the book is set in a particular time and region. To state the obvious, this background characterization carries implications about the contents of the book. For instance, the book was much more likely to refer to Ephraim or northern Israel than to Judah, to Assyria and Egypt rather than to Babylon and Egypt. The issue is not one of historical reality (Aram played a crucial role in the decades leading to the fall of Samaria, but is not mentioned), but of constructions of the past. This being so, the search for the most likely setting of the production of the present book and its original target readership is to focus on general thematic matters that are neither a requirement of the world of the book nor suit it easily.

Although absolute certainty is impossible, a number of features tend to support the position that a postmonarchic setting for the present book of Hosea is most likely. To begin with, there is widespread agreement that Hos 1:1 reflects postmonarchic Judahite readership (see Hos 1:1 STRUCTURE). The same holds true for Hos 14:10. Both serve as the main interpretative keys for the book, and as such they are certainly an integral part of it.

As it will be demonstrated in this commentary, Exile is a central and pervading motif in the book of Hosea. Of course, claims that numerous passages in the book of Hosea refer to the return from Exile such as those advanced in this commentary are not new. There is a long history of early interpretation that understands them as pointing to such a return or to the conditions during and after such a return (e.g., see Abrabanel on Hos 2:18-22; 2:23-25). The argument here, however, is not only that they point at and elaborate on these matters, but that the fact that they do so contributes to the evaluation of the date for the composition and first readings of the book of Hosea, as it stands, in postmonarchic rather than monarchic times.

It bears particular notice that the intended and primary rereaders of the book of Hosea are often asked to imagine Exile (hereafter, exile) in terms of either a reversal of the Exodus from Egypt or as a return to the wilderness, or both. The latter is construed as a purification process (see already Hosea 2, which along with Hosea 1–3 serves to introduce the readers to the book and sets its ideological tone). Thus the future reversal that will lead Israel to its ideal situation is construed to follow the exile, and the dissolution of the monarchy. Certainly these themes are not only common, but also central to the story of Yehud about itself and appear in numerous postmonarchic texts (see Ben Zvi, "What Is New in Yehud?" and bibliography). (Concerning the motifs of "Exodus" and "wilderness" in the book of Hosea cf. and ct. the approach of this commentary with those advanced in Hoffman, "North Israelite," and Dozeman, "Hosea." See, for instance, discussions of Hosea chapters 2, 3, 8, 9, 11, 12, 13).

It is to be stressed that if the exile is to be imagined in terms that set it as both a reversal of the Exodus from Egypt and an event that sets in motion a second Exodus, as it were, it has to involve at least notionally "all Israel" or "YHWH's people." That is, it must involve an Israel that encompasses the people who lived in the northern and southern monarchical polities: those who were at the Exodus from Egypt, those who went into exile, and the readership of the book — which, if the setting proposed here is correct, consists of the literati living in Persian Yehud. Significantly, within this discourse, the return from exile and the glorious future that will ensue are ideologically associated with the reunification of Israel and Judah (i.e., "all Israel"). Further, in Hosea 3, this return is explicitly associated with a future Davidic king, and the rereaders of Hosea 1–3 most likely understood in similar terms the reference in Hos 2:2 (see discussion there).

To be sure, it is possible to maintain that the Davidic king was Josiah and that the text is a kind of political propaganda for his attempt to annex the territory of the former kingdom of Israel. However, there is no evidence that Josiah annexed such a territory; to the contrary, it is clear that he did not (see Na'aman, "Kingdom"). The fallback position that he planned to do so, but never did, is unverifiable, and one cannot support it by assigning to his days texts that seem to support the unification of north and south under a Davide without engaging in circular thinking (I discussed at length elsewhere the Josiah of the prophetic books and scholarly proposals to associate several prophetic texts with the Josianic period. See Ben Zvi, "Josiah and the Prophetic Books: Some Observations.")

In addition, one may notice that, for instance, the rereadership of Hosea 1–3 was asked to imagine a future in which YHWH will make "a covenant for them with the wild animals, with the birds of the air and the creeping things of the ground," and will "break the bow and the sword and war from the land," and will "make them lie down in safety" (see Hos 2:20). Further, they were asked to imagine the ideal future associated with the return of the monarchy, and the reunification of Israel as standing in the faraway future (see 3:3-5). Are these rhetorical and ideological requests best explained in terms of propaganda for a supposedly planned campaign of conquest by Josiah aimed at his own contemporaries?

The combination of themes of the returning of the exile, of the future reunification of Israel and Judah, of the rule of a highly elevated Davide — one may say a quasi-messianic Davide (see 3:5 and cf. Isaiah 11 — and notice the expression in 11:10; cf. Mal 3:1) — of a future, eternal, and peaceful covenant, and of Israel's being YHWH's people that appear in Hosea 2 clearly resonate with Ezek 34:24-28; 37:15-28; and Isaiah 11; and partially with Jer 50:4 (notice also the motif of seeking YHWH and cf. Hos 3:5) or, despite some tension concerning the question of the leader, Obadiah (esp. vv. 14-18). All these texts are most likely postmonarchic, and the same holds true for other prophetic texts in which the themes of the gathering of the exiles (e.g., Mic 2:12-13; 7:12) and salvation after exile (e.g., Mic 4:10; 7:11-13) appear. Finally one may mention that the exile of Judah is referred to in Hos 2:2.

There is also a reference to the House of YHWH, which in any case — be it in the Josianic or postmonarchic period — was understood by the readers of the book as pointing to the temple in Jerusalem. Significantly, in both occasions (8:1; 9:4), the text plays with the meanings of Israel, and shifts from the northern kingdom to that of the southern, to that of trans-temporal Israel. In one case, danger to the temple of Jerusalem is envisaged; in the other (9:4), the cessation of offerings is referred to. (On 8:1 and 9:4 see respective READINGS.)

To be sure, it is possible to advance hypothetical redactional proposals to explain the composition of the present text, but, in any event, even if for the sake of the case one were to grant them a high probability of being correct, they are irrelevant for the purpose of the present study since the readers of the book were not asked to read the text according to these proposals. The present text of the book of Hosea as read by its intended and primary rereaderships is the object of this study.

The same holds true for the implications of several studies about the language of the book of Hosea. It is obvious that the speaking characters — both divine and human — express themselves in a manner that is somewhat different from that in other prophetic books, including the book of Amos, in which the speakers are constructed as addressing a northern Israelite readership, and the books of Micah and Isaiah, whose superscriptions set the world of their books in a period more or less overlapping that in which the book of Hosea is set. To be sure, this atypicality contributes to the characterization of the implied author of the book, and of the book itself. It bears note in this regard that, as observed before, the books of Hosea and Job are among the most atypical from the perspective of language (e.g., Rabin, "Language"). (In ancient Israel, YHWH's voice was construed as carrying the linguistic style of different implied authors and books.) But can this atypicality contribute to the dating of the present book of Hosea?

It has been proposed that the strangeness of the Hebrew in Hosea is due to the fact that forms common in Israelian Hebrew are embedded in the text. This might be the case to some extent. One may notice, however, that some of the most obvious markers of the northern dialect (e.g., שׁ instead of אשׁר — though on this matter see also Young, "Northernisms" — or שׁת for "year") are not present, and above all that most of the scholars who maintain this position assume also that the Israelian Hebrew of Hosea underwent some changes during the editing of the book in Judah (Yoo, *Israelian Hebrew,* 178-79). Most importantly, even if one were to grant the argument advanced by these scholars, this would not make the *book of Hosea* as a whole and in its present form a northern Israelite document, nor would it provide grounds to date it to the monarchic period. To illustrate, one of the recent proponents of the presence of Israelian Hebrew in Hosea maintains that almost half of the verses in Hosea contain some IH feature (Yoo, *Israelian Hebrew*, 177-78), but it is worth stressing that the same scholar explicitly maintains "the book of Hosea was shaped by . . . Judaean editors or scribes" (Yoo, *Israelian Hebrew*, 179).

A few examples should clarify the point advanced here. The features referred to by Yoo include, to mention the first three: (a) the use of דבר ב meaning "speak to" in Hos 1:2; (b) ממלכת meaning "kingdom, reign" in Hos 1:4, and (c) אל חי meaning "the living god" in 2:1. Concerning (a), Yoo (op. cit, 36-38) brings the comparable case of 2 Sam 23:2, but even if the text there includes some IH as advanced by Rendsburg, it does not follow from that observation that "the last words of David," and more fitting to the present study, the book of Samuel, were written in northern Israel (nor does Yoo suggest that such is the case). Concerning (b) Yoo cites Josh 13:12; 1 Sam 15:28; and Jer 26:1. Since the first reference concerns the kingdom of Og, he suggests that use of the word ממלכת there reflects "native usage." The second is placed in the mouth of Samuel, an Ephraimite, and the third appears in a text that reflects the Benjamite border dialect (Yoo, op. cit, 38-40). Needless to say, the books of Joshua, Samuel, and Jeremiah were not written in the northern kingdom, nor likely in the monarchic period. As for the example (c), Yoo refers to Josh 3:10; Amos 8:14; Ps 42:3; 84:3. Significantly, he states that explicitly Josh 3:10 seems to be a Judahite text, but this phrase occurs in words spoken by Joshua, an Ephraimite (op. cit., 41). Yoo's observations, and similar observations advanced by other scholars, including the presence of a significant number of Aramaisms (following Yoo, Greenfield, and Driver, and in contrast to Morag and Macintosh; for a review of the debate, see Yoo, op. cit., 180-81; also cf. "as is well known Hosea is replete with linguistic usages that find their congeners in either Phoenician or Aramaic," Greenfield, "Aramaic hnṣl," 117), are important for understanding characterization in biblical books in general, and the way in which the readers of the book of Hosea were required to imagine the speakers in the authoritative voices in the text — both YHWH and the prophetic character speak in a similar "odd" Hebrew. To be sure, from the perspective of the intended readers of the book, the high density of "odd" Hebrew features within a book whose language on the whole is similar to that of other prophetic books (cf. Rabin, "Language"; Young, "Northernisms," 67-68) certainly impacted their characterization of the mentioned personages. It is even likely that they were supposed to understand these odd linguistic forms as pointing to Israelian Hebrew. In addition, these observations might be helpful for the purpose of detecting the presence of embedded sources, for redactional critical purposes. Yet, they cannot serve to date the book of Hosea.

In addition, one may mention that an examination of the wording of the book may lead also to comparisons with postmonarchic texts as well. To illustrate, a poetic string (see 2:21-22) is based on the associations between צדק "righteousness" and משפט "justice," and חסד "hesed" and משפט (e.g., Hos 12:7; Mic 6:8; Zech 7:9; for the previous three see Ps 33:5; 89:15), חסד and

רחמים "mercy" (e.g., Isa 63:7; Jer 16:5; Zech 7:9; Ps 25:6; 40:12; 51:3; 69:17; 103:4; Dan 1:9), חסד and אמונה "faithfulness" (e.g., Ps 36:6; 88:12; 89:3, 25; 98:3), אמונה and משפט (e.g., Deut 32:4; Jer 5:1; Ps 119:30, 75), צדק and אמונה (e.g., Ps 96:13; 119:75, 138; Prov 12:17), and משפט and רחמים (Ps 119:156). The expression את ה׳ אלהיהם ואת דוד מלכם "YHWH their God and David their king" appears in Hos 3:5 and in Jer 30:9, a text usually associated with postmonarchic times. See also the masc. form of the qal infinitive construct of the root אהב in 9:10 and elsewhere in the HB only in Qoh 3:8, and, in the same chapter, the occurrence of קמוש "nettles" in 9:6 (elsewhere only in Isa 34:13 and Prov 24:31). These examples may be multiplied. (Illustrative references to these matters are included in the discussion of particular READINGS.)

The presence of the so-called "deuteronomist" ideas in the book of Hosea, such as the rejection of the worship of Baal and other gods, also cannot be used to date the text to the Josianic period. These ideas were integral to the discourse of postmonarchic Yehud as well as that of late monarchic Judah, *if* the Josianic reform as described in the book of Kings actually occurred, which is in itself a highly debatable and debated matter. In any event, their presence certainly does not necessitate a Josianic date for the composition of the present form of the book (cf. the book of Chronicles, which shares many of these ideas). Similarly, one may add that many of the characteristic features of the horizon of thought implied and reflected in READINGS within the book of Hosea clearly occur in postmonarchic texts (e.g., Jer 31:31-34 and see Hos 2:3-25 Setting; and see many of the discussions under Setting).

As with other prophetic books (e.g., the book of Micah or Zephaniah) the monarchic setting of the world of the book communicates to the postmonarchic readership that some of the events foreseen by the speaker or speakers in the text have come to pass. Since the events already fulfilled point to judgment and destruction, and those yet to be fulfilled to salvation for Israel, the pattern of partial fulfillment serves to enhance the authority and validity of the text, and accordingly, its ability to provide hope to Israel in general, and surely to the direct readership of the book.

The monarchic setting of the book shaped and to some extent reflected an already existing image of the past among the readership of the book, more precisely an image of the days of the kings Uzziah, Jotham, Ahaz, and Hezekiah of Judah, and those of King Jeroboam son of Joash of Israel (see Hosea 1:1). To be sure, this image of the past interacted with other images of the same past that existed in the community of readers. These images reflect that which the target readership of the present book of Hosea, a readership that lived many years (and in fact, centuries) apart from the time in which the world of the book is set and under substantially different conditions than those described in the world of the text, was told or could have learned about that period of time from their reading and rereading of the book. Such constructions of the past had to be consistent with some core "facts" about the past that were agreed among the literati of the time (e.g., the sequence of kings of Judah), but they cannot be taken as a reliable source for an understanding of the history of monarchic Judah, from Uzziah to Hezekiah, nor of that of the northern kingdom in the days of Jeroboam. To begin with, to be coherent with a few core facts about the past agreed upon by a group of literati that lived centuries apart is not necessarily a guarantee for the historical referentiality of their text.

Further, there is a question of genre. These are literary and theological texts, not historical compositions in our present understanding of the term. They are not and do not present themselves as true snapshots of any social reality, but represent that which their authors wanted, or at best allowed, their readers to think of these circumstances (cf. Carroll, "Prophecy," 206-08). It is worth stressing also that the book of Hosea itself does not show much interest in historical, particular events, nor does it attempt to convey a strong sense of mimesis. Rather than asking the readers to historize its READINGS, the book is written so as to read them against their *Sitz im Buch,* and against more general circumstances. (On these matters, cf. Davies, "Audiences," 51; Ben Zvi, *Micah,* 10-11.)

For the study of the Settings of the different READINGS, both in terms of the world of the book and that of the intended readership, see the particular discussions under Setting in this commentary.

Intention

Prophetic books were used to educate or, better, socialize the communities that accepted them as authoritative texts. They encouraged particular sets of theological outlooks, norms, constructions of the past, and discouraged others. As it is the case in all prophetic books, the most general primary intention of the book as it stands is to instruct the intended community of readers. Through their reading and rereading of the book of Hosea, these readers are supposed to learn about YHWH and YHWH's attributes as well as YHWH's relationship to Israel. The book explains YHWH's punishment of Israel in the past and above all communicates hope by pointing to an ideal future. See the particular discussions of Intention in this commentary.

One should take into account not only that which the text said, but also that which the reading, rereading, and reading to others of these books did. For instance, these activities served to shape, among others, a shared past, a shared explanation of this past, a shared future, a shared hope, a shared space within which the literati could let their imagination play, and a shared set of authoritative texts. The reading and rereading of these texts socializes a group as such, and creates ideological boundaries among Israel and the other groups who do not have similar texts, and sociological boundaries among the literati who actually read, reread, and meditated upon these texts. Further, within a worldview in which YHWH's word is a written text, such as the book of Hosea, only the literati can have *direct* access to YHWH's word, and by implication to YHWH's mind. They become, therefore, within their own discourse and through the reading and rereading of these books, brokers of divine knowledge and indispensable mediators between YHWH, the provider of knowledge, and Israel, who needs that knowledge to maintain its ways and to fulfill its obligations to YHWH (see Ben Zvi, *Micah,* 11).

Finally, it is worth stressing that within a commentary of the (present) book of Hosea, the term Intention does not address the putative intentions of a historical prophet who is hypothetically constructed by assigning him certain sections of the book and disassociating him from others, nor the intentions of a flesh-and-blood author of the book. First, it is unlikely that there was ever one single author who wrote the book out of whole cloth. Second, the matter of whether a particular message was conveyed knowingly or unknowingly is irrelevant to any historical study, aside from a biographical note on the author. The stress here is on those which the intended and primary rereadership of the book could have considered as possible messages encountered or developed through the reading, rereading, reading to others, and studying of the book of Hosea. To be sure, such messages involve and necessitate a shared intellectual setting or outlook between the primary readerships and their construction of the implied author of the book. This intellectual setting is, as mentioned above, imagined as shared by the readership, that is, the literati of the time, and such an author. Thus, the latter is construed as similar to the *general self-image* of the literati of the time; among them one has to find those individuals responsible for the composition of the present book and its intended and primary rereaders. At another level, this general *Weltanschauung* is also conceived as shared between the readership and any godly voice, and mainly YHWH's. One of the main intentions of the text of Hosea, and other prophetic books, is to socialize through continuous rereading the literati themselves and their society in a way that internalizes the claim that the literati's *Weltanschauung* is authoritative, because it is YHWH's. Each prophetic book and each READING within the book of Hosea bring to the forefront particular aspects of this generalized intellectual and theological (or ideological) outlook as the text is read again and again, against different circumstances. See particular discussions under Setting and Intention.

Bibliography

R. Albertz, "Exile as Purification. Reconstructing the 'Book of Four,'" P. L. Redditt and A. Schart (eds.), *Thematic Threads in the Book of the Twelve* (BZAW 325; Berlin: de Gruyter, 2003) 232-51; L. J. Braaten, "God Sows: Hosea's Land Theme in the Book of the Twelve," P. L. Redditt and A. Schart (eds.), *Thematic Threads in the Book of the Twelve* (BZAW 325; Berlin: de Gruyter, 2003) 104-32; R. P. Carroll, "Prophecy and Society," R. E. Clements (ed.), *The World of Ancient Israel* (Cambridge: Cambridge Univ. Press, 1991) 203-25; R. E. Clements, "Understanding the Book of Hosea," *RevExp* 72 (1975) 405-23; P. R. Davies, "The Audiences of Prophetic Scrolls: Some Suggestions," S. B. Reid (ed.), *Prophets and Paradigms. Essays in Honor of Gene M. Tucker* (JSOTSupS 229; Sheffield: JSOT Press, 1996) 48-62; T. B. Dozeman, "Hosea and the Wilderness Tradition," S. L. McKenzie and T. Römer (eds.; in collaboration with H. H. Schmid), *Rethinking the Foundations: Historiography in the Ancient World and in the Bible: Essays in Honour of John Van Seters* (BZAW 294; Berlin/New York: de Gruyter, 2000) 55-70; J. C. Greenfield, "Aramaic hnṣl and Some Biblical Passages," I. Seybold (ed.), *Meqor Hajjim. Festschrift Georg Molin zu seinem 75. Geburtstag* (Graz, Austria: Akademische Druck- u. Verlagsanstalt, 1983) 115-19; Y. Hoffman, "A North Israelite Typological Myth and a Judaean Historical Tradition: The Exodus in Hosea and Amos," *VT* 39 (1989) 169-82; J. Jeremias, "The Interrelationship Between Amos and Hosea," P. House and J. W. Watts (eds.), *Forming Prophetic Literature: Essays on Isaiah and the Twelve in Honor of John D. W. Watts* (JSOTSupS 235; Sheffield: JSOT Press, 1996) 171-86; idem, "Die Anfänge des Dodekapropheton: Hosea und Amos," J. A. Emerton (ed.), *Congress Volume Paris 1992* (VTSup 61; Leiden: E. J. Brill, 1995); D. C. Kraemer, "The Intended Reader as a Key to Interpreting the Bavli," *Prooftexts* 13 (1993) 125-40; S. Morag, "On Semantic and Lexical Features in the Language of Hosea," *Tarbiz* 53 (1984) 489-511 (in Hebrew); N. Na'aman, "The Kingdom of Judah under Josiah," *TA* 18 (1991) 3-71; C. Rabin, "The Language of Hosea and Amos," B. Z. Luria (ed.), *Studies on the Book of the Twelve* (Jerusalem: Kiriat Sepher, 1981) 117-36; P. L. Redditt and A. Schart (eds.), *Thematic Threads in the Book of the Twelve* (BZAW 325; Berlin: de Gruyter, 2003); J. Vermeylen, "Osée et les prophètes du VIIIe siècle," R. G. Kratz, T. Krüger and K. Schmid (eds.), *Schriftauslegung in der Schrift. FS für Odil Hannes Steck zu seinem 65. Geburstag* (BZAW 300; Berlin/New York: de Gruyter, 2000) 193-206; I. Young, "The "Northernisms" of the Israelite Narratives in Kings," *ZAH* 8 (1995) 63-70.

Every work of a scholar is interwoven with some of her or his previous other works. I, for one, have been working on questions related to the production and reading and rereading of prophetic texts in ancient communities for a while. So, at times, this commentary on Hosea deals with matters that I have discussed elsewhere at some length or with matters that directly relate to issues discussed in these works. This commentary certainly follows the basic methodological premises that guided my commentary on Micah in this series and reaches some similar conclusions, as any reader of this introductory chapter could have easily noticed. Such a similarity between the two books, in their present form, is to be expected since there are no substantial differences in their respective intended and primary readerships. Both were prophetic books written to be read by the same type of highly literate, postmonarchic readership. The following works of mine are at one point or another referred to in this commentary. They are gathered here because they too are *not* included in the bibliographic lists attached to each of the following sections in this commentary.

Ehud Ben Zvi, "'The Prophets' — Generic Prophets and Their Role in the Construction of the Image of the 'Prophets of Old' within the Postmonarchic Readership of the Book of Kings," *ZAW* 16 (2004) 555-67; "Josiah and the Prophetic Books: Some Observations," L. L. Grabbe (ed.), *Good Kings and Bad Kings: The Kingdom of Judah in the Seventh Century in History and Tradition* (LHBOTS; European Seminar in Historical Methodology, 5; London: T&T Clark International, 2005) 47-645; "Observations on the Marital Metaphor of YHWH and Israel in Its Ancient Israelite Context: General Considerations and Particular Images in Hosea 1.2," *JSOT* 28 (2004) 363-84; "Analogical Thinking and Ancient Israelite Intellectual History: The Case for an 'Entropy Model' in the Study of Israelite Thought," T. J. Sandoval and C. Mandolfo (eds.), *Relating to the Text. Interdisciplinary and Form-Critical Insights on the Bible* (JSOTSupS 384; London: T&T Clark International, 2003) 321-32; "The Secession of the Northern Kingdom in Chronicles: Accepted 'Facts' and New Meanings," M. P. Graham, S. L. McKenzie and G. N. Knoppers (eds.), *The Chronicles as a Theologian: Essays in Honor of Ralph W. Klein* (JSOTSupS 371; London: T&T Clark International, 2003) 61-88; *Signs of Jonah: Reading and Rereading in Ancient Yehud* (JSOTSupS 367; Sheffield: Sheffield Academic Press/Continuum, 2003); "The Prophetic Book: A Key Form of Prophetic Literature," M. A. Sweeney and E. Ben Zvi (eds.), *The Changing Face of Form Criticism for the Twenty-First Century* (Grand Rapids, MI: Eerdmans, 2003) 276-97; "Malleability and Its Limits: Sennacherib's Campaign Against Judah as a Case Study," L. L. Grabbe (ed.), *'Bird in a Cage': The Invasion of Sennacherib in 701 BCE* (JSOTSupS 363; European Seminar in Historical Methodology 4; Sheffield: Sheffield Academic Press/Continuum, 2003) 73-105; "What Is New in Yehud? Some Considerations," R. Albertz and B. Becking (eds.), *Yahwism after the Exile* (STAR 5; Assen: Van Gorcum, 2003) 32-48; "Shifting the Gaze: Historiographic Constraints in Chronicles and Their Implications," M. Patrick Graham and J. Andrew Dearman (eds.), *The Land That I Will Show You: Essays on the History and Archaeology of the Ancient Near East in Honor of J. Maxwell Miller* (JSOTSupS 343; Sheffield: JSOT Press, 2001) 38-60; "Introduction: Writings, Speeches, and the Prophetic Books — Setting an Agenda," E. Ben Zvi and M. H. Floyd (eds.), *Writings and Speech in Israelite and Ancient Near Eastern Prophecy* (Symposium 10; Atlanta: Society of Biblical Literature, 2000) 1-29; *Micah* (FOTL XXIB; Grand Rapids, MI and Cambridge, UK: Eerdmans, 2000); "About Time: Observations About the Construction of Time in the Book of Chronicles," *HBT* 22 (2000) 17-31; "A Deuteronomistic Redaction in/among 'The Twelve'? A Contribution from the Standpoint of the Books of Micah, Zephaniah and Obadiah," L. S. Schearing and S. L. McKenzie (eds.), *Those Elusive Deuteronomists* (JSOTSupS 268; Sheffield Academic Press: Sheffield, 1999) 232-61; "The Urban Center of Jerusalem and the Development of the Literature of the Hebrew Bible," W. G. Aufrecht, N. A. Mirau and S. W. Gauley (eds.), *Aspects of Urbanism in Antiquity* (JSOTSupS 244; Sheffield: Sheffield Academic Press, 1997) 194-209; *A Historical-Critical Study of the Book of Obadiah* (BZAW 242; Berlin/New York: de Gruyter, 1996); "Studying Prophetic Texts Against Their Original Backgrounds: Pre-ordained Scripts and Alternative Horizons of Research," S. R. Reid (ed.), *Prophets and Paradigms. Essays in Honor of Gene M. Tucker* (JSOTSupS 229; Sheffield: JSOT Press, 1996) 125-35; "Twelve Prophetic Books or 'The Twelve': A Few Preliminary Considerations," P. House and J. W. Watts (eds.), *Forming Prophetic Literature: Essays on Isaiah and the Twelve in Honor of John D. W. Watts* (JSOTSupS 235; Sheffield: JSOT Press, 1996) 125-156; "Inclusion in and Exclusion from Israel as Conveyed by the Use of the Term 'Israel' in Postmonarchic Biblical Texts," S. W. Holloway and L. K. Handy (eds.), *The Pitcher Is Broken: Memorial Essays for Gösta W. Ahlström* (JSOTSupS 190; Sheffield: JSOT Press, 1995) 95-149; "A Sense of Proportion: An Aspect of the Theology of the Chronicler," *SJOT* 9 (1995) 37-51; "Prophets and Prophecy in the Compositional and Redactional Notes in I-II Kings," *ZAW* 105 (1993) 331-51; "Understanding the Message of the Tripartite Prophetic Books," *ResQ* 35 (1993) 93-100; "History and Prophetic Texts," M. P. Graham, J. Kuan, and W. P. Brown (eds.), *History and Interpretation: Essays in Honor of John H. Hayes* (JSOTSupS 173; Sheffield: JSOT Press, 1993) 106-20; "Isaiah 1,4-9, Isaiah, and the Events of 701 BCE in Judah. A Question of Premise and Evidence," *SJOT* 5 (1991) 95-111; *A Historical-Critical Study of The Book of Zephaniah* (BZAW 198; Berlin/New York: de Gruyter, 1991).

Chapter 2

The Individual Units

Superscription, 1:1

Structure

I. Main Characterization of the Book (Genre Identification)	1aα
II. Particular Characterization of the Book (Individualization)	1aβ-1bβ
A. Relative clause identifying the prophetic book by its association with Hosea, the son of Beeri	1aβ
B. Relative clause pointing to the temporal setting of the world of the book	1b
1. In terms of the reigns of the kings of Judah	1bα
2. In terms of the reigns of the kings of Israel	1bβ

The opening of the book fulfills a most important function. It tells its readers about the genre of the book, provides a title, and, above all, introduces them to the book they are about to read. It serves to create a set of expectations, but also a set of assumptions, that are supposed to govern the readers' approach to the text (see Genre). To be sure, theoretically, the readers could have rejected all these guidelines and questioned the reliability of the opening. But whereas this approach may be consonant with the worldview, and the socially accepted norms of some contemporary readerships, it is extremely unlikely that such was the case for the ancient readership for which it was intended and the historical, primary readership that read, reread, and accepted this book as authoritative. Had they thought, for instance, that the book is not "YHWH's word," they would not have read, meditated on, passed from generation to generation, and included it among their corpus of authoritative, prophetic books.

The book opens with the expression "YHWH's word." This is a textually inscribed, unequivocal semantic marker that provides the readers of the book with a most significant interpretative key: They are asked to read the ensuing text (i.e., the book of Hosea) in a way that is governed by a characterization of the book as nothing less than YHWH's word. The expression thus provides the readers with a genre characterization (see Genre) that carries a claim to legitimacy and authority. The expression as a whole may be seen as answering the implied question of why a person should read this text, and why such a person should care about what the text says.

"YHWH's word" characterizes the book in broader terms. It certainly fails to fully identify it, since more than one prophetic book is so presented to its readers (see Joel 1:1; Mic 1:1; Zeph 1:1; and cf., for instance, with Jer 1:2). Each of these books is set apart from the others, and fully characterized by a set of relative clauses. Thus Hos 1:1 claims that the following text is a particular instance of YHWH's word, the one that (a) came to Hosea, the son of Beeri and (b) was in the days of Uzziah, Jotham, Ahaz, and Hezekiah, kings of Judah, and Jeroboam, the son of Joash, king of Israel.

The association of YHWH's word with a *particular* personage is the first and most salient way that served to set apart one prophetic book from another. All prophetic books were associated with a prophetic main character, but significantly, no prophetic book was ever associated with more than one main prophetic character, no matter how many redactional layers and authors may have been at work during the composition and redaction of the book (cf. Ben Zvi, "Twelve").

This being the case, the combination of the main clause ("YHWH's word") and the first relative clause ("that came to Hosea, the son of Beeri") may have functioned for generations as a code-expression (signifier) pointing to the book of Hosea (the signified of the signifier). Against this background it seems clear that "YHWH's word that came to Hosea the son of Beeri" was considered the title of the book. The interpretation of this expression as the title of the book rests on (a) the fact that the information included in "YHWH's word that came to Hosea, the son of Beeri" is enough to characterize this book within the biblical repertoire, but also (b) the tendency to refer to a text by its first words, which is found in Mesopotamian literature (and later on, in Jewish, biblical literature). Significantly, such a tendency is already suggested by the way in which particular speeches (or types of speeches) are referred to in 1 Kgs 22:28//2 Chr 18:27; Jer 7:4; 23:38; Ezek 22:28.

Moreover, it is unlikely that it is by accident that the full (and precise) expression rendered in English by "YHWH's word that came to X" (X = the prophet) occurs *only* in four related texts in the HB, namely in Hos 1:1; Joel 1:1; Mic 1:1; and Zeph 1:1. The fact that the occurrence of this seemingly natural expression in biblical Hebrew is restricted to the first words of these four prophetic books strongly suggests that its presence there is dependent on conventions and expectations associated with that literary context. It is reasonable to assume that for the intended audience of these books (and their actual first readers) the aforementioned combination of the main and first relative clauses functioned as a clear marker about the character of the book that provided them with the most significant interpretive key as they began reading the book, and at the same time as a "title" to refer to the book in settings other than its reading or rereading.

Certainly, Hos 1:1 does not claim that Hosea himself wrote the book. Rather it claims that the book is associated with Hosea, the son of Beeri; that is, that this personage is its central prophetic character. The name Hosea is from the root ישע ("salvation"), and could have served as a signpost for the readers and rereaders of the book concerning two main themes in the book. First, Israel's eventual "salvation" whose magnitude is rhetorically augmented by the plethora of reported announcements of judgment within which the hope for and certainty of an ideal future of reconciliation between the LORD and Israel are communicated to the readership. It is worth mentioning that even today portions of Hosea are used in Jewish liturgy because of this element of hope against a background of apparent hopelessness. Second, it points at the theme about the existence of only one true savior, namely YHWH. Kings and mighty nations are explicitly presented as false and misleading "saviors" who lead only to disaster. See the use of verbal forms of this root in Hos 1:7; 13:4 on the one hand, and Hos 13:10; 14:4 on the other (see commentary there).

Whether by accident or design, the later collection of "the Former Prophets" begins with the book of Joshua, that of the "Latter Prophets" with Isaiah, and the collection of the twelve prophetic books with Hosea; all the relevant names are from the root ישע (cf. Abma, "H-Hour").

Although there are other Hoseas in the HB, including Joshua the son of Nun (see Num 13:8; Num 13:16; 2 Kgs 15:30; 17:1, 3, 4, 6; 18:1, 9, 10; 1 Chr 27:20; Neh 10:24), none of them is the son of Beeri. There have been attempts to associate the Hosea of the book with Hosea, the son of Elah, the last king of Israel (see, for instance, Itzhaqi, quoted in Ibn Ezra's commentary), but such a reading would require considering Beeri as something other than the name of Hosea's father. The latter is extremely unlikely. X son of Y is the most typical biblical Hebrew expression to characterize a man by his own name and by the name of his father. In sharp contrast, the expression "son of X" is unlikely to mean "inhabitant of X" or "originally from X," which is the only possible alternative to Beeri as the name of Hosea's father. (In addition, although it is theoretically possible that there was a place called "Beeri," no such place is attested in the HB, but Beeri is attested as a personal name elsewhere; see Gen 26:34 and Elephantine Papyri, Cowley 53, l. 3). Of course, we know nothing about Beeri except that he was the father of Hosea, so a reference to him adds neither information nor constraints to any image that the intended readership of the book could have developed of Hosea. (There is no reason to assume that within this readership Beeri was identified as a prophet, or an influential figure, or with Beerah, בְּאֵרָה, the chief of the Reubenites who according to 1 Chr 5:6 was exiled by Tiglath-Pileser. All these identifications have a place in the history of readings of the text but are not relevant to the study of the likely understanding of the book of Hosea within the community of literati within and for which it was composed.)

From the name of the prophetic character the ancient readership learned that the prophetic character was a male. Significantly, this datum did not constrain the ancient literati's reading beyond the already agreed borders of their discourse. In fact, all the personages with whom prophetic books were associated were male, despite the fact there were female prophets in Israel (see 2 Kgs 22:14; 2 Chr 34:22; Neh 6:14). The literati also learned that Hosea was the son of Beeri. On the surface, this datum may seem to limit to some degree the possible ways in which the readers constructed the prophetic figure, and, to be sure, Hosea could have been identified only by his name, without any reference to that of his father (cf. Obad 1; Amos 1:1; Mic 1:1; Nah 1:1; Hab 1:1). But, first, nothing is known about Beeri, and, second and more important, had the character been identified only as Hosea, the readers could have pondered whether this character might be identified with the other well-known Hosea, the last king of Israel (cf. the case of Obadiah; Jonah; and notice that despite the unequivocal identification of the man as a son of Beeri, some later readers still pondered whether he was the son of Elah). In other words, the reference to Beeri serves to free the construction of the figure of Hosea from any possibility of attachment to that of the king — on the mention of the father's name to avoid another potential ambiguity in characterization, see also below — but not to bring any information that may narrow their ability to imagine Hosea, after all; nothing is mentioned or known about Beeri.

The ancient readers were also not told of Hosea's place of origin (ct. Jer 1:1; Amos 1:1; Mic 1:1; Nah 1:1) nor where any of the divine communications reported in the book took place. It is likely that they imagined him as a person from northern Israel, but not necessarily because of the predominance of references to northern Israel, since even a strong prevalence of prophecies against/ about the North does not necessarily require the intended and primary readers of prophetic books (i.e., those later called "latter prophets") to imagine the prophet as a northern Israelite (cf. Amos). More important is the occurrence of unusual language, along with typical, common linguistic markers that communicated to the readership a sense of slight foreignness to the book and its main human character (cf. Job, and contrast with Amos). It is likely that the intended and primary readers were to understand the oddity of language as pointing to a northern background (on the language of the book see Introduction, Setting). It is worth stressing that if the intended and primary readership imagined him as a northern Israelite, which is most likely, then such an identification conveyed an important meaning, as it pointed at a truthful, northern Israelite prophet who lived in a different polity but shared and expressed (and probably "must have shared and expressed") the basic ideological viewpoints of the later Judahites, or better, Yehudites, among whom one is to find the authorship and intended readership of the present book. Just like them, the prophet is described as thinking that only the Jerusalemite-centered Davidic dynasty and its polity are legitimate for Israel in the sight of YHWH. Similarly, the prophet is also described as holding an unequivocal vision of a renewed unified kingdom ruled by a Davide (see Hosea 1–3, Hos 1:2–2:3; Hos 3:1-5, STRUCTURE; for an analogous case see, for instance, the characterization of Elijah in 2 Chr 21:12-15).

It is worth noting that the readers of the prophetic books were not asked to identify or consider the possible identification of any other of the main prophetic characters in the prophetic books as a northern Israelite, except Jonah — in a book that is actually metaprophetic. It cannot be overstressed that also Jonah is characterized as a northern prophet who shares the ideological viewpoint of the Judahites or, better, Yehudites, that is, the authorship and intended readership of the present book. (On Jonah see Ben Zvi, *Signs of Jonah*.) The lack of main prophetic characters in the prophetic books stands in contrast with the sit-

26

uation in other biblical genres. The books of Kings and Chronicles show no problem associating true prophets with the northern kingdom.

Even if the readers were asked to, and most likely did, imagine Hosea as northern Israelite, there are no particular grounds to assume that they had to imagine the personage as originally from Samaria. (Scholars and early traditions have advanced different claims about the historical prophet; for the position that he was from Samaria, see G. I. Davies, *Hosea,* 24, and cf. b. Hag 15a; for the position that he was from the tribe of Issachar and, to be more precise, from Belemoth in the land of Issachar, see *Life of the Prophets,* 5; some scholars have also claimed that he was a Benjaminite or even a Judahite — for a summary of some of these positions, see Rowley, *Men of God,* 74).

Further, the readers and rereaders are also not told of Hosea's profession or status (contrast with Jeremiah, Ezekiel, Amos). Contemporary scholars have tried to fill that gap. For instance, according to S. L. Cook ("Lineage Roots," 146) Hosea seems "to have descended genealogically from those who had an active clerical role" within Israel's traditional ritual system. According to Cook and Wolff, he was a Levite. See also,

> There is no reason to assume from the images of nature and animals that he employs that he was a farmer and cattle breeder (Sellin), from his knowledge of the priestly milieu (4:1ff.; 5:1ff.) that he was a priest (Duhm), or from the taunt in 9:7 that he belonged to the guild of nebiim (Eissfeldt*, Sellin-Rost*). He was, however, a member of the intelligentsia, as his knowledge of the past, his judgment upon history and the present, and his mode of expression all show (T. H. Robinson). When we also note the way wisdom has influenced his language, we may conclude that he was educated in a wisdom school, which serves primarily the training of royal officials (Fohrer, *Introduction,* 419).

Although Fohrer is correct in his refutations, he is actually constructing the implied author of the book rather than the historical prophet Hosea. (Fohrer, as most scholars of his generation, confuses the two, in part because he assigns most of the book to the historical, monarchic period prophet.) In any event, it is self-evident that none of these observations diminishes the fact that the intended readers of the book are not given information about Hosea's profession or status, in sharp contrast with the situation in the case of the intended readership of the books of Jeremiah, Ezekiel, or Amos.

In sum, Hos 1:1 leaves much to the readers and rereaders of the book in terms of the construction of their first image of the prophetic personage. Yet not everything is open; there is a clear temporal restriction to their freedom to imagine the character Hosea (cf. the book of Amos, ct. the book of Joel). He and the divine communications reported in the readings included in the book are set in a particular time of Israel's past. (Needless to state, Hos 1:1 does not claim that the book was written at that period, but rather that it is to be read as set in it.) There are two temporal clauses. According to the first, the book is set in precisely the same time in which the world of the book of Isaiah is set (see the *precise* repetition of the wording in Hos 1:1 and Isa 1:1). Although this world partially overlaps that of the book of Micah, its temporal span is explicitly longer (see Mic 1:1), and certainly much longer than the one of the book of Amos (Amos 1:1).

According to the second temporal clause, the world of the book is not only in the period of the mentioned Uzziah, Jotham, Ahaz, and Hezekiah, kings of Judah, but also in the times of Jeroboam, the son of Joash. To be sure the explicit mention of the name of the father of Jeroboam — ct. with the names of the kings of Judah that are presented without patronyms — serves to set him apart from the best-known Jeroboam within the world of knowledge of the readership and authorship of the book, namely, Jeroboam, the son of Nebat, the first king of northern Israel. The reference to Jeroboam II immediately raises an important question and provides a substantial clue about the way in which these temporal clauses were meant to be read. All historians agree that the reign of Jeroboam II was not coterminous with those of Uzziah, Jotham, Ahaz, and Hezekiah. Even a cursory reading of 2 Kings 14–18 shows that only a portion of Jeroboam II's reign was coterminous with a portion of Uzziah's reign, and that kings other than Jeroboam reigned during the period leading to the downfall of the northern kingdom, which occurred in Hezekiah's time. Historians today assign the period of Jeroboam II to the dates 790/89-750 (Na'aman), 790-50 (Galil), or 788-48 (Hayes and Hooker); and 787/86-686/5 (Na'aman), 788-698/7 (Galil) or 785-699 (Hayes and Hooker) to the Uzziah-Hezekiah period. It is extremely unlikely that the literati among whom and for whom the book was written were *un*aware that the reign of Jeroboam II was not coterminous with the period from Uzziah to Hezekiah. To assume that they did not recognize the chronological tension requires the validity of a set of unlikely premises, such as that the literati were not minimally aware of the basic narrative about Israel's past reflected in Kings, of the chronology it advances, and, needless to say, of basic facts about Israelite history. Moreover, if for the sake of argument one were to agree that this might be the case, then what purpose could have served to associate the prophetic character with the regnal periods of Uzziah, Jotham, Ahaz, Hezekiah, and Jeroboam II, and from where would such historically illiterate literati have gathered their information about the names of the kings, the kingdom in which they reigned, their temporal sequence, and even the name of the father of Jeroboam?

In sum, it was rather obvious to the ancient authorship and readerships of the book of Hosea that the mentioned periods were not coterminous. This being so, two issues come to the forefront. The first concerns the implicit assumptions shared by authorship and intended (and primary) readership about the text that governed the latter's reading. The second concerns the explicit message that the temporal clauses conveyed to the readers of the book. The simultaneous presence of two temporal clauses that are clearly not coterminous assumes the readership (and authorship) did not approach the claims of Hos 1:1 and by extension the world of the book it opens (i.e., the entire book of Hosea) with an eye to clear-cut chronology, to precise historical links to reigns and events. This position is consistent with a key element in the book: none of its reports of divine communications is dated or unequivocally associated with historical events. The intended and primary readers are allowed freedom to associate the world of the text and its reports with more than one period, within the limitations provided by the temporal clauses.

References to particular historical periods also assume that the world of knowledge of the readership and authorship included information about these periods (cf. Trotter, *Reading Hosea*, 170-73). This information contributes to the organization of the world of the past that is to be associated with the book. Insofar as it concerns (northern) Israel, the mention of Jeroboam's reign along with the explicit absence of any reference to any king later than him indicates that northern Israel within the world of the book is still a major power, that its downfall stands in the future and, accordingly, that the divine communications that the ancient readers were supposed to learn about through their reading of the book predated the fall of Jehu's dynasty, the polity's disintegration process, the confrontations with Assyria, and overall took place in a relatively calm period (cf. 2 Kgs 14:23–18:12; and 2 Kgs 10:30). Thus, according to this temporal clause, the prophetic character and YHWH's references to judgment and destruction are not construed as referring to current events in the world of the book, but to events that will actually take place in the future of that community.

As it concerns Judah, the list of Judahite kings points at a pre–late monarchic environment in contrast with, for instance, the environment in which the books of Zephaniah, Jeremiah, and Ezekiel are set. The main power in the area within the world of the two books that share the same Judahite list of kings (i.e., Isaiah and Hosea) is Assyria. Moreover, in both books Assyria is confronted by Egypt. It is worth stressing that the theme of reliance on Egypt vs. Assyria (and later, Babylon) is common in prophetic literature. Historically, however, the debacle of the northern kingdom followed its disastrous alliance with Aram, the main regional power that opposed Assyria at the time. Egypt's intervention in these events was quite marginal. But the theme of reliance on Aram vs. Assyria is found nowhere in the world of the book of Hosea. In other words, the world of the book follows and reflects more closely a common (and later) prophetic theme than the historical events of that portion of the past that serves as the general setting of the book.

The reference to the Judahite kings and the fact that they are mentioned first serve multiple purposes (see Intention). These purposes include the shaping of an ideological world in which time is construed in terms of the legitimate kings (cf. Ben Zvi, "About Time"), who, accordingly, are given textual and ideological precedence. This mention of the Judahite kings first also directly and saliently links the world of the book, and the references to Judah within it, to the Judahite worlds in which the books of Isaiah and Micah are set, and thus re-create a past populated at the same time by these prophetic characters and their messages.

In addition, as the text was read and reread, the references to these regnal periods allowed a double vision, as it were. If read with an eye to the (northern) Israelite temporal clause, the book becomes anchored in the last period of strength of the northern kingdom; but if it is read from a viewpoint that is informed by the Judahite temporal clause, it might be understood as anchored in a period in which (northern) Israel moves from a political position of strength to its demise in the days of Hezekiah. These two readings allow the readership to

29

approach the book in more than one way, and each of these ways contributes to the meaning of the book within the discourse of the literati who read, reread, meditated upon the book.

It should be noted that the detailed structure of v. 1 mentioned above is not the only one possible, or the only one that could have arisen through the process of continuous reading, rereading, meditating upon, and reading to those who could not read by themselves for which the book was composed. One can easily recognize that, for instance, this structure differs significantly from the one hinted at by the masoretic, cantillation markers. These markers show the main division of the verse after "kings of Judah." Although these markers are late, the mentioned division might have reflected some possible nuances of ancient readings of the text. For instance, the division suggests and reflects a close association of the prophetic character, and those who are supposed to identify with him, with the regnal years of the kings of Judah, and with Judah (see Intention). In addition, it suggests a reading of the verse that is in line with that of Mic 1:1. If so, the reference to Jeroboam, *king of (northern) Israel* — notice that the phrase stands at the conclusion of the verse — not only identifies the period, but also connotes a strong hint about the contents of the book — that is, that it contains readings in which divine announcements of judgment against (northern) *Israel* are reported. It is worth noting that already in the first verse of the book we face a case of possible multiple structures. A multiplicity of possible outlines is a central feature of many prophetic texts. It contributes to the ability of the community to read, reread, and continually study the prophetic book. It also allows the readership to emphasize one aspect of the book in one reading and another in a different reading. All in all, this multiplicity creates a situation in which partial readings based on particular outlines inform each other and all together communicate a meaning much richer than any one of them separately.

Whereas the references to the kings of Judah along with their salience point to an intended Judahite readership that at least potentially could have lived during either the late monarchic or postmonarchic period, the spelling of Hezekiah, יחזקיה, in 1:1 is far more congruent with a postmonarchic than a monarchic date for the superscription. Macintosh (2-3) dates the (present) superscription to "some time between the mid-sixth century BC and the mid-fourth century BC," whereas Wolff (*Hosea,* 3-4), who associates it with deuteronomistic groups, dates it to the exilic period (see already Harper, and Wellhausen). Although the language of the superscription does not require the hypothesis that a particular group in society, "the deuteronomists," wrote it (see Ben Zvi, "A Deuteronomistic Redaction in/among 'The Twelve'"), there is widespread agreement that Hos 1:1 reflects postmonarchic Judahite readership.

This being so, there is a clear tension between the postmonarchic and Judahite-centered character of Hos 1:1 and hypotheses about a monarchic date for the book or its forerunner (see Introduction to the book of Hosea), about a northern audience as the main target of the work, about a northern Israelite viewpoint (as opposed to Judahite) shaping the text, or any combination of these. Many scholars have attempted to solve this tension and maintain the validity of the mentioned hypotheses by redactional means; that is, by maintaining that the present Hos 1:1 is indeed late, but also an end-result of a redactional process, or that Hos 1:1 or its forerunners were added to a forerunner of the book of Hosea (e.g., Wellhausen, Harper, Wolff, Yee, Jeremias, Nogalski, Watts).

To be sure, to maintain the positions mentioned above requires much more than a surgical treatment of Hos 1:1. For instance, the claim that the original text was not Judahite-centered requires not only the removal of the names of the kings of Judah in 1:1, but also that the many references to Judah within the body of the book (1:7; 2:2; 4:15; 5:5, 10-14; 6:4, 11; 8:14; 10:11; 12:1, 3) be considered late additions, and that, for instance, the image of a Davidic king who will rule the North and South together and related texts be also considered a late addition (see the explicit and characteristic argument advanced here: "Thus we would say that 1,10–2,1 is not from Hosea ben Beeri. This is not because it is full of hope, but because it looks forward to the hope of an Israel and a Judah unified with one common head. This is a southern expectation. No northerner could possibly look forward to anything of this kind. The vision of a united kingdom with a Davidic king belongs to the south. All dreams of Davidic Messiah are southern dreams. Similarly the last phrases of 3,5 are from a later writer, because they look forward to a Davidic king. No northerner in his senses would write or say a thing like that. . . . We think that the whole of chapter 3 is late and not from Hosea"; Snaith, *Mercy and Sacrifice,* 50). Similarly other widely agreed postmonarchic texts (e.g., Hos 14:10) are often removed to allow for the positions mentioned above.

Although it is possible that the superscription had a redactional history and that it was added later to an already existing, but unrecoverable forerunner of the book of Hosea or to one of its written sources, one has to keep in mind that such proposals do not arise in response to any intrinsic difficulties in Hos 1:1, but to particular assumptions about the monarchic date or Northern origin of Hosea. In other words, these proposals are not made necessary by the text, but by the assumptions already held by those who advance them. The same holds true for scholars who link their proposals for the redactional history of the superscription to their hypothetical reconstruction of the redactional history of the "Book of the Twelve" (e.g., Nogalski, Watts): a "book" whose very existence in antiquity is in any case very doubtful (see Ben Zvi, "Twelve Prophetic Books or 'The Twelve'"). For an early critical perspective according to which "the title as it stands is about what might be expected if the late author of the book wished to date his work back in the earlier time," see Day, "Is the Book of Hosea Exilic?" (quotation p. 110).

As it stands, the type of superscription present in Hos 1.1 not only appears in other prophetic books, and in some cases in a very similar way, but also serves as one of the usual ways to indicate the genre of these books, namely, "prophetic books." Its occurrence at the beginning of the book of Hosea is fully consistent with the genre requirements of the prophetic books. Moreover, there is nothing in the book of Hosea — in its present form — that required or even asked its intended or primary rereaders to approach the superscription as a secondary addition. In fact, the opposite is true: They are requested to approach the superscription/title as a major interpretative key for their reading of the book, namely, as an introduction to the book that provides not only information about the book they are about to read, but also a crucial signpost for successive rereadings (see Genre). Needless to say, the ancient readers and rereaders of the book were also asked to understand the superscription as a superscription to Hos 1:2–14:10, and not to any particular section of the book (e.g., Hosea 1–3) (see Genre).

Genre

Hos 1:1, as is the case with similar units in other prophetic books, introduces the book to its readers. It conveys to them a clear message about the genre of the book (namely, "YHWH's word," likely connoting the meaning of YHWH's instruction) and its authority. In addition it particularizes the book in relation to similar instances of "YHWH's word," that is, "prophetic books," by associating it with the figure of Hosea, the son of Beeri. It also informs the readers about the world in which the book is set and against which they were supposed to read and reread it. In addition, it communicates some hints about its contents. All these elements together provide a frame of reference, a scheme that not only allows but also strongly informs the subsequent reading of the text. In sum, from a "functional" vantage point, Hos 1:1 is to be considered an INTRODUCTION.

It is customary to refer to Hos 1:1 and similar written introductions as SU-PERSCRIPTION. Such a characterization is correct if one keeps in mind that Hos 1:1 and similar passages should not be considered the superscription to the book, but to the *main body* of the book (in this case, Hos 1:2–14:10; see STRUC-TURE). Hos 1:1 and similar SUPERSCRIPTIONS are an integral — and a most significant — part of their respective books as a whole. In fact, they provided the rereaders with authoritative, interpretative keys that, to a large extent, governed the set of potential interpretations that the texts were allowed to carry. Not only do they not stand apart from the book (a position that is implied in the distinction between superscript and script), but it is also misleading to characterize them in such a way. In fact, they characterize and look at the book as a whole, and as such they contribute substantially to the cohesiveness of the book, and to its separate status vis-à-vis all other works within the repertoire of the community/ies of readers and rereaders (cf. Ben Zvi, "Twelve Prophetic Books").

Setting

The social setting of the actual writing, reading, and rereading of this integral unit of the book is that of the actual writing, reading, and rereading of the entire book, namely, it involves a social group or groups that are characterized by high literacy, by an interest in prophetic literature, in its authority, and in the (claimed to be divine) theological and ideological message that this literature conveyed. These groups imply also a social organization in which resources were allocated to develop and maintain bearers of high literacy. It stands to reason that such groups (or group) comprised a very small portion of the total population (see Ben Zvi, "Introduction: Writings, Speeches, and the Prophetic Books —Setting an Agenda," and bibliography mentioned there).

The authorial voice responsible for the introduction also reflects this milieu. It evokes and reflects a scribal milieu, one in which people refer to and classify written works by titles that carry, among other things, genre information (cf. Tucker, "Prophetic Superscriptions" and cf. "Instruction of the Mayor of the City, the Vizier Ptahhotep"). Significantly, the authorial voice, the intended rereadership, and the actual writers and audience seem familiar with such classifying and cataloguing activities. This fact implies a system of archiving and retrieving texts for reading, rereading, reading to, and, of course, copying if necessary. In other words, it implies some kind of (personal, public, or temple-centered) library.

From the information provided by this verse, one may learn something about the world of knowledge of these literati. They were aware of historical traditions. They shared some reconstruction of Israel's and Judah's past that included knowledge of the names of kings and of the (constructed) circumstances of their times.

Although it is possible or even likely that shaped and reshaped traditions about an ancient prophet named Hosea were existent and even cherished among these literati, for them YHWH's word that came to Hosea *signified* a written book, to be read, reread, studied, and whose message, as understood by them, was supposed to be communicated to the vast majority of the people, who were not bearers of high literacy. The claim that divine knowledge is in a written book turns them into absolutely necessary brokers of knowledge for those who cannot access directly a highly literate text such as the book of Hosea.

Intention

The main role of Hos 1:1 is to introduce the book to the readers or, in other words, to help them develop their first concept about what the book is about. This first concept is then highly influential in the shaping of their reading of the book. The emphasis here is on the basic and most categorical proposition that the text *is* a particular instance of YHWH's word (or perhaps, YHWH's instruction). The issue of authority and the related question of why this text is supposed to be read and reread (and copied, and edited, and the like) are addressed by this proposition.

It is worth stressing also that YHWH's word or teaching is individualized by a reference to a human personage called Hosea, and that this personage and YHWH's word are explicitly anchored in a certain section of the construed image of the past shared by the community of writers and readers within which the book was not only composed but also first read and reread (see STRUCTURE). The primacy of the organization of time according to the regnal periods of the kings of Judah reinforces the assumption that legitimate kings are Davidic (cf. Hos 3:5) and that Judah, which is understood from an ideological perspective as "Israel," stands at the center of the concerns of the intended readership. This is consistent with the repeated references to Judah, and the substantial ubiquitous explicit notes about the relevance for Judah of the reported events, divine communications, and messages conveyed by the book, even in a text that on the surface focuses on the northern kingdom (cf. Amos).

Bibliography

R. Abma, "H-Hour for the Kingdom of Israel? Hosea 1:1 in the Light of Two Paradigms of Interpretation," A. Brenner and J. W. Van Henten (eds.), *Recycling Biblical Figures. Papers Read at a NOSTER Colloquium in Amsterdam,* 12-13 May 1997 (STAR 1; Leiden: Deo, 1999) 93-126; R. P. Carroll, "Prophecy and Society," R. E. Clements (ed.), *The World of Ancient Israel* (Cambridge: Cambridge Univ. Press, 1991) 203-25; S. L. Cook, "The Lineage Roots of Hosea's Yahwism," *Semeia* 87 (1999) 145-61; P. R. Davies, "The Audiences of Prophetic Scrolls: Some Suggestions," S. B. Reid (ed.), *Prophets and Paradigms. Essays in Honor of Gene M. Tucker* (JSOTSupS 229; Sheffield: JSOT Press, 1996) 48-62; E. Day, "Is the Book of Hosea Exilic?" *American Journal of Semitic Languages and Literature* 26 (1909/10) 105-32; G. Fohrer, *Introduction to the Old Testament* (Initiated by E. Sellin; ET D. E. Green; Nashville: Abingdon, 1968); G. Galil, *The Chronology of the Kings of Israel and Judah* (Studies in the History and Culture of the Ancient Near East IX; Leiden: E. J. Brill, 1996); J. H. Hayes and P. K. Hooker, *A New Chronology for the Kings of Israel and Judah* (Atlanta: J. Knox, 1988); G. Loughlin, "Using Scripture: Community and Letterality," J. Davies et al. (eds.), *Words Remembered, Texts Renewed. Essays in Honour of John F. A. Sawyer* (JSOTSupS 195; Sheffield: Sheffield Academic Press, 1995) 321-39; S. A. Meier, *Speaking of Speaking. Marking Direct Discourse in the Hebrew Bible* (VTSup 46; Leiden: E. J. Brill, 1992); N. Na'aman, "Historical and Chronological Notes on the Kingdoms of Israel and Judah in the Eighth Century B.C.," *VT* 36 (1986) 71-92; J. Nogalski, *Literary Precursors to the Book of the Twelve* (BZAW 217; Berlin: de Gruyter, 1993); S. Parpola, *Assyrian Prophecies* (SAA IX; Helsinki: Helsinki Univ. Press, 1997); H. H. Rowley, *Men of God* (London: Nelson, 1963); N. Snaith, *Mercy and Sacrifice. A Study of the Book of Hosea* (London: SCM Press, 1953); J. M. Trotter, *Reading Hosea in Achaemenid Yehud* (JSOTSupS 328; Sheffield: Sheffield Academic Press, 2001); G. M. Tucker, "Prophetic Superscriptions and the Growth of a Canon," B. O. Long and G. W. Coats (eds.), *Canon and Authority: Essays in Old Testament Religion and Theology* (Philadelphia: Fortress, 1977) 56-70; idem, "Hosea Commentaries," Review Article, *RSR* 7 (1981) 132-36; J. Vermeylen, "Osée et les prophètes du VIIIe siècle," R. G. Kratz, T. Krüger and K. Schmid (eds.), *Schriftauslegung in der Schrift. FS für Odil Hannes Steck zu seinem 65. Geburtstag* (BZAW 300; Berlin/New York: de Gruyter, 2000) 193-206; H-M Wahl, "Die Überschriften der Prophetenbücher," *ETL* 70 (1994) 91-104; J. D. Watts, "Superscriptions and Incipits in the Book of the Twelve," J. D. Nogalski and M. A. Sweeney (eds.), *Reading and Hearing the Book of the Twelve* (Symposium 15; Atlanta: Society of Biblical Literature, 2000) 110-124; J. Wellhausen, *Prolegomena to the History of Ancient Israel* (Cleveland: Meridian Books, 1957).

First Set of Readings:
Hope for the Future and Explanation of Past Judgment through Metaphors of Hierarchical Family Relationships, 1:2–3:5

Structure

I. First Reading	1:2–2:3
II. Second Reading	2:3-25
III. Third Reading	3:1-5

This set of closely related and intertwined readings sets the tone for the book. The set introduces the readers to the main issues addressed in the book and brings to the forefront the use of sexual imagery to portray apostasy (cf. Davies, *Hosea*, 36).

The extent of the unit is demarcated by the presence of the introduction in 1:1 and by the clear beginning of a new set of readings marked by a relatively common opening for new units, namely, שמעו דבר ה' "hear YHWH's word" in 4:1. The internal borders among the readings in this set are, however, porous, although each reading moves from an explanation of the terrible judgment that stood in the past of the community of readers of the book to explicit notes of assurance and hope for the future (2:2-3; 2:16-25; 3:5).

Verse 2:3 serves as an integral part of two readings and acts as a bridge between them. Verse 3:1 presupposes 1:2–2:25 (see the explicit textual marker עוד "again" in 3:1). In addition, not only do the three readings address similar matters, but main themes and imagery present in the first reading are further developed and clarified in the second (see Hos 1:2–2:3 STRUCTURE). Therefore, they serve to some extent as a single unit of meaning and particularly so as the book of Hosea was read again and again, and some of the terms and imagery in Hos 1:2–2:3 activated the memory of those in Hos 2:3-25; i.e., served as signposts. One may notice also that issues and imagery present in Hos 1:1–2:3 are addressed from a slightly different perspective in Hos 3:1-5. In all these cases, a web of meanings is created mainly through the use of marital or father/children metaphors for the representation of the past and future relation between YHWH and Israel. It is this web of meanings that carries the message of the set of readings, rather than any partial reading of each one of them. (On the discursive marginalization of the present exemplified here and common in prophetic literature, and on the correlated strengthening of the position of "self-effacing" literati responsible for these texts, see E. Ben Zvi, "What Is New in Yehud?")

The use of a family and particularly a marital metaphor for a representation of the history of the relations between the deity and Israel was made possible by (a) the common conceptualization of the relation of husband/wife as asymmetrical and associated with patron/client-like relations, such as king/subject, master/servant, father/child, and the like, and (b) the ability of a marital narrative to represent metaphorically the ideologically construed history of Israel in which the latter behaves sinfully, is severely punished, but eventually because of divine mercy is not only forgiven but exalted again through a loving relation with YHWH. For this narrative to work, Israel/the wife must be construed as

35

ıd sinful, later as punished and eventually as being taken again by
ıWH (Jer 2:1–3:5; 13:26-27; Ezek 16:15-58; 23:1-49).
ıning of the marriage/betrothal represents a problematic matter
‒‒‒. Jn the one hand, one expects some reference to "youthful love"
(cf. Hos 2:16-17); on the other, Israel's sin is construed as an integral part of her
nature: she is אשת זנונים "a promiscuous woman" (see Hos 1:2). At times,
such rhetorical constructions are actually reinforced by the motif of youthful-
ness: see, for instance, the imagery of Ezek 23:19-21. Notice that the text here
associates this youthful period with the stay, or slavery in Egypt, but not with
the Exodus motif, and cf. Hos 2:16-17.

To be sure, within the metaphorical realm of a family, the narrative and
ideological position of the subordinate could be fulfilled also by children
(YHWH/husband is to Israel/wife as YHWH/father is to Israel/children). The
two images co-exist and complement each other in this set. Of course, marital
imagery carries some potential problems too. For one, polygamy (or better,
polygyny) existed in ancient Israel, and in the ancient Near East as a whole.
Moreover, polygyny was more common among powerful, male members of rul-
ing elites (e.g., kings). Thus, in principle, YHWH could have taken and could
still take more than one wife, that is, nations other than Israel, in addition to the
latter. Of course, even under such conditions, not all wives would be necessarily equal. The partner of "youth" was regarded as the most important (cf. Isa
54:6; Joel 1:8; Mal 2:14-15; Prov 2:17; 5:18). Significantly, many of these texts
pointed at and stressed the early relation between the two. To be sure, the wife/
Israel could not have married YHWH/her husband when the latter was young,
but rather when she was young. Her adultery then becomes even more poignant, because she betrayed the husband of her youth. At the same time, since
within the discourse of Israel, YHWH had no "wives" when he metaphorically
married Israel, the latter cannot be other than the first wife of YHWH, and
therefore Israel symbolically takes the role of the wife of YHWH's youth. It
bears notice that the marriage to the wife of youth is associated elsewhere with
a sacred covenant (see Prov 2:17; Mal 2:14). Within this symbolic and metaphorical discourse, even if YHWH were to have some personal relation to another people, Israel's unique role, as the wife of youth, remains solid, unless
YHWH divorced his wife/Israel. The ideologically threatening possibility of a
divorce is a strong concern within this type of imaginative discourse, and much
effort is placed in this text to show that no matter how much the wife/Israel may
have given YHWH reasons for divorce, he will never do that (cf. Isa 50:1-3).
Instead he will remain with Israel forever, despite its past (and perhaps future,
but see 2:3-25, Setting) unfaithfulness. It is precisely the certainty of this position that provided the intended and primary readership with the hope that is
central to the message of this section in the book and of the book as a whole.
(On many of these and related issues see Ben Zvi, "Observations on the Marital
Metaphor," and Hos 1:2–2:3, Intention).

It goes without saying that the marital metaphor associates YHWH with
the male and the land but also Israel (i.e., the children of Israel) with a female
counterpart. Although the land is usually associated with female figures, the
children of Israel are not. They are usually coupled with male imagery. Yet one

has to remember that male/female or, better, gender-related imagery, served also to express power relations in the discourses of ancient Israel and in biblical texts. In fact, it is because gender reflects power that in the marital metaphor YHWH, who can only be the superordinate partner in relation to Israel, will always remain the husband; and Israel, who can only be the subordinate partner, will remain a female character. Thus, within this discourse, if Israel is characterized as sinful, "she" will be described as adulterous, and conversely if Israel is pious, then "she" will be described as a faithful, chaste, fruitful (and probably wealthy, because of her husband's gifts) wife. On these matters cf. D. Seeman, "Where Is Sarah Your Wife?"; and also G. Yee, "She Is Not My Wife," esp. pp. 368-71; and, here, Hos 3:1-5, Setting; for a different approach, see Schmitt, "The Wife of God"; and cf. Braaten, "God Sows." (Outside the marital metaphor, but still within a family metaphor, Israel may be construed as a "male" character provided that "he" is not imagined as the head or patriarch of the family. Thus, Israel may be "male," but if so it must be a "minor"; see Hos 11:1.)

The intended and primary readers, for their part, are asked to identify with the position advanced by the superior and sovereign partner (i.e., YHWH/ husband) but they are also and certainly Israel/wife/children. As such their hope is to be accepted again by YHWH/husband/father to restore the proper family relationship. The necessary step is for them to understand that their actions in the past were sinful and accept the justice of the divine punishment that followed them. To be sure, within the world of the book punishment is still in the future — after all, Hosea is associated with the times of Jeroboam II — but from the perspective of the readers of the book of Hosea, as we know it, the punishment has already occurred. The new ideal relationship that is imagined here and which involves a Davidic restoration and the re-union of (northern) Israel and Judah is certainly in the future of this readership, be it Josianic or, as is most likely, postmonarchic (on the time of the primary readership of the book of Hosea, see Hos 1:1–14:10 INTRODUCTION).

Obviously, all the mentioned discursive constructions of family relations are part and parcel of a clearly patriarchal point of view. But within a historical commentary on the book — such as this one — it has to be stressed that such viewpoints were prevalent in ancient Israel, and particularly so among the authorship and readership of the prophetic books that consisted for the most part of males. This is not to deny that contemporary readers of the book may feel uncomfortable with such constructions of the family realm or that this imagery carries connotations that are very troublesome for many contemporary readers, and especially painful for those who cannot but associate their reading of the text with their or their acquaintances' personal experiences (see particularly Hos 2:3-15). For many contemporary readings of the book that address these matters, see Bibliography.

Some scholars have maintained that Hos 1:2–3:5 or a closely related forerunner existed as a literary unit independent of, and prior to, the existence of the present book of Hosea (cf. Y. Kaufmann, *Toldot* 3, pp. 93-146; H. L. Ginsberg, *Israelian Heritage*, 97-98; idem, *Enc. Judaica* 8, cols. 1010-24; Wolfe, "Editing of the Book of the Twelve," 92). Many others have advanced different proposals for the redactional history of this unit (for a summary of common proposals, see Daniels, *Hosea and Salvation History,* 24-28; and among many others see Harper, Wellhausen, Renaud, Ruppert, Vermeylen, Wolff, and Yee; Watts ["A Frame for the Book of Twelve"] wonders if Hosea 1–3 was composed for its position at the beginning of the Book of the Twelve). To be sure, it is possible and even likely that the text underwent some redactional process. It is less likely that we will be able to reconstruct the original text of each layer in a conclusive or even widely accepted manner. (Proposals include one of three redactional levels: (a) disciples of Hosea, (b) Levites from Josiah's time, and (c) exilic-judaic; or alternatively (a) Hoseanic kernel, (b) deuteronomistic, and (c) priestly.) It is worth noting that most of these proposals are more a corollary of presuppositions about authorship, date, and short oral delivery than a response to actual tensions that are incompatible with a written, sophisticated prophetic book, as the book of Hosea certainly is (see STRUCTURE in the discussions of each of these readings; and see already, Day).

In any case, since this is a commentary on the "book of Hosea" (as opposed to any hypothetical forerunner), it is worth stressing that the intended and primary readers of the book of Hosea were *not* asked to read it in a way that was informed by any of these (hypothetical, contemporary) proposals. The readers of the book were asked to read a set of readings that although closely associated with one another were also part and parcel of the book of Hosea. Not only did they serve as a general opening to the book that introduced many of the themes that were to be found in the ensuing reading, but they were also strongly linked to the following readings in the book by textual and semantic markers and by metaphors. Thus, for instance, the metaphor of adultery appears elsewhere in Hosea (see already chapter 4) and so does the imagery associated with the motif of "wandering in the wilderness" (cf. Grätz; "Die vergebliche Suche nach Gott; Dozeman, "Hosea and the Wilderness Wandering Tradition"). As mentioned in the introduction, these cross-references serve well as texts to be read and reread. They create signposts for the readers that remind them of particular issues dealt with in the book as a whole. They also contribute to the creation of networks of various readings continuously informing each other, and to some extent, shaping the meaning of each other in various ways, and thus create multiple potential meanings, as expected in texts to be read and reread.

Genre

Each of the texts included in this unit is a DIDACTIC, PROPHETIC READING about (a) the hopeful future and (b) the reconstruction of Israel's history through the metaphor of family relations between YHWH, the father/lord, and his wife or children. The genre of the unit as a whole is SET OF READINGS.

Setting

The setting of the production of these written literary units as integral parts of the book of Hosea and of its primary reading and rereading is that of a group of literati who were aware of ideological constructions of Israel's past, and shared a strong hope for its future. The precise ways in which the latter is imagined, along with singular aspects of the past that were recalled in each unit, will be discussed along with each of these readings. The temporal setting of these social groups is likely to be the postmonarchic period (see Introduction to the Book of Hosea).

The setting of the events within the world of the book is left open. For instance, where and when, within that world, did YHWH speak the words reported in 3:1? Does the report in Hos 1:2 inform the readers of the book that YHWH spoke to Hosea when he was alone, or in a public place? Did others hear the divine command? All these issues are left open to the imagination of the readers and rereaders of the book. The lack of specificity is not accidental. In fact, it characterizes all readings in the book of Hosea — and most of the readings in prophetic literature in general. The lack of all these details shows that the thrust of the text is not toward historical mimesis (or historicity). The text is not designed to help the readers reconstruct the actual sequence of events in the life of the historical Hosea (ct. Macintosh, *Hosea,* 117-19; and notice the title of the section there, "Historical Conclusions"), but to lift the imagination of the readers toward the portrayed ideal future and to allow it to set the readers in the place of Hosea. For even centuries later than the time in which the book was set, people could have imagined, even for a moment, that they were like that man and see themselves in the role of husband of a promiscuous woman and having the mentioned children (see FIRST READING) and be at once fulfilling the role of YHWH as it were, and at the same time reconsidering the entire history of Israel and its great future. Or in another rereading of the book of Hosea, they may imagine themselves as and identify with the Hosea of chapter 3. Significantly, none of the actions attributed to Hosea actually necessitate a particular setting. In addition, and in a quite complementary way, they may identify themselves with Hosea's children, and their offspring, who are Israel too, just as they are (and cf. Hos 5:7). The latter not only involves no particular setting, but also suggests a kind of transtemporal setting.

The text contains also an important textual marker (Hos 1:1 and see Hos 1:1 Genre) that alerts its intended and primary readerships that these READINGS, as any other READINGS in the book, are an integral part of YHWH's word — that is, a written, prophetic book. First, such a reference reminds the readers that there is always a gap between report and portrayed event, that there is a narrator whose presence is made explicit in the text (see also Hos 1:2a). Second, and more important, it keeps reminding the readers to set the world of the book in a particular period in Israel's history, in the days of Kings Uzziah, Jotham, Ahaz, and Hezekiah of Judah, and in the days of King Jeroboam son of Joash of Israel.

Of course, the readers' construction of the monarchic past during the period mentioned above is both shaped and reflected by these readings. Such a construction has to be coherent with some set of basic "facts agreed upon" regarding that period within the community of postmonarchic literati. It should be stressed, however, that this type of constraint is not directly associated with the most likely historical reconstruction of any of the days of these kings, but rather with what the literati thought was the case in these days. Significantly, even there, the constraints allow flexibility, and particularly so if ideological issues are involved (see the list of kings in Hos 1:1). Moreover, the literati's construction of that past included reference not only to certain kings (e.g., Jehu) but also to agrarian socio-economic systems that existed for centuries, including the time of the readers of the present book of Hosea. The considerations advanced here and in the preceding paragraph undermine attempts to take the monarchic world portrayed in these chapters as reliable reflection of historical circumstances in the monarchic period during the days of the kings mentioned in 1:1.

It is worth stressing at this point that the world portrayed in the book in general and in Hosea 1–3 in particular consists of many layers, or worlds. The latter includes the world of the narrator who presents the story and appears not infrequently in chapter 1 reporting events (and commenting on them), the monarchic world associated with Hosea, but not necessarily with the narrator, and of course, the "messianic" future world/s that take(s) center stage at the conclusion of each of the READINGS in the set.

(For a different approach to the question of setting, see, for instance, G. Yee, "She Is Not My Wife.")

Intention

The intention of the text is not only to ask its intended and primary readers to attempt to imagine in human terms the relation between YHWH and Israel, but to communicate hope to the readers (that is, Israel), to interpret their past and offer them ways to ponder about what the ideal future should be. The intention, to be sure, is not to offer one single, unequivocal picture of that future. Three different descriptions balance each other and inform each other in this set of readings, but all instill certainty in the readers that this will be a glorious future.

The text is written so as to strongly communicate to its intended readers that its main concern is *not* with the reported sexual sins and marital life of Gomer (or of the unnamed woman in chapter 3 [see already the final clause of v. 2]) or even the fate and actions of Hosea, but rather that which they symbolized. These descriptions point on the one hand to the "harlotry of the land and its inhabitants" — that is, the worship of gods other than YHWH — and on the other, to the construction of a literary and ideological image of a prophetic personage who on the one hand represents YHWH, but with whom Israel is also supposed to identify. The motif of the harlotry of the land and its inhabitants not only allows for the narratives mentioned above, but also reflects ideological discourses in which there was some sense of mental overlap between cultic and sexual defilements. In ancient Israel, and in other ancient Near East societies, both repel the divine presence. In fact, they may be considered anti-sacrifices since they undo that which proper sacrifices are supposed to do, namely, to attract the divine presence (cf. Klawans, "Pure Violence: Sacrifice and Defilement in Ancient Israel," and bibliography cited there).

The constant reference to the worship of deities other than YHWH served

40

well to explain the reasons for the divine judgment against the monarchic polities. This feature is consistent with the similar use of these references in, for instance, the so-called deuteronomistic history, the chronistic history, and the books of Jeremiah and Ezekiel. It is very doubtful, however, that one of the main intentions of the book of Hosea was to teach the literati for whom it was written in its present form (i.e., most likely Yehudite, Jerusalem-centered literati) that they should worship YHWH alone. This readership most likely consisted of people who followed the ideology of the Jerusalemite center of the Persian period in any case, and were not likely at all to worship Baʿal or any other deity except YHWH. Moreover, they were unlikely to have worshiped the latter in a way that was unacceptable to the Jerusalemite center of the time. It is possible, nonetheless, that portions of the book of Hosea (or perhaps even the book as a whole) were read to other groups who could not read it by themselves and who may have been more prone to worship either "other gods" or YHWH but not in the exclusive way in which YHWH's cult was understood by the Jerusalemite center and its elite (cf. Isa 57:3-13; 65:1-12). On these matters cf. Trotter, *Reading Hosea,* 163-65.

It is beyond any doubt, however, that the book assumes that reading about Israel's punishment in the past is a way of acquiring knowledge about the divine and YHWH's wishes and, thus indirectly, that YHWH's severe punishment of Israel in the past served a pedagogical purpose, possibly from the perspective of the generation that is under judgment (cf. Hos 5:15; 11:10-11; 14:2-4 which seem to indicate that this is YHWH's hope), but above all as an everlasting process relived as social memory that enriches, educates, and warns Israel (cf. Albertz, "Exile as Purification," 248).

Although it is not the "intention" of the book, it is certainly true that, indirectly, it legitimized the patriarchal ideologies concerning gender and family roles that existed within the discourse shared by its authorship and intended and primary readerships by referring to a set of marital relations, and the respective roles of the husband and wife within it, as the normative frame around which metaphors about the relation between YHWH and Israel are presented in this book that claims to be and is accepted as YHWH's word. To be sure, the text was not written to create or even support these ideologies, but a text written by males for males within the common ancient Near Eastern discourses of the time was, as one would expect, a carrier of these ideologies.

Bibliography

R. Abma, "H-Hour for the Kingdom of Israel? Hosea 1:1 in the Light of Two Paradigms of Interpretation," A. Brenner and J. W. Van Henten (eds.), *Recycling Biblical Figures. Papers Read at a NOSTER Colloquium in Amsterdam,* 12-13 May 1997 (STAR 1; Leiden: Deo, 1999) 93-126; R. Albertz, "Exile as Purification. Reconstructing the 'Book of Four'," P. L. Redditt and A. Schart (eds.), *Thematic Threads in the Book of the Twelve* (BZAW 325; Berlin: de Gruyter, 2003) 232-51; G. Baumann, *Liebe und Gewalt. Die Ehe als Metapher für das Verhältnis JHWH-Israel in den alttestamentlichen Prophetenbüchern* (SBS 185; Stuttgart: Verlag Katholisches Bibelwerk, 2000); idem,

"Die Metapher der Ehe für das Verhältnis JHWH-Israel in den alttestamentlichen Prophetenbüchern — (nicht nur) feministisch-kritisch betrachtet," M. Oeming (ed.), *Theologie des AT aus der Perspektive von Frauen* (BVB 1; Münster: LIT, 2003) 173-77; P. Bird, "'To Play the Harlot': An Inquiry into an Old Testament Metaphor," P. Day (ed.), *Gender and Difference in Ancient Israel* (Philadelphia: Fortress, 1989) 75-94; E. Bons, "Osée 1,2. Un tour d'horizon de l'interprétation," *RevScRel* 73 (1999) 207-22; C. D. Bowman, "Prophetic Grief, Divine Grace: The Marriage of Hosea," *ResQ* 43 (2001) 229-42; L. J. Braaten, *Parent-Child Imagery in Hosea* (PhD dissertation; Boston University, 1987); idem, "God Sows: Hosea's Land Theme in the Book of the Twelve," P. L. Redditt and A. Schart (eds.), *Thematic Threads in the Book of the Twelve* (BZAW 325; Berlin: de Gruyter, 2003) 104-32; A. Brenner, "Pornoprophetics Revisited: Some Additional Reflections," *JSOT* 70 (1996) 63-86; M. J. Buss, "Hosea as a Canonical Problem: With Attention to the Song of Songs," S. B. Reid (ed.), *Prophets and Paradigms. Essays in Honor of Gene M. Tucker* (JSOTSupS 229; Sheffield: Sheffield Academic Press, 1996) 79-93; E. Day, "Is the Book of Hosea Exilic?" *American Journal of Semitic Languages and Literature* 26 (1909/10) 105-32; A. Dearman, "YHWH's House: Gender Roles and Metaphors for Israel in Hosea," *JNSL* 25 (1999) 97-108; idem, "Interpreting the Religious Polemics Against Baal and Baalim in the Book of Hosea," *OTE* 14 (2001) 9-25; J. L. del Valle, "La sexualidad: Simbología matrimonial en los escritos proféticos," *ByF* 18 (1992) 37-50; L. O. Dorn, "Is Gomer the Woman in Hos 3?," *The Bible Translator* 51 (2000) 424-30; T. B. Dozeman, "Hosea and the Wilderness Wandering Tradition," S. L. McKenzie and T. Römer (eds.), *Rethinking the Foundations: Historiography in the Ancient World and in the Bible: Essays in Honour of John Van Seters* (BZAW 294; Berlin: de Gruyter, 2000) 55-70; C. S. Ehrlich, "The Text of Hosea 1:9," *JBL* 104 (1985) 13-19; J. C. Exum, *Plotted, Shot, and Painted: Cultural Representations of Biblical Women* (JSOTSupS 215; Sheffield: Sheffield Academic Press, 1996); C. R. Fontaine, "Hosea," A. Brenner (ed.), *A Feminist Companion of the Latter Prophets* (Sheffield: Sheffield Academic Press, 1995) 40-59; idem, "A Response to 'Hosea'," A. Brenner (ed.), *A Feminist Companion of the Latter Prophets* (Sheffield: Sheffield Academic Press, 1995) 60-69; T. Frymer-Kensky, *In the Wake of the Goddesses* (New York: Free Press, 1992); H. L. Ginsberg, "Studies in Hosea 1–3," M. Haran (ed.), *Y. Kaufmann Jubilee Volume* (Jerusalem, 1960) 50-69; idem, *The Israelian Heritage of Judaism* (New York: Jewish Theological Seminary, 1982); J. Goldingay, "Hosea 1–3, Genesis 1–4 and Masculinist Interpretation," A. Brenner (ed.), *A Feminist Companion of the Latter Prophets* (Sheffield: Sheffield Academic Press, 1995) 161-68; E. N. Good, "The Composition of Hosea," *SEÅ* 31 (1966) 21-63; R. Gordis, "Hosea's Marriage and Message," *HUCA* 25 (1954) 9-35; N. Graetz, "The Haftarah Tradition and the Metaphoric Battering of Hosea's Wife," *Conservative Judaism* 45 (1992) 29-42; idem, "God Is to Israel as Husband Is to Wife: The Metaphorical Battering of Hosea's Wife," A. Brenner (ed.), *A Feminist Companion of the Latter Prophets* (Sheffield: Sheffield Academic Press, 1995) 126-45; S. Grätz, "Die vergebliche Suche nach Gott. Traditions- und kompositiongeschichtliche Überlegungen zu Herkunft und Funktion der Strafvorstellungen in Hos. 1v 1–vi 6," *VT* 50 (2000) 200-17; M. I. Gruber, "Marital Fidelity and Intimacy: A View from Hosea 4," A. Brenner (ed.), *A Feminist Companion of the Latter Prophets* (Sheffield: Sheffield Academic Press, 1995) 169-79; J. A. Hackett, "Can a Sexist Model Liberate Us? Ancient Near Eastern Fertility Goddesses," *JFSR* 5 (1989); Y. Hoffman, "A North Israelite Typological Myth and a Judaean Historical Tradition: The Exodus in Hosea and Amos," *VT* 39 (1989) 169-82; T. J. Hornsby, "'Israel Has Become a Worthless Thing': A Re-Reading of Gomer in Hosea 1–3," *JSOT* 82 (1999) 115-28; A. A. Keefe, "The Female Body, the Body Politic and the Land: A Sociopolitical Reading of Hosea 1–2," A. Brenner (ed.), *A Feminist Companion of the Latter Prophets* (Sheffield: Sheffield Academic Press, 1995) 70-100; J. Klawans, "Pure Violence: Sacrifice and Defilement in Ancient Israel," *HTR* 94 (2001) 133-55; P. A. Kruger, "Israel, the Harlot," *JNSL* 11 (1985), 107-16; idem, "Prophetic Imagery: On Metaphors and Similes in the Book of Hosea," *JNSL* 14 (1988) 143-51; F. Landy, "In the Wilderness of Speech: Problems of Metaphor in Hosea," *BibInt* 3 (1995) 35-59; idem, "Fantasy and the Displacement of Pleasure: Hosea 2.4-17," A. Brenner (ed.), *A Feminist Companion of the Latter Prophets* (Sheffield: Sheffield Academic Press, 1995) 146-60 (cf. F. Landy, *Hosea*, pp. 31-41); M. J. Leith, "Verse and Reverse: The Transformation of the Woman, Israel, in Hosea 1–3," P. Day (ed.), *Gender and Difference in Ancient Israel* (Phildelphia: Fortress, 1989) 95-108; M. Malul, *Knowledge, Control and Sex. Studies in Biblical Thought, Culture and Worldview* (Tel Aviv-Jaffa: Archaeological Center Publication, 2002); R. D. Nelson, "Priestly Purity and Prophetic Lunacy: Hosea 1.2-3 and 9.7," L. L. Grabbe and A. O. Bellis (eds.), *The Priest in the Prophets: The Portrayal of the Priests, Prophets and Other Religious Specialists in the Latter Prophets* (JSOTSup 408; London: T&T Clark International, 2004) 115-33; F. S. North, "Solution to Hosea's Marital Problems by Critical Analysis," *JNES* 16 (1957) 128-30; idem, "Hosea's Introduction to His Book," *VT* 8 (1958) 429-32; M. S. Odell, "I Will Destroy Your Mother: The Obliteration of a Cultic Role in Hosea 4:4-6," A. Brenner (ed.), *A Feminist Companion of the Latter Prophets* (Sheffield: Sheffield Academic Press, 1995) 180-93; R. C. Ortlund Jr., *Whoredom. God's Unfaithful Wife in Biblical Theology* (Grand Rapids, MI.: Eerdmans, 1996); B. Renaud, "Genèse et unité redactionnelle de Os. 2," *RevScRel* 54 (1980) 1-20; idem, "Le Livret d'Osée 1–3. Un travail complexe d'edition," *RevScRel* 56 (1982) 159-78; idem, "Osée 1-3: analyse diachronique et lecture synchronique, problémes de methode," *RevScRel* 57 (1983) 249-60; idem, "Fidélité humaine et fidélité de Dieu dans le livret d'Osée 1–3," *Revue de Droit Canonique* 33 (1983) 184-200; H. H. Rowley, "The Marriage of Hosea," H. H. Rowley, *Men of God: Studies in Old Testament History and Prophecy* (London: Thomas Nelson and Sons, 1963) 66-97 (= *BJRL* 39 [1956-57] 200-33); L. Ruppert, "Erwägungen zur Kompositions- und Redaktionsgeschichte von Hosea 1–3," *BZ* NF 26 (1982) 208-23; A. Scherer, "'Gehe wiederum hin' zum Verhältniss von Hos. 3 zu Hos. 1," *BN* 95 (1998) 23-29; J. J. Schmitt, "The Wife of God in Hosea 2," *Biblical Research* 34 (1989) 5-18; B. E. Scolnic, "Bible Battering," *Conservative Judaism* 45 (1992) 43-52; D. Seeman, "'Where Is Sarah Your Wife?' Cultural Poetics of Gender and Nationhood in the Hebrew Bible," *HTR* 91 (1998) 103-25; T. D. Setel, "Prophets and Pornography: Female Sexual Imagery in Hosea," L. M. Russell (ed.), *Feminist Interpretation of the Bible* (Philadelphia: Westminster, 1985) 86-95; Y. Sherwood, "Boxing Gomer: Controlling the Deviant Woman in Hosea 1–3," A. Brenner (ed.), *A Feminist Companion of the Latter Prophets* (Sheffield: Sheffield Academic Press, 1995) 101-25; M. S. Smith, *The Early History of God. Yahweh and the Other Deities in Ancient Israel* (2nd ed; Grand Rapids: Eerdmans, 2002); M. A. Sweeney, "A Form-Critical Rereading of Hosea," *Journal of Hebrew Scriptures* 2 (1998), available at http://www.jhsonline.org and http://purl.org/jhs; A. Szabo, "Textual Problems in Amos and Hosea," *VT* 25 (1975) 500-24; S. Talmon, "The Desert Motif in the Bible and in Qumran Literature," S. Talmon (ed.),

Literary Studies in the Hebrew Bible. Form and Content (Jerusalem/Leiden: Magnes Press/E. J. Brill, 1993) 216-54; D. A. Tushingham, "A Reconsideration of Hosea, Chapters 1–3," *JNES* 12 (1953) 150-59; J. Unterman, "Repentance and Redemption in Hosea," *SBLSP* 21 (1982) 541-50; F. van Dijk-Hemmes, "The Imagination of Power and the Power of Imagination. An Intertextual Analysis of Two Biblical Love Songs: The Song of Songs and Hosea 2," *JSOT* 44 (1989) 75-88; J. Vermeylen, "Osée et les prophètes du VIIIe siècle," R. G. Kratz, T. Krüger, and K. Schmid (eds.), *Schriftauslegung in der Schrift. FS für Odil Hannes Steck zu seinem 65. Geburtstag* (BZAW 300; Berlin/New York: de Gruyter, 2000) 193-206; W. Vogels, "Diachronic and Synchronic Studies of Hosea 1–3," *BZ* 28 (1984) 94-98; idem, "'Osée-Gomer' car et comme 'Yahweh-Israël' Os 1–3," *NRT* 103 (1981) 711-27; M.-T. Wacker, "Traces of the Goddess in the Book of Hosea," A. Brenner (ed.), *A Feminist Companion of the Latter Prophets* (Sheffield: Sheffield Academic Press, 1995) 219-41; L. Waterman, "Hosea, Chapters 1-3, in Retrospect and Prospect," *JNES* 14 (1955) 100-09; J. D. Watts, "A Frame for the Book of Twelve: Hosea 1–3 and Malachi," J. D. Nogalski and M. A. Sweeney (eds.), *Reading and Hearing the Book of the Twelve* (Symposium 15; Atlanta: Society of Biblical Literature, 2000) 209-17; R. J. Weems, "Gomer: Victim of Violence or Victim of Metaphor," *Semeia* 47 (1989) 87-104; R. E. Wolfe, "The Editing of the Book of the Twelve," *ZAW* 53 (1935) 95-129; G. A. Yee, "'She Is Not My Wife and I Am Not Her Husband': A Materialistic Analysis of Hosea 1–2," *BibInt* 9 (2001) 345-83.

First Didactic, Prophetic Reading That Imagines Israel's Trajectory from Divine Judgment to the Ideal End-Situation through Metaphors of Family Relationships, 1:2–2:3

Structure

I. Introduction	1:2a
II. Four sets of reported ongoing divine communication to Hosea pointing at judgment and relating it to family imagery	2b-9
A. First Set	2b-3
1. Direct speech formula	2bα
2. Divine command	2bβ1
3. Explicit explanation of the divine command: interpretative key for the report	2bβ2
4. Report about beginning of the fulfillment of the divine command	3
B. Second Set	4-5
1. Direct speech formula	4aα
2. Divine command	4aβ
3. Explicit explanation of the divine command	4b
4. "On that day . . ." unit — expansion of the preceding explanation	5
(a report about the fulfillment of the divine command is implied)	

The unit shows a clear and well-organized structure. Following an introduction that legitimizes the unit and sets it within the temporal world of the book as first among the others, it moves into four sets that each include a report of a divine command to Hosea, an explicit or implicit note about its fulfillment, and above all an explanation of the meaning of the command in terms of a characterization of Israel's behavior and of its consequences in the divine economy. These explanations are addressed to Hosea in the world of the book, but also, of course, to the primary (and intended) readers and rereaders of the book in the actual world. From their perspective, this section recapitulates and represents, through the metaphor of disrupted family relations, a construction of Israel's sinful past and the destruction of its polity/ies.

As expected in the prophetic books, the unit then moves to construct an image of Israel's future in terms of a reversal of fortunes, as restoration becomes the salient motif in the conclusion of this unit. Already the names present in the previous section (see especially "She-is-not-pitied" and "Not-my people," but also "Jezreel," which carries multiple meanings — see below) clearly developed within the primary and intended readership an anticipation of reversal. As expected, "Not-my-people" turns into "My-people," and "She-is-not-pitied" into "She-is-pitied." But the conclusion goes further. Son "Not-my-people" turns actually into *brothers* about whom Israel says "My-people" (cf. 2:1), and daughter "She-is-not-pitied" is transformed into *sisters* about whom Israel says "She-is-pitied." The singular in vv. 6, 8, 9 turns into the plural in 2:3 — there is no substantial reason to emend the text here to disallow the plain reading of it (cf. Barthélemy, *Critique Textuelle,* vol. III, 498-99). This shift is consistent with the image of a shift from a small group to the very populous one of an ideal future.

45

as the shift is envisaged, there is a clear allusion to the/a divine
ıe patriarchs concerning the multiplication of their "seed" (Gen
; for "like the sand of the sea" see also Gen 41:49; Isa 10:22). This
gs to the readers of the book not only a sense of reaffirmation of the
ı-   t by setting it in the future, it creates a sense of a new beginning after
the punishment that is clearly consistent with, and related to the message of, the
next reading in the set (2:4-25), which explicitly carries the image of a new beginning in the desert (another pentateuchal motif). Significantly, there are textually inscribed markers that ask the readers to closely relate the new future depicted in 2:16-25 with that in 2:1-3, and see the language of 2:25 and the
repetition of the motif of the three children (Jezreel, Not-my-people/My-people,
She-is-not-pitied/She-is-pitied) in 2:24-25.

Martin Buss once wrote, "A paradoxical union of attitudes occurs in Hosea's naming of Gomer's children, at divine command. . . . Hosea, by giving
them names, accepts them into his family. Yet the names themselves say the opposite" (Buss, "Tragedy and Comedy," 75). The above observations show that
although, for obvious rhetorical purposes, the names defamiliarize the situation, they in fact do tell the readers of the book that YHWH (as represented by
Hosea) has accepted Israel (/the children) as his children, for the names carry
the seed of their reversal and certainly draw the attention of the rereaders and
evoke among them the memory of their reversal. Indirectly, by doing so these
names serve as markers pointing at the irrevocable character of the relation of
these children (/Israel) to their father (/YHWH), for nothing they may do, or
have done — according to the text — may lead to a final estrangement from
their father. Within the full context of the book and the rereaders for whom it
was intended, the names carry as it were a built-in promise of hope.

The term יזרעאל (Jezreel) not only is the name of another son, but also
serves a variety of roles within the text. A secondary structure of the unit is conveyed by the inclusio created by the word יזרעאל (Jezreel) in 1:4-5 and 2:2. It
centers on the theme of the day of Jezreel. The day associated with Jezreel in
1:4-5 is a judgment day on Israel, whereas the one explicitly called "the day of
Jezreel" in 2:2 is of redemption. Thus the text's shift from punishment to redemption is encapsulated by the contrasting inclusio. Further, it also conveys
that the two days are, from a more general perspective, two faces of one ideological entity, already existing as it were in the mind of YHWH even before the beginning of the downfall of the northern kingdom, which in turn was seen as the
first step in the downfall of all Israel, including Judah in the monarchic period.
This being the case, it is not by chance that the readers are asked to imagine restored Israel in terms of a new polity including both northern Israel and Judah.

The name Jezreel itself serves, among other things, to encapsulate the entire trajectory from punishment to ideal future. It is the name of a city and a valley, but it also carries the meaning "El/God sows" and, accordingly, has numerous positive connotations, some of which are directly associated to the theme
around the allusion to divine promise to the patriarchs concerning the multiplication of their "seed" (see above). Yet, "sowing" means "scattering seed," and
as such it points at exile (cf. Zech 10:9). The first occurrences of the term in this
reading point to the realm of destruction, exile, and desolation of the land (see

below); the second to restoration, to increased "seed," both in the sense of population and agrarian produce.

Since Jezreel is the name of one of the children but also that of a city and a valley, it connotes a sense of association between the children who stand for the people and the land. That which is connoted in this reading is explicitly advanced in the conclusion of the next reading (see 2:24-25; see commentary there), to which the present one is closely related.

On another level, Jezreel in 1:4-5 is directly associated with and points to the fall of the House of Jehu, which was a historical fact from the perspective of the readership of the book, but stood in the future of the speaker and audience within the world of the book. Thus, the text comforts the readership by conveying certitude that just as the first part of that day came to pass, so the second part of the divinely created day of Jezreel will come to pass. (On the potential for the "personification" of a day in ancient Israel, see T. Jacobsen and K. Nielsen, "Cursing the Day.")

The reference to the House of Jehu carries several additional but crucial messages to the readership. (On the claim that the text read "House of Jehoram instead of "House of Jehu" see Kaufmann, *Toldot* III, 97-99; the LXX reads "House of Judah" instead of "House of Jehu.") The text assumes that the intended readership of the book of Hosea has some knowledge of the traditional history of Israel (see 1:1, the very reference to Jehu and Jezreel, and, of course, the reference to pentateuchal traditions). Moreover, given the date of 1:1, the spelling choice for the name Hezekiah made there, and other features in the book, it is also likely that the readership was acquainted either with the book of Kings or a closely related forerunner. This being so, it is worth noting that the House of Jehu was the only dynasty in northern Israel about whom a number of positive remarks were made (e.g., 2 Kgs 10:18-28, 30; 13:4-5; 14:10, 26-27), even if they are always qualified in one way or another, as one would expect given the ideological position advanced by the book of Kings (e.g., 2 Kgs 10:29, 31-33; 13:6-7; 14:14, 24). Moreover, given the focus on purging the cult that exists in the book of Hosea as a whole, and particularly the explicit references to the worship of Baal/Baals in the next and closely related reading in this set (see 2:10, 15-19; cf. 11:2; 13:1), it is worth stressing that Jehu is depicted as the one who "wiped out Baal from Israel" (2 Kgs 10:28). The text not only conveys the message of but also brings particular emphasis on the partial and temporary success of Jehu's actions, in contrast to the final process that the text metaphorically construes as "bringing Israel back to her husband, YHWH," a process that is located in the ideal future. Some of the differences are developed in the next reading in the setting; for instance, Israel must go back to the "desert," to its very beginning outside the fertile land, and there YHWH "will speak to her heart" and "betroth her forever" (2:16, 21). The imagery is, of course, a far cry from that of Jehu's rebellion and its historical circumstances. The difference between the two is also addressed and brought to salience through the two metaphorical references to "breaking the bow." In the first one (1:5), on the day of Jezreel that is associated with Jehu and the "blood of Jezreel," the breaking of the bow points at the destruction of Israel's military might (cf. Jer 49:35; the expression "to break the bow" appears also in other ancient Near Eastern texts; such as the so-called "Vassal Treaties" of Esarhaddon and the Sefire inscription; on the motif of breaking weapons, see Hillers, *Treaty Curses,* 60), precisely that which brought Jehu to power, allowed him to "wipe out Baal from Israel," and associated him with bloodshed at Jezreel (2 Kgs 9:24-37). The instance of the future "breaking the bow" in 2:20 is associated with the complete cessation of warfare, with a new peaceful covenant, with a new world, as it were, in which YHWH will be able to "betroth Israel forever" and which is brought about by YHWH. Cf. with the world described in Ps 46:7-11; 76:1-4, and notice the explicit use of the theme of "breaking the bow" in 46:10; 76:4. It is worth noting that these two psalms belong to a discourse or discourses in which Zion figures prominently; that is, they are the part and parcel of the discourse of Judah/Yehud. (See also Zech 9:9-10.) On the expression "breaking the bow," see Waldman. (For the position that the reference to the banishing of the bow, sword, and war signifies a rejection of Baal's attributes, see M. J. Winn Leith, "Verse and Reverse," 104.)

One may notice that this imagery of the future transformation, and the reference to the uselessness of the *bow,* or of any other weapon, in Hos 1:7, i.e., within the same literary context, is quite incompatible with any understanding of the text as pointing to or supporting real political or militaristic plans or campaigns by Judahite kings, such as Hezekiah or Josiah, aimed at annexing the former territories of northern Israel to their realm (for alternative approaches to Hosea, see Sweeney, *King Josiah*). In fact, the considerations advanced here suggest that the text was less at home with the discourses advanced by royal centers than with those of the non-royal center of postmonarchic Jerusalem. One may notice, for instance, the ideological similarity between the way in which YHWH is to save Judah in 1:7 and the promise in Zech 4:6. The precise language of 1:7 is also reminiscent of Ps 76:4 and particularly connected to that of Hos 2:20, because of the close, serial combination קשת-חרב-מלחמה ("bow," "sword," and "war") that appears in these texts and elsewhere only in 1 Chr 5:18. (The other two terms in 1:7 consist of the ubiquitous pair סוס-פרש "horse" and "rider"; Psalm 76 is a Zion-centered psalm that is most likely postmonarchic, and it shows the pan-Israelism discussed under Intention. Cf. also Zech 9:9-10.)

Another matter related to Jehu: Although from the perspective advanced in the book of Hosea, he can only be the best king of northern Israel, within this discourse he can only lead to a dooming and doomed leadership, because only a polity that encompasses both northern Israel and Judah can be associated with a divinely ordained ideal future. In other words, there is no room for a separate northern polity, and, accordingly, the readers of the text are told that the day of Jezreel leads to the fall of the northern monarchy, not simply of Jehu's dynasty (1:4; cf. 10:15).

Moreover, although the identity of the leader at the time of the latter day of Jezreel is left open in 2:2, the readership of the closely related set of readings (Hosea 1–3) within which the text stands cannot but contextually relate it to 3:5. Thus, when it comes to envisaging the ideal future there is no room for a separate northern polity, or for any non-Davidic king, even if he is a Jehu-like king, within the discourse of this set of readings. The book of Hosea is not substantially different in this regard from a number of postmonarchic, Jerusalem-centered works.

The considerations advanced above provide not only an exp
the thematic choice of Jezreel and Jehu, but also show how the text
own purposes, and intertwines within its discourse, some historical fa
by the authorship and readership (such as the reference to Jehu, h
Jezreel) but is not bound at all to reconstruct history. After all, if the ....is
knew about Jehu, Jezreel, Jeroboam, Uzziah, Jotham, Ahaz, and Hezekiah, they
knew that there were kings after Jeroboam and that the last house of the northern kingdom was not that of Jehu. Both the authorship and intended readership
of the book of Hosea (1:1–14:10) did not view historical referentiality as a major requirement for the communication of what they perceived to be ideological
truths, such as the construction of Israel's trajectory from punishment to future
existence in a renewed world. (For alternative understandings of historical
referentiality in Hosea and of the references to Jezreel, see Irvine, "Threat of
Jezreel"; Sweeney, *Twelve Prophets*, 18-20; Simian-Yofre, *Desierto*, 32-36.)

Additional partial structures at the verse level are clearly indicated in the
unit and convey particular meanings. For instance, a somewhat literal translation of 1:2 would be ". . . Go take for yourself a wife of whoredom and children
of whoredom, for the land whores, whores away from following the LORD." The
emphasis on the motif of "whoredom and committing whoredom" is clearly expressed by the quadruple repetition at the center of the verse. Around the center, one finds the references to the woman and the land, that is, to those who
commit whoredom, and at the beginning of the verse, one finds the "wronged
husbands," namely, the LORD and Hosea. Within this metaphorical world of the
text the people of Israel are construed as the children of the land of Israel and of
her husband (the LORD), which is consistent with observations about the ideology of the link between the land and the people that is conveyed by the book,
even if, and perhaps because, the same ideology requires the people to be sent
outside the land, to the desert, before they can be re-established in the land, in
the ideal future.

It also bears note that within the ideological horizon of the text, even if
the father clearly acknowledges that the children are his, he can justifiably reject them because of the behavior of the mother (cf. Hos 2:6). It is the choice of
the husband/father to re-accept them.

A few comments on several expressions and references are in order. To
begin with, the link between people and land and YHWH as merciful provider
of fertility would be enhanced if the root רחם connoted a secondary meaning of
"rain" (see Rendsburg, "Hebrew RHM = 'Rain,'" and cf. Isa 49:10), in addition
to its widely known associations with womb.

The "strange" expression ואנוכי לא אהיה לכם in Hos 1:9 is most likely a
well-crafted construction meant to allow a double reading. On the one hand, it
clearly connotes the meaning of "I am not your God," even if it is elliptic (see
already Ibn Ezra); moreover, the text of its reversal in Hos 2:25 ensures that
such a connotation was not missed by the intended readership. On the other
hand, it certainly evokes the text in Exod 3:14 (in which אהיה serves as a noun),
and as such it raises the image of circumstances that were just opposite to those
that existed at the time leading to, and during, the Exodus. The precise choice
of words here serves to anticipate issues and themes that are to be developed in

the next reading. Significantly, there is no reason within the text to assume that this precise choice of words must be due to a late editorial change (cf. and ct. Ehrlich and bibliography mentioned there), unless one assumes beforehand that much of the second reading (and esp. 2:16-25*) is in itself redactional, or that the text in Hosea cannot be later than the wording of Exod 3:14.

The expression ועלו מן הארץ in Hos 2:2 has been translated in modern English Bibles in many different ways. For instance, the NRSV reads, "they shall take possession of the land" (also see Wolff, *Hosea*, 28); the RSV and other English translations, "they shall go up from the land"; whereas the NAB has "[they shall] come up from other lands" (cf. Wellhausen who understands the text as stating ". . . from the land of their exile," see Wellhausen, *Kleinen Propheten*, 97 and Szabo, ". . . they shall go up from the land of exile" or "from the foreign land," Szabo, "Textual Problems," 508). Similarly, translations in modern commentaries or monographs on Hosea offer different understandings of the phrase. For instance, Macintosh (*Hosea*, 30) renders it "they will flourish in the land," whereas Buss (*Prophetic Word*, 8) translates it as "[they will] come up (to the central sanctuary or Jerusalem) out of the land" (also see Sweeney, *Twelve Prophets*, 24). Andersen and Freedman (*Hosea*, 4, 208-9) understand the text as "they will come up from the land," with "land" carrying a double meaning of (simple) "land" and "underworld" that associates the text both with the Exodus and resurrection (and cf. Holladay, "ERETS — Underworld"). Finally, some scholars have advanced the possibility that the text refers to a situation in which Israel and Judah are united under one leader and "go from the land to battle against other nations" (Blakenbaker, *Language of Hosea 1–3*, 147).

It is worth noting, however, that Macintosh admits that the text was understood from the exilic period onwards as "they will go up (to the land of Israel) from the land (of their captivity)." The implications of his admission are clear if one considers the phrase as an integral part of the book of Hosea in its present form, which is a postmonarchic document. In fact, there is much in favor of this understanding. First, the text in Hosea 2 unequivocally resonates with Ezekiel 37. One may notice easily that the themes of a future reunification of Israel and Judah, of a Davidic ruler over them, of a future, eternal, and peaceful covenant, and even of Israel's being YHWH's people are all there, as is the reference to returning from the exile. See also Ezek 34:24-28, and see Hosea 3, Setting. Second, not only is עלה "to go/come up" the usual expression for coming to the land of Israel, but X עלה מן is widely used for leaving the land of X to come to Israel/Canaan (e.g., Gen 13:1; 45:25; 50:24; Exod 3:8, 17; 17:3; 32:1, 4, 7, 8, 23; 33:1; Num 16:13; 20:5; 21:5; 32:11; Deut 20:1; Josh 4:16, 17, 19; 24:32; Judg 6:8, 13; 11:13, 16; cf. Exod 1:10, "escape from the land"; 3:17), and in particular in reference to the Exodus from Egypt (Exod 3:8, 17; 17:3; 32:1, 4, 7, 8, 23; 33:1; Num 16:13; 20:5; 21:5; 32:11; Deut 20:1; Josh 24:32; Judg 6:8, 13; 11:13, 16; 19:30; 1 Sam 8:8; 10:19; 12:6; 15:2, 6; 2 Sam 7:6; 1 Kgs 12:28; 2 Kgs 17:7, 36; Isa 11:11; Jer 2:6; 11:7; 16:14; 23:7; Hos 2:17; 12:14; Amos 2:10; 9:7; Mic 6:4; Ps 81:11) and associated related themes or descriptions (e.g., Gen 13:1; 45:25; 50:24; Josh 4:16, 17, 19). Third, the book of Hosea alludes numerous times to, and assumes a readership that is well aware of, pentateuchal traditions. Fourth, the next reading in Hosea, which is clearly interwoven with the present one — see above — explicitly and prominently links the motif of the (past) Exodus/Wandering and that of the future redemption (2:16-17). Fifth, the main objection to this understanding is that 2:2 shows the term הארץ, "the land," which usually refers to Israel, rather than Egypt, or any other country. But from a postmonarchic perspective, it is easy to understand why the text had "the land" instead of "the land of Egypt." The lack of specification of which land it refers to (is it "the land of Egypt"? or Babylon? or "all the lands of their exile"? or some paradigmatic place of exile?) serves better the ideological purpose of closely linking all the traditional imagery of the Exodus, that is, the first coming out of exile, associated with X עלה מן (go/ bring out from the land of X = Egypt or references to Egypt), with that of the future coming out from exile (see Hos 2:16-25 and esp. vv. 16-17, and cf. Ezekiel 37). A similar rhetorical approach led to the choice of "one head" in the same verse, over the alternative "king." The use of the former allows an allusion to Moses (cf. Num 14:4, where the "Anti-Moses" is referred to as "head"), whereas the term "king" would have not. Yet, the readers of this set of prophetic readings know also that this "head" of the ideal future will be like Moses, but also a Davidic king. (See 3:5, and discussion above. For a different approach, see Daniels, *Hosea and Salvation History,* 112. It goes without saying that in periods later than the Persian era, the image of a future Messiah who will combine features of a Davide with those of Moses fulfilled important roles and influenced among others the characterization of Jesus.) Sixth, the lack of specification of the land allows the connotation of "earth" or "underworld" (see 1 Sam 28:13; cf. Gen 2.6; and again cf. Ezek 37:4-14; for an example of the probable use of connotation to enrich the meaning of this text, see the example of רחם discussed above). Seventh, the concept of and the images evoked by the ideological theme of the "return from exile" in the discourse/s of Achaemenid Yehud tend to be multivalent. On the one hand, the return has taken place and stands at the base of the community (see Ben Zvi, "Inclusion in and Exclusion from"), but on the other the community is still in exile and the earth-shaking event of its "return" stands in the future; in fact, it stands as the opening event of an ideal future. The reference to "head" (instead of "king") and the association of this head with the Davides allow for the ideal, messianic images of the future to come. It also, at least by connotation, allows for a reference to the story of the return under Sheshbazzar (as represented in Ezra 1:8, 11; cf. 1 Chr 3:18) or to the stories of the return and rebuilding of the temple associated with Zerubbabel. Thus, the prophecy was considered as (partially) fulfilled in the return and foundation of the temple, but still unfulfilled, and therefore looking towards and defining an ideal future that from the perspective of the readers is certain to come; a future that carries hope and solves any problems with cognitive dissonances (see Carroll, *When Prophecy Failed;* see also Hosea 3, Setting). Eighth, the main alternatives either run counter to the text (עלה מן) such as those represented by the NRSV and Wolff in his Hosea commentary (see Macintosh, *Hosea,* 31; Rupprecht, "עלה מן הארץ," 443), or are based on the image of cultic pilgrimage to a particular place in the land (Jerusalem?) about which nothing is said in Hosea 1–3, or result from attempts to solve tensions raised by the assumption that the text must come from the monarchic period or even the period in which the book is set, and therefore it was unlikely to refer to a future, idealized return from exile. (For the understanding that וְעָלוּ מִן הָאָרֶץ in Hos 2:2 refers to return from exile see, among others, Peshiṭta, Targum, and on this and related aspects of the discussion cf. B. Renaud, "Osée II"; see also Pentiuc, *Long-Suffering Love,* 35 for a general discussion and particularly for a brief but illustrative survey of Christological interpretations. For messianic — but not Christological — interpretations within Jewish medieval interpreters, see, for instance, Radak.)

It is worth stressing that although Hosea 2 and Ezekiel 37 share a large number of motifs and ideological tendencies, the former is clearly marked as Hoseanic and the latter as Ezekianic by their respective language and imagery. Moreover, each fits well its own *Sitz im Buch.* Although these texts share common concerns and ideological stances and reflect a similar discourse, the literati responsible for the prophetic texts clearly allowed each to talk as it were in its own Hoseanic or Ezekianic "voice" and within the literary set that characterizes each book (cf. Ezek 34:24-28).

Another matter to take into account, despite the high use of sexual metaphors: the text consistently avoids the expected formulas "X knew/came to/approached his wife/Y and she conceived and bore . . ." or some variant of them (e.g., Gen 4:1, 17; 16:4; 30:4-5; 38:18; 1 Sam 1:19-20; Isa 8:3; Ruth 4:13; 1 Chr 7:23). Although an explicit reference to Hosea's intercourse with Gomer may seem unnecessary in 1:3 (see Exod 2:1-2), the consistent avoidance of such references is noticeable. The point cannot be that the text wishes to suggest that the children are not Hosea's (for a different position see Simian-Yofre, *Desierto,* 31). Had this been the case, "Hosea-children" would not be comparable to "YHWH-Israel," and then within that metaphorical world Israel would not have to respect and follow its father. Clearly such a meaning would have been contrary to the main thrust of the text. Rather, it seems that the absence of explicit references to Hosea's intercourse is due to the close link that the text creates between the character of YHWH and Hosea. As such, it reflects the uneasiness among the authorship and readership of the book of Hosea with the implied image of YHWH (through Hosea) having sexual intercourse with a woman; cf. Hos 3:1-5 (see STRUCTURE).

It is worth stressing also that despite the sexual imagery in Hosea, neither here nor elsewhere can one find the ideological construction of "sin as sex and sex as sin." This construction did exist in later times (see Wilson and bibliography there), but not in those of the authorship and intended and primary readerships of Hosea. Within their discourses, the ideological construction was "sin as *illegitimate* sex and *illegitimate* sex as sin."

Many (but not all) scholars who maintain that parts of this reading go back to the time in which the book is set, and perhaps even to the historical Hosea, as well as scholars who not only associate the text with an oral address by the historical Hosea but also assume that the prophet could not have spoken of imminent judgment and restoration on the same occasion, have considered some or even many verses in Hos 1:2–3:5 as secondary. In general, verses 1:7 (because of its explicit Judahite perspective; see Wolff, *Hosea,* 20; "verse 7 is easily recognizable as a gloss on v 6") and 2:1-3 have very often been considered late additions (according to Vogels the majority of the scholars consider 2:1-3 an addition; see Vogels, "Osée-Gomer" and idem, "Diachronic and Synchronic"). See also the redactional proposals advanced by Yee, Renaud, and Ruppert, and the reconstruction of the original text advanced by North; for a brief history of interpretation, see Blakenbaker, *Language of Hosea 1–3*, 129-34, and for relatively early proposals, see, for instance, Harper). Although the book of Hosea may have been composed on the basis of written sources or be the *result* of a process of punctuated literary growth, these reconstructions are certainly hypothetical. More important for the present study is the fact that neither the intended nor the primary readers of the book of Hosea were asked to read the book in a way informed by any redactional proposal. To the contrary, they are asked to read it as a unit held together by a title, a conclusion, and numerous markers of textual coherence. From the perspective of the post-monarchic readership of the book of Hosea, there were no reasons to assume that the text shows lack of "unity." Nor is there any proof that any ancient readership ever read the book in the light of any proposed redaction theory.

(The same considerations apply to Nelson's recent claim [Nelson, "Priestly Purity and Prophetic Lunacy in Hosea," esp. pp. 122-30] that Hos 1:2-9 is a tightly constructed and self-contained narrative that is supposed to be read without any reference to Hosea 2 and 3, and that if it is read in that way, the marriage between Gomer and Hosea has nothing to do with the marital metaphor of YHWH and Israel. Yet the intended and primary readerships of the book of Hosea were never asked to read Hos 1:2-9 as independent from Hosea 2 and 3; in fact, the opposite is true.)

Genre

This text is a DIDACTIC, PROPHETIC READING, that is, a text that is meant to be read and reread by ancient readers and that claims it should be read as part of YHWH's word, the part associated with a prophetic character of the past named Hosea. It is also not a regular prophetic reading, however. It is one that was supposed to be read not only within the general context of the book of Hosea, but also as an integral part of a closely related set of readings (Hosea 1–3).

The text is also a narrative. There are two main speakers, the narrator and YHWH, although most of the text is assigned to the latter. As a rule, the narrator confirms and fulfills the divine speech (for instance, cf. vv. 2 and 3) and provides continuity to the narrative. From the perspective of the book as whole, the text is YHWH's word (see Hos. 1:1), whether attributed to the speaker YHWH or to the narrator. So, even when it takes the form of a seemingly simple narrative (e.g., v. 6aα), it is still an integral part of YHWH's word.

The text activated the expectations that the readership associated with several literary topoi. It shows the usual sequence of marriage, giving birth to children, and naming them, but also defamiliarizes this sequence in more than one way. For instance, as mentioned above, the wife is a promiscuous woman, and explicit references to the husband's sexual activity are omitted. Moreover, neither the wife nor the children stand as heroes by themselves (contrast with

Gen 4:1; 21:2; Exod 2:2; 1 Sam 1:20, etc.) but only as symbols of what they are supposed to personify. In this regard, the text follows a particular topos in prophetic literature, that of the symbolic children (cf. Isa 7:14-17; 8:3-4; the case of Isa 9:5-7 is different again, because the child is not only a carrier of a symbolic name, but is to become the hero). It is worth noting also that even the prophetic character, Hosea, bears a name that carries a symbolic meaning too; it connotes deliverance.

(It is likely that גמר בת דבלים "Gomer daughter of Diblaim" carried some symbolic connotation too, but the case is less clear — many readers who lived later than the primary readership carried that expectation and had no problem assigning one to her name associations; see, for instance, b. Pes. 87a-b; Ibn Ezra. Originally גמר might have pointed, ironically, to "perfection," whereas the vocalization of the name could have carried a pejorative connotation [cf. Anderlini, "GMR BT DBLYM," 306, n. 6; Fensham, "Marriage Metaphor," 71; Mays, *Hosea,* 26; Rudolph, *Hosea,* 50]; דבלים might have evoked the image of either "fig" or "fig cakes" [cf. 1 Sam 25:18; 30:12; 2 Kgs 20:7; Isa 38:21; 1 Chr 12:41] and see Hos 2:14. But, as stated above, the case is not as clear as in all the other names. On the possible meanings of the name Gomer, see also Scibona "Gomer.")

It is important to stress that the narrative here carries also a mythical dimension, which is developed in the next reading in the set and informs the understanding of this text in the continuous rereading of the community/ies among which it was intended to undergo this process. Moreover, already in this reading itself, there are clear references to a future ideal world that will be fulfilled on a day that has already been formed, as it were. At that time, former divine promises will be fulfilled, and the world known to the Judahites and the intended readership of the book will change dramatically. Within this reading, the changes are within the inner-group envisaged by the community (or "nation"), but as it is reread in a manner informed by the next reading, it involves changes in nature too, and in the relation between YHWH and nature. Moreover, these changes do not seem reversible within the world communicated by the book. To be sure, there is no doubt whatsoever that neither this text nor the following unit (2:3-25) is an apocalypse, but, nonetheless, messianic and perhaps eschatological-like elements are present. They are present already in this reading, even if they become more prominent in 2:16-25, and the more so given that the latter text did inform the way in which the intended, and most likely the primary, readers of the book of Hosea approached 1:2–2:3.

The fulfillment of these elements was imagined to be in history, in social realia, but also particularly in the light of verses such as 2:20, this history or social realia was conceived within a larger mythical frame. Myth was not out of their "(hi)story," but a part of it. To some extent, this unit as it was read and reread in the light of 2:3-25 may be considered as a mythical formulation of Israel's (hi)story that extends well into the future of the community of readers, into a future whose date is unknown and probably irrelevant but whose certainty is strongly emphasized. (On general questions of apocalypse/apocalyptic elements and prophetic texts see in particular Collins and Grabbe's contributions in Grabbe and Haak [eds.], *Knowing the End from the Beginning.*)

The account in this section bears also the thematic markers of prophetic stories that report about prophets of old who have behaved in ways that, on the surface, seem to be odd and even "anti-social," such as marrying Gomer and giving children "strange" names. From the perspective of the readers of the book of Hosea — and other prophetic books — such seemingly outlandish behavior was not so odd among prophets of old (cf. Isa 20:3; Ezek 4:9-12). In fact, references to it further legitimize and enhance Hosea's status as a true prophet (compare and contrast with Nelson, "Priestly Purity and Prophetic Lunacy in Hosea"; see also Rowley, *Men of God,* 92-93). To be sure, reports of odd, symbolic actions also serve to call the attention of the readers of the book to the future reality that they signify.

These reports and above all the characterization of prophets that they convey (i.e., seemingly "odd" personages) are informed by a long ancient Near Eastern tradition that associates some prophetic personages with symbolic actions meant to signify a future reality. (See already ARM [Archives royales de Mari] 26 206 [= A. 3893] which appears with translation and a selected bibliography in Nissinen, *Prophets and Prophecy,* 38-39; cf. Isa 20:3; Jer 19:10; passim.) The communicative efficacy of some of these symbolic actions, whether enacted in the actual world or narrated in a book, is related to awareness in society of a principle of analogy (e.g., *shattering* a bottle signifies *shattering* of the people and the city). Although a similar principle is at the center of sympathetic magic, it is worth stressing that the point here is certainly not one of manipulation of future events, but to the contrary one of a representative embodiment of either (a) a future that is (rhetorically) presented as unavoidable or (b) a strongly characterized past, or (c) both. Literary accounts of symbolic actions in the prophetic books of the HB tend to be relatively brief, and to include three main components: (a) a report of the commission to perform the act, (b) a report of its performance, and most importantly, (c) an explicit, reliable explanatory remark about its meaning. On the surface, this reading seems to fulfill the expectations of the target readership that these components be included and that they be reliable (see vv. 2-9), but this seeming fulfillment serves to catch the attention of readers to the way in which the text undermines both the message conveyed by the explanatory notes in these verses and the convention of a self-contained, relatively brief report including accounts about commission, performance, and a reliable explanation. The profound significance of the actions referred to in vv. 2-9 (both marriage and naming of children) is by no means circumscribed or even faithfully represented by the explanations advanced in these verses. In fact, any understanding of these actions in terms of explanations given in vv. 2-9 alone would be not only partial, but also fundamentally misleading. The full significance of these actions and names becomes clear to the readers of the book only when the expected "format" is broken and the reported actions are understood in the light of 2:1-3, chapter 2 as a whole, and, to some extent, in the light of chapter 3 as well. (On these reports of symbolic actions see Hals, *Ezekiel,* 354-55; Sweeney, *Isaiah,* 536-37, and bibliography cited there. For other accounts involving symbolic naming of children in HB prophetic literature see Isa 7:14; 8:3; and cf. 7:3.)

Setting

The book of Hosea provides no clear setting within and for this narrative. Where did Hosea receive this divine communication? Was it private? Were other people able to "listen" to it? Within the world of the book the addressees in 1:9, 2:3 are the people, in the second person plural. The text shifts addressees, but there is no indication at all that the setting of the speech act changes. In fact, this is a typical strategy in a written text and serves to bring the intended readers into the text; after all, they are Israel too. Significantly, this strategy is not compatible with a report of a speech that presents itself as fully mimetic of an external reality.

It is worth stressing that there is nothing to anchor this narrative to any *Sitz im Leben* within the world of the book. There is nothing to anchor the narrative to any historical event outside the world of the book, besides the claims advanced in Hos 1:1, which inform the entire book. Moreover, the narratorial voice does not mention the circumstances of the narration or any aspect of those who are addressed. The text requires from the readers only to accept the sequential, internal logic of the narration. But there are no temporal markers beyond that, nor is any social or historical precise background given.

This openness is not accidental. This narrative is not presented to its intended readers as one about historical or biographical events, dependent on a particular *Sitz im Leben,* or meaningful only against a precise set of socio-historical circumstances. The readership is asked to go above and beyond these concerns, and particularly so as the narrative turns into a basic meta-narrative: a mythical reconstruction of a terrible past that will be transformed into a great future, and that serves to encapsulate and shape an authoritative understanding of Israel's understanding of its (own terrible) past as well as its hopes and certitude for the future.

The setting of the activities of reading, rereading, studying, and meditating on this section of the (present) book of Hosea, however, is clear. It concerns a very small group of literati in Persian Yehud who were bearers of high literacy. The social settings in which these literati could have read to others this section, or a portion of it, or perhaps the entire set of readings are difficult to reconstruct. It is likely that they involved public performance and, given the authority of the text, that such performances, whether in the form of public teaching, ceremonial reading, or the like, were controlled in some way or another by the center of power in Jerusalem. On these matters see Ben Zvi, "Introduction: Writings, Speeches, and the Prophetic Books — Setting an Agenda."

Another important element in the setting is that which may be called the general discourses or the mindset of these literati. What can be learned on these matters from this didactic reading? The ideological constructions that the text reflects and reinforces are part and parcel of their worldview. For instance, the text deals with the self-image of Israel as one who because of its own nature is ready and willing to sin (metaphorically, a "promiscuous" woman), with the ideological construction of the futility of seeking support from any ruler or deity other than YHWH (metaphorically, the "other men" whose work is implied in the text), and with the construction of YHWH as a merciful ruler that despite all is willing and certainly will take Israel back.

One of the main messages of the text is the implicit exhortation to follow YHWH's ways, which within the world of the images of the text is presented as an exhortation not to be a "promiscuous woman," but rather like "Hosea." The text contrasts the behavior of the "promiscuous woman" and the man "Hosea" who did as commanded, even if it meant to endure that which misleadingly could have been interpreted by his contemporaries as dishonor (cf. Abraham's test). Of course, one must keep in mind that the text was written by male literati for a male primary readership within a patriarchal society. Another, and just as important, communicative role of this passage is to evoke among its readers images of an ideal future that are associated with pentateuchal traditions (e.g., Exodus, Moses), but that go well beyond a repetition of the mythological past agreed upon by authorship and readership. These images involve messianic aspirations, return from exile, and a reshaping of Israel's polity, its leadership, and even the world to some extent. The text assumes the fulfillment of divine judgment/punishment, but uses references to the past associated with them (e.g., the fall of Jehu's dynasty) to communicate to the readers a sense of certitude about the fulfillment of this future (see STRUCTURE).

Needless to say, references to pentateuchal traditions in this context not only reflect but also contribute to the shaping of a shared culture in which these traditions serve as basic meta-narratives for understanding Israel's world and circumstances.

Finally, the text reflects, shapes, and inculcates the Judahite or Yehudite ideological position that the separate existence of northern Israel is not in accordance with the divine will, that the latter is consistent with one polity that is centered on Judah and their kings. The references to Judah in 1:7 and 2:2 reflect this Judahite or Yehudite perspective in which pan-Israelism is conceptualized as an extension of the Jerusalemite polity (cf. Ben Zvi, "Inclusion in and Exclusion from"). In this regard it is worth noting the multiple uses of the term "Israel" in this text. In v. 1 it certainly means the northern kingdom, to the exclusion of Judah. In v. 4 it signifies the northern kingdom, but the Yehudite readership of the book of Hosea might have wondered whether it carried a secondary connotation that encompasses Judah as well, and particularly so since the reversal of the earlier day of Jezreel involves both Judah and (northern) Israel and is to carry out the fulfillment of the Judahite/Jerusalemite ideology (2:2), and in any case, the earlier day of Jezreel could be interpreted as the beginning of the process of the destruction of the monarchic period polities. Verse 7 seems to refocus the reader on the northern kingdom, but in v. 9 it is impossible to understand "my people" as excluding the Judahites and those who thought themselves to be their direct successors, including the intended and primary readership of the book of Hosea. So the child stands not only for the northern Israelites, but also for the theological concept of YHWH's people. The same holds true for 2:1. Although 2:2 brings back the meaning of Israel as exclusively pointing to the descendants of the northern kingdom, it does so to include it explicitly in a Judah-centered ideological future (cf. Jer 50:4); see also the identity of those addressed in 2:3. In other words the meaning of the term "Israel" has shifted within the reading itself from a socio-political unit that existed at some point to an ideological Israel whose trajectory leads into the ideal future, and with whom the intended readership of the book fully identifies. In a similar way the term "land" has shifted: whereas at least theoretically it could have been interpreted as the land of the northern kingdom alone in 1:2, it surely does not exclude Judahite territory in 2:2. Significantly, as the rereadership moves into the next unit in this set of readings, the inclusive, ideological constructions of Israel (YHWH's people, child, unfaithful wife, future bride, the people of the Exodus) and of the land take full control. As they move into the conclusion of the set (3:4), they find a strong reminder that these ideological conceptions are all part and parcel of the discourse of Judah/Yehud, to the exclusion of both the historical discourse of the northern kingdom and that of Persian period Samaria. Such a conclusion is more poignant given the rhetorical association of the ideal future with the day of Jezreel (2:2, 24).

(For a very different understanding of Hos 2:2, according to which it "refers to the co-operative effort of Hoshea and King Ahaz of Judah to overthrow Pekah, see Hayes and Kuan, "Final Years," 155.)

Intention

This reading has caused much debate and uneasiness for centuries, because of the divine command given to Hosea to marry a prostitute or a "promiscuous woman" (see below). Did YHWH actually command him to marry a "real" prostitute? Or was she not a prostitute at all (e.g., North, "Hosea's Introduction"), or at the very least not at the time of the marriage? (Cf. Harper, *Hosea,* 206 ["a man of sensitive temperament marries a young woman who later proves unfaithful to her marriage vows"]; Andersen and Freedman, *Hosea,* 165; cf. Macintosh, *Hosea,* 9 — the opposite has also been suggested that Gomer was a harlot before her marriage to Hosea, but was not unfaithful later [cf. Sweeney, *Twelve Prophets,* 38].) Perhaps she was a "young Israelite woman, ready for marriage, who had demonstrably taken part in the Canaanite bridal rite of initiation that had become customary" (see Wolff, *Hosea,* 15 and cf. Simian-Yofre, *Desierto,* 29-32). Or perhaps she was a "temple prostitute" or simply a Ba'al worshiper (see Andersen and Freedman, *Hosea,* 163) or even just a woman worshiping as any common Israelite worshiper of the time (e.g., Waterman, "Hosea, Chapters 1–3"). Or is it inconceivable that YHWH would command anyone, and least of all a faithful prophet, to marry a real prostitute, and, therefore, the story of the marriage is a matter of a divine message conveyed through a dream or the like, but involving no real matrimony and human sexual contact? (For the first main alternative, despite all their differences, see, for instance, Cyril of Alexandria, Irenaeus, bab. Pesahim, Rashi, Abrabanel; for the second, for instance, Augustine, Luther; for the third, for instance, Ibn Ezra, Rambam, Radak, Calvin). Or should the text be understood allegorically? As expected the tension created by the association of a true prophet with a prostitute, in the context of the values and discourse of the traditional, patriarchal communities of readers of the text, led to a variety of interpretative approaches that sought to attenuate the tension. For a summary and discussion of many of these attempts see Y. Sherwood, *The Prostitute and the Prophet,* esp. pp. 19-82; cf. Bons,

"Osée 1,2." For an example of a redactional-critical approach to the problem that associates all the "problematic" expressions with a later stage, see, for instance, North, "Hosea's Introduction."

If one focuses on the ancient readers and rereaders for whom the book was composed, it is obvious that the discursive necessity of running a marital narrative parallel to that of YHWH's relationship with Israel requires the image of a marriage between a prophet and a "promiscuous woman" — which is the best English translation for אשת זנונים (see Keefe, *Woman's Body,* 18-21 and bibliography; Ben Zvi, "Observations on the Marital Metaphor"). Moreover, the point of the text here is that YHWH knew from the beginning that Israel because of its very nature would go astray (see Ben Zvi, "Observations on the Marital Metaphor"). This being so, the narrative of the text demands a story about such a marriage. It is worth noting that within the discourse of these ancient literati, YHWH may give commands that, within the shame and honor system of the period, would seemingly undermine the honor of the person who follows them (cf. Isaiah 20 and Ezekiel 4), but which for the readers of the books clearly enhanced their status, because these prophets show unequivocally that they follow YHWH's will by performing these actions, and therefore, are worthy of much honor. Their message is thus reinforced. The literary character of Hosea does not lose honor by doing as he was commanded, nor is one to expect that YHWH (whose structural slot is shared by Hosea in this text) be imagined as actually — as opposed to seemingly — losing honor, even if he metaphorically married such a promiscuous wife as Israel.

Of course, within the discourse/s of the period, YHWH's particular relation with Israel could have led *theoretically* to a perceived diminished status of YHWH, at least among the nations. Such a theological position not only would be consistent with those that assume that the nations will understand the actions and above all the destruction wrecked upon Israel as a dishonor for YHWH (see, for instance, Exod 32:12; Jer 14:21; Joel 2:17; Ps 25:10-11; 143:11-12), but also would seem to explain in theological terms the reality of the readership in which all peoples, except one considered quite insignificant from the perspective of worldly might, worship and thus honor YHWH. Within the ideological world reflected and shaped by the text, of course, YHWH cannot really lose status. For one thing, there is no one to whom YHWH's status may be lost. If the honor-shame game is eventually a zero-sum game, it is impossible to lose any if no one can gain any. Within this discourse, YHWH's real honor is actually incommensurable. When all of this is taken into account, the issues raised here and the explicit characterization of Israel as a promiscuous woman suggest a particular construction of self that on the one hand is strongly self-deprecatory, but on the other maintains that there is a special, everlasting relation between YHWH — the only deity — and Israel that is not contingent on any possible Israelite behavior. No action of Israel can break this relation, as Hosea 1–3 clearly shows, as it results from a fully unexplainable love of YHWH for Israel (see Ben Zvi, "Observations on the Marital Metaphor").

This commentary deals with the book of Hosea from the perspectives most likely to belong to the primary and intended readership — as opposed to other readerships, ancient or contemporary. Within this frame of reference, the most important observation is that all textual markers (see the salience of the explanation notes, and how they take over the story towards the end of the unit) suggest that the main intention of the text was not to provide the readers with a kind of (personal life) biography of a particular man, Hosea, nor to elicit thoughts about *his* supposed prophetic growth through his difficult family or marital experiences. Instead, it was to instill a hope for the future based on the theme of obeying YHWH and following YHWH's lordship and on an explanation of Israel's (hi)storical disasters in terms of a just retribution for Israel's rejection of YHWH. In this regard, despite all the smiles that the "sanitized" version of Hosea that appears in the Targum raises today, it still conveys at least some of the intention of the book.

> ". . . Go and speak a prophecy against the inhabitants of the idolatrous city, who continue to sin. For the inhabitants of the land surely go astray from the worship of the Lord. So he went and prophesied concerning them that, if they repented, they would be forgiven; but if not, they will fall . . ." (Tg. Hos 1:2-3). "And from the land where they were exiled among the nations, when they transgressed the law . . . they shall return and be made great. . . ." (Tg. Hos 2:2).

For a contemporary reconstruction of the historical circumstances of Hosea's life, see Macintosh, *Hosea,* 117-19; for a premodern construction of the process of prophetic growth associated with his experiences, see b. Pes 87a-b. It is worth emphasizing that neither this SET OF READINGS (i.e., Hosea 1–3), nor any of the three individual READINGS shows any particular interest in Hosea, or any other human character for that matter, as a hero. On the contrary, Hosea, Gomer, the woman in ch. 3 — who may or may not be Gomer, see commentary there — the children, or the lovers of the woman for that matter, appear in the text only in so far as their presence and actions stand as a metaphor for facets of the relation between YHWH and Israel (or the land associated with Israel). One may note also that "there is no evidence . . . of the usual interest of a legend in the person of a hero, who in prophetic stories ordinarily appears as an able prognosticator or determiner of the future, as a miracle worker, or a sufferer, with an ultimate emphasis on divine action through or in him" (Buss, *Prophetic Word,* 55; Buss is referring to ch. 1, but his considerations apply to chs. 1–3 as well). Of course, texts communicate more than one message. For instance, our text undoubtedly reinforces the ideological constructions discussed under Setting.

Bibliography

G. Anderlini, "GMR BT DBLYM (Os 1,3)," *Rivista Biblica* 37 (1989) 305-11; M. J. Buss, "Tragedy and Comedy in Hosea," *Semeia* 32 (1984) 71-82; R. P. Carroll, *When Prophecy Failed. Cognitive Dissonance in the Prophetic Traditions of the Old Testament* (New York: Seabury Press, 1979); C. S. Ehrlich, "The Text of Hosea 1:9," *JBL* 104 (1985) 13-19; F. C. Fensham, "The Marriage Metaphor in Hosea for the Covenant Relationship Between the Lord and His People (Hos. 1:2-9)," *JNSL* 12 (1984) 71-78; L. L. Grabbe and R. D. Haak (eds.), *Knowing the End from the Beginning: The Pro-*

phetic, the Apocalyptic, and Their Relationships (JSPSupS 46; London: T&T Clark International/Continuum, 2003); R. M. Hals, *Ezekiel* (FOTL 19; Grand Rapids, MI: Eerdmans, 1989); D. J. H. Hayes and J. K. Kuan, "The Final Years of Samaria (730-720 BC)," *Bib* 72 (1991) 153-81; R. Hillers, *Treaty-Curses and the Old Testament Prophets* (BibOr 16; Rome: Pont. Bib. Inst., 1964); W. L. Holladay, "ERETṢ — Underworld: Two More Suggestions," *VT* 19 (1969) 123-24; S. A. Irvine, "The Threat of Jezreel (Hosea 1:4-5)," *CBQ* 57 (1995) 494-503; T. Jacobsen and K. Nielsen, "Cursing the Day," *SJOT* 6 (1992) 187-204; E. H. Maly, "Messianism in Osee," *CBQ* 19 (1957) 213-25; T. E. McComiskey, "Prophetic Irony in Hosea 1.4: A Study of the Collocation על פקד and Its Implications for the Fall of Jehu's Dynasty," *JSOT* 58 (1993) 93-101; M. Nissinen (with contributions by C. L. Seow and R. K. Ritner), *Prophets and Prophecy in the Ancient Near East* (Writings from the Ancient World 12; Atlanta: Society of Biblical Literature, 2003); F. S. North, "Hosea's Introduction to His Book," *VT* 8 (1958) 429-32; B. Renaud, "Osée II: 'LH MN H'RṢ: Essai d'interprétation," *VT* 33 (1983) 495-500; G. Rendsburg, "Hebrew RḤM = 'Rain,'" *VT* 33 (1983) 357-62; K. Rupprecht, "עלה מן הארץ (Ex. 1:10, Hos. 2:2): 'sich des Landes bemachtigen'?" *ZAW* 82 (1970) 442-47; R. Scibona, "'Gomer' (Os 1,3) Nota Critica (Area filologica sumerica e semitica)," *BeO* 43 (2001) 3-28; D. J. Slager, "The Figurative Use of Terms for 'Adultery' and 'Prostitution' in the Old Testament," *The Bible Translator* 51 (2000) 431-38; M. A. Sweeney, *Isaiah 1–39 with an Introduction to Prophetic Literature* (FOTL 16; Grand Rapids, MI: Eerdmans, 1996); N. M. Waldman, "The Breaking of the Bow," *JQR* 69 (1978) 82-88; W. W. Wilson, "Sin as Sex and Sex with Sin: The Anthropology of James 1:12-15," *HTR* 95 (2002) 147-68.

Note: Bibliography mentioned in Hosea 1–3 is not repeated here.

Second Didactic, Prophetic Reading:
Israel's Trajectory from Divine Judgment to the Ideal End-Situation through Metaphors of Family Relationships in a Reported Divine Monologue, 2:3-25

Structure

It is obvious that most of the literary space in this didactic, prophetic reading was devoted to (a) the description of YHWH's punishment and the substantiation of its reasonability and (b) images of future reconciliation. In other words, the bulk of the text deals with both the judgment of monarchic Israel (and from the perspective of the primary readership, also of Judah) and the hopes and expectations of the postmonarchic community for a divine reconciliation with Israel (i.e., the community of [rightful] servants/worshipers of YHWH) that has earthly implications. Defamiliarizing introductions and the continuation of family imagery for the description of the past and future relations between the superordinate (YHWH, father/husband) and Israel (wife/sons and daughters) also play substantial roles.

The text as a whole is presented to the readers as a divine monologue. The text leaves open the circumstances in which YHWH spoke (thought?) these words and who was in the audience. Although here and there within the monologue there are references to a supposed addressee in the second person (e.g., the children of the mother in v. 4, the wife in v. 18), the same addressee is referred to in the third person in close textual proximity (see vv. 6-7, 17). Although shifts between second and third person are common in poetry, and in the prophetic books, they still suggested to the readers of the book that they should not take the report as mirror of a particular speech of YHWH to a particular group or individual at a particular time and against particular circumstances. Rather, it is a monologue to be read by an intended readership, which is supposed to identify with the "you"s in the text, that is, Israel (see below). (The occurrence of the expression 'ה םאנ, often translated "thus says the LORD," also does not necessarily mean that the words of a "narrator/commentator" interrupted the divine monologue. YHWH may refer to YHWH in the third person; see, among others, Judg 6:26; 1 Sam 10:19; 2 Sam 12:9; 1 Kgs 17:14; 2 Kgs

20:5; Isa 49:7; Jer 14:10; 17:5; 23:16; 26:2; 27:16; Mic 2:5; 4:7, 10; Zeph 3:12; Mal 1:4.)

The immense majority of scholars consider v. 4 the beginning of the unit. (For an exception, see Sweeney, *Twelve Prophets,* esp. 27-28.) On the surface, such considerations make sense thematically. Moreover, units in prophetic books may certainly begin with imperatives (e.g., Zeph 2:1). Yet within the world of the book of Hosea the identity of those who are asked to remonstrate, that is, those identified indirectly by the reference to *"your* mother" in v. 4 is most likely the same as those identified in v. 3 by the similar *"your* brothers . . . *your* sisters" (and it points to Israel). Moreover, and particularly given this identity of the addressee, the text in v. 3 may connote the following meaning, "Say to your brothers, Ammi ('my people'); say to your sisters, Ruhamah ('she-is-pitied'); remonstrate with your mother, remonstrate. . . ." Needless to say, this understanding defies the familiar expectations of the readers, who might have assumed that following the first two calls, the third would have been positive too. Defamiliarizing introductions and texts written so as to run at some point opposite to the expectations they create are not strange to prophetic literature, or to literature in general. They serve to draw attention to the text (see also 16aα in this same unit) and enhance its "punch." Moreover, in this instance, there are additional levels at which the "defamiliarizing" introduction makes sense. One of them will be discussed below. It suffices to say at this point that for the children to be able to contend with their mother in the name and as per the direct instructions of their father (YHWH) they have to identify themselves — at the very least at some level — with the latter and his (just) claims, but if they do so, they are "my people" and "she-is-pitied."

It is worth emphasizing that both the mother and the children are Israel and so are the readers of the book. Of course, they are Israel in the theological/ ideological, trans-temporal sense of the term. From their perspective, Israel has sinned, was punished, reads and learns about its past which from its perspective is a reflection of the status of its relation with YHWH. This Israel encompasses the people who lived in the northern and southern monarchical polities, those who were at the Exodus from Egypt, those who went into exile, those living in Persian Yehud; that is, "all Israel." This Israel, of course, can read about itself, can be called to remonstrate with itself, and can imagine itself as both "she-is-pitied" and "she-is-not-pitied," as YHWH's people, and as a people who rejected and were rejected, or better, who seemingly (or metaphorically) were rejected and are certainly worthy of being rejected by YHWH.

If the text is understood as a direct representation of words that the historical prophet Hosea actually said to a group of (northern) Israelites at a particular event, a tendency to separate the mother from the children is likely to develop. For instance, some have understood the latter as referring to a group of pious, or potentially pious Israelites who were addressed by the historical prophet, and the former as the sinful majority (e.g., G. I. Davies, *Hosea,* 69-70; and see already the Targum that associates the latter with "the prophets" and the former with the "congregation of Israel"). For the position that "the speech beginning in 2:4 is not some abstract theological meditation on Yahweh's relationship with Israel that uses the allegory of Israel as Yahweh's wife . . . rather the speech is Hosea's proclamation of Yahweh's 'divorce' from the Asherah and his 'disinheritance' of his own people for supporting the sexual rites between Asherah and Ba'al," see Whitt, "Divorce" (quotation from p. 66); for the position that the "wife" stands for the city of Samaria, see J. J. Schmitt, "The Wife of God." These two last positions have not received much support. For one thing, neither Asherah nor Samaria is mentioned in this unit. For a critique of Schmitt's position, see A. Dearman, "YHWH's House."

Despite the fact that both the children and the mother are Israel, the metaphors evoke in the readership a different spectrum of images. Among these two, only the mother/wife can be treated as adulteress, as having lovers, and as a bride-to-be of YHWH. Only the mother/wife can be construed metaphorically as "the land." These metaphorical constructions play a most significant role in the present report of a divine monologue. As for the children, they may be seen as kids pleading with their mother to improve her behavior, lest their father will abandon and punish her and them — a family imagery that may have carried emotional power within the world of the intended readership. The children can also be construed as the "children of the land." The land is supposed to nourish them, but if it is unproductive because of drought, their fate will be sealed. Certainly, the close association of Israel and "the land" reflected and shaped by the metaphor carried ideological overtones, and as such was coherent with main meta-narratives existing in the central discourse of Yehud and was ubiquitous in prophetic literature in general. (On "the woman" as "the land," cf. Keefe, *Woman's Body,* 213-20 and see below.)

The beginning of a new subunit in 2:16 can be securely inferred from the change of tone, theme, and the concluding נאם ה׳ "utterance of YHWH" in 2:15; cf. Hos 11:11. The expression נאם ה׳ appears also in Hos 2:18, 23, but in a non-final position and within references to circumstances that will hold on ביום ההוא "on that day"; in these cases it conveys stress and legitimacy to the text but does not serve as a major macrosyntactical marker. (On נאם ה׳ see Meier, *Speaking,* 298-314, and concerning its discourse functions see also Parunak, "Some Discourse Functions," 510-12.) Awareness of the beginning of a new subunit after v. 15 is reflected not only in the MT system of paragraph markers, but already in 4QXIIc (Russell, *The Twelve,* 239). It bears stressing, however, that the intended and most likely primary readers of the book are asked to read the two sections as part of one reading. First, there is the opening in v. 16, לכן "therefore" that presupposes a preceding text. Second, a comprehensive set of textually inscribed references conveys to the intended and primary readerships a sense of coherence and serves them as an interpretative key. For instance, the reference to מדבר ("desert") in 2:5 evokes and serves as a signpost for the readers of the book that points at מדבר ("desert") in 2:16. The readers are asked to imagine that Israel/wife/land becomes a desert, but also that the desert is where YHWH/husband/provider of land will transform Israel/ adulterous wife into a faithful wife. The imagery of punishment carries in itself that of a new ideal future. Similarly, images of parched land and thirst in 2:5 are associated with that of YHWH as the future provider of rain in 2:23. Further, the expression והיא לא ידעה "she did not know" referring to the wife's/Israel's lack of knowledge of YHWH's/husband's attributes and his past actions on her behalf in v. 10 reverberates and is turned around in וידעת את ה' "she will know YHWH" in v. 22 (ct. also with "and me [YHWH] she forgot" in v. 15; for a somewhat similar message that evokes some of the wording in Hosea 2 see Jer 24:7). Significantly, already the scribe responsible for 4QXIIg who left an interval after 1:9 and 2:1 (and accordingly closely links 2:1 to 2:2-15?) left none between 2:15 and 2:16, contrary to the scribe responsible for 4QXIIc (see Russell, *The Twelve*, 239, 276-77).

The language of Hos 2:10 also reverberates in Hos 11:3. The literati who were supposed to read and study the book were asked to perceive the link that this reverberation creates between these two verses, and inform their knowledge of one with that of the other. One may notice also the tapestry of meanings that are created by a comparison of Hos 2:3-25 and Hosea 11:1-6, and the shared references to the beginning of Israel, YHWH's relation to Israel, the latter's familial, but subordinate character (e.g., wife/bride — child).

The expression וידעת את ה' ("and you [fem. sing.] shall know YHWH") in Hos 2:22 may also carry sexual connotations, even if it does not seem to be used to denote a sexual encounter when the subject is a woman (see Hos 3:1-5 Setting). The expression "to know YHWH" carries also the connotation of acknowledging an obligation and ties to YHWH that, within the discourses of the time, could only be imagined in terms of superordinate/subordinate (i.e., suzerain/vassal; husband/wife; etc.) and could only be understood to include a forceful demand to follow the instructions of the superordinate (i.e., YHWH). Conversely "not to know YHWH" or "not to know a deity" connotes that such ties are non-existent, have been abrogated, or that the subordinate decided not to acknowledge them; cf. Hos 5:4 and 6:3 (also cf., among many others, Jer 7:9; Ps 79:6; and see Malul, *Knowledge*, 220, 226). Of course, Hos 2:22 points to the ideal, future situation that involves a new world (see 2:20). Hos 5:4 points to monarchic Israel. Hos 6:3 (at least in one reading of it) suggests a failed return to YHWH that is initiated by Israel rather than by YHWH and that does not include a fundamental change in the nature of Israel (i.e., to be endowed with the features mentioned in 2:21-22). See Hos 5:1–7:2 Setting.

The mention of the devouring חית השדה ("wild animals") in v. 14 brings home not only the terror of YHWH's punishment. Through the process of the anticipated and closely related reversal at work in the text, it evokes in the readers the ideal image of the future in v. 20. Significantly, the same expression חית השדה opens the imagery that characterizes this new world. To this example one may add, among others, the references to "grain, wine, and oil" in v. 10 (cf. also 11) and v. 24. The point is, of course, to emphasize that even the description of the divine punishment which stands in the future of the world of the book, but in the past of the readership, carries in itself the seed of hope and renewal for the future (cf. the motif of the "day of Jezreel" discussed in 1:2–2:3). Thus the "defamiliarizing" introduction in v. 3 is not totally out of order, but reflects the main message of the text as a whole, to its intended readership.

A secondary message deeply interrelated to the first is that Israel's suffering at the hand of YHWH was well deserved. Since this was the case, and since Israel is by definition liable to "fornicate" (see 1:2), the readership community may wonder and worry whether the mentioned restoration would be ephemeral, just as the early period in which Israel's and YHWH's "love" for each other blossomed. The text explicitly assuages these concerns (see v. 21). On the particularities of the images of misbehavior and the future ideal world see Setting and Intention.

The text is also explicitly related to the preceding reading (i.e., Hos 1:2–2:3). See, for instance, the reference to בני זנונים "children of whoredom" in 2:6 and ילדי זנונים "children of whoredom" in 1:2; the references to רוחמה "She-is-pitied" and the occurrence of pi'el forms of the root רחם "show pity" in 1:6, 7; 2:3, 6, 25; references to "not my people" in 1:8; 2:2, 25; to Jezreel (1:4, 5; 2:24); and the reverberation of the separation statement in 1:9 (here, father-child) and that in 2:4 (husband-wife) (see Hos 1:2–3:5; STRUCTURE). Verse 25 also serves as a signpost of the meaning of 1:2–2:3 within the entire set of rereadings from 1:2 to 2:25 (see Hos 1:2–2:25) and to some extent may be seen as a conclusion to that reading. The text of Hos 2:2-25 is linked thematically also to the following reading, 3:1-5 (see Hos 1-3; STRUCTURE).

Subunits, or subdivisions within these subunits, may appear at times clearly demarcated, but even if so their borders are often transgressed. For instance, the reference to "your mother" and "their mother" in Hos 2:4 and 2:7 creates a potential envelope, but "your mother" and "your brothers" in Hos 2:4 and 2:3 are also clearly linked, and 6b with its reference "children of whoredom" suggests an envelope whose second part is in Hos 1:2. The "final" references to She-is-pitied in v. 25 and v. 3 (see also above) may be suggestive of some structural construction, but there is the clear reference in 1:6 too. Likewise, one may notice the instances of "Not-my-people" that link together Hos 2:1 and 2:25 (but see also 1:9). In addition, readers may wonder whether there is a thematic envelope concerning the forced nakedness of the woman/wife/Israel in Hos 2:5 and Hos 2:11a-12b. All in all, the text clearly conveys a sense of overlapping envelopes and overlapping structures, each of which conveys only a partial meaning of the text. The intended and primary readers are asked to take into account the way these different possible structures and their meanings inform each other.

At times, however, clustered repetitions of words and sounds in close proximity serve not only the rhetorical purpose of emphasis that draws the attention of the intended and primary readers to leading words or concepts, but also may connote a sense of a closely knit textual subunit. In this category one may include the three-fold repetition of וארשתיך ("I will take you for my wife") in vv. 21-22 and the five-fold repetition of verbal forms of ענה in the qal ("answer") in vv. 23-24 (the emphatic usage of this verbal form here is preceded by that in v. 17; in the latter the restored ["new"] wife/Israel is the subject; in the former, it is YHWH and his subordinates). See also the eleven-fold repetition of the 3rd person feminine suffixes in vv. 4-6. Yet prominent repetitions may also occur in not such a close textual proximity, as the four-fold reappearance of the term "lovers" in 2:9, 12, 14, and 15 shows. It is worth stressing that word play and in particular repetitions of sounds, including a concern for the sonorous quality of the text, are very common in this reading (e.g., the repetition of final "i" sound in תקראי אישי ולא תקראי לי עוד בעלי "you will call me 'my husband,' and no longer will you call me 'my Baal'" in v. 18; the play on the roots זכר and כרת in vv. 19-20; and the repetition of the same initial letter in ציה "parched [land]" and צמא "thirst" in Hos 2:5, and cf. Ezek 19:13). Such considerations most likely also influenced the choice of words in the text. For instance, see מפתיה and פתח in vv. 16-17 and the unique expression תקוה פתח "door of hope"; considerations of word play influenced word choices elsewhere in the Hebrew Bible, see already Gen 1:1 and see Rendsburg, "Word Play." Another example spans over the entire set of 1:2–2:3 and 2:3-25. It is obvious that there is a textually inscribed bond between 2:1b and 2:25b of which the readers of the book were supposed to be aware (see the explicit reference to "my people"). The second part of this dyad (v. 25b) concludes with a reference to how Israel will call YHWH אלהי "my God"; the sound concluding the sentence is likely to have influenced the choice of words in the ending of v. 1b, which mentions how Israel will be called בני אל חי "children of the living God," even if the expression "living God" appears elsewhere (e.g., Josh 3:10; Ps 42:3; 84:3). (Yoo has noticed that the word חי appears associated with Baal in Ugaritic. *If* the intended and primary readership of the book were aware of such a use, then they would have seen the verse as anticipating or implicitly conveying that which is explicit in v. 18. Yoo, *Israelian Hebrew* [p. 41] associates the occurrence of the expression with Israelian Hebrew in Hosea. On the possible implications of the language of the book of Hosea see Hosea 1:1–14:10 Setting.)

Common word pairs or triads have also influenced the choice of words. For instance, "heaven and earth" (v. 23), "grain, wine, and oil" (v. 24), חיה "beast" and יער "forest" (v. 14; cf. Ps 50:10; 104:20; Isa 56:9). A poetic string is based on the associations between צדק "righteousness" and משפט "justice," and חסד "hesed" and משפט (e.g., Hos 12:7; Mic 6:8; Zech 7:9; for the previous three see Ps 33:5, 89:15), חסד and רחמים "mercy" (e.g., Isa 63:7; Jer 16:5; Zech 7:9; Ps 25:6; 40:12; 51:3; 69:17; 103:4; Dan 1:9), חסד and אמונה "faithfulness" (e.g., Ps 36:6; 88:12; 89:3, 25; 98:3), the latter and משפט (e.g., Deut 32:4; Jer 5:1; Ps 119:30, 75), צדק and אמונה (e.g., Ps 96:13; 119:75, 138; Prov 12:17), and משפט and רחמים (Ps 119:156). These lexical pairs and triads not only provide common expressions but also, from the perspective of a rereading community in the postmonarchic period, raise the possibility of connections with images (and ideological perspectives) that are associated with these expressions in the general discourse of the literati. For instance, and particularly given the context of Hosea 1–3, the associations of צדק "righteousness" and משפט "justice" expressed in Isa 1:21 may be relevant. Perhaps more importantly, Ps 97:2 associates the same attributes with the divine realm, and references to the other attributes in relation to YHWH are numerous (e.g., Ps. 25:6; 33:5; 36:6; 40:12; 89:15; etc.). In other words, the text is likely to connote a sense that future Israel will share, through YHWH's betrothal gifts, many of YHWH's attributes. The future wife becomes closer as it were to her husband. (The basic idea that Israel was supposed to imitate YHWH to some extent belongs to the general horizon of thought of postmonarchic Yehud; cf. Lev 19:2 and see Klawans, "Pure Violence.")

The text also contains references that relate this unit to others in the book of Hosea. For instance, the motif of Israel seeking a deity — or what symbolizes a deity — and not finding it and the related motif of not seeking YHWH appear in Hos 2:9; 3:5; 5:6, 15; 7:10. The continuous reading, rereading, and study of the book bring to the forefront these interconnections and the tapestry of meanings they convey.

Several expressions in this unit deserve particular consideration. (On "she is not my wife, and I am not her husband" see Genre.) The reference to killing the wife by thirst in v. 5 is surely not based on any ancient Near Eastern mode of execution of "wayward" wives. It makes sense only because the woman (/YHWH's wife) *is* the land, and her thirst is drought. Thus YHWH is construed as the provider of rain. Moreover, as a provider of rain he (/husband) fertilizes the land (/wife), clothes her (drought is associated with nakedness, v. 5), and thus allows her children to live. Moreover, since he feeds them through the process that begins with the husband's provision of rain, he serves as the provider of the children, and as such he becomes their patron/father whom they, the children, should acknowledge and serve/worship. This trend of thought and imagery is brought to bear quite explicitly in the emphatic ending of the unit in vv. 23-25.

It is worth noting that this construction of YHWH shares its main attributes with that of Baal (see also Hos 6:2-3). Therefore, it is not surprising that the text does not deal with these attributes per se, but with the question of the identity of the deity who carries them. Thus, the text advances an opposition between the reliable husband/provider and the lover unable to provide. Within these discourses, the true provider/husband is, of course, the one the woman/land/wife is supposed to acknowledge and serve/worship, whereas she is supposed to completely remove even the memory of the others (see vv. 18-19). (On the asymmetrical, non-egalitarian, ideological character of the imagery of marriage implied and expressed here, see Hosea 1-3, STRUCTURE and Ben Zvi, "Observations on the Marital Metaphor of YHWH").

The use of the expression וזרעתיה לי בארץ "I [YHWH] will sow her for myself in the land" in v. 25 is particularly significant given the central role that v. 25 plays for the set of readings from 1:2 to 2:25 (see Hos 1:2–2:3 STRUCTURE). On the one hand the expression is a pun or further development of what is implied in the term Jezreel, which at one level connotes the sense of "El/God sows" and also "El/God scatters seed" (see Hos 1:2–2:3 STRUCTURE). Now YHWH seeds her (Israel) in the land as opposed to the previous scattering of Israel, that is, to its exile from the land (cf. Radak). YHWH seeds her/the land so that it can produce agricultural goods which in turn will provide for the material needs of its people. In addition, the text probably hints at a secondary (metaphorical) connoted imagery, that of YHWH impregnating his wife/land, which in turn stands for Israel — even if the *qal* is used instead of the expected זרע hiphil form. (For a variety of positions concerning the meaning of the phrase, see, among others, Macintosh, *Hosea,* 89-91; Rudolph, *Hosea,* 83; Andersen and Freedman, *Hosea,* 288; Sweeney, *Twelve Prophets,* 37.)

There is one important instance of Janus parallelism in Hos 2:3-25. It involves the word וענתה in 2:17. וענתה conveys the meaning of "answer" in the sense of (a) the willing sexual response of the bride — the sexually charged atmosphere of the section is already clear from the beginning; see מפתיה "I will seduce her" in 2:16 and cf. Exod 22:15, and also (b) that of the responsiveness of the field, that is, being fruitful, growing grain; cf. Hos 2:24. (On these matters, see Frisch and the bibliography mentioned there, and especially Morag, "The Great Metaphor"; cf. idem, "On Semantic and Lexical Features," 494-96.) This case of Janus parallelism clearly serves to further intertwine the images of the woman/bride of YHWH, Israel and the land.

Many scholars have assigned much of the material in 2:3-25, and especially 2:4-17, to the prophet Hosea although the tendency has been to maintain that redactional processes have shaped the present form of these verses. Some assign to Hosea himself some of these processes. The statement of Wolff, as well as the argumentation he advances to support such a reconstruction, is illustrative: "The transmission of these verses [2:4-17] probably goes back to Hosea himself. Later editors (cf. 1:2-9; 2:18-25) could not have taken older rhetorical units and created a literary structure that is such a completely indivisible kerygmatic unit. According to 3:1 Hosea was responsible for some of the written tradition. And chap. 3 represents the continuation of a preceding section, the beginning of which is most likely to be found in 2:4-17" (p. 33). It is worth noting that the claim that one may learn from 3:1 that the historical prophet was responsible for some of the written tradition is dependent on the fact that the text refers to him in the first person. This, however, is hardly a sound basis for identification of actual authors of biblical books or of any books for that matter. To be sure, many other redactional proposals have been advanced. For instance, Yee (1987) has suggested that only vv. 4*, 5, 7b and 12 are Hosea's sayings, and the rest of the material belongs to three different redactional levels.

Several scholars have also advanced the position that vv. 8-9 originally followed v. 15 (e.g., Rudolph, *Hosea*, 68-69). It is obvious that v. 9 ("I [Israel/wife] will go and return to my first husband [YHWH] . . .") may be seen as a first step towards reconciliation, and the more so since the choice of words placed in the mouth of the wife clearly evokes those in v. 18, and may seem like Israel's (/wife's) attempt to reverse the situation reflected in v. 4. But the text as a whole clearly communicates that this future change of mind does not really constitute the change of behavior required by YHWH/husband. In fact, the presence of v. 9b in this literary context would lead the intended, postmonarchic readers of the text to imagine that such a change will be achieved only through the agency of YHWH/husband, as vv. 16-25 explicitly outline, and will represent a "new beginning." It bears notice that from the perspective of the readership of the Book of Hosea the mentioned change of mind of "Israel" towards YHWH — as understood by them — and away from (the worship of) other gods was identified with postmonarchic times (cf. Radak). Yet from their perspective, this shift has not yet resulted in the much-anticipated reconciliation with YHWH that they envisaged and that is addressed in vv. 16-25.

Genre

This unit is a DIDACTIC, PROPHETIC READING. It is a reading to be read and re-read, meditated upon, and read to others by the literati. It is also a reading that is to be understood as part and parcel of a prophetic book. This particular reading is set as a divine monologue.

The monologue is written in such a manner that it evokes images associated with other genres and settings in real life. For instance, 2:4a is evocative of both a divorce and a family quarrel, and it also carries a sense of legal litigation. Of course, it can do that because it does not follow closely any of these "settings." For instance, the formula "she is not my wife, and I am not her husband" is likely to evoke in the readers the image of a divorce (cf. Elephantine papyri B3.3 lines 3-4 and B6.4 line 4 [according to *TAD* numbers; B28 and B36 respectively, according to B. Porten, *Elephantine Papyri in English*]; cf. Geller, "Elephantine Papyri"; Weinfeld, "Patterns," 187-88), but a statement that he has already divorced her cannot sit well with the request to the children to plead with his wife so she may turn away from her ways and save herself from his future punitive actions. In fact, the text here defamiliarizes the use of the formula by advancing an attempt to avoid divorce (cf. Hunter, *Seek the Lord,* 128-29; Macintosh, *Hosea,* 40-41). This is consistent with the tendency to show that YHWH will never divorce Israel, even if such an action would be fully justified within the discourse. In fact, the entire unit emphasizes that YHWH not only will not divorce her, but even will do his best to seduce her back (2:16-25). (On the metaphor of YHWH not divorcing his wife/Israel, and on her symbolic status akin to that of the "wife of youth," see Hosea 1–3, Setting; notice also that Hosea is not described as having another wife before marrying Gomer; the latter is to be understood as his wife of youth.)

The request from the children to plead with her is evocative, in turn, of a family quarrel (cf. Gen 31:36; Macintosh, *Hosea,* 41). From the perspective of the readership, this is a family quarrel that belongs to an odd and quite regrettable past, when they (i.e., the wife in the story) betrayed YHWH rather than reading, rereading, and meditating upon YHWH's word — that is, a prophetic book such as the book of Hosea. Of course, the latter is that which the readership of the book is actually doing.

In addition, one may note that the opening with רִיבוּ ("plead" but also conveying the meaning of "contend") as well as details of the text that resemble (legal) cases of adultery in the ancient Near East (cf. Greengus, "Textbook Case"; Huehnergard, "Biblical Notes on Some New Akkadian Texts," and texts and bibliography cited there) may lead the readers to associate the text with mental images of a judicial action. Yet the reference to the children as those addressed by the request to plead, among other features, is inconsistent with that image. In other words, the text plays with images associated with genres and settings in life within the world of knowledge of the intended readership. This "playfulness" is with purpose. It attracts the attention of the readers, leads them to ponder its possible meanings, contributes to rereading, and serves to communicate a multi-layered message, which includes:

(a) The family quarrel imagery brings home the image that YHWH and Israel are a family, even if it is a quarreling family because of the dissolute behavior of the wife/Israel.

(b) The so-called divorce formula raises the potential of divorce and reminds the readers of other formulas seemingly disassociating YHWH and Israel employed in Hosea 1–3 (Hos 2:8), as well as of their eventual reversal (2:1, 25).

(c) The legal flavor not only justifies YHWH's punishment of Israel that led to the end of the monarchic period, but also leads the readers to ponder about images of punishment and the possible extent of the punishment against the woman/wife/Israel. Is this a final divorce? Does it mean death for the woman/Israel/land? What about her children/inhabitants of the land/Israel? In addition it raises questions about the punishment of her lovers. Does it mean death for her lovers? Obliteration? One may notice v. 19 that moves from "I will remove the names of the baals from her [wife/Israel/land] mouth," indicating her separation from the "baals," to the more general claim about the negation of even the memory of the baals, which is tantamount to total obliteration (cf. Zech 13:2). See "they [the baals] shall be invoked/remembered [root זכר, "remember"] by their name [Heb שם "name" and notice the word pair זכר + שם; cf. Blau, "Reste des I-Imperfekts von *zkr, qal*," 85] no more."

(d) The imagery of the legal avenues for the husband/YHWH to punish his wife/Israel/land may be seen against the background of the actions that, within the discourse of the readership, the husband/YHWH could inflict upon his adulterous wife/Israel/land (e.g., the fall of the monarchic polities, depopulation — the land loses her sons — diminished agricultural production, and the like).

It bears notice that the expression "she is not my wife, and I am not her husband" has led to a vivid debate about its precise meaning. For a very good summary of research and for a proposal see Dass, "Divorce (?) Formula in Hos 2:4a." For an association of the motifs of "divorce" and "vassal lawsuit" see Weinfeld, "Patterns," 187-88.

Setting

The setting of the writing and reading of this portion of the book of Hosea is the same as that of the book as a whole. Both writers and readers are among the literati of Yehud. These literati may also have read the unit or portions thereof, or portions thereof within a larger textual context, to the immense majority who were not able to read for themselves.

Within the world of the book, the divine monologue is not set in any particular *Sitz im Leben*. Moreover, it is not set in any particular time within the monarchic period referred to by the time-frame communicated to the readers in Hos 1:1. This openness of the text is worth stressing. The intended readers are not asked to tie it to any singular historical event or circumstances. The text is presented as a kind of trans-temporal speech within certain limits.

The world of the book belongs to that which may be described as a pre-judgment era, which by inference is constructed as a time of substantial well-being (note references to fertility of the land, gold, etc.). The text, of course, communicates to the readers that such "good times" were essentially unstable, because the people betrayed their provider, YHWH, and worshiped other gods. It is worth noting that the text does not convey a critique of good economic times per se. The opposite holds true. The text clearly reinforces the belief that the material abundance that the Israelites enjoyed at the time was granted by YHWH. It is only because the recipients of these material goods failed to recognize their provider that they were bound to lose them. Needless to say, within the world of the book such a characterization of YHWH as a provider is ideationally related to, and leads to that of, YHWH as husband (and father).

It is worth stressing that this implied ideological discourse not only permeates the world of the book, but also reflects and shapes that of the primary readership of the book. In this sense, it is part and parcel of the setting of the book. Indeed, it serves to reconstruct the ideological horizon of the group within which and for which the book was written in its present form, and within which it was first read, reread, and meditated upon.

The same holds true for other ideological constructions that underlie the horizon of ideas that characterize the world of the book. Among them, one may mention the reflection of male concerns (or insecurities) about female fidelity within husband-wife relations, and above all the implicit ideological construction of the roles of husband and wife in such a relation. One may notice, for instance, that the provider (YHWH/husband) is to be served/worshiped by the one being provided for, that his voice is the dominant one in the relation. He seduces, marries, rejects, condemns, punishes, or restores *his* wife. He has the power of death and life over her (cf. v. 5) and possibly over her sons. Needless to say, he also re-creates her speech and condemns her for it. She is unable to speak for herself in her own defense. Significantly, the wife takes the initiative, according to the husband's recount, only to do evil (that is, to follow other men/ providers/gods).

Moreover, according to 2:10 YHWH the husband/provider/superordinate provides Israel/his wife/subordinate with agrarian goods, and silver and gold. The implicit cultural assumption of both the world of the text and its target (male) readership that informs vv. 9-11 is that women/wives (the land/Israel) are not supposed to gain access to these and related goods (e.g., clothes, see v. 11) directly, but be given them by their male providers who may give but also take back these goods, as explicitly expressed by the semantic wordplay with נתתי "I have given" in v. 10 and ולקחתי "I will take back" and והצלתי "I will remove" in v. 11 (see Greenfield, "Aramaic hnṣl"; incidentally, the sophisticated craftsmanship of the writer is evident here: First there is a verbal form of נצל carrying the meaning "remove" and associated by the mentioned semantic link with the previous נתן [v. 11], and then there is a second verbal form of the same root but this time carrying the meaning "save"). It is worth stressing that these are ideological constructions of marital relations and not necessarily a faithful reflection of the actual circumstances governing all or even most of these relationships in historical Yehud (or monarchic Judah for that matter); contrast, for instance, with Prov 31:10-31. (On some of these matters see Ben Zvi, "Observations on the Marital Metaphor.")

Another important ideological construction in this category is that of the desert/"outside the land" as an area of beginnings or new beginnings. This is consistent with the foundational role of the notion of the "return from exile" in the discourse of Achaemenid Yehud and its conceptual association with the motif of the Exodus from Egypt, which is clearly manifested in v. 17. It is also directly associated with the "mythical" position of the land as the eco-theological place where a proper relation with YHWH is meant to be maintained — and, accordingly, as a place of prosperity and well-being; see above — but at the same time as one that is always in danger of being overrun by its opposite, the "desert." There are numerous attestations to the ideological construction that paradoxically turns the "desert" into a "systemic" purification and preparation place for those deemed unfit to dwell in the land, and further, given the inhospitable character of the desert, metaphorically into one in which YHWH's love (i.e., protective patronship) abides. See Ben Zvi, "What Is New in Yehud?" and T. L. Thompson, "Historiography in the Pentateuch," esp. 265-71; cf. Talmon, "Desert Motif."

It is also important to stress that the motif of the return to the desert is presented to the readership as both a return and a novelty. The historical readers are not supposed to imagine the future experience in and of the desert as simply a replay of the old one. For one thing, Israel (both the woman and the readers) is now older and has an awareness of the deeds described before. More importantly, the future, ideal relation between Israel and YHWH involves a change in the order of creation itself and in the life of humanity (2:20; cf. Isaiah 11; Zech 9:9-10). In addition, the bridewealth or betrothal capital that YHWH will endow Israel with at that time will consist of righteousness, justice, mercy, faithfulness, or fidelity. A woman endowed with this wealth of attributes is able to "know" YHWH (2:21-22; for the general motif and variants of "adorning the bride" with wisdom and other "godlike" features in the ANE and later literature, see Lapinkivi, "Adorning the Bride," and notice the possible associations of this topos with mythological motifs of ascent and descent; cf. Hos 6:2). In others words, the new betrothal results in a new Israel, one that, given all her new attributes, is unable to go astray again. The horizon of thought here is very similar to that in Jer 31:31-34 (notice also the emphasis on a relation that is presented as different from the old covenant, on the motif of YHWH as husband and the clear emphasis on knowing YHWH). This element of a new and different beginning is a response to an implicit fear of circularity, namely, that YHWH marries/enters into covenant with Israel, the latter is a promiscuous woman/tends to go astray from YHWH's ways (Hos 1:2) and away from YHWH (e.g., 2:7), then sooner or later she does so, and as a result YHWH punishes her (exile, destruction of the polities, cessation of proper worship), then YHWH takes her back to the desert and reconciles with her, and the circle begins again. For the circle to stop, and for the readership to image a stable bliss for YHWH's wife Israel, she has to change substantially. She cannot be a promiscuous woman anymore, but one whose essential character is defined by righteousness, *hesed,* faithfulness, and the like. (Cf. with the matters discussed in Ben Zvi, "Analogical Thinking and Ancient Israelite Intellectual History.")

Finally, it is worth stressing that the text not only is consistent with but supports the discourses in Yehudite Israel concerning the "return." From the perspective of the readers, YHWH's monologue as reported in the book may be seen as fulfilled not only in regards to punishment, but also and to some degree concerning hope. From their viewpoint, Israel (as represented by the intended and primary readership of the book) is back in the land (and cf. v. 25), after an exile in the "desert" that within their discourse is compared to the one associated with the exodus from Egypt (and cf. v. 16; this association is very common in postmonarchic literature; see E. Ben Zvi, "What Is New in Yehud?"). The very produce of the fields in Yehud suggests some fulfillment of the promises in vv. 22-25, and, of course, the reversal of that which is stated in vv. 11 and 14 — after all they (and the land) have vines and fig trees. In addition, the existence of a Temple in Jerusalem means that there was a reversal of v. 13 — after all, they have festivals and cultic occasions. From this perspective, YHWH had shown pity on Israel (and the land); see v. 25. Yet the text is clearly double-headed, as is much of the construction of the "return" in Yehudite Israel. The "return" has happened and it is still the future (for a similar case see 1:2–2:3 STRUCTURE). The text here unequivocally indicates to these readers that the ideal world associated with that "return" (see, for instance, v. 20; see discussion on v. 5 in 1:2–2:3 STRUCTURE) and described in YHWH's monologue is nowhere to be seen yet. The text is more about hope for a future change than an evaluation of the (from their perspective, meager) return that led to the establishment of Persian Yehud (see Ben Zvi, "What Is New in Yehud?"). For references in Hosea to the Exodus as construed in an ideal past or the closely related second exodus see Hos 2:17; 11:1, 11; 12:10, 14; 13:4; the images of a second Exodus from Egypt are often associated in this book with those of returning to Egypt, because of the sins of Israel; see 7:13; 8:13; 9:3, 6 and ct. 11:5. The theme/s of coming into and out of Egypt through YHWH's agency informs the entire book of Hosea; for particular comments see discussion of relevant units.

As for the references to "Baal" or "Baals," it is worth stressing that the text does not identify the deity or deities involved (see 2:10, 15, 19; cf. 11:2; 13:1), except in one case in which its referent is YHWH (2:18). (For the unequivocal use of B/baal in reference to YHWH see 2 Sam 5:20; 1 Chr 14:11; in Hos 2:18 the reference to YHWH as "my baal" is placed in the mouth of sinful Israel, who eventually, once it is reconciled with YHWH, will call him "my husband" rather than "my owner/baal.") The lack of markers of particular identity in references to "Baal" or "Baals" (or to "her [Israel's] lovers" in 2:12, 14, 15) is consistent with the tendency of the book to dissociate its world from narrow historical circumstances. Baal, Baals, and "lovers" stand in the text for deities that should not be worshiped or served and who are absolutely powerless (cf. the semantic range of the common expression אלהים אחרים "other gods") except in 2:18. There, the use of the epithet "baal" in reference to YHWH by sinful Israel shows that she does not really know YHWH, that for her YHWH is like one of the baals. Thus, according to the text, when she will finally know him she will call YHWH "her husband," rather than her "baal(-type deity)" (cf. 2:22). Needless to say, the use of the term "baal/baals" in Hosea as general code words for the mentioned type of deities allows multiple readings under different circumstances, and allows multiple identifications with "foreign" deities, or even with the YHWH that wrongdoers imagine to exist, according to the book.

Significantly, the same holds true for references to Baal in other prophetic books (e.g., Jeremiah). From the perspective of the readers of these books, it was irrelevant whether the "baal" in the text refers to Baal Zaphon, or to Baal Shamem, or to any other deity or deities — including YHWH, as per the perception of those who according to the text do not know YHWH — that could be understood as the referent of the term "baal." Instead, for them the crucial ideological and rhetorical matter was that monarchic Israel (or the Israelites) should not and ought not to worship any "baal" deities, but they did anyway. (See also Hos 13:1–14:1 Setting.)

It is worth mentioning that Baal/baals imagery here, in the book of Hosea and in the Hebrew Bible, focuses on meteorological/fertility attributes. The martial attributes of Ba'al are not mentioned (cf. Smith, *Early History,* 79). In these discourses, the military (doomed to fail) "competitors" of YHWH, whom the Israelites may wrongfully trust, are foreign kings and nations (cf., among others, Hos 5:13; see there Setting).

The considerations mentioned above, along with others (e.g., the clearly biased approach of the book), make the world portrayed in the book of Hosea a less than reliable source for the reconstruction of the history of the religious and cultic activities of Israelites during any period in the Iron Age. For these purposes, archaeological, iconographical, and inscriptional evidence are much more helpful. (Cf. Keel and Uehlinger, *Gods;* Keel, *Goddesses and Trees;* Dearman, "Interpreting"; and for ba'als, see also Koch, "Ba'al Ṣapon.")

To be sure, the ideal, "eschatological" future portrayed in 2:18-25 is clearly associated in 2:20 with the complete cessation of warfare, with a new peaceful covenant, a new world, as it were, in which YHWH will be able to "betroth Israel forever" and which is brought about by YHWH. Cf., among others, with the world portrayed in Isaiah 11; Ezek 34:25-30; Ps 46:10-11. Significantly, in these cases, the proclamation of this new world follows a description of a period of destruction. There seems to be a general assumption within the ancient discourses of the literati that such an ideal world requires a period of severe destruction. Significantly, from the perspective of the postmonarchic readership for which the book of Hosea, as we know it, was composed, that destruction has already happened, and thus they situate themselves in a pre-eschatological period, hoping and waiting for the fulfillment of worlds such as the one portrayed in Hos 2:18-25.

Finally, a word about goddesses is in order. The text contains no reference to Asherah, or to any other goddess, but it develops a metaphorical world in which YHWH has a spouse. Significantly, within that world, when YHWH will be finally united with her (Israel, the land) in a permanent, proper manner (2:21-25), then the land will be fruitful because YHWH (the male) will cause rain to fall upon her (the land) from the heavens. The text adapts and revises common ancient Near Eastern mythological constructions, with one most substantial change: Israel (/land) now stands in the mythological slot of a goddess (/land). The text thus conveys an ideological frame of mind that not only removes the place of the/any goddess as the spouse of the deity of heavens, but also elevates Israel (and, indirectly, its land; see also Hos 9:3; cf. Ps 85:2) well above the level of that which may be considered worldly (cf. Weinfeld, "Feminine Features," esp. 323-24; also cf. Malul, *Knowledge*, 245-46; Lapinkivi, "Adorning of the Bride," Smith, *Early History*, 74-75). Needless to say, YHWH's spouse is certainly conceived as trans-temporal Israel, and surely not the (temporary) monarchic period polity that carried that name. Significantly, it is this trans-temporal Israel with whom the readers of the book identify.

There is another aspect of this construction of Israel and the land that bears particular note. The prosperity of Israel and the land becomes tied to a cosmic order, but one that advances a substantial variant on the usual, ancient Near Eastern model of deity/ies-king-people/land. In this model, the king serves as a cosmic mediator between "earth and heavens," and the proper conduct of the king is the key determinant of the well-being of the people and land. This model removes the proper king from the realm of the ordinary humans and makes any opposition to him an attack on the basic cosmic order whose consequences will be felt in the land and by the people (cf. Cohen, "Dehistoricizing"). Here it is Israel (and by association, the land) that is removed from the realm of ordinary humans (see also Hos 8:4 STRUCTURE), and any activity that is considered within the world of the book to be contrary to that which is construed as Israel's obligations to YHWH as wife (and son, or essentially subordinate to YHWH in a hierarchical relation) is seen as an attack on the basic cosmic order. Within this ideological world there cannot be any dissention against that which the authorial voice in the book considers appropriate Israelite behavior. It is worth stressing that this is presented as an a-historical condition since it existed outside the vicissitudes of time from the moment of YHWH's first liaison with Israel. These are central messages of the book, as well as central tenets of the ideological horizon of the world within which the book was written. Moreover, reading the text as an authoritative text cannot but produce a reader who is subordinate to the way in which the book assumes YHWH commanded Israel to behave. At the same time, one must keep in mind that the literati were, at the very least, the readers, authors, editors, and interpreters of YHWH's word.

To be sure, the elimination of the role of the king in the traditional ancient Near Eastern model carries implications regarding the way in which even a messianic king (see Hos 3:5) was imagined (see also Hos 5:1–7:2 Setting).

Intention

The main intention of this reading is to communicate hope for an ideal future. The text not only ends with vv. 16-25, but also consistently looks towards them, and so does the previous reading. Notice the reference to "She-is-Pitied." As many other texts within the repertoire of Yehud, it focuses on both the promise of the ideal future and an explanation of the fall of the great monarchic past. The latter serves not only as an explanation for traumatic historical memories, but also as a warning for Yehud. As such it serves the purpose of socializing the community around the main ideological tenets of its center, and around the memories and traditions that carry these tenets. In addition, it serves to reflect, shape, and strengthen particular images of the past, of traditions and of ideological constructions and worldviews such as those mentioned under Setting.

Bibliography

B. F. Batto, "The Covenant of Peace: A Neglected Ancient Near Eastern Motif," *CBQ* 49 (1987) 187-211; J. Blau, "Reste des I-Imperfekts von *zkr, qal*. Eine Lexicographische Studie," *VT* 11 (1961) 81-86; W. S. Boshoff, "Yahweh as God of Nature. Elements of the Concept of God in the Book of Hosea," *JNSL* 18 (1992) 13-24; A. C. Cohen, "Dehistoricizing Strategies in Third-Millennium B.C.E. Royal Inscriptions and Rituals," T. Abusch et al. (eds.), *Historiography in the Cuneiform World. Proceedings of the XLVe Rencontre Assyriologique Internationale* (Bethesda, MD: CDL, 2001) 99-111; T. J. Connolly, "Metaphor and Abuse in Hosea," *The Journal of the Britain and Ireland School of Feminist Theory* 18 (1998) 55-66; M. Dass, "The Divorce (?) Formula in Hos 2:4a," *Indian Theological Studies* 34 (1997) 56-88; C. J. Dempsey, *The Prophets. A Liberation-Critical Reading* (Minneapolis: Fortress, 2000) 155-56; L. de Regt, "Person Shift in Prophetic Texts. Its Function and Rendering in Ancient and Modern Translations," J. C. de Moor (ed.), *The Elusive Prophet. The Prophet as a Historical Person, Literary Character and Anonymous Artist* (OudSt 45; Leiden: E. J. Brill, 2001) 214-31; A. Frisch, "וענתה (Hosea 2:17) — An Ambiguity," *Tarbiz* 69 (2000) 445-447 (in Hebrew); M. J. Geller, "Elephantine Papyri and Hosea 2,3," *JSJ* 8 (1997) 139-48; J. C. Greenfield, "Aramaic ḥnṣl and Some Biblical Passages," I. Seybold (ed.), *Meqor Hajjim. Festschrift Georg Molin zu seinem 75. Geburtstag* (Graz, Austria: Akademische Druck- u. Verlagsanstalt, 1983) 115-19; S. Greengus, "A Textbook Case of Adultery in Ancient Mesopotamia," *HUCA* 40 (1969) 33-44; J. Huehnergard, "Biblical Notes on Some New Akkadian Texts from Emar (Syria)," *CBQ* 47 (1985) 428-34; A. V. Hunter, *Seek the Lord* (Baltimore: St. Mary's Seminary and University, 1982); O. Keel, *Goddesses and Trees, New Moon and Yahweh. Ancient Near Eastern Art and the Hebrew Bible* (JSOTSupS 261; Sheffield: Sheffield Academic Press, 1998); O. Keel and C. Uehlinger, *Gods, Goddesses and Images of God in Ancient Israel* (Minneapolis: Fortress, 1998); Jonathan Klawans, "Pure Violence: Sacrifice and Defilement in Ancient Israel," *HTR* 94 (2001) 133-55; K. Koch, "Baʿal Ṣapon and Baʿal Šamem and the Critique of Israel's Prophets," G. J. Brooke, A. H. W. Curtis, and J. F. Healey (eds.), *Ugarit and the Bible. Proceedings of the International Symposium on Ugarit and the Bible, Manchester, 1992* (UBL 11; Münster: Ugarit Verlag, 1994) 159-74; C. J. Labuschagne, "The Similes in the Book of Hosea," *OTWSA* 7-8 (1965) 64-76; P. Lapinkivi, "The Adorning of the Bride: Providing Her with Wisdom," S. Parpola and R. M. Whiting (eds.), *Sex and Gender in the Ancient Near East. Proceedings of the 47th Rencontre Assyriologique Internationale, Helsinki, July 2-6, 2001* (The Neo-Assyrian Text Corpus Project; Helsinki: University of Helsinki, 2002), I. 327-35; S. A. Meier, *Speaking of Speaking. Marking Direct Discourse in the Hebrew Bible* (VTS 46; Leiden: E. J. Brill, 1992); S. Morag, "The Great Metaphor of Hosea," *Tarbiz* 68 (1999/2000) 5-11 (in Hebrew); idem, "On Semantic and Lexical Features in the Language of Hosea," *Tarbiz* 53 (1984) 489-511 (in Hebrew); H. Van Dyke Parunak, "Some Discourse Functions of Prophetic Quotation Formula," R. D. Bergen (ed.), *Biblical Hebrew and Discourse Linguistics* (SIL; Winona Lake, IN: Eisenbrauns, 1994) 489-519; B. Porten, *The Elephantine Papyri in English. Three Millennia of Cross-Cultural Continuity and Change* (DMOA 22; Leiden: E. J. Brill, 1996); B. Porten and A. Yardeni, *Textbook of Aramaic Documents from Ancient Egypt* (hereafter, TAD; Jerusalem: Hebrew University, Dept. of the History of the Jewish People/Winona Lake, IN: Eisenbrauns, 1986-89); G. A. Rendsburg, "Word Play in Biblical Hebrew: An Eclectic Collection,"

S. B. Noegel (ed.), *Puns and Pundits. Word Play in the Hebrew Bible and Ancient Near Eastern Literature* (Bethesda, MD: CDL Press, 2000) 137-62; M. Roche, "The Reversal of Creation in Hosea," *VT* 31 (1981) 400-409; K. A. Tängberg, "A Note on Pištî in Hosea II,7, 11," *VT* 27 (1977) 222-24; T. L. Thompson, "Historiography in the Pentateuch: Twenty-five Years after Historicity," *SJOT* 13 (1999) 258-83; M. Weinfeld, "Feminine Features in the Imagery of God in Israel: The Sacred Marriage and the Sacred Tree," *VT* 46 (1996) 515-29; idem, "Ancient Near Eastern Patterns in Prophetic Literature," *VT* 27 (1977) 178-95; W. L. Whitt, "The Divorce of Yahweh and Ashera," *SJOT* 6 (1992) 31-67.
Note: Bibliography mentioned in Hosea 1–3 is not repeated here.

Third Didactic, Prophetic Reading That Imagines Israel's Trajectory from Divine Judgment to the Ideal End-Situation through Metaphors of Family Relationships, 3:1-5

Structure

The structure already shows that most of the literary space in this didactic, prophetic reading was devoted to the explanation of the meaning of the reported (symbolic) acts, not to the acts themselves. The reason for this is obvious. The meaning of these acts provides hope for the future of the intended and primary readerships and supplies them with an explanation for the fall of the monarchies' polities and for their present situation. Furthermore, this explanation socializes the community/ies of readers as well as those who identify with their discourse to accept the importance of following the ideology advanced by the socio-politico-religious center in postmonarchic Israel (/Yehud).

Although this is a human monologue, it is presented as being as authoritative as the preceding divine monologue (see Genre). The human monologue is in itself embedded in YHWH's word (that is, the book of Hosea; see Hos 1:1 STRUCTURE), and in turn it explicitly embeds YHWH's words (as authoritatively reported by the speaker in the book, see Hos 3:1), which now in turn become clearly distinct from YHWH's word (i.e., the prophetic book). It is worth noting that the human monologue includes not only a report of YHWH's words to the prophet, but also the self-reported words of the prophet to the woman. The "conversation" between the two also becomes part of YHWH's word. To be sure, the conversation is not symmetrical. Because of the hierarchical nature of their relationship, the conversation consists of his address to her, but her response is not reported. (The response of the subordinate in a hierarchical relation is often not voiced; see Ben Zvi, "Observations on the Marital Metaphor.") Yet there is much at stake in his speech to her. It serves to characterize her, in the sight of the readership that is supposed to identify with the voice of the husband/YHWH, but also with the actual situation of the woman, Israel.

Although it is possible to understand the reported speech of the man as coming to a close by the end of v. 3, some markers in the text point in a different direction. These include:

(a) the multiple links between vv. 3 and 4, and with 5 as well — see above;
(b) the dependent character of the clause that begins in v. 4; and
(c) the absolute lack of any textually inscribed marker pointing at the end of his address to her in v. 3.

The cumulative weight of these markers surely increases the likelihood of readings of the text in which the man's address to her concludes only by the end of v. 5. If so, within these readings, how does the speaker characterize the woman, and how does a historical readership that accepts the speaker's authority characterize her? She is certainly a woman to whom it is sensible to explain, and who will be able to understand, that her situation parallels that of Israel, and above all one for whom the hope for a Davide monarch, a full return to YHWH, and a full restoration of YHWH's worship to be materialized in a distant future (far beyond the span of her own and Hosea's lives) are issues of central importance. Thus, she is surely not imagined as a common, adulterous woman; she is imagined as Israel.

As with the other two readings in this set, Hos 3:1-5 concludes with a note of high hope. The unit is clearly demarcated by the *wyqtl* verbal form that introduces the reported new command and that note of hope. Yet it is also related to the other two readings. It shares the basic themes, namely, the explanation of the fall of monarchic Israel, the assurance that YHWH will bring a glorious future to Israel, and the use of the marital metaphor. Moreover, the readers are already alerted to the link between 3:1-5 and 1:2–2:3 by the explicit textual choice in 3:1, namely, עוד אלי ה׳ ויאמר, "YHWH said to me *again*" (italics mine). It is worth noting that the word עוד "again" here serves a double duty that creates two levels of meaning. It points at the meaning mentioned above, and also at "Go again, love a woman who. . . ." It is to be stressed that the double meaning serves to convey and strengthen an unequivocal meaning.

"Again" brings to the forefront an awareness of the previous texts in the book to the ancient readers as well as a sense that the unit here is not to be read as "independent." On the contrary, the language of the unit implies that it is a literary unit within a larger book, and that the readers are supposed to approach it in a way that is informed by its *Sitz im Buch* rather than by any hypothetical social setting in which the prophet proclaimed his monologue. Such a setting is actually completely erased in the world of the book, which assigns no room for any reference to the place, occasion, or the nature of the addressee or addressees of the human monologue (see Setting).

The approach mentioned above is to be contrasted with that of some redactional critical scholars who maintain that the writer of chapter 3 does not presuppose any knowledge of chapter 1 (see, for instance, Wolff, *Hosea,* 59; Macintosh, *Hosea,* 95). These scholars tend to deal with a text that differs at times from that in the present book of Hosea. They are interested in Hosea, the historical man, rather than the character Hosea as it is construed in the book associated with him.

Scholars who approach the text as a true reflection of the life of Hosea would understand this mode as asking them to deal with the matter of Hosea's marital life in general and to begin with questions about the identity of the woman in chapter 3. Is she Gomer or is Hosea asked twice to "take" a "problematic" woman? And if so, did he already divorce Gomer? If not, did he have two "problematic" wives? And if so, did he marry them sequentially? If he divorced Gomer, how could he remarry her (see Deut 24:1-4), or does the rule in Deut 24:1-4 not apply to her since although she prostituted herself, she did not marry another man? If Gomer is not to be identified with the second woman, who in any case was the "first wife" of the prophet, Gomer or the other woman? Did the actions mentioned in chapter 3 occur before those in chapter 1? Or vice versa? (On these matters, see, among many others, Andersen and Freedman, *Hosea,* 294-95; G. I. Davies, *Hosea,* 98-99; Harper, *Amos and Hosea,* 215; Macintosh, *Hosea,* 113-26; Mays, *Hosea,* 55-56; Rowley, *Men of God,* 66-97; Sweeney, *Twelve Prophets,* 38-39; Törnkvist, *Use and Abuse,* 165.)

Yet the emphasis on the meaning of the mentioned acts and the absolute lack of any reference to these "details" in the world of the text strongly suggest that the intended and primary readers were not asked so much to focus on the already dead for centuries prophet or his marriage/s, but rather on the fate and hope of Israel. The portrayal of Hosea's marriage/s is in the service of making a didactic point about the past, the eventual fate of Israel, and the hope that its (certain) future provides to the readers. The details of Hosea's life are important only as metaphors and imagery that illuminate these matters. In other words, the readers were asked to understand the story in ch. 3 as expressing another way of imagining the marital metaphor associated with the fate, history, and hope of Israel. Of course, this brings the readers back to Hosea 1–2. Biblical literature includes many other examples of returning to a basic starting point to develop an image, scene, concept, or symbol in a manner different from that which was developed before. This holds true in the patriarchal narratives (see, for instance, the case of the "matriarch in danger"; Gen 12:10-20; 26:1-11), but also numerous times in the prophetic books. In these instances the readers face a kind of "loop" in which themes addressed before are revisited and developed in different ways (see, for instance, Mic 2:11; 6:15; Obad 7, 12; Zeph 3:1-8; I discussed these matters in Ben Zvi, *Micah,* 61, 161; idem, *Zephaniah,* 335-36; idem, *Obadiah,* 73, 144-45). This concept is particularly helpful in the case of Hos 3:1-5 since it seems to revisit most of the points or issues mentioned in the previous readings in the set. For instance, Hosea's/YHWH's love for the unfaithful woman/Israel (3:1) has an obvious counterpart in Hos 1:2; 2:4; 7:10). Moreover, a network of similar terms serves to emphasize the bonds between the units. There is, for instance, נאפופיה "her adultery" in 2:4 and מנאפת "who commits adultery" in 3:1; מאהביה "her lovers" in 2:9 (see also 7) and a concentration of forms from the root אהב "love" and related terms in 3:1. Notice also "go, marry a woman . . ." and "go, love a woman . . ." in v. 1:2 and 3:1 respectively, and also "you shall not be promiscuous" (root זנה; sometimes also translated "you shall not play the whore" [NRSV]) and the multiple uses of this root in Hos 1:2–2:25. Verse 3:2 may be seen as matching 1:3a, and 3:3 matches to some extent 2:7-9, and also v. 10 (and cf. 23-24). Certainly, the note about a period without a king in 3:4a has a counterpart in 2:4; whereas the reference to a lack of temple and cultic services (3:4b) has one in 2:13. The ideal future in 3:5 has also a clear counterpart in 2:2 (to some extent 3:5 is equivalent to vv. 16-25 as well) (On these matters, cf. Ginsberg, "Studies in Hosea 1–3.") Yet from an even ubiquitous presence of matches and counterparts between two units, it does not follow that they convey the same message. In fact, these two (didactic) READINGS are present in the book because they force the intended and primary rereaderships to revisit and reshape previous images, and suggest new possible meanings, which in turn inform and interact with those associated with the previous READING. See Intention.

Repetitions and puns on words contribute to the internal coherence of the unit. This is particularly true of the crucial section in which the text shifts from the metaphorical reference to Israel by means of the woman to an explicit reference to the former. Thus, one finds a textually binding repetition of ימים רבים "many days" (see vv. 3 and 4). Likewise, there is a textually based link between תשבי ("she will sit") and ישבו ("they will sit") in the same verses. The first refers to the woman, the second to Israel; the singular feminine reference is thus transferred to the masculine plural (they, the children of Israel), and yet metaphorically, both are one and the same.

Undoubtedly, from the perspective of the readership of the book, the textually inscribed action of closely binding together these verses strengthens the link between the metaphor of Hosea and the woman and its discursive counterpart, of YHWH and Israel. Moreover, the sense of a quasi-parallel structure creates an interpretative expectation that sections in v. 3 will have a counterpart in v. 4. There is also an expectation that the meanings of vv. 3-5 are related because of the envelope created by ימים רבים "many days" at the beginning of v. 3 and אחרית הימים "days to come" or "faraway days" at the end of v. 5. Furthermore, the additional envelope created by ימים רבים at the beginning of v. 5 and אחרית הימים "days to come" or "faraway days" at the end of v. 5 suggests to the readers that vv. 4 and 5 are also closely related.

These expectations are fulfilled. A set of balanced meanings, already hinted at in the conclusion of v. 3 connects vv. 3 and 4. Thus "you shall not commit harlotry, nor shall have intercourse with a man, not even I with you" (v. 3) is the counterpart of "without king and without officers, without *zebach* sacrifice and without pillar, without ephod and teraphim" (v. 4). Just as the latter points to a transitory situation during which Israel is denied, because of its improper use of them, central political and cultic referents with which it was endowed, so the woman who according to the text put her sexuality to wrong use, is denied sexual intercourse. (For a different understanding of 3:3, see Geller, "Elephantine Papyri," but see Ginsberg, "Studies in Hos 1–3," 53). The reference to "many days" in 3:3 communicates also the certitude that in the future the woman will engage in sexual intercourse with her proper man (Hosea). This certitude serves as an interpretative key for v. 4. Thus the text deals with Israel's sinful past and the consequent punishment, but also points at the reversal of Israel's condition to its ideal future, all of which are implied but certain at the end of v. 3. (The implicit but certain message of hope in v. 4, becomes explicit and is elaborated further in v. 5.) Thus, within this discourse the woman serves as mirror for Israel, Hosea for YHWH, sex with an improper partner for the past conduct of Israel (cultic and political elite, both of which are notionally brought together in the text). Similarly, sex with the proper partner corresponds to either trembling towards YHWH (see Abma, *Bonds of Love,* 205) or a connoted joyful thrill towards YHWH (see Isa 60:5 for this shade of meaning of the verb פחד in the qal; the verb usually means "fear") and with restoration; and the certitude that Hosea will have intercourse with his woman mirrors the certitude that YHWH will bring Israel to its ideal status. Needless to say, within this discourse, just as the woman is not endowed with the right to choose sexual partners — Hosea makes the choices for her — so Israel is conceived as having no choice but to accept YHWH and worship YHWH alone. On other aspects of the worldviews shared by the characters in the book, the authorship, and primary and intended readerships of the book, see Setting.

Certain terms and expressions in the text demand some explanation. For instance, אהב אשה אהבת רע ומנאפת in 3:1 is probably better understood as "love a woman who is beloved by another and [yet] commits adultery" (cf. "Go, love a woman who has a lover and is an adulteress," NRSV). For discussion of the phrase that leads to the conclusion that a literal translation is to be rendered, "une femme aimée d'un epoux et se livrant à l'adultère," see Barthélemy, *Critique Textuelle,* vol. III, 503-04. The point is not the logical precision of language (e.g., how can she commit adultery if she is not married?) but its metaphorical, evocative character. How did the text ask its intended and primary readers to imagine the woman/Israel? First, she is loved by someone, who takes the structural and associative slot of YHWH in the discourse of the intended rereadership, for Israel is loved by YHWH. Yet she is also involved in sexual interactions with men who do not (and cannot) love her. The following section in the verse conveys to the readers the absurdity of the situation, "as YHWH loves the children of Israel, while they turn to other gods and love raisin cakes!" Whatever may be the best translation of the expression rendered here as "raisin cakes" (some claim the meaning of the relevant Hebrew phrase is "flagons of wine"), and whatever sexual (cf. Song 2:5) or religious imagery or connotations it might carry (for the latter, cf. 2 Sam 6:19//1 Chr 16:3 and perhaps Isa 16:7; Jer 7:18; 44:19 are often mentioned in this regard), the point of the text is that it would be absurd for the woman to love cakes instead of fulfilling her obligations to a loving husband/provider. (For a summary and good critical evaluation of meanings and connotations often proposed for "raisin cakes" see Tooze, *Framing the Book of the Twelve,* 155-56; for a different approach, see Jeremias, *Hosea,* 54.)

It is worth stressing that the term "love" here points not only to an emotional state, but also and perhaps mainly to a sense of commitment to, and complete fulfillment of, the required roles of a husband or wife towards each other, according to the way in which they were represented in the ideological discourse informing the world of the book, and which is probably a reflection of that held, at least, by the literati for whom the book was composed. See Setting below.

The same expression אהב אשה אהבת רע ומנאפת in 3:1 may have, in addition, connoted or evoked secondary meanings. For instance, it may have connoted, "Love a woman who loves another and commits adultery." This potential, secondary meaning reflects an understanding of the passive participle as carrying an active meaning. There is no doubt that passive participles in biblical Hebrew may carry active meanings, as a number of instances clearly show (see Talmon and Fields, "Collocation")." For this understanding, see already Ibn Ezra. One may note that some scholars propose the same meaning, but by means of an emendation of the Hebrew text, e.g., Wolff, *Hosea,* 56. This emendation is not necessary since the passive participle can carry an active meaning. In any event, this secondary and complementary approach to the text is consistent with the characterization of the woman/Israel/the land in 2:7, 9 and again sets an opposition between YHWH and the other gods. In this case, rather than stating ba'al or ba'alim (e.g., 2:10, 15, 19), the text states אלהים אחרים "other gods" (on the expression see Setting). (If Israel was conceived as loving "the other gods" rather than vice versa, then the imagery would carry a pejorative connotation concerning "the other gods," and this would be consistent with the evaluation of "the other gods" by the implied authorship of the book and its intended and primary readerships. For the hierarchical attribution of the "slots" of lover and loved see Ackerman, "The Personal Is Political"; see also Setting, below.) The text is written to suggest a further connotation. The textual choice of רע, which here denotes a male neighbor or friend and basically, a male member of the same community (Macintosh, *Hosea,* 94), carries the same consonants of nouns or adjectives meaning "evil" or "disaster" (see Hos 7:15; 9:15). Thus, it evokes among the intended readership a complementary sense of "love of woman who loves evil (cf. Mic 3:2; Ps 52:5) and commits adultery (cf. love a woman that loves evil things, an adulteress; Hos 1:3 LXX)." In doing so, the text not only asked its historical readership to strongly characterize the woman, but also to associate "evil" with the slot of the "lover" that is, "the other gods" (see above). (For another example of multilayered, complementary meanings connoted by a careful choice of a word in prophetic literature see Zeph 3:8; see Ben Zvi, *Zephaniah,* 220-23.)

The gradation of the temporal expressions from ימים רבים "many days" in v. 3, to ימים רבים in v. 4 but to אחרית הימים "the end of (or, the latter) days" (i.e., a faraway future) in v. 5 serves to keep a careful balance that maximizes the coherence of the text, the thematical coherence of the metaphor, and also serves to convey an important ideological message. As mentioned above, the first two bring together vv. 3 and 4, the use of the second expression serves a similar purpose (see above), but one can easily note that (a) obviously it could not have been used for a simple mortal (i.e., only ימים רבים could be used for the woman if the metaphor is to have some "logical" consistency) and (b) it serves to emphasize that Israel (including the readership of the book) is to wait patiently for a long and indeterminate period for its glorious future (cf. Hos 2:2). In this sense it disambiguates ימים רבים; the readers are not supposed to think in terms of "many days" within the frame of the life of a single human being (that is, that of the woman), but in terms of the indefinite number of generations of the children of Israel that the woman represents. (In addition אחרית in אחרית הימים at the end of v. 5 creates an envelope with אחר at the beginning of the verse; another instance of a carefully thought choice of words.)

In another case of careful writing, the text does not inform the reader about the identity of the (implied) person from whom Hosea buys the woman (v. 3:2). This erasure of identity is again part and parcel of a sophisticated attempt to maximize the relation between the metaphor and its referent. In the human world, Hosea has to purchase from another man who has rights over her, who legally "owns" her; but in the ideological world of YHWH and Israel, there is no room for another deity who has rights over Israel. The absence of such a deity finds its counterpart in the erasure of the figure of the previous "owner" of the woman. "Historical" attempts to bring back the previous owner into the text — was he her father? her pimp? — are therefore misguided. Yet erasures are never complete. The shadow of the absence remains perceptible. One may wonder whether an implied imagery of "other nations" as "owners" from whom Israel is bought by YHWH (cf. Isa 11:11; and to some extent Deut 7:8) and accordingly some imagery of exile and return, as in Hos 2:2, can be discerned among these shadows.

(On the textual discussion of the verb often translated as "bought" in v. 2, see, among others, Rowley, *Men of God,* 68-69; Andersen and Freedman, *Hosea,* 298-99; Vogels, "Hosea's Gift," 412-12 and bibliography; Macintosh, *Hosea,* 99-101. The possibility that Hosea only "hired" her, that is, that "he took over the management of the woman/prostitute" has been raised by several scholars for a long period of time, and found its way in some English translations, see NJPSV. Yet "bought" is more likely than "hired" in this case.)

Some scholars have proposed that the value of the goods mentioned in Hos 3:2 amounts to (about) thirty shekels of silver, which is according to Exod 21:32 the price to be paid as compensation for a slave killed by one's ox, and according to Lev 27:4, the equivalent for a female, twenty to sixty years of age. If the intended and primary readership considered thirty shekels to be the price of purchase of a female slave, then they might have wondered whether Hosea/YHWH would be "freeing" her to become "his." In any case, these calculations involve a characterization of the woman as a slave, or alternatively, as one who can be bought very cheap, that is, one of "low status." Of course, these characterizations have bearings on the ideological setting in which the book was composed and read.

It is to be stressed, however, that the calculations involved in the value in silver of "a homer of barley and a letek of barley (following the LXX some English translations read, ". . . and measure/*nebel*/skin of wine"; but see, among others, Rowley, *Men of God,* 83) are very hypothetical. Moreover, there is no clear indication in the text that would have required the intended or primary readership to calculate the value of the goods according to a valuation that leads to the mentioned thirty shekels instead of understanding these goods in terms of their market value in their own time — or that which they could have imagined them to be worth at the time in which the book is set. There is no clear indication that the amount of thirty shekels by itself would have evoked the imagery of buying a female slave, or that such was the "market" value of female slaves within the community of readers for which the book was composed. Moreover, even if for the sake of argument one were to accept that a simple reference to thirty shekels would immediately bring to mind among the historical readers of the text the price of a female slave, then it is worth stressing that the text does not say thirty shekels, which is what one would expect the text to say in such a case, had it been meant to raise the issue of the female slave within its historical readership (cf. Rowley, *Men of God*, 83). For the calculations, see, for instance, Wolff, *Hosea*, 61; Pentiuc, *Long-Suffering Love*, 48, 66-67; on this matter see also, Abma, *Bonds of Love*, 207; Andersen and Freedman, *Hosea*, 300; Rudolph, *Hosea*, 91-92; Macintosh, *Hosea*, 99.

Some scholars have used the reported mode of paying (i.e., in goods) and the amount paid by Hosea to characterize not only the literary personage in the world of the book but also the historical prophet, and to maintain the historicity (in modern terms) of the text. For instance, Wolff writes, "The amount comprising the purchase price indicates not only the event's historicity, but also suggests that Hosea was not particularly wealthy" (*Hosea*, 61). Pentiuc follows Wolff and writes, "the intricate way in which the payment was done sheds some light on Hosea's modest financial status and, at the same time, underlies its historicity" (*Long-Suffering Love*, 48). Even Mays maintains, "the breakdown may suggest that he [Hosea] had some trouble in getting the required sum together" (*Hosea*, 57).

Surely, the price is not too high, but it characterizes the value of the "merchandise" (i.e., the woman; i.e., Israel), and the latter could not have been high, given what is said about her (both the woman and Israel) and its impact on the discourses of the period. As for historicity, any transaction that was within the realm of possibility in the world known to the literati was also a transaction that such literati could write about, or include in their writing. A literary report about a transaction embedded in a didactic and theological piece is by no means a proof of the historicity (in modern terms) of the transaction. As for the characterization of Hosea within the world of the book, the amount does not serve to characterize him (but her), and the way in which the payment was made, by means of both goods and silver. This combination of goods may have carried some literary and ideological symbolism (see Abma, *Bonds of Love*, 207-8; cf. Vogels, "Hosea's Gift"). This combination of goods is not a necessary marker of the poverty of the one paying (Hosea, and indirectly and metaphorically, YHWH). For further discussion see Setting, below.

Some of the expressions in this unit are very uncommon in the HB. Among them, X פחד אל ("coming trembling toward X" where "X" stands for YHWH or God) appears nowhere else. The verb פחד may be understood in terms of Mic 7:17, but there "they [the nations] shall lick dust like a snake, like the crawling things of the earth; they shall come trembling out of their fortresses; they shall turn in dread to the LORD our God, and they shall stand in fear of you [Israel]" (NRSV). It may also connote or even denote a sense of joyful thrill as in Isa 60:5, "then you shall see and be radiant; your heart shall thrill and rejoice" (NRSV). On the matter of "seeking" both YHWH and David in v. 5, rather than YHWH alone, see Setting below.

Many scholars have attributed this section to the historical Hosea because of the use of the first person (but see, among others, Ward, *Hosea,* 52), the details of the "purchase" in 3:3 (see above), and because of the assumption that the text goes back to Hosea unless convincingly proved otherwise. This supposition is a reflection of a still deeply ingrained assumption in historical critical studies that texts in the prophetic books go back to the historical person or the time of the prophetic character with whom the book is associated unless proven otherwise. (I argued against this assumption elsewhere; see, for instance, Ben Zvi, "Studying Prophetic Texts.")

Significantly, most of the scholars who attribute the text either to Hosea or his times have it found necessary to expunge some key phrases from the text of Hos 3:1-5, as it stands in the book of Hosea, and to assign them to later redactors. The most common among these key phrases are "and David their king" and "to his goodness in the latter days" (or "in the latter days") in v. 5. For these and related approaches see, among others, Davies, *Hosea,* 98, 104-5; Macintosh, *Hosea,* 108-112; Mays, *Hosea,* 54; Rudolph, *Hosea,* 93-94; Wolff, *Hosea,* 63). For a discussion on the lateness of the entire v. 5 see Harper, *Amos and Hosea,* 216, 223-24; for the contrary position see Emmerson, *Hosea,* 101-5. The latter stance seems to be clearly in the minority. Buss considers vv. 4-5 later than the rest, and ch. 3 as a whole as an "afterthought" (Buss, *Prophetic Word,* 34, 70). There have also been many voices that assign the entire chapter or most of it to days later than those in which the world of the book is set, including postmonarchic times. For these approaches, see, among many others, Day, "Is the Book of Hosea Exilic?" esp. 113; Wolfe, "Editing of the Book of the Twelve," esp. pp. 93-95; Yee, *Composition and Tradition,* esp. 57-64 and see bibliography cited there. Zulick (and others) associate most of Hos 3:1-4 with a post-722 BCE Judahite voice, but v. 5 with a "restorationist," most likely postmonarchic voice (Zulick, *Rhetorical Polyphony,* 132-39).

From the methodological perspective advanced here, it is worth stressing that clear markers of textual coherence particularly bind together vv. 3-5 in their present form (see above) and that the references to a lack in political and cultic areas in v. 4 are meant to lead the readers to an expectation of the resolution of that lack. The reference to the future Davide certainly provides a resolution to the mentioned lack. In other words, there are good reasons to assume that the readers of the book were asked to approach Hosea 3:1-5 in its present form as a literary unit. On the construction of the image of a future Davide that serves as one of the highest elements of hope in the unit see Setting, below. It would suffice here to state that the same Hebrew expression את ה' אלהיהם ואת דוד מלכם "YHWH, their God and David, their king" (and with both serving as direct object of a verb whose governing subject is the children of Israel) appears in Jer 30:9, a text widely accepted as postmonarchic and in which a future Davide is also envisaged.

In addition, it is worth stressing that the text of Hosea 3:1-5 as it stands (as opposed to proposed, but hypothetical, forerunners) asks its readers to approach it as a reading within a set of readings (Hosea chs. 1–3) and as part of the entire book of Hosea, namely, 1:1–14:10. Such a text therefore cannot exist separately from the book of which it is an integral part, and therefore, it cannot predate it.

Genre

Whereas the preceding unit in this set of readings (Hos 2:3-25) is presented to the readership as a divine monologue, Hos 3:1-5 is presented as a prophetic monologue, that is, as a human monologue. Significantly, a human monologue is considered an integral part of YHWH's word (see Hos 1:1), just as a divine monologue (Hos 2:3-25) is. Explicit human words become YHWH's word within this discourse and for those who accept it. To be sure, these are human words, but not the words of a common person. They are presented and ideologically accepted by the readership as the words of a true prophet of old who prophesied about a divine punishment that was in his future, and which was not only fulfilled, but whose fulfillment is directly associated with one of the most important events in their story about themselves. The readership of the book of Hosea is all too aware that children of Israel dwelled many days without king or prince or temple, and from their perspective, still dwell without a king. Yet the fulfillment of the prophetic words not only provides legitimization to the interpretation of the past events they advance, but also conveys a sense of certitude that the announcements of hope that were also prophesied will be fulfilled as well (see also below, Setting).

Finally, one may add also that just as in the case of Hos 1:2–2:3, this section bears the thematic markers of the stories that report about prophets of old who behaved in a manner that seems odd (e.g., buying the woman and refraining from having intercourse with her for an extended period of time). As mentioned in Hos 1:2–2:3 Genre, from the perspective of the readers of the book, seemingly odd behavior was not so odd in the case of prophets of old. From their perspective, it would even further legitimize and rhetorically enhance Hosea's authority as a true prophet of old.

Setting

The setting of the writing and reading of this portion of the book of Hosea is the same as that of the book as a whole. Both writers and readers are among the literati of Yehud. Within the world of the book, the human monologue is not set in any particular *Sitz im Leben* or time, except for the general monarchic period frame of Hos 1:1. Needless to say, had the monologue been set in a postmonarchic period, it would have lost all authority. After all, prophets whose voices are supposed to carry rhetorical weight cannot be construed as prophesying about events in their own past. On the surface, however, the monologue could have been addressed to a defined group and at a particular time within the world of the book. The fact that it does not is an indication that the monologue was not meant to be understood by the readers of the book as closely anchored to a supposed moment or circumstances of delivery. The latter are presented as basically irrelevant to the message of the text. The readership of the book, however, being (trans-temporal; theological) Israel, is supposed to be identifying itself as the addressees of the monologue; they "are" these addressees.

What does this didactic reading contribute to our understanding of the worldview of the literati within whom and for whom the book of Hosea (including, of course, Hos 3:1-5) was composed? Turning to the mindset that characterized the setting of the composition and reading of the book, it is worth noting that Israel's period of judgment is construed through the metaphor of sexual estrangement between husband and wife. A period in which there is no sexual activity between husband and wife is imagined as the counterpart of a period in which Israel has no king and no temple. Consequently, the imagery makes sense within a discourse in which sexual activity between legitimate partners is considered extremely positive and so is the proper attitude towards temple and cult (cf. Levine, "Essay on Prophetic Attitudes Towards Temple and Cult"). On these issues also see STRUCTURE.

To be sure, within these ideological discourses, the partners were not and could not be imagined as equal (see Ben Zvi, "Observations on the Marital Metaphor," and Hos 1:2–2:3, Intention). Hos 3:2 constructs the husband/Hosea/YHWH as "buying" the woman/wife/Israel. Regardless of the actual market value of the goods mentioned in 3:2, the point is that taking a woman/wife/Israel involves (or is akin to) a purchase. Such a construction expresses and reflects a hierarchical understanding of the relations between men and women, husbands and wives.

A combination of several expressions in the text particularly contributes to the shaping of the character Hosea, and of his mindset, from the perspective of the postmonarchic readership of the book of Hosea. Although "to seek (Heb. בקשׁ) YHWH/God" is not uncommon in prophetic literature (e.g., Isa 65:1; Jer 29:13; 50:4; Hos 5:6; 7:10; Zeph 1:6; 2:3; Zech 8:21-22), "to seek YHWH and David" (see v. 5) is very unusual, even if deity and king may appear as the objects of a single verb elsewhere (see 1 Kgs 21:10; and above all in Jer 30:9 which uses the same expression). The reason is simple: within the authoritative discourses of ancient Israel, people were supposed to seek the deity, not human beings. (Jer 30:9 speaks of "serving" [Heb. עבד] both YHWH and king. Certainly, there is no ideological difficulty with the notion of people serving a king, since subjects and vassals served their kings, willingly or unwillingly, e.g., Judg 3:14; Jer 25:11; 27:17; 40:9.) The text of Mal 2:7 is illustrative of the ideological difficulties of imagining people seeking their king: "people should seek (Heb. בקשׁ) instruction from his [the priest's] mouth, for he is the messenger of the LORD of hosts" (NRSV). Even if the priest is a messenger of God, people are not supposed to seek the priest, but the instruction from his mouth (cf. Amos 8:12). A text that states explicitly that people are to seek "X" cannot but characterize X as something more than a human being essentially similar to all those who populate the earth (cf. Isaiah 11 — and notice the expression in 11:10; cf. Mal 3:1). In other words, the text connotes that the future David, the king of the children of Israel (meaning here trans-temporal Israel) is not another king to reign on earth but an elevated figure, a messianic figure. The text here conveys an image of a Davide even more elevated than the one in Jer 30:9. The readers for whom the book of Hosea was intended and who were asked to approach Hosea 1–3 as a set of related readings closely informing each other most likely brought together the related motifs in the preceding unit. The result is clear: a cluster of images including that of the "head" that will bring back Israel from the exile (2:2), the re-unification of Israel (2:2), the peaceful new world (2:20), the fertility of the land/provision of rain (2:23-24), and the new David (3:5). Significantly, many of the motifs in this cluster appear together in other prophetic books, in one way or another (e.g., Isaiah 11; Jeremiah 31; Ezek 34:24-28; 37:15-28; Zechariah 9; cf. Zech 10:6-12). The text here reflects a set of ideas or images that belonged to a discursive or mental realm associated with the ideal future.

It is particularly worth noting that although in these texts the future Davide is strongly elevated, none of them connotes a message that David is, as it were, YHWH-like. The ideological distance between the new David and YHWH is always maintained in some way or another. In 3:5 this is achieved by the final stress: Although Israel shall seek YHWH their God, and David their king, "they shall come in awe to/trembling towards YHWH (not YHWH and David) and to his (YHWH's, not YHWH's and David's) goodness." The text unequivocally distinguishes between the participants in the pair YHWH–(future) David.

As mentioned in Hos 1:2–2:3 STRUCTURE, the association of this head with the Davides still allows for a double reading. The ideal, messianic images of the future to come are precisely that: images of a distant future that bring hope to the readership. Yet, the text may, at least by connotation, loom in the background of the story of the postmonarchic community of readers of the book of Hosea about themselves, and somewhat, in a partial way impact their understanding of the foundation narratives about the return under Sheshbazzar (as represented in Ezra 1:8, 11; cf. 1 Chr 3:18) and those of the return and rebuilding of the temple associated with Zerubbabel. Thus Hosea's prophecy was not yet fulfilled and the people should wait for the time envisaged by the prophet long ago. At the same time, the prophecy was partially fulfilled in the foundation of their own community. A partial fulfillment that does not stand instead of the complete fulfillment still to come, but rather as a kind of precursor, or minor prefiguration. Yet, significantly, this partial fulfillment represents a return to temple and sacrifices.

The reference to David in 3:5 also indicates a construction of the monarchic past in northern Israel in which true prophets recognized (just as did the readership of the book of Hosea) that the kingship does not belong to any non-Davide and, therefore, that any single king and dynasty of the northern kingdom was contrary to the long-term will of YHWH (as well as the very existence of the kingdom, see 2:2).

Texts to be read and reread tend to carry multiple layers of potential meaning. For instance, in addition to all the meanings discussed above, "seeking" (בקש) David, or the Davidic king — with the meaning communicated by v. 5, and contrast with that in 1 Sam 24:3; 26:2; 2 Sam 5:17 — may have served to evoke the image of the elders of Israel seeking David as their king (2 Sam 3:17 and note also 2 Chr 9:23).

The emphasis on "love" and above all the explicit reference to YHWH's love of Israel shape the image of a Hosea for whom this concept was obvious and salient (see v. 1), and relate him to other characters or implied authors in a substantial number of texts (see Deut 7:8, 13; 23:6; 1 Kgs 10:9; Isa 43:4; 48:14; 63:9; Jer 31:3; Zeph 3:17; cf. Mal 2:2). The concept appears elsewhere in the book of Hosea itself, in Hos 9:15; 11:1; 14:5, and thus conveys a sense of ideological coherence, at least in relation to this basic concept. It is worth stressing that whereas the fluidity of the concept of love that may belong to interpersonal relations as well as covenantal/politico-religious relations (e.g., YHWH-Israel) stands at the center of the metaphor developed in chapter 3 (and to a large extent in Hosea 1–3, and other sections of the book), the text here shows a clear lack of fluidity concerning the identity of the subject and object of the love. The (ideologically) superordinate or hierarchically superior partner is always referred to as loving the subordinate member, rather than vice versa or reciprocally (see Ackerman, "The Personal Is Political"). Thus, Hosea is commanded to love the woman, YHWH is said to love Israel, and Israel is said to love "raisin cakes," and perhaps at a connoted level, "other gods."

The expression אלהים אחרים "other gods" (see v. 1) is common in the HB, but its distribution is not random. It appears, for instance, in Exod 20:3; 23:13; numerous times in Deuteronomy; Josh 23:16; 24:2, 16; Judg 2:12, 17, 19; 10:13; 1 Sam 8:8; 26:19; 1 Kgs 9:6, 9; 11:4, 10; 14:9; 2 Kgs 5:17; 17:7, 35, 37, 38; 22:17; Jer 7:6, 9, 18; 11:10; 13:10; 16:11, 13; 19:4, 13; 22:9; 25:6; 32:29; 35:15; 44:3; 44:8, 15. The term associates the world of the text with constructions of the history of Israel, according to which (trans-temporal) Israel (northern Israel, Judah) worshiped or followed "other gods" instead of YHWH and as a result were eventually punished with destruction and exile. The term "other gods" may also provide Hosea with a "deuteronomistic" bite, but one can notice easily that in this text terms such as מצבה "pillar" or תרפים "teraphim" in v. 4 are presented along with terms such as king, officers, and *zebach,* none of which is an essentially — as opposed to a contingently — negative feature in the life of Israel. In fact, their presence in one single list seems to suggest that, just as the existence of a king, officers, and *zebach* sacrifices are essentially positive features in the life of Israel (i.e., a royal polity and cult), even though they have been perverted in monarchic times to the extent that led to terrible consequences, the same is likely to hold true for "pillars" (and contrast with, for instance, Deut 16:22; 2 Kgs 18:4; 23:14, 24; Hos 10:1-3 partially revisits and "corrects" the theme of pillars in 3:4) or ephod or teraphim (ct. 2 Kgs 23:24).

Significantly, the term pillar may carry very positive associations (Gen 28:18-22; 31:13; Exod 24:4), particularly in narratives about early Israel but also in notes about the ideal future such as Isa 19:19. Of course, it carries clearly negative connotations in other — and particularly deuteronomic or deuteronomistic — texts (see, for instance, Deut 12:3; 2 Kgs 18:4). Similarly, ephod may connote very positive associations (e.g., Aaron, the High Priest, pious priests; see, among many others, Exod 28:4, 26-30; Lev 8:7; 1 Sam 2:28;

14:3; 22:18), but may also be associated with Israel's sins (see Judg 8:27; also cf. Judg 17:5; 18:14-18). The teraphim themselves may appear at least in neutral contexts (e.g., 1 Sam 19:13-16, and see also Gen 31:19, 34-35; significantly, in none of these texts is the holder of teraphim even indirectly condemned for idolatry), but see also texts such as 2 Kgs 23:24. The combination of teraphim and ephod in v. 4 might suggest a sense of divination (and see Ezek 21:26 [cf. Zech 10:2] and see Exod 28:30) but even if this is the case, it would not be necessarily a negative feature, for not all divination is considered in negative terms (see, for instance, Joshua 7, Jonah 1, and above all the references to the urim and thummim, e.g., 1 Sam 28:6; Ezra 2:63; Neh 7:65). The ambiguity and openness of the text attributed to Hosea are remarkable. The text is consistent with, and evokes the positive or neutral images of, the pillar and teraphim as well as the salient association of ephod with priest, while at the same time, because of its context in v. 4, it alludes to the social memory of the (mis)use of all these elements in Israel in the past. In addition, because of the choice of terms, it serves to characterize the voice of Hosea in chapter 3:1, 4-5 (and by implication, the voice of Hosea in general) as not necessarily a "deuteronomistic" one, but rather as a voice that carries some "deuteronomistic flavor" while at the same time being a rather nuanced voice that reflects a much larger and balanced perspective of the historical memory of Israel (and ct. with Deut 16:22). Furthermore, it points at a future that is still not fully realized at any time in the second temple period (see also v. 5).

It is also worthy of notice that the voice of this Hosea in his monologue serves as a kind of (human) counterpart to that of YHWH in the divine monologue in chapter 2. Both show a similar awareness of, and reflection on, the history of Israel, and subtly choose their words to connote meanings within the accepted discourses of the period (cf. the choices made in v. 4 with those concerning "head" in 2:2). Hosea is also construed by the text as a prophet who does not expect the materialization of the ideal future in his own days or any time soon. This has to wait till אחרית הימים, a faraway future (though certainly not "the end of days"; cf. among others, Gen 49:1; Deut 4:30; 31:29). In other words, the postmonarchic readers of the book are asked to construe the character of Hosea in the book as a person who did not expect a full restoration in the monarchic period, and whose vision of the future is still open. He is construed as a true prophet who is able to contemplate centuries of wait and to convey hope at the same time.

As mentioned above (STRUCTURE), the authorship and the intended and primary rereaderships of the book of Hosea as well as the characters in the book itself (and any society in the ancient Near East) share a worldview in which men initiate marriage and men must pay to initiate marriage, and in which women are "purchased" (see below) by their future husbands. Moreover, the price of women is conceived as proportional to their perceived (market?) quality.

It is likely that the intended readers of the book constructed the price of the woman (/Israel) in Hos 3:2 as a *mohar* or bride price or bride wealth (see Geller, "Elephantine Papyri"), that is, as the amount that the future husband is supposed to pay to the father of the bride. This social institution was part and parcel of ancient Near Eastern kinship organization (and is or has been attested in many societies all over the world). Usually it is better understood not as a real "purchase" per se, but as a way to bind together, in patriarchal, agrarian societies, the families of the bride and groom through an exchange of goods that often carry symbolic value. In addition, it carries a deterrent against any action or attitude from the side of the family of the bride (i.e., her former household) that may destabilize her marriage (i.e., her new household). Yet in the case of Hosea/YHWH and the woman/Israel there cannot be a real family of the bride (see above) to whom she legally belonged until the prospective groom married her. Nor does the exchange of goods bind Hosea's/YHWH's new family to the former family of the woman/Israel. The "purchase" in Hos 3:2 is thus a rhetorical, ideologically necessary, and defamiliarized version of the common social institution of bride price that the text evokes among the intended readership. What does one make, therefore, of the actual detail concerning the bride price in Hos 3:2, and how does it help to reconstruct the worldview that informs the setting of the world of the book as well as that of the authorship and primary readership? It seems that the question is one of valuation of the bride, and evaluation of Israel. As the intended and primary rereaderships approached Hos 3:2 in the context of Hosea 1–3, the contrast becomes clear. The bride price of sinful Israel is as paltry and based on material goods as the one in Hos 3:2; the one of renewed, purified Israel in 2:21-22 is divine righteousness, justice, steadfast love, mercy, and faithfulness. (Within the social context of the ancient Near East, the image of betrothal evokes and often encompasses that of the payment of the bride price.)

(Braaten has written extensively about the relation between bride wealth and the husband's right to the offspring of the couple. This relation has obvious implications within a metaphorical world in which the husband is YHWH, and the woman/wife is Israel and so are the children [see previous discussions]. But Braaten claims that the payment in Hos 3:2 is not to be associated with bride-wealth. See Braaten, *Parent-Child,* 135-219.)

It is worth mentioning that the impossibility of attaching the woman/Israel explicitly to her original family, and binding the "new couple" to the original family of the bride, is conducive to the ideological and rhetorical construction of a pre-marriage woman/Israel who is independent of any male/patriarchal household. The latter in turn is conducive to the characterization of the woman/Israel as a prostitute.

In all these matters the mindset of both the character Hosea as shaped in the book and that of the implied author of the book not only inform the ideological setting of the world of the book, but also provide a window into the worldviews of the literati among whom and for whom the book was composed.

Intention

The general intention of Hosea 3 is to provide hope and convey certitude about the establishment of an ideal future among the intended readers of the book of Hosea. It also urges the readership to imagine that future as one in which Israel will seek and tremble towards YHWH, will have a "messianic" Davide as king, and will enjoy prosperity. It also urges the readership to understand that such a time may be still far away. The ideal future is also imagined as one in which sacrifices and temple functions are conducted in a proper manner. The text looks back at the past history of Israel and explains the fall of the monarchic period in terms of Israel's sin (and to some extent, inexplicable stupidity, for instance, in loving "raisin cakes"). In addition, the text indicates to its readers that they should understand the period in which Israel is without king, officers, sacrifices, and priests — that is, without monarchy and without temple — as a purification period. Tooze correctly writes concerning 3:4, "the language of separation and the deprivation of political and cultic practices conjure up the images of the Babylonian exile" (Tooze, *Framing the Book of the Twelve*, 157). Images of exile and return to the land appear elsewhere in Hosea (see 2:2) and are similarly associated with quasi-messianic imagery (cf. Tg to Hos 3:3). Yet it is to be stressed that from the perspective of the readership in Achaemenid Yehud, the "exilic" period is not over yet, even if the temple has been partially restored, and the more so since the latter has not been restored to its (hoped to be) full glory. The readers of Hosea 3 certainly cannot consider themselves as living under the conditions of v. 5; rather they are still in those described in vv. 3-4, hoping for the time in which YHWH will metaphorically and finally consort with Israel, thus ending the period of lack of intimacy referred to in v. 3.

Needless to say, scholars who associate Hosea 3 with the Josianic or Hezekianic period would propose that the intention of the text has to do with the efforts of either Josiah or Hezekiah to take over the territories of northern Israel, after the fall of its monarchic polity. From their perspective, the text serves as a propaganda piece for the actual Davidic monarch reigning in Judah at the time. An excellent example of this approach is Sweeney, *King Josiah of Judah* (see particularly p. 272). Yet the association of this and related prophetic texts with the time of Josiah (or Hezekiah) is problematic (see Ben Zvi, "Josiah and the Prophetic Books"). Clearly, the association with the "messianic" king in a faraway future, that is, אחרית הימים "the end of (or, the latter) days" (i.e., a faraway future), does not buttress the claim that these texts reflect propaganda for an expansionist policy of a reigning king. When claims related to contemporary policies are made, they tend to emphasize the identity of the ruler and are unlikely to set the actions in a very distant future. This is particularly so if the speaker is not set in a very distant past. In any case, there is nothing in the text that asks the readers to understand that the future Davide is Josiah (or even less likely Hezekiah, during whose reign the world of Hosea is partially set; see Hos 1:1); contrast the situation here with that in 1 Kgs 13:2.

Clearly the intention of Hosea 3 is not to provide a historically reliable (auto)biography of Hosea. His actions are important because they are symbolic, because they stand as a representation of the trajectory in time of YHWH's relation to Israel, and the latter's behavior towards the former. The numerous constraints on the range of possible characterizations of Hosea and the woman that are imposed by rhetorical and ideological motifs — e.g., the woman cannot be associated with a family prior to her engagement to YHWH, the latter is not expected to socially relate to the original family of Israel, any reference to that family is to be erased, common constructions of women independent of patriarchal custody, and the like — along with the explicit metaphor for which the actions of Hosea (and the woman) stand raise numerous questions about any possible degree of full social mimesis or historicity.

Hosea 3:1-5 serves to reflect, shape, and strengthen particular images of the past, socializing the community of readers with interpretations of the past and hopes for the future, both of which, in part, serve to characterize YHWH. In addition, it advances claims about the future David and his quasi-messianic character, which, particularly because of the latter, and the references to faraway times, need not be associated with any practical expectation that the new David will appear soon, but which certainly convey a sense of rejection of any legitimacy of the monarchic period polity of northern Israel and of those who do not expect such a Davide (e.g., worshipers of YHWH who do not share the ideology propagated by the Jerusalemite center in the Achaemenid period). In this sense it is a typical product of the period (cf. Ben Zvi, "Inclusion in and Exclusion from"). Further, and to state the obvious, the text reinforces the ideological constructions, social views, and general worldviews that were associated with the authoritative voices in the book, such as those mentioned under Setting.

Bibliography

S. Ackerman, "The Personal Is Political: Covenantal and Affectionate Love ('ĀHĒB, 'AHĂBÂ) in the Hebrew Bible," *VT* 52 (2002) 437-58; M. J. Geller, "Elephantine Papyri and Hosea 2,3," *JSJ* 8 (1997) 139-48; J. Krizpenz, "Das 'ehebrechereisch veranlagte Weib' und der 'gott-identifizierte Mann' in Hosea 3," M. Oeming (ed.), *Theologie des AT aus der Perspektive von Frauen* (BVB 1; Münster: LIT, 2003) 155-71; Sh. Talmon and W. W. Fields, "The Collocation משתין בקיר ועצור ועזוב and Its Meaning," *ZAW* 101 (1989) 85-112; W. Vogels, "Hosea's Gift to Gomer (Hos 3,2)," *Bib* 69 (1988) 412-21.

Note: Bibliography mentioned in Hosea 1–3 is not repeated here.

Second Set of Readings:
Hope for the Future and Explanation of Past Judgment by References to Sinful Worship, Leadership, and General Behavior of the People, 4:1–11:11

Structure

The tripartite division of the body of the book of Hosea, namely, chs. 1–3 (except 1:1); 4–11, and 12–14 (except 14:10) is *one* of the structures that the book suggests, and so the internal division of chapters 4–11 is advanced here. The text of the book also suggests a second, complementary bipartite structure (chs 1–3 — except 1:1 — and 4–14 — except 14:10). In either case, the second section begins with lengthy descriptions of Israel's rejection of YHWH and YHWH's way, contains multiple references to severe punishment, and culminates in strong expressions of hope. (To a large extent, the portrayals of punishment carry the seed of their own reversal and, consequently, remind the readership of the future hope; see below and cf. Hosea 1–3.) One of the main structural differences between the bipartite and tripartite structures is that if one follows the bipartite, the seventh reading (see above) would fulfill a role similar to that of Hos 2:16-25 as a commanding expression of hope, whereas chapters 12–14 would fulfill that of chapter 3 in the first set, namely, a kind of loop or additional READING that goes back to address issues already discussed in the preceding READINGS, but from a different perspective. In this case, the concluding expression of hope in Hos 14:5-9 would fulfill the rhetorical slot of Hos 3:5. These two structures are not alternative but complementary, and it is likely that both were activated in the process of continuous rereading of the book of Hosea, for which process it was composed. On multiple structures, see E. Ben Zvi, "Prophetic Book," and the discussions of STRUCTURE of these seven READINGS mentioned above, and particularly that of Hos 5:1–7:2.

The section Hos 4:1–11:11 is marked off by an initial דבר ה' בני ישראל "hear the word of YHWH, O Children of Israel," that calls attention to and characterizes the ensuing text in the book (see Hos 4:1-19 STRUCTURE) and by a final נאם ה' "YHWH's saying" in Hos 11:11, as well as by the return of the motifs of sinful past and judgment in Hosea 12. (נאם ה' contributes to the demarcation of the unit but above all marks the preceding text as direct quotation of YHWH, legitimizes it, and functions in a way similar to a focus marker in the sense that it draws the attention of the readers to the marked text; cf. Parunak, "Some Discourse Functions," and Meier, *Speaking,* 298-314.)

Hos 4:1–11:1 explores further some of the main themes advanced in the first set (1:2–3:5). In turn Hos 12:1–14:9 explores further some of the main themes advanced in 4:1–11:11. Although Hos 4:1–11:11 continues to employ metaphors associated with whoring, the marital metaphor/s that plays such a central role in Hos 1:2–3:5 is not continued in this set. Like the first SET of READINGS, it deals with constructions of the past, proclaims an exile from the land that stands in the future of the world of the book (as specified in Hos 1:1), emphasizes monarchic Israel's sin, justifies YHWH's actions against Israel, and even characterizes the punishment as positive for Israel, since it leads to the removal of kings, monarchic elites, high places, calves, idols, and the like that lead Israel to sin (see 10:1-15 Setting). The lengthy pedagogical (see Intention) reports and condemnations of the sins of Israel in the monarchic period lead to a strong expression of hope (Hos 11:8-11) that includes explicit references to the return to the land and a new idyllic relation between YHWH and Israel (cf. Hos 2:1-3, 16-25; 3:5; 14:5-9). These hopeful notes carry strong affective components and are most salient particularly against the background of the description of Israel's sins that takes most of the space in the book.

Both Hos 1:2–3:5 and Hos 4:1–11:11 deal with the reported and ideologically construed apostasy of Israel. The role fulfilled by references to other males in the first set of readings is taken over in this set by references to other gods, idols, foreign powers, and kings. Yet the latter are obviously implied in the first set, and the second keeps playing with images of Israel's "whoring." Similarly, although the second set of readings focuses more on kings and political elites, these are not absent from the first set of readings (see Hos 3:4-5). In fact, as pointed out by Alonso Schokel and J. L. Sicre Diaz (*Profetas,* II, 882), there are a number of clear correspondences between these two sets of readings. As it will be shown in the individual discussions, there are numerous connections between the different READINGS in this set (Hos 4:1–11:11).

Commentaries that propose a tripartite division of the book into 1–3*, 4–11, 11–14* include those by G. I. Davies, Wolff, and Pentiuc. Those that emphasize a division of the book into 1-3*, 4-14* include those by Rudolph, Andersen and Freedman, and Mays, as well as the monograph of Buss, *Prophetic Word.* Other proposals for understanding the structure of the body of the book of Hosea in general, and Hosea 4–14 in particular, have been advanced. For instance, Simian-Yofre *(Desierto)* proposes Hos 1:2–3:5; 4:1–7:16; 8:1–10:15; and 11:1–14:9/10. Sweeney (*King Josiah,* 258) refers to a tripartite structure: "Hosea 1–3, which presents Hosea's marriage to Gomer as a paradigm for YHWH's relationship with Israel; Hosea 4–11, which articulates Hosea's message of judgment against Israel and concludes with YHWH's passionate outcry that denies the Deity's capacity to give up Israel or allow it to be destroyed; and Hosea 12–14, which reiterates the history of YHWH's relationship with Israel by employing elements of tradition that rehearse the grounds for Israel's punishment and call for Israel's return to YHWH." But Sweeney rejects this viewpoint in favor of a bipartite structure of the main body of the book that is unlike the one mentioned above. He proposes two blocks: 1:2–2:3 and 2:4–14:9 (see Sweeney, *King Josiah,* 258-63; idem, *The Twelve,* 12-140 (12-13); idem, "Form-Critical Rereading of Hosea").

It goes without saying that each of these proposals includes subdivisions within the major structural blocks they advance, and at times the matter at stake concerns the relative hierarchy of a structural break in the text. In other words, the question involves whether a particular break is indicative of a division of first order (i.e., separates the major blocks of material within the book), second order (i.e., separates particular blocks within a major block of material), or third order (i.e., separates blocks of material within a particular block of material that belongs to a major block of material). Yet these matters of hierarchy often involve or shape particular emphases within the range of messages that the text may convey to its readerships. It is to be stressed again that since the book of Hosea was meant to be reread and studied, and read to others on different occasions and under different circumstances, many of these possible understandings of the book were likely realized and contributed each to the tapestry of meanings that the book conveyed to its primary readerships. These issues will be discussed under STRUCTURE in the ensuing pages.

It is also worth noting that there are structural proposals that depart more radically from the others. For instance, Qyl has proposed a division into (i) Hos 1:2–3:5; (ii) 4:1-19; (iii) 5:1–6:11; (iv) 7:1–8:14; (v) 9:1–10:8; (vi) 10:9–11:11; (vii) 12:1–13:11; (viii) 13:12–14:1; and (ix) 14:2-9. For a recent proposal that the structure of the book of Hosea is shaped around six sections ([i] Hosea 1–3; [ii] Hos 4:1–5:7; [iii] Hos 5:8–7:16; [iv] Hos 8:1–9:9; [v] Hos 9:10–10:15] and [vi] Hos 11:1–14:10) see Braaten, "God Sows." For earlier proposals see the masoretic division of the book into open and closed paragraphs, and Abrabanel, according to whom the text contains five prophecies: (a) Hos 1:1–2:25; (b) Hos 3:1-5; (c) Hos 4:1–5:7; (d) Hos 5:8–9:9; and (e) Hos 9:10–14:10.

Genre

Each of the texts included in this unit is a PROPHETIC READING. The genre of the unit as a whole is SET OF READINGS. It is to be stressed that these READINGS do not exist independently of each other, but as part and parcel of the BOOK of Hosea. As such the meaning conveyed by each one of them to their intended and primary readerships is informed by the others, and at times even choices of words and metaphors in one READING are heavily influenced by those appearing elsewhere in the book.

Setting

The setting of the production and the primary reading and rereading of these literary units is that of the book as a whole. It involves a group of (postmonarchic) literati who were aware of ideological constructions of Israel's past and shared a strong hope for its future. Many elements of the intellectual world of these literati will be explored as the different READINGS that constitute this SET OF READINGS are discussed in the following chapters of this commentary.

Intention

The main intention of the text is to communicate hope to the readers (that is, Israel). It reaffirms their hope that it is YHWH's will that they (= Israel) will achieve that ideal future at some point. It enhances this hope without advancing any concrete, worldly (or other-worldly) scenario for the process that would narrow the expectations or allow them to be too closely identified with any particular historical event. This openness for the future bears particular notice and allows multiple possible understandings that serve to maintain the readability and rereadability of the book under different circumstances. The same degree of openness does not exist concerning the nature of the ideal future. The text encourages readers to ponder about the future and allows for socially shared imaginations, but within some clear discursive limits: the ideal future involves YHWH's reconciliation with Israel, Israel's full and unconditional acceptance of YHWH's rule over her — as this rule is understood by the literati among whom one finds the authorship of the book as well as its primary readership — and a return to the land. As expected, since this set of readings is part and parcel of the book of Hosea, and since the latter is part and parcel of a general authoritative discourse or set of discourses shared by the mentioned literati and those who support them or are influenced by them (postmonarchic Israel/Yehud), this range of imagination of the ideal future is not unique to this SET OF READINGS, but is widely shared within the mentioned discourse or set of discourses.

As the book of Hosea as a whole — and as prophetic literature in general — this SET OF READINGS assumes that reading about Israel's punishment in the past is an important way of acquiring knowledge about the divine and YHWH's wishes. Thus indirectly, YHWH's severe punishment of Israel in the past serves pedagogical purposes. This is present at the level of the world of text (cf. Hos 5:15; 11:10-11, which seem to indicate that this is YHWH's hope, and cf. Hos 14:2-4), but above all at the level of the intended readership of the book, for whom YHWH's punishment becomes an everlasting process which is relived as social memory as they read the book, and which enriches, educates, and warns Israel (cf. Albertz, "Exile as Purification," 248).

It is also worth noticing that the strong emphasis on an abysmally negative construction of Israel's past serves not only to justify YHWH's punishment — after all, the idea that YHWH was a just deity was probably not a continuous item of debate among the literati — but also to strongly communicate to the intended and primary readers that Israel will continue to exist forever. In other words, that no matter how much Israel has sinned or will sin in the future, no matter how much they were punished because of their sins, or how low their (perceived) status is in the world, YHWH will never destroy Israel. Rather YHWH will keep it and eventually raise it to the ideal status in which it will enjoy the proper relationship with YHWH that these readers hope for. Significantly, this central message is forcefully conveyed by the three sets of readings in the book of Hosea, by the book as a whole, and by much of prophetic literature.

Bibliography

R. Albertz, "Exile as Purification. Reconstructing the 'Book of Four,'" P. L. Redditt and A. Schart (eds.), *Thematic Threads in the Book of the Twelve* (BZAW 325; Berlin: de Gruyter, 2003) 232-51; S. A. Meier, *Speaking of Speaking. Marking Direct Discourse in the Hebrew Bible* (VTSup 46; Leiden: E. J. Brill, 1992); H. H. Van Dyke Parunak, "Some Discourse Functions of Prophetic Quotation Formula," R. D. Bergen (ed.), *Biblical Hebrew and Discourse Linguistics* (SIL; Winona Lake, IN: Eisenbrauns, 1994) 489-519; M. A. Sweeney, "A Form-Critical Rereading of Hosea," *Journal of Hebrew Scriptures* 2 (1998), available at http://www.jhsonline.org and http://purl.org/jhs.

First Didactic Prophetic Reading:
About a Particular Case of YHWH's Word Embedded in a Larger Instance of YHWH's Word (i.e., the Book of Hosea), 4:1-19

Structure

This first didactic, prophetic READING opens the SET OF READINGS that comprises Hos 4:1–11:11. The reading raises fundamentally the same type of matters as Hosea 1–3. From the perspective of the postmonarchic readers of the entire book, it serves to construct the past, explain YHWH's judgment of Israel, and provide hope for the future. It does so, however, in a different manner. There is a clear shift in tone and style. The use of the marital life of Hosea as a metaphor for the relation between YHWH and Israel disappears, though the text continues to employ, quite extensively, imagery of sexual "whoring" or promiscuity (זנה), and marital metaphors.

It is reasonable to assume that the boundaries of the present unit (4:1-19) are demarcated by the call to hear in 4:1 and the one in 5:1 that opens the new unit. (A break between 3:5 and 4:1 is marked not only in the MT tradition of paragraphs, but already in 4QXIIg; see Russell, *The Twelve,* 278.) Calls to hear, expressed by imperative forms of שמע ("hear"), are common introductory elements in the HB/OT in general and in prophetic literature in particular (see, for instance, Deut 6:4; Judg 5:3; 2 Kgs 7:1; Isa 1:2; 7:13; 48:1; 49:1; Jer 10:1; Amos 3:1; 4:1; 5:1; Mic 1:2; 3:1; 6:1; Ps 49:2; Prov 1:8; 4:1; Job 34:2).

It is important to note that here (as in some other places in prophetic literature, e.g. Amos 3:1; 4:1; 5:1) the call to hear serves as both a macrosyntactical and a rhetorical marker that sets the proceeding unit apart from the preceding, and as a contextual, literary marker that links the two. In fact, the structure of the two openings is very similar. Each begins with the plural imperative שמעו "hear" followed by a reference that identifies that which the addressees are supposed to hear (here, "YHWH's word"), followed by the vocative that identifies the addressees (here, "the children of Israel"), followed by a series of explanations, each of which opens with כי "for," and each of which includes the shortest and most general reason as the first item in the series.

For other possible macrosyntactical roles of expressions beginning with imperative forms of שמע see Mic 1:2; 3:1; 6:1, 2. To be sure, שמעו "hear" is not actually a "call to hear" but a call to "hear" what is reported in a written document. The same holds true for all the readings in the book. Thus, for instance, the text includes only reported condemnations or expressions of hope for Israel by YHWH, and the like. For the implications of these considerations, see Genre. For practical purposes the term "reported" is almost always omitted in discussions under STRUCTURE, but it is implied in all these cases.

In most instances in the HB the imperative calling to hear is immediately followed either by a vocative (i.e., by a reference to the one who is called to hear) or by a reference to the object of the "hearing," i.e., what is to be heard (see Isa 48:1; Jer 10:1; Hos 5:1; Amos 3:1; 4:1; 5:1; Micah 3:1). In any case, the main speech to be heard in the world of the book is placed in the text in close proximity to the imperative (e.g., Deut 6:4). In the present case, the situation seems, on the surface, obvious. Those who are supposed to hear are "the children of Israel," and that which they are supposed to hear is YHWH's word, which points to the text that follows. Issues concerning the referents of "the children of Israel" will be discussed below. But what is meant by YHWH's word? Is this a multivalent term? It certainly points at 4:1-19, but does it point at that text only?

Hos 4:1-3 certainly serves as introduction to Hos 4:4-19, but at the same time to Hosea 4:4–11:11, or perhaps to Hosea 4:4–14:9 (cf. Neef, *Heilstraditionen Israels*, 193-94; Naumann, *Hoseas Erben*, 19; Daniels, *Hosea*, 345; Eideval, *Grapes in the Desert*, 52; Wolff, *Hosea*, 69; Limburg, *Hosea*, 15; Good, "Composition," 33, 61-63). In fact, Zeph 1:2-3 provides a somewhat similar introduction to Zeph 1:4–3:20. (For further discussion on Zeph 1:3 and Hos 4:3 see Setting; double-duty words or sections are not uncommon in prophetic books.) It is worth stressing that from the perspective of a rereading of the book of Hosea that considers 4:1 the opening of a larger set of readings that concludes with 11:11, the term YHWH's word refers to this particular reading (i.e., Hos 4:1-19), but also to 4:1–11:11. Moreover, when the text is read in such a way, readers take notice of the envelope, דבר ה' (4:1) — נאם ה' (11:11). Significantly, within the range of Hos 4:1–14:10, this expression occurs only in 11:11 in a final position (cf. Andersen and Freedman, *Hosea*, 331-32). It also bears note that the precise wording of the beginning of the reading that introduces the set of readings in Hosea chapters 4–11, immediately after the "call to hear," includes כי ריב לה׳ עם ישבי הארץ "for YHWH has a quarrel/indictment against the inhabitants of the land." The same expression is used at the beginning of the next SET OF READINGS in the book (Hos 12:1–14:9), for Hos 12:3 reads עם יהודה ריב לה׳ "for YHWH has a quarrel/indictment against Judah." The difference, of course, is that monarchic Judah now replaces "the inhabitants of the land." Moreover, the context in Hos 12:3 associates Judah with Jacob and its traditions, that is, with Israel. The readers are confronted with multiple images informing each other within a general discursive world. Judah, Israel, the inhabitants of the land, and also Ephraim (see 12:1) are all interconnected, and all point in different ways to facets of trans-temporal Israel, the ideological group with whom the readers of the book identify. (On this matter see also below.)

It is worth stressing at this point that summons to hear such as the one in Hos 4:1 (and cf. Mic 1:2; 3:1; 6:1, 2, among many others) serve an affective function in regards to the readership of the text. The call to hear is addressed not only to the addressees that populate the world of the book but above all to the readership. They are supposed to pay attention to the text, to overhear the voices of the textually inscribed speakers, and to identify with the addressees.

Several expressions in this reading evoke other sections in the book, and contribute to the creation of additional networks of various rereadings continuously informing each other. For instance, the reference to the lack of faithfulness, *hesed*, and knowledge of God in v. 1 links the verse to Hos 2:21-22. In addition, within the discourse of the period some of the referents explicitly mentioned in only one place evoke those explicitly mentioned only in the other (see Ps 89:15). In other words, the terms mentioned here serve as code words that raise an entire horizon of thought. In any event, at the very least, the intrabook connection with Hos 2:21-22 is clearly reinforced by the references to חית השדה "the beasts of the field" and עוף השמים "the birds of the sky" in both 2:20 and 4:3. This linkage of Hos 4:1-3 and Hos 2:20-22 creates a contrast between past and future; a contrast between a realm in which divine and ideal human attributes are shared to some extent and one in which there is clear dissonance and separation. This contrast, in fact, goes beyond Hos 2:22, because 2:23-24 surely serves as a contrast figure to the devastating draught imagery of 4:3 (which in turn, recalls that of 2:5). This is an excellent example of the general principle that from the perspective of the intended and primary readership, the meanings of particular readings (or "small textual units") in the book are dependent on the meanings of other readings or units within the book. No one unit stands alone. It is worth noting that additional motifs such as whoring/sexual promiscuity (זנה) and adultery (נאף) also link this reading to the previous set of readings (for these motifs see vv. 10, 11, 12, 13, 14, 15, 18). Of course, references to X and connections with X do not convey identity with X; to the contrary, their point is to relate texts that at least at one clear level communicate something different. (See Setting and Intention.)

One can easily notice clear word links between this and the following section in the book, i.e., Hos 5:1–7:2. See, for instance, רוח זנונים "a spirit/impulse of sexual promiscuity/whoredom" (in 4:12 and 5:4 and nowhere else in the HB); the motif of stumbling (כשל) in Hos 4:5, 5:5, which reinforces the bonds and partial overlapping of images of priests (and prophets) and those of Israel created in this reading (see below). See also the set of כשל "stumble" references in the book of Hosea (4:5; 5:5; 14:2, 10), which from the perspective of the readers are illuminated by the interpretative key of 14:10: those who stumble (in YHWH's ways) do so because they are פשעים "transgressors" (cf. Hos 7:13; 8:1) as opposed to צדקים "righteous" (cf. Macintosh, "Hosea and the Wisdom Tradition," 124). Compare also Hos 4:1 and 6:6. The first text characterizes the situation to be portrayed in the chapter in the most general and generalizing terms: "There is no hesed (Heb., חסד), and no knowledge of God (דעת אלהים) in the land." In 6:6 the readers are told that what YHWH desires is "hesed and not (just) zebach sacrifice, the knowledge of God (דעת אלהים) more than olah sacrifices." Of course, the readers of the book are aware of 6:6 when they read 4:1 and vice versa. As they begin to reread chapter 4, which deals among others things with priests and cult, they keep in mind that under the circumstances portrayed in 4:1 no sacrifice can be proper (and efficacious) in the sight of YHWH. On Hos 6:6 and on hesed, see Hos 5:1–7:2 STRUCTURE and Setting. One may also note that Hos 4:1 refers also to faithfulness (אמת). חסד and אמת are a common word pair in the HB (e.g., Exod 34:6; 2 Sam 2:6; Mic 7:20; Ps 25:10; 61:8; 69:14; 86:15; Prov 3:3).

Not only are Hos 4:1 and Hos 6:6 related, but the next verse in this READING, Hos 4:2, informs (and is informed by) the next READING in the book (see Hos 5:1–7:2, STRUCTURE). In addition, one may compare Hos 4:7 and 10:1a, and note the motif of the "foolish people" in Hos 4:7, 10b-12, 14 and 7:11; 8:7; 9:7; 12:2; 13:13 (see Seow, "Hosea 14:10 and the Foolish People Motif").

Numerous textual connections also contribute to internal coherence within this READING, some within an immediate literary context and others within the frame of the entire subset. For instance ריב "contention, grievance, indictment" and ירב "contend" link the introduction to the opening of the first section (cf. also the use of the motif of knowledge in vv. 1 and 6).

Markers of internal coherence within respective sections of this reading are also present. For instance, there is the reference to יושבי הארץ "those who dwell in the land" and כל יושב בה "all who dwell in her [the land]" in vv. 1 and 3. Parallel structures, the repetition of איש "man/person" or forms of כשל "stumble," or forms of דמה "destroy" (and in addition, probably at the connoted level also דמם "silence"; for the same combination of connotation and denotation, see Hos 10:15), as well as usual pairs "day" and "night" or "priest" and "prophet," contribute to a sense of coherence within vv. 4-6a. At times, the basic style of a short section is clearly chosen for its rhetorical power. For instance, the clear parallel structure (and verbal repetition) highlights the point of "measure for measure" that v. 6b communicates.

The readership of the text is presented with numerous shifts from second to third person in reference to Israel or groups associated with the latter (e.g., priests). Similarly, references to YHWH appear in the first and in the third person. It does not follow from this observation that the unit was not understood as a rhetorical unit or that its style is "jagged" or that it is in need of repairs by means of redactional hypotheses (ct. Wolff, *Hosea*, 74; Yee, *Composition*, 158-70). Although it is true that such shifts are not likely in actual life, oral communication, and particularly so in extremely brief speeches, the same does not hold true for sophisticated, written works such as the prophetic books. In fact, shifts from second to third person and vice versa are not uncommon in these books (e.g., Obadiah, passim; Mic 1:2). They contribute to the message and, at times, the rhetorical appeal of the text. In the present case, the predominance of the address in the second person, and of direct speech in general, serves to enhance the identification of the readers with those addressed in the world of the book. The "you" in the world of the text may refer to the children of Israel (v. 1), or an "individual" whose people is Israel (v. 4b, on this verse see below), or those for whom "Israel" is their "mother" (v. 5), or likely priests (v. 6), or those whose daughters and daughters-in-law behaved as reported in v. 13, or northern Israel (v. 15). In every single case, from the perspective of the primary and intended readership, the shifts from second to third person convey a careful balance. Surely, the text speaks of monarchic Israel, of priests and other Israelites long dead, but it speaks also about (trans-temporal) Israel, of which the ancient Israelites in the world of the book (and in the discourse of the community of readers) as well as the intended and primary readerships of the book are an integral part. In this sense, they, these readerships are required to identify with the "you" in the text (cf. the pervasive use of "you" in Deuteronomy; for the rhetorical use of grammatical person to convey this sense of belonging to trans-temporal Israel, see, among others, Exod 13:8).

Likewise, there is nothing odd about the shift in the reported speech from a focus on the priest (vv. 5-9) to the people (9-15). From an ideological perspective, the failure of the priest (along with the prophet's failure, see v. 5; cf. Odell, "Prophets," and see also discussion in Hos 9:1-17 Setting) points at the inability of the people to "communicate" correctly with the divine. Accordingly, it points at a people at fault in its relation with the divine. Moreover, the text purposefully and emphatically blurs the boundaries separating priests and "people." It does so explicitly: "like people, like priest" (v. 9a). In addition, it does so by means of a careful literary construction. Within a clearly unified unit, the text moves seamlessly to focus on the condemnation of the people (v. 4), the priests (6-8; and explicitly mentions the relation between the two, see v. 9). Then it reaches a Janus portion that if it is read in relation to the preceding verses, it points to the priests (v. 9b); but, if read in relation to the proceeding verses, it points to the people. From that Janus portion, the text moves to a subunit that clearly points to the people. Priests and non-priests become discursively intertwined; boundaries are transgressed. Ideologically, this is exactly the point of the text. Priests are not supposed to become indistinguishable from non-priests, within the proper order. At the same time that the text is shaped to maximize this rhetorical goal, it uses it to enhance the ability of the readership to identify with the "you-s" of the text, for the more the priest becomes not only a representative of Israel, but like Israel, the more those in the primary readership who are not priests may identify with them. As mentioned above, all are part and parcel of "trans-temporal" Israel. It is worth stressing in this regard the precise wording of v. 9 and the network of meanings that it suggests. Immedi-

ately after the statement "like people like priest," it reads ופקדתי עליו דרכיו
ומעלליו אשיב לו "I [YHWH] will punish him [the priest; but also the people,
as a connotation] for his ways and repay him for his (mis)deeds." Significantly,
an extremely similar expression appears in Hos 12:3. The text there reads,
ולפקד על יעקב כדרכיו כמעלליו ישיב לו ". . . punish Jacob according to his
ways and he will repay him for his (mis)deeds." The explicit, textually inscribed cross-reference between the two texts suggests to the intended and primary readership that when they read, reread, and study these texts, their understanding of one of them is to be informed by the other. In this case, such an
informed rereading, at the very least, leads to and reinforces the identification
of priest and people already suggested in Hos 4:9.

This reading includes two deeply intertwined readings. The first (vv. 4-
11) focuses in particular on religious leadership, mainly priestly, though prophets are mentioned. This section concludes with a saying that serves as an explanation for Israel's behavior, "(love of) sexual promiscuity and wine, and new
wine take away understanding/capture the heart." An Israel that indulges in
both cannot show wisdom in its choices (cf. Hos 4:14; see below). The motif of
the negative power of wine and of women in general, and in particular, of
women other than their wives over men — from the perspective of men, to be
sure — is relatively common in "wisdom" literature, which usually admonishes
against them (see Proverbs 5; 20:1; 23:31-34; and for instance, the story of the
three guardsmen in 1 Esd 3:1–5:6; also cf. Isa 28:1-3). The combination of the
themes of sexual promiscuity and drunkenness is quite common in this book.
References to sex and wine together, however, are not unique to the book of
Hosea (cf. Ruth; and see Hos 9:1-2). In fact, the association of sexual activity
with drinking, and particularly wine, is a common literary topos; see, for instance, Song 2:4, which may have reflected in some way actual life. (On the
wording of 4:10 see below.)

In the book of Hosea, drunkenness and sexual promiscuity (or whoredom) do not stand by or for themselves, but rather serve to convey a sense of
wrongful cultic behavior, as the extensive use of metaphors of sexual promiscuity and whoredom, and the repeated use of terms from the root זנה for the portrayed rejection of YHWH by Israel (cf. Jer 2:20; 3:6, 13) show. To be sure, the
ideological and literary connection between cultic activities considered highly
improper and sexual activities also considered highly improper — and often involving activities in the field, or under the trees (see Hos 4:13) — is a common
motif in the HB (see, for instance, Exod 32:6; Ezek 18:6, 11, 15; 22:9; Isa 57:5;
Prov 7:14-20). For the claim that these, and similar verses, "paint an appropriate, comprehensive picture of the cultic activity of Baalism" see Wolff, *Hosea,*
86. On the possibility of reconstructing historical baalism, see Setting below,
and the previous discussion of Hos 2:3-25. It is worth noting here, however,
these references are not necessarily circumscribed to portrayals of northern Israel, or to texts usually assigned to the monarchic period (see mentioned
verses). For the particular wording in 4:13, see below.

The explanation for Israel's behavior in terms of sexual promiscuity/
whoredom and wine creates a thematic and ideological link to the second main
reading, in which a similar explanation is advanced. There, the reason is רוח

זנונים "a spirit/impulse of sexual promiscuity/whoredom" (see 4:12; cf. 5:4 and nowhere else in the HB; cf. אשת זנונים in 1:2, ילדי זנונים "promiscuous children or children of promiscuity" and בני זנונים "promiscuous children or children of promiscuity" in 1:2 and 2:6, which are also expressions that appear in Hosea but nowhere else in the HB). The first main reading includes a section in which the rhetorical principle of measure for measure plays a central role (4:6-10), and that leads to a futility clause (cf. Lev 26:16; Deut 28:30-34, 38-42; Amos 5:11; Mic 6:15; Zeph 1:13 and for their reversals see Ezek 28:26; Isa 65:21). This clause leads to the saying in v. 11, which in turn connects to the text in v. 12 (on vv. 12-19 see below).

The precise wording of Hos 4:10a is worth noting. The text assumes the validity of the comparison between eating and not being sated with acting in a sexually promiscuous manner (cf. Macintosh, *Hosea,* 147-48) and not being fertile, that is, failing to conceive or give birth to children. This comparison involves not only an action and anticipated result, but also a desired result (cf. also other futility curses, Lev 26:16; Deut 28:30-34, 38-42; Amos 5:11; Mic 6:15; Zeph 1:13; cf. Ezek 28:26; Isa 65:21). The sexual activities envisaged here are strongly condemned, but implicitly they are construed as having procreation as their desired goal.

The precise wording כי את ה' עזבו לשמר (for meaning see below) in Hos 4:10b is also worth noting for it allows the expression to carry more than one complementary meaning. By placing the direct object at the front of the clause it brings salience to the reference to YHWH. But in addition, it allows the expression to convey, on the one hand, a meaning akin to either (i) "because they have ceased paying attention to YHWH" or (ii) "because they have ceased to observe the obligations of [/demanded by] YHWH," or (iii) "because they have ceased to observe YHWH's ways (or 'commandments' or the like)" or better, a combination of them all; and on the other hand, to link this verse with the beginning of the next one and thus convey a meaning akin to "because they have abandoned YHWH to observe (/practice/give themselves to) whoredom/ sexual promiscuity (and perhaps, "whoredom and wine"). From the perspective of the readers of the book, both meanings are complementary and together convey the meaning of the text. Of course, this double meaning closely links v. 10 and v. 11 and creates a sense of double local structure, as well. See above.

It is worth noting that the textual choice of YHWH or זנות "whoredom" (or "sexual promiscuity") as the object of the verb שמר "observe" is, in fact, very unusual — neither appears elsewhere in the HB — but it is crucial here to the ability of the text to convey its multilayered meaning. The text defamiliarizes to some extent common linguistic expectations in order to call attention to itself and above all to enrich the meaning it conveys through the intertwining of those mentioned above. It bears note that the first main group of meanings is attested in the Vulgate, the Targum, followed in, for instance, KJV, NASB, and in central translations in languages other than English, e.g., the Luther Bibel; Reina Valera Actualizada and Reina Valera 95. It is supported, for instance, by Calvin, Luther, Ibn Ezra, and among contemporary scholars, see, for instance, Rudolph (*Hosea,* 98); Simian-Yofre (*Desierto,* 66). Alternative (i) is supported by the use of שמר in texts such as Ps 31:7; (ii) is supported by the use of שמר

in texts such as 1 Kgs 11:11; Hos 12:7; (iii) assumes that the text is elliptic and urges the readership to fill in the "missing object" in a manner informed by their knowledge of common ideology evoked here with terms such as דרך "way/ways" (cf. Gen 18:19; 2 Sam 22:22; Ps 18:22), or מצות "command-ments" (cf. Deut 4:2; 8:6; 10:13; 28:9; 2 Kgs 17:19) or similar terms (cf. Deut 4:40; 1 Kgs 2:3; Amos 2:4; Ps 119:5, 8, 17, 34, 55, 136, passim). The second main group of meanings (i.e., "because they have abandoned YHWH to prac-tice sexual promiscuity" and the like) is supported by the LXX, represented in English translations such as the NRSV, NJB, NAB, NJPSV; was already ad-vanced by R. Saadia Gaon (as quoted by Radak) and among contemporary scholars see, for instance, Macintosh (*Hosea*, 147-48, 151); Wolff (*Hosea*, 72). The usual stance here has been to accept one group of meanings and reject the other. The point advanced here is that to the contrary, this is a "both and" situa-tion. Both groups of meanings are correct, but partial; only together do they convey the full meaning of the text to its intended and primary readership.

The second main reading (vv. 12-19) strongly intertwines images of sex-ual promiscuity and of improper cultic practices. For some of the ideological constructions involved see Setting. In addition to explicit imagery, it is also possible that the reference to his "wood" — עץ — and his "rod" — מקל — carry a double meaning; on the one hand, they point to divinatory items, but on the other to "his penis" (cf. Ginsberg, "Lexicographical Notes," 74).

In a way similar to that of 1:7, the text construes an image of northern Is-rael/Ephraim as separate from Judah, refers explicitly to northern sanctuaries but not to Jerusalem, and expresses a divine hope that Judah will not follow the steps of Ephraim (4:15). Of course, the intended and primary readership of the book knows all too well that such an expectation was not fulfilled (as, inciden-tally, clearly expressed in the book: see Hos 5:5, which is linked by textually in-scribed choices to 4:5; see above). It is worth stressing that the world portrayed in this reading is consistent with the world in which the book is set in Hos 1:1, and the on-the-surface focus of the book on northern Israel, while at the same time it carefully connotes a sense of Judah's centrality in YHWH's mind. After all, when YHWH talks about the northern Israel, this deity cannot but think about Judah and care about its future. (For a different approach to v. 15 — and to the book of Hosea — see Hunter, *Seek the Lord*, pp. 135-42.)

As the intended and primary readership of the book knew well, northern Israel fell many years before Judah. The gap in time between the destruction of these two polities was interpreted in postmonarchic discourse in terms of Ju-dah's inability to learn from northern Israel's behavior and fate. The point that Judah failed to understand, that following the northern polity's ways leads to destruction, and, accordingly, it was eventually destroyed, occurs in numerous texts (e.g., 2 Kgs 17:18-20; 21:1-9; Jer 3:6-13; Ezek 16:46-52; 23:1-48). Fur-thermore, the judgment against northern Israel serves to draw attention to that of Judah in several prophetic texts (see Micah 1). From the perspective of the intended and primary readers of the book and their discourse, the separate con-struction of Ephraim, along with the explicit reference to YHWH's hope that Judah will behave differently, function as explicit interpretative keys for the reading. Ephraim's fall was a lesson to monarchic Judah that was not learned, because the latter was not different in a substantive way from monarchic Israel in its rejection of YHWH and YHWH's ways, and therefore, YHWH executed appropriate judgment against it too.

Significantly, no prophetic book refers only to northern Israel, although there are some that refer only to Judah, or Yehud. References to Ephraim as separate from Judah do not necessitate a monarchic period setting for the composition or reading of the present book; cf. Zech 9:10, 13; 10:6-12; Obad 18.

The second main reading contains two sections that show a somewhat different style and thematic focus. The first section opens with a reference to עמי "my people" (4:12) and concludes with a proverbial note that opens with עם "a people" (4:14b). Not surprisingly, the next section opens with a reference to Israel and Judah (v. 15), and provides not only an important interpretative key for the significance of the text (see above) but also serves to connect the two sections. The conclusion of a section with a proverbial note is, of course, structurally reminiscent of the conclusion of the first main reading (4:11). Thematically, however, because of its possible double meaning, it evokes both the conclusion of the book of Hosea as a whole, 14:10, and 4:11, for it may be understood as "a people without understanding are inflamed by passion" (for this understanding of לבט see Morag, "On Semantic and Lexical Features," 504-5, and cf. 4:11), but may also mean "a people without understanding shall come to ruin/stumble" (cf. most English translations; see Prov 10:8, 10, which significantly are the only other instances in which this verb appears in the HB); cf. Hos 14:10. For a review of positions about the meaning of the expression, see Macintosh, *Hosea,* 159.

The second unit of the second section in this reading suggests to the readers that the text is moving towards a climax, through an emphatic series of six short, strongly condemnatory, asyndetic statements consisting of only two words in Hebrew, except for the first which is headed by a short construct chain (vv. 17-18; verse 16 leads the reader into the style of this string of statements). The series, which in English translations is often and understandably smoothed over, communicates a sense of immediacy, gravity, and fragmentation. It includes plenty of Hebrew emphatic forms (see esp. v. 17; cf. Macintosh, *Hosea,* 169-71), as well as some expressions and words that appear here but nowhere else in the HB. Emphatic conclusions tend to show this feature. The series leads to a concluding and elliptical statement that may be translated as "a wind has confined her [i.e., Israel, see below] in its wings; they will be ashamed of their sacrificial feasts" (cf. Macintosh, *Hosea,* 172-73). The meaning "being ashamed of X" (בוש מן) in the second section may be illuminated by its use in verses such as Jer 2:36; 12:13; 48:13; Isa 20:5; Hos 10:6; Mic 7:16; cf. Ps 119:116. It communicates that "X" was considered a secure source of support, protection, or strength but that "X" completely failed to fulfill this expectation. In the context of 4:19 it indicates to the readers that Israel thought that their sacrificial feasts would protect them (by ensuring divine favor), but they failed to do so. Israel is disappointed, confounded because their actions did not work in its favor and did not preempt the punishment referred to in the first part of the verse. What is the punishment that the latter suggests to the readership of the book of Hosea? The wind is to be understood as carrying the punishment, as an

107

agent of YHWH (cf. Hos 13:15; Macintosh, *Hosea,* 174), by confining them/ her (see below) under its wings. But the wind/bird imagery seems elliptical, since it is difficult to assume that it describes a final situation per se. Is Israel to remain in the air? Or does the bird/wind have some destination? Given that the latter is more likely, the readers of the text are left to wonder which destination was meant. The text is clearly open. But of all possible destinations, one is excluded, given the context of Israel's judgment, namely, the land from which the "wind/bird" wrapped them/her up. This being so, the text probably evoked an image of exile among the intended and primary readers of the book, in the postmonarchic period (cf. Eidevall, *Grapes,* 66-67; Macintosh, *Hosea,* 173-74; and Rashi). In other words, the text announces that, contrary to the participants' expectations, the sacrificial feasts of Israel did not protect her/them from exile. The entire cycle of portrayals of cultic wrongdoing is thus summarized in a concluding sentence. Exile was upon them, their cultic actions did not produce the results Israel expected, and as the readers know well, Israel was led to exile, because of their actions. For alternative understandings of v. 19, see, for instance, Simian-Yofre, *Desierto,* 75-76; Sweeney, *Twelve Prophets,* 51.

As is often recognized, the text in v. 19 skillfully plays with association and disassociation of terms (e.g., רוח "wind/spirit" is a divine agent, as opposed to רוח זנונים "spirit of whoredom/promiscuity," which governs the people, but both lead Israel to its punishment to exile), images (wings and sacrificial feasts do not provide protection but relate to punishment), and multiple meanings (see below). A major feature of 17-19 is the literary fluidity of the gender of Israel. Israel/Ephraim is referred to in the third person masc. plural and singular, as one may expect, but also in the third person feminine, which is at least on the surface less expected. Yet, the partial feminization of Israel in vv. 17-19 is consistent with the metaphor of "whoring" and promiscuity, and with the characterization of Israel as a sinful woman associated with this metaphor. In fact, a similar instance of feminization of sinful Israel appears in Hos 5:7. See Hosea 5, STRUCTURE. For alternative approaches whose result is the erasure of the feminization of Israel in Hos 4:17-19, see, for instance, Emmerson ("Fertility Goddess"), McLaughlin (*Marzeah,* 137-42), and Davies (*Hosea,* 134-35) who, among others, maintain that the text here includes a reference to a goddess (cf. Wacker, "Traces"). Another approach that effectively erases the feminization of Israel here involves textual emendations that delete the feminine suffixes in the Hebrew text; see, for instance, Mays, *Hosea,* 76.

A few expressions in this reading are worthy of particular notice. The expression in v. 4b that is at times translated "for with you is my contention, O priest" (NRSV) or the like, actually means in the Hebrew text, "your people are like those who contend [with] the priest" (see above). Many English renditions of the expression reflect textual emendations (e.g., NRSV), but see Barthélemy, *Critique Textuelle,* vol. III, 507-08. On the importance of the expression for an understanding of the ideological horizon of thought of the authorship and primary readership see Setting. Two related expressions appear in vv. 5-6, "I will destroy your mother. My people are destroyed." The people, YHWH's people, are associated again with a feminine form, but this time Israel is imagined as a "mother" (see above). Within this metaphorical world, the sin of her children causes her destruction (ct. Hosea 1–2).

The expression אלה וכחש ורוצח וגנב ונאף "cursing, perjuring, murdering, robbery and adultery" in v. 2 is somewhat similar to Lev 19:11; Jer 7:9; cf. also Exod 20:13-17//Deut 5:17-20. The choice of words in Hosea, however, is unique, and as in other instances (see below), it serves to create a particular Hoseanic voice (also cf. INTRODUCTION). It bears note that each of the five words has a kind of counterpart somewhere in Hosea 4–11 (see Hos 10:4; 9:2; 6:9; 7:1; and 4:13, 14; 7:4, respectively). The conceptual (and ideological) similarities between Exod 20:13-17; Lev 19:11; Deut 5:17-20; and Jer 7:9 point to a general understanding of these types of actions as paradigmatic of those that lead a society to its destruction. (One cannot learn from Hos 4:2 that the precise text of Lev 19:11, of the Decalogue, or Jer 7:9 existed or did not exist by the time of the writing of Hos 4:2; both positions have been advanced in research.) It is worth stressing that just as in 4:2, also in Jer 7:9 the series of sins is intertwined with unacceptable worship. The issue is developed later in this reading.

The contents and wording in v. 13, יקטרו תחת אלון ולבנה ואלה על ראשי ההרים יזבחו ועל גבעות "they sacrifice on the tops of the mountains, and make offerings upon the hills, under oak, poplar, and terebinth" (NRSV) are noteworthy. The text joins many others in condemning forms of worship upon hills and under trees (cf. Deut 12:2; 1 Kgs 14:23-24; 2 Kgs 16:4; 17:10; Isa 57:5; 65:7; Jer 2:20; 3:6, 13; 17:2; Ezek 6:13; 2 Chr 28:4). The wording in Hosea, however, is unique.

Several other expressions in this reading are clearly unique. For instance, one may mention חבור עצבים, probably "bound to the idols"; כבש במרחב "lamb in a broad pasture; and ויבשו מזבחותם, which, vocalized as in the MT, may be translated "they will be ashamed of their sacrificial feasts," but which also connotes the meaning "they shall be ashamed because of their altars" (NRSV) in vv. 16, 17, 19, respectively. The connoted reference to their altars may evoke associations with Hos 10:2, 8; 12:12 among the intended and primary readership. The reference to פרה סררה "stubborn cow" (cf. Deut 21:18) may evoke associations with Hos 10:11; on the possible meanings of the shift from "cow" to "lamb" in v. 16, see Labuschagne, "Similes," 67-68 (cf. Nwaoru, *Imagery,* 159-61).

One may notice also the hapax legomenon הבו conveying a sense of "give" or "desire" or perhaps "love" in v. 18; as well as the intransitive use of זנה ("be promiscuous" or "playing the whore") in the hiphil, which is present only in Hos 4:10 and 5:3; and even the unusual orthography of ואמאסאך "I reject you" with its aleph. (For a discussion of most of these features, see Yoo, *Israelian Hebrew,* 160-64 and bibliography cited there.) Clearly, all these are textual markers that point at and contribute to the construction of the uniqueness of the book. They serve to characterize the sound of the book (not necessarily the voice of the character Hosea, since YHWH is portrayed as uttering at least some of these expressions) as different from other prophetic books.

Redactional hypotheses have been advanced in relation to Hosea 4, as with any other section of the book of Hosea. As one may anticipate, either the reference to Judah in v. 15 or the entire verse is often taken as a later editorial,

Judahite addition (e.g., Emmerson, *Hosea,* 77-83; Wolff, *Hosea,* 72, 74; Macintosh, *Hosea,* 162-63; J. Jeremias, "Die Anfänge"). Several other verses or portions of verses in Hosea 4 have been considered secondary. For instance, Buss, among others, has proposed that v. 10 is a (later) expansion (Buss, *Prophetic Word,* 36). See also Wolfe, "Editing," and Jeremias, *Hosea,* 59, 62-63. Yee has proposed three main levels in Hosea 4 (see Yee, *Composition,* 142-44, 158-70, 262-72, 315). For another redactional, comprehensive proposal for Hosea 4, see Diefenderfer, *Rhetorical Polyphony,* 151-73, 265-67; see also Good, "Composition." None of these proposals has achieved any kind of consensus, and none is verifiable in any way. It is worth noting that neither changes from second to third person, nor references to Judah, nor the presence of expressions carrying multiple levels of meaning, nor that of shifts in the characters being addressed by the speaker in the world of the book requires redactional explanations. Without denying that the text may have, or likely did, undergo redaction, or that some written sources or portions thereof may be embedded or reflected in the text, from the perspective of a study of the (present) book of Hosea as read and reread by its ancient readership, none of the hypothetical textual reconstructions is particularly helpful. Not only is this readership not asked to read the book in any way that is informed by these proposals, but it also is asked to read and meditate upon the text in a way that is informed by other sections in the book in its present form. Thus, the meanings carried by each particular subunit are intertwined with those of other units and set within the context of the book as whole. To be sure, the approach advanced here does not and cannot answer any questions about the message of a historical Hosea. It shows, however, how uncertain are the premises used to reconstruct any of the hypothetical texts used to achieve this goal, and therefore raises questions about the entire enterprise.

It is important to stress that other structural outlines or divisions of the text have been proposed for this section. For instance, Simian-Yofre (*Desierto,* 63-76) proposed (a) 4:1-3; (b) 4:4-14 and (c) 4:15-19; Eidewall (*Grapes,* 52-77) considers 4:1–5:7 as one large discourse unit divided into 4:1-3; 4:4-19 and 5:1-7; Mays (*Hosea,* 60-79) divides 4:1-19 into 4:1-3; 4:4-10; 4:11-14; and 4:15-19; whereas Pentiuc (*Long-suffering Love,* 70-82) divides it into 4:1-3 and 4:14-19. The MT "paragraph" division indicates an understanding of 4:1-19 as one unit. It is to be stressed that most of the proposed readings implied by these divisions are possible. In fact, Hos 4:1-19 not only allows alternative structures — or alternative partial substructures — to be discerned (and to be subverted as well), but also seems to be written so as to encourage the intended and the primary readerships to develop a set of complementary rereadings, each based on one of these structures. Of course, each of these structures provides a certain perspective on the matters, emphasizes some aspects and de-emphasizes others. This situation is quite common in prophetic literature and is expected in texts written to be read and reread continuously. The result, of course, is a series of partial, perspectival understandings of the unit informing each other and contributing all together to the rich tapestry that we may call the possible meaning of the text within the primary readerships of the book of Hosea (cf. Ben Zvi, "Prophetic Book").

Genre

This is the first reading in a much larger set of readings (Hos 4:1–11:11). The two main sections in this reading are explicitly presented as an instance of (or part of an instance of) YHWH's word that is a part of the larger instance of YHWH's word that we call "the book of Hosea." As with the other readings in the book, those included in this subset show an array of sophisticated literary techniques. The presence of these techniques is indicative of the existence of a target readership able to decode them (see Setting). It is worth stressing that these techniques include textually inscribed networks of meanings, the span of which goes far beyond the limits of the subset and of any reading therein. They presuppose an understanding of this unit as an integral part of a larger unit, that is, the prophetic book as a whole. The readings here are didactic readings, in the sense that their intention is to instill a teaching about YHWH, Israel, and their relations to the readership (see Intention). Of course, the call to hear that opens this particular unit shows that the text, to achieve its didactic purposes, invites the readers of the book to imagine a world of verbal communications in ancient, monarchic Israel, while at the same time making the full meaning of the words reportedly said in that verbal communication dependent on words written elsewhere in the book.

If the section was read to others unable to read by themselves — that is, the immense majority of the population, a literati would have embodied and re-enacted as it were the literary world of the unit. Yet the message of that literati to that audience would have been dependent on the context in which the text was read, the co-texts being read, the intonation and body language of the reader, and certainly would have been different from that of the reading of the book as a whole, with attention to the vast sea of meaningful networks that links the book as a whole through continuous rereadings.

Although no part of a prophetic book, being a written work, can be equated with any oral genre, it is possible for the text to evoke, and in prophetic books often defamiliarize multiple "genres" of social intercourse. For instance, some scholars have suggested that at least 4:1-3 is a "prophetic lawsuit," to a large extent because of the use of the term רִיב, which they understand as an important marker of a lawsuit (cf. Mays, *Hosea,* 61; Wolff, *Hosea,* 65-66. But contrast with the more nuanced study by Daniels ["Is There a 'Prophetic Lawsuit'?"], who in turn develops further ideas first advanced by M. De Roche). A reading within a larger book cannot be a called a lawsuit in any real sense, but it is likely that the text in v. 1 served to evoke or play with common images associated with legal proceedings that existed in the world of knowledge of the readership. Yet, the same text also likely evoked an image of quarrel, not necessarily involving legal procedures, and perhaps even of a "family" quarrel (see 2:4). The term "evoke" is crucial here. The text is not attempting to convey mimesis with proceedings of a real court, or with those of a quarrel. Instead it creates multiple, alternative, and, in terms of continued rereading of the text, complementary images from within the world of knowledge of the readership to serve as possible backgrounds for readings. Moreover, it de-stabilizes these images not only by allowing more than one, but also by the profound way in

111

which the text here is intertwined with other texts in which such images cannot apply. To illustrate, textually inscribed markers of coherence bind together 4:1 and 4:4. The present text of 4:4 would clearly and strongly subvert any possible understanding of 4:1 as an attempt at mimesis of a legal procedure.

The authorship and intended and primary readership of the book accessed their knowledge of other literary genres (or sets of literary expressions) as they composed, edited, read and reread this reading. The most obvious example is the proverbial short saying; see 4:11, 14b. The relatively common "summons to hear" (4:1) is another case.

Setting

The setting of the writing and reading of this, or any portion of the (present) book of Hosea for that matter, is the same as that of the book as a whole. Both writers and readers are among the literati of Yehud. But what can one learn from this reading about the worldview of the literati within whom and for whom the book of Hosea was composed? This reading is indicative of many aspects of the intellectual and ideological atmosphere within which it was written and which permeates it.

The initial summons to hear shows that, within their discourse in the world of monarchic Israel — the world in which prophets communicated to their audiences — oral communication prevailed. The text does not say "read, O children of Israel," even if this is precisely what the literati were supposed to do, but says "Hear, O children of Israel." This situation creates a disjoint between the literati who compose and read books and the oral prophets of the past that populate their texts and whose words they shape and voice, and between YHWH's word imagined as oral speech and its identification in the present with a written text. In addition, this situation colors the style of the text that purports to be a representation of an oral speech. Thus, one does not find, for instance, many and long clauses, but many deictic markers (cf. Polak, "Style"). Yet, at the same time the text, among other things, shifts and mixes deictic referents, addressees, topics, and images, in addition to creating a tapestry of textual connections with other readings in the book, none of which is typical or even compatible with a situation of oral communication. Thus, the text both reflects and destabilizes aspects of orality and aurality within the text. This multi-layered approach is consistent with the actual social setting of the literati and the society within which they work (cf. Ben Zvi, "Introduction: Writings, Speeches, and the Prophetic Books — Setting an Agenda").

Hos 4:3 and Zeph 1:3 reflect a tripartite spatial division of the world and express this division in similar terms. In fact, the expression עוֹף הַשָּׁמַיִם "the birds of the air" is immediately followed by דְּגֵי הַיָּם "the fish of the sea" only in these two texts (cf. Ezek 38:20; Ps 8:9; Job 12:7-8). Both Hos 4:3 and Zeph 1:3 follow the principle that each area is represented by a single type of animal, and vice versa, and that one type of animal corresponds to a particular area. Although the organization of the world into land, air, and water (e.g,. Ps. 96:11) is not uncommon, the order in which they appear in Hos 4:3 and Zeph

1:3 and, above all, the one-to-one correspondence between basic realms and animal kingdoms are not universal in the HB. For instance, there are texts that include more than one animal type in the category of land and, most pointedly, explicitly mention the reptiles as a separate class (see Gen 1:24-25; Ezek 38:20). Then there is the question of humanity and its place. In Zeph 1:3 the text refers to אדם ובהמה "human and animals"; Hos 4:3 refers to חית השדה "wild animals." Such a choice of words helps the reader understand that the situation described here is much worse than the one in Hos 2:14 (cf. Lev 26:22), but also serves to characterize that part of the dry land as outside human control and culture (cf. Deut 7:22). In Hos 4:3 humanity represents the area of human control and culture, and notice the reference to כל יושב בה "all who dwell on her [the land]." Significantly, the domesticated animals have no representation at all in the system in Hos 4:3 and plants are only implicitly referred to, as the necessary background for the existence of the animals/humanity, as the reference to the drought alludes to a process that leads to extinction through lack of available water. It is worth stressing that the very subsistence of the agrarian society within which the literati lived was based on grains, and secondarily on herds and the produce of orchards. But these are not mentioned, or not mentioned explicitly in the description and organization of the world in Hos 4:3. The horizon of discourse of this group is *not* that of homo economicus. Economy and actual life do not play the central role with the typology of the world; abstract classifications of "land, air and water" do. At the same time, the land is imagined as carrying two alternative representatives, "humans" and "wild animals," cultured and uncultured worlds. This is another important observation about the ideological setting within which and for which the book of Hosea was composed. Similar ideological constructions permeate other books (e.g., Zephaniah). The book of Hosea is not unique, nor can it be expected to be unique in these matters. Much of its intellectual setting is similar to that of others.

The descriptions in both Hos 4:3 and Zeph 1:3 are equivocal about the geographical extent of the described, future destruction (see Ben Zvi, *Zephaniah,* 51-58). Certainly the text may refer to the land in which Israel dwells (cf. Ezek 38:20; see Radak on Hos 4:3), but also to the whole earth. The phrase כל יושב בה "all who dwell on her [the land]" may also point to all the inhabitants of the earth (see Isa 24:6). The ambiguity around the meanings of "land" and "earth" reflects an implicit mental association of these two realms within the discourse of the community, and, as such, it is consistent with claims about the cosmic significance of the land and what Israel does on it. Significantly, the text accuses no people except the children of Israel (see Hos 4:1-2) of the sins that lead to the destruction of the natural world (Hos 4:3) on a scale that seems at least at a secondary, connoted level to be universal. (Scholars who think that the text here portrays a total reversal of creation, such as De Roche, maintain that this understanding of the text is neither secondary nor connoted, but the main meaning of the text.) In any event, it bears notice that the text is unequivocal on one point, namely, the sins of the children of Israel can and will cause a serious disruption, even destruction of the natural world, of the natural order. (Simian-Yofre raises the possibility that the

113

phrase כל יושב בה "all who dwell on her [the land]" conveys a reference to the Canaanites. For the claim and some possible implications see Simian-Yofre, *Desierto,* 65.)

It is worth stressing that the sins mentioned there are described, purposefully, in the most general terms. "Cursing, perjuring, murdering, robbery and adultery" are not bound to any period in history or social memory. The readers for whom the book was written (and any other readers thereafter) could associate it with numerous periods and social circumstances. Significantly, the text does not associate these circumstances with any particular period within the world of the book, nor does it anchor these within the conditions of any period in history or memory. The openness of the text is maximized in this regard, so as to allow readers to imagine different periods and societies as fulfilling these conditions.

The series of sins that occurs in Hos 4:2 and the similar one in Jer 7:9 lead to references of unacceptable worship. In the case of Hosea 4, the entire second section deals with this matter. The common association of sins such as those mentioned in 4:2 with cultic "anti-worship" points to an ideological discourse in which both types of sin are seen as deeply intertwined. This ideological or theological atmosphere permeates Hosea 4, and the book of Hosea as a whole.

The second main reading strongly intertwines images of sexual promiscuity and improper cultic practices (see above). To understand the social "mindset" of the groups within which and for which the book was composed, it is worth noticing that women are construed as the active participants when it comes to sexual promiscuity. As v. 13 clearly suggests, it is they who either commit adultery, or who "commit harlotry" (if they are still not married or betrothed; that is, if they are under the control of their father). The text also suggests that the patriarch of the family is supposed to "take care" of the situation (see the reference to "daughters" and "daughters-in-law"), and that if the heads of the families (i.e., the patriarchs) fail to do so, then YHWH is supposed to take up the "job," and restore the proper social order. The rhetoric of the text takes for granted these social and ideological expectations within the readership, as it comes with the "surprising" answer that carries the punch of this subunit, YHWH will not punish the female transgressors, because males (probably not the heads of the families, who are referred in the second person) associate with prostitutes and eat sacrifices with the קדשות *"qedeshot"* (v. 14).

The reference to *qedeshot* in v. 14 has raised considerable debate. Until recently, the most common understanding of the term has been "(female) cultic prostitutes" — this led to common English translations such as "temple prostitutes" (NRSV) or "sacred prostitutes" (NJB). It is highly doubtful that this is the correct understanding. It is not only a matter of whether there was cultic prostitution in ancient Israel — relatively common scholarly reconstructions of a wide practice of cultic prostitution in ancient Israel are well off target — but also of whether the term *qedeshah* per se means cultic prostitute. The latter is also unlikely. (See Frymer-Kensky, *In the Wake of the Goddesses,* 199-203, 273 n. 19; Hackett; Gruber, "Hebrew QĔDĒŠĀH"; but also cf. Macintosh, *Hosea,* 157-60; Bird, "'To Play the Harlot,'" and Oden, *Bible*

Without Theology, 131-53; see also Van der Toorn, "Female Prostitution." For a typical example of earlier scholarship on the matter, see Wolff, *Hosea,* 86-88.) Within the context of Hos 4:14, it is likely that the term *qedeshah* conveys a pejorative meaning of prostitute. It refers to "unattached" women — unlike the mentioned daughters and daughters-in-law, who are "attached" women (though in different kinds of attachments; the former can only be promiscuous, the latter commit adultery) — who engage in sex with male partners. The general context also evokes some kind of festival as the setting for sexual activity. Associations between sexual activities and festivals, which were also town parties involving eating and heavy drinking, dances and the like — i.e., a quite carnivalesque atmosphere — are certainly not unprecedented in the ancient Near East (cf. Judg 21:10-23; MAL A 55-56; see, for instance, Van der Toorn, "Female Prostitution," 202-3; for festivals in the ancient Near East, see also G. Pinch, "Private Life," 369-70). From the perspective of the readership of the book, it is worth stressing that males (not necessarily male priests, see Macintosh, *Hosea,* 160-61) are condemned here for having sex with consenting (at least, within the world of the text) unattached women. Although such activities are not exalted anywhere in the HB, they do not constitute wrongdoing by themselves within the range of worldviews represented in the HB, unless they involve a transgression of purity laws. The point the text conveys is that such behavior is tantamount to wrongdoings that justify the mentioned punishments if they are associated with cultic activities. In others words, the text is advancing the point that sex and proper cult cannot take place together, and that passions obscure the necessary understanding of worshipers/the people (and see "sexual promiscuity and wine, and new wine take away understanding/capture the heart" [v. 11] and "a people without understanding are inflamed by passion" [v. 14]; see above). For the problematic relation of sex in general with cult within the general outlook on purity of ancient Israel in the postmonarchic period see Klawans, "Pure Violence."

The expression "your people are like those who contend [with] the priest" in 4:4 sheds light on another aspect of the general outlook shared by the authorship and intended and primary readerships of the book. Contending with the priest is wrong in principle. Priests are criticized because they are (or behave) like "people" (i.e., non-priests), because they do not fulfill their duties. The text reflects the viewpoint that in an orderly world, priests are not like non-priests, that their authority should be accepted by the non-priests; of course, conversely, that they fulfill their duties properly, such as teaching the people "the instruction of YHWH" (v. 6). This outlook is actually very similar to that in the book of Malachi, and other books in the Hebrew Bible. A shared perspective on these matters permeated the world of ancient Israel (and leaving aside the motif of YHWH's instruction, the ancient Near East as a whole) and was integral to the intellectual setting of Hosea 4, and the book of Hosea as a whole.

It is worth noting that from the perspective of a postmonarchic readership, the choice of words in the references to the priest in the singular in 4:6 could have been understood as an allusion to the high priest and his sons (cf. Exod 28:1, 3, 4; 28:41; 29:1, 44; 30:30; 40:13, 15; Lev 7:35). If this is the case, the text conveys on the one level a general condemnation of the priests of old, including those of northern Israel. But on another level, at least by connotation, it also conveys a condemnation of the rightful high priests who served in Jerusalem; i.e., the priest whose *torah* is supposed to be YHWH's *torah* and whose decisions people were supposed to follow rather than contend with. (The issues raised in 1 Kgs 2:27; Ezek 44:13; 2 Chr 11:14 might have also informed the readers of 4:6; cf. Nissinen, *Prophetie,* 203-4).

Within the world of the book, the human monologue is not set in any particular *Sitz im Leben* or time, except for the general monarchic period frame of Hos 1:1 (see below). The openness of the text in this regard is a very salient and significant feature and relates directly to the message it conveys. The teaching it conveys is not to be understood as anchored in particular (and narrowly construed) social or political events or circumstances, or in the details of a specific instance of human communication (i.e., a particular speaker talking to a clearly identified group of people on a certain occasion, in a particular place, time, and the like). Rather, the book construes the teaching it communicates as something that transcends all the above, and as such it provides a reading that is relevant to the communities within whom and for whom the book of Hosea as we know it was composed.

Yet the world of the book is also set in a general time frame that associates it with the past of the community of readers and with their "classical" monarchic period. No prophetic book as a whole is set in a world that is portrayed as in the future of its readership (like science fiction today), or in the present. These books are about prophets of old, who prophesied about the future — from the perspective of the world of the book — and whose prophecies were understood as partially fulfilled.

The reference to Gilgal and Beth-Aven (i.e., a pejorative term for Beth-el that may be translated as "Iniquitytown") in Hos 4:15 characterizes the world of the book as one in which these two places are active cultic centers — cf. Hos 9:15; 10:5; 12:12; Amos 3:14; 4:4; 5:5-6; see also Jer 48:13 that explicitly points at Bethel from the perspective of a period later than the fall of the northern polity — and in fact, centers that might attract Judahites and lead them into sin (in Zechariah 7, it is the people of Bethel who properly consult Jerusalem; see Zech 7:2). Whether monarchic period Judahites were attracted to Bethel (rather than to Jerusalem?) was ever true or not (notice the reversal of the motif in 1 Kgs 12:26-27), there is no dispute that Gilgal and Bethel served as major cultic centers in monarchic northern Israel, and the memory of their existence remained within Israel after the destruction of the northern polity. One has to assume that the intended readers of the book of Hosea and the actual literati who read, reread, and studied it knew about these centers. (For Bethel in the neo-Babylonian and Persian periods see Blenkinsopp, "Bethel," and Lipschits, "History," 171-72, and bibliography cited there)

It has often been claimed that the portrayal of cultic activities in Hosea 4 corresponds to the historical situation in the northern kingdom of Israel, and that it is a true description of "Baalism," as opposed to "Yahwism" (e.g. Limburg, *Hosea,* 22-26), or historical Canaanism as opposed to pure "Israelite" behavior, and as actually practiced in ancient Israel. There are numerous problems with this claim, but a few points will suffice. First, the old dichotomy "Canaanite" vs. "Israelite" is not actually a historical construction but an ideological one that served theological purposes. Second, even if the book were a historiographical work, it aims clearly at setting the reader against that which it describes, and therefore its "historical accuracy" should be questionable. But Hosea 4 is a prophetic, didactic reading that is an integral part of a prophetic book associated with a prophet of old, not a historiographical work. Moreover, the book continuously demonstrates to its intended and primary readers not only that mimesis is not its goal, but also that they should not read the world of the book (and its reports) as strongly anchored in any particular social or historical circumstances however construed they may be in the memory of the community beyond the general reference in Hos 1:1. It consistently, however, asks the readers to understand its units in a way that is strongly informed by the book as a whole, and by other units in the book. (And it significantly undermines the borders separating different units, allowing and suggesting multiple structures informing each other [see STRUCTURE].) Moreover, given that Hosea 4 calls the readers of the book to identify with those addressed in the text, and with trans-temporal Israel, including both Judah and (northern) Israel, it is worth stressing that much of the description seems to fit general portrayals of Israel's (including both kingdoms and their peoples) cultic sins known to the primary readership and authorship of the book. In particular, the world described in 4:13 is comparable to that in 1 Kgs 14:23-24; 2 Kgs 16:4; 17:10; Jer 2:20; 3:6, 13; 17:2; Ezek 6:13; 2 Chr 28:4. The features mentioned there are neither specifically northern nor "Baalistic." In fact, in most cases, they appear in relation to a kind of worship of YHWH that, from the perspective of the authorship and intended readership, is totally flawed, and which is tantamount, within that perspective, to rejecting YHWH. Moreover, although Hosea 4 clearly and strongly condemns the cultic world that it portrays, the text contains no reference to Baal, despite the fact that the book of Hosea explicitly mentions Baal in other occasions (Hos 2:10, 15, 18, 19; 11:2; 13:1). Nowhere are the readers told that the sinful worshipers and their priests actually served Baal. In fact, the text strongly suggests that they did not. One may notice, for instance, that the condemnation of the priests, and the people, does not involve any claim that they worship "other gods" (ct. Hosea 2). Moreover, people are urged not to swear "As YHWH lives." In other words, they are imagined as sinful, but still swearing in such a manner (4:15).

The text shows a "northern flavor" (see the references to Gilgal and Bethel), but a southern "heart" too (see v. 15), and above all portrays a general situation of cultic disarray characterized by lack of wisdom, discernment, correct knowledge/YHWH's instruction, and which is closely associated with the common topoi of cult, sex, wine, and parties in the natural world and in the neighborhood of towns and villages. To be sure, it is very likely that town festivals took place in Israel and Judah during the monarchic period, and for that matter that trees had a place in Israelite worship at least in some occasions and circles (cf. Josh 24:26 and the material mentioned in Keel, *Goddesses and Trees;* for reconstructions of Israelite worship on the basis of iconographic and inscriptional matters, see also Keel and Uehlinger, *Gods, Goddesses and Im-*

ages of God), but the text of Hosea 4 by itself cannot be used as an accurate historical document for the reconstruction of these practices, nor of the common cultic situation in northern Israel, and certainly not for that of "Baalism" (see also Hos 2:3-25 Setting; cf. Koch, "Ba'al Ṣapon").

Finally, it is worth stressing that nothing in the world portrayed in Hosea 4 can be correlated with any particular event or narrow set of circumstances in the history of monarchic Israel, or Judah for that matter. For instance, claims that the reference for "cursing, perjuring, murdering, robbery and adultery" and the like refer to the days of Jeroboam II and northern Israel and reflect the reality of the time go far beyond the claims the text makes, and beyond any historical evidence. How do we know that there were more cursing, adultery, and the like in these days than in other days? Can we reconstruct historical circumstances on the basis of the assumption that people curse, murder, rob, and commit adultery more during "seemingly prosperous" times as some scholars would phrase it (i.e., during the days of Jeroboam) than when economic conditions worsen and destruction follows? For a different approach on the matter, see Macintosh, *Hosea,* 131. Significantly, it has been proposed also that the text of Hos 4:1-3 must be dated and clearly reflects the period from Zechariah to Pekah (i.e., kings not mentioned in Hos 1:1), because Jeroboam's time was one of peace and security (e.g., Harper, *Hosea,* 249). Pentiuc suggested that ודמים בדמים נגעו, "bloodshed follows bloodshed," in v. 2 may refer to the circumstances of Jehu's revolt; he also mentions the (pre-critical) position of Julian of Eclanum that associates the reference with the persecutions of prophets in the time of Elijah. See Pentiuc, *Long-Suffering Love,* 71. The basic fact is that text is open and allows readers to imagine it as referring to different sets of historical and social circumstances.

Similarly, as seen above, the cultic situation portrayed in Hosea 4 is not unequivocally marked for one historical period or set of circumstances. In fact, a postmonarchic readership would find much of it relevant to several periods and regions within their (constructed) memory of past events associated with trans-temporal Israel (cf. Deut 12:2; 1 Kgs 14:23-24; 2 Kgs 16:4; 17:10; Isa 57:5; Jer 2:20; 3:6, 13; 17:2; Ezek 6:13; 2 Chr 28:4).

Intention

The general intention of Hosea 4 is to provide instruction about YHWH, Israel, the relation between the two, and to justify in the sight of the readership the divine judgment that befell Israel in the past. It also serves to communicate and reinforce numerous positions that characterized the general horizon of thought of the authorship and readership (see Setting).

The text here communicates the importance of elites that bear divine knowledge, and the responsibility of those who carry such knowledge. In this regard, although the text does not talk about literati, it instills in its readership a sense of duty, proper behavior, and the terrible price that their society (and indeed, perhaps the whole world, see v. 3) may pay if they fail to fulfill their duties (cf. Limburg, *Hosea,* 19-22).

Bibliography

P. Bird, "'To Play the Harlot': An Inquiry into an Old Testament Metaphor," P. Day (ed.), *Gender and Difference in Ancient Israel* (Philadelphia: Fortress, 1989) 75-94; J. Blenkinsopp, "Bethel in the Neo-Babylonian Period," O. Lipschits and J. Blenkinsopp (eds.), *Judah and the Judeans in the Neo-Babylonian Period* (Winona Lake, IN: Eisenbrauns, 2003) 93-107; D. R. Daniels, "Is There a 'Prophetic Lawsuit' Genre?" *ZAW* 99 (1987) 339-60; A. Dearman, "Interpreting the Religious Polemics Against Baal and Baalim in the Book of Hosea," *OTE* 14 (2001) 9-25; M. DeRoche, "The Reversal of Creation in Hosea," *VT* 31 (1981) 400-409; idem, "Yahweh's *rib* Against Israel: A Reassessment of the So-called 'Prophetic Lawsuit' in the Preexilic Prophets," *JBL* 102 (1983) 563-74; G. I. Emmerson, "The Fertility Goddess in Hosea IV 17-19," *VT* 24 (1974) 492-97; P. N. Franklyn, "Oracular Cursing in Hosea 13," *HAR* 11 (1987) 69-80; T. Frymer-Kensky, *In the Wake of the Goddesses* (New York: Free Press, 1992); H. L. Ginsberg, "Lexicographical Notes," *Hebräische Wortforschung. Festschrift zum 80. Geburtstag von Walter Baumgartner* (VTS 16; Leiden: E. J. Brill, 1967) 71-82; F. Gangloff, "À l'ombre des Déesses-arbres? (Os 4:12-14)," *BN* 106 (2001) 13-20; F. Gangloff and J.-C. Haelewyck, "Osée 4,17-19. Un Marzeah en l'honneur de la déesse 'Anat?," *ETL* 71 (1995) 370-82; E. N. Good, "The Composition of Hosea," *SEÅ* 31 (1966) 21-63; S. Grätz, "Die Vergebliche Suche nach Gott. Traditions- und kompositionsgeschichtliche Überlegungen zu Herkunft und Funktion der Strafvorstellungen in Hos iv 1–vi 6," *VT* 50 (2000) 200-217; M. I. Gruber, "Hebrew QĔDĒŠĀH in Her Canaanite and Akkadian Cognates," M. I. Gruber, *The Motherhood of God and Other Studies* (Atlanta: Scholars Press, 1992) 17-47 = *UF* 18 (1896) 133-47; idem, "Marital Fidelity and Intimacy: A View from Hosea 4," A. Brenner (ed.), *A Feminist Companion of the Latter Prophets* (Sheffield: Sheffield Academic Press, 1995) 169-79; J. A. Hackett, "Can a Sexist Model Liberate Us? Ancient Near Eastern 'Fertility Goddesses,'" *Journal of Feminist Studies in Religion* 5 (1989) 65-76; A. V. Hunter, *Seek the Lord* (Baltimore: St. Mary's Seminary and University, 1982); J. Jeremias, "Die Anfänge des Dodekapropheton: Hosea und Amos," J. A. Emerton (ed.), *Congress Volume Paris 1992* (VTS 61; Leiden: E. J. Brill, 1995); O. Keel, *Goddesses and Trees, New Moon and Yahweh. Ancient Near Eastern Art and the Hebrew Bible* (JSOTSupS 261; Sheffield: Sheffield Academic Press, 1998); O. Keel and C. Uehlinger, *Gods, Goddesses and Images of God in Ancient Israel* (Minneapolis: Fortress, 1998); J. Klawans, "Pure Violence: Sacrifice and Defilement in Ancient Israel," *HTR* 94 (2001) 133-55; K. Koch, "Ba'al Ṣapon and Ba'al Šamem and the Critique of Israel's Prophets," G. J. Brooke, A. H. W. Curtis, and J. F. Healey (eds.), *Ugarit and the Bible. Proceedings of the International Symposium on Ugarit and the Bible, Manchester, 1992* (UBL 11; Münster: Ugarit Verlag, 1994) 159-74; C. J. Labuschagne, "The Similes in the Book of Hosea," *OTWSA* 7-8 (1965) 64-76; O. Lipschits, "The History of the Benjamin Region Under Babylonian Rule," *TA* 26 (1999) 155-90; J. R. Lundbom, "Contentious Priests and Contentious People in Hosea IV 1-10," *VT* 36 (1986) 52-70; A. A. Macintosh, "Hosea and the Wisdom Tradition: Dependence and Independence," J. Day, R. P. Gordon, and H. G. M. Williamson (eds.), *Wisdom in Israel. Essays in Honour of J. A. Emerton* (Cambridge: Cambridge Univ. Press, 1995) 124-32; J. L. McLaughlin, *The Marzeah in the Prophetic Literature. References and Allusions in Light of the Extra-Biblical Evidence* (VTSup 86; Leiden: E. J. Brill, 2001);

S. Morag, "On Semantic and Lexical Features in the Language of Hosea," *Tarbiz* 53 (1984) 489-511 (in Hebrew); idem, "The Great Metaphor of Hosea," *Tarbiz* 68 (1999/ 2000) 5-11 (in Hebrew); K. Nielsen, *Yahweh as Prosecutor and Judge. An Investigation of the Prophetic Lawsuit (*Rîb *Pattern)* (JSOTSupS 9; Sheffield: Dept. of Biblical Studies, University of Sheffield, 1978); M. S. Odell, "Who Were the Prophets in Ho-sea?" *HBT* 18 (1996) 78-95; idem, "The Prophets and the End of Hosea," P. House and J. W. Watts (eds.), *Forming Prophetic Literature: Essays on Isaiah and the Twelve in Honor of John D. W. Watts* (JSOTSupS 235; Sheffield: JSOT Press, 1996) 158-170; idem, "I Will Destroy Your Mother: The Obliteration of a Cultic Role in Hosea 4.4-6," A. Brenner (ed.), *A Feminist Companion of the Latter Prophets* (Sheffield: Sheffield Academic Press, 1995) 180-93; R. A. Oden Jr., *The Bible Without Theology* (San Fran-cisco: Harper & Row, 1987); H. Pfeiffer, "Zechen und Lieben. Zur Frage einer Göttin-Polemik in Hos 4,16-10," *UF* 28 (1996) 496-511; G. Pinch, "Private Life in Ancient Egypt," *CANE*, 363-81; F. H. Polak, "Style Is More than the Person: Sociolinguistics, Literary Culture and the Distinction Between Written and Oral Narrative," I. M. Young (ed.), *Biblical Hebrew: Chronology and Typology* (JSOTSupS; Sheffield/London: Sheffield Academic Press/Continuum, 2003); C. L. Seow, "Hosea 14:10 and the Fool-ish People Motif," *CBQ* 42 (1982) 212-24; K. R. Shrofel, "No Prostitute Has Been Here: A Reevaluation of Hosea 4:13-14" (MA Thesis, University of Winnipeg, 1999); Y. Suzuki, "On Yahweh's Court in Hosea 4:1-3," D. Ellens et al., *Reading the Hebrew Bible for a New Millennium* (Harrisburg, PA: Trinity Press, 2000) 253-63; A. Szabo, "Textual Problems in Amos and Hosea," *VT* 25 (1975) 500-524; M.-T. Wacker, "Traces of the Goddess in the Book of Hosea," A. Brenner (ed.), *A Feminist Companion of the Latter Prophets* (Sheffield: Sheffield Academic Press, 1995) 219-41; K. Van der Toorn, "Female Prostitution in Payment of Vows in Ancient Israel," *JBL* 108 (1989) 193-205; R. E. Wolfe, "The Editing of the Book of the Twelve," *ZAW* 53 (1935) 95-129.

Second Didactic Prophetic Reading:
YHWH's Condemnation of (Monarchic) Israel and Its Implications, 5:1–7:2

Structure

I. Introduction   5:1
   A. Summons to Hear "This" (YHWH's Word): Call to Hear and
      Identification of Those Summoned to Hear   1aα
   B. Reason for the Summons: Judgment for a Leadership That Fails to
      Implement Justice   1aβ
II. First Main Section: Further Condemnation of Israel I   1-7
   A. Introduction with Imperatives   1
   B. Main Body   2-6
   C. Concluding עתה "now" Note: Because of their dealings with
      YHWH, they and their lands will be destroyed   7
III. Second Main Section: Further Condemnation of Israel II   8-14
   A. Introduction with Imperatives   8

*Verses 6:1-3 serve double duty. They stand by themselves as an interlude in the series of condemnations, and as a human response to IV. At the same time, the section is deeply intertwined with 6:4-6. The reported divine speech in 6:4-6 stands in fact as the response either to a well-meaning human voice that is, however, unable to bring a long-lasting change of attitude in Israel in vv. 1-3, or perhaps to YHWH's ironic construction of the human voice of ungodly Israel, according to another possible reading of vv. 1-3 (see below).

There are numerous possible proposals for the structure of Hosea 5–7. In fact, the situation here is such that it presents an excellent case for broad considerations about STRUCTURE in the book of Hosea, and in prophetic books in general. The proposal advanced above takes into account, among others:

(a) The use of imperative calls in Hosea as markers for the beginning of new units: first, the one in 5:1 that is similar too, and parallel in function to, the one in 4:1; and second, the references to the blowing of a ram's horn (Heb. שופר) in 5:8 and 8:1 — which on the surface may suggest the beginning of a new literary unit of a higher order in 5:8 than the one reflected in the preceding outline, but see below.

(b) The close connection between 5:1-7 and 5:8–6:7 created by key shared conclusions expressed in explicitly the same language, בה׳ בגדו "they have broken faith with YHWH" in 5:7 and בגדו בי "they have broken faith with me" in 6:7.

(c) The double duty of 6:7, as conclusion of the preceding verses and as the opening for the following unit, as explicitly shown by its reference to "there" (see Barthélemy, *Critique Textuelle,* vol. III, 527-31, esp. 531).

(d) The close thematic link, enhanced by word choice, between 5:15 and 6:1; notice אלך ואשובה "I will return" in 5:15 and לכו ונשובה "let us return" in

6:1; in addition to those between 5:13-14 and 6:1 (notice references to רפא "heal," טרף "tear, devour," and the general semantic field in which there are references to sickness, wound, blow, and heal; cf. Isa 1:5-6; cf. Sweeney, *Twelve Prophets*, 69).

(e) Several links connect verses in this reading to 7:1, among them, the motif of YHWH's healing in 6:1 and 7:1; the reference to "gangs" (Heb. גדוד) in 6:9 and 7:1 and פעלי און "doers of evil; evildoers" in 6:8; and פעלו שקר (often translated as "they deal falsely") in 7:1.

(f) The significant link created between 5:4 ואת ה' לא ידעו "and they did not know YHWH" and ונדעה נרדפה לדעת את ה' "let us know, let us press on to know YHWH" in 6:3.

(g) Textual coherence markers involving the first and last section in this reading, such as the envelope created by similar expressions carrying similar meanings in 5:3 and 6:10b, the similar rhetorical use of explicit or connoted references to geographical places, and the references to priests, the house of Israel in 5:1 and in the last section of this reading (6:9-10).

(h) Similar structural patterns involving key interpretative verses at the end of main sections, and particularly at the conclusion of the first and last sections.

As mentioned above, many other proposals for the structure of Hosea 5–7 have been advanced. It is certainly possible to divide this section of the book into 5:1-15 and 6:1-11 and 7:1-16. The masoretic division seems to be 5:1-7; 5:8–6:11; 7:1-12; 7:13–8:14. Abrabanel maintained that this section of the text is contained within two "prophecies," namely, 4:1–5:7 and 5:8–9:9. He further divides 4:1–5:7 into two units, 4:1-19 and 5:1-7, and 5:8–9:10 into 5:8–6:11; 7:1-12; 7:13–8:14; and 9:1-10. Among modern critical scholars, some maintain that Hos 5:8–6:6 is a separate unit, and they tend to consider 5:1-7 as another unit (e.g., Jeremias, *Hosea,* 73-89), though for some it is part of a larger unit 4:1–5:7 (e.g., Eidewall, *Grapes,* 51-101; Landy, *Hosea,* 53-83). Wolff divides the text into 5:1-7 and 5:8–7:16 (see Wolff, *Hosea,* 94-130; cf. Limburg, *Hosea,* 26-30), Mays into 5:1-2; 5:3-7; 5:8–6:6; 6:7–7:2; 7:3-7; 7:8-12 and 7:13-16 (Mays, *Hosea,* 79-113), Davies into 5:1-7; 5:8–6:3; 6:4–7:16 (Davies, *Hosea,* 135-93), Stuart into 5:1-7; 5:8–7:1ac and 7:1ad-16 (Stuart, *Hosea,* 87-125), Wendland into 5:1-7; 5:8–6:3; 6:4-11a; and 6:11b-7:16 (Wendland, *Discourse Analysis,* 126-27), and Andersen and Freedman into 5:1-7; 5:8-11; 5:12-15; 6:1-3; 6:4-6; 6:7–7:2; 7:3-7; 7:8-16 (Andersen and Freedman, *Hosea,* 10-15, 380-480). Qyl divides the relevant text into two sections, chapters 5-6 on the one hand and 7-8 on the other (Qyl, *Hosea,* 10), and Pentiuc into 5:1-7; 5:8-15; 6:1-6; 6:7–7:2; 7:3-7 and 7:8-16 (Pentiuc, *Long-Suffering Love,* 82-111). The scribe responsible for 4QXIIg left an interval after 6:3 and another after 6:11 (see Russell, *The Twelve,* 280).

The bewildering number of proposals, of which those mentioned above are only a few examples, bears consideration. To be sure, at times, proposals reflect redaction-critical concerns associated with the endeavor of reconstructing the actual words of the historical prophet rather than with a study of the likely ways in which the (present) book of Hosea was probably read by its intended and primary readerships. Yet, even if one takes into account these considerations, major differences remain. These differences may be accounted for, in part, in terms of the variety of criteria that may be used to determine the opening of a new unit and closures of units (cf. Wendland, *Discourse Analysis,* 30-70), and by questions associated with how to evaluate links created by markers of textual cohesion (cf. Wendland, *Discourse Analysis,* 71-118) in terms of unit demarcation. Has the search for structure become a meaningless exercise of picking and choosing criteria that leads to no additional knowledge of the text?

The answer to the preceding question is a clear "no." Structural analysis is and remains a helpful tool, but its goals should be more realistic. Even a brief survey of the seemingly perplexing variety of positions shows that there is a certain degree of convergence. For instance, many consider 5:1-7 a unit, although they may disagree on the hierarchical level of such a unit. Is it an independent unit within the book, or a subunit within a larger unit, and if the latter, what is the extent of such a unit, or is it, by itself, a subunit of an even larger unit within the book? The fact that 5:1-7 is largely considered a unit of some sort reflects an awareness of the existence of some textually inscribed markers, such as openings and closures. To be sure, there may be debate about the hierarchical level marked by the relevant opening, or it may be proposed that other markers supersede its "structural" message. Yet, its presence is acknowledged more often than not, and the same holds true for an awareness of the presence of additional markers in the text that may point at other possible divisions of the text.

At this point it is worth stressing that particular readings and structures of the text go hand in hand. Every structural outline emphasizes particular meanings and de-emphasizes others. For instance, if Hos 6:6 is considered the concluding verse of a large unit, the unequivocal emphasis falls upon "For I [YHWH] desire *hesed* and not (just) *zebach* sacrifice, the knowledge of God more than *olah* sacrifices." *Vice versa,* a reading of the text that assigns to these words the highest importance would tend to understand the text in terms of a structure in which 6:6 represents the heightened conclusion of a section. (*Hesed* may be translated as "fidelity"; the term often conveys the meaning of "loyalty" and "interpersonal duty," and it may refer to the interpersonal obligation of the client to the patron — cf. Lemche, "Kings and Clients," 125-26; Malina, "Patron and Client" — it is often translated as "steadfast love.") Conversely, a reading of this portion of the book according to which its main communicative message is (monarchic) Israel's lack of loyalty to YHWH would tend to consider 6:7 as the heightened, concluding, key interpretative note of an important subunit or of the unit as a whole (see above; within the structure advanced above, the last section of this reading is a confirmation or elaboration of the conclusion advanced in 6:7).

The point is not only that (a) here as in many other instances in prophetic literature, the borders that demarcate units are very porous or even fluid, or (b) networks of meanings span across them and suggest additional meanings that inform those that the readers could have abstracted from this reading alone, but mainly that (c) the text is written in such a way that it allows for multiple structures or outlines that complement each other and that are enacted through the interaction of the ancient readers and the text as the former keep studying, and as the literati not only keep reading and reading it among themselves, but also keep reading it to others against different circumstances and in different contexts. This being so, claims for the existence of a single valid structure — and the rejection of other structures — are misleading. In fact, they are an impediment to a better understanding of the meaning of the text in its primary context of readings and readings. Instead, the text shows a set of possible structures informing and complementing each other. The structure set out above is simply one of these possible structures. The notes that accompany this discussion — below and above — show that the text both supports and subverts this structure by hinting at other possible structures, other links to other units, and by raising questions of hierarchical level. For instance, one may wonder whether Hos 5:1-7 is a main section of a reading, or an independent reading within a larger set of readings. And for whom and when? It is most likely that the ancient literati for whom the book was composed approached the matter not as an "either — or" but as a "both-and" proposition, from the perspective of multiple readings among the literati, and including also full or partial readings of the text to those unable to read.

Prophetic books, except for their opening and concluding notes, show fluid and multiple structures. But this does not mean that structures such as the one mentioned above are meaningless. It is still worthwhile to propose one among the several possible structures provided that its limitations are discussed, as has been done in all the discussions on STRUCTURE in this commentary. Should multiple structures, and multiple and partially overlapping units, be shown side by side and each commented upon separately in terms of STRUCTURE, Genre, Setting, and Intention in a commentary such as this? The answer is again a clear no; this time, at least in part, for practical reasons associated with printed commentaries. Only a very sophisticated and complex hypertext may attempt to do so. In fact, it is more practical and methodologically sound to present *one* of the several possible structures as a *heuristic* device: to study it, and to raise continuously matters of complementary structures and unit arrangements that may have influenced the way in which the book was read in ancient times, by studying links that point to its textual cohesiveness as well as those that subvert its set boundaries.

Returning to the structure mentioned above. The command to hear "this," which given the text it preceded and the literary context created by Hos 4:1 is likely to be understood as YHWH's word, serves as an introduction to both the entire reading (5:1–7:2) and its first main section (5:1-7). Certain verses or versets may belong to more than one unit at the same time and fulfill double duties. For instance, 5:15 may be considered the beginning of a prophetic, didactic reading or the main structural section of a reading that either consists of or includes 5:15–6:11 (cf. Macintosh, *Hosea,* 214-15; Rudolph, *Hosea,* 131-35; Jeremias, *Hosea,* 83-85; Simian-Yofre, *Desierto,* 90-92; Kidner, *Hosea,* 62-65; among many others). Verse 5:15 may be considered also the heightened conclusion of an independent prophetic reading (5:1-15) — within the set of readings of Hos 4:1–11:11 — whose structure may be envisaged as follows:

Prophetic Reading:
YHWH Punishes, Awaits for Israel's Penitence,
and Above All Teaches, 5:1-15

Of course, 5:15 is clearly connected to 5:14 by the careful choice of words in 5:14b and 5:15a. Most noticeable are the numerous words that begin with the Hebrew letter aleph. Numerous examples of assonances, including alliteration, occur throughout the book of Hosea (see Buss, *Prophetic Word*, 38-40) and are unlikely to be the result of random chance. At the same time, the language of 5:15aα certainly resonates in 6:1a (לכו ונשובה and אלך אשובה). In other words, two types of repetitions are at work here: one linking 5:14 to 5:15 and the other 5:15 to 6:1. Both should be taken into account. In other words, if one considers 5:15 to "belong" to 5:1-15, one has to consider also the same verse as "belonging" to the literary subunit that begins with 6:1.

Returning to the main proposal of STRUCTURE, verse 6:6 may be translated as "I [YHWH] desire *hesed,* not (just) *zebach* sacrifice; the knowledge of God (Heb. דעת אלהים) more than *olah* sacrifices." The text here is clearly related to Hos 4:1, "there is no *hesed* or loyalty, and no knowledge of God (Heb. דעת אלהים)." Under these circumstances, sacrifices are not acceptable. (The pair *zebach* — *olah* is common in the HB and conveys the sense of sacrifices as a whole. See, for instance, Exod 18:12; 1 Sam 10:8; 15:22; 2 Kgs 5:17; Isa 56:7; Jer 7:21-23.) Interestingly enough, Hos 6:6 seems to assume that the Israelites actually offered sacrifices to YHWH (cf. Hosea 4; on the relation between 4:1 and 6:6 see Hos 4:1-19 STRUCTURE). It is worth stressing that the text in itself is not a condemnation of the cult *per se,* but a restatement of the common principle that fidelity to YHWH and acceptance of YHWH's guidance have priority over sacrifices (e.g., 1 Sam 15:22; Jer 7:21-23). The latter, in turn, is simply a version of the widespread ideological topos of "the primacy of morality over sacrifices," which is well known both in the HB (e.g., Isa 1:11-17; Amos 5:21-24; Mic 6:8; Ps 40:7-9; 50:8-23; 51:18-19; Prov 15:8; 21:3, 27) and in other ancient Near Eastern texts and discourses (e.g., "The Instruction addressed to King Merikare" and "The Tale of the Shipwrecked Sailor"; see M. Lichtheim, *Ancient Egyptian Literature,* 106, 214). On these issues see, among others, Weinfeld, "Ancient Near Eastern Patterns." Remarkably 6:6 represents an upside-down world from the perspective of a "pious" readership. In 6:6 Israel does not know YHWH and does not show *hesed* in relation to YHWH; the readers hope that they or Israel would know YHWH and that YHWH will show *hesed* to them (see Ps 36:11; cf. Jer 9:23).

Verse 6:7 serves both as a kind of second conclusion for the preceding section (6:1-6) and the beginning of the next (6:7–7:2). In fact, it is a (if not "the") pivotal text in this reading. It can be understood with a meaning akin to "but, they, as Adam (or, as a human being/in the manner of human beings), there they have transgressed the covenant, they have broken faith with me [YHWH]" (cf. Ps 82:7; Job 31:33; and cf. Barthélemy, *Critique Textuelle,* vol. III, 527-31). As a conclusion it directly refers the reader to 5:7, and with the reference to Adam/human beings it reinterprets the reported situation of Israel in terms of human condition (on these matters, see Setting). (One may also notice that when the verse is read in relation to the preceding text, "there" seems to point, implicitly, to the lands of Judah and Ephraim (v. 4), and accordingly, it seems to create a mental association between them and the mythological Garden of Eden; see Setting.) When the verse is read from the perspective of the following verses, "there" clearly points at "Gilead" (v. 8) and accordingly brings the text "back to earth" as it were, to the reported, wrongful behavior of monarchic Israel, i.e., to a kind of "historicized-mythology." Further, the text likely connotes, "but, they, at Adam [see Josh 3:16; likely, modern ed-Damiyeh, on the east bank of the Jordan, north of the Dead Sea], there they have transgressed the covenant, they have broken faith with me [YHWH]," in which case, the text integrates itself with the following verses by its references to a northern location, while at the same time keeping its connection to the preceding verses by its explicit referent to "they have broken faith with me."

The conclusive and emphatic statement of the deity, "they have broken faith with me," is confirmed by an additional section in this literary unit (6:7–7:2), which is connected in several ways to the first one in this reading (5:1-7). For instance, in addition to thematic links (e.g., YHWH knows the sin of Israel), they share references to toponyms (5:1b; 6:7-9; see Setting), to "the House of Israel" (5:1; 6:10), to sinful priests (5:1b; 6:9), and cf. הזנת אפרים נטמא ישראל (NRSV, "Ephraim, you have played the whore; Israel is defiled") in 5:3 and זנות לאפרים נטמא ישראל (NRSV, "Ephraim's whoredom is there, Israel is defiled") in 6:10b. In addition, one may notice the "also Judah" (Heb. גם יהודה) clauses in 5:5 and 6:11. Significantly, both of these sections conclude with עתה ("now") clauses. The first one in 5:7 announces the destruction of Israel and its fields; the second one in 7:2 announces that their crimes surrounded Israel (cf. Ps 17:11-12; 22:13-14, 17; for the metaphorically active and crucial role of their wrongful "deeds" [Heb. מעלל] see Hos 5:2; cf. Jer 4:18) and that they ("their deeds") stare, as it were, YHWH in the face (lit. "stand before YHWH's face"; cf. Isa 1:16; and ct. Ps 16:8; 18:23; and from a slightly different perspective, see also Isa 65:6). The two together bring forward a construction of the fall of the monarchic polities and an explanation for it, both in terms of the deeds of Israel and of YHWH's seeming inability (cf. 6:4) to act in a way that would have exempted Israel from heavy punishment.

Language and motifs link some aspects of this reading to previous readings in the book. The explanation for the wrongful behavior of Israel in terms of רוח זנונים "a spirit/impulse of sexual promiscuity/whoredom" in 5:4 reminds the readers of the text and message of Hos 4:12. The reference to Israel's lack of knowledge of YHWH also in 5:4 reminds them of 2:10, 22, and 4:5 but resonates, even if ironically, in 6:3. The imagery of seeking and not finding YHWH in 5:6 is reminiscent of the image of Israel's seeking other deities ("lovers") and not finding them in 2:9. In addition, the image of marital/sexual misconduct (see chapters 1–3 and also 4) is also present in 5:3, 7; 6:10. In fact, the sudden, but explicit feminization of Israel in 5:7a — the Hebrew text does not say "they fathered" but "they gave birth"; see below — just as the text moves back to deal with sexual misconduct bears particular note and provides further links with previous chapters in the book of Hosea in which Israel is represented metaphorically as a woman.

Of course, language and motifs link some aspects of this reading also to readings that follow it within the structure of the book. Significantly, at times they do so in ways that show an awareness of the text of other sections within the book of Hosea. For instance, it seems that the text of Hos 4:2 illuminates this and the immediately following reading in the book. For the triad of "murder, stealing, and committing adultery," see 6:9; 7:1; and 7:4. The term כחש "lying" appears in 7:3, and it is possible to approach the אלה "swearing" of 4:2 in terms of swearing a covenant; see 6:7 (cf. Hos 10:4). One may notice also the reference to the shedding of blood in 6:8 (cf. Hos 4:2a). In other words, the text of 5:1–7:4aα may have conveyed to its intended readership a sense of implementation and illustration of the more generic words of Hos 4:2. Significantly, it does so by cutting across proposed units. The text not only carries multiple possible structures, but also connotes a sense that the intended readers can (and perhaps should) cut across their boundaries. Incidentally, one may notice also the image of YHWH being surrounded by Ephraim's lying (Heb. כחש) in 12:1; cf. Hos 7:2-3. (It is worth mentioning that while Hos 4:2 illuminates this and the immediately following reading in the text, Hos 4:1 directly and explicitly relates to Hos 6:6; see below.)

Additional markers of textual coherence within 7:2-4 are present. The most obvious of them is the pronominal reference to "their" at the very beginning of the new reading (7:3) that points back to similar references in 7:2 and eventually to Israel. Notice also the repetition of רעתם "their wickedness" in 7:2, 3 (and cf. רעות שמרון "the wicked deeds of Samaria" in 7:1).

For additional markers of textual coherence between other sections of this reading and other readings in the book, see 7:9-10 and the combination of motifs and word choices that appear there and in 5:7-9. In particular, notice the occurrence of the expression ענה גאון ישראל בפניו "the pride of Israel testifies against its face" in 5:5 and 7:10 (and nowhere else in the HB), and the motif of seeking (Heb. בקש) YHWH as well as the references to "foreigners" (Heb. זרים). See also the construction of a foreign king as מלך ירב (often translated as "the great king," but see below) in 5:13 and 10:6; the precise repetition of the expression כענן בקר וכטל משכים הלך "like a morning mist/cloud or like dew that goes away early" in Hos 6:4 and 13:3, which appears nowhere else in the HB — on the meanings of this repetition see Hos 13:1–14:1 STRUCTURE — or the possible set of signposts for readings marked by references to רעתם "their wickedness" in Hos 7:1, 2, 3 and 9:15 and 10:15; or by those to עון אפרים in Hos 7:1 and 13:12, and cf. 4:8; 5:5; 8:13; 9:7, 9; 10:10; 12:9; 13:12; and esp. 14:2 and 14:3.

These and previous markers of textual coherence, particularly at the seams between units as is the case in 7:1-4, emphasize to the intended and primary readers the unity of the book. As much as it is profitable and even necessary to focus on units and multiple possible structures and their meanings, none of these units exists outside the confines of the book, and none of them exists in a way that is not interwoven into the full tapestry of the book. From the perspective of the readers of the book, any attempt to extract literary units from that literary tapestry so as to deal with them as independent units runs contrary to the explicit mode of reading indicated by the book itself.

Markers of textual coherence within and among sections of this reading are also clearly present. Some were mentioned above, and one may add the frequent reference to Ephraim and Judah, or Israel. In addition to them, one may note also that the first and second main sections (subunits II and III above) share not only an opening imperative call, but also a similar structure. Among the markers of textual coherence within subunit II, one may mention the four openings with כי "for." As for subunit III, there is the salient parallel structure that governs vv. 8-14 and which is disturbed only by a rhetorically emphatic, pleonastic double repetition of אני "I [YHWH, metaphorically imagined as a lion]" in "I, certainly I, I will myself tear and go away . . ." in v. 14b. There are also two related sets of imagery of YHWH's punishment based around two divine sets of comparisons, namely, YHWH is like עש "maggots" and רקב "rottenness" in vv. 12-13; and like שחל "lion" and כפיר "young lion" in v. 14. Both sets show the same basic structure. A double comparison referring to YHWH introduces them, followed by a development of that imagery as it affects Israel/Judah (properly, the imagery of the first set leads to "sickness and wound," the second to "being torn apart by the lion"), and concluded by a reference to the unavailability of rescue from such a situation. Both include some rhetorical feature towards the conclusion that serves to accentuate the message. In the case of 12-13, it is the change from third to second person in 13b (see below); in that of 14, it is the pleonastic double "I" in 14b. It is worth noting also that the beginning of this set of two comparisons is also clearly linked to the preceding verses in subunit III; note עשוק "oppressed" and עש "maggots" in vv. 11 and 12, respectively, and their association with Ephraim. The third main section (subunit VI) consists of two structural components. The second serves as an explanatory note to the first (cf. the case of 2:9b and its following verses). The first part is marked by a (direct or indirect) human speaker representing Israel and above all by its use of cohortative verbal forms (6:1, 3). The voice of the human speaker can be associated with that of the main human character in the book (i.e., Hosea), the people, or the priests. This holds true whether the words are sincere or not. More likely, these words may be understood as embedded in YHWH's speech, that is, as YHWH's quote (and construction) of Israel's speech (see below), and accordingly, as a (human) sub-voice embedded in YHWH's. The second part (6:4-7) is thematically deeply related to the first. It is bound together also by the contrastive reference to their (i.e., Israel's) *hesed* ("fidelity" or "loyalty") in v. 4 and the *hesed* that YHWH requires (see v. 6). One may also notice the similar grammatical constructions in 6:11b and 7:1 and the mentioned repetition of רעתם "their wickedness" in Hos 7:1, 2 (and cf. 7:3).

It is worth noting that this reading as a whole shows fluidity in regards to the identity of the godly speaker. The words that the implied author put in the mouth of the speaker in some verses indicate that the readers are supposed to understand the speaker as none but YHWH (see 5:3, 9, 10, 12, 14, 15; 6:4-7; 6:10; 6:11b; 7:1, 2). References to YHWH in the third person in other verses (see vv. 5:4, 6, 7) give the impression, though by no means the necessity (see Judg 2:22; 6:26; 1 Sam 10:19; 2 Sam 12:9; 1 Kgs 17:14; 2 Kgs 20:5; Isa 49:7; Jer 14:10; 17:5; 23:16; 26:2; 27:16; Mic 2:5; 4:7b, 10; 6:5; Zeph 3:12; Mal 1:4; and cf. Revell, *Designation,* § 27.3), that the speaker is likely to be other than YHWH — that is, a human, prophetic voice. If the latter is the case, then the most salient observation is that the two voices are constructed and imagined as fully interwoven. The result is one "godly voice" that carries the "godly message" that the text conveys. Significantly, the godly voice may also report the voice of the ungodly in a way that, as it were, mimics their speech (according to one possible reading of 6:1-3 [see above]; cf. 2:7, 9; as mentioned before, the ungodly does not have an independent voice in the book; the godly voice always constructs the discourse of the ungodly).

The identity of the formal addressees of the godly voice is fluid for rhetorical purposes. The priests, the house of Israel, and the house of the king are referred to in the second person in 5:1-2, but Ephraim and Israel (and even Judah) are referred to in the third person in 5:3-7. Similarly, some less identifiable group clearly associated with Israel is referred to in the second person at the beginning of the second main section; then Ephraim, the tribes of Israel, the officer of Judah, Ephraim, and the house of Judah or Judah — all are referred to in the third person. In 6:4-5, Ephraim and Judah (that is, Israel) are explicitly addressed in the second person, but they appear in the third in v. 7.

An address in the second person bears a particular affective, rhetorical power. This is the most likely reason for the imperative openings in 5:1, 8; and numerous other imperative openings in prophetic literature. Perhaps more interesting is the fact that this power leads to "unexpected" shifts to the second person. For instance, there is significant shift to the second person in 5:13b as the text reads "but he is not able to cure *you* or heal *your* wound." The result is a more emphatic, more affective text, from the perspective of the readership (see Setting). Another interesting case: The formal addressee in 6:8-10 is unclear, and the text may be formally categorized as a representation of a monologue of the divine voice (Gilead, Ephraim, the House of Israel — all appear in the third person), but towards the end of the structural section, in v. 11a, one finds a reference to a second person, which might refer to Judah, but most likely to a general addressee who stands for trans-temporal Israel, with whom the readers of the book identify. Conversely, the text may refer to Ephraim and Judah in the second person, but shift to the third person when a rhetorically impersonal, general, "objective," summary comment about them is advanced (see 6:7). Significantly, in the structurally similar, general comment in 7:2, Israel is also presented in the third person, and the same holds true for 5:7.

As expected, the craftsmanship reflected in the composition of this reading includes the use of common pairs and expressions, but at times with a particular twist. There is the call to "hear" (see above) and the call to "blow the trumpet" (תקעו); see Joel 2:1, 15. One finds lexical pairs such as בקש "seek" and מצא "find" (e.g., Deut 4:29; Josh 2:22; Jer 29:13; Hos 2:9; Song 3:1) and ידע "know" and לא נכחד "not hidden" (see Ps 69:6; 78:3-4; 139:14-15). But word pairs may serve to develop contrastive, rather than supporting, images. Such is the case in 6:3-4. There one finds שחר "dawn" in 6:3 and בקר "morning" in 6:4 (cf. Job 38:12); טל "dew" in 6:4 and "rain or showers" in 6:3. (The common Heb. word for the second term in these cases is מטר "rain"; e.g., Deut 32:2; 2 Sam 1:21; 1 Kgs 17:1, but it is substituted here by the semantically related term גשם — for the two terms, see Zech 10:1; and notice the additional association of גשם "rain" with מלקוש "late rain" and יורה "early rain" in Jer 5:24 and cf. Joel 2:23 and Zech 10:1.) Of course, in addition to their role within their respective word pairs, some of these words are part of "long range" networks of meanings across the book that serve well their readers. For instance, the *hesed* of the people in relation to YHWH is likened to quickly disappearing "dew" (טל) in 6:4 (and cf. Hos 13:3; see Hos 13:1–14:1 STRUCTURE), but YHWH will be like a nourishing dew that does not fail to appear and whose effects are long-lasting in the ideal future the book promises to its readers in Hos 14:6. For a study of the "dew" metaphors see Oestreich, *Metaphors,* 157-89. Within the world of postmonarchic literati, dew may raise connotations of bringing those who are dead to life (see Isa 26:19); see 6:2; needless to say, a dew such as Israel's *hesed* in 6:4 is not capable of fulfilling this role. Does the text connote a vague satirical note pointing at the failure of Israel's repentance in 6:1-3 to achieve such return to life?

Words pairs also provide opportunities for a very sophisticated, careful wordplay that allows for the construction of multiple meanings, and some level of de-familiarization that serves as an attention-getter for the readership and focuses it on the particular meanings conveyed by the relevant section. An excellent example is in 5:11. The relevant expression is based on the word pair עשוק "oppressed" and רצוץ "crushed" (see Deut 28:33). But the text in Hosea replaces the expected "Israel" or "house of Israel" or perhaps "Judah/house of Judah" with משפט "justice" (cf. Ps 103:6; 146:7) and additionally, at least in the MT tradition of vocalization, has רצוץ in the construct, as opposed to the absolute as expected. The results of these seemingly minor changes are far-reaching. First, the text states, "Ephraim is oppressed, crushed in respect to/by justice" (cf. Macintosh, *Hosea,* 204, and bibliography). Second, the text certainly connotes to the readers, "Ephraim is oppressed, justice is crushed" (cf. Wolff, *Hosea,* 104; Mays, *Hosea,* 85, 91). Third, the text conveys and implies an anticipated association between Ephraim/Israel and justice, and uses it to highlight that the opposite of such expectation holds true in this case. Fourth, it augments that reversal of expectation by associating עָשׁוּק "oppressed" and מִשְׁפָּט "justice," not in the usual way — that is, justice will liberate the oppressed (Israel?) — but to the contrary that justice is at the root of oppression in this case. Fifth, it is still possible to understand the passive participle as carrying an active meaning; in which case, Ephraim is characterized as an oppressor who crushes justice (cf. "Ephraim oppresses his opponent and treads justice under foot"; LXX Hos 5:11). These denoted or connoted meanings are not alternative but complementary from the perspective of the literati who formed the primary and target readership of the book of Hosea (see also the discussion on 5:7b, below). It may be mentioned also that the reason for all the meanings associated with Ephraim conveyed by 5:11a was emphatically portrayed. Verse 11b most likely meant "because he [Ephraim] was determined to go after dung" (cf. Emerton, "Some Difficult Words"; cf. Isa 28:10, 13). The literati among whom the book was composed were clearly able to balance multiple connoted and denoted meanings with some unequivocal, strong statements, if they so wished, while at the very same time keep the text open to the imagination of the intended readership, for more than one negative image of "going after dung" can be developed within the discourse embedded in the unit and the book as a whole (cf. Hos 2:7, 15), as well as in the general discourse of these literati (cf. (a) Jer 3:17; 9:13; 16:12; Amos 2:4; (b) Deut 4:3; 6:14; 8:19; 11:28; 13:3; 28:14; Judg 2:12, 19; 1 Kgs 11:5, 10; 18:18; Jer 2:5; 7:9; 8:2; 9:13; 11:10; 13:10; 16:11; 25:6; 35:15; (c) Ruth 3:10; Prov 7:22; (d) 1 Sam 17:14 and ct. 1 Kgs 14:8; 2 Chr 34:31; and Jer 2:2).

Another word pair worthy of particular notice is Ephraim — (house of) Israel. This pair is common in the book of Hosea as a whole (see 5:5, 9; 6:10; and cf. 11:8; 12:1; 13:1). The terms are not interchangeable, however. It is not by chance that the term "house of Ephraim" does not occur but "house of Israel" and "house of Judah" do appear in Hosea. (The same holds true elsewhere: the only instance of "house of Ephraim" in the HB is Judg 10:9; the other two terms are very common.) The word pair Ephraim — Israel serves here to rhetorically create a mental (and ideological) domain to which both terms (and Judah; see 5:3-5, 11-12; cf. 12:1-2) belong. This domain serves to highlight certain properties of Ephraim and downplay others, to draw the attention of the readers to the most prototypical term in the domain and its main features (i.e., Israel). By doing so it encourages the intended and primary readers to identify with the people mentioned in the world of the book, for monarchic Ephraim, as well as monarchic Judah, become part and parcel of "trans-temporal Israel." Similar considerations apply to the quartet "my [YHWH's] people — Israel — Ephraim — Samaria" in 6:11b-7:1, which in the minds of the readers they themselves associate with monarchic Israel, Ephraim, and Samaria, as all are part and parcel of trans-temporal Israel, i.e., (and ideologically) YHWH's people. It bears notice that the construction of this mental domain, its inner logic, and certainly its repeated use are conducive to the development — or reinforcement of existing — ideological expectations and ideal images of a future of reunification of north and south; see Hos 2:2; 3:5. (Some text-critical scholars have proposed a forerunner of the present text of 6:10 in which the triad "House of Israel — Ephraim — Israel," which communicates the message discussed above, is replaced with "Beth-el — Ephraim — Israel.")

The word pair רפא "heal" and חבש "bind" (i.e., binding up wounds and the like) is clearly recognizable in Hos 6:1 (for the pair see Isa 30:26; Ezek 34:4; Ps 147:3; Job 5:18 and also Barré, "Bullutsa-rabi's Hymn"). The message conveyed by the pair רפא — חבש is reinforced by the central word pair in the next verse (Hos 6:2), namely, חיה "restore to health" and קום "raise" (cf. Isa 26:16, 19; see also 2 Kgs 13:21 and see Barré, "New Light"). Hos 6:2 is thus to be understood as "in two days he will restore us to health; on the third day he will raise us [from our sickbeds/from our sickness] that we may live on in his presence" (cf. Macintosh, *Hosea*, 220; Barré, "New Light"; idem, "Bullutsa-rabi's Hymn"). The temporal reference is in the pattern of "x, x+1" (see Roth, "Numerical Sequence") and here serves to convey a sense of a brief period; it should not be taken literally (cf. the medical omen texts mentioned in Barré, "New Light"; cf. 2 Kgs 20:5). Hosea 6:1-2 therefore reaffirms the image of YHWH as the powerful healer (or "physician") of the speakers portrayed in the book (see esp. Barré, "New Light"; idem, "Bullutsa-rabi's Hymn").

At the same time, from the perspective of the readers, the text may connote a secondary sense of national resurrection (i.e., "return from exile," and cf. Hos 2:1-3) similar to that of Ezekiel 37. In fact, one may say that the metaphorical image of "resurrection" is a heightened version of that of sickness and healing, in which sickness turns into "death" and, correspondingly, "healing" into "resurrection."

It is worth noting that the pair חיה "restore to health" and קום "raise" does not appear in the mythological sense of the dying and rising of deities. The speakers in their speech of repentance, and Israel who identifies with them, do not convey any sense that they take the structural slot of any deity in Hos 6:2. Of course, from the perspective of a Persian period readership, the theme of an ideal return from "the exile" points not only to the establishment of the province of Yehud, according to its main meta-narrative about itself, but above all, carries in itself a hope for a messianic future (cf. Targum). The pair חיה "restore to health" and קום "raise" allows also a further development in the text. The first verbal form of חיה with YHWH as a subject leads to a second and concluding verbal form of the same root, with the speakers/Israel as subject. YHWH's restoration to health (חיה Piel) carries a purpose, "that we may live (חיה qal) before him" (cf. Gen 17:18 and also the themes conveyed by Ps 6:6; 30:10; 88:11-13; of course, contrast with YHWH's reported assessment of the reality at the very conclusion of this reading, "their wrongful deeds are before me"; Hos 7:2b). Moreover, the shift from piel to qal serves to reinforce the image of the relation between YHWH and Israel/the speakers as a relation between the one who "causes" the other to live, who gives and maintains life, and the one who is given life, and consequently is alive and may stand before the life-giver, YHWH. To be sure, Hos 6:2 could have used חיה qal to communicate a sense of reviving the sick or the dead (e.g., Num 21:8-9; 2 Kgs 1:2; 8:8-14; 13:21; Ezek 37:3-14), but had that been the case, the text would have lost the mentioned piel-qal contrast. On early Christian readings of Hos 6:2 see Macintosh, *Hosea*, 222-23, and Pentiuc, *Long-Suffering Love*, 95-97.

One more example of sophisticated play with word pairs may be mentioned: מלקוש "late rain" or "spring showers" and יורה "early rain" are a known semantic pair (see Deut 11:14; Jer 5:24 — and for the same pair with related form מורה "early rain" see Joel 2:23). The text in 6:3, however, defamiliarizes the pair; for יורה here is not a noun, but a verb, which in this context means "water." Thus 6:3b can be translated, "he [YHWH] comes to us like rain, like spring showers that water the land." Moreover, one has to take into account that because יורה may also mean "teach, instruct," the text advances a secondary connotation of "he [YHWH] comes to us like rain, like spring showers that instruct the land" (cf. Hos 10:12 and Joel 2:23). Thus, it evokes an imagery of YHWH's words and teaching as leading to the fertility of the land (for the basic imagery see Isa 55:10-11; and cf. with Deut 32:2 in which Moses is the teacher and with Ps 72:6 in which the image most likely refers to a messianic king — see Gerstenberger, *Psalms, part 2,* 67-68).

A few expressions in this reading require a brief comment. The opening explanation for the summons to hear in 5:1ab כי לכם המשפט carries a double and complementary meaning. Within its context in the book, it certainly carries the ominous sense of "the judgment is yours" (i.e., you will be judged, found guilty, and punished), but the "natural" meaning of the expression is "it is you who have justice in your care" (NJB; "justice" here carries a sense of "proper or just government/order/practices"). The two meanings are complementary and the text actually conveys to the readers that YHWH will judge the leadership, because they were responsible for justice and failed. In other words, YHWH is imagined as a kind of mirror image of the leadership: What they failed to do, YHWH does, and necessarily within discourse, through executing punishment against it. These considerations about the language of 5:1 along with some to be discussed in Setting provide a good example of the use of carefully crafted language aimed at conveying multiple meanings.

Another example is in 5:2b. The Hebrew text reads ואני מוסר לכלם, meaning literally "I am discipline to all of them," which is an elliptic expression (cf. Ps 109:4) meaning something akin to "I am a force for discipline to all of them," and in less abstract form, "I will discipline all of them" (cf. Tg; Pesh; NRSV; see Macintosh, *Hosea,* 178-80, 182 and for alternative proposals, Andersen and Freedman, *Hosea,* 388-89). The ellipsis carries rhetorical power by itself, and is consistent with constructions of YHWH's discipline elsewhere (Deut 11:2; Prov 3:11), with the background image of YHWH as father of Israel (see Hos 11:1 and Hosea 1–2; and cf., among others, Prov 1:8; 4:1; 8:33; 13:1; 15:5), and with the presence of other wisdom expressions in this reading. The ellipsis also allows a secondary connotation of "bond" or "fetters" (Isa 28:22; 52:2; cf., among others, Garret, *Hosea, Joel,* 143-44), which also suit and enrich the context as well as carry associations of absolute inability to free oneself, of being captive, and of exile.

Verse 5:7b is introduced by עתה "now," a phrase which often leads to the main issue being addressed in a text and carries a soft consequential meaning (cf. Waltke and O'Connor, *Biblical Hebrew Syntax,* § 39.3.4.f). The issue is how to understand what follows "now." The text, unless it is emended, can be translated as, "the new moon (Heb. חדש) will devour them along with their fields/allocated portions of land" (Heb. חלק; see, for instance, Num 18:20; Deut 12:12; Josh 18:5-7; 19:9; Mic 2:4; Zech 2:16). For the imagery of YHWH devouring חלק see Amos 7:4. If the primary readers of the book of Hosea followed this understanding, they most likely did not imagine the new moon actually devouring fields, but probably understood the text to mean that the wrongful rituals of Israel during "new moon" — as implied by the literary contexts of Hos 5:1-7 and the book of Hosea as a whole; and cf. Isa 1:13-14 — were the cause that led to the destruction of the people and of their fields. Rather than save Israel and their produce through proper human behavior towards the deity, these rituals caused the opposite result (cf. Barthélemy, *Critique Textuelle,* vol. III, 520-21; Simian-Yofre, *Desierto,* 82; Garret, *Hosea,* 146-47). Moreover, within the present literary context, given that a prophetic book is read and reread and meant to be read and reread, and taking into account the discourse of a postmonarchic community, the richness of mental and lexical associations carried by the term חלק is worth noting. For instance, the term may have evoked in the readership a figurative connotation of חלק "portion." Israel is YHWH's חלק in Deut 32:9 and a righteous person's חלק may figuratively be YHWH (see Ps 73:26; 119:57; Lam 3:24; cf. Ps 16:5, and notice the binding together of these two ideological images in Jer 10:16; 51:19). If these meanings are evoked by the text, then verse 7a carries a strong connotation that when Israel and YHWH are in effect each other's חלק then Israel's חלק is safe, but when Israel deals treacherously against, or commits adultery (Heb. בגד ב; see Jer 3:20) against her husband, YHWH, and gives birth to "alien/bastard" children (on the feminization of Israel in v. 5:7 see above), then Israel's חלק, that is, her fields and territory, will be devoured, which is not incidentally a repeated motif in the book of Hosea. In addition, as verse 5:7b was read again and again by the literati for whom the book of Hosea was written, it could have been interpreted in a complementary manner. These literati may have considered it elliptic, in which case the subject would be YHWH and the meaning of v. 5:7b would be "Now YHWH will devour them and their חלק at the new moon [i.e., soon, in less than a month] (cf. Andersen and Freedman, *Hosea,* 11). Finally, the readers may have also understood the text as meaning "a new time will destroy them and their חלק." In which case, "the new time" serves as a personification of a "new period." In sum, the present discussion shows how the multiple meanings were likely conveyed and constructed by the postmonarchic readership of the book of Hosea — in its present form — through their reading and rereading of some verses. Most significantly, all of these meanings are consistent with the general worldview of these literati, and it is the tapestry created by them as they inform each other — rather than any one of these readings alone — that conveys that which may be called the "meaning" of the verse for this readership. For a similar case see discussion on 5:11, above.

Hos 6:1-3 can be and has been understood in several ways. As mentioned in the structure advanced above, these verses serve a double structural role. On the one hand, 6:1-3 are an integral part of 6:1-6. Thematic and textually inscribed markers (see above) provide a strong sense of coherence to 6:1-6 and bind 6:1-3 to the subsequent verses in the book. At the same time, 6:1-3 serve as a kind of inner response to the claim advanced in 5:15. If YHWH is a deity that waits for Israel's repentance, then 6:1-3 provides at least an attempt at response. The readers know that YHWH actually "devoured" monarchic Israel (both Ephraim and Judah) so Israel's response was not adequate. Verses 6:4-6 explicitly explain that Israel's response in 6:1-3 was ephemeral and not informed by knowledge of YHWH (cf. Hos 2:9b-10, and for similar portrayed circumstances, see Ps 78:34-37; Jer 3:10; for the general worldviews involved in these matters see Setting).

Verses 6:1-3 also serve as a kind of interlude within YHWH's words. As such, they may be understood as carrying a human voice that urges repentance and correctly characterizes YHWH within the ideological horizons of the intended and primary readerships. (This holds true whether the human voice is understood as embedded in the divine voice or not [see above]. In any case, a human speech reported by YHWH is certainly a reliable version of the contents — hypothetical or not — of human speech from the perspective of the intended and primary readerships.) Significantly, within the world of the book, such a voice and such a call are not anchored to any particular circumstances, event, or any group of addressees at a certain occasion. This feature allows the voice to speak in non-contingent terms and to address directly the postmonarchic readership of the book, for they too expect YHWH to heal and revive (transtemporal) Israel. They too trust YHWH and they too should seek to know YHWH. The message of hope that the text carries, along with the explanation for the past destruction of Israel, is clear and to some extent provides a summary of the book as whole. Yet, at the same time, neither Israel in the world of the book, nor the Israel of the readers can be imagined as healed Israel. So to a large extent, 6:1-3, even if read in this way, calls for 6:4-6 or something similar. For the implicit horizon of thought informing the text, see Setting.

(For a survey of ways of understanding 6:1-3, see Davies, *Hosea,* 149-51; see also Buss, *Prophetic Word,* 74; Rudolph, *Hosea,* 134-38; Limburg, *Hosea,* 27; Simian-Yofre, *Desierto,* 90-93. It is also possible to understand 6:1-3 as ironic or satiric; see, among others, Hunter, *Seek the Lord,* 143-52; Wendland, *Discourse Analysis.*)

Several redactional hypotheses have been advanced in relation to Hosea 5–7. For comprehensive redactional proposals concerning these texts, see Yee, *Composition,* 170-80; Diefenderfer, *Rhetorical Polyphony,* 173-88, 265-67. As one may anticipate, some scholars have considered references to Judah a later editorial, Judahite addition. For instance, Buss — among others — has suggested that one should read "Israel" instead of "Judah" in 5:10, 12, 13, 14; 6:4, and that the term "Judah" was later written into the text (Buss, *Prophetic Word,* 13-14, 37 — he also proposes that this is the case in, for instance, 10:11 and 12:3). Ginsberg maintains that "in a copy of the (North) Israelite Book of Hosea which reached Jerusalem after the fall of Samaria the word *yśr'l* was frequently represented by the initial y, which in a number of instances was misunderstood by a Judite [sic] copyist as the initial of some other proper name as that of *yhw'* in i 4; *yhwdh* in v 12, 13, 14, vi 4, x 10 (sic), xii 13; and of *yhwh* in viii 1" (Ginsberg, "Lexicographical Notes," 76 n. 2). Similarly, Harper claims that the original text read "Israel" instead of Judah in almost every case, except

Hos 4:15 and 5:5 (see Harper, *Hosea,* 263, 270, 275, 277, 278, 286-87, 350, and 378-79). To be sure, there are also other scholars who consider many of the references to Judah as part and parcel of the original text or words of the historical prophet. See, for instance, Emmerson, *Hosea,* 62-77, and Simian-Yofre, *Desierto,* 255-61, both of whom conclude that the references to Judah in Hos 5:10, 12, 13, 14, among other references to Judah, go back to the first layer of the text. Simian-Yofre (op. cit.) and Macintosh (*Hosea,* 202, 208, 213, 229) add to them the one in 6:4 too.

Significantly, if the reference to the officers of Judah in 5:10 reflects a particular historical event, in this case, a supposed incursion of Judah in Ephraimite territory that according to most, but not all, occurred shortly before 733 BCE (notwithstanding minor differences, see Alt, "Hosea 5:8–6:6"; Thompson, *Situation and Theology,* 66-67; Wolff, *Hosea,* 110-114, esp. 114; Andersen and Freedman, *Hosea,* 401-3, 408; Macintosh, *Hosea,* 202), then other portions of Hosea 5–7 may point to later events (concerning 5:1-2, see Alt "Hosea 5:8–6:6," 187 n. 1). These proposals are deeply interrelated with the hypothesis that much of these texts and in particular Hos 5:8–6:3/6, or at the very least 5:8-14, relate to the circumstances around and during the Syro-Ephraimite war, but see Setting.

Genre

This is a didactic, prophetic reading. It contains main sections as well as sections that introduce, connect, interpret, or comment on these main sections (namely, "INTRODUCTION," "INTERPRETATION," "SUMMARY," "INTERLUDE"). As a whole, the different sections are associated, though not exclusively, with each other by textually inscribed markers. As all other readings in the text do, the present one shows an array of sophisticated literary techniques. The presence of these techniques is indicative of the existence of a target readership able to decode them (see Setting). This reading, on the whole, serves to advance the condemnation of monarchic Israel through a manifold description (and constructions) of its sins and thus to explain the fall of the monarchic polities and YHWH's role and reasons for the deity's assault on these polities.

Several sections in this reading were composed to evoke in the readership some genre expectations, which may, at times, be partially fulfilled but also defamiliarized in more than one way, and for rhetorical purposes. This may involve matters of style that convey meaning or the unequivocal foiling of thematic expectations. For instance, the summons to hear in 5:1 serves to introduce the readers to 5:1-7, and to create a set of expectations (e.g., a divine address in the second person conveying either condemnation or hope). The text follows the literary expectations associated with the call in v. 1 (see above), but rapidly moves to the third person and conveys a sense of distancing between YHWH and Israel. A more dramatic case of play on expectations appears in 6:1-3. The unit resembles a song or psalm that, although opening as a summons to worship (e.g., Isa 2:3; Mic 4:2; Ps 95:1), particularly given the context, seems in fact to be an invitation to lamentation, which functions as an exhortation to return to YHWH (see Hunter, *Seek the Lord,* 147; cf. Lam 3:40; Jer 31:18-19) and has been described as a liturgy of repentance (e.g., Barré, "New Light," 136). In any case, the text is written so as to create an expectation that "returning" Israel will be delivered, at least in some way, by YHWH. This anticipation is negated in the following verses.

Stuart refers to the implicit legal nature of Hos 5:1-7 (Stuart, *Hosea,* 93). He may be correct in the sense that there might be a certain legal scent, as it were, in that section. Yet, as he admits, there is not much of legal language or of a language that evokes legal proceedings.

Good ("Hosea 5:8–6:6") senses that 5:8–6:6 "is highly reminiscent of the 'covenant lawsuit'" (op. cit., 284), but also notes, "we do not have all the formal ingredients of a 'covenant lawsuit'" (284). He maintains that 5:8–6:6 is a poem that "had a function in the cult" (285) and which includes legal and theophanic elements that not only point at a covenant festival (likely, in the fall), but also to the cultic role of the "covenant" prophet as the mediator of the covenant lawsuit in such a festival. In fact, he writes, "our poem [5:8–6:6] may be an instance of the occupation of such office" (286). Yet, whereas Good exposes many of the problems with Alt's discussion of the text, his own proposal is highly hypothetical. Leaving aside questions about the genre of covenant lawsuit and their relation to the proposed fall covenant festival — both of them problematic — the text clearly does not ask its readers to approach it as a cultic, liturgical poem, nor explicitly associates it with a festival or a prophetic performance in a cult festival. Moreover, even if for the sake of argument, one were to grant these claims, it would have only evoked the genre of "cultic poem," because the text does not stand alone as record of a liturgy. Instead, it is an integral part of a prophetic book and is intertwined in very profound ways with other readings in the book that can hardly be associated with such a cultic liturgy. Franklyn ("Oracular Cursing") in turn exposes problems that beset both Alt's and Good's discussion of the text. But his own solutions for an association of Hoseanic texts and the cult is problematic as well, for the reasons mentioned above.

At times it is more helpful to focus on scenes, rather than on literary genres. Yet one may notice that even these scenes tend to be de-familiarized at times. The second section of this reading opens by asking the readership to image a scene of military alarm with horns and trumpets alerting the population of towns that an enemy is on their doorsteps. Yet, although the scene serves as an attention-getter for the readers, it soon disappears into the background of the story.

Setting

The setting of the writing and reading of this or any portion of the (present) book of Hosea for that matter, is the same as that of the book as a whole. Both writers and readers are among the literati of Yehud. But what can one learn from this didactic, prophetic READING about the worldview of the literati within whom and for whom the book of Hosea was composed? This reading is indicative of many aspects of the intellectual and ideological atmosphere within which it was written and which permeates it.

Before addressing these matters, it should be noted that several proposals for the redactional history of this reading (or, better, of texts included in this reading) have been advanced. It is quite common to associate Hos 5:8–6:6, or at the very least 5:8-14, either as a compositional or redactional unit, with the circumstances of the Syro-Ephraimite War. See, for instance, Alt, "Hosea 5,8–6,6"; Arnold, "Hosea"; Mays, *Hosea*, 85-98; Andersen and Freedman, *Hosea*, 399-431; Stuart, *Hosea*, 97-102; Lind, "Hosea 5:8–6:6," but see also Good, "Hosea 5:8–6:6" and Utzschneider, "Situation und Szene." For examples of scholars who worked within a general, similar "historical" approach, but reach very different conclusions, see, among others, Tadmor, "Historical Background"; Ginsberg, "Hosea."

Within the form-critical and historical-critical approach followed in this commentary, setting does not refer to the hypothetical circumstances in which the historical prophet — to be distinguished from the literary character Hosea as portrayed in the book as a whole — may or may not have uttered the words, or any portion thereof, that the book ascribes to the literary character, Hosea. Rather it refers to the setting of the world of the writing and primary reading of the (present) book of Hosea. To be sure, to understand the message conveyed by the book to its intended and primary readership, one must also take into consideration the setting within the world of the book of the relevant, reported speeches — mainly uttered by YHWH — which are embedded in the various PROPHETIC READINGS or SETS OF PROPHETIC READINGS.

It is worth stressing, however, that the text does not directly associate any of these speeches with particular events, or more precisely, the construed memory of any particular event in Israel's history. Yet it is clear that a general setting in the world of the book does exist. In fact, the present didactic reading illustrates the way in which the text keeps a fine balance between the literary northern Israelite, monarchic setting of the world portrayed in the book and the setting of the readership of the book and the latter's web of identification. A few examples will suffice. At one level, the reference to the priests, the house of Israel and the house of the king in 5:1 points to the priests of YHWH in the northern polity, the northern royal establishment (i.e., the royal court including its high officers), and the (male) "citizens" or landowners of that kingdom who were in a position of power (see discussion on 5:1aβ, above) referred to as "the house of Israel" (for a possible, similar use of that expression, see Jer 2:26). The choice of words, however, is very thoughtful. One would have expected, for instance, the leadership list to include "the elders of the house of Israel" or the like rather than "the house of Israel" (cf. Wolff, *Hosea*, 97). Yet the reference is to the "house of Israel." This term ("the house of Israel") points on the one hand to the powerful segment of the northern Israelite society in the world portrayed in the book (see above), but, on the other, allows the readership to further identify with the addressees in the world of the book. The use of the term "house of Israel" connotes to them the message that the entire house of Israel bears the responsibility for justice, for failure to behave in a just manner, and for divine punishment, in the past as well as in the present. The message is all the more poignant since they, just as monarchic Ephraim or Judah, are (part of) the house of Israel. The reference to Judah in 5:5 serves again to reinforce a sense of identification. For the people in Yehud are Israel and are also, from their own perspective, the continuation of exilic Judah which in turn stands in continuation with monarchic Judah (see Ben Zvi, "Inclusion in and Exclusion from Israel").

The references to places in northern Israel in 5:1b and 6:7-9 emphasize the setting of the world of the book in northern Israel, but many of them carry additional connotations. The readers could certainly identify Mizpah with Benjamin, the late kingdom of Judah and the central town of Judah in the neo-Babylonian period, and probably above all, with a central place in the story of Israel about itself within the discourse of the readership (e.g., Judges 20–21; 1 Samuel 7; 10:17-25; 2 Kings 25; on Mizpah see, for instance, McKenzie, "Mizpah of Benjamin" and, from a different perspective, Zorn, "Estimating," and Lipschits, "History," 165-70; and see also Edelman, "Did Saulide-Davidic Rivalry" for a reconstruction of the Benjamin-Judah relations in Early Persian Yehud). For the intended and primary readerships Tabor is symbolic of a high mountain (see Jer 46:18; Ps 89:13; cf. Tg), which is a necessary feature for the literary gradation of height in the text from Mizpah to Tabor that eventually leads to the contrastive "they have made/gone/dug deep" (Heb. העמיקו) in 5:2a. At the same time, it evokes episodes in the readership's story about itself (see Judges 4). The connoted pun on Shittim (the term "Shittim" is not in the Hebrew text) is part and parcel of a strong repetition of sounds aimed at carrying an additional emphasis, but it also evokes in the readership the circumstances of Numbers 25 (and see Hos 9:10 and discussion there) as well as Joshua 2 and 3 (and cf. Mic 6:5). Similarly, central stories in Israel's construction of its past are evoked by references to Bethel (Beth Awen), Gibeah (cf. Hos 10:9), Ramah, Gilead, and Shechem (5:8; 6:8-9) in this reading, and in a very salient manner for the first and last in the series. (The choice of Adam in 6:7 is due to another feature: it is the only toponym in the northern kingdom that allows for the double meaning Adam (i.e., a geographical place — human beings; and see below).

In other words, the list of places is careful crafted and serves multiple purposes: It contributes to (a) the literary artistry of the book (e.g., its multiple meanings, gradations, emphatic repetitions and the like), (b) the portrayal of the world of the text as set in northern Israel, and (c) the creation of an ideological geography with which the readers of the book can identify, and of much value in the context of their social memory. In addition, the negative characterizations of Shechem, Mizpah, and Bethel are influenced by the ideological construction of Jerusalem among its literati during the Persian period, as the only legitimate religio-political center. This list of places is a product of sophisticated, literary craftsmanship. It is relevant to the setting of the world portrayed in the book and at the same time to the setting of the intended and primary readerships of the book of Hosea. Because of its multiple functions it sheds light on the setting of the writing and reading of the book in its present form. The list contributes to our understanding of their world of knowledge, their social memories as Israel, the importance given to these social memories in their discourse, and, of course, the sophisticated level of the bearers of high literacy who wrote these books.

Many scholars have focused on the supposed circumstances in which their proposed forerunner of the historical prophet said the words that the book attributes to its literary character Hosea. This forerunner is often constructed on the basis of either textual emendations or redactional proposals. Among these scholars, many have proposed a historical setting around the Syro-Ephraimite War and its immediate preceding and following time (e.g., Alt, "Hosea 5:8–6:6"; Wolff, *Hosea,* 108-16; Thompson, *Situation and Theology,* 63-78; Andersen and Freedman, *Hosea,* 401-10; Macintosh, *Hosea,* 193-213; Davies, *Hosea, 145-48,* 154-55). It cannot be overstressed, however, that the text itself does not ask its intended and primary readerships to imagine that war or the period surrounding it as the background against which they had to understand the reported speeches. In fact, any reconstruction of that war that was either shaped or reflected by the relevant sections in the books of Kings and Isaiah (2 Kgs 15:29, 37; 16:5-9; Isa 7:1-9) would be incongruent with the world portrayed in this reading within the book of Hosea, and incidentally, the same holds true for the most likely historical reconstruction of the Syro-Ephraimite War itself. To begin with, in Hosea 5:1–7:2 there is no reference to Aram. The latter was the main ally of northern Israel during the war and the main regional player that confronted Assyria. Second, according to Hos 5:13aβ, Ephraim asked Assyria's help, but Ephraim fought with Aram against Assyria. Significantly, whereas Judah stood in Assyria's camp and asked for its help, Judah is not explicitly, if at all, accused of doing so.

Neither the references in 5:8-9 require an unequivocal association of the text with the historical events of the Syro-Ephraimite War or their memory in later generations, nor does the expression הָיוּ שָׂרֵי יְהוּדָה כְּמַסִּיגֵי גְּבוּל "the officers of Judah have acted like shifters of field boundaries" (NJPSV) in 5:10. In fact, it is very unlikely that the intended readers of the book would have imagined that the latter refers to a Judahite annexation of territories held by the northern kingdom, following the failure of the Aramean-Israelite coalition to conquer Jerusalem — an annexation that is not, incidentally, reported elsewhere. The text was most likely read against the common ancient Near East topos of shifting field boundaries (see Prov 22:28; 23:10; see also Deut 19:14; 27:17 and the Instruction of Amenemope, ch. 6). Moreover, in all these cases, the point centers on inner social oppression rather than territorial annexation by polities (cf. Wellhausen, *Die kleinen Propheten,* 112; Premnath, *Process of Latifundation,* 158-60). Significantly, as one would anticipate given this meaning, the text in Hos 5:10 assigns such an attitude not to "Judah" nor to its king, but to the "officers," i.e., high-class individuals in the court that are often admonished not to use their power to the detriment of the powerless in society (cf. Isa 1:23; 3:14; this is a common topos in ancient Near Eastern literature).

It is not surprising therefore that numerous generations of readers of the book of Hosea (who knew about the Syro-Ephraimite War from the mentioned references in the books of Kings and Isaiah; and cf. 2 Chronicles 28) did not advance a reading similar to that of Alt, and those who follow his approach, of the key verse in 5:8, or of 5:10. The text as it stands does not lead to such a reading. Significantly, such proposals have been put forward only in relatively recent times, when a new set of critical assumptions was advanced. This new set focused on the goal of reconstructing the words of the historical prophet within his historical circumstances, rather than reading the book as it is, and often came along with a willingness to emend the text so as to allow coherence between the reconstructed words and the reconstructed historical setting of the prophet. Macintosh's final comments on Hos 5:10 are worth quoting in this regard, "Indeed it is unlikely that Hosea would condemn the social injustices of a neighboring state in the context of sayings concerning a political crisis" (*Hosea,* 203-4). Macintosh here focuses on the historical prophet Hosea — as he reconstructs him — rather than on the ancient readership's understanding of the literary character Hosea portrayed in the book of Hosea. This literary character certainly can, and in fact does, repeatedly refer to Judahite matters in the context of seemingly northern Israelite matters. Moreover, from the perspective of the literary character — and of the book as a whole, and of its implied author — the main focus of the text is not a political crisis, whose main characters or circumstances go, significantly, unmentioned in the text. But it is rather on matters of divine judgment, of construction of a sinful past, and the like. (For a critique of Alt's and similar proposals from a different perspective see Good, "Hosea 5:8–6:6," esp. 273-76; and for a brief but pointed critique of "historicist" approaches to this text, see Simian-Yofre, *Desierto,* 85.)

Of course, if one holds beforehand the following two assumptions: (a) the text here directly reflects the particular, oral speeches of the historical prophet Hosea who lived within the time-frame of Hos 1:1 (and in particular, its Judahite time-frame), and these speeches and their communicative message to the addressees can be fully reconstructed, and (b) these speeches were directly and unequivocally related to and addressed political circumstances in late monarchic Israel, then it follows, (c) there must be a sub-period within the mentioned time-frame that either suits well or at least is coherent with a particular reconstruction of each speech of the historical prophet and vice versa — that is, there must be a reconstruction of these historical speeches that suits the historical circumstances of their proclamation, as envisaged by the scholar. Given that there are only a limited number of political events during that period that are known and potentially relevant, the only question is which one would fit better a particular speech. Thus, for instance, Alt and others have suggested the events during and around the Syro-Ephraimite War for 5:8–6:6, and Pentiuc concludes that 6:7–7:2 "echoes Pekah's rebellion in 736 B.C., when supported by fifty Gileadites (2 Kgs 15:25), Pekah succeeded in overthrowing king Pekahiah" (see also his logic of selection of possible events that illustrate the point advanced here; see Pentiuc, *Long-Suffering Love,* 100-101). The intensity, the general claims about the meaning associated with these attempts, and the willingness to reconstruct an "original" speech — through textual emendation and redactional proposals — on the basis of the historical circumstances that the scholar associates with the reconstructed original speech are a relatively recent phenomenon. It is to be stressed, however, that attempts to tie some of the sayings in this reading to historical events are certainly *not* a recent phenomenon. For instance, Rashi associated the reference to "Ephraim went to Assyria" (Heb. וילך אפירם אל אשור) in 5:13 with king Hoshea (2 Kgs 17:3), but the contiguous verset וישלח אל מלך ירב (and "he sent [envoys] to the patron king"; on the meaning and connotation of the expression see below) as pointing to Ahaz's request of help from Assyria against Ephraim (2 Kgs 16:5-7). R. Qara agrees with Rashi concerning Ahaz, but associates "Ephraim went to Assyria" with king Menahem (2 Kgs 15:19-20). Radak agrees with Qara regarding "Ephraim went to Assyria" but also adds a comment that the case of Ahaz was similar. Of course, Rashi's exegesis does not rely on textual emendations, and is careful to be consistent with the narrative in 2 Kings 16, but it involves separating two closely related versets and assumes that the subject of the verb in "he sent . . ." is Judah rather than Ephraim, contrary to the explicit claim of the text. But the fact remains: the same book of Kings may be used to relate "Ephraim went to Assyria" to the reign of two different kings (Hosea and Menahem). This points only to the fact that the text here — and elsewhere in the book of Hosea — is written in a way that preempts its readers from making any categorical historical identification. By avoiding particular historical details, the text requires the intended and primary readerships to approach "Ephraim went to Assyria" as a generic, or better, generalized, example: the folly of asking for Assyrian help rather than YHWH's help (see below). (Of course, this example stands in turn for a more general category: the folly of asking help from mighty persons or polities rather from YHWH — see below.) For these purposes, the identity of the Israelite king who asked for Assyrian help is not only absolutely irrelevant, but also even distracting.

This generalizing principle still must take into account the general construction of the period within the discourse/s of the readership. It bears note, however, that the authorship and ancient readerships of the book of Hosea are not dependent on the historical events *per se* — or better, the most likely reconstruction of these events that contemporary historians are able to develop. For instance, Aram, the main regional power allied with Israel (in fact, Pekah was more likely a subordinate of the Aramean king) and confronting Assyria at the time, is not mentioned in the text. Its absence, however, is easily explained. The book of Hosea seems to be written in a way that is informed by the very *general* construction of the pre-late monarchic period shared by the literati among whom one is to find the authorship and readership of the book. The book of Hosea as a whole (7:11; 9:3; 11:5, 11; 12:2) reflects (and construes) a general world of memory in which there were two main powers in the region: a northern power and a southern one, which in the pre-late monarchic period (see Hos 1:1; cf. Isa 1:1 and Mic 1:1) were Assyria and Egypt, respectively — Aram is not construed as playing the role of the main alternative power to Assyria in the books of Micah and Isaiah, nor in the book of Hosea. (In the late monarchic books, Babylon takes the place of Assyria, as was the case historically.)

At the same time, it bears note that Hos 1:1 asks the readers to approach the text not only from that perspective, but also from a northern Israelite one in which the world portrayed in the book is assigned to the days of Jeroboam II. From this perspective, the reported godly words of which the book consists were communicated at that time, no matter when the book of Hosea was composed. If the intended and primary readership of the book associated the time of Jeroboam with stability and prosperity, then they were asked to understand the reported godly words as pointing to an end of this stability and prosperity at their own height.

An excellent example of recent scholarship that rests on the presuppositions that (a) the text here directly reflects the particular speeches of the historical prophet Hosea and (b) these speeches were directly and unequivocally related to and addressed political circumstances in late monarchic Israel can be found in Arnold, "Hosea and the Sin of Gibeah." Arnold suggests, for instance, that an original text read "officers of Israel" rather than "officers of Judah," and thus interprets the verse as an indictment of "the approaching Syro-Ephraimite invasion" of Judah (458-59). Not only does his interpretation suffer from the problems mentioned above, but it requires a textual reconstruction that is not a necessity of the text but rather of Arnold's assumptions. For the same reasons he suggests, albeit cautiously, that the passage "because he [Ephraim] was determined to go after dung" in 5:11 may be a reference to Pekah's alliance with Rezin of Aram (459). He thus proposes to insert into the text that which the text does not state, namely, a reference to Aram — ct. with the explicit textual references to Assyria and Egypt in the same text. In any case, Arnold, and others before him, is not reading the present book of Hosea, but reconstructing and analyzing a hypothetical prophetic indictment advanced by a historical prophet, as opposed to a literary character within the world of the book. To be fair to Arnold, he is certainly not alone, but he exemplifies well a methodological issue. Wolff (*Hosea,* 144) and Thompson (*Situation and Theology,* 67), among others, also consider "to go after dung" a reference to Ephraim's alliance with Rezin, and the latter as the referent of the term "dung" — or "what is worthless" as they translate the Hebrew צו. The identification of "dung" with Rezin does not arise from the text at all, but results from an assumption held beforehand that it *must* refer to the Syro-Ephraimite War.

Resuming the analysis of the intellectual setting of the primary readership of the book, the image of the king of Assyria is for them not only a distant memory, but also a paradigmatic figure. The king of Assyria is referred to as מלך ירב in 5:13 — the same expression is used in Hos 10:6; there is no substantial reason to assume that it is a result of textual corruption as the NRSV and NJB, among others, seem to assume. Particularly in the light of Isa 51:22, this expression should probably be translated "a king who champions" or "who may contend for you," or perhaps in better English, "a protecting king" or "a patron king" (NJPSV). (On these matters, see Ginsberg, "Hosea," 1017; Good, "Hosea 5:8–6:6," 278; and above all, Barthélemy, *Critique Textuelle,* vol. III, 524-26). Of course, Israel's decision to accept the Assyrian king as a protecting or patron king is absolute folly from the viewpoint of the discourse of the literati within whom and for whom the book of Hosea was written. From their perspective, Israel's patron king, the only one able to protect and heal Israel, is YHWH. The contrast between YHWH and the Assyrian king is explicitly conveyed by the double use of verbal forms from רפא "heal" in 5:13; 6:1; and 7:1. The Assyrian king cannot "heal," but when Israel shows wisdom (6:1), it recognizes that YHWH is the only one who can heal (cf. Hos 11:2-3), as well as punish those who accepted other kings over YHWH. Hosea 7:1 reaffirms the basic characterization of YHWH as Israel's healer. In other words, YHWH is the only champion of Israel (cf. Isa 51:22). No human king, not even the most powerful, can fulfill that role. This theme is explicitly brought back to the attention of the readers of the book in Hos 14:4-5; moreover, the explicit reference to YHWH's healing (רפא) serves as a signpost that reminds the readers that this reading and the one in chapter 14 inform each other. (On the construction of YHWH as the only healer, cf. these texts particularly with Deut 32:39, which reflects the same theological approach. For a study on the "healing metaphor" in the book of Hosea see Oestreich, *Metaphors,* 57-87; cf. Nwaoru, *Imagery,* 155-59.)

The motif of Assyria — or Egypt, and if the text is set in a later period, Babylon — or their kings vs. YHWH is common in prophetic literature (e.g., Isa 30:1-5; 31:1-3; 36:13-20; Ezekiel 31; Hos 14:4). This motif leads in Hosea, in other prophetic books (e.g., Isaiah), and in biblical historiographical works, including Kings and Chronicles, to the ideological construction of voluntary servitude to foreign powers as categorically sinful and to a portrayal of the past that is informed by this belief. (The motif is explicit in Chronicles and Isaiah; for its presence in Kings see Na'aman, "Deuteronomist"; for prophetic books that do not follow this approach, see, for instance, the book of Jeremiah.) The motif itself may be seen as a variation of the typical ancient Near Eastern motif of the enemy who trusts in earthly kings or his own power as opposed to the pious king who places his trust in his gods (cf. Liverani, "KITRU, KATARU," and cf. Hos 10:13-14 and, among others, Deut 28:52; Jer 5:17). Of course, in this variation, (a) the image of the king as trusting in earthly powers is supplanted with that of Israel as a people, and (b) the rhetorical contrastive comparison of YHWH with foreign kings as competitors for Israel's attention raises a mocking characterization of them as false gods but, above all, of Israel and its reported foolishness. Point (a) is particularly important since it is very influential in the discourses of the postmonarchic literati. It is reflected, for instance, in the motif of YHWH making a covenant with all Israel rather than with a king or kingly figure, and above all it is part of an ideological worldview that undermines the usual heavenly king–earthly king–people hierachical organization, by removing the necessity of the earthly king, because of a shift of ideological slots associated with the earthly king in part to Israel (see above) and in part to YHWH (see Deut. 13 and cf. P. E. Dion, "Deuteronomy 13:2: The Suppression"). If this general worldview is present also among the intended readers and rereaders of the book of Hosea, as is likely the case, then it sheds light on the way in which they imagined the Davidic king of chapter 3. See also Hos 2:3-25 Setting.

Hosea 6:1-7 makes an important contribution to the understanding of the horizon of thought of the literati among whom one is to find the social setting for the composition and the readings of the text for which it was composed. On the one hand, 6:1-3 represents what postmonarchic Israel should think and do. As an interlude, it provides an important teaching to the community. Nothing in the text per se suggests that Israel is insincere in 6:1-3. Yet within the literary context 6:1-3, in a seemingly unexpected manner, leads to YHWH's negative response in 6:4-7.

To be sure, if the postmonarchic readers of the book approached 6:1-3 as the words of monarchic Ephraim and Judah (see 6:4), they already know that YHWH did not accept them or, at least, not in any manner that would produce significant lasting effects. They knew all too well that the monarchic polities were destroyed. From this perspective, one may conclude that YHWH's response was anticipated by their world of historical knowledge. Even if this explanation is accepted, this does not mean that YHWH's rejection of monarchic Israel's attempt to turn back to YHWH carries no theological message. Moreover, the text in 6:1-3 is carefully crafted in such a way that the intended and primary readerships can see it as a model for what they and trans-temporal Israel are supposed to think and do. The emphatic first person in 6:1-3 and the second person in 6:4-6 reinforces this trans-temporal message as the target readership identifies with the characters in the book (cf. the significant shift to the second person in 5:13b as the text reads "but he is not able to cure *you* or heal *your* wound," which is meant to enhance the affective appeal of the text from the perspective of its readership). This being so, what is the central message and which intellectual setting does the report of YHWH's rejection of a sincere attempt of Israel to return to YHWH reflect?

Hosea 6:4 opens YHWH's verbal response to such an attempt. Within this context, the text connotes an image of YHWH as a father who laments his inability to help wayward sons (Ephraim and Judah). YHWH, the father, asks himself "what can I do for you?" or, and probably a better translation of the question, "what can I do about you?" (cf. Gen 31:43; 1 Sam 10:2; and metaphorically, Exod 17:4), although it also carries the ominous meaning of "what will I do to you?" (cf. Exod 33:5). The implied answer in this context seems to be "nothing." YHWH explains that this is the case, not because Israel is insincere in 6:1-3 (ct. Jer 3:10), but because its return to YHWH is ephemeral. The claim for the transient character of Israel's response is repeated, though in different ways, in 6:6, in which YHWH expresses an unfulfilled wish for Israel's *hesed* and for their knowledge/acknowledgement of their relation with YHWH (see above), both of which imply permanence. (On 6:5, see below.) But why is Israel's response ephemeral within this theological discourse? The reference to Adam/human beings in 6:7 explains this in terms of a human condition. I maintained elsewhere that the Israelite/Yehudite literati — and probably larger sectors in their community — behaved as if they had held an implied concept of social entropy, and as if it played a central role in their worldviews. In other words, they assumed that spontaneous interactions among humans lead to increased social entropy or disorder in human society. The latter was understood as parting ways from YHWH and from the society and social behavior that YHWH wishes and commands for humanity (Ben Zvi, "Analogical Thinking and Ancient Israelite Intellectual History"). Clearly the reference to the human condition in Hos 6:7 is consistent with this pervading concept, but it also raises the question of whether YHWH will ever be able to do anything for Israel, since the latter consists of humans who sooner or later will reject YHWH and this deity's ways, and therefore is not capable of *hesed*/loyalty and consequentially will eventually abrogate its relation with the deity even if it keeps carrying sacrifices (6:6). Other sections in the book of Hosea suggest a positive and hopeful answer to this question (see Hos 2:20-25; 3:5; 10:12; see also Hos 10:1-15 Setting). This answer, however, involves a dramatic change in the nature of Israel and of the existing world, which will be replaced with an ideal or messianic one. Significantly, similar matters are expressed in Psalm 78 (see esp. 78:34-72, and for the "messianic" solution there, cf. Hosea 3:5). It bears note, however, that within this type of discourse, the expectation for a positive solution in the ideal future of the readership does not detract from that which, from their perspective, is an already fulfilled, severe, divine punishment for sinful Israel. (Of course, such a punishment is in the future of the world portrayed in the book.) Significantly, the tendency is to stress the harshness of the punishment; see 6:5. (On its characterization of the prophets, see below.)

It is worth noting also that when 6:7 is read in relation to the preceding text, "there" seems to point, implicitly, at the lands of Judah and Ephraim (v. 4). Accordingly, it seems to create a mental association between these lands and the mythological Garden of Eden. This association may well be part of the intellectual setting within which the book and for which the book was composed. The ideological elevation of the land was already perceived in the basic metaphor of Israel/the land as YHWH's spouse and is consistent with language and imagery about Zion, Jerusalem, and the land in other pieces of prophetic literature (e.g., Mic 4.1-5//Isa. 2.2-5; Ezekiel 40–48; Zechariah 14, and see the expression אדמת הקדש "holy land" in Zech 2:16).

Hosea 6:5 provides an interesting window on one of the constructions of the prophets of old among the literati within whom and for whom the book of Hosea was written (cf. and ct. Hos 12:11). On one level it is consistent with some of the ways in which prophets of old were imagined in the postmonarchic period (see Ben Zvi, "'The Prophets' — References to Generic Prophets and Their Role in the Construction of the Image of the 'Prophets of Old' within the Postmonarchic Readership of the Book of Kings"). At another level, it is worth noting that according to Hos 6:5, YHWH associates "the prophets" not only with "the words of YHWH's mouth," as expected, but also and unequivocally with death for monarchic Israel. In fact, YHWH reportedly describes both the words and the prophets as the deity's instruments to kill and hack to pieces monarchic Israel. As is well known, the prophetic books were associated with restoration and hope (cf. Sir 49:10) mainly because the prophetic characters with whom these books are associated were imagined as those who proclaimed and explained a doom that already happened and an ideal future still to come, which was a source of hope for them. Within the horizon of thought reflected in Hos 6:5, proclamations of doom are crucial active agents. Once they are uttered, that is, created by an act of speech, they become effective entities whose role is to fulfill the semantic content of that which was uttered (cf. Isa 55:10-11; Malul, *Knowledge,* 122-23; 421-22; Rofé, *Prophetical Stories,* 169-70). From the perspective of a readership that understands the divine judgment announced in the world of the book as already fulfilled, the effectiveness of YHWH's words can only be a measure of hope, for it means that YHWH's words of hope have already been created and are working their inexorable way towards fulfillment. As such, they provide hope and certainty to the readers.

The repertoire of metaphors and images of the authorship and readership activated in this reading is consistent with those informing other biblical books, but in particular Psalms (e.g., see Hos 5:14 and cf. Ps 50:22; and see Buss, *Prophetic Word,* 84-86). It is even possible that the deeds associated with the cities in Hos 6:8-9 might have evoked, in part, images reminiscent of those of the typical "evildoer" in Psalms; cf. Kruger, "The Evildoer." This situation is to be expected, not only because of the existence of a widespread, general ancient Near Eastern set of metaphors, but also because of the very restricted number of bearers of high literacy in Jerusalem that did not allow for the creation of separate, self-sustaining socio-cultural groups.

Finally, it bears stressing that the writers, readers, and rereaders of this didactic, prophetic READING imagined YHWH in many different ways. Along with images of YHWH as rain and as the one who refreshes the earth and makes it fertile (i.e., "baalistic" images; cf. Lemche, "God of Hosea,") and as a healer of Israel (cf. Exod 15:26; Isa 57:18-19; Jer 33:6; Hos 11:3; and see also Isa 19:22; Ps 30:3), YHWH is thought of as (a force for) discipline, on a connoted level as physical fetters. YHWH is imagined as a lion that tears a prey, but also as maggots and rottenness — in fact, according to the text it is YHWH who imagines himself in such ways. This vast range of metaphors shows that each cultural setting may develop different metaphors about the deity and a different sensitivity for that which is permitted in that regard in a particular society. Moreover, the existence of a vast range of metaphors within literati who seemed to have accepted the command not to create a (plastic) image of YHWH bears notice. (On the motif of knowing YHWH in Hos 5:4 and 6:3, cf. Hos 2:22 and see Setting there.)

Intention

The general intention of Hosea 5:1–7:2 is to communicate and reinforce the positions and the general horizon of thought of the authorship and readership as represented in these texts (see Setting) and to socialize the literati through their shared reading of the material and the larger society through the literati's reading to others of this reading. Such an activity informs the readers (or listeners if read to) of Israel's monarchic past, of its shortcomings, of the shortcomings of its leadership, worship, and the like, while at the same time it encourages their identification with that sinful Israel, as part and parcel of transtemporal Israel. As such it serves as a lesson to the readership about themselves. At the same time, within the context of the book of Hosea as a whole, from which it is inseparable (see multiple connections, STRUCTURE), it provides hope.

Bibliography

A. Alt, "Hosea 5,8–6,6: Ein Krieg and seine Folgen im prophetischer Beleuchtung," *Kleinen Schriften zur Geschichte Israels* (München: Chr. Beck, 1953) 163-87; idem, "Micha 2,1-5. *Ges Anadasmos* in Judah," *NTT* 56 (1955) 13-23; P. M. Arnold, "Hosea and the Sin of Gibeah," *CBQ* 51 (1989) 447-60; M. L. Barré, "New Light on the Interpretation of Hosea 6:2," *VT* 28 (1978) 129-41, idem, "Bulluṭsa-rabi's Hymn to Gula and Hosea 6:1-2," *Or* 50 (1981) 241-45; J. Day, "Pre-Deuteronomic Allusions to the Covenant in Hosea and Psalm LXXVIII," *VT* 36 (1986) 1-12; M. DeRoche, "The Reversal of

HOSEA

Creation in Hosea," *VT* 31 (1981) 400-409; P. E. Dion, "Deuteronomy 13: The Suppression of Alien Religious Propaganda in Israel during the Late Monarchical Era," B. Halpern and D. W. Hobson (eds.), *Law and Ideology in Monarchic Israel* (JSOTSupS 124; Sheffield: Sheffield Academic Press, 1991) 147-216; D. Edelman, "Did Saulide-Davidic Rivalry Resurface in Early Persian Yehud," J. A. Dearman and M. P. Graham (eds.), *"The Land I Will Show You": Essays on the History and Archaeology of the Ancient Near East in Honor of J. Maxwell Miller* (JSOTSupS 343; Sheffield: Sheffield Academic Press, 2001) 69-91; J. A. Emerton, "Some Difficult Words in Isaiah 28.10 and 13," A. Rapoport-Albert and G. Greenberg (eds.), *Biblical Hebrew, Biblical Texts. Essays in Memory of Michael P. Weitzman* (JSOTSupS 333; Sheffield: Sheffield Academic Press, 2001) 39-56; P. N. Franklyn, "Oracular Cursing in Hosea 13," *HAR* 11 (1987) 69-80; E. Gerstenberger, *Psalms, Part 2, and Lamentations* (FOTL 15; Grand Rapids, MI: Eerdmans, 2001); H. L. Ginsberg, "Lexicographical Notes," *Hebräische Wortforschung. Festschrift zum 80. Geburtstag von Walter Baumgartner* (VTS 16; Leiden: E. J. Brill, 1967) 71-82; E. M. Good, "Hosea 5:8–6:6: An Alternative to Alt," *JBL* 85 (1966) 273-86; idem, "The Composition of Hosea," *SEÅ* 31 (1966) 21-63; S. Grätz, "Die Vergebliche Suche nach Gott. Traditions- und kompositionsgeschichtliche Überlegungen zu Herkunft und Funktion der Strafvorstellungen in Hos iv 1–vi 6," *VT* 50 (2000) 200-217; A. V. Hunter, *Seek the Lord* (Baltimore: St. Mary's Seminary and University, 1982); P. A. Kruger, "The Evildoer in Hosea 6:8-9," *JNSL* 17 (1991) 17-22; C. J. Labuschagne, "The Similes in the Book of Hosea," *OTWSA* 7-8 (1965) 64-76; N. P. Lemche, "The God of Hosea," E. C. Ulrich et al. (eds.), *Priests, Prophets and Scribes: Essays in the Formation and Heritage of Second Temple Judaism in Honour of Joseph Blenkinsopp* (JSOTSupS 149; Sheffield: Sheffield Academic Press, 1992) 241-57; idem, "Kings and Clients: On Loyalty Between the Ruler and the Ruled in Ancient 'Israel'," *Semeia* 66 (1995) 119-32; B. A. Levine, "An Essay on Prophetic Attitudes Toward Temple and Cult in Biblical Israel," M. Z. Brettler and M. Fishbane, *Minhah le-Nahum* (JSOTSupS 154; Sheffield: Sheffield Academic Press, 1993) 202-25; M. C. Lind, "Hosea 5:8–6:6," *Int* 38 (1984) 398-403; O. Lipschits, "The History of the Benjamin Region Under Babylonian Rule," *TA* 26 (1999) 155-90; M. Liverani, "KITRU, KATARU," *Mesopotamia* 17 (1982) 43-66; A. A. Macintosh, "Hosea and the Wisdom Tradition: Dependence and Independence," J. Day, R. P. Gordon, and H. G. M. Williamson (eds.), *Wisdom in Ancient Israel. Essays in Honor of J. A. Emerton* (Cambridge: Cambridge Univ. Press, 1995) 124-32; B. J. Malina, "Patron and Client. The Analogy Behind Synoptic Theology," *Forum* 4 (1988) 2-32; M. Malul, *Knowledge, Control and Sex. Studies in Biblical Thought, Culture and Worldview* (Tel Aviv-Jaffa: Archaeological Center Publication, 2002); Y. Mazor, "Hosea 5:1-3: Between Compositional Rhetoric and Rhetorical Composition," *JSOT* 45 (1989) 115-26; S. L. McKenzie, "Mizpah of Benjamin and the Date of the Deuteronomistic History," K. D. Schunck and M. Augustin (eds.), *"Lasset uns Brücken bauen." Collected Communications to the XVth Congress of the International Organization for the Study of the Old Testament, Cambridge* (BEATJ 42; Frankfurt am Main: Lang, 1998) 149-55; N. Na'aman, "The Deuteronomist and Voluntary Servitude to Foreign Powers," *JSOT* 65 (1995) 37-53; M. S. Odell, "Who Were the Prophets in Hosea?" *HBT* 18 (1996) 78-95; idem, "The Prophets and the End of Hosea," P. House and J. W. Watts (eds.), *Forming Prophetic Literature: Essays on Isaiah and the Twelve in Honor of John D. W. Watts* (JSOTSupS 235; Sheffield: JSOT Press, 1996) 158-70; D. F. O'Kennedy, "Healing as/or Forgiveness? The Use of the term רפא in the

148

Book of Hosea," *OTE* 14 (2001) 458-74; S. M. Paul, "שרים מלך משא Hosea 8:8-10 and Ancient Near Eastern Royal Epithets," *Scripta Hierosolymitana* 31 (1986) 193-204; L. Perlitt, *Bundestheologie im Alten Testament* (WMANT 36; Neukirchen-Vluyn: Neukirchener Verlag, 1969); E. J. Revell, *The Designation of the Individual. Expressive Usages in Biblical Narrative* (CBET 14; Kampen: Kok Pharos, 1996); A. Rofé, *The Prophetical Stories. The Narratives about the Prophets in the Hebrew Bible. Their Literary Types and History* (Jerusalem: Magnes Press, 1988); W. M. W. Roth, "The Numerical Sequence x/x+1 in the Old Testament," *VT* 12 (1962) 300-311; A. Szabó, "Textual Problems in Amos and Hosea," *VT* 25 (1975) 500-524; H. Tadmor, "The Historical Background of Hosea's Prophecies," M. Haran (ed.), *Yehezkel Kaufman Jubilee Volume* (Jerusalem: Magnes Press, 1960) 84-88; M. E. W. Thompson, *Situation and Theology. Old Testament Interpretations of the Syro-Ephraimite War* (Prophets and Historians 1; Sheffield: Almond Press, 1982); J. Unterman, "Repentance and Redemption in Hosea," *SBLSP* 21 (1982) 541-50; H. Utzschneider, "Situation und Szene. Überlegungen zum Verhältnis historischer und literarischer Deutung prophetischer Texte am Beispiel von Hos 5,8–6,6," *ZAW* 114 (2002) 80-105; M. Weinfeld, "Ancient Near Eastern Patterns in Prophetic Literature," *VT* 27 (1977) 178-95; E. R. Wendland, *The Discourse Analysis of Hebrew Prophetic Literature* (Lewiston, NY: E. Mellen Press, 1995); J. Wijngaards, "Death and Resurrection in Covenantal Context (Hos. VI 2)," *VT* 17 (1967) 226-39; J. R. Zorn, "Estimating the Population Size of Ancient Settlements: Methods, Problems, Solutions and a Case Study," *BASOR* 295 (1994) 31-48.

Third Didactic Prophetic Reading:
Wrongful Leadership Leads to Disaster, 7:3-16

Structure

This is one among several possible proposals for the structure of Hosea 7:3-16. Some scholars have associated 7:3-16 with sections of the preceding reading (see STRUCTURE Hos 5:1–7:2). In addition, questions concerning the hierarchical level within the structure mentioned above may be raised. For instance, the two units in vv. 8-12 may be considered to be separate sections within this reading, in which case the interpretative note in v. 10 would become the center of a set of four sections. Conversely, I, II, III can be read as constituting a single section, in which case vv. 3-12 would be seen as preparing the ground for the "Woe to" section (vv. 13-16). All these proposals are not really alternative, but complementary, and each highlights certain aspects of the structure of this literary unit. All are mindful of textually inscribed markers, and are consistent with the world of ideas of the primary readership of the book of Hosea.

Textually inscribed markers include the fact that verses 3-4aα, 8, and 11 serve as introductions to their structural units as well as bridges connecting them to those that precede them in the text. Bridges, however, not only link places but also call attention to the gap between them. These units link to the previous ones but also alert the reader to some new elements, to a shift towards something different.

The "their" in 7:3 points back to similar references in 7:2 and eventually to Israel. In addition, the salient repetition of רעתם "their wickedness" creates a sense of textual coherence between verses 7:2 and 7:3 (and cf. רעות שמרון "the wicked deeds of Samaria" in 7:1). Thus the text allows the intended and primary readers to "slide" as it were from one reading into the other, or, better, to read 7:3-4a as both part of the preceding reading and the initial section of another. Support for multiple and partial readings that inform each other and contribute to a carefully interwoven tapestry of meanings is expected in a sophisticated written work to be read, reread, and studied.

When 7:3-4aα is approached from the perspective of the preceding texts, the influence of Hos 4:2 becomes clear. The latter includes the triad of "murder, stealing, and committing adultery" — see Hos 6:9; 7:1 and 7:4. The term כחש "lying" appears in 7:3, and it is possible to approach the אלה "swearing" of 4:2 in terms of swearing a covenant — see 6:7 (cf. Hos 10:4). Perhaps more importantly, when the text is read from that perspective, the readers are faced with YHWH's conclusion: "all of them [i.e., all the members of the establishment elites mentioned since 5:1, and in fact, all the people] commit adultery" (7:4aα; cf. Jer 9:1-2). Adultery becomes the general metaphor for all improper activity in which people are involved. It expresses or reflects an abrogation or lack of acknowledgement of their obligations to their superordinate partner (e.g., husband, proper king, and, above all, YHWH). Significantly, this understanding of adultery serves also as an introduction for the main theme of 7:3-16 as a whole. The text begins with the lack of loyalty towards superordinate leaders in the worldly realm and interweaves it with a lack of loyalty to the ultimate superordinate of Israel, YHWH, their king, husband, and redeemer. (On "redeemer" see explicitly 7:13 — cf. Hos 13:14, in which YHWH certainly can redeem, but refuses to do so. On the general issue of the interwoven lack of loyalties see below and

Setting, and cf. the similar but less developed motif in Hos 4:4, where people are condemned for contending with the priest, that is, for not acknowledging his proper role in society.) The reference to adultery and its obvious sexual connotations closely associates the text with preceding readings in the book of Hosea (e.g., Hosea 1–3, and 4) and vice versa.

Hos 7:3-4b introduces this READING (Hos 7:3-16; see above) and also, in particular, 7:3-7 (that is, the first section of this READING). The latter also begins with a lack of loyalty in the worldly realm and concludes with lack of loyalty to YHWH. See the emphatic concluding note of this unit, אֵין קֹרֵא בָהֶם אֵלָי "none of them calls to me [YHWH]" in 7:7bβ.

Hos 7:3-4b also introduces the intended and primary readers to the portrayal of the relations between king and officers in late monarchic Israel, and prepares them for the oven metaphor. One may easily notice the linking occurrence of the term "king" in 7:3, 5, 7 and of "officers" in 7:3, 5, and the pun on sounds (and words) between מְנָאֲפִים "they commit adultery" and מֵאֹפֶה "by a baker" or "without a baker." Further, the term מְנָאֲפִים was likely to have evoked a pun on the root אנף "to be angry," along with its common associations with heat and fire (e.g., Num 11:1; Deut 32:22; Isa 30:27; Jer 15:14; Zeph 3:8; Ps 2:12; 79:5; Lam 4:11), which directly relate to the metaphor of the blazing oven.

The multiple functions that the term מְנָאֲפִים "they commit adultery" plays in this READING point at both the craftsmanship of the implied author of the text and the expected sophistication of the intended readership of the present book of Hosea. For text-critical proposals that would remove the term מְנָאֲפִים from a forerunner of the present book of Hosea, see, for instance, Paul, "Image of the Oven," 115. Paul advances a reconstruction of a text prior to Hos 7:4-10 in its present form. See also Szabó, "Textual Problems," 513.

The reference to the "cake" in 7:8 creates a thematic bridge with the image of the baker and the oven in 7:3-7. Moreover, Hosea 7:8 opens with אֶפְרַיִם בָּעַמִּים הוּא יִתְבּוֹלָל "Ephraim! he shall be mingled with the nations," which may carry a connotation of "Ephraim! he shall be kneaded among the nations" (cf. Paul, "Image of the Oven"; but ct. Macintosh, *Hosea,* 267-68 and bibliography). Macintosh translates the expression "through the nations Ephraim is vitiated." According to Paul, "Image of the Oven," Andersen and Freedman, *Hosea,* 467, and see NJPSV, the culinary metaphor continues in v. 9. According to them the relevant expression does not mean "gray hairs are sprinkled upon him" (NRSV) but "mold is scattered over him/it," meaning "the cake/Ephraim grew moldy." (On 7:9 see also Yoo, *Israelian Hebrew,* 167-68 and bibliography there.)

Verses 11 and 13aα also contain textually inscribed bridges to the respective literary units they follow. In v. 11, the verbal form וַיְהִי (usually not translated in this case) and the reference to Ephraim fulfill this role; in v. 13aα לָהֶם "to them" implies the presence of the preceding text; and "me" (YHWH) tells the readers that there is certainly no change of speaker between vv. 12 and 13. In addition, the term נָדְדוּ "they have fled" plays on the bird/dove metaphor of vv. 11-12 (cf. Isa 10:14; 16:2; Jer 4:25; Prov 27:8). It bears notice that from the perspective of the rereaders of the book, the occurrence of נָדְדוּ here may have reminded them of the text in Hos 9:17, in which exile is mentioned, and vice versa.

Markers of textual coherence are also present within the units at different levels. They may involve thematic motifs such as the interweaving of the images of the baker/oven and those of the interactions in the monarchic elite (7:3-7), the cake motif (7:8 or 7:8-9?), the dove/bird-net motif (7:11-12), and the emphatic repetition of the name Ephraim in 7:8-11. One may notice also the pun between אפרים "Ephraim," אפרוש "spread" and שמים "skies" both in v. 12 and the refrain "but he did not know" in 7:9 that links two versets within the same verse.

An interesting case in 7:14-15 entails a phonetic pun that involves two different Hebrew roots but still conveys an emphatic sense of failed reciprocity that evokes the one in the previous subunit within the "Woe to" section. Verse 14 concludes with יסורו בי "they have rebelled against me [YHWH]" (Heb. root סור), and v. 15 begins with ואני יסרתי "I [YHWH] trained (/disciplined) . . . [their arms, i.e., them] (Heb. root יסר)." The pun is clear. It points to the stark dissonance between YHWH's (previous) treatment of Israel and Israel's response, a theme that comes explicitly to the forefront in 7:13b and 7:15 (cf. Isa 1:2; Hos 2:10).

Verses 14-15 are, in addition, linked through an envelope created by the repetition of אלי "to me [YHWH]" that encapsulates the response of the people to YHWH, namely "they did not cry out אלי [to me] (7:14a) . . . but אלי [against me] they plot evil" (7:15b; cf. Mic 2:1). The text within the envelope elaborates and further contrasts the people's actions and YHWH's support of them. It is worth noting that the language that opens 7:14-15, namely, לא זעקו אלי "they do not cry to me [YHWH]" not only serves to communicate this envelope, but also serves to link this text with 8:2, which opens with לי יזעקו "to me [YHWH] they cry out." Whereas 7:14 asks the intended readership to imagine Israel as not willing to cry out — that is, to repent sincerely to YHWH (on 7:14 see below), its counterpart in 8:2 asks them to imagine Israel as crying out to YHWH but showing no repentance whatsoever, as shown by their claim that they know YHWH (cf. Hos 5:4; 6:3). Israel's words in 8:2 stand in sharp contrast with the divine (and therefore authoritative, from the perspective of the intended and primary readership) evaluation of Israel. According to Hos 8:1-3, YHWH states explicitly "they [Israel] have transgressed my covenant . . . against my teaching they have rebelled. . . . Israel has spurned the good." In other words, ancient rereaders who approached 7:14 in a way informed by 8:2 and vice versa, because they followed textually inscribed markers, were likely to relate the two in terms of a relatively common figure of speech, namely, Israel did not cry to YHWH to express its repentance; and when Israel cried to YHWH, it expressed no repentance (cf. "for there is no food and no water, and we detest this miserable food" in Num 21:5; cf. O'Connor, "Pseudosorites"). This figure of speech serves here to emphasize the lack of true repentance (and in Num 21:5, the speakers' absolute disgust with the food they were provided). A closely related variant of this figure of speech appears in Hos 8:7, and see also Hos 9:11-12. As for the matter of "knowing YHWH," the message of the book of Hosea is that eventually Israel will truly know YHWH, but for that they have to wait till the messianic, ideal future described in Hos 2:22. At that time, they will recognize and accept YHWH as their patron/husband, and be fully and permanently devoted to YHWH.

The discussion above points at one of several instances of language and motifs that link some aspects of this reading to others in the book. As mentioned before, it seems that the text of Hos 4:2 illuminates this and the preceding READING in the book. (For the triad of "murder, stealing, and committing adultery," see Hos 6:9; 7:1 and 7:4.) The term כחש "lying" appears in Hos 7:3, and it is possible to approach the אלה "swearing" of Hos 4:2 in terms of swearing a covenant; see Hos 6:7 (cf. Hos 10:4). One may notice also the reference to the shedding of blood in Hos 6:8 (cf. Hos 4:2a). In other words, the text of Hos 5:1–7:4aα may have conveyed to its intended readership a sense of implementation and illustration of the more generic words in Hos 4:2. Additional markers of textual coherence in Hos 7:2-4 are present. The most obvious of them is the pronominal reference to "their" at the very beginning of the new reading (7:3) that points back to similar references in Hos 7:2 and eventually to Israel. Notice also the repetition of רעתם "their wickedness" in Hos 7:2, 3 (and cf. רעות שמרון "the wicked deeds of Samaria" in 7:1).

The presence of אכל "consume" in 7:7 is related to its occurrence in 7:9, and the two together convey a clear meaning, namely, "the inner group consumes its leaders — foreigners consume their strength" (cf. the latter expression with Prov 5:10). In addition, the references to foreigners' consumption in 7:9 link the text here to 8:7 (and cf. Isa 1:7; 61:5; and Lev 26:16). The ancient readers who approached 7:7 in a way informed by 8:7 and vice versa, because they followed textually inscribed markers, were likely to recognize a rhetorical shift widely attested elsewhere in the book of Hosea (see Hosea 1–3) between "people" and "land," as the text moves back and forth — from the perspective of rereaders of the book — from the strength of the people that is consumed (Heb. אכל) by the foreigners (7:7) to the "strength/yield of the land" (cf. Job 31:39) that is consumed (Heb. בלע) by the foreigners in 8:7. For the word pair אכל and בלע see also Num 16:34-35; Jer 51:34; Ps 21:10. In the present case the word pair is divided into two related READINGS within a single book.

One may also compare 7:9-10 and the combination of motifs and word choices that appear there and in 5:7-9. In particular there are the expression ענה גאון ישראל בפניו "the pride of Israel testifies against its face" in 5:5 and 7:10 (and nowhere else in the HB), and the motif of seeking YHWH (Heb. בקש in 5:6).

From the perspective of the ancient readers of the book, the references to a king of northern Israel in 7:3 and 5 likely evoked those in Hos 10:3, 7, but above all that in Hos 8:4. ברעתם ישמחו מלך in 7:3 likely conveyed to these readers something akin to "in their wickedness they promote the rise of a king" (as translated by Macintosh, *Hosea*, 255) or "in their evil they elevate kings" (Greenfield, "Lexicographic Notes," 148-49; cf. Ibn Ezra; "The Accepted Commentary"; Simon, *Abraham Ibn Ezra*, 78; Wellhausen, *Skizzen*, 115, proposed a similar meaning, but he assumed that the original text read ימשחו instead of ישמחו); cf. Hos 8:4, "They made kings, but not through me [YHWH]" (NRSV). The usual translation of ברעתם ישמחו מלך in 7:3, namely, "by their wickedness they make the king glad" (NRSV) or "in malice they make a king merry" (NJPSV), represents a secondary meaning that is linked to the theme of the motif of the drinking feast (Hos 7:5). This seems to be another case of inter-connected multiple levels of meanings.

From the perspective of intended and primary readers of the entire book, the references to "grain and new wine" in 7:14 likely informed and were informed by those in 2:10-11, 24; and within the context of evil deeds, they were associated with much drinking (see 7:5) and the general theme of adultery (see 7:4) — cf. Hos 4:11; 9:1-2 and their central messages. The presence of שד "destruction" or "violence" and כזב "falsehood" in 7:13a and 13b, respectively, at the beginning of the "Woe to" section, was likely to evoke כזב ושד "falsehood and violence" in 12:2, which in turn is thematically related to 7:11 — see the central references to foolish alliances with Assyria or Egypt. Significantly, the pair שד and כזב is very uncommon; in fact, it appears only in these two texts within the HB (e.g., Hos 7:13 and 12:2).

The observations made above, and similar observations in discussions of structure throughout this commentary, unequivocally point at the interrelated character of the literary units discussed here. They are written READINGS within a book. As their language clearly indicates, they do not stand alone, separate from the other units in the book, nor do they exist outside the book of Hosea.

To be sure, common word pairs also play a significant role in the shaping of meanings and textual cohesion within the sections that comprise this reading. One may mention, for instance, bow and sword in 7:16 (cf. Gen 48:22; Josh 24:12; Ps 7:13; 37:14, 15; etc.); שוב "return" and בקש "seek" in 7:10 (and cf. Hos 3:5; 5:15; 2 Chr 7:14); and king and officers (Heb. שרים) in 7:3, 5. The reference to the officers at the beginning of the reading creates an envelope with that to them at its end (7:16). An important thematic trajectory within this reading is encapsulated in the relation between first and last references to שרים: from the officers' wicked deeds (7:3) to their future demise by the sword (7:16). In addition, the prominent role in this reading of officers and kings and in particular the reference to kings and שופטים "rulers/judges" in 7:7 were likely to recall the only other mention of שופטים and kings in the book, that is, Hos 13:10. The latter belongs to a unit that revisits the issue of kingship and in which YHWH reportedly repudiates the office of king as one of a false, improper savior (in contrast to YHWH, who is the only real savior), and, moreover, does so from the very outset, in a manner that evokes the memory of the events narrated in 1 Sam 8:6 (cf. the choice of words there and in Hos 13:10, and see also 13:11; cf. 8:4).

Another interesting case involving a common word pair occurs in Hos 7:14a and is based on a pair of verbal forms of זעק "cry" and ילל "wail" (cf. Isa 14:31; 15:3; Jer 25:34; 47:2; 48:20, 31; Ezek 21:17; also cf. Isa 65:14; Jer 49:3) and the associations carried by the terms "heart" and "bed" (cf. Ps. 4:5). The result is that verse 14a may be understood in several different, but complementary ways. For instance, v. 14a is usually translated, "they do not cry (זעקו) to me from the heart, but they wail (ייללו) upon their beds" (NSRV), in which the first clause means "they do not cry to me in sincerity" and the latter may mean they wail rather than sleep in their beds, probably due to distress (cf. Ps 107:13, 19). According to Macintosh (*Hosea,* 280) the text actually conveys the meaning of "they have not cried out to me in sincerity, rather they howl about their couplings." Macintosh understands the reference to "their beds" (Heb. מִשְׁכְּבוֹתָם) as pointing to sexual intercourse (cf. Judg 21:11-12; Isa 57:8; Ezek 23:17). This reading would be consistent with the common use of sexual imagery in the book of Hosea, and in particular with the general characterization in Hos 7:4aα, "all of them commit adultery," and perhaps with the mental frame evoked by the reference to "grain and new wine"; and see discussion of Hosea 4.

Barré ("Hearts, Beds and Repentance") advances another main understanding of v. 14a by focusing on the pair "heart — bed" and pointing out that it serves to shape an image of a private as opposed to public realm. There is only one person who knows one's thoughts in one's heart/mind, that is, oneself. The same holds true for one's thoughts upon one's bed (cf. Mic 2:1). The basic idea is that, since no one can know about them, these thoughts are sincere. Barré also raises the issue that to "cry to YHWH" under distress often carries a sense of repentance for the wrongful behavior that led YHWH to bring distress upon the person or group in the first place (see, for instance, Judg 10:10 — and implicitly in Judg 3:9, 15 — 1 Sam 12:10; Neh 9:4). Accordingly, YHWH is described as authoritatively maintaining that they (i.e., those representing Israel) lack any true repentance, for they expressed none in their innermost thoughts, and even under considerable distress. In sum, the play on the mentioned two pairs created within a text meant to be read, reread, studied, and read to others on different occasions and circumstances at least three complementary meanings, those suggested by the NRSV, Macintosh, and Barré.

It bears notice that given the possible sexual connotations of the reference to "their beds," some scholars associate the text in 7:14a with "baalistic" rituals of fertility, involving some sexual activity or connotation (e.g., Garret, *Hosea;* Wolff, *Hosea,* 128). This position is usually buttressed by the possible existence of an (original) Hebrew text that read יתגדדו "they gash themselves" in v. 14b (and cf. 1 Kgs 18:28) rather than יתגררו, which means either "they gather together for grain and new wine" or "they fear for themselves (III גור, 'be afraid') concerning grain and new wine," though it might carry a connotation of committing adultery as well (see NJPSV; Ginsberg maintained that יתגררו — יתגודדו — means "fornicate" or the like, see Ginsberg, "Lexicographical Notes," 77-75, and cf. idem, *Israelian Heritage,* 59). Barré, who supports the reading "they gash themselves," sees in v. 14b *alone* a reference to a "forbidden mourning rite connected with obtaining 'grain and wine,' probably from Baal"; see Barré, "Hearts, Beds and Repentance," 57-58. The word Baal, however, does not appear in the text, and YHWH was also considered the provider of "grain and wine' — see 1 Kgs 18:28, but also Zech 13:5-6. Given the emphasis on the private realm of "heart" and "bed," it is difficult to maintain that 7:14a refers to a public ritual.

From the perspective of the ancient readers of the book, the identity of the (godly) speaker would have seemed fluid. The close link between 7:2 and 7:3 may have suggested to them that the identity of the speaker has not changed as they move from one reading to the other. But in v. 5 it becomes clear that the speaker cannot be YHWH, since they probably did not imagine the deity refer-ring to "our king." When did YHWH stop being the speaker in the text? It is possible, but not necessary, that this happened in v. 3. As they continued to read, it became apparent that the deity is the speaker in v. 7. Again, when did the human voice cease to be the speaker in the text? It is possible that this hap-pened at the end of v. 5, but certainly is not necessary. It is possible but again not necessary that a human voice is the speaker in v. 10, but certainly YHWH is the speaker in vv. 12-15. All in all, the text shows again a sense of partial over-lapping and blurring of identity among the godly speakers, and by doing so it communicates to the intended and primary readers that, for the most part, YHWH and the human voice constitute as it were one voice, the authoritative voice reported in a text that is characterized as YHWH's word.

Significantly, the text does not identify the addressees to whom the godly speeches were delivered within the world of the text. This is consistent with the tendency not to anchor the message of the text in particular circum-stances and in particular groups of Israelites in the monarchic past. The text would have conveyed to its primary and intended readerships that the particu-lar identity of the addressees and the precise time or circumstances of the proclamation of the reported words — beyond the general setting of late mo-narchic (northern) Israel — are immaterial to their message to the target read-ership. (Of course, the language, metaphors, references, and messages of the text assume much of and characterize the intended readership of the book. On these matters, see Setting.)

Although by no means written in Northern Hebrew (see, for instance, יין "wine"), a number of expressions serve to characterize the reported language of YHWH (and of the human voice) in this reading as a bit unusual. The most commonly mentioned case in this section of the book is the use of זו "this" in 7:16 that in the HB appears only in Ps 132:12 — for the ideological setting of this Psalm see vv. 10-13 — but is common in later Hebrew (cf. Rabin, "Lan-guage," 124; for the proposed Israelian link, see Yoo, "Israelian Hebrew," but also cf. Macintosh, *Hosea*, 287). Other instances of somewhat unusual lan-guage involve the use of the hitpolal form of בלל in 7:8 (see above) and זרק ב in 7:9 (see above), among others. To be sure, the same holds true for other sec-tions of the book. On these matters see INTRODUCTION.

Some scholars have argued that 7:10a is the work of an interpolator who took the text from 5:5a, and that possibly 7:10b is also an interpolation (e.g., Wolff, *Hosea*, 126; according to Zulick, 7:10 is "a Judahite refrain" [see Zulick, *Rhetorical Polyphony*, 187]). The same holds true for זו לעגם, which may be translated "this is their derision" (according to Macintosh, *Hosea*, 286, 186-87, "this is their blasphemy"). For a redaction critical proposal for Hosea 7 accord-ing to which the text is based on an Hoseanic tradition and the work of a final, second editor (R2) who was strongly informed by the exile, see Yee, *Composi-tion*, 179-89. See also the redactional proposals for 7:11-16 advanced in Zulick, *Rhetorical Polyphony*, 191-94, 269-71. For proposed textual emendations that substantially impact the meaning of verses and of the text and its intellectual setting see, for instance, the treatment of Hos 7:16 in Wyatt, "Of Calves and Kings," 85-88.

Genre

Hos 7:3-16 is a didactic, prophetic reading that is closely interwoven with other prophetic readings in the book of Hosea.

This reading includes an extended and multi-layered metaphor and a "Woe to" unit. The intricate baker metaphor serves to draw the attention of the readers to the portrayal of Israel that it advances and channels their imagination as they construct the Israel of the book. "Woe to" units usually evoke a sense of (true or sarcastic) dread or lamentation (cf. Hos 9:12; and see, for instance, Num 21:29-30; 1 Sam 4:7-8; Isa 3:11; 6:5; 24:16; Jer 4:13; Ezek 16:23). Here it is used to evoke a sense of divine sorrow or grief over Ephraim's dreadful situation as well as condemnation against it. Whatever the original setting or genre associations of the expression אוֹי ל, it substantially contributes to the characterization of YHWH. The deity is portrayed not only as just — Ephraim and their leaders are portrayed as deserving the divine punishment — but as caring and lamenting over Ephraim's situation. On אוֹי ל see Wanke, "אוֹי und הוֹי"; cf. Janzen, *Morning Cry*, esp. 18-27; see also Hillers, "Hôy and Hôy-Oracles"; Gerstenberger, "Woe-Oracles."

Setting

The setting of the writing and reading of this, or any portion of the (present) book of Hosea for that matter, is the same as that of the book as a whole. Both writers and readers are among the literati of Yehud.

The world portrayed in the book as standing in the present of the textually inscribed speaker is one of political instability. This is a world in which leaders are devoured as well as one characterized by Ephraim's "incomprehensible" rejection of YHWH, who was the redeemer of the people and the one who strengthened it. Instead of YHWH, they foolishly sought Egypt and Assyria (cf. Hos 12:2). The world portrayed in the book as standing in the future of the textually inscribed speaker is one of divine punishment of Israel and its leadership, which significantly includes the motif of derision in Egypt.

As is well known, political instability and violent inner struggle characterized the last decades of the northern polity, from the reign of Zechariah to that of Hoshea. Memories and constructions of that period were strongly influenced by these events (see, for instance, 2 Kgs 15:8–17:23; as anticipated in biblical discourses, rejection of YHWH is the central component in these construed memories). The world portrayed in the present of the speaker in the book is not only consistent with these memories but also most likely meant to evoke them.

From none of these considerations does it logically follow that the circumstances of the world portrayed as being in the present of the textually inscribed speaker in a literary unit within the book must be those of the composition and primary reading and rereading of the book or any of its units. Nor does it logically follow from these considerations that the intended readers were supposed to go beyond the general atmosphere of the period portrayed in the relevant readings and attempt to approach them in a way that is strongly informed by a close and unequivocal relation between the circumstances described in the world of the book — either in the present or future of the (godly and mostly divine) speaker — and precise, particular events in the history of the northern polity. It is not by chance that the scholarly debate about the precise "historical referent" of Hos 7:3-7 has reached no conclusion. Does the text refer to the assassination of king Zechariah, king Shallum (cf. Sweeney, *Twelve Prophets,* 79), king Pekahiah (e.g., Macintosh, *Hosea,* 256; cf. Pentiuc, *Long-Suffering Love,* 106), or king Pekah (e.g., Mays, *Hosea,* 104; Wolff, *Hosea,* 124) or to none of them (e.g., Rudolph, *Hosea,* 149)? Significantly, the text of Hosea is unequivocal on one point: it does not provide the readers with any clear indication of the identity of the king, nor does it anchor the world portrayed in the book in any particular historical event or any construction of such a particular event in the memory/ies of Israel. The text of Hosea does not ask the intended and primary readers to read the text in a way strongly informed by any such particular event, but also it unequivocally indicates to them in v. 7 by means of ואכלו את שפטיהם כל מלכיהם נפלו "they have consumed all their rulers (/ judges); all their kings have fallen" that the preceding text is to be understood in terms of a general construction of the monarchic period, rather than in terms of a single reign (cf. Hos 13:10 and STRUCTURE, above), and perhaps even connotes a sense that failed (non-Judahite?) leadership goes back into the time of the judges (cf. Pentiuc, *Long-Suffering Love,* 107).

It bears note that the baker's metaphor works on multiple levels of meaning. It is certainly based on the topos of the destructive, blazing oven/furnace (e.g., Isa 31:9; Mal 3:19; Ps 21:10). Some of its details convey or conjure up a sense of continuous instability associated with hot-minded high officers continuously involved in secret, political conspiracies (7:6, 7). Moreover it is interwoven into the images of drinking parties (notice חמת מיין "the heat of [caused by] wine" in 7:5). The metaphor carries a sense of reversal: that which is meant to produce "bread," that is, to provide sustenance, becomes a symbol of destruction. This reversal is associated with the activity of the elite and calls attention to it. Whereas family ovens were more often than not in the hands of women (Lev 26:26), the one portrayed here seems to be a "professional" or "court" oven run by a male baker (Hos 7:6). Constructions of gender and gender roles within the world of the elite are also involved in the portrayal of reality here. All in all, within the general setting of Hos 7:3-16, it is self-evident that members of the elite will fall because of these conspiracies, but the elite as a whole will fall because of YHWH's actions. The wrongful destruction caused by the former leads to the just destruction to be carried by the latter (notice also the presence of verbal forms of נפל "fall" in 7:7 and 16). The destructive power of the "oven" is thus associated with YHWH (cf. Isa 31:9; Ps 21:10). (For the claim that the reference to the "oven" is related to the affluence of the high stratum of the society in the northern Kingdom during and immediately after the reign of Jeroboam II see Premnath, *Process of Latifundation,* 161-62 [cf. M. Silver, *Prophets and Markets,* 93-96]; of course, as one would expect, the elite is portrayed in the world of the book as affluent, but nothing more follows from that observation.)

The construction of worldly powers such as Egypt and Assyria as the (false) "competitors" of YHWH to be patrons, redeemers, and protectors of Israel was discussed before in this commentary (e.g., Hos 5:1–7:2 Setting). Aram is again not mentioned (see above). There is, of course, a historical kernel for such an ideological construction, and without it, the construction would have lost any persuasive power. It is certainly not by chance that there are no texts in the HB that describe any Israelite leadership pondering whether to rely on king Pannammû II of Sam'al (a king who was a vassal of Assyria, and contemporary with Tiglath-pileser III and the world in which the book of Hosea is set) or on his enemies, or to mention a slightly earlier powerful opponent of Assyria that did not intervene in Palestinian affairs, to rely on Sarduri of Urartu or not.

The intellectual setting of the text here is certainly informed by a world of knowledge that includes memories of confrontations between northern kingdoms (Assyria and later Babylon) and Egypt, and of the policy choices regarding the two that faced leaders in Syro-Palestine during the neo-Assyrian period, and particularly since the fall of Aram Damascus. This question was more acute given that there is no room for "neutrality"; polities were asked or forced to take sides (cf. Na'aman, "Forced Participation"). Neither this lack of any possible neutral position, nor the historically obvious fact that any ruler in the area would not have even contemplated a rebellion against one of the two superpowers without support from the other plays any role in the construction of the past advanced by this book. Instead, for ideological considerations discussed above — which are also communicated by and reflected in books other than Hosea, e.g., Isaiah; Chronicles, Kings; see also 5:1–7:2 Setting — construed reliance on any of the superpowers is a breach of trust with YHWH that could lead only to defeat. Historically, substantial Egyptian support was provided only twice and only to Judahite kings, Hezekiah and Zedekiah, who rebelled against their northern overlords. Significantly, since Hezekiah was construed as successful in later Israelite discourses — though historically, he failed — there is a strong emphasis in biblical works on his characterization as one who did not rely on Egypt, but on YHWH (see 2 Kings 18–19), and whose "salvation" was not effected in any way by the Egyptian army (see 2 Kgs 19:35).

Historically, no late northern Israelite king received any substantial support against Assyria from Egypt, nor was the latter in any position of providing such help in the years just preceding the takeover of Egypt by the 25th dynasty. Lack of military capability did not preclude political involvement in, and agitation of, the area against Assyria to the detriment of the polities and leaders who followed Egypt's advice (see 2 Kgs 17:4 and notice that Yamanni of Ashdod and Hanun of Gaza fled to Egypt after rebelling against Assyria). The point in Hosea 7, however, is not that Egypt was powerless to help or was deceitfully projecting a power it did not have (ct. 2 Kgs 18:21; Isa 36:6) as opposed to Assyria, which actually had it, but that YHWH alone can save Israel. The image of the past that is construed and communicated through this book is not historically accurate in contemporary terms but strongly shaped the "memory" of later communities of Israel and as such created a past that carried a strong significance to them.

It bears particular note that this reading concludes or reaches its climax with Israelites in Egypt, where they will be derided because of their "offensive," gibberish language (cf. Hos 8:13; 9:3; cf. Paul, "Gibberish"). Two aspects of the horizon of thought of the intended and primary readers of the book of Hosea are relevant and shed light on the world of ideas and knowledge that characterize the literati among whom and for whom, primarily, the book was composed. The first deals with the image of Egypt, the second with the importance of proper speech, discourse, and the honor that they bestow within society.

In this reading Egypt is not merely a country and a people or polity. Egypt (as well as Assyria) is a contender of YHWH for Israel's trust, but above all a central player in the story of the Exodus from Egypt that serves as the model for the image of a new Exodus from exile. With the intertwined character of the past and future — from the perspective of the readership and authorship of the book — deliverance is a central theme in the book of Hosea (see Hos 2:2, 16-25; 11:1-11; 12:10-11) and among the literati for whom it was first composed. This world of images and ideas requires that in this book even Ephraim's exile into Assyria be somewhat associated with exile in Egypt (see Hos 9:3). Needless to say, from the fact that the second exodus is imaginatively seen in terms of the first, it does not follow that they are envisioned as one and as a replay of the other, or that their expected results must be identical. (See the discussion on Hos 1:2–3:3; 2:3-25.) In addition, the book keeps communicating its messages at two levels. On the first level, it deals with Ephraim's (i.e., northern Israel's) exile and with Assyria (and Egypt), as expected from the circumstances in which the world of the book is set. The readership certainly knew that the northern polity fell at the hands of the Assyrians, not the Babylonians, and that the Assyrians deported "Ephraim." Yet, the readership of the book is urged to associate Ephraim with trans-temporal Israel, including themselves and the people of monarchic Judah. From that perspective, the exile of Ephraim to Assyria is nothing but the first movement in YHWH's punishment of both north and south, and YHWH's eventual redemption of trans-temporal Israel, including the unified descendants of both in the ideal future characterized in terms of the fulfillment of central themes in common Judahite/Yehudite discourses (e.g., the role of the Davidic king, Temple, etc.; see Hos 2:1-3; 3:5; and see discussion there).

One may mention that, according to Yee, the idea of the derision of the people in the land of Egypt "seems to have its background in the events of the exile." She attributes the idea to a postmonarchic editor (her R2) who prepares for "later editorials where he affirms that the One who first brought Israel out of Egypt will bring Israel home from exile in a New Exodus" (Yee, *Composition,* 189). From a different perspective, Simian-Yofre maintains that the reference to the leavened dough in 7:4 carries an association with slavery in Egypt and serves as the opposite to "unleavened" which stands for freedom (cf. Exod 12:15, 19, 34, 39; 13:3, 7; Deut 16:3). According to him "the baker of Hosea has allowed the unleavened dough to become leavened dough, a sign of oppression." He suggests that the dough stands for the Israelite society that was corrupted by a negligent leadership. See Simian-Yofre, *Desierto,* 105-6 (translation from Spanish is mine).

As for the role of proper language in the horizon of thought reflected and conveyed by the text, one may note that this reading concludes with a note that does not emphasize exile *per se,* or being in Egypt in particular, but derision and the consequent lack of honor that is associated with incomprehensible language. Moreover, in 7:13 the main claim against Israel is that they דברו עלי כזבים "they speak lies against me." The reference to cry out indicates speech too (cf. 1 Sam 28:12; 2 Sam 19:5; Jer 20:8; Ezek 9:8; Ps 142:2, 6), and in the case of Hos 7:14, absence of proper speech. In addition, the word רמיה "deceit" in 7:16 was likely to evoke secondary associations with (deceitful) speech (cf. Mic 6:12; Ps 120:2, 3; Job 13:7; 27:4). Furthermore, these references appear in a book that contains numerous references that evoke or are associated with wisdom literature (e.g., Hos 8:7a; 13:13; cf. Macintosh, "Hosea and the Wisdom Tradition") and which concludes with "those who are wise understand these things; those who are discerning know them. For the ways of YHWH are right, and the upright walk in them, but transgressors stumble in them" (Hos 14:10; modified NRSV). Emphases on speech and understanding are typical markers of the worldview of literati, who tend to associate these features with being upright. Their presence here is consistent with the careful, highly sophisticated use of language that characterizes this book. Emphasis on speech is characteristic of wisdom literature, within which it abounds, but also appears in prophetic books (see Mic 6:12; Zeph 1:9; 3:13; and see Ben Zvi, *Micah,* 161; idem, *Zephaniah,* 235-37). The reason is simple: both prophetic and wisdom literature are the product of the literati.

This reading sheds light on additional features of the horizon of thought of those involved in the production of the book of Hosea and its target readership. For instance, the text suggests a succession of kings, none of whom is characterized in positive terms in these readings. Moreover, one should keep in mind that the rereadership of the book was also informed by texts such as Hos 13:10-11. Yet (human) revolt against these kings is not viewed in positive terms (cf. Hos 4:4) either. This position is consistent with the image of adultery as a metaphor for all improper activity in which people are involved and that expresses or reflects an abrogation or lack of acknowledgement of their obligations to their superordinate partner.

It bears note also that the fall of Israel is here (and in fact, in the book of Hosea as a whole) construed and explained in internal terms. Foreign powers play no significant role, except as the potential target of Israel's hope in the mind of Israelites and as the source of dishonor for Israel outside YHWH's land (7:16; 9:3). Assyria is not even unequivocally characterized as a powerful invader that destroyed cities and exiled Israel. On the surface, one might tend to attribute this characterization to the setting of the world described in the book within which the events of 722-20 BCE stand in the future, but such explanation fails to take into consideration that prophetic speakers in prophetic (and other) books may be and were portrayed as describing events in their own future (e.g., Deut 28:64-65). A better explanation is that the text here reflects and communicates a central viewpoint: Israel's relation with YHWH, its acknowledgement in the course of its life of its obligation to YHWH, decides its fate. All external powers are essentially irrelevant, except as minor participants in Israel's decision to acknowledge or reject their superordinate, YHWH.

Tadmor and Ginsberg explained the lack of references to Assyria as a conqueror and a power that exiled Israel in terms of a dating of the actual prophecies of the historical prophet Hosea, or, more precisely from their perspective, Hosea B (chs. 4–14) prior to 738 BCE. See Tadmor, "Historical Background," and Ginsberg, "Hosea." These scholars are involved in a debate with Kaufmann (*Toldot*, 108) who considers Hosea B to be later than 732 BCE because it does not mention Aram; in fact, Kaufmann dates Hosea B to 732-25 BCE. For the position that יום מלכנו "the day of our king" refers to a particular royal, annual celebration held during the autumn festival in the northern kingdom, see Hayes and Hooker, *New Chronology*, 13.

Intention

The general intention of Hosea 7:3-16 is to communicate and reinforce the positions and the general horizon of thought of the authorship and readership as represented in these texts (see Setting) and to socialize the literati through their shared reading of the material and the larger society through the literati's reading to others of this reading. This reading reinforces the belief that the fate of Israel (and its polities and societies) is decided by the people's full acceptance of YHWH as their only patron and by its observance of what follows from that acknowledgment. This belief serves to condemn the society of the northern kingdom and its leadership, to explain their fall, but also to give reason for hope to (trans-temporal) Israel and the readers of the book who identify with this Israel. Unlike the people in northern Israel and their leadership, they know that actions of the latter were foolish and led to a justified destruction. Moreover, they know this because they read and accept as authoritative the book of Hosea and books carrying a similar message (cf. Hos 14:10).

Bibliography

M. L. Barré, "Hearts, Beds, and Repentance in Psalm 4,5 and Hosea 7,14," *Bib* 76 (1995) 53-62; H. J. Cook, "Pekah," *VT* 14 (1964) 21-35; G. Galil, *The Chronology of the Kings of Israel and Judah* (SHANE 9; Leiden: E. J. Brill, 1996); E, Gerstenberger, "The Woe-Oracles of the Prophets," *JBL* 81 (1962) 249-63; H. L. Ginsberg, *The Israelian Heritage of Judaism* (New York: JTS, 1982); idem, "Lexicographical Notes," *Hebräische Wortforschung. Festschrift zum 80. Geburtstag von Walter Baumgartner* (VTS 16; Leiden: E. J. Brill, 1967) 71-82; J. C. Greenfield, "Lexicographic Notes II," *HUCA* 30 (1959) 141-51; J. H. Hayes and P. K. Hooker, *A New Chronology for the Kings of Israel and Judah and Its Implications for Biblical History and Literature* (Atlanta: John Knox, 1998); D. R. Hillers, "Hôy and Hôy-Oracles: A Neglected Syntactic Aspect," C. L. Meyers and M. O'Connor (eds.), *The Word of the Lord Shall Go Forth: Essays in Honor of David Noel Freedman in Celebration of His Sixtieth Birthday* (Winona Lake, IN: Eisenbrauns, 1983) 185-88; W. Janzen, *Morning Cry and Woe Oracle* (BZAW 125; Berlin: de Gruyter, 1972); P. A. Kruger, "The Divine Net in Hosea 7,12," *ETL* 68 (1992) 132-36; C. J. Labuschagne, "The Similes in the Book of Hosea,"

OTWSA 7-8 (1965) 64-76; A. A. Macintosh, "A Consideration of the Hebrew גער," *VT* 19 (1969) 471-79; idem, "Hosea and the Wisdom Tradition: Dependence and Independence," J. Day, R. P. Gordon, and H. G. M. Williamson (eds.), *Wisdom in Ancient Israel. Essays in Honor of J. A. Emerton* (Cambridge: Cambridge Univ. Press, 1995) 124-32; N. Na'aman, "Forced Participation in Alliances in the Course of the Assyrian Campaigns to the West," M. Cogan and I. Eph'al (eds.), *Ah, Assyria: Studies in Assyrian History and Ancient Near Eastern Historiography Presented to Hayim Tadmor* (Jerusalem: Magnes Press, 1991) 80-98; idem, "Historical and Chronological Notes on the Kingdoms of Israel and Judah in the Eighth Century B.C.," *VT* 36 (1986) 71-92; M. O'Connor, "The Pseudosorites: A Type of Paradox in Hebrew Verse," E. R. Follis (ed.), *Directions in Biblical Hebrew Poetry* (JSOTSupS 40; Sheffield: Sheffield Academic Press, 1987) 161-72; S. M. Paul, "The Image of the Oven and the Cake in Hosea 7:4-10," *VT* 18 (1968) 114-20; idem, "Hosea 7:16: Gibberish Jabber," D. P. Wright, D. N. Freedman, and A. Hurvitz, *Pomegranates and Golden Bells: Studies in Biblical, Jewish, and Near Eastern Ritual, Law, and Literature in Honor of Jacob Milgrom* (Winona Lake, IN: Eisenbrauns, 1995) 707-12; C. L. Seow, "Hosea 14:10 and the Foolish People Motif," *CBQ* 42 (1982) 212-24; M. Silver, *Prophets and Markets: The Political Economy of Ancient Israel* (Boston/The Hague/London: Kluwer-Nijhoff Pub., 1983); A. Szabó, "Textual Problems in Amos and Hosea," *VT* 25 (1975) 500-524; H. Tadmor, "The Historical Background of Hosea's Prophecies," M. Haran (ed.), *Yehezkel Kaufman Jubilee Volume* (Jerusalem: Magnes Press, 1960) 84-88; M. A. Tate, "The Whirlwind of National Disaster: A Disorganized Society (Hosea 7–10)," *Review and Expositor* 72 (1975) 449-63; M. E. W. Thompson, *Situation and Theology. Old Testament Interpretations of the Syro-Ephraimite War* (Prophets and Historians 1; Sheffield: Almond Press, 1982); R. J. Tounay, "Le Psaume 149 et la "vengeance" des pauvres de YHWH," *RB* 92 (1985) 349-58; G. Wanke, "אוי und הוי," *ZAW* 78 (1966) 215-28; N. Wyatt, "Of Calves and Kings: The Canaanite Dimension in the Religion of Israel," *SJOT* 6 (1992) 68-91.

Fourth Didactic Prophetic Reading:
(Monarchic) Israel's Unfaithfulness and Its Punishment, 8:1-14

Structure

I. Introduction	8:1a
II. First Section	8:1-3
III. Transitional Verse	8:4
IV. Second Section	8:5-8a
V. Third Section	8:8b-13bα
V. Concluding Note	13bβ
VI. Additional Concluding Note	8:14

The outline above is one among several possible proposals for the structure of Hos 8:1-14. Questions of hierarchical structure may be raised. For instance, it is also possible to consider this reading as part and parcel of a subset of readings within Hos 4:1–11:11 that comprises all of Hos 8:1–10:15. These texts

convey a godly displeasure with monarchic Israel, focus on the northern kingdom (although Judah is always in some way in the mind of the implied author of
the text), deal with judgment, and tend to conclude with heightened messages
that point at Israel's punishment, or the like. In addition, some markers of textual
coherence bind them together. This is more pronounced in the case of 8:1-14 and
9:1-9, which are bound by numerous lexical and thematic bonds (notice the repetition of חטאתם ויפקוד עונם יזכר "he will remember their iniquity, and punish
their sins" [NRSV] in 8:13 and 9:9; for a comprehensive list see Eidewall,
Grapes, 125-26). These considerations have led Eidewall to consider Hos 8:1-14
as a subunit within 8:1–9:9. Landy, on the other hand, has pointed to a structural,
thematic parallelism between 7:2-12 and 8:2-10 (Landy, *Hosea,* 105-6). These
literary features link chapter 7 to 8 and vice versa. It has also been proposed that
Hos 8:1-14 is the opening unit of a larger structural section that concludes in
14:8 (see, for instance, Garret, *Hosea,* 177-78), but for Good, Hosea 8 is closer
to 5:8–7:16 than to Hosea chapters 9–10 (Good, "Composition," 41-43). In addition, the paragraph divisions in the MT tradition suggest an understanding of
Hos 7:13–8:14 as one unit. Although this position has not received much support, at least at some point, some readers interpreted the text as supporting this
understanding of the structure.

It is also possible to advance proposals for complementary inner structures of 8:1-14. For instance, Simian-Yofre (*Desierto,* 114-19) suggests a subdivision of the unit into 8:1-6, 7, 8-14, whereas Wendland (*Discourse Analysis,*
128) proposes five strophes: 1-3, 4-6, 7-10, 11-13, and 14. Stuart (*Hosea,* 129)
divides the unit a bit further, into 1-3, 4-6, 7-8, 9-10, 11-13, and 14, but Good
("Composition," 42-43) thinks in terms of 8:1-7, 8-10, and 11-13 — v. 14 was
an addition according to him. It is worth stressing that each of these proposals
is consistent with, and highlights a possible understanding of, Hosea 8; moreover, most of them are based on some linguistic or thematic markers and represent complementary rather than alternative readings. As I develop an explanation of the structure proposed above, it must be taken into account that
structures or outlines were meant to be fluid, so as to allow the intended and
primary readers of the book to develop multiple rereadings informing each
other. The outline mentioned above is certainly *not* meant to preclude the possibility that some ancient readers followed, at least in some of their readings of
the book, the inner structure advanced by Simian-Yofre, for example, or the understanding of 8:1-14 as a subunit of 8:1–9:9 (as per Eidewall's proposals).

Most scholars, however, agree that verse 8:1 points to the beginning of a
new unit, be it an independent unit within 4:1–11:11 or a subunit of, for instance, 8:1–9:9 or 8:1–10:15. Verse 8:1 does not elaborate further the matters
discussed in 7:13-16. Although 8:1a is clearly elliptic, it carries a clear imperative sense that is only strengthened by the sharp, short, elliptic utterances. This
feature also serves to mark the beginning of a new unit. Verse 8:14 represents
the heightened conclusion of the unit that begins in 8:1. The next verse, 9:1, indicates the beginning of a new unit, by means of the opening with a negative
imperative (or better, vetitive), which serves as a textual marker of break with
the previous unit, and the change of topic. The impression that this new beginning was meant to be understood, at least on one level, as standing at the same

structural level as 8:1 is strengthened by the alliteration created by the openings אל "not" in 9:1 and אל "to" in 8:1.

As is the case in all other readings in the book of Hosea, textual markers interweave this READING and its meanings with others in the book, and thus shape a richer tapestry of meanings. A few examples will suffice. The theme of the return to Egypt (see 8:13 and cf. 9:3, 6 and 7:11 and ct. 11:5), which associated with its ideal past and future reversals (see 2:17; 11:1, 11; 12:10, 14; 13:4), serves as a central theme throughout the book. The verbatim repetition of יזכר עונם ויפקוד חטאתם "he will remember their iniquity and he will punish their sins" in 8:13 and 9:9 creates a circle of interpretation linking unfitting worship and sacrifices to moral corruption and the latter to historical antecedents in the traditional memory of the readers, and associates all with divine punishment, including a return to Egypt. The signpost in 8:4 suggests a possible link between the gifts of gold and silver for the Baal in 2:10 and the making of עצבים "idol images" (cf. 13:2; 14:9). One may notice also the way in which Hos 10:5 leads the readers of the book to associate the calf mentioned in 8:5-6 with the well-known calves of Bethel (for a different understanding of both 8:5-6 and 10:5 see Hayes and Kuan, "Final Years," 167). In addition, one may compare 8:4 and 7:3 in their approach to the matter of kings and officers. The subtle differences between the instances of עבר ברית "transgress covenant" in Hosea, namely, 6:7 and 8:1, are also worth notice. In the former, the reference to Adam/human beings reinterprets the reported situation of Israel in terms of human condition; the latter brings Israel back to the center.

The language that opens 7:14-15, לא זעקו אלי "they do not cry to me [YHWH]," links this text with 8:2, which opens with לי יזעקו "to me [YHWH] they cry out." The rhetorical point is clear: The literati who read and studied the book are told to imagine (monarchic) Israel as one that did not cry to YHWH. Even if or when it cried to the deity, Israel could not do so without advancing a false cry, that they know YHWH (cf. Hos 5:4). Significantly, the issue of knowing YHWH is raised also in Hos 6:3, which just like Hos 8:2b brings to the readers a report of YHWH's report of Israel's (misleading and wrong) response. On these matters see discussions under STRUCTURE in Hos 5:1–7:2; Hos 7:3-16).

In addition, one may note that the זנח "spurn" in 8:3 (on 8:5a see below) reverberates with the common use of forms from זנה "play the whore" (e.g., Hos 9:1 and passim in the book), and particularly since the matter not only is of alliteration but involves also the message conveyed by the expression, namely, alienation and rejection of YHWH. This association between זנח and זנה may also be at work in 8:5a. The meaning of the text there is highly debated. The text reads זנח עגלך שמרון חרה אפי בם. It is possible to understand the text as meaning "your calf has spurned you, Samaria; my anger burns against them" or "your calf has spurned Samaria; my anger burns against them" (see Simian-Yofre, *Desierto*, 113), but it is probably more likely that the text conveyed the sense of "My [YHWH's] anger has spurned your calf, O Samaria, my anger burns against them" (cf. Lundbom, "Double-Duty Subject"; Barthélemy, *Critique Textuelle*, vol. III, esp. 549). If this second reading is correct, then the text advances a measure for measure (cf. Hos 4:6 — STRUCTURE) approach that binds together 8:3 and 8:5, while at the same time it calls attention to an important difference: Israel has spurned טוב "the good," whereas YHWH has spurned Samaria's calf, not Israel. "The good" stands for either YHWH (cf. Ps 73:1 — see, among others, Ibn Ezra, Abrabanel, Radak, Qyl, *Hosea*, סא; Davies, *Hosea*, 198) — or an attribute or gift from, or associated with, YHWH (cf. Ps 73:28; cf. Garret, *Hosea*, 181; Pentiuc, *Long-Suffering Love*, 113; Davies, *Hosea*, 198; Simian-Yofre [*Desierto*, 111-12] associates "the good" with the covenant). The somewhat odd language of the text allows it also to evoke in the readers cultic images and evaluations associated with זנה "(to) whore" (with an implied, elliptic אחרי "after"), that is, to construe an echo of the common expression "prostitute to/with" a (false) deity, an idol, "other gods," or the like (e.g., Exod 34:15; Lev 17:7; Deut 31:16; Judg 2:17; 8:33; 1 Chr 5:25 — the latter refers to the reasons for the fall of northern Israel). If this is so, the text would reverberate with an echo stating, "he has prostituted to your calf"; that is, "he went astray by worshiping the calf"; cf. 9:1. It is worth noting that there have been many proposals for textual emendation in Hos 8:5 (for a summary and bibliography see Barthélemy, *Critique Textuelle*, vol. III, esp. 548), and that the LXX points to an imperative reading, "Spurn your calf, O Samaria," which some scholars assume to have been the original version of the Hebrew text (e.g., Wolff, *Hosea*, 132).

From the perspective of the readership of the book, the characterization of Israel as sowing רוח "wind" in 8:7 and as shepherding wind in 12:2 evoke each other. Both contribute to the characterization of sinful Israel as unnaturally foolish, and, significantly, both texts associate its behavior with covenants and agreements with foreign nations (cf. C. L. Seow, "Hosea 14:10 and the Foolish People Motif"; and ct. with the characterization of the intended readers of the book in Hos 14:10).

Perhaps the most interesting case of the tapestry of meaning involves 8:1aα and 5:8. Although the choice of words in 8:1aα, "to your palate, *shofar/ horn!*" (i.e., set the horn to your lips! blow it!; the LXX here most likely reflects a different Hebrew text), is different from that in 5:8 ("blow the horn!"), the text is meant to evoke the call there. Yet, bridges to and signposts connecting different readings often serve to foreground their differences. While 8:1aα and 5:8aα recall each other, 8:1aβ and 5:8aβ explicitly bring forward a very significant difference. Instead of the geographical locations mentioned in 5:8, the reader faced another heightened, elliptical statement, "as an eagle over the house of YHWH." The image of the eagle (or perhaps, vulture) conveys a sense of a swift, imminent attack by an enemy that leaves no tracks and just falls on its prey from above (cf. Deut 28:49; Jer 4:13; 48:40; 49:22; Ezek 17:3, 7; Hab 1:8; Lam 4:19). More important, however, is the reference to בית ה' "YHWH's house." The most common and likely primary understanding of בית ה' "the house of YHWH" is in the sense of temple rather than kingdom or land of YHWH. It is worth stressing that from the perspective of the (postmonarchic) readership of the book of Hosea, YHWH, who is the speaker in v. 1 — see 1b — could not have referred to any temple aside from the temple in Jerusalem as YHWH's house (בית ה') at the time in which the book is set (cf. Targum; R. Qara; Radak; and among modern critical researchers, Day, "Is the Book of Hosea Exilic?" 124). To be sure, within the authoritative discourse/s of the community, other religious sites or institutions could have been identified as YHWH's house provided that they were associated with periods prior to the building of the temple in Jerusalem (see Josh 6:24; Judg 19:18; 1 Sam 1:24; 3:15; cf. Exod 23:19; 32:26), but the expression בית ה' signifies the temple in Jerusalem in the numerous instances in which it appears in settings that post-date the establishment of the temple in Jerusalem (e.g., Isa 2:2; 37:1; 66:20; Jer 7:2; 17:26; 19:4; Ezek 8:14, 16; 10:19; Joel 1:14; Mic 4:1; Ps 122:1, 9 and, of course, numerous instances in Kings and Chronicles). The same considerations apply to other occurrences of בית ה' in the book of Hosea, namely, in Hos 9:4, and probably to "my [YHWH's] house" in 9:15. The double connotation of the call of the shofar, to raise a military alarm but also as a call for a ritual convocation, plays well with the understanding of בית ה' as YHWH's temple (see Simian-Yofre, *Desierto,* 112).

It is also worth mentioning that בית could have *also* connoted in 8:1 the household of YHWH, that is, the polity and the territory that the readership imagined as belonging to YHWH (cf. Hos 9:3; such an imagery of YHWH's house is a metaphorical variant of the common and basic construction of the "house of the father," which was common in the ancient Near East; cf. Schloen, *House*). The imagery of household and house is notably porous and may lead to ambiguity (cf. Jer 12:7). Moreover, if the image here is that of an enemy coming against Jerusalem, then the enemy must have been imagined as coming against the land/kingdom too (see already Radak). In any event, the reference to YHWH's house could have also been understood in a secondary sense as a case of synecdoche or even metonymy without losing its primary meaning of the temple of YHWH. In any case, the reference would have reflected and contributed to the ideological elevation of the status of the land in the book of Hosea (see 9:3 and also 2:21-25 and 2:3-5 Setting as well as 6:7 and 5:1–7:2 Setting).

Some scholars have proposed that בית ה' here refers to, and actually denotes, only the land (e.g., Wolff, *Hosea,* 137; Mays, *Hosea,* 115-16; Macintosh, *Hosea,* 292). Other scholars have proposed that it refers indeed to YHWH's temple, but not to that in Jerusalem, but rather to a temple in Bethel (Emmerson, "Structure," 708-9) or perhaps Samaria (Sweeney, *Twelve Prophets,* 85). These proposals depend to a large extent on the assumption that the historical Hosea, as a northern prophet who prophesied about and to the northern kingdom, would not refer to the temple in Jerusalem. Yet, the ancient readers of the book of Hosea did not interact with the historical Hosea, however he is hypothetically reconstructed, but with the prophetic character Hosea within the book of Hosea, and as they constructed him through their reading and rereading of the (present) book of Hosea. Not only did the book (i.e., the word of YHWH that was associated with Hosea) include references to Judah, but this Hosea would have had no problems whatsoever prophesying concerning Judah, Jerusalem, its temple, or about events far away from those in which the book is set, such as the eventual destruction of the Jerusalemite temple by the Babylonians. In fact, from the perspective of the intended and primary readers of the book, it would have been very odd if this Hosea had not mentioned Judah at all, since, after all, all prophetic books in their present form refer in one way or another to Judah or Jerusalem. Surely, it would have been extremely unusual had this Hosea been imagined as unable to prophesy about events in the far future of his own circumstances. No prophetic character in the Hebrew Bible is construed in such a manner.

Moreover, Hos 8:1 opens a subunit (8:1-3) that addresses not only the single individual who is called to blow the shofar — who most significantly is neither identified nor characterized in any way, but rather kept generic and unattached to any known historical event — but above all the intended and primary readerships of the book. It conveys to them a message that is not restricted to a particular period but subsumes their understanding of the monarchic period, and the relation of cause and effect in the divine economy. It also serves as a strong warning for the primary readers themselves. If they forsake YHWH's covenant and instruction, even if they cry to and claim to have knowledge of YHWH, YHWH will give them into the hands of enemies, and the temple and the land will swiftly fall. (See also Setting.)

The first section (8:1-3) expresses clearly the general character of the period. It is a period of imminent catastrophe, transgression of the covenant with YHWH, rebellion against YHWH's torah (/instruction), and false hypocritical claims to know and acknowledge YHWH. The rest of the reading provides examples that illuminate this general characterization. (On these matters see Setting.)

According to the inner structure proposed here the next section in this reading consists of a transitional verse, v. 4 (for other possible and perhaps complementary inner structures see above). This verse creates a bridge between the reported, general and generalizing, divine evaluation of Israel's conduct in 8:1b-3a and its consequences (3b — even here notice the general and generalizing reference to אויב "enemy"). This bridge directly warns the intended and any future rereaders of the book of the world in which the book itself is set. It brings forward, again, the matter of the illegitimacy of the northern kings and by direct association their elite (i.e., their officers); see 7:3 and discussion there. In the light of 3:5 it points to all northern Israelite kings. In fact, there seems to be not only an echo of Hosea 2:10 (see above), but also an echo of the traditional (Jerusalemite) image of king Jeroboam I, the first and paradigmatic king of the north (cf. 1 Kgs 12:28-30; Exod 32:1-35). In any case, v. 4 serves to bring together the common motif of wrongful political leadership and wrongful cultic activities, a theme very common in Hosea and much of biblical literature (cf. Kings, Chronicles, passim) and which is based on the traditional ancient Near Eastern understanding of the king as responsible for the cult. Yet, one may easily notice a major difference. Although no (northern) Israelite king can be pious, the emphasis in the present discourse is on Israel. It is *they* who crown kings in disobedience of YHWH; *they* who appoint officers that YHWH does not accept and acknowledge; and *they* who make idols with *their* gold and silver. (On the ideological substitution of "king" by "Israel" see 2:3-25 Setting.) Given the message of 8:4, it is worth noting the repeated use and the sonorous effect of the numerous occurrences of מ in crucial positions in the verse, namely, "they [Israel]," "made kings," (not) "from me [i.e., not from YHWH]," "their silver," "their gold," "for them/themselves [i.e., for Israel]," (made) "idol images," and "for the purpose that (it might be cut off)." The "it" in "it might be cut off" stands for Israel or the idol images, or both — and perhaps also the sil-ver and gold, seen as a collective representing Israel's wealth.

Although verse 8:4 is thematically closely related to the following section in the reading, as a linking verse it shows also markers of textual coherence with the preceding verses. First, the opening "they" in v. 4 refers back to the third personal suffix that concludes v. 3 and whose referent is "Israel." Second, one may notice the rhetorical, modified "tit for tat" conveyed by the two occur-rences of the verb ידע "know": Israel foolishly claims that it knows YHWH (v. 2), but YHWH does not state that YHWH does not know *Israel,* but rather that the deity does not know/acknowledge Israel's officers (and within this con-text, its kings too). These features are consistent with the characterization of the verse as a bridge between units.

The second section (8:5-8a) and some of its main themes are suggested by the linking verse. It focuses mainly on the calf — which in turn is associated in the traditional memory of Israel with its kings, its evaluation as an idol (see 8:4 and 8:6 and cf. Ps 115:4), and the consequences of Israel's association with the calf, which led to Israel's being swallowed by זרים "foreigners" (cf. Hos 7:9; see Hos 7:3-16 STRUCTURE). The emphatic characterization of the calf as an idol is conveyed in v. 6 by (a) ולא אלהים הוא "it is not a god" (cf. 2 Kgs 19:18; Isa 37:19; Jer 16:20 and above all, 2 Chr 13:9, which may have been in-fluenced by this verse or, in any case, reflects a similar approach to the matter at stake here) and by (b) the mention that a חרש "artisan" עשהו "made it." (For the world of thought that is consistent with this statement, see Setting.) The עשהו here serves on the one hand to link the verse with v. 14 (see below) and on the other leads to two other verbal forms of the same Hebrew root עשה "make, do, produce, yield" that play a central role in the verse immediately fol-lowing v. 6, namely, the two יעשה, which the NRSV translates as "it shall yield" and "it were to yield" in v. 7. The reference to a חרש "artisan" also links v. 6 to 7. This reference works on a sophisticated pun on the double meaning of the root חרש "engrave," but also "plough." Although the meaning "artisan" (/ "engrave") is the only one activated in v. 6, the dormant secondary meaning is used to create a defamiliarized and unexpected form of the pair זרע — חרש "sow" (see v. 7 and cf. Hos 10:11-12; Isa 28:24; Job 4:8). The mentioned fea-tures shed light on the craftsmanship of the authorship of the book and also contribute, from the perspective of the readers, to the cohesion of the text. The conclusion of this section is marked by the emphasis conveyed by the repetition of verbal forms from בלע "swallow" (vv. 7b and 8a) and by the (interpretative) explicit association of the metaphor of the standing stalk without "sprout" (i.e., "head" or "ear") and flour to Israel as a referent marking the end of the unit. (On the metaphor see Setting.) Verse 8:7bα provides also another instance of the use of pseudosorites (see O'Connor, "Pseudosorites"; and 7:3-16 STRUC-TURE and 9:1-17 STRUCTURE) whose rhetorical role is to lead to and emphasize the concluding note of the section: "Israel is swallowed up" or "Israel has itself been swallowed."

The next section (8:8b-13) is enclosed by the envelopes created by the עתה "now" openings in v. 8b and 13b and המה עלו אשור "they [Ephraim/Is-rael] have gone up to Assyria" in v. 9a and המה מצרים ישובו "they shall return to Egypt" at the conclusion of v. 13 (and the section). On the messages and ideological world reflected and conveyed by this contrast see Setting. It is sufficient at this point to stress that the expression "they shall return to Egypt" connotes a sense of ending to the period in the traditional memory of Israel that began with leaving Egypt (i.e., the Exodus; see Hos 2:17; 11:1; 12:10-14; 13:4 and cf. Hos 7:16; 9:3, 6; 11:5 — on the LXX see Setting). As such this heightened reference serves as a conclusion to both this section of the reading and to the reading itself, even if the latter shows a second, additional conclusion. For the classical example of the presence of an additional concluding note following the main, heightened conclusion, see Isa 66:23-24; cf. Leviticus 27 and on additional concluding notes see below.

Markers of textual coherence based on repetition of words and sounds are prominent in this section (8:8b-13). For instance, one may notice (a) בגוים "among the nations" in vv. 8 and 10; (b) מזבחות לחטוא "altars for sinning" twice in v. 11 (on this expression see below); (c) the seven-fold repetition of the מ in שרים מלך ממשא מעט meaning "because of [or 'under'] the tribute [and connoted, 'burden'] to the King of Princes/Kings [i.e., the Assyrian king]" in v. 10 — this sound repetition contributes to the foregrounding of the terms "tribute" and "king" (of Assyria); on this expression see below; and (d) the multiple sonorous repetitions in זבחי הבהבי יזבחו to be translated either "they continually sacrifice/slaughter sacrifices" (see Macintosh, *Hosea,* 327-29) or "they sacrifice the sacrifices of my offerings" (that is, "they sacrifice the offerings which should be offered to me," see Barthélemy, *Critique Textuelle,* vol. III, esp. 554-57) or "they sacrifice my burnt-offerings" (following Barr, *Comparative Philology,* 233-34, and Yoo, *Israelian Hebrew,* 102-4) in v. 13. To be sure, repetitions of sounds are not unique to this section (e.g., קמה — צמח — קמח "standing grain" — "sprout" — "flour" in 8:7) but are one of the prominent features of this section and contribute to the textual coherence.

The reading ends with a second concluding note (Hos 8:14) that brings to the readers an additional perspective. Supplementing the reference to the "return to Egypt" and the (temporary) undoing of the Exodus, the readers are asked to imagine the fate of worldly monarchic Israel *and Judah,* in terms of YHWH's destruction of its palaces and fortified cities. On the ideological world reflected and communicated by this note see Setting. Textual markers closely relate this additional concluding note to the preceding section and the reading as a whole. Among them are three pairs that serve to encapsulate central matters in this reading: (a) the pair זכר "remember" and שכח "forget" in vv. 13-14 — YHWH remembers their sins, but they forget their maker; (b) עשהו in v. 6 meaning "he [an artisan] has made it [the calf]" and עשהו in 14 meaning "he [YHWH] has made it [Israel]" — the contrast between the two "makers" is clear, and so is the comparison and association between the two products "Israel" and "the calf," neither of which is a deity nor should take any of the roles associated with the deity; and (c) הרבה אפרים מזבחות "Ephraim multiplied altars" in v. 11 and יהודה הרבה ערים בצרות "Judah multiplied fortified cities" in v. 14; neither altars for wrongful cult nor fortified cities provide any protection; quite the opposite since they stood instead for acknowledgment and trust in Israel's maker whom it forgot (v. 14). In other words, within this context these building activities serve as (ideological) markers of disaster. The ancient and common characterization of the (doomed) enemy of the deity who trusts either in false worship or military force stands in the background (see 2 Kgs 18:19-25//Isa 36:4-10).

The text's use of the word היכלות in v. 14 is noteworthy. The term היכלות carries a double meaning: "temples" (cf. 1 Sam 1:9; Isa 6:1; 66:6; Jonah 2:5; Ps 5:8), which fits well with the preceding reference to "altars," and "palaces" (cf. 1 Kgs 21:1; 2 Kgs 20:18//Isa 39:7), which fits the following reference to building ערים בצרות "fortified cities." The latter expression may have evoked the memory of cities given to Israel after the Exodus, according to the construction of the past held by postmonarchic communities (see Deut 3:5; Neh 9:25). Ancient readers who approached the text in this manner would have understood it, at one level, as constructing Judah (and theologically, Israel) as attempting to take the role of YHWH (see above) and build for itself that which YHWH has given; that which follows the Exodus is now contrasted with that which precedes the reversal of the Exodus (v. 13bβ and see above).

Of course, the expressions הרבה אפרים מזבחות "Ephraim multiplied altars" in v. 11 and יהודה הרבה ערים בצרות "Judah multiplied fortified cities" in v. 14 also play on אכתב לו רבי תורתי (Ketiv; Qere אכתוב לו רבו תורתי) in v. 12, which connotes — but most likely does not denote, see below — "I [YHWH] write for it [Israel] the multitude of my instructions" (NRSV). Thus the text conveys at the connoted level a secondary contrast: whereas Ephraim/Judah/Israel multiplied (false) altars and cities, YHWH multiplied for Israel the deity's instructions (cf. among others, Tooze, *Framing*, 212).

A few expressions in this reading require a brief comment. Verse 9aβ-b reads פרא בודד לו — אפרים התנו אהבים. This may be understood as "a wild donkey on its own [lit. 'alone by itself']; Ephraim hired lovers" or perhaps, "a wild donkey on its own; Ephraim celebrated love-affairs" (cf. Macintosh, *Hosea*, 316-17; Morag, "On Semantic and Lexical Features," esp. 498, 503). The crucial point in the latter interpretation is its understanding of אהבים as an abstract noun; see Prov. 5:19; within this view, התנו is approached as a hiphil form of the root תנה meaning "recount/celebrate" (cf. Judg 5:11) rather than "hire" or more precisely "arrange or pay a whore's wage" — a denominative verbal form from אתנה/אתנן "whore's wage"; cf. Hos 2:14; 9:1; among others, see Paul, "משא מלך שרים Hosea 8:8-10," 194. Of course, even if "celebrate love affairs" was the primary meaning of the text, the other would remain a connoted meaning. Verse 10 explicitly refers to Israel as sending/giving harlot's fees among the nations (cf. Labuschagne's ["Similes," 68] understanding of the simile of the wild donkey; see also Nwaoru, *Imagery*, 161-62). The construction of the world, of Israel and other nations in particular, is strongly reminiscent of that in Hosea 1–3 (see Setting there and relevant bibliography). However, here Israel — or its leadership, or both — is not depicted as a woman, but rather as a man who buys sexual favors (i.e., support) from lovers (i.e., "the nations"; for the opposite position see Wolff, *Hosea*, 143, but see also Eidewall's critique, Eidewall, *Grapes*, 135-36). Israel's characterization as a male is consistent with the implicit, but continuously present, thread of its self-positioning in the role of a deity (see above). It is in this context of

Israel's trusting in its own power to make alliances that it is compared to a wild donkey on its own (cf. Job 39:5-8). Israel's independence is presented as sinful and leading to disaster; it is an attempt to show or gain independence from YHWH. It is worth notice that the same expression פרא בודד לו carries an additional connoted meaning that was likely actualized through the process of reading and rereading the book of Hosea. If it is slightly revocalized, it would have meant "he [Ephraim] has sprouted up on his own" (cf. LXX). This reading is consistent with the other puns on words with Ephraim in the book (Hos 9:16; 13:15; 14:9; and cf. Gen 41:52) and certainly reinforces, even if it is a secondary connoted meaning, the mentioned thread. (Irvine, "Politics" maintains that this last reading is the original one.) Of course, this attempt at independence from YHWH is fruitless within the world of the book, and the ideologies that inform it. Already by the end of v. 10a YHWH is depicted as gathering "them." This "them" stands on the one hand for Israel, but on the other, at least in a secondary, connoted meaning, for Israel's payments. Within these discourses rather than facing the "lovers" Israel will face YHWH with obvious and expected results.

As mentioned above, the expression מעט ממשא מלך שרים "because of (or 'under') the tribute (connoted, 'burden') to the King of Princes/Kings (i.e., the Assyrian king)" in v. 10 carries a seven-fold repetition of מ that contributes to the foregrounding of the terms "tribute" and "king" (of Assyria). It also carries a three-fold repetition of שׁ that evokes the image of the שרים "princes" or "officers." In fact, the paired expression is meant to evoke in the readers the usual pair מלך — שרים "king — officers" (see Hos 3:4; 7:3; and particularly 13:10). This time, however, it does not refer to the Israelite king and his officers, but to the king of Assyria, and as such it expresses his power. Thus, the choice of words communicates a sense of "poetic (or divine) justice" as it shifts the usual meaning from the royal Israelite elite to the figure that will take over its role, the mighty king of Assyria; from the royal Israelite elite that was not appointed or acknowledged as legitimate by YHWH to a foreign king whose actions are consistent — in a way unbeknownst to him, but known to the readers of the book — with the divine economy; from a local elite whose policies towards Assyria led to their replacement with the one who replaces them. Significantly, this is the second time in Hosea in which the text chooses a way of referring to the Assyrian king that is fully consistent with its titles but that at the same time conveys important messages to the readership of the book (see the use of מלך ירב in 5:13; see Setting; and see also 10:6). To be sure, this feature already points at the degree of literary sophistication and superior education in both the authorship and the intended readership of the book. It also bears notice that the very word preceding the expression מעט ממשא מלך שרים is ויחלו (notice the repetition of the ל here and in the word "king" and cf. the case with the שׁ in officers). In the process of reading, rereading, and studying the text, this word could have helped to convey all the following meanings: "they will soon begin (to bear) . . . ," "they will soon begin to waste away . . . ," "they shall soon writhe . . ." (NRSV), "they shall soon grow sick. . . ." It is likely that all these possible meanings came to bear within that process of reading and rereading, thus adding a rich texture of multiple complementary shades of meaning to the text. (On this expression in its context in the book and on its ancient Near Eastern background see in particular Paul, "משא מלך שרים Hosea 8:8-10.")

The expression מזבחות לחטוא "altars for sinning" appears twice in close textual proximity in v. 11. The repetition certainly conveys a strong emphasis. In addition, it may connote a range of shades of meaning. For instance, a slight emendation to the present vocalization of the text renders "altars for expiating sin" and "altars for sinning" — see NRSV; cf. NJB, NAB. It is possible and even likely that this approach to the text was raised through the ancient process of reading, rereading, and studying the (unvocalized) text within the community of literati for whom the book of Hosea was written. Another possible and complementary reading of the text here, and one that is particularly compelling from the perspective of a postmonarchic readership, is that Ephraim's multiplications of altars is in itself a sin — because there should be only one altar to YHWH, that in Jerusalem. Thus, "Ephraim has increased the number of altars to sin" and "the altars themselves are a sin and so is their use."

Verse 14 refers to Israel, meaning both the northern kingdom and the theological, trans-temporal concept of Israel in postmonarchic communities. It also refers to Judah, which stands here for the monarchic kingdom of Judah, but serves also as representative of trans-temporal Israel. It concludes however, with the following expression: ושלחתי אש בעריו ואכלה ארמנתיה "I will send fire on *his* cities and it will consume *her* fortresses" (cf. Amos 1:4, 7, 10, 12; 2:2; 2:5). The pronoun "his" points to Israel and Judah, and "her" to the cities. Such a stylistic choice serves to underscore that "Judah and Israel" belong together, and so do their attributes. In other words, it is neither Judah alone that multiplied fortified cities — with all the connotations and implications mentioned above — nor Israel alone that built palaces/temples. Both were together in sin, and both were implicated in the actions and attitudes portrayed in the text. In fact, both are one, temporal representatives of the trans-temporal concept of Israel, just as the readers of the book are.

The reference to Amos 1:4, 7, 10, 12; 2:2; 2:5 made above is one of several cases in which expressions in this prophetic reading are similar or reminiscent of expressions in other prophetic books. For instance, compare Jer 14:10 and Hos 8:13, or Hos 8:8 and Jer 22:28. The latter case is particularly interesting since it points at the set of possible, metaphorical referents of כלי אין חפץ בו "a vessel no one wants" (NRSV). It may serve to describe Israel (Hos 8:8) or the king (Jer 22:28). The implied horizon of thought is one in which images of people and kings are interrelated (see Setting). Although it has been proposed that some of these cases point to literary dependence (e.g., according to Ginsberg "8:1-2; 7-14 obviously served as a model for Isaiah 58:1-4" ["Hosea," col. 1020]; for Jer 14:10 and Hos 8:13, see below), certainly from the perspective of the community of readers of the books in their present form, it is better to approach the matter in terms of an intellectual setting of literati who shared much in terms of worldviews and repertoires of images (see Setting). The same holds true for the possible relation between Hos 8:13 and Deut 12:15. (Ginsberg maintains that "this passage in Hosea [Hos 8:11-14] was a factor in giving rise to the law in Deut. 12" and sees a confirmation of his position in the relation between יזבחו בשר ויאכלו "they continually slaughter and eat meat"

[Macintosh, *Hosea,* 327] in 8:13 and ותזבח ואכלת בשר "you may slaughter and eat meat" in Deut 12:15. See Ginsberg, *Israelian Heritage,* 21.)

It bears mention that, as in other readings, here too YHWH is generally presented to the readers in the first person — as the explicit and unequivocal speaker — but at times the text shifts to references to YHWH in the third person. For instance, in the first two versets of v. 13a YHWH is presented in the first person (as in most of the reading), but the reference shifts to the third person towards the end of 13a and 13b (cf. Jer 14:10) and then again to the first person in v. 14 (or at the very least, v. 14b). This is a stylistic feature. (Notice that, for instance, references to Samaria may shift from second person to third person even within a short unit for rhetorical purposes, see 8:5-6 — the LXX homogenizes here; see de Regt, "Person Shift," 218.) It is very unlikely that these shifts led the readers of the book to approach the text as spoken by two different characters with two separate voices. Moreover, when the voice of (sinful) Israel is reported (v. 2b), it is conveyed through YHWH's speech and not as an independent voice.

Redactional proposals and substantial textual emendations of the text of Hosea 8 have been advanced. According to Wolff, "verse 14 bears the characteristics of a secondary addition" (*Hosea,* 136; cf. Good, "Composition," 42-43). Comparisons between the text referring to YHWH in the third person in v. 13 and Jer 14:10 have led to proposals that Jeremiah is quoting Hosea, or that the book of Jeremiah contains a citation taken from the book of Hosea (e.g., Mays, *Hosea,* 123; Wolff, *Hosea,* 136), but have also led to redactional proposals. The sentence usually translated as "YHWH does take delight in them" or "YHWH does not accept them" is often considered a gloss (e.g., BHS). The third person references in the rest of the verse are at times familiarized by means of textual emendation that renders them into first person references to YHWH (e.g., Weiser, *Die Propheten,* 67; BHS). Much more important for the overall meaning of the section is the fact that the crucial "they shall return to Egypt" has also been considered a later gloss (e.g., Weiser, *Die Propheten,* 67; BHS), perhaps originating as a marginal note taken from Jer 14:10. It bears notice that this proposal has been strongly criticized, among others, by Wolff (*Hosea,* 136, 145). In v. 13, there is also the matter of the addition to the verse in the LXX that brings the issue of the eating of unclean food; see MT Hos 9:3 — scholars who think that versets should be of a similar length noticed that "they shall return to Egypt" is briefer than those preceding it. But even if it is likely that the text of the LXX here is not original and results from the influence of the text in 9:3, the question remains: did some Hebrew readers of the book of Hosea complement the reading in 8:13 with that in 9:3? It is likely that some did so. Of course, even if this is the case, the fact remains that a short ending was preferred in 8:13. This preference is probably due to the fact that the short ending calls attention to itself and to the central significance within the text of the message it carries. Another proposed change has a substantial impact on the characterization of the intellectual setting of the text. Some scholars have proposed that v. 1b with its reference to YHWH's *torah* and covenant (see Setting) is also an addition, and in particular, a deuteronomistic addition (see Perlitt, *Bundestheologie,* 146-49; Clements, *Prophecy and Tradition,* 41-45; cf.

Wellhausen, *Prolegomena,* 418; Harper, *Hosea,* 308; for a critique of this position, see Day, "Pre-Deuteronomic," 7). For a brief summary of the discussion on possible instances of a dtr. edition of a forerunner of the present book of Hosea see Albertz, "Exile as Purification," 246). A possible, but still hypothetical text that carries no reference to the latter two concepts or to the return to Egypt is, however, substantially different from that of (present) Hosea 8.

As for comprehensive redactional proposals, Yee assigns 8:8-10 to the Hoseanic layer, 8:1-4a, 5aBb-6*, 11-12 to "R1" (a redactor from the Josianic period close to the "DTR1" approach as putatively expressed in the deuteronomistic history) and 8:4b-5aA, 8*-7, 13-14 to "R2" (an exilic period redactor whose approach is similar to that of the putative "DTR2" layer of the deuteronomistic history). See Yee, *Composition,* 189-97, 316. For another comprehensive, redactional proposal, see Zulick, *Rhetorical Polyphony,* 194-200.

Genre

Hos 8:1-14 is a didactic, prophetic reading interwoven with other prophetic readings in the book of Hosea. It uses typical scenes such as that of the sentry raising the alarm in the city by blowing the shofar, but utilizes them in ways that go far beyond that associated with that very particular setting in actual life (see discussion on Hos 8:1, STRUCTURE and Setting). The text assumes a readership and authorship for whom, when YHWH's report states that Israel cries to YHWH saying, "My God, we — Israel — know you" (Hos 8:2, NRSV), the words evoke not only images of a liturgy of communal complaint but also and in particular the central role of liturgical expressions of trust (for "knowing YHWH" as communicating trust in YHWH and YHWH's deliverance see Ps 9:11; 36:11; expressions of trust are also important in "thanksgiving"). The strategy of the text is to evoke these images so as to turn them around and communicate through them Israel's lack of trust in YHWH, and the ironical situation that their complaint will fail to achieve its goal (at least in part) because of their mistaken confidence in their relationship with YHWH, against whom they have sinned and added even to their sins by their very claim "we know you."

Some of the scholars who attempt to reconstruct the words of the prophet have proposed that Hosea 8 contains a series of brief oracles proclaimed by the historical prophet Hosea at different occasions. For instance, Weiser (*Die Propheten,* 67-71) proposes that 8:4a+8-10 was proclaimed during the reign of king Hoshea and 8:11-13 during the reign of Jeroboam II. (For a critique of the division of the text into brief oracles see Gnuse, "Calf, Cult and King.") As it stands, as a part of the Book of Hosea, chapter 8 not only provides a reading, but also suggests itself to the readers as a report of a divine monologue of complaint against Israel (cf. Garret, *Hosea,* 177) rather than as a series of separate, oral oracles. Significantly, the book does not ask the readers to imagine any circumstances associated with the issuing of an oracle as part of an oral communication event such as those involving a clearly identified speaker, a set of addressees, place and time of the oral communication, or for that matter any of the issues associated with the preservation of the supposed oral communication (e.g., someone writing and copying the oracle, attaching it to other oracles, editing the text, and the like). The readers of the book are presented with a written report of a divine communication (mostly if not all in the first person) that is part and parcel of, and closely interwoven with other units in a written work that is characterized as YHWH's word (i.e., the book of Hosea).

Setting

The setting of the writing and reading of this, or any portion of the (present) book of Hosea for that matter, is the same as that of the book as a whole. Both writers and readers are among the literati of Yehud.

To be sure, if a scholar wishes to attempt to reconstruct the sayings, message, and historical situation of a historical prophet Hosea, who lived in the last decades of the northern kingdom — to be distinguished from the character in the book — and assumes that these sayings and messages directly addressed particular, although crucial, political events and decisions of these decades, then she or he has to deal (a) with what s/he assumes to be the actual words of the historical prophet or the closest possible approximation to them (as opposed to the present book of Hosea that does not even claim to be a compilation of the words spoken by Hosea during the reign of Jeroboam II over northern Israel and Uzziah, Jotham, Ahaz, and Hezekiah over Judah) and (b) with one of three basic scenarios of crises between Israel and Assyria as reported in Kings, namely, the 738 BCE, the 735-732 and the 725-22/20 scenarios, or alternatively, a period of alliance between Assyria and Israel that predated 738 BCE.

An excellent example of this approach is in Irvine's work. Irvine repoints and more importantly transposes to 8:8a the following פרא בודד לו אפרים "a wild donkey on its own" (but see above) in v. 9, and then advances the claim that the original vv. 8-10 that he has proposed relates to the circumstances in Samaria in 725-24 BCE as described by Hayes and Kuan ("Final Years"). In a nutshell, Hayes and Kuan maintain that Hoshea rebelled against Assyria (727 BCE) and was captured (725 BCE), that the sanctuary of Bethel was looted (725 BCE) and the order for the kingdom to be annexed as a province to Assyria was given (725 BCE), but when the Assyrian army left for Tyre in the summer or fall of 725, Samaria rebelled again, installed a new king, and set up a new sanctuary with a new calf. According to these scholars Hos 8:4-5a attests to the latter action. (For other reconstructions of the period see Becking, *Fall of Samaria,* 21-60; Na'aman, "Historical Background.") Irvine writes:

> In v. 8a, the prophet looks back on the initial subjugation of Israel in the spring of 725 BCE. The Assyrian measures against the country, including the provincialization order, are summarized metaphorically: "Israel was devoured." Hosea then focuses on present circumstances and refers to the renewed revolt of Israel: "Ephraim has sprouted up on his own." The last part of v. 8 refers to the country's efforts to acquire allies against Assyria. If so the text indicates the reluctance of the other states to support the rebellion: "Now

they [the Israelites] are among the nations like an unwanted vessel." Verse 9 contrasts the current rebellion with Israel's earlier, voluntary submission to Assyria: "although they themselves went up to Assyria, (now) they have bargained for lovers." The first clause probably alludes to the embassy and tribute that Hosea sent to Tiglathpileser III in 730 BCE. . . . Verse 10 declares that the effort to acquire allies against Assyria is futile. . . . The threat against Israel is elaborated in v. 10b: "they will shortly writhe because of the tribute of the king of kings." The prophet here anticipates that Shalmaneser V will crush the Israelite revolt and impose harsh conditions on the survivors. (Irvine, "Politics and Prophetic Commentary," citation from p. 294)

Macintosh, however, chooses a different political scenario, as he associates 8:8 with the situation in 735-732 (*Hosea*, 315). He maintains that in 8:9 "Hosea had in mind specifically Hosheah's tribute paid to Assyria in 732/1 BC, soon after he had deposed Pekah" (*Hosea*, 318), and that relates v. 10 to v. 9. See also, among others, Wolff, *Hosea*, 142-43; Stuart, *Hosea*, 134-35; Pentiuc, *Long-Suffering Love*, 117; cf. Kaufmann *Toldot*, 108-9. The third scenario (Menahem's payment of tribute to Tiglathpileser III in 738 BCE — cf. 2 Kgs 15:19-20) is preferred by, for instance, Simian-Yofre (*Desierto*, 114-20, and already Radak). Finally, those scholars who associate Hosea 4–14 with Hosea B, a historical prophet who lived and proclaimed his message before Menahem's payment of tribute, had no problems in associating these verses (and all Hosea 4–14) to a period prior to 743-39 BCE (see Tadmor, "Historical Background").

The fact that many possible scenarios could fit the world portrayed in the book is proof positive that the text is written in such a way that is not strongly anchored into any particular historical event, but rather is written so as to be consistent with and to reflect as well as shape the intended readership's "memory" of the late monarchic period in northern Israel, while at the same time to convey a sense that the situation in Judah in the late monarchic period was not different in that which matters the most, according to the authorship and intended readership of the book of Hosea, namely, both did not follow YHWH, though they should have done so.

From the perspective of a study of the book of Hosea — to be distinguished from any hypothetical study of the historical prophet Hosea or Hosea B — there is no point in trying to narrow down that which the book refuses to narrow down; that is, there is no point in assuming that the particular description in this reading, or section thereof, was meant to and was understood by the intended and primary readerships to precisely point to their knowledge of the events in northern Israel from 725-24 BCE, as opposed to those of, for instance, 735-732 BCE, 738 BCE, or 743-39 BCE. The text is not interested in communicating precise political history — as per our understanding of the term — but in making a theological point. For that purpose, a general characterization of the past is more effective than any narrow vignette associated with this or that set of characters to the exclusion of others. Significantly, despite all the focus on the royal elite, the book of Hosea does not name any king except those mentioned in the general introduction to the book in Hos 1:1, nor does it associate any of them with any reported saying.

The setting of the world of the speaker within the book is the same past mentioned above. The general character of the period is expressed clearly in the first section of the reading (8:1-3). The world of the speaker is portrayed as facing an imminent catastrophe, and is characterized by Israel's transgression of the covenant with YHWH, its rebellion against YHWH's torah (/instruction), and its false hypocritical claims to know and acknowledge YHWH. As mentioned above, the rest of the reading provides examples that illuminate this general characterization. These involve idolatry, crowning kings contrary to YHWH's wishes, trust in the efficacy of a cult that is improper and sinful, trust in earthly powers and structures, and the like. The rest of the reading brings forward a number of aggravating circumstances and slightly elaborates the more general claims advanced in the reading: YHWH has given YHWH's written torah/instruction — so they cannot claim not to know it; see 8:12 and below. Israel did not forget any deity but its own maker when it made idols/ false gods for itself (see 8:14). Images of exile (and reversal of the Exodus) are prominent.

This reading sheds some light on aspects of the ideological setting of the literati for whom the book of Hosea was composed. Leaving aside the obvious (e.g., they considered themselves an instance of trans-temporal Israel, just as the northern Israelites and Judahites of the world portrayed in the book, worshiped YHWH, considered the book authoritative, considered the character of YHWH as portrayed in the book reliable, shared a memory of Israel as coming from Egypt, and the like), one cannot but notice that two terms are crucial in the ideological discourse reflected and communicated by 8:1-3, namely, the pair תורה "torah/instruction" and ברית "covenant." The pair itself appears in Ps 78:10 (most likely a postmonarchic Psalm which seems to reflect a horizon of thought similar to that of the book of Hosea as a whole); cf. Isa 24:5; Jer 31:33; and to some extent with Josh 24:25-26. Both terms appear elsewhere in the book of Hosea. But whereas תורה in Hos 4:6 seems to denote the priestly instruction (see commentary there), here a more general concept of torah is evoked, as its association with covenant shows. The referent of the term ברית here is the general concept of YHWH's covenant with Israel (cf. with but notice the differences between the text here and Hos 6:7 and 2:20, respectively).

The intended readership of the book is also asked in this reading to refer to the concept of תורה in terms of a comprehensive concept and to associate it with a written text that YHWH wrote and which, significantly, bears (only) the principles of YHWH's torah. See 8:12a, which conveys the meaning of "I [YHWH] write for it [Israel] the weightier matters of my torah/instruction." This understanding of the verse follows in the main Macintosh, *Hosea,* 325-26; see discussion there. In other words, תורה refers to a divine torah/instruction that is written, read, interpreted (by the authorities of the period), and complemented with less weightier matters that are not written in the text, and which one would assume remain in the hands of the accepted authorities of the period (cf., for instance, Deut 4:8; 17:11, 18-19; 29:28; 30:10; 31:11; Josh 1:7-8; 23:6; 24:25-26; 1 Kgs 2:3; 2 Kgs 17:34, 37; Isa 30:9; 51:4; 2 Chr 23:18; 31:3; and esp. Ps 1:2; 2 Chr 17:9 and Nehemiah 8; and cf. E. Ben Zvi, "Analogical Thinking" and "Introduction: Writings, Speeches, and the Prophetic Books").

For complementary modes of conveying YHWH's message/instructions and for a similar argument that YHWH took great pains in conveying that message/ instruction to Israel, but the latter refused to accept it, see Hos 12:11 and discussion under Hos 12:1-15 STRUCTURE. The combined message of 8:12a and 12:11 to the intended readership of the book of Hosea seems to mirror and show the influence of the ideological pair: YHWH's Torah and Word.

Metaphors often offer a window into the imagery and the worldview of the authorship and target readership; e.g., the metaphor in v. 7, namely "they sow the wind, they will reap the whirlwind; stalk without ear, it will never yield flour — or if it does, foreigners will swallow it" (cf. NJB). The image of "sowing" may be used to portray negative circumstances through a variety of futility clauses (within prophetic literature, see Isa 17:10-11; Jer 12:2; Mic 6:15; Hag 1:6; cf. Lev 26:16; Judg 6:3 — and see the conclusion of Hos 8:7; Job 31:8). In all these instances, the point is that common cause-and-effect expectations are thwarted because of YHWH's response to the behavior of the sower, planter, or the like (cf. Deut 28:30-34, 38-42; Hos 4:10; Amos 5:11; Zeph 1:13). In other words, within the worldview reflected here there is a normal sequence of events governed by cause-and-effect considerations, but the deity may occasionally turn it upside down. Significantly, there is no automatic, "natural" system of punishment and rewards. Yet the very expectation of a normal sequence of events may be used rhetorically to portray wrongdoers as unnatural and absolutely unreasonable characters that contrary to any possible expectation of sowers would knowingly sow that which will by necessity be harmful to them and their community. Here, the speaker characterizes the wrongdoers as those who sow wind. Wind is often associated with fruitlessness, rootlessness, ephemerality, and destructive movement that leave nothing of consequence (cf. Isa 26:18; Hos 12:2; Ps 1:3-4; and notice in Jer 22:22 the reversal of the image of herding wind in Hos 12:2 that brings forward the destructive associations of wind). To sow wind is mentioned because it describes a preeminently foolish action, particularly so in an agrarian society. Of course, the anticipated, natural order of events keeps working in the background of the metaphor and leads the readers to imagine that sowing wind would lead to the harvest of mighty winds of a storm, unless YHWH decides to stop the natural process to save Israel. Although the intended and primary readerships are well aware of the reassurances of hope that serve for them as interpretative keys for their reading of the book of Hosea, within the context of this particular reading, the reference to the "harvest" of the "seeded wind" could only be destructive, and therefore the "wind" becomes a "storm" (for the word pair רוח "wind" and סופה "storm" see Isa 17:13; Job 21:18) and, by doing so, the text reaffirms the readership's assumptions concerning the natural process that serve as notional ground for the metaphor. For a similar system of metaphor and worldviews see Prov 22:8, and for its positive mirror image see Prov 11:18 and Hos 10:12. Wolff (*Hosea*, xxiv, 142), among others, sees here an example of the influence of wisdom on Hosea; it is probably better to approach the case in terms of shared worldviews and repertoires of metaphors among the few literati able to compose, edit, and study the book that eventually was included in the HB.

As mentioned above, motifs such as sowing in this context may serve to portray negative circumstances if they are integrated into a futility motif. The latter is not at work in 7a, but, significantly, it stands at the center of 7b, which although not explicitly associated with sowing, still implies that action. The text thus sheds light on the world of mental associations and options at work in the process of producing the text of this prophetic reading and of reading and rereading it. (To be sure, the ancient literati may well have been unaware of their own network of mental associations, but even if this is the case — as is likely — it does not undermine the importance of such a world and its role in shaping the setting of the authorship and primary readership of the book of Hosea.) The agrarian imagery underlying the comparison of Israel's existence with that of the standing stalk without sprout and an unlikely flour that in any case fails to feed also sheds light in the world of images and social realities (e.g., the ever-present danger of famine) of the literati.

As mentioned above, the section comprising verses 8:8b-13 is enclosed by the envelopes created by the עתה "now" openings in v. 8b and 13b and המה עלו אשור "they [Ephraim/Israel] have gone up to Assyria" in v. 9a and המה מצרים ישובו "they shall return to Egypt" at the conclusion of v. 13 (and the section). The text here points, as in numerous other cases in the book, to an intellectual setting that is certainly informed by a world of knowledge that includes social memories of a world in which there were two main polities, Assyria and Egypt (as always, no references to Aram), and in which northern Israel attempted to stand in Assyria's camp so as to avoid destruction and, accordingly within these discourses, ensured it. But there is more that can be learned about the intellectual setting of the book from this section. The first geographical move involves the political elite, since only members of the elite probably עלו "went up" (notice also the associations of "Israel went up" [from Egypt/to YHWH's temple/etc.] which convey an ironical message to the readership) to negotiate treaties, but the result of their actions affects the entire people, for the return to Egypt evokes the undoing of the Exodus. In other words, the theological worldview that is reflected and shaped here may be summarized: The sins of the leaders are visited on the whole people.

In verse 14 the readers are asked to imagine the fate of worldly monarchic Israel and Judah in terms of their palaces and fortified cities (which are, to be sure, associated with central elites, rather than "all the people"). The text here does not reflect a particular interest in building activities, as the lack of any details of the products of such activities shows, nor in history as understood today. Instead, it serves to advance a historiographical, theological principle of causation. The character YHWH communicates to the implied addressees of YHWH's speech in the world of the book, and above all to the readers of the book, that the palaces (temples?) and fortified cities will be destroyed because Israel forgot its own maker. From the perspective of the postmonarchic readership of the book, this is a causal explanation of their history, which incidentally is expressed elsewhere and particularly developed in Chronicles. To be sure, from this observation it does *not* follow that Chronicles influenced the composition of the book of Hosea, but rather that a set of general principles illuminated the horizon of thoughts and theological explanations of the writers and primary readers of these books. The thread of Israel's independent actions and of its "tak-

180

ing care of itself" that was mentioned above is directly relevant to these matters. Any thought that Israel can successfully take care of itself without resorting to YHWH is, within these discourses, beyond the pale. The problem is not with foreign alliances *per se,* but with trusting foreign alliances instead of trusting and following YHWH, and with attempts to use foreign powers to prevent the fulfillment of YHWH's judgment against Israel, because it broke trust with YHWH. Within this discourse, reliance on foreign powers is both a result and an expression of Israel's unfaithfulness. Significantly, this is another common motif in, among others, prophetic literature (e.g., Isaiah, passim) and Chronicles.

There is a general and strongly polemical stance against the construction of images representing the divine in 8:6 (and cf. 13:2). After all, all images are made by human hands and, therefore, according to the logic of 8:6 cannot "be" deities. The general outlook is comparable to stances, and the pejorative, though more developed, rhetoric at work in, for instance, Isa 44:9-20; Jer 10:1-16; Hab 2:18; Ps 115:2-8; 135:15-18 and cf. among others Deut 4:12-20. It indicates a theological mindset in which aniconic worship was seen as such a central tenet that iconic worship of any kind is strongly derided. Such a setting is consistent with that of the Jerusalemite-centered literati in Yehud, though also, most likely, with that of late monarchic Judah as well (concerning the latter, see Na'aman, "No Anthropomorphic Graven Image" and bibliography cited there — the matter is strongly debated as shown by the mentioned bibliography). The cultic association of northern Israel with calf imagery reflected in the book is consistent with both (a) the portrayal of the situation in the northern kingdom in the repertoire of texts available to postmonarchic literati (1 Kgs 12:28-31) and certainly evokes their shared "memory" or construction of monarchic (northern) Israel and (b) the most likely historical reconstruction of the situation in the northern kingdom (see, among others, Smith, *Early History of God,* 83-85 and bibliography; Keel and Uehlinger, *Gods, Goddesses and Images,* 191-95 and bibliography).

A number of expressions and choices of words in this reading serve to characterize the reported language of YHWH (and of the human voice) as a bit unusual. Among these one may mention שבבים (meaning unclear; it may mean "splinters, fragments," or "sparks" or perhaps even "banishment") in v. 6, a hiphil form of תנה in v. 9 (which may mean "recount/celebrate," or "hire" or "arrange or pay a whore's wage"; see above), and הבהבי in v. 13 whose meaning is also unclear (see above). For a discussion of these cases see, among others, Yoo, *Israelian Hebrew,* 98-107, and Macintosh, *Hosea,* 308-10, 316-17, 327-39 and the bibliography mentioned in both works.

Finally, it is worth noting that a particular but relatively ancient rereading of the references to Israel's return to Egypt in the book of Hosea most likely led to textually inscribed changes in the LXX translation of Hosea. The LXX in Hos 8:13; 9:3, 6; 11:5 shifts the references to a return to Egypt from the future to the past tense. Thus, it construes the world portrayed in the book as one in which Israel is already in Egypt. In other words, Israel/Ephraim has symbolically returned to Egypt because of its sin. Divine announcements of judgment associated with Assyria are, however, kept as pointing to future punishment. Some degree of historicizing was likely involved — northern Israel actually fell to the Assyrians in both history and the social memory of Israel's past among the literati — the main point is ideological characterization. On Egypt in the LXX see Pisano, "Egypt."

Intention

The general intention of Hos 8:1-14 is to communicate and reinforce the positions and the general horizon of thought of the authorship and readership as represented in these texts (see Setting) and to socialize the literati through their shared reading of the material and the larger society through the literati's reading to others of this reading. In particular, it contributes to the characterization of monarchic Israel in terms of idolatry, foolishness, and replacement of trust in YHWH with attempts at salvation based on alliances with other nations, improper worship, or fortresses. The reading serves not only to explain the fall of monarchic Israel (and Judah too) as fully justified, but also to enhance the awareness of readership of the dangers and expected results associated with the activities of which northern Israel is accused by YHWH. The text conveys, among other things, the importance of YHWH's torah, of YHWH's temple, and of accepting as kings only those that YHWH accepts, which within the context of the book of Hosea are Davides. It also constructs the weightier matters of torah as matters expressed in written documents. This reading also communicates a theological theory of causation in history and deals with matters of cause and effect, deeds and reward or punishment.

Bibliography

R. Albertz, "Exile as Purification. Reconstructing the 'Book of Four'," P. L. Redditt and A. Schart (eds.), *Thematic Threads in the Book of the Twelve* (BZAW 325; Berlin: de Gruyter, 2003) 232-51; J. Barr, *Comparative Philology and the Text of the Old Testament* (Oxford: Clarendon Press, 1968); B. Becking, *The Fall of Samaria: An Historical and Archaeological Study* (SHANE 2; Leiden: Brill, 1992); idem, "Assyrian Evidence for Iconic Polytheism in Ancient Israel?" K. van der Toorn (ed.), *The Image and the Book. Iconic Cults, Aniconism, and the Rise of the Book Religion in Israel and the Ancient Near East* (Leuven: Peeters, 1997) 157-71; H. Cazelles, "The Problem of the Kings in Osee 8:4," *CBQ* 11 (1949) 14-25; R. E. Clements, *Prophecy and Tradition* (Oxford: Basil Blackwell, 1975); E. Day, "Is the Book of Hosea Exilic?" *American Journal of Semitic Languages and Literature* 26 (1909/10) 105-32; J. Day, "Pre-Deuteronomic Allusions to the Covenant in Hosea and Psalm LXXVIII," *VT* 36 (1986) 1-12; L. de Regt, "Person Shift in Prophetic Texts. Its Function and Rendering in Ancient and Modern Translations," J. C. de Moor (ed.), *The Elusive Prophet. The Prophet as a Historical Person, Literary Character and Anonymous Artist* (OudSt 45; Leiden: E. J. Brill, 2001) 214-31; G. I. Emmerson, "The Structure and Meaning of Hosea VIII 1-3," *VT* 25 (1975) 700-710; H. L. Ginsberg, *The Israelian Heritage of Judaism* (New York: JTS, 1982); R. Gnuse, "Calf, Cult, and King: The Unity of Hosea 8:1-13," *BZ* 26 (1982) 83-92; J. H. Hayes and J. K. Kuan, "The Final Years of Samaria (730-720 BC)," *Bib* 72 (1991) 153-

81; R. S. Hendel, "Aniconism and Anthropomorphism in Ancient Israel," K. van der Toorn (ed.), *The Image and the Book. Iconic Cults, Aniconism, and the Rise of the Book Religion in Israel and the Ancient Near East* (Leuven: Peeters, 1997) 157-71; Y. Hoffman, "A North Israelite Typological Myth and a Judaean Historical Tradition: The Exodus in Hosea and Amos," *VT* 39 (1989) 169-82; S. A. Irvine, "Politics and Prophetic Commentary in Hosea 8:8-10," *JBL* 114 (1995) 292-94; O. Keel and C. Uehlinger, *Gods, Goddesses, and Images of God in Ancient Israel* (Minneapolis: Fortress, 1998); C. J. Labuschagne, "The Similes in the Book of Hosea," *OTWSA* 7-8 (1965) 64-76; J. R. Lundbom, "Double-Duty Subject in Hosea VIII 5," *VT* 25 (1975) 228-30; idem, "Poetic Structure and Prophetic Rhetoric in Hosea," *VT* 29 (1979) 300-308; T. N. D. Mettinger, *No Graven Image: Israelite Aniconism in Its Ancient Near Eastern Context* (Stockholm: Almqvist & Wiksell, 1995); idem, "Israelite Aniconism: Developments and Origins," K. van der Toorn (ed.), *The Image and the Book. Iconic Cults, Aniconism, and the Rise of the Book Religion in Israel and the Ancient Near East* (Leuven: Peeters, 1997) 173-204; S. Morag, "On Semantic and Lexical Features in the Language of Hosea," *Tarbiz* 53 (1984) 489-511 (in Hebrew); N. Na'aman, "The Historical Background to the Conquest of Samaria (720 BC)," *Bib* 71 (1990) 206-25; idem, "No Anthropomorphic Graven Image. Notes on the Assumed Anthropomorphic Cult Statues in the Temples of YHWH in the Pre-Exilic Period," *UF* 31 (1999) 391-415; E. W. Nicholson, "Problems in Hosea VIII 13," *VT* 16 (1966) 355-58; H. Niehr, "In Search of YHWH's Cult Statue in the First Temple," K. van der Toorn (ed.), *The Image and the Book. Iconic Cults, Aniconism, and the Rise of the Book Religion in Israel and the Ancient Near East* (Leuven: Peeters, 1997) 73-95; M. O'Connor, "The Pseudosorites: A Type of Paradox in Hebrew Verse," E. R. Follis (ed.), *Directions in Biblical Hebrew Poetry* (JSOTSupS 40; Sheffield: Sheffield Academic Press, 1987) 161-72; S. M. Paul, "משא מלך שרים Hosea 8:8-10 and Ancient Near Eastern Royal Epithets," *Scripta Hierosolymitana* 31 (1986) 193-204; L. Perlitt, *Bundestheologie im Alten Testament* (WMANT 36; Neukirchen-Vluyn: Neukirchener Verlag, 1969); S. Pisano, "'Egypt' in the Septuagint Text of Hosea," G. J. Norton, S. Pisano, and C. M. Martini (eds.), *Tradition of the Text: Studies Offered to Dominique Barthélemy in Celebration of His 70th Birthday* (OBO 109; Fribourg: Éditions universitaires, 1991) 301-8; J. D. Schloen, *The House of the Father as Fact and Symbol. Patrimonialism in Ugarit and the Ancient Near East* (Winona Lake, IN: Eisenbrauns, 2001); C. L. Seow, "Hosea 14:10 and the Foolish People Motif," *CBQ* 42 (1982) 212-24; Mark S. Smith, *The Early History of God,* 2nd ed. (Grand Rapids: Wm. B. Eerdmans, 2002); A. Szabó, "Textual Problems in Amos and Hosea," *VT* 25 (1975) 500-524; H. Tadmor, "The Historical Background of Hosea's Prophecies," M. Haran (ed.), *Yehezkel Kaufman Jubilee Volume* (Jerusalem: Magnes Press, 1960) 84-88; W. I. Toews, *Monarchy and Religious Institutions under Jeroboam I* (SBLMS 47; Atlanta: Scholars Press, 1993); M. Tsevat, "Some Biblical Notes," *HUCA* 24 (1952-53) 107-14; C. Uehlinger, "Anthropomorphic Cult Statuary in Iron Age Palestine and the Search for Yahweh's Cult Images," K. van der Toorn (ed.), *The Image and the Book. Iconic Cults, Aniconism, and the Rise of the Book Religion in Israel and the Ancient Near East* (Leuven: Peeters, 1997) 97-155; J. Wellhausen, *Prolegomena to the History of Ancient Israel* (Cleveland and New York: World Publishing Company, 1961; 1st published, Berlin, 1883); E. R. Wendland, *The Discourse Analysis of Hebrew Prophetic Literature* (Lewiston, NY: E. Mellen Press, 1995); N. Wyatt, "Of Calves and Kings: The Canaanite Dimension in the Religion of Israel," *SJOT* 6 (1992) 68-91.

Fifth Didactic Prophetic Reading:
On YHWH's Sentencing Israel to Exile for Its Failings, 9:1-17

Structure

The above outline is one among several possible proposals for the structure of Hosea 9:1-17. A common understanding of the text is well reflected in the masoretic tradition of paragraph division (9:1-9; 9:10-17, see Aleppo Codex) and today is illustrated in the work of several scholars. For instance, Davies (*Hosea,* 211-31) refers to 9:1-9 and 9:10-17 under the rubrics of "The end of festal worship" and "A sinful history begets a barren future," respectively. Macintosh (*Hosea,* 335-82) refers to them under the titles of "The effects of Yahweh's sentence of judgement" and "What must be contrasted to what was and might have been." Simian-Yofre (*Desierto,* 120-34) entitles them "Inutilidad del culto y los profetas" (i.e., "uselessness of cult and prophets") and "Infidelidad de Efraím" (i.e., "Ephraim's infidelity"). Stuart (*Hosea,* 138-55) refers to them as "From festival days to punishment days," "Ephraim rejected, exiled, unloved." It is worth noting that, at times, the perceived break in 9:9 is even interwoven as an important component in a hypothetical narrative of the life of the historical prophet Hosea (see Wolff, *Hosea,* xxx, 161; Pentiuc, *Long-Suffering Love,* 125).

To be sure, other proposals for the understanding of these verses have also been advanced. Weiser (*Die Propheten,* 71-77) puts forward 9:1-6, 7-9, 10-14, 15-17. Sweeney (*The Twelve,* 102-3) disassociates v. 17 from the preceding text and associates it with 10:1-8. He also divides the rest into 9:1-9, 10-13, 14, and 15-16 (op. cit., 95-102). Qyl (*Hosea,* 10) considers the whole of 9:1–10:9 as a unit, which he refers to under the rubric גלות וחורבן "exile and destruction," whereas Wendland (*Discourse Analysis,* 128) maintains that 9:1-17 is a single oracle, in which he notices five different strophes, namely, 1-3, 4-6, 7-9, 10-14, 15-17. (See also Good, "Composition.")

Even within the general approach adopted here, questions concerning the hierarchy of the proposed sections may be raised. For instance, one may argue that some sections, and especially 9:1-7a (or 9:1-7), are readings by themselves, within the set of readings of Hosea, chapter 4–11. In addition, given that Hos 10:1-8 is closely connected to 9:1-17 (see below), one may wonder whether it is not to be considered a section of this reading rather than a reading by itself.

As the rubrics mentioned above — including those in the above outline — clearly show, proposals concerning structure are related to, and in fact often intensify, some possible readings of the text. But significantly, more than one understanding of the text is allowed by any of the basic proposed structures, and conversely different structures do not preclude converging readings. The sure fact is that the text is written in such a way that allows readers — including the primary readership of the book — to find more than one possible outline and more than one single meaning to an outline. This situation permits a sophisticated interweaving of meanings and structures that emerge through the continuous reading and rereading of the book of Hosea. Yet, of course, not every outline is possible. The suitability of an outline to the text has to be argued. Below I will argue for the plausibility of the one advanced above, as one of the possible structures.

Despite the numerous links between 8:14 and 9:1-9 (see 8:1-14 STRUC-TURE), it is still reasonable to consider verse 9:1 as the opening of a new reading, at least as one among several possible structures. Verse 9:1 suggests the beginning of a new reading within this set of readings because of its opening with a vetitive, the way it evokes the beginning of the previous unit in 8:1 (see STRUCTURE there), the presence of a pair of concluding notes in 8:13bβ and 8:14, and the change of topic and tone. One may wonder also whether 10:1-8 is better understood as a kind of additional section to this reading or as an independent reading within Hosea 4–11. Both positions can be argued. The one preferred here is based on the fact that 10:1-8 represents, to some extent, a kind of thematic loop that revisits a number of matters or images mentioned in 9:1-7, but also in other readings. Moreover, 10:1-8 may be construed as the first part of a "double-headed" reading (10:1-15) that also revisits matters or images mentioned before. To some extent, because of its character as a loop and because of thematic considerations, the text of this section may be seen as leading the intended and primary reader towards the conclusion of the entire sets of reading (Hosea 4–11) in 11:1-11 and particularly 11:8-11. The multiplicity of possible structures is consistent with the nature of the text, that is, sections within a book meant to be read, reread, and studied continuously.

As for the internal structure advanced here, the first section (9:1-7a) begins with Israel (9:1) and concludes with Israel (9:7a). It is shaped around a triple negation, "they will not live in YHWH's country anymore . . . will not come to YHWH's temple anymore . . . will not be able to celebrate YHWH's festival." The rhetorical strategy is also clear: It begins with YHWH's land and moves to its ideological center (YHWH's temple), and then to its role in terms of necessary worship. At the same time, the very same section construes an image of agricultural disaster. Thus, the text reflects the common idea of "no (proper) worship, no produce of the fields" (see Setting). The triple negation, and particularly the motif of exile, is then elaborated in terms that evoke the negation of the Exodus, and the unit concludes with the heightening and ominous line, "the days of punishment have come, the days of recompense have come" (NRSV, 7a)

The unit begins with a subunit (9:1) that interweaves this reading into the preceding one (cf. 9:1aα and 8:1a; 8:9-10 and 9:1b). This subunit is unified by the pairs ישראל — עמים "Israel — nations [other than Israel]" (cf. Hos 7:8; and passim in the HB; cf. Hos 8:8 — see Setting) and שמח and גיל "rejoice — be glad" (cf. Isa 25:9; 66:10; Ps 14:7; 16:9; 21:2; 31:8; 32:11; 48:12; 53:7; Song 1:4). On this pair in Hos 9:1 see below. Verse 1b concludes thematically the first mini-unit, but it is closely interlinked with v. 2 by explicit word-pairs. Verse 1 concludes with a reference to גרנות "threshing floors," which in the context of this verse may evoke sexual connotations (cf. Ruth 3), that is taken in v. 2 as part of the word pair יקב — גרן "threshing floor — [wine] vat" (Num 18:27, 30; Deut 15:14; 16:13; 2 Kgs 6:27; Joel 2:24) and which leads to the reference to תירוש "new wine" (cf. Prov 3:10). This תירוש along with דגן "grain" at the end of v. 1 points to a second word pair, דגן — תירוש "grain — new wine" (see Hos 2:10, 24; 7:14 and particularly 4:11; and cf. Gen 27:28, 37; Num 18:12; Deut 28:51; 33:28; 2 Kgs 18:32; Isa 36:17; Joel 1:10; Zech 9:17 — note the gender differentiation in the latter — etc.), that is semantically similar to the "threshing floor — [wine] vat" and which reinforces the imagery of the text. (The reference to דגן in v. 1 also allows for a reading of the verse in a way informed by Hos 2:14). These word pairs substantially contribute to textual cohesion. The subunit concludes with the first of the three negations mentioned above, the one referring to YHWH's land (see Setting).

The next subunit is bound to the preceding one, and the intended readers are asked to approach both as part and parcel of one single reading. Among the most obvious formal markers linking the two are the endings ארץ ה' and ה' בית and the rhetorical trajectory from ישב "dwell/live/sit" to בוא "enter/come" (see conclusions of vv. 3 and 4, respectively; and cf. Ps 26:4; see also 2 Kgs 19:27). Not only does the conclusion of this subunit link it to the preceding, but so does its opening. The sonorous pun in ישבו and שב ("they shall live — they shall return") in 3a and 3b is obvious, and so is the semantic contrast: "they shall not live in YHWH's country" and "they shall return to Egypt."

Since this subunit leads to the negation associated with the temple, it is fitting that the agricultural imagery evoked in the preceding subunit becomes more centered in, and more explicitly associated with, the role of produce in the cult. Numerous markers of textual cohesion are present in this subunit. Among them, the pair "Egypt — Assyria" (v. 3b), טמא יאכלו "they shall eat unclean [food]" and אכליו יטמאו "those who eat it shall be unclean [/defiled]" in vv. 3 and 4, respectively, the repetition of the word לחם "bread" (and notice the sonorous pun, לחם — להם "for them" in 4aβ).

The two references to X ליום, which here may be translated as "the day of X," contribute to the shaping of textual coherence in the additional note. The note stands apart from the two previous negation subunits because of its structure; it is much briefer than the others, and it opens with direct address, מה תעשו "what will you do?" Yet it is clearly linked to the other two by its ending 'חג ה' "the festival of YHWH," and by the thematic thread that keeps the three negation subunits together. This note takes its thematic clue from, and elaborates further the issue of, the future impossibility of YHWH's (proper) worship that is raised in vv. 3b-4.

Two central threads shape the tapestry created by the preceding subunits, namely, exile and the associated impossibility to maintain YHWH's worship (see Setting). The next subunit in this section elaborates further the former. Significantly, the subunit opens with a multivalent expression כי הלכו משד that the intended and primary rereaders could have understood as leading, among other things, to meanings such as "even if they escape destruction . . ." (NRSV), "behold, they have departed because of the destruction/devastation . . ." (cf. Simian-Yofre, *Desierto*, 121), "behold they have departed from the devastated land . . ." (cf. Wolff, *Hosea*, 150, 156), "for behold, they come from devastation . . ." (Garret, *Hosea*, 194), or more likely, from the perspective of the primary rereadership/s, a combination of all of the above. The openness of this text is counterbalanced by its univocality that is central to the message, namely, that they will be gathered and destroyed in Egypt, whereas their homes and land will become uninhabited, a place outside human culture (see Isa 34:13; 1 Sam 13:6; cf. Job 31:40). From the viewpoint of style, this central message is emphasized by the salient repetition of the מ sound in the sequence of eleven words that begins with משד and concludes with באהליהם lit. "in their tents," but here meaning in "their dwellings" (cf. Ps 132:3). Ten of these eleven words contain the מ sound. The end of this sequence — along with shift in contents and sentence structure — points to the conclusion of this subunit.

The final subunit in this section consists of the concluding note of the section. It comprises three versets of similar structure, and in the case of the first two, of similar beginning. The first two versets enhance the message of the section by stressing that the days of judgment "have come" (concerning the first verset, see Isa 10:3; cf. Jer 46:21; Mic 7:4). The second verset (cf. Isa 34:8) adds to that message the sense that the punishment is a requital of evil deeds, thus subtly shifting the focus to Israel, which stands at the center of the third verset, namely, ידעו ישראל "[then] Israel shall know." The implied question posed to the readers of the book is, *what* shall Israel know at that time? It is unlikely that the main answer to this question is "the prophet is a fool" as in Hos 9:7b; in fact, the latter functions as the beginning of a new section within the reading. Israel is supposed to know then that which has come to happen to it as well as the reasons for the punishment. In this manner, Israel, both as a character inscribed in the book and as trans-temporal Israel with whom the intended and primary readers of the book identify, shall come to know through these events, or through the reading about these events in the book, about YHWH and YHWH's ways. In other words, the message of the text is not too different from the conclusion of, for instance, Psalm 83 (see Ps 83:19), and cf. Ps 109:20-29 (esp. v. 27). Within these discourses, the concept of "to know about YHWH" partially overlaps and can only lead to that of "to know YHWH," which is a basic concept in the book of Hosea involving not only theological, abstract knowledge but an acknowledgment of YHWH, YHWH's proper position, and Israel's obligations concerning YHWH. (On these matters see Malul, *Knowledge,* esp. 119-20; and for a similar understanding of this verset, Sweeney, *Twelve Prophets,* 97; many scholars have proposed emendations to the text here, involving claims of a different wording or a different location of this verset; see, for instance, Wolff, *Hosea,* 150; NRSV — but not RSV, or the KJV; the LXX of Hosea differs at this point from the Hebrew MT.)

The next two sections focus on the present of the Israel that is portrayed in the book, and on the past history of that Israel and of trans-temporal Israel. The beginning of the second section is marked by the shift in the grammatical structure and theme. The conclusion of the unit is marked by the verbatim repetition of יזכר עונם ויפקוד חטאתם "he will remember their iniquity, and punish their sins [NRSV]" (see 8:13 and discussion there) and the presence of a new opening with a focal noun phrase and a new theme in 9:10. Markers of textual coherence are abundant in the first subunit of this section (7:7b-8). They include word pairs, word repetitions, and puns on words (e.g., נביא "prophet" — איש הרוח "the man of the spirit," רוב "great" — רבה "great," משטמה "animosity/hostility" vv. 7 and 8; צופה "watchman" and fig. "prophet" [e.g., Ezek 3:17; 33:7] — נביא). The short note in 9a summarizes the situation in Israel and is elaborated later in the book (see below). In addition it generalizes the sin of Israel, and by doing so this note facilitates the use of an expression that occurs in Hos 8:13bα as the concluding phrase in 9:9b (see below).

The conclusion of the first subunit in this section, בבית אלהיו "in the House of his God" in 9:8, also points back to the second negation in the first section, and provides another reason for it. Thus, the conclusion creates one of the many thematic loops that appear in the book of Hosea; its aim is to revisit something explicitly referred to or implied in a preceding section within the reading or the book; see discussion above.

A reference to אלהי "my God" occurs in v. 8 and in v. 17. Both references serve to stress the particular connection between the speaker and YHWH at one level, between the authorial voice and YHWH at another, and above all between the readership who embodies the authorial voice as they read the book and YHWH, on a related, third level. All of these connections are based on and reflect a discursive necessity to set these voices as "other" in relation to the Israel portrayed in the book and to see the clear opposition between the construction of the "I" in "my God" and that of the "they" in v. 17. (It goes without saying that, if the voices and identities of the two were identical, then the text would never be reliable or worth reading as an authoritative instance of YHWH's word.) It does more, however. It allows the readership, that is, Israel, to construe itself as standing with YHWH and apart from the particular manifestation of trans-temporal Israel that is monarchic Israel. Moreover, as they read and reread the book, the text allows them to associate themselves with those who will say אלהי "my God" in Hos 2:25 (and ct. Hos 8:2; see discussion there; see also discussion of the imprecation in v. 14 below).

188

The third section in this reading reaches back into the past of the relationship between YHWH and Israel, then characterizes Ephraim and portrays its punishment, and finally leads to a concluding note about exile. The beginning of the section is marked by the shift in topic, and by the introduction of a focal noun phrase. The existence of a break of some level between 9:9 and 9:10 is widely agreed upon, and already the MT division into paragraphs recognizes it. The same holds true for the one between 9:17 and 10:1, for similar reasons. In fact, 9:10 is somewhat reminiscent of 10:1 (see above).

The analysis of the inner structure of this third section owes much to Eidewall, *Grapes,* 148-49. In v. 10a YHWH is portrayed as reporting the beginning of YHWH's relationship with Israel (cf. v. 13; 10:11; 11:1). The text here sheds light not only on the characterization of YHWH but also on the construction of ideal Israel, of Israel before its rejection of YHWH. Verse 10a is characterized by a high density of markers of textual coherence, including parallel structures, similar beginnings, repetitions of sounds, and word pairs. (On the constructions of Israel's past and of the divine attitude towards early Israel that the text conveys, see Setting.) YHWH's report of Israel's apostasy follows immediately in 10b. The text here further elaborates on the memory of the event in Israel's memory likely referred to in Hos 5:2 (see Num 25:1-5, and cf., among others, Num 31:26 and Ps 106:28). A similar and complementary reference to Israel's memory is advanced in v. 15, a subunit clearly held together by patterns of repetitions of words and sounds similar to those observed before, and which is the structural counterpart of v. 10b. (On the significance of the mention of Gilgal and Baal Peor, see Setting.) Two subunits (vv. 11-13 and v. 16) deal explicitly with Ephraim's childlessness as punishment, and, implicitly, with its lack of future. Moreover, since without making children Ephraim/Israel will soon cease to exist, then the text also deals with YHWH's reported, future cancellation of the deity's relationship with Israel that began as portrayed in v. 10. The imagery of Ephraim (/Israel) fading as a flock of birds that flies away in 11a accentuates both the sense of complete disappearance to the point of leaving no trace and the swiftness of the process (cf. Ibn Ezra, "Accepted Commentary"; cf. Labuschagne, "Similes," 69-70; Nwaoru, *Imagery,* 168). It also introduces a spatial dimension, insofar as the birds leave a certain place when they fly away. (On of the meanings of v. 11a see below.) Both of these subunits share a similar rhetoric and are shaped, at their core, by more or less explicit pseudosorites. (Pseudosorites are a type of paradox, that is, a set of assertions that is self-contradictory. In particular it creates a powerful rhetorical message through illogical or self-contradicting negatives, e.g., a curse such as "you will never have children, and if you were to have any, they will die young." If the person will never have children — a point stressed by the "were" — then it is illogical and self-contradictory to speak about the death of these children. The combined rhetorical power of these assertions, however, is hard to miss.)

The first one, however, focuses on the female side of the failed reproductive process, "no giving birth, no pregnancy, no conception" (11b); whereas the second one focuses on the male side of that failed process, "their [Ephraim's] root is dry, they produce no fruit" (16a). (On these matters see O'Connor,

"Pseudosorites," esp. pp 165-68.) The completeness of the failure of the basic process of reproduction is conveyed by the pseudosorites as well as by reference to both the failure of male and female reproductive roles. It is worth noting that although Ephraim is construed as directly associated with the male side by the reference to "their root" (v. 16 — notice the absence of "their giving birth" and similar terms in v. 11b), it is also and explicitly associated with the female side by "the precious things of [or, 'in'] their [Ephraim's] wombs" (i.e., children). The main point is not that gender constructions of the concept of Ephraim (/Israel) are not necessarily male (cf. Hosea 1–3) but that the completeness of the failure of Ephraim to reproduce is conveyed to the intended and primary rereadership in part by this double association of the character with both male and female gendered roles and biological features. (The reference to שרש "root" in v. 16 is also related to the pun on פרי-אפרים "Ephraim-fruit" — see above — and the common pair שרש — פרי "root — fruit"; see 2 Kgs 19:30//Isa 37:31; Ezek 17:9; Amos 2:9; and cf. Isa 14:29. The pair works, in part, by raising a kind of cause-and-effect relation between the two terms, e.g., if the root is rotten, there will be no fruit. This cause-effect pattern is consistent with the interpretations advanced here.)

Both of these subunits show textually inscribed markers that set them partially apart from the rest. One may mention three micro-units beginning with "Ephraim" (vv. 11, 13a, 13b) and two with כי (vv. 12a, 12b), which in English cannot be translated by the same word. (On the image in v. 13a and its relation with 10a, see Setting.) The second subunit shows, for instance, a repetition of the sound ש that brings together "their root" — "dry" — "[not] produce" in 16a and a pun on אפרים "Ephraim" and פרי "fruit." This later pun is central to the meaning of the text here for it is directly reminiscent of "he [Jacob/Israel] named Ephraim, 'for God has made me fruitful'" (Gen 41:52). From the perspective of a readership that is aware of the "meaning" of the name Ephraim, the central role of childlessness in this section of the reading can only shape a sharp contrast: nomen — anti-omen and through it a sense of a world upside down, that is, one in which that which is or is to be actually stands for the exact opposite of that which should have been. As such it eloquently expresses the main gist of the section, and to a large extent the book as a whole. (It is likely that the imagery of childlessness was included here, to begin with, to convey such a meaning.)

The imprecation in the middle of the childlessness/punishment section brings a human voice into the text. However, not only is the message of this human voice consistent with and strongly supportive of the divine voice reported in the reading, but its wording is reminiscent of that of the divine speech (cf. משכיל "bereaving" [v. 14] and ושכלתים [v. 12a] "I will bereave them"; and notice the word pair בטן "belly, womb" [vv. 11, 16] — רחם "womb" [v. 14], and cf. Isa 46:3; 49:15; Jer 1:5; Ps 58:4; Job 3:11; 31:15; and esp. Ps 22:11). Likewise, the human speech contains repetitions of words and sounds similar to those found in other subunits within this reading. Because of these features the human voice, on the one hand, converges into the general godly voice of the speaker in the text and, on the other hand, reinforces the rhetorical case of the divine voice by suggesting that any godly person who listens to or reads

YHWH's (reported) words and YHWH's case cannot but join YHWH in his proclamation of punishment over Israel (ct. with the figure of Abraham in Genesis 18).

The text states that any godly person in Israel (notice the lack of any markers of particular identity) including the intended readers of the book cannot but shout, as it were, "Give them (monarchic Israel) a bereaving womb. . . ." The text not only reinforces the sinful construction of past Israel, but also allows the readers who are also Israel to identify with YHWH and separate themselves from the sinful manifestation of trans-temporal Israel that is portrayed in the book, and which is part of their social memory and story about themselves (see discussion on "my God" in vv. 8 and 17 above.) Although somewhat obvious, a significant difference between the human and the divine voice is communicated by the verse: the former cannot "bereave" by itself. YHWH, of course, can and did.

The concluding unit in this section (v. 17) and in the reading as a whole is assigned again to a human voice. (For the reasons for this choice and its implications see above.) The final statement encapsulates much of this reading and of the book of Hosea: (a) (monarchic and even pre-monarchic) Israel did not listen to YHWH; thus (b) YHWH must reject them, and as a consequence (c) Israel shall become a fugitive among the nations, that is, exiled. From the perspective of the readers of the book, this simple conclusion encapsulates the basic tenets of their understanding of their past. As for the particular choice of words in the verse, it was likely to evoke in the rereaders of the book Hos 7:13 and vice versa. The linkage between the two verses conveys a clear message: Since Israel/Ephraim has wandered away (נדד) from YHWH, they will be wanderers among the nations. The language of v. 17 demands some scrutiny. A message very similar to the one mentioned above is shaped by a reading of Hos 9:17 that is informed by 2 Kgs 17:15 and vice versa: since they have rejected (מאס) YHWH's statutes . . . , YHWH has rejected (מאס) them. Cf. Hos 9:17 with 2 Kgs 17:20 and notice the use of the same verb (מאס), the same subject of the verb (YHWH = my God), and, from the perspective of the readership, the same object (all the seed of Israel = them). The reference to "not listening to YHWH" in this particular context seems consistent with those in 2 Kgs 18:12 and Jer 43:7. All of these instances may point to a common discursive and ideological horizon.

It is perhaps worth mentioning that Hos 9:17 has a long history of Christian (and at times, anti-Jewish) interpretation in which this verse is associated in some way or another with the image of the "eternal Jew" wandering among the nations. Obviously, no literati in postmonarchic Judah (or late monarchic Judah for that matter) would have ever understood the verse in such a way. Moreover, although the verse itself refers only to punishment and exile, it does not exist by itself. Rather, it is part and parcel of a book and a set of readings (Hosea 4–11) that, while offering an explanation for the past including the exile, also provide one of the strongest expressions of hope for an ideal future of reconciliation between Israel and YHWH. The literary setting of such expressions of hope — i.e., hope against a background of apparent hopelessness — serves to heighten such hopes rather than eliminate them. (For a critique of this interpretative tradition, see Macintosh, *Hosea*, 382-83, and cf. Sweeney, *The Twelve*, 102-13; for relatively recent reverberations of the mentioned interpretative tradition, see, for instance, Wolff, *Hosea*, 168; Hubbard, *Hosea*, 169.)

Before concluding this discussion of the possible structures of Hosea 9, some further observations are in order. Verse 6 seems to elaborate further the motif of the return to Egypt from Hos 8:13. (Macintosh [*Hosea*, 350] suggests that it is a "meditative expansion of the terse judgment of 8.13b.") From the perspective of the rereaders of the book, המה ישובו מצרים in Hos 8:13bβ serves as a signpost that evokes texts such as Hos 9:6, just as the reading of Hos 9:6 evokes that of 8:13b. The same considerations apply to Hos 10:9-15, which elaborate the theme of "the days of Gibeah" that is very briefly mentioned in Hos 9:9a. Notice the almost verbatim repetition of the key phrase here and cf. with the verbatim repetition between 8:13bα and 9:9b. All of these considerations cannot be explained as products of random choice. They point at the deep interrelatedness of different readings within the book of Hosea, and to a composition and authorial voice that explicitly ask the intended readers of the book to pay careful attention to such a feature by means of clear textually inscribed markers. These considerations suggest, of course, that the main structural unit is "the book of Hosea," rather than any of the (complementary) sets of particular readings according to which the book may be divided and outlined.

The presence of some textual markers linking different sections of the reading was acknowledged above. It is worth stressing that these markers are numerous and meaningful. For instance, one may notice the envelope created by עמים "peoples/nations" in 9:1a and גוים "nations" in 9:17 (since Israel behaved like the "nations," it shall be wandering among the "nations"). Similarly the set of references to בית ("house, temple") in vv. 4, 8 and 15 is salient, and one is to keep in mind that בית denoted "Temple" there, but may have also connoted a sense of the household of YHWH, that is, the polity and the territory that the readership imagined as belonging to YHWH (see Hosea 8:1-14, STRUCTURE; cf. Lohfink, "Hate and Love"). The result is, of course, a multilayered message to which both the denoted and connoted meanings contribute. For instance, this approach would have led the intended and primary readers to understand in particular v. 15 as referring to both their "exile" from the Temple *and* from the land, and thus linking v. 15 also to vv. 2-3 and enhancing the theological outlook that binds Temple and land. (Sweeney [*The Twelve*, 101-2] maintains that בית in 9:15 may refer also to "the house of the husband" and, accordingly, that the meaning of the verse may be approached through the prism of language and imagery associated with divorce, i.e., the husband sends away his wife from his house.)

A few observations about the text of Hosea 9 and its implications are also in order. The text of Hos 9:1 (at least the MT) defies the common expectations of the primary readership concerning שמח "rejoice" and גיל, which is often translated as "rejoice" or "exult," as it uses the nominal form of גיל, commonly understood as "exultation," and the preposition אל־ rather than the negation אל. Although the text is frequently emended, in the light of Job 3:22 and given the tendency to unusual language in the book of Hosea, there is no substantial reason to emend it (see Macintosh, *Hosea*, 337). The root גיל likely carries the meaning of "physical agitation," and is most often associated with joy. It may be used also in relation to sadness or affliction that involve physical agitation; see Hos 10:5; Ps 2:11; Macintosh, "Considerations of Problems," and idem, *Hosea*, 337, 400. The expression זנית מעל אלהיך in 9:1 (lit. "you have whored from [upon] your God") is also slightly odd and, in fact, unique in the HB (see Setting). Significantly, from the perspective of a readership that continuously reads and meditates upon the text, this expression is reminiscent of the general form זנה אחרי ה' (lit. "whore after YHWH") that appears in Hos 1:2 (Exod 34:15, 16; Lev 17:7, etc.) and the expression ויזנו מתחת אלהיהם (lit. "they whored [from] beneath/under their God") in Hos 4:12 (cf. Ezek 23:5). Although the shift in the prepositions might perhaps be fortuitous, the sequence in the book may be taken as suggestive of the completeness of Israel's whoring behavior as these prepositions evoked in the intended and primary readers the meanings of "up" (מעל), "down" (מתחת), and "behind" (אחרי). Needless to say, if this is the case, the message conveyed by this particular way of pointing at that completeness would certainly be consistent with and supportive of the main thrust of the book.

There is no widespread agreement about the meaning of Hos 9:8. The position advanced here is that the text plays with two main possible meanings to convey a multilayered message. At the very center of the pun one finds a careful use of two possible meanings of צפה. The term carries here the meaning of "to watch" in the sense of "to confront" or "to stand in confrontation with/against" (cf. Ps 37:32), and עם אלהיו can be understood as "against my God" (see Deut 9:7, 24; 31:27; and cf. Gen 32:29). The resulting reading of 9:8 would be akin to "Ephraim stands in confrontation with my God; as for a/the prophet, he is a fowler's snare in all his [double meaning, both the prophet's and Ephraim's] ways." At the same time, צפה אפרים was likely to evoke the meaning "the watchman of Ephraim," which would have purposefully led the intended rereadership to construe a possible meaning of 9:8a akin to "Ephraim's watchman is with my God [i.e., YHWH]"; cf. Exod 34:28; 1 Sam 2:21. The expectations created by this salient possible meaning are, however, contradicted by the following note in 9:8b, which again denigrates the figure of the prophet — צופה "watchman" may also point at the meaning "prophet" (e.g., Ezek 3:17; 33:7). Thus, rather than being a source of hope, the prophet is a snare (see 7b). The rhetorical point is to raise the hope associated with the traditional assumptions about the role of prophets, and then to trash them. For some partially similar and different interpretations of this verse, see, among others, Macintosh, *Hosea*, 354-57; Wolff, *Hosea*, 151, 157-58; Barthélemy, *Critique Textuelle*, vol. III, 564-66; Simian-Yofre, *Desierto*, 121-25; Sweeney, *The Twelve*, 97-98; Pentiuc, *Long-suffering Love*, 124; Dobbie, "Text of Hosea IX 8." See also Radak, Ibn Ezra, both "Accepted Commentary" and "Alternative Commentary" (Simon, *Abraham Ibn Ezra*, 94, 280-81); and from a different perspective, Limburg, *Hosea-Micah*, 32-34. For a different approach to the verse, see Driver, "Linguistic and Textual Problems," 159.

Verse 9:11a is a typical case of the use of a multivalent expression to articulate a meaning that is constructed by interweaving the different partial meanings it conveys into a single whole. One of the partial meanings of 9:11a is

akin to "Ephraim is like a flock of birds, their population flies away" (for popu-
lation/multitude as the referent of כבודם see Radak; Qyl, *Hosea,* עג; Rudolph,
Hosea, 181-82; Macintosh, *Hosea,* 365; Simian-Yofre, *Desierto,* 130). This
meaning suits the immediate literary context. The text also bears an associated
meaning, namely, "Ephraim is like a flock of birds, their nobility flies away" in
which "nobility" stands for the elite of the people (cf. Isa 5:13), which in turn
stands for the people. In addition, it carries the (related) connotation of
"Ephraim is like a flock of birds, their wealth flies away" (and for references to
the loss of the wealth on which Ephraim/Israel is portrayed as trusting cf. 9:6b).
Images of Ephraim as a bird appear elsewhere in the book of Hosea; see Hos
7:11-12; 11:11. Another partial meaning conveyed by the expression in 9:11a
may be translated as "As for Ephraim, like a bird their glory [i.e., YHWH] will
fly away," or in more idiomatic English, "Ephraim's Glory will fly away" (see,
Davies, *Hosea,* 227-28; cf. Andersen and Freedman, *Hosea,* 542; for similar
uses of "glory" see Jer 2:11; Ps 106:20). This understanding of the text is directly linked to, and explicitly supported by, "when I [YHWH] turn aside [i.e.,
depart from] them" in 12b. All of these partial meanings complement and inform each other, and shape the full meaning of the text. As a whole, they point
to the disaster that is expected from YHWH's departure, including lack of human fertility, and to the related, anticipated end of Israel/Ephraim that results
from YHWH's departure and the cessation of the relationship between YHWH
and Israel. These partial meanings revisit the ideological constructions of
(a) Ephraim/Israel as trusting in their power (glory), which within this discourse necessarily leads to its loss, and (b) the elite as representing the people
as a whole. Significantly, they reintroduce in this reading the image of the land
and temple mentioned above, this time not from the perspective of the people
who will not be able to dwell in the land or come to the Temple, but from the
viewpoint of YHWH, who is leaving the land. Perhaps more importantly, they
associate the image of exile (flying birds) with that of (national) death, and convey and reflect a land/temple centric theology comparable to that widely attested in the book of Ezekiel. This type of sophisticated writing is consistent
with the general setting of the book of Hosea, that is, a book written by literati
for other literati's continuous rereading and studying.

It is worth noting the ways in which the shifting of speakers and referents
contributes to the communication and construction of meanings in this reading.
For instance, the "her" at the end of Hos 9:2 instead of an anticipated "them" (as
expected, some scholars propose to emend the text, see BHS) can only refer to
the land — YHWH's land — and contributes to the construction of an ideological overlap of images between people and land. References to Israel shift from
the second to third person and vice versa in the first section to maximize the rhetorical power of the text. These shifts contribute to the shaping of the affective
appeal of the reported words on the unnamed addressees within the world of the
book, but above all on its intended and primary readers, and on those to whom
these literati, who embodied the voice of the text and its characters, read the text.
Similar shifts appear elsewhere in the reading (e.g., על רב עונך "because of
your great iniquity" in v. 7) and are common in written literature.

Numerous proposals for textual emendations of words and expressions in this reading have been advanced (see, for instance, BHS). For a summary and critique of many of them, see Barthélemy, *Critique Textuelle,* vol. III, 558-69; see also Macintosh, "Hosea. Rabbinic Commentators," 77-78, and his numerous analyses of these matters in idem, *Hosea;* and, from a different perspective, Daniels, *Hosea and Salvation History,* 53-55.

For proposed reconstructions of the redactional history of Hosea 9 or as often proposed, Hos 9:1-9 and Hos 9:10-17, see, among others, Yee, *Composition,* 198-207, 316; and Zulick, *Rhetorical Polyphony,* 201-13. A general tendency is to relate texts that clearly deal with exile to a postmonarchic redaction. For instance, Yee assigns 9:2-4, 6, 17 — among other verses — to her R2. Concerning Hos 9:10-17, see the summary and proposals in Daniels, *Hosea and Salvation History,* 55-56. For summary references and a critique of earlier suggestions along with some proposals, see Harper, *Hosea,* 326-41.

Genre

Some of the scholars who attempt to reconstruct the words of the historical prophet — and accordingly, the historical prophet himself — have proposed that Hosea 9 contains at least two oracles or speeches proclaimed by the historical prophet Hosea at different occasions. For instance, Wolff associates Hos 9:1-9 with the words of the historical prophet in a disruption of a jubilant celebration of the festival of Sukkoth in a northern Israel city or cities — and esp. Samaria — in a year between 733 and 727 BCE in which the harvest was "apparently plenteous" (see Wolff, *Hosea,* 153). According to Sweeney (*The Twelve,* 93-98), the historical Hosea asks the people not to rejoice at the festival of Sukkoth, but he understands Hos 9:1-9 as the initial speech in a lengthy discourse by the prophet (Hos 9:1–14:1). Davies (*Hosea,* esp. 211), who also associates the text with Sukkoth, divides Hosea 9 into Hos 9:1-9, a prophetic diatribe, and 9:10-17, a prophetic oracle.

Hos 9:1-17, however, is not an oral work, nor can it be separated from the book of Hosea. In fact, as demonstrated above, it is closely intertwined with other units in the book, even at the textual level, a fact that implies written compositional activity. Even Hos 9:1-7 is neither an orally proclaimed oracle given at a particular occasion nor anywhere an independent unit.

From the perspective of the book of Hosea (as opposed to any hypothetical proposal concerning the putative words and public life of a historical figure reconstructed on the basis of these proposals), Hos 9:1-17 can only be considered a non-independent, sophisticatedly written portion of a prophetic book that is deeply interwoven with other portions within the book of Hosea. Within this commentary, such units are called PROPHETIC READINGS, and as such, it may be claimed that 9:1-17 is included in a set of prophetic readings that begins in Hos 4:1 and concludes in Hos 11:11. One is to keep in mind the discussion under STRUCTURE, however, and recognize that prophetic readings are fluid units, and that the intended and primary readerships are allowed to develop different but complementary structures of the book, each with its own set of slightly different "prophetic readings."

It bears particular notice not only that the book is a holistic, written document, but also that neither the book as a whole nor Hos 9:1-17 asks the intended readership to imagine a particular set of circumstances against which the proposed oral communication took place. The text shifts and partially conflates two speakers, YHWH and a human speaker, and provides the readership with no information on the addressees, the place, the circumstances, or the time of the oral communication. To be sure, readers may identify the situation in the world of the book as the festival of Sukkoth, but they are certainly not required to do so. In fact, the text remains as open as possible within the time limitations and general scope of the world in which the book is set, as one would expect from a written text composed for continuous reading and rereading by literati in the postmonarchic period, and for the literati's interpretative readings to others unable to read by themselves at different occasions and for different reasons. Some of the approaches mentioned above seem to go against the grain of the written text by attempting to narrow its meaning to particular historical occasions in monarchic Israel.

Setting

As the previous discussion shows, questions of setting and genre are linked. The setting of the writing and primary reading of this, or any portion of the (present) book of Hosea for that matter, is the same as that of the book as a whole. Both involve writers and primary readers who are among the very few, sophisticated literati of Yehud.

The basic setting of the world portrayed in the reading is consistent with that of other readings in the book. It is a monarchic, agrarian world. Ephraim still exists as an independent polity, Israel is still in the land, and the two main political-military powers of the period are Assyria and Egypt. Israel worships YHWH and offers sacrifices to YHWH, but in a way deemed improper and therefore offensive by YHWH (cf., among others, Hosea 8; see also below).

As is the case with other readings in the book, Hosea 9 also contributes to the characterization of the language of the speaker — divine and human — as somewhat odd in relation to that expected to be found in prophetic books set in the monarchic period (cf. the books of Amos, Micah, and Isaiah and see their superscriptions). This portrayal indirectly contributes to the characterization of the implied author of the book, and of the book itself (see INTRODUCTION). The intended and primary readerships of the book sense, in the main, this shade of strangeness in the language through the presence of unique or uncommon expressions. One may mention, among others, צפה עם in v. 8 (for a discussion of the meanings conveyed by this expression see STRUCTURE above); קמוש "nettles" in v. 6 — elsewhere only in Isa 34:13 and Prov 24:31; יקוש "fowlers" in v. 8 — the vocalization is unique, and the form appears elsewhere only in Ps 91:3 and Prov 6:5; משטמה "animosity" or "hostility" — it occurs in the HB in Hos 9:7, 8 but nowhere else; as is well known, the term is important in the War Scroll; the masc. form of the qal infinitive construct of the root אהב "love" in v. 10 — it appears elsewhere in the HB only in Qoh 3:8; the common feminine form occurs also in the book of Hosea; see 3:1; 9:15. (Yoo ["Israelian Hebrew"] attributes most of these linguistic features to a northern Israelian dialect; on this matter see INTRODUCTION.)

Several key aspects of the worldview that Hosea 9 associates with the godly speakers clearly reflect the viewpoint of the implied authorship and of the literati of the period. Verse 9:1a certainly does not convey a sense that rejoicing is forbidden in general, but rather that Israel is not supposed to rejoice because it (/he) has "whored" (cf. Hosea, chs. 1–7; on the particular expression see below), departing from its (his) deity. The text, however, also plays with and advances a world outlook based on a dichotomy of "self" vs. "other," of "Israel" vs. "the nations (other than Israel)." This dichotomy contributes to the construction of boundaries around the identity of the primary readerships. The issue of boundaries comes to the forefront in the reference to the unclean food that the Israelites will have to eat in exile (in Assyria, but by extension anywhere outside YHWH's land; see v. 3; cf. Ezek 4:13) and reflects a theological discourse in which ethno-social-cultural and geographical boundaries are deeply interwoven (see below).

In addition, on the one hand, Hos 9:1 seems to suggest that unlike the other nations, Israel departed from its deity (cf. Jer 2:11 for a similar idea). On the other hand, it seems to suggest an inner circle image of the "other" that associates it with "exuberant rejoicing" that has no place in Israel. The immediate literary context in the book of the relevant expression אל גיל כעמים (which may translated as "do not rejoice exuberantly like the [other] peoples," see above) may have also suggested to the rereaders that such an exuberant rejoicing of the other involves some form of improper sexual behavior. (The text, however, does not refer to the Canaanites, nor to their supposed ritual activities, contra Rudolph, *Hosea,* 170-71; Harvey, "Rejoice Not.")

As mentioned above in the expression זנית מעל אלהיך (9:1), the "whoring" party, Israel, is referred to by a masc. sg. "you" (cf. Hos 4:15). Authoritative texts within the repertoire of the postmonarchic communities include numerous texts in which Israel is addressed in that manner. These texts tend to carry a strong affective appeal for their intended and primary male readership — it is likely that most literati were men — (see, for instance, the similar appeals that occur so often in Deuteronomy). At the same time, one may note that a construction of "errant" Israel in terms associated mainly with prostitutes carried connoted "feminization" of the errant (cf. previous discussion of Hos 4:1-19; for a different approach see Ginsberg, "Hosea," 1018-19).

Hos 9:2 reflects and reinforces the central element of the world outlook of ancient Israel — and other nations in the ancient Near East: "no (proper) worship, no produce of the fields." Numerous references to this view occur in the Hebrew Bible. Heavy attestation does not detract but reflects its centrality in agrarian societies. Proper worship and, therefore, the necessary knowledge and infrastructure, including proper personnel, are thus construed as the most basic components necessary for the physical survival of the group. This READING develops further the mental images and metaphors through the shift from "no proper worship — no produce of fields" to no produce of human wombs, the ultimate metaphor for the group's lack of physical survival.

This triple negation at the center of the message of the first section, and to a large extent of the entire reading, focuses the attention of the readers on the theme of exile: exile from the land of YHWH and the Temple of YHWH, and the concomitant inability to participate in YHWH's festival. Indirectly, it reflects and reinforces a conceptual characterization of Israel and its boundaries in which YHWH and YHWH's relation with Israel carry a conceptual close association between a land that is portrayed as YHWH's land, its geographical boundaries, and the Temple of YHWH within it, or better, at its center. These themes permeate much of the HB and are reflected in manifold ways across different literary genres (e.g., Ezekiel 37; Ps 137:1-4). It is worth noting that here they are set within a reading that focuses to a large extent on a particular manifestation of Israel, namely, Ephraim (i.e., the northern kingdom) in the monarchic period. From the perspective of the postmonarchic readership, it is obvious that the text intimated to them that (a) Ephraim was supposed to worship in Jerusalem even during monarchic times, and (b) YHWH's land includes not only the territory of Judah/Yehud but rather the lands of Judah *and* the northern kingdom, at whose center was the temple in Jerusalem. These are central themes in much of the Jerusalem-centered discourse of Yehud (cf. Ben Zvi, "Inclusion and Exclusion") and are consistent with the image of the future ideal unification of "all Israel" around Jerusalemite ideological tenets and related discursive concepts (e.g., the Davide kingship, and see Hosea 3 and 2:1-3). These themes reflect a discursive necessity of Judahization (or Yehuditization) of northern Israel both in the past and in the future. Since the memory of northern Israel does not conform to that image, the former substantially contributes within postmonarchic discourses to the general image of northern Israel as sinful. The latter is, of course, part of the idyllic image of a certain, but not soon to be attained, hopeful future. It bears notice that the necessity of the Judahization (or Yehuditization) of northern Israel is a result of the conceptualization of trans-temporal Israel in Judahite, Jerusalem-centered ideological terms, but still including northern Israel as one of its temporal manifestations. The book of Hosea contributes much in this regard. (Incidentally, this reading provides clear examples of the smooth textual slippage between references to Ephraim and Israel (cf. vv. 8 and 10) that characterizes the book as a whole and reflects and reinforces the ideological positions mentioned above.)

Of course, this reading's stress on the impossibility of maintaining YHWH's worship in a foreign land or without the Temple of YHWH carried a direct message to postmonarchic communities in Yehud (cf. Ezekiel 37; Haggai).

On a different matter, verse 7 characterizes the prophet as אֱוִיל "fool" and by doing so brings along the common associations of the term (see, for instance, Prov 1:7; 7:22; 10:8, 10, 14, 21; 12:15; 14:9; 16:22 and cf. Jer 4:22). In other words, it associates the prophet with foolishness, rejection of godly attitudes and behaviors, and ruin and destruction. The text here revisits the bond between destruction and prophets mentioned in Hos 6:5 from a very different perspective that imagines the prophet as part of a corrupted system of intermediaries between people and the deity that includes both priests/the Temple and prophets (cf. Hosea 4 and in particular 4:5). In addition the characterization of the (common) prophet as an active agent for ruin אֱוִיל leads the readership to imagine a counterpart, that is, a person who may save Israel if he (or less likely, she) is heeded as "wise" (and see the construction of the intended readership of the book in Hos 14:10). The overall tendency towards a negative characterization of prophets in the book (see Hos 4:5; 6:5; 9:7-8; 12:11) conveys a significant differentiation between "the prophets" on the one hand and the character Hosea in the book and the prophetic book on the other (cf. Odell, "Who Were" and "The Prophets"). For a positive characterization of a prophet, see Hos 12:14. Significantly, however, even the prophet referred to in Hos 12:14 (i.e., Moses) and his teachings failed to prevent Israel's rejection of YHWH and YHWH's paths.

Wolff (*Hosea*, 150-57), among others, emends the text in v. 7 from יֵדְעוּ יִשְׂרָאֵל "Israel shall know" or "let Israel know" to יָרִיעוּ יִשְׂרָאֵל and, accordingly, they understand the relevant part of the verse as follows, "Israel shouts: 'The prophet is a fool! The man of the spirit is mad!'" Although the proposed emendation is very problematic (see, for instance, Macintosh, *Hosea*, 351-52), it allows those who approach the passage as a faithful representation of a historical event — another highly problematic assumption — to assume that the (historical) prophet Hosea was involved in some kind shouting match with his (historical) opposition. Once one accepts this proposal then one can decide to assign the words "the prophet . . . is mad" to those who in that reconstructed historical event confronted the prophet Hosea. If one accepts that this is the case, one would be able to reconstruct different situations in the life of the historical Hosea, before and after his confrontation with angry Israelites who shouted at him that he was mad. See below. Even if one does not follow the research approach advanced here, there are numerous disadvantages to this serial hypothesizing. See also the very different approach taken in Odell, "Who Were."

Verse 10 provides a significant window into the ideological understanding of the first stages of YHWH's relationship to Israel and vice versa, as they were reflected and shaped by this reading. It is to be stressed, however, that this image, expressed in Hos 9:10 and 9:13, is like a thread woven into a larger tapestry to which Hos 10:11 and Hos 11:1 also contribute important threads (see also Hos 2:17bβ). Each of them advances tentatively ways in which the community of readers may image and construe such a beginning, and all together convey a more complete, multi-layered image that is more representative of the horizon of thought of the authorship and primary and intended readerships (see Hos 11:1-11 Setting). Turning to Hos 9:10, the first comparison is strange, since there are no grapes in the desert. Of course, within the existing discourses the relationship had to begin outside the land, and be associated with the related motifs of the exodus from Egypt and the stay in the desert under the leadership of Moses (cf. Hos 2:5, 16-18; 11:1; 12:10, 14; 13:4). Thus, the mention of the desert is easily understandable, but why an explicit reference to "grapes" in the context of desert (and contrast with Ps 80:9)? To be sure, the mention of grapes is probably linked to the usual association of grapes and figs, vines, and fig trees (e.g., 1 Kgs 5:5; 2 Kgs 18:31; Isa 34:4; Jer 8:13; Hos 2:14; Joel 1:7, 12; Mic 4:4; Zech 3:10; Ps 105:33; Song 2:13), and to the metaphorical uses of images of the vine signifying Israel (e.g., Ps 80:9; Ezek 19:10; and Hos 10:1). But even if this is the case, still the expression "grapes in the desert" carries meaning in and of itself. Moreover, its startling oxymoron serves to draw the attention of the readers to the expression itself and its possible meanings. It seems that "grapes in the desert" carries a sense that includes a combination of elements: (a) an extreme, miraculous rarity (i.e., the way in which YHWH found Israel compared to other nations at that time; cf. the theme of "self-other" mentioned above), (b) an extremely pleasant surprise for the personage who finds them (i.e., YHWH was extremely pleased with Israel at the time), and (c) intrinsic value (i.e., YHWH was extremely pleasant with Israel because of its intrinsic worth at the time). (Cf. the expression here with Num 20:5 and Judg 9:13, and cf. the position advanced here with Eidewall, *Grapes in the Desert,* 150-51, and Macintosh, *Hosea,* 361-63, and see the summaries of research in both.) In addition, it may connote some erotic flavor to the meeting between YHWH and Israel (see Song 2:13; 7:13; and cf. Hosea 2:16-25).

The reference to the early-ripening fig reinforces some elements of the message conveyed by the reference to the grapes. Early figs were considered particularly tasty (that is, of intrinsic worth; cf. Isa 28:4; Jer 24:2), and it was considered pleasant to find them. In Jeremiah 24, people who are valued are compared to early figs. In addition, the term might have also carried some erotic connotations (Song 2:13). Unlike the grapes' imagery, however, the early (בכורה) fig metaphor drives the attention of the readers to the sense of "early," and even evokes a sense of "firstborn" (בכור); Israel is the "firstborn" of YHWH in biblical traditions. In addition, the grapes and figs are representative of settled land as opposed to the desert (cf. Num 20:5; 13:23-24). Moreover, the construction of a space in the desert that contains these markers of settled land at the time of "the first encounter" serves to transgress the austerity of the setting in the desert, while at the same time to suggest the possibility of miraculous plenty. The shifting of images of the settled land into that scene is even more salient given that the entrance to the settled land serves to mark the end of the idyllic period and the beginning of Israel's transgressions, a point that the text immediately develops.

Before we turn to this aspect, it is worth noting that verse 13 offers a kind of thematic loop. The verse revisits the beginning of the relationship between YHWH and Israel to offer a slightly different emphasis through another metaphor, "Ephraim, when I saw it, it became as a young palm planted in a [lovely] meadow" (cf. Ezek 19:10). For this understanding of Hos 9:10a see, among others, Macintosh, *Hosea,* 370-72; Dozeman, "Hosea," 65; NRSV. Thus, verse 13a brings forward an image clearly associated with fertility (i.e., the palm tree), as required by its immediate literary context and the emphasis on the opposition between that which should have been and that which is to be, due to Israel's actions. In both cases, however, the text shapes and reflects an understanding of Israel's potentiality, of Israel's past history as a deviation from its fulfillment, and of YHWH as a deity who justly punished Israel. (Substantially different translations of v. 13 have been offered. The RSV translates the relevant section as "Ephraim's sons, as I have seen, are destined for a prey." The RSV reading is based on the LXX. According to Kuan the verse [Hos 9:13] means, "Ephraim, just as I have seen Tyre planted in a pleasant place . . ."; cf. NIV, NASB, NJB, NAB. According to Szabó ["Textual Problems," 517], the verse means, "Ephraim, as far as I see, is planted for the flint [or, 'for the edge of the knife'] in the field.")

The significances of the mention of Baal Peor in v. 10b and Gilgal in v. 15 have been debated at length in scholarly literature. It is clear, however, that the reference to an incident in Baal Peor in Hos 9:10b was likely to have evoked among the intended and primary readerships of the book of Hosea (in its present form) images associated with constructions of the past or "agreed memories" such as those reflected in Num 25:1-3, 18; 31:16; Deut 4:3; Josh 22:17; Ps 106:28. Four features of these "memories" are particularly worth noting and illuminate the matters they evoked within the world of discourse of the intended and primary readerships: (a) The sin of Baal Peor occurred before Israel entered the land and in a location that was geographically close to the land; accordingly, the text suggests that the Israel of the desert transformed itself into a transgressor at the boundary region between the desert and the land, between "wandering" and "settlement" — see below and Setting Hos 2:3-25; (b) within these discourses, this is the first and perhaps archetypal case of explicit Baal worship by Israel — on the latter see Hos 2:10; 13:1; the expression וינזרו לבשת "they consecrated [in Baal Peor] to Shame" in 9:10 may stress in particular the beginning of, and turning point of, the event; בשת "Shame" stands for Baal; needless to say, within these memories the "calves" preceded the episode in Baal Peor, but the matter there is idolatry; cf. Hos 8:4-6; 13:2; (c) the sin of Baal Peor involves and interweaves apostasy with improper sexual activity, a recurring topic in the book of Hosea — in this case, it is improper male sexual activity (see 9:1 and 4:15); and (d) the entire population of sinners was destroyed — cf. the announcements of judgment against Israel/Ephraim in this reading. These features explain the suitability of that image for the book, this READING, and the images it evoked. (Boudreau ["Hosea and Pentateuchal Traditions"] contends that the reference to the Baal Peor incident in Hos 9:10 is not related to the traditions mentioned above, points at idolatry *after* the settlement, and reflects the historical participation of Transjordanian Israelites in the cult of Baal at the site of Peor in the eighth century. To some extent his claim is based on the assumption that the text in Hos 9:10 is from the eighth century and therefore earlier than [exilic] Num 25:1b-5 and the other texts.)

The reference to Gilgal in v. 15 strengthens and complements some of these images. Gilgal is in the land but close to the edge of the land and on the other side of the border from Baal Peor. In other words, the text conveys to the readers that just as Israel consecrated itself to Baal at the outer edge of the land, Israel's calamities/evil deeds — the two concepts are deeply intertwined in this type of discourses, see also below — began as soon as they entered the land (at Gilgal; see Josh 4:19-20; 5:9-12), because YHWH hated Israel (i.e., the opposite of "love" and marker of rejection of bond, be it imagined as marital, covenantal, or both; see Hos 9:15). (The possible explanation for the relation between being in the land and sin and future calamity is elaborated in Hosea 10.) To be sure, the expression כל רעתם בגלגל conveys two different, though related and complementary, meanings. The first one, which is reflected above, is akin to "all their calamity (or distress) began at Gilgal"; the other is akin to "all their evil began in Gilgal" or "all their wickedness appeared in full at Gilgal" (cf. NJB). These meanings evoke evil acts done by Israel in Gilgal. Again a double set of images is suggested to the readers. Within the discourse of the book, the name Gilgal is linked with improper worship of YHWH (cf. 4:15, 12:12), which is polemically associated with that of Baal (a matter that is implicitly reflected in the coupling of Gilgal and Baal Peor in this READING; cf. Setting 2:3-25). In other words, from this perspective Gilgal serves a discursive role parallel to that of Beth-el/Beth-Aven; see Hos 4:15; cf. Hos 10:5, 15. One may notice also that some elements of the language of Hos 4:16 are reminiscent of those at the conclusion of 9:15 and vice versa. At the same time, the text here likely evoked the failure of the first king of Israel, because he disobeyed YHWH (see 1 Sam 13:11-15; 15:12-25, and see also 1 Sam 11:14-15 and cf. 1 Sam 8:7-8 and Hos 7:3; 8:4; 13:10-11). Saul in this case may be seen as paradigmatic of northern kings, and of all non-Davide kings (cf. Hos 13:11). The reference to "officers" in v. 15 may be seen as supportive of some connotation that the text may be associated (also) with the political elite. The combination of wrongful worship and political elite conveyed by the combination of these two meanings is, of course, very common in the book of Hosea.

It is worth noting that the reference to Gibeah in 9:9 seems to point to a third place that fulfills discursive roles similar to those of Baal Peor and Gilgal. The matter is not expanded in this READING, but significantly, it is taken over in the next one: "from the days of Gibeah you have sinned, O Israel" (Hos 10:9). Surely, this observation strengthens the claim advanced under Genre for the interdependence of these READINGS within the book. (On Gibeah see Hos 10:1-15 Setting; for another approach on Baal Peor, Gibeah, and Gilgal in the book of Hosea see *Simian-Yofre, Desierto*, 246-53.)

The text here represents one of many instances of an important ideological meta-narrative that is widely attested in the discourses of the literati. According to this meta-narrative, YHWH and Israel enjoyed initially an ideal relationship that is associated with pre-settlement, either the Exodus or the wilderness, and which vanished when Israel settled in the land, sinned, and abandoned YHWH. Within this meta-narrative the ancestors who first sinned in the land and the much later people who inhabited the monarchic period are brought together as manifestations of sinful Israel. It is worth noting that this meta-narrative includes two additional stages that may appear explicitly in some of its particular manifestations, but are in any case implicitly conveyed by the general literary and ideological context, and well known to the readership of texts that involve this meta-narrative. The first of these stages is YHWH's just punishment of sinful Israel — most often explicitly associated with separation from land (exile). The second addresses promises of hope concerning a new beginning, a new renewal associated with being outside the land, but that eventually leads back to the land. The latter stage is also a systemic, social, political, and ideological necessity of the discourses of the leadership of postmonarchic Israel, for none of them could have accepted a status construed as separation from YHWH and exile as the final and eternal destination of Israel. Examples of this meta-narrative, each with its own particularities and each intertwined in its own way with its larger literary contexts, appear in texts such as Deuteronomy 32; 2 Kings 17; Jeremiah 2; Hosea 2, 10, and 11.

A brief comment on another aspect of the intellectual setting of the book: Exile and distress are construed here as, and explained in, internal terms. Foreign powers play no significant role in the process.

Scholars who are involved in the reconstruction of the life and words of the historical prophet Hosea have proposed several settings for Hos 9:1-17 or 9:1-9, 10-17. Some of these proposals were briefly mentioned in Genre, above. Among many others, one may mention Wolff's contention that,

> For the first time Hosea's words [9:10-17] are addressed exclusively to the circle who transmitted his sayings. . . . The preceding context in 9:7-9 explains why Hosea's audience is now reduced to a smaller group. The literary affinity between 9:7-9 and vv. 10-17 suggests that only a short period of time separated them [Wolff assigns 9:1-9 to 733 BCE or the years immediately following, and in any case, before 727 BCE]. Thus, e.g., the "flying away" of Ephraim in v. 11 (cf. v. 15) recalls the flight to Assyria and Egypt in 9:3. This audition account would then confirm our interpretation that at sometime after 733, the leaders and many of the people became so hostile to Hosea that he could no longer speak publicly. The closing sentence alludes to this: "They have not listened to him" (v. 17). Now he addresses his words to the inner circle of the opposition. . . . Moreover, this sketch of the prophet's audition indicates that his public rejection led him to a new, personal struggle with his God. (Wolff, *Hosea*, 163)

Intention

The general intention of Hosea 9:1-17 is to communicate and reinforce the positions and the general horizon of thought of the authorship and readership as represented in these texts (see Setting) and to socialize the literati through their shared reading of the material and the larger society through the literati's reading to others of these readings.

This READING explains the reasons for exile, stresses the importance of the land, being in the land, and of temple and temple worship, which are possible only in the land. Moreover, it constructs the land as *YHWH's* land.

This READING offers also a general interpretation of Israel's history from the very beginning of Israel's inception, which is understood in terms of YHWH's encountering them, to the exile. It is a story of continuous sin and rejection of YHWH that is consistent with the tone of the READING, and which deals not only with exile but with the threat of a divinely caused, and fully justified, total annihilation of Israel. Of course the readers know well that Israel did not disappear, they themselves embody a positive proof for the continuity of Israel, and that the exile was at least in part overcome. This READING, when set in proper context within the book of Hosea, and within its own set of READINGS in the book, serves to portray a picture of the depths of the disaster and wrongful behavior of past Israel that in itself serves to enhance the rhetorical and persuasive appeal of announcements of hope and reversal (see Hosea 11), which is the heightened conclusion of this set of READINGS.

Bibliography

P. M. Arnold, "Hosea and the Sin of Gibeah," *CBQ* 51 (1989) 447-60; G. R. Boudreau, "Hosea and the Pentateuchal Traditions. The Case of Baal of Peor," M. P. Graham, W. P. Brown, and J. K. Kwan, *History and Interpretation. Essays in Honour of John H. Hayes* (JSOTSupS 173; Sheffield: Sheffield Academic Press, 1993) 121-32; R. Dobbie, "The Text of Hosea IX 8," *VT* 5 (1955) 199-203; T. B. Dozeman, "Hosea and the Wilderness Tradition," S. L. McKenzie and T. Römer (eds., in collaboration with H. H. Schmid), *Rethinking the Foundations: Historiography in the Ancient World and in the Bible: Essays in Honour of John Van Seters* (BZAW 294; Berlin/New York: de Gruyter, 2000) 55-70; G. R. Driver, "Linguistic and Textual Problems: Minor Prophets. I," *JTS* 39 (1938) 155-66; E. N. Good, "The Composition of Hosea," *SEÅ* 31 (1966) 21-63; D. W. Harvey, "Rejoice Not, O Israel," B. W. Anderson and W. Harrelson (eds.), *Israel's Prophetic Heritage. Essays in Honor of James Muilenburg* (New York: Harper, 1962) 116-27; Y. Hoffman, "A North Israelite Typological Myth and a Judaean Historical Tradition: The Exodus in Hosea and Amos," *VT* 39 (1989) 169-82; D. Krause, "A Blessing Curse: The Prophet's Prayer for Barren Womb and Dry Breasts in Hosea 9," D. N. Fewell (ed.), *Reading Between Texts. Intertextuality and the Hebrew Bible* (Louisville, KY: Westminster/John Knox Press, 1992) 191-202; P. A. Kruger, "Prophetic Imagery, On Metaphors and Similes in the Book of Hosea," *JNSL* 14 (1988) 143-51; J. K. Kuan, "Hosea 9.13 and Josephus, *Antiquities* IX,277-87," *PEQ* 132 (1991) 103-8; C. J. Labuschagne, "The Similes in the Book of Hosea," *OTWSA* 7-8 (1965) 64-76; N. Lohfink, "Hate and Love in Osee 9,15," *CBQ* 25 (1963) 417; A. A. Macintosh, "A Consideration of the Problems Presented by Psalm II.11 and 12," *JTS* (1976) 1-14; idem, "Hosea. The Rabbinic Commentators and the Ancient Versions," A. Rapoport-Albert and G. Greenberg (eds.), *Biblical Hebrew, Biblical Texts. Essays in Memory of Michael P. Weitzman* (JSOTSupS 333; Sheffield: Sheffield Academic Press, 2001) 77-82; M. Malul, *Knowledge, Control and Sex. Studies in Biblical Thought, Culture and Worldview* (Tel Aviv-Jaffa: Archaeological Center Publication, 2002); J. L. McLaughlin, *The Marzēaē in the Prophetic Literature. References and Allusions in Light of the Extra-Biblical Evidence* (VTSup 86; Leiden: E. J. Brill, 2001); M. O'Connor, "The Pseudosorites: A Type of Paradox in Hebrew Verse," E. R. Follis (ed.), *Directions in Biblical Hebrew Poetry* (JSOTSupS 40; Sheffield: Sheffield Academic Press, 1987) 161-72; M. S. Odell, "Who Were the Prophets in Hosea?" *HBT* 18 (1996) 78-95; idem, "The Prophets and the End of Hosea," P. House and J. W. Watts (eds.), *Forming Prophetic Literature: Essays on Isaiah and the Twelve in Honor of John D. W. Watts* (JSOTSupS 235; Sheffield: JSOT Press, 1996) 158-70; S. Pisano, "'Egypt' in the Septuagint Text of Hosea," G. J. Norton, S. Pisano, and C. M. Martini (eds.), *Tradition of the Text: Studies Offered to Dominique Barthélemy in Celebration of His 70th Birthday* (OBO 109; Fribourg: Éditions universitaires, 1991) 301-8; W. Schutte, "Hosea 9,7-9 — Eine crux interpretum?" *BN* 114-115 (2002) 57-60; A. Szabó, "Textual Problems in Amos and Hosea," *VT* 25 (1975) 500-524; E. R. Wendland, *The Discourse Analysis of Hebrew Prophetic Literature* (Lewiston, NY: E. Mellen Press, 1995).

Sixth Didactic Prophetic Reading:
The Vine and the Heifer. Agricultural Images Pointing at
Israel's (Past) Failure and Consequent Judgment, 10:1-15

Structure

I. Introduction	10:1a
II. First Section: Revisiting Israel's Fault and Calamity	10:1-8
A. Fault and Calamity: From Greatness to Improper Worship — Altars and Pillars	10:1-2
B. Fault and Calamity: King and Royal Elite	10:3-4
C. Fault and Calamity: Improper Worship — Calves	10:5-6
D. Fault and Calamity: King	10:7
E. Fault and Calamity: *Bamot* and Altars	10:8
III. Second Section	10:9-15
A. Fault and Calamity: Sin since Gibeah and Its Consequence: Devastation by War	10:9-10
B. Israel's Fault in the Light of YHWH's Actions	10:11-13a
C. Fault and Calamity in the Form of Devastation by War	10:13b-14
D. Conclusion	10:15

This READING represents to some extent a thematic loop in this SET OF READINGS. As in other cases in prophetic literature, this thematic loop explores some of the issues mentioned before in the book from a different perspective and using a somewhat different imagery. The result is that the book bears multiple explorations of similar themes. These explorations inform each other and together convey a multi-faceted, interwoven meaning to the intended and primary readership. In particular, Hosea 10 re-explores matters advanced in Hosea 8 and 9 and prepares the readers for the climactic conclusion of the SET OF READINGS with the message of hope in Hosea 11. Significantly, the strength of that message of hope is in part grounded in the setting of the proclaimed message in the world of the book, namely, the worst possible circumstances that result from the (theologically) intertwined character of evil deeds and calamity.

The structure proposed above is one among several possible alternatives. It is certainly possible to approach the two sections (i.e., 10:1-8 and 10:9-15) as independent READINGS (cf. already the masoretic division of the book of Hosea into open and closed paragraphs) within the SET OF READINGS that comprises Hosea 4:1–11:11. Given that Hos 10:1-8 is in some ways closely connected to 9:1-17, it is also possible to approach 10:1-8 as a section within a READING that comprises 9:1–10:8 (see 9:1-17 STRUCTURE) and belongs to the same SET OF READINGS. It is worth mentioning, however, that there is a relatively widespread tendency to acknowledge the existence of two large units, Hos 10:1-8 and Hos 10:9-15 (e.g., Simian-Yofre, *Desierto,* 134-45; Eidewall, *Grapes,* 155-63; Davies, *Hosea,* 231-50; Wolff, *Hosea,* 178-89; Stuart, *Hosea,* 156-73; Landy, *Hosea,* esp. 130; Pentiuc, *Long-Suffering Love,* 129-39).

Other general external boundaries and, above all, numerous slightly different internal structures have been advanced. Sweeney, for instance, divides the text into 9:17–10:8 ("Hosea's Allegorical Statement of YHWH's Intention to Reject Israel"); 10:9-11 ("YHWH's Chastisement of Israel for Sins from Gibeah"); and 10:12-15 ("Hosea's Announcement That War Will Overtake Beth El and Israel"), all of which he relates to a larger discourse, Hos 9:1–14:1 (see Sweeney, *Twelve Prophets,* 93, 101-12). Weiser (*Die Propheten,* 77-83) proposes a division into the following units, 10:1-2, 3-4, 5-8, 9-10, 11-13a, 13b-15 (see also Rudolph, *Hosea,* 191-208). Wendland (*Discourse Analysis,* 128-29) proposes a slightly different internal structure. According to him, the oracle of 10:1-8 consists of four strophes, vv. 1-2, 3-4, 5-6, 7-8, whereas the oracle of Hos 10:9-15, of the aforementioned triad, vv. 9-10, 11-13a, and 13b-15. Other proposals are possible (e.g., Hos 10:1-8 and 10:9-15 as separate units of a larger discourse unit that encompasses Hos 9:10–10:15; see Eidewall, *Grapes,* 147-65). Good ("Composition," 46-47) wonders whether "we have one, two, or three poems" in Hosea 10. If there is one poem, then according to him the structure would be: (1) Introduction (vv. 1-2), (2) King (vv. 3-4), (3) Calf (vv. 5-6), (4) King (vv. 7-10), (5) Calf (vv. 11-13a), and (6) King (vv. 13b-15). If there are three poems, then the first would consist of vv. 1-2, the second of 3-8 and the third, 9-15. If there are two poems, which is the position he eventually favors, then the first one consists of vv. 1-8, and its subunits are vv. 1-2, 3-4, 5-6 and 7-8, whereas the second consists of vv. 9-15 and is subdivided into vv. 9-10, 11-13a — itself divided into three subunits, vv. 11, 12 and 13a — and 13b-15.

As in the case of other READINGS, the text of this literary unit is written so as to allow more than one possible structure — though not infinite structures. This feature allows the literari to develop complementary readings and meanings that are reflective of these possible structures and that inform each other within the literati's larger discourse.

Turning to the structure mentioned here, the first main section (10:1-8) opens with גפן בוקק ישראל (v. 1aα), often translated as "Israel is (or was) a luxuriant vine." גפן בוקק ישראל marks a break from the preceding text in the book, not only by introducing a new theme, but also by clearly opening a new (independent) sentence. The comparison of Israel to a vine creates a link between the text here and "like grapes . . ." in 9:10 and, indirectly, between the literary units that each of them opens. On the expression גפן בוקק ישראל and its structural roles, see below. The first section (10:1-8) is surrounded by an envelope, ישראל — חטאת ישראל — ישראל "Israel — the sin of Israel," which to some extent encapsulates the theme of the section (cf. discussion on גפן בוקק ישראל below). It bears note that the word Israel occurs relatively often at the beginning and ending of literary units or subunits in the book of Hosea (e.g., Hos 3:5; 4:1; 5:1; 9:1, 10; 10:15; 11:1; 12:1); or Israel is referred to in some other form (e.g., Hos 2:3; 2:25; 11:11). Cf. Andersen and Freedman, *Hosea,* 548. This feature is not random, but reflects the centrality of "Israel" in the book. This book is about Israel, YHWH, and their relationship, as chs. 1–3 already show.

The first section (10:1-8) shows, mainly, a concentric thematic structure (see Simian-Yofre, *Desierto,* 136; Eidewall, *Grapes,* 155; Jeremias, *Hosea,* 127), albeit a slightly distorted one, and, as shown below, distorted for a purpose. An external concentric ring is shaped by verses 1b and 8. They evoke images of prosperous and desolate agrarian worlds, respectively, and these images are closely associated with cultic infrastructure, the setting up of altars and pillars in v. 1b, and the destruction of high places and altars in v. 8. An inner ring is shaped by vv. 3(-4) and 7, which refer to the lack of kingly leadership. At the center of these rings one finds vv. 5-6 that deal with the calves.

Turning to the two textual pieces that stand outside the mentioned ring system that shapes the unit, namely, vv. 1a and 2, the expression גפן בוקק ישראל in v. 1aα — often translated as "Israel is (or was) a luxuriant vine" — represents an excellent example of the use of careful wording to convey a multiplicity of meanings. This multiplicity enhances the rhetorical appeal of the text and shapes its message. On the one hand, given the occurrence of words from the root בקק elsewhere in the HB (e.g., Isa 19:3; 24:1, 3; Nah 2:3; Jer 19:7; 51:2) that carry a sense of to "empty," "damage," "ruin," and the like, it is clear that the expression at the very least evoked a sense of "Israel is a damaged vine." Many scholars maintain that this is its meaning here. See, for instance, Macintosh, *Hosea,* 383; Simian-Yofre, *Desierto,* 134-35, 137; and already Ibn Ezra (both the Accepted and Alternative Commentaries), Radak, and Tanhum HaYerushalmi (Shy, *Tanhum HaYerushalmi,* 32) and the Targum; for English translations that follow this interpretation, see NJPSV and KJV. On the other hand, particularly given the explicit reference to כרב לפריו "when its fruit was abundant" in 1b and the existence of a possible cognate, it seems reasonable that the text was understood, at least on one level, as meaning "Israel is (or, was) a prolific vine." See the LXX, Syriac, Vulgate; and among modern scholars, for instance, Eidewall, *Grapes,* 156; Wolff, *Hosea,* 170; Morag, "On Semantic and Lexical Features," 493. (For a summary of research on both and other proposals, see Yoo, *Israelian Hebrew,* 117-21.) It is likely that בקק was one of the roots that carried contrasted meanings (see Morag, "On Semantic," 493; cf. Gordis, "Studies," 49). But if this is the case, the text draws the attention of the readers to a situation of textual ambiguity (cf., among others, Zeph 1:7; 3:1; and see Ben Zvi, *Zephaniah,* 82-86, 184-87; idem, *Signs of Jonah,* passim). The readers are left with two answers, both correct. Israel was conceived and presented to the readers as both a luxuriant vine and a damaged one, and the two readings enhance and inform each other. The process continues in 10:1aβ, because פרי ישוה לו also evokes more than one meaning. It carries by denotation or connotation, (a) "the fruit is similar to it [Israel, the vine]" (cf. Prov 26:4 and see, for instance, Simian-Yofre, *Desierto,* 134-35, 137) and, therefore, either damaged or luxuriant according to the two meanings of בקק; (b) "it yields/makes fruit for itself" (see Morag, "On Semantic," 493-94; Sweeney, *The Twelve,* 103; and cf. Hos 9:16; contrast also with Hos 14:9), which may be understood again in a positive and negative sense, according to the two meanings of בקק; and at least in a connoted sense (c) "its fruit turns out empty" (cf. Hos 9:2, 16; notice the root שוא that conveys a sense of "emptiness, vanity" and either evokes here that sense because of its similar sound, or might reflect a case of exchange between the third letters (א and ה); cf. Macintosh, *Hosea,* 386; Sweeney, *The Twelve,* 103). (Other proposals have been advanced, including emendations of the text.) In sum, in a very sophisticated way, v. 10:1a draws the attention of the readers and evokes in them two images of Israel. According to one, "Israel is a luxuriant vine that yields its (equally luxuriant) fruit." This image is consistent with the construction of Israel as entering into the cultivated land and becoming prosperous there (see Hos 2:4-15; passim). Of course, within this ideological construction of Israel's past, economic prosperity became intertwined with rejection of YHWH and YHWH's ways — as interpreted by the implied authorship of the book of Hosea and its intended and likely primary readership. This motif is immediately developed in the READING and addresses some of the issues raised by Hosea 9 (see there STRUCTURE). At the same time, as soon as Israel transgressed its obligations towards, and dealt treacherously with its patron YHWH, it is, for all intents and purposes, a vanished vine, and its fruits are just as worthless. The message of the book to its intended and primary rereadership carries a meaning that results from the interconnectedness of the two main reading approaches mentioned above.

This stylistic feature not only points to a sophisticated target rereadership (see Setting) but also has implications for structural analysis. Verse 1aα is a subunit that stands in close relation to v. 1b and accordingly that serves to develop one of the mentioned lines of thought, but also in a meaningful way as a subunit by itself that draws the attention of the readers to its possible meanings and asks them to study and relate them to each other. Two salient textually inscribed markers point at this double situation. The "his" in fruit in 1bα requires an antecedent, namely, Israel, the vine (on גפן "vine" as a masc. noun see Setting below), and closely links vv. 1a to 1b. At the same time, the envelope created by the two sets of מזבחות "altars" — מצבות "pillars" sets 1b-2 apart from 1a. The relation of 1a to the thematic rings that shape 10:1b-8 contributes to and reflects their sense of standing aside and looming over the following text when v. 1a is understood as pointing to a vanished vine, while it allows it to be grasped as an integral part of the external ring when v. 1a is understood as pointing to a luxuriant vine. In sum, a careful combination of textual and structural markers conveys a double, complementary message. Verse 1a serves as (a) a subunit closely related to vv. 1b-2, and as such it opens the first subunit of the first section of this READING; and (b) as a unit by itself that opens and serves as an interpretative key for this entire READING, and perhaps even for the one preceding it in the book (i.e., as an additional concluding note that asks its readership to interpret the entire preceding text in its light, cf. Hos 14:10).

The envelope created by מזבחות "altars" — מצבות "pillars" draws attention to the text that stands at its center. The multiplicity of meanings carried by this text (i.e., 10:2a) serves as an additional attention getter. Given the meanings evoked by both חלק and יאשמו in v. 2a, the text conveys the following meanings: (a) "their (Israel's) heart is false; now they must bear their guilt" (NRSV; cf. Hos 4:15; 13:3; 14:1 and contrast the message conveyed by the text here with that in Hos 5:15 — both inform each other from the perspective of the intended and primary rereaderships of the book); (b) "their (Israel's) heart is false; now they will be desolate" (cf. Hos 14:1); (c) "their (Israel's) heart is divided (i.e., they are duplicitous); now they must bear their guilt"; and (d) "their (Israel's) heart is divided (i.e., they are duplicitous); now they will be desolate." In addition, "bear their guilt" connotes both a sense of "bear their punishment," and a necessity to expiate the guilt. The latter involves sacrifices for which altars are required. Ironically, the multiplication of altars (and pillars) is not presented here as something that facilitates the remedy of guilt but to the contrary as the cause of guilt. In other words, this subunit re-elaborates the basic theme present in Hos 8:11. (Ironically again, the verb that the text uses to express YHWH's destruction of the altars is עָרַף, which usually means to "break the neck." Rather than Israel "breaking the neck" of animals for proper sacrifices, YHWH "breaks the neck" of their altars.)

Significantly, within this sea of complementary readings informing each other, a salient and unequivocal "rock" remains standing high: the pun on Jacob (i.e., Israel), who was חָלָק both in the sense of "smooth" (Gen 27:11) and "duplicitous" (passim). In other words, the text hints that Israel's future behavior can already be discerned in Jacob. (Cf. Sweeney, *The Twelve*, 103-4.) Significantly, the theme is later elaborated in 12:4.

Conversely, Hos 10:1-8 shows a number of instances in which motifs and above combinations of motifs that appear in a text preceding Hos 10:1-8 in the book are further elaborated. The case involving 8:11 has been discussed above, and so the role of 10:1 as an explanation of the theological notion that Israel's sin is directly associated with its being in the land (see Hosea 9 Setting). In addition, one may mention that verses 2-4 move from the removal of pillars and the destruction of basic material structures needed for sacrifices and, therefore, of the possibility of sacrifices, to an image of monarchic Israel becoming kingless. The text here either elaborates further on themes present in Hos 3:4, or at the very least creates a series of signposts that lead the rereaders of the book to relate one text to the other. These interrelationships carry important meanings. The references to the uselessness of past monarchs and to their disappearance are set in proportion by the expectation of and hope for a Davidic, quasi-messianic, future king expressed in Hos 3:4-5. Furthermore, the association of the improper and ineffectual leadership of kings with salient references to the calves and idolatry in vv. 3-6 evokes that of 8:4-5, and both elaborate the same conceptual combination and its associated meanings in slightly different ways. (For a different approach to the correlations between Hosea 3 and Hosea 10, see Jeremias, *Hosea*, 127-28. For kings and salient references to the calves and idolatry see also Hos 13:1-11.)

At times, particular choices of words might have suggested to the intended readers that they should relate one text to another, let one inform the other, at least in some of their rereadings of the book. The case of verses 5:13 and 10:6 provides a good example. Israel (foolishly and sinfully) relies on the king of Assyria, referred to as מֶלֶךְ יָרֵב in both 5:13 and 10:6 but nowhere else in the HB. The king, of course, cannot (יוּכַל) heal Israel (5:13), but significantly the calf on which Israel (foolishly and sinful) relies will be sent (יוּבַל) to him as a (forced) tribute. A circle of folly, futility, and sin is thus construed. Within this discourse, the entire circle could have been easily preempted had Israel relied on YHWH — as conceived and worshiped by the intended and primary readerships of the book of Hosea.

The second section of this READING is set apart by the thematic and syntactic breaks in 10:9 and 11:1. There are textually inscribed markers, however, that closely link this section to the preceding one (10:1-8) and therefore support the contention advanced here that the text suggested to its intended rereaders that, among other possible alternatives, both could be read as two sections within a READING (see above). Among these markers one may mention the clear link between חטאת ישראל "the sin of Israel" in v. 8 and חטאת ישראל "You, have sinned, O Israel," in v. 9; and that of גבעות "hills" in v. 8 to הגבעה "The Hill, that is, Gibeah") in v. 9. Similarly, there are נדמה שמרון מלכה, which may be translated "as for Samaria, its king will perish," in v. 7 and נדמה נדמה מלך ישראל at the conclusion of the READING in v. 15, which may be translated as "the king of Israel will surely perish."

As mentioned above, the second section also takes up the motif of the calves of the first section and develops it in a very different manner, as it identifies Israel with a heifer (v. 11; cf. 11:4). On a more general level both sections deal with the history of Israel and with the way in which this history leads Israel to calamity. The first focuses negatively on the king and on cultic infrastructure, the second mainly on the king, but there is a salient reference to Beth-el at the crucial v. 15. ככה עשה לכם בית אל in v. 15 carries among its multiple meanings, "so has Beth-el done to you" and "so it has been done to you, O Beth-el." Both meanings, in any case, raise the realm of sinful cult and its consequences (cf. v. 15 and v. 5 — Beth-aven, or better translated "Iniquitytown," is a pejorative reference to Beth-el). (Textual emendations of v. 15 have been proposed, including removing the reference to Beth-el or its replacement with one to "Beth-Israel," that is, the House of Israel; see also LXX.)

Like Hos 10:1-8, Hos 10:9-15 also revisits a number of themes present in other units in the book. Already its introduction (Hos 10:9) suggests to the readers that it deals with a theme like that addressed in Hos 9:10b and 15, namely, the beginnings of Israel's sin and their relationship to common constructions of Israel's (hi)story. In this case, rather than associate the beginning of its sin and calamity with Baal Peor or Gilgal, the text goes back to another central episode within Israel's past as known among the literati, that is, in their shared "memory" of the past. This is the Gibeah episode. (On the latter see Setting.) As it does so, it elaborates further the reference to the "days of Gibeah" in 9:9.

Metaphors, imagery, and particular word pairs also serve as textually inscribed markers that suggest to the intended and primary readers that Hos 10:12-13 and Hos 8:7 are to be understood as related readings informing each other. Hos 10:12-13 elaborates Hos 8:7 and complements it by advancing a reading of the combined passages in which there is a clear opposition between YHWH's view of that which should be Israel's sowing and reaping, and that which Israel actually sows and reaps. Moreover, as shown below, Hos 10:12-13 also revisits the theme of YHWH's early choice of Israel and its eventual rebellion (cf. Hos 2:17bβ; 9:10, 13; see below and Setting; and see also Hos 11:1-4). Further, the concluding image in Hos 10:12 revisits or is at least clearly linked to 6:3 (see discussion there, and Setting below).

Hos 10:9-15 shows some form of concentric thematic structure (10:9-14) to which a conclusion (Hos 10:15) is attached. The first and third units (i.e., 10:9-10 and 10:13-14) point at Israel's fault and a calamity that takes the form of a devastating war (on the descriptions of these wars, see Setting). Encircled within these two units one finds a highly elaborate agrarian image of the patronship of YHWH that encapsulates a deeply interrelated set of central ideological themes: (a) Israel's selection — though this time by implication in a cultivated land, (b) YHWH's high hopes of Israel's potential, (c) YHWH's instructions and expectations for Israel's behavior, and (d) the latter's rebellious response (see Setting). The final note brings back the matter of improper cult, Israel's evil deeds, and links them to the removal of the king. The latter is intertwined in a series of notes about kingship (see above).

Markers of internal cohesion in the subunits such as similar structures, word pairs, and repetition of sounds are abundant within the subunits of this READING. A few examples will suffice. A case of clear parallel structure, sonorous repetitions, and use of a typical word pair, along with a level of stylistic variation, occur in 1b. There the expression כי רב לפריו הרבה למזבחותיו is followed by כטוב לארצו היטיבו מצבות. The former can be translated as "when its fruit [פרי; pun on אפרים 'Ephraim'; see 10:1aβ] was abundant, it multiplied altars" (notice the "unnecessary" inclusion of the preposition ל in למזבחותיו that is meant to follow the form of כי רב לפריו; see Macintosh, *Hosea*, 387); the latter as "when its land was rich, they [notice the change from the singular to the plural reference, without any real change in the referent] enriched its altars."

Another obvious case of sonorous and, in this case, consonantal repetition occurs in v. 10. The text contains ואסרם, from the root יסר and meaning here "I [YHWH] will chastise them," and באסרם, from the root אסר and meaning here "when they [Israel] bound themselves." The similarities in sound draw attention to the close, causal relation between Israel's actions and YHWH's. (In addition, ואסרם might evoke the image of a parent disciplining a child [cf. Prov 19:18; 29:19: 31:1]; see Hos 11:1.) There has been much debate on the meaning of Hos 10:10 as a whole, and several proposals of textual emendations have been advanced. On these matters, see, among others, Macintosh, "Hosea and the Wisdom Tradition," esp. 129-31; idem, *Hosea*, 414-17; Barthélemy, *Critique Textuelle*, vol. III, 577-82; Andersen and Freedman, *Hosea*, 565-66.

For an additional and interesting case of sonorous repetition see that created by the pun on verbs from גיל and גלה in v. 5, and the repetition of the consonants ל — ג, which not accidentally appear in the same order in the word עגלה commonly translated here as "calf" (see below), that is, the one whose forced departure caused extreme distress (גיל) to its people and its "priestlings" (כמרים). This instance is particularly interesting. It involves the root גלה in its usual meaning "go into exile/depart," but גיל, which usually is used for "rejoice," here means "to show distress." In other words here the sonorous value of the repetition influenced the choice of a term rarely used to convey the rhetorically necessary meaning (cf. Simian-Yofre, *Desierto*, 138; Andersen and Freedman, *Hosea*, 557; Tsevat, "Biblical Notes," 111). There are two additional advantages to the use of a verbal form from the root גיל in Hos 10:5 that are discussed under Setting.

The root גיל likely carries a sense of physical agitation in both cases; see Ps 2:11; for the understanding of the expression advanced here see Macintosh, *Hosea*, 400; idem, "Consideration," 3; and among medieval commentators,

Tanhum HaYerushalmi — see Shy, *Tanhum,* 34; for a different approach and a survey of research including proposals for textual emendation, see Barthélemy, *Critique Textuelle,* vol. III, 570-71; see also Wolff, *Hosea,* 171; and cf. LXX, the Vg, and among modern English translations, NJB, NIV, and the creative explanation of Jerome for his understanding of the גיל as "rejoice," namely, "they [the priests] rejoiced for their fraud [i.e., the replacement of the golden calf with bronze calves] would never be disclosed or discovered"; translation according to Pentiuc, *Long-Suffering Love,* 133.

The word עגלה, commonly translated as "calf" (see above), usually denotes and at the very least connotes here a sense of "heifer" or "female calf" (cf. Hos 10:11, in which Israel is compared to a heifer). Moreover, the expected word for "male calf," עגל, is clearly attested in the book (see Hos 8:5, 6; 13:2) and associated with the cult of Samaria/Ephraim elsewhere (1 Kgs 12:28-29; 2 Kgs 10:29; 17:16; and cf. Exod 32:4, 8, 19, 20, 24, 35; Deut 9:16, 21; Ps 106:19; Neh 9:18; none of these texts refers to a female calf). If so, what is the message that the intended and primary readers of the book could have associated with the use of the feminine form "heifer" instead the expected masculine form עגל "male calf" in 10:5? Within a patriarchal society such as the one for which the book was written, such an explicit feminization of the statue/idol representing the high deity might be understood as polemical and even derogatory (cf. Radak; Luther; and notice that El and Baal are represented by bulls not heifers in the ancient Near East). Alternatively, one may understand עגלה as an abstract noun meaning "calfery/the calf cult" (see Macintosh, *Hosea,* 399-400; Rudolph, *Hosea,* 195), but even if this approach is taken, the connotation "heifer" remains. (The reference to a female calf shapes a contrastive link between early Israel/Ephraim as portrayed in Hos 10:11, that is, "a trained young, female calf," and later Israel/Ephraim who worships a human-made representation of a young, female calf instead of YHWH [see 10:5]. But this link neither removes nor hinders but strengthens the portrayed feminization of the divine statues in 10:5.)

Incidentally, just as the text of v. 1b discussed above attests to an instance of a shift from a singular to a plural reference without changing the identity of the referent, in vv. 5-6 references to the calf/calves shift from a female plural form to a masculine singular form, without any noticeable change in the identity of the referent. (For possible explanations and explanatory proposals that separate between the two see Macintosh, *Hosea,* 399-400.)

Common word pairs are easily recognizable in the text (e.g., הרים "mountains" and גבעות "hills" in v. 9 — and cf., among others, Prov 8:25). On some examples of word pairs and their implications for the intellectual setting of the literati among whom and for whom, primarily, the present book of Hosea was composed see Setting. It bears note that some of these instances contribute to the cohesion of the READING, including its two sections. See below.

Some expressions in the text demand particular consideration. The expression והמלך מה יעשה לנו "what can/could a king do for us?" in v. 3 serves a rhetorical purpose similar to that of the pseudosorites, namely, "we have no king . . . and even if we had one, what can a king do for us?" On another level, the intended readership that is supposed to continuously study the book and pay

attention to its carefully crafted language would likely relate the expression to
6:4 מה אעשה לך אפרים מה אעשה לך יהודה "What can I [YHWH; that is, the
King] do for you, Ephraim? What can I do for you, Judah?" and vice versa. The
resulting message is, of course, that the King cannot do anything good for Israel
(i.e., save it from punishment), because, among other things, they followed a
king who cannot do anything for them in any case. It is possible that the unique
use of the word קצף in v. 7 is related to the mentioned, conceptual opposition
between King and king. The word is usually understood as "stick," "chip,"
"twig," or as Labuschagne ("Similes," 72) claims, "a piece of wood or a
branched plucked off a tree rather than a splinter or chip resulting from chop-
ping." It is more likely that the term here means "foam" (see Cohen, "Foam";
idem, *Biblical Hapax,* 24-25; NAB and KJV), but the image remains unique. At
least from the perspective of the readership, some pun on words is meant. The
king is קצף "foam," while the King's קצף "wrath" is extremely powerful (e.g.,
Jer 10:10). For the opposition between King and king see also 1 Sam 8:7. As
mentioned before, this and similar references throughout this commentary are
not meant to suggest that one text is citing or taking the necessary cue from another, but that both texts reflect a general, shared worldview. (On קצף in Hos
10:7, see also Macintosh, *Hosea,* 406-7; and idem, "Hosea: The Rabbinic Commentaries," 78-79.)

This ideological construction of the opposition between King and king is
conceptually related to and partially overlaps that of human and King/YHWH,
which is expressed in texts such as Ps 56:5, 12; 118:6-8 (and cf. Ps 118:6-12).
A conceptually related and particularly common image in descriptions of the
enemy, or the side constructed as justly losing a war, is that it foolishly did not
trust the deity, but human power and products (see vv. 13b, 14a). From the
viewpoint of the intended and primary readership these connections contribute
to the conceptual coherence of the text (see also Setting).

The reference to "Ephraim . . . Judah . . . Jacob" in 11b serves as an unequivocal marker to the readership that the totality of Israel (i.e., trans-temporal
Israel) is involved. This is consistent with the structural emphasis on Israel in
this READING (see 10:1 and 15; and cf. 10:8, 9 — see discussion above). Moreover, such identification is required because in its absence the reference to
Ephraim in the "selection" motif in 11a might have carried an implication that
only Ephraim — or northern Israel to the exclusion of Judah — is indicated (cf.
with case in 9:10 and 9:13; see also 2:16-17; 11:1; 13:4-5, which refer to "all
Israel" rather than Ephraim alone). The point the text makes here is likely to
have influenced the reading of the intended and primary readerships in other literary units within the book and contributed to their identification with Ephraim.
After all, both are instances of transtemporal (all) Israel. The three kinds of
plowing in verse 11 suggest the initial breaking up of the ground, then plowing
to cover the seed, then plowing (or "harrowing" [cf. NRSV]) to clear the
ground for the next cycle. The imagery, therefore, provides again a sense of
completion and wholeness.

Numerous proposals for emendations of the text of Hosea 10 have been
advanced (see, for instance, BHS; Driver, "Linguistic and Textual"). For instance, Wolff (*Hosea,* 180) proposes to read an original דעת "knowledge" in-

stead of ועת "for/and it is time of" in v. 12. His position is influenced by the LXX, but see Joosten, "Exegesis," 65-67, and Macintosh, *Hosea,* 222, 224. For a summary and critique of many other proposals, see Barthélemy, *Critique Textuelle,* vol. III, 569-88.

Many claims concerning the "secondary" character of some subunits or words have been advanced as well. For instance, Harper maintains that Hos 10:3 cannot go back to the time of the historical prophet and must be a late addition, which he assigns as probably from the exilic period because among other things, it states "we have no king" and "no Israelite of Hosea's time could have acknowledged that they did not fear Yahweh" (see Harper, *Hosea,* 344-45, citation from 345). Wolfe associates all the references to Judah including 10:11 with a "Judaistic editor" who, among other things, replaced an original "Israel" with "Judah" (Wolfe, "Editing," 91). In fact, many scholars have considered that the reference to Judah in 10:11 does not belong to the "original" text (see BHS; Willi-Plein, *Vorformen,* 191-92, 276). Another example is the expression נירו לכם ניר "till for yourself a tilling" ("break up your fallow ground" in NRSV) in v. 12, which also appears in Jer 4:3. Some scholars proposed that it is "more original" there (see Harper, *Hosea,* 357; cf. Wolfe, "Editing," 93; Yee, *Composition,* 153, 157-58, Willi-Plein, *Vorformen,* 192-93).

For comprehensive reconstructions of the redactional history of Hosea 10 within the frame of the redactional history of the book of Hosea, see, among others, Yee, *Composition,* 152-53, 157-58, 207-14, 316. Yee assigns 10:9-10, 12, 13b-14 to a postmonarchic redactor (R2) and 10:1-8 to a previous redactor whose ideological horizon is similar to that of the proposed DTR1 of the so-called Deuteronomistic History. See also Zulick, *Rhetorical Polyphony,* 213-20. See also the explanation of the process of the composition of the book of Hosea advanced by Good ("Composition of Hosea") and by Willi-Plein *(Vorformen).*

Genre

Hos 10:1-15, as other READINGS in the book of Hosea, neither is an oral work, nor can it be separated from the book of Hosea. In fact, as demonstrated in STRUCTURE and Setting, it is closely intertwined with other units in the book. Thus it is neither a series of actual individual sayings, nor oracles. It is a DIDACTIC PROPHETIC READING within a set of READINGS that exists only as part and parcel of a prophetic book.

One may also notice that Hos 10:1-15 does not ask its readers to associate the reported utterances with any typical scene or set of scenes. (See also Setting.) This is true even if it uses a language that is fitting within the conventions of the time to the meaning evoked by each of the subunits within the READING. Thus, for instance, one may consider Hos 10:12-13a to be an "accusation" (cf. Hunter, *Seek the Lord,* 155-57), but the divine speech is not set in the book as a typical scene of a court procedure or the like, nor necessarily evokes images of a judicial trial like those with which the readers of the book were most likely acquainted.

Setting

The setting of the writing and primary reading of this, or any portion of the (present) book of Hosea for that matter, is the same as that of the book as a whole. Both involve writers and primary readers who are among the very few, sophisticated literati of Yehud. A number of verses shed light on the intellectual setting of the literati or the setting of the world portrayed in the book. For instance, verse 10:3 can be translated, "For now they will say/If they would say: 'We have no king, for we do not fear/have not feared YHWH, and a king, what can/could he do for us?'" Who are "they" and who was supposed to identify with them? On the surface, the answer is obvious, given that v. 3 follows v. 2 and "they" and "their" in that verse clearly point at Israel: Israel is the "they" referred to in v. 3. But when can Israel be imagined to say "we have no king"? Or as in v. 7, when can a reliable speaker state that נדמה שמרון מלכה כקצף על פני מים "as for Samaria, its king fades away as foam in the water"? Does the text suggest that the world of the book must necessarily be understood as later than the capture of the last king of Samaria, Hoshea? The answer is no. First, "we have no king, for we do not fear/have not feared YHWH, and a king, what can/could he do for us?" is in itself open to interpretation concerning the actual existence of a king (cf. already Radak). But second, and more importantly, the text is not actually marked for a particular temporal situation. In fact, it is written in such a way that allows the readers to imagine the citation reported by the authoritative speaker in v. 3, and the words of the authoritative speaker in v. 7, as being pronounced before the fall of monarchic (northern) Israel and its last king. Whereas the setting of the words within the world of the text remains open, it is clear that they resonate within the world of the postmonarchic literati who read, reread, and study this text. Yet, there is a difference. From their perspective, and as they identify as Israel, the lack of a king cannot refer only to Hoshea's capture and the downfall of the northern kingdom, but also to their own situation, to their being without a king, and implicitly to the downfall of the last Judahite monarch. From this perspective, the saying "we have no king, because we have not feared YHWH" voices also their assessment of their own situation and the reasons for it, that is, their ancestors/Israel have not feared YHWH and this led to the present circumstances. Such expressions are tantamount to a general construction of the monarchic past but also shape and reflect a self-identification with trans-temporal Israel as a community that stretches over different periods of time.

It is worth stressing that this READING (cf. Hos 8:1-14) asks its intended and primary readers to imagine YHWH's punishment as a process that removes the stumbling blocks that lead Israel to sin, among them wrongful altars (in places other than Jerusalem), pillars (cf. Lev 26:1), king and elite (the latter implied in the plural verbal forms used in v. 4a), the calves, the *bamot* of "Iniquitytown" (which is a good translation of the polemic reference to Beth-el as בית און), which are explicitly characterized as "the sin of Israel" (notice the double meaning of v. 15 above). People are implicitly described as trusting not only Beth-el and its cult (cf. Jer 48:13) but also their fortresses instead of relying on YHWH. This being so, it is probably expected that the text explicitly reports that the latter will also be destroyed (vv. 13b-14a). Thus this READING communicates to the intended and primary readership that the divine punishment carried a positive component of purging that which is either sinful or causes Israel to sin or both. Of course, this purification is of limited scope because it does not address the real reasons for Israel's pursuit of sin in the manifold ways constructed and reported in the book. These reasons are, however, discussed elsewhere in the book; see for instance, Hosea 1–3, 4:12; 5:4 and discussions there; for a larger heuristic frame, see Ben Zvi, "Analogical Thinking." A full and permanent purification is envisaged in Hos 2:16-23; cf. Hos 14:5-9. It bears notice that the image of YHWH's removing stumbling blocks or second-level reasons for, and circumstances associated with, manifestations of Israel's rejection of YHWH's ways is relatively common in prophetic books (see, for instance, Zeph 1:4-6; 3:11-12), and both the destruction of the Temple in Jerusalem and the (purifying) exile that removes Israel from the land so it can come back to it renewed can easily be understood from this perspective. Similarly, images of full purification appear not only in Hos 2:16-23 but also elsewhere in prophetic literature (e.g., Jer 31:31-34 and cf. Ezek 36:26). Needless to say, the images are not identical, but they deal with similar ideological needs within a basically shared set of discourses (see Ben Zvi, "Analogical Thinking"). (For a redactional-critical approach to some of these matters, see Albertz, "Exile as Purification.")

The use of a verbal form from the root גיל in Hos 10:5 has been discussed above. In addition to the considerations advanced under structure, two observations on the matter directly relate to the ideological setting of the book. First, the use of a verbal form from the root גיל in Hos 10:5 connotes a sense of incoherence that befits the evaluative perspective of the implied author and the intended rereadership on the reported actions. Second, it contributes to a connoted sense of correlation between chapters 9 and 10 (cf. Landy, *Hosea*, 128-29) that suggested to the intended and primary postmonarchic readerships to read one in a way informed by the other, at least as one of their multiple reading strategies. When the two chapters are taken together, an underlying, polemical conceptual parallelism between the sinful people (in ch. 9) and the cultic infrastructure (e.g., calves, altars) that leads to sin emerges. Symbols of wilderness take over tents in 9:6 and altars in 10:8; in 9:11 Ephraim's כבוד (on the meanings of the term in 9:11 see Hos 9:1-17 STRUCTURE) departs; in 10:5 it is the calf's כבוד that departs. The discursive association of (constructed) unfaithful Israel with calves and improper altars polemically parallels that of faithful Israel or representatives of faithful Israel with YHWH, as properly conceived and worshiped from the perspective of the implied authorship and intended readership (cf. the figure of Hosea in chs. 1–3 and the attribution of godly attributes to Israel in 2:21-22). It is worth noting that neither the calves, nor the altars, nor the *bamot,* nor the pillars are attributed in Hosea 10 to Baal. Nor does the use of the pejorative term כמריו "its [the calf's] priestlings" point at priests who worship gods other than YHWH (see 2 Kgs 23:5; on the term כמר in Zeph 1:4 see Ben Zvi, *Zephaniah*, 67-69; in Jewish-Aramaic of Elephantine, however, כמר is used only for non-Yahwistic priests). The most one can say is that the text here conveys perhaps a polemic "baalistic" shade to what was known to be

YHWH's cult, even if it was considered to be a totally improper form of YHWH's cult from the perspective of the speakers in the book, its implied authorship, and its intended and primary readerships. Of course, there is a strong element of polemic against the calf/ves and against idolatry in general (cf. Hos 8:6; 13:2). For instance, the "priestlings" are not characterized as priests of a deity (in this case, YHWH, even if wrongfully worshiped), but only of a statue of a calf. It is likely, however, that from northern Israelite cultic perspectives, the calf/ves (or bull/s) was conceived as both a statue and a deity; a representation of the deity or a pedestal for the deity as well as an immanent manifestation of the deity itself, in this case, YHWH; cf. with similar cases in the ancient Near East.

From the fact that vv. 5, 6, and 8 deal with the cultic matters it does not follow that "its [Samaria's] king" in 10:7 is a reference to Baal or the bull-image rather than to the human king. Against such a proposal one may mention, among others, the common use of the Hebrew term מלך, the concentric structures mentioned above, the contrast between the king and the King discussed above, the common association between (northern) king, elite and improper worship conveyed by the book and which leads to the idea that the two will disappear together, the meaning of the explicitly similar expression in Hos 10:15 — see STRUCTURE — and the lack of any necessity to interpret the term in such unusual manner. For a different approach see, among others, Mays, *Hosea,* 142; Andersen and Freedman, *Hosea,* 558; Rudolph, *Hosea,* 197-98. For an approach similar to the one advanced here, see, for instance, Macintosh, *Hosea,* 407-8.

The information about the fate of the calf of Beth-el — that it was sent as (forced) tribute to Assyria (perhaps during the reign of Hoshea) — might be correct but is unverifiable. The statue or its metal could also have been pillaged, even if it is highly debatable whether the relevant section of the Nimrud Prisms of Sargon refers to the calves (as suggested in Cogan, *Imperialism,* 104-5) and even whether the information in the Prisms is historically reliable (see Na'aman, "No Anthropomorphic Image," 395-404 and bibliography). What can be said is that a readership aware of 2 Kgs 23:15-16 would have to conclude that there were no cultic calves when Josiah purged Beth-el and accordingly, they had to be removed by the Assyrians before Josiah's conquest, either as pillage/booty or as a forced tribute.

Hos 10:9 recalls the social memory of the "days of Gibeah." It also emphasizes in a negative manner the location by alluding to and connecting with the *bamot* of Iniquitytown and Iniquitytown itself (Beth-Aven/Bethel); see the pun on חטאת ישראל "the sin of Israel" in v. 8 and חטאת ישראל "you, have sinned, O Israel," in v. 9. Moreover, it seems to elaborate, within the literary setting of 10:9-15 and its emphasis on war, the reference to Gibeah in 9:9. This reference is part and parcel of a concerted effort to damage the reputation of main locations in the northern kingdom (cf. Hos 4:15; 5:1, 8; 6:7-9; 7:1; 8:5-6; 9:9, 15; 10:5, 15; 12:12; 14:1), and above all those most likely associated with important cultic activities. It is worth noting at this point that Dan (cf. 1 Kgs 12:28-30) is not mentioned in the book of Hosea and rarely mentioned in the prophetic books as a whole (see Jer 4:15; 8:16; and Amos 8:14); contrast with the numerous references to Beth-el and their salience in Hosea and in prophetic literature in general. The matter may have more to do with the inclusion of Beth-el within the realm of Judah/Yehud, since the reign of Josiah to the end of the Persian period and beyond, than with the historical cultic roles of Beth-el and Dan in the northern kingdom.

On the other hand, the references to the "days of Gibeah" (here and in 9:9) are meant to evoke the construction of particular events in the social memory shared by the target readership, just as the reference to the events of Baal Peor in 9:10 does. The references to the "days of Gibeah" seem to bear a double meaning. For one, the references evoke the social memory reflected in Judges 19; cf. the explicit evaluation of the event in Judg 19:30 that considers it the first of its kind in wickedness since the exodus from Egypt. This evaluation explains in part why references to the "days of Gibeah" were included. In addition, it is worth stressing in the case of Hos 10:9 the association of the event with extremely destructive wars which significantly almost blotted Benjamin out of existence but did not do so; just as the readers of the book know for a fact that YHWH's punishment did not fully remove Israel from existence and are assured that he will never do so (see Hos 4:1–11:11 Intention, Hos 11:1-11 Intention, and also Sweeney, *The Twelve,* 108). Yet, the social memories reflected in Judges 19 are also associated within the discourses of these literati with the lack of a king and raise the question of whether a king is necessary for the well-being of a society and to preempt Israel from committing this type of sin. The answer to that question within the book of Hosea can only be negative — the same holds true in many other biblical books, e.g., Deuteronomy, Zephaniah, Obadiah, Chronicles. Within the book of Hosea, kings (and royal elites) were among the reasons for Israel's sin and had to be removed — the only good king is the future, quasi-messianic, Davidic king of 3:5. It is in this context that the second social memory evoked by the reference to "the days of Gibeah" comes into play. It points precisely at the establishment of the monarchy in the days of Saul (1 Sam 10:26-27; 11:4; see, among others, Mays, *Hosea,* 131); cf. the reference to Gilgal in 9:15 and see Setting there. (For another approach on the matter of Gibeah and Gilgal in Hosea see Simian-Yofre, *Desierto,* 247-51.)

As mentioned above, Hos 10:9-14 shows some form of concentric thematic structure, to which a conclusion (Hos 10:15) is attached. The first and third units point at Israel's fault and a calamity that takes the form of a devastating war. The way in which these wars are described is worth noting. The first unit (vv. 9-10) advances an interplay of a previous and a future war that fits with a rhetorical (and ideological) position that past, present, and future are deeply intertwined — notice "since the days of Gibeah, you have sinned, O Israel . . ." and its implications for the future, as well as the reference to the social memory of a war of the tribes of Israel against Benjamin. Significantly no war is described in any detail. One reads about war against בני עלוה "children of badness" (Buss, *Prophetic Word,* 21) and about a (future) war for which peoples (other than Israel) will be gathered. The first is consistent with the presence of general wisdom-like elements in this READING (see below), and the other is a common motif. The result, of course, is that the future war is construed around typological terms rather than being anchored into precise historical circumstances. The first unit develops the common ancient Near East motif of the foolish enemy that trusts in its own military power, its soldiers and fortresses (cf. Liverani, "KITRU, KATARU," and, among many other biblical texts, Deut 28:52; Jer 5:17; Obad 3), and describes the fall of these unworthy objects of trust. The reference to the terrible fate of the children and mothers is a relatively common motif in the depiction of defeat (cf. 2 Kgs 8:12; Isa 13:16; Nah 3:10; Ps 137:9 and Hos 14:1). It is grounded in the possible result of defeat in the ancient Near East, carries strong emotional value and an extremely harsh ideological message in an honor-shame patriarchal society. In the present text the murder of children and mothers is associated with the destruction of the fortresses and, of course, implies the destruction of the multitude of warriors (רב גבוריך) that were supposed to defend them. The readers of the book are asked to compare both the murder of children and mothers and the destruction of fortresses to that which seems to be taken as a paradigmatic case, the destruction of Beth-Arbel by Shalman. It is possible that the reference evoked social memories within the readership about a particular event in the past. These memories, however, are not reflected anywhere in the biblical corpus (or outside it, for that matter). It is unclear which city is Beth-Arbel and to whom "Shalman" refers. Is he Shalmaneser III, Shalmaneser V, Salamanu, king of Moab, or someone else? From the perspective of the postmonarchic readership of the book of Hosea in its present form it is most likely that the name Shalman evoked at least that of Shalmanesser V, king of Assyria (727-22 BCE), who attacked and defeated Israel. Significantly, neither Salamanu nor Shalmaneser III is referred to by name if at all in the HB, and one wonders if the literati of the postmonarchic period knew anything about them. In contrast, Shalmaneser V is explicitly mentioned by name in 2 Kgs 17:3; 18:9, fulfills a central role in the events narrated in 2 Kgs 18:1-12, and certainly was known to these literati. It is worth noting, however, that Hos 10:14 does not read Shalmaneser, nor does it refer to Samaria, but to Beth-Arbel. Thus from the perspective of these readers the text remains open in regards to geography, time, and particular protagonists. Significantly, it is not open at all concerning the main issue the text wants to convey. The event is paradigmatic of the pitiless consequences that follow military defeat and, by emphasizing the killing of mothers and children, the impact that such an event would have for the very physical continuation of Israel. Here one can see a common thread in the book of Hosea in which images of birth, mothers, and the production of children, or the children themselves, are impaired or destroyed to illustrate the point of the physical destruction of Israel's future (e.g., 4:5; 9:14; 14:1 and cf. 4:10; 9:16 and of course, Hosea 1–3). To be sure, the book of Hosea also informs its readers that such a trend will not reach completion, and that in fact Israel's progeny will be numerous and countless (see 2:1-3 and cf. 14:7).

A common component of the mentioned motif of the enemy foolishly trusting that which must not be trusted from an ideological/theological perspective is not present here, namely, that of relying on a foreign power such as Egypt or Assyria (among others, cf. Isa 36:6). This theme is prominent in other READINGS within the book of Hosea, but absent here, perhaps because of the stress on the early behavior of Israel as deeply intertwined with the present and future. In any event, it is worth stressing that a READING does not have to de-velop fully all its potentiality through an image or ideological construction be-ing used in the READING. Not every aspect of the theological or ideological set-ting within which the book in its present form was produced and first read and reread has to come up in every READING, even if the text would have allowed for its presentation and development.

Hos 10:12-13 also revisits the theme of YHWH's early choice of Israel and its eventual rebellion (cf. 2:17bβ; and above all Hos 9:10, 13; see below and Setting, and Hos 11:1-4). At the center of the concentric structure mentioned above, one finds a highly elaborate agrarian image of the patronship of YHWH that encapsulates Israel's selection — though this time by implication in a culti-vated land — YHWH's high hopes of Israel's potential, YHWH's instructions and expectations for Israel's behavior as well as the latter's rebellious response. First, Ephraim — representing here itself but also all or trans-temporal Israel; see above — is compared with a trained heifer (ct. Jer 31:18) that loves to thresh. To be sure, a heifer no matter how trained it may be does not work by it-self. It requires a patron figure in the form of a farmer and owner, here soon to be identified with YHWH. In fact, it needs the farmer (soon, YHWH) to do that which it (in its ideal state) loves to do. Moreover, the results of the heifer's threshing benefit the farmer. So Israel's ideal, initial love for threshing is clearly a love to do the farmer's/YHWH's will, to serve the farmer/YHWH (cf. Nwaoru, *Imagery,* 85). The farmer/YHWH is described as mindful of these positive features of Ephraim/heifer and of its fine neck, that is, its potential for excellent work at the more difficult job of ploughing for him, as YHWH re-counts, ואני עברתי על טוב צוארה "it was I [emphatic, pleonastic 'I'] who happened upon her fine neck" (for the translation see Macintosh, *Hosea,* 417-18). Then YHWH decides, "I shall harness Ephraim, Judah shall plough and Ja-cob should engage in harrowing," letting the implied listeners of YHWH's tell-ing in the world of the book, and above all the readers know that Ephraim stands for all, trans-temporal Israel (see above). Thus, the text conveys a con-struction of the selection of Israel and of the beginning of the relationship be-tween YHWH and Israel not in terms of husband/wife, or father/son (cf. al-ready Hos 11:1 and cf. Hosea 1–2), but in terms of other asymmetrical, patronship relationships. Like the descriptions of "first contact" in chapter 9, Israel is described initially as holding important positive characteristics (ct. Hos 1:2 and Hos 11:1-4 and discussions there). But the image of the farmer un-avoidably evokes and carries in itself that of arable land, as opposed to the desert. Thus the text constructs an ideal image of Israel in the farmer's land (i.e., YHWH's land) in the idyllic past that serves as a counterpart for that of the ideal future of reconciliation, also in the land. (For other treatments of Hos 10:11-13a see Holt, *Prophesying the Past,* 77-81; Morris, *Prophecy,* 95-97.)

The recurrence of images taken from the natural world here and in this set of reading as a whole (see 4:16; 8:7; 9:10, 13, 16; 10:1, 4, 11; cf. 14:6) is worth mentioning. On one level, it is a reflection of the actual world within which the authorship and primary rereadership of the book lived, namely, the world of a small agrarian society. On another level, it is indicative of an intellectual setting in which there was a general, implied, positive approach to the world of what

we may call "nature," and which is for the most part centered around the culti-
vated land (i.e., the result of "culture"), and human activity within that realm as
potential sources of knowledge for those who observe and mediate on them. It
is possible to relate this approach to elements usually associated with wisdom
that appear in this READING, though also elsewhere in the book (e.g., Hos 8:7).
For instance, the same logic that governs the saying in Hos 8:7 governs the one
in 10:12aα. In addition, one may consider also the presence of a word registrar
that contrasts עלוה/עולה "badness" in vv. 9, 13 (including children of badness
in v. 9) and רשע "wickedness" in v. 13 and associates them with כחש "falsehood" on the one hand, and with צדקה/צדק "righteousness" and חסד "hesed"
in v. 12 on the other, as well as the reference to "chastise" in v. 10. These observations certainly do not prove, nor are meant to prove, that the "wisdom tradition" influenced the book of Hosea; rather, they seem to reflect a simple sociological fact that the writers and primary readers of the book of Hosea were a
very small group of bearers of high literacy, and among them one is to find the
"sages" of the period. Although these literati were mindful of the existence of
different genres, it is only expected that works produced for (and among) these
circles would share more than a few linguistic and conceptual realms, and that
this sharing would be reflected in, for instance, a prophetic book, proverbs, or
psalms. (For studies on wisdom and Hosea, see, among others, Macintosh,
"Hosea and Wisdom Tradition," and see Hosea 4 STRUCTURE; Hosea 7:3-16
Setting; Hosea 14 Setting.)

The precise choice of the words וְיֹרֶה and דרך (for the meanings of these
two words see below) in vv. 12 and 13 bears particular notice as it sheds light
on the intellectual setting of the production and primary reading of the book of
Hosea. The first word appears in the expression ועד יבוא וירה צדק לכם
(12bβ). The expression can be understood "until he [YHWH] comes and rains
[וְיֹרֶה] righteousness [צדק] down for you." Understood this way, the text
(a) continues the combination of an agrarian metaphor with abstract objects and
particularly "sow for yourself righteousness [צדקה]") in v. 12a; (b) relates to
the general ideas expressed in Hos 2:21-23 about the godly characteristics that
YHWH will "shower" on Israel in the ideal time (see, for instance, "I will betroth you to me with righteousness [צדק]" in 2:21 and even the reference to
rain; see discussion of Hos 2:3-25); (c) directly relates to one of the possible
understandings of 6:3 (notice the explicit use of the rain metaphor and even of
the verbal form יֹרֶה = יורה and see the discussion on 6:3 in 5:1–7:2 STRUC-
TURE); and (d) contributes to the creation of signposts for reading, and within
the system of continued reading and studying of the book of Hosea, of readings
of a text within the book in a manner informed by another text. Such an approach to these texts would immediately reveal a significant difference. The
failed approach (6:3) is characterized by human initiative failing to result in
YHWH's rain; the successful one still in the future (10:12) is characterized by
divine initiative (cf. Hos 2:16-25; 11:8-11; 14:5-9). At the same time the particular choice of the verb allows this expression to be understood as "until he
[YHWH] comes and teaches [וְיֹרֶה] you righteousness." The connection with
6:3 would remain in this case, and the same holds true for the identity of the ini-
tiator. Yet references to a divine teacher subtly raise a different set of matters

and images (see, for instance, Ps 119:102; cf. Isa 28:26). They also raise the question of what will this teacher teach in that ideal future, which in this case is "righteousness" (cf. among others, Jer 31:33). They also raise the issue of the correlation between this act of teaching and the contents of previous acts of teaching by the same teacher (cf. Hos 8:12).

One of the implications of the mentioned interrelation between 6:3 and 10:12bβ — and many other similar interrelations discussed in this commentary — is that from the perspective of the readers for whom the book of Hosea, in its present form, was composed and who were supposed to read and reread it, not only do meanings take shape as a tapestry of partial meanings and interrelations between different texts within the book, but also the book itself shows textually inscribed markers that lead them to approach it in that particular way. Of course, these considerations strongly influence their understanding of the intention of the implied author of the book that they, as readers, construe. If this author intended to create all these connections, then none of the subunits can really be considered "individual sayings" or the like, for even at the level of word choice, they were meant to achieve their significance within the frame of the entire book.

As for the use of דרכך in v. 13, it is likely that it denotes "your power" here, as many English translations recognize. (Some translations and many scholars emend the Hebrew text to רכבך "your chariots.") Yet the word דרך is rarely used in this sense; in fact, the only other potential example is Prov 31:3. The word certainly connotes at least the sense of "your way" and, therefore, within this context a very negative sense (cf. Ps 37:5; 143:8) that locates the "you" in opposition to YHWH and YHWH's ways. See also "his ways" in Hos 12:3. It is possible also to understand דרכך as meaning "your policy" (see Barthélemy, *Critique Textuelle,* vol. III, 585, and Macintosh, *Hosea,* 425-27). This understanding would not substantially affect the analysis advanced here, but it may add an additional layer. It is obvious that the term connoted at least a sense of "your way," and that within its context, the "you" in the world of the book is portrayed as considering it a source of strength (see the parallel structure with warriors).

One may also easily notice that some combinations of word pairs seem to reflect word and conceptual associations that existed among the literati for whom and among whom the book, in its present form, was composed. For instance, one finds the pair זרע "sow" — קצר "harvest" in 10:12. The same pair appears metaphorically in relation to abstract concepts in Prov 22:8. Significantly, the two terms associated with the pair in Prov 22:8 are עולה "iniquity" (see 10:13; cf. v. 9) and און "wickedness," which also appear in Hosea 10 (see v. 5). Moreover, עולה "iniquity" occurs in a contrastive pair with צדק "righteousness" (see Ps 58:2-3; and Isa 59:3-4); see Hos 10:12 (notice also צדקה "righteousness" in this verse). One may even notice that עולה is often associated with false speech (e.g., Isa 59:3); cf. 10:4. To be sure, none of these observations point at direct textual dependence. But they point at something much more important: a shared network of words, word associations, and mental conceptual associations. Such networks underlie the use of language and the discourses of those who bear them. To be sure, shared networks of this type do not necessarily point to a common date, but they *do point* to a shared conceptual, linguistic map. From the perspective of the readers, the presence of the mentioned mental networks contributes to the textual cohesion of the text.

Finally, it is worth stressing that the book does not associate the utterance of the words reported in this READING with any historical event. As usual in the book of Hosea, there is no reference to when or where or even to whom, in practical terms, and against which circumstances these words were uttered. Within the basic limits set in Hos 1:1 and a construction of a past world in which the Assyrians were the main power and the Israelite cult included (northern) altars, *bamot,* and, of course, the calf/calves, the world of the text is as generalized in this regard as it can be. Even the characterization of the "moral" wickedness of Israel, here and elsewhere, remains open and generalized (cf. Buss, *Prophetic Word,* 98-102) and applicable to any period. The intended and primary readers are given no clue about particular historical events and their potential relation to the world of the text, nor is there any textually inscribed sign that may suggest that they were urged to bring into the text this type of historical question. In other words, this READING or any portion thereof is not presented as closely anchored in historical circumstances, nor are the intended readers asked to approach it in a manner that is strongly informed by concrete historical events and circumstances, such as those of 731 BCE as opposed to those of 722, 727, or 738 BCE. One may contrast this situation with the plethora of textually inscribed markers that asked them to approach this READING in a way that is strongly informed by other READINGS within the book.

All this said, many scholars focus on the historical Hosea, as opposed to the character in the book or the book itself, and they identify most of the text with Hosea's reaction to, or his stance against, the background of concrete historical events during the last decades of the northern kingdom. These scholars have proposed corresponding settings. Wolff, for instance, dates the sayings in 10:1-8 to sometime after 733 BCE, "when the disturbances of 733 had begun to recede in the public mind" (*Hosea,* 173), and associates v. 3 with the reign of Hoshea (731-25; see also Macintosh, *Hosea,* 393). Wolff also maintains that the words in 10:9-15 were probably proclaimed in Samaria and after 733 BCE (see also Pentiuc, *Long-Suffering Love,* 134), when the people felt secure against hostile attacks, when they had begun to think that they could rebel against Assyria, and in particular towards 727 BCE (Wolff, *Hosea,* 183), and again most likely during the reign of King Hoshea. Of course, not everyone agrees with these dates. For instance, Simian-Yofre assigns the activity of the historical Hosea to the reigns of Zechariah, Shallum, and Menahem, and sees no reason to assign any (original) text to any time later than the reign of the latter (cf. Simian-Yofre, *Desierto,* 120, 218); and Tadmor ("Historical Background") maintains that Hosea 4–14 is to be dated between 743 and 739 BCE.

At times these approaches tend to develop an incipient biography of the historical Hosea. For instance, Pentiuc, who assumes a period of withdrawal of the historical Hosea on the basis of 9:1-9 and associates 9:10-17 with that period after 733 BCE, concludes that "his [Hosea's] withdrawal did not last very long given the same expression 'days of Gibeah' found in 9:9 and 10:9" (Pentiuc, *Long-Suffering Love,* 134).

It is also worth noting that Sweeney associates the entire discourse of Hos 9:1–14:1 with the festival of Sukkoth. Such an understanding influences interpretation. For instance, after stating that "the allegorical portrayal is established in Hos 10:1, which presents Israel as 'a luxuriant vine that yields its fruit,'" he maintains that "the vine, of course, presupposes the celebration of Sukkoth when the grape harvest is brought in" (Sweeney, *Twelve Prophets,* 103).

As other readings in the book, Hosea 10 contributes to the characterization of the language of the speaker/s as somewhat odd in relation to that expected to be found in prophetic books set in the monarchic period (cf. the books of Amos, Micah, and Isaiah and see their superscriptions). One may notice, for instance, that גפן "vine" appears in 10:1 as a masculine noun instead of the usual feminine. Significantly, תנור "oven" is treated as a feminine noun in Hos 7:4, instead of the expected masculine. Similarly, the syntax of נדמה שמרון מלכה in v. 7 is unusual. A different type of oddity is the spelling קאם instead of the usual קם in וקאם "it will arise" in 10:14 (the presence of the א may have been influenced by that of an א in שאון "tumult," and a desire to achieve alliteration; see Qyl, *Hosea,* 30). Significantly, none of these instances involve hapax legomena, but a slightly different use of a common, shared vocabulary. The book of Hosea contains roughly twice the number of hapax (absolute and non-absolute) it would have had if the distribution of hapax were random. Although this figure sets it apart from other prophetic books later included in the Twelve except for Habakkuk and Nahum, it is in the "middle range" and certainly much lower than Songs, Job, or Isaiah for that matter. Moreover, the relatively small size of the book of Hosea raises some questions about the statistical value of these observations. (On these matters, see Greenspahn, *Hapax Legomena.*) These features do not necessarily indicate that the speaker is construed as speaking northern Israelite Hebrew, but that the book characterizes its speakers (and mainly YHWH) as carrying a different voice than is usual in prophetic books. (On some of these features, cf. Morag, "On Semantic and Lexical Features," 493; Rudolph, *Hosea,* 191; Yoo, *Israelian Hebrew,* 173-74.)

Intention

The general intention of Hosea 10:1-15 is to communicate and reinforce the positions and the general horizon of thought of the authorship and readership as represented in these texts (see Setting) and to socialize the literati through their shared reading of the material and the larger society through the literati's reading to others of these readings.

Among others, this READING shapes a general interpretation of Israel's history, evoking its promising beginnings as well as its downfall. It advances a causal relation between Israel's fault and its calamities that come into being through the agency of YHWH. Yet punishment is construed also as a purifying and even educative process necessary to ensure Israel's proper behavior (cf. Jer 5:17-19). Past cultic and kingly faults are stressed, along with "foolish" worldviews that fed them, but hope is also implied.

Bibliography

R. Albertz, "Exile as Purification. Reconstructing the 'Book of Four,'" P. L. Redditt and A. Schart (eds.), *Thematic Threads in the Book of the Twelve* (BZAW 325; Berlin: de Gruyter, 2003) 232-51; P. M. Arnold, "Hosea and the Sin of Gibeah," *CBQ* 51 (1989) 447-60; M. Cogan, *Imperialism and Religion. Assyria, Judah and Israel in the Eighth and Seventh Centuries B.C.E.* (SBLMS 10; Missoula: Scholars Press, 1974); H. R. (Chaim) Cohen, "'Foam' in Hos 10:7," *JANES* 2 (1969) 25-29; idem, *Biblical Hapax Legomena in the Light of Akkadian and Ugaritic* (SBLDS 37; Missoula, MT: Scholars Press, 1978); G. R. Driver, "Linguistic and Textual Problems: Minor Prophets. I," *JTS* 39 (1938) 155-66; E. N. Good, "The Composition of Hosea," *SEÅ* 31 (1966) 21-63; R. Gordis, "Studies in Hebrew Roots of Contrasted Meanings," *JQR* 27 (1936) 33-58; F. E. Greenspahn, *Hapax Legomena in Biblical Hebrew. A Study of the Phenomenon and Its Treatments Since Antiquity with Special Reference to Verbal Forms* (SBLDS 74; Chico, CA: Scholars Press, 1984); A. V. Hunter, *Seek the Lord* (Baltimore: St. Mary's Seminary and University, 1982); J. Joosten, "Exegesis in the Septuagint Version of Hosea," J. C. de Moor (ed.), *Intertextuality in Ugarit and Israel* (OtSt 40; Leiden: E. J. Brill, 1998) 62-85; P. A. Kruger, "Prophetic Imagery, On Metaphors and Similes in the Book of Hosea," *JNSL* 14 (1988) 143-51; C. J. Labuschagne, "The Similes in the Book of Hosea," *OTWSA* 7-8 (1965) 64-76; B. A. Levine, "Review of H. Louis Ginsberg, *The Israelian Heritage of Judaism*," *AJSReview* 12 (1987) 143-57 (150-55); M. Liverani, "KITRU, KATARU," *Mesopotamia* 17 (1982) 43-66; A. A. Macintosh, "A Consideration of the Problems Presented by Psalm II.11 and 12," *JTS* (1976) 1-14; idem, "Hosea and the Wisdom Tradition: Dependence and Independence," J. Day, R. P. Gordon, and H. G. M. Williamson (eds.), *Wisdom in Ancient Israel. Essays in Honor of J. A. Emerton* (Cambridge: Cambridge Univ. Press, 1995) 124-32; idem, "Hosea. The Rabbinic Commentators and the Ancient Versions," A. Rapoport-Albert and G. Greenberg (eds.), *Biblical Hebrew, Biblical Texts. Essays in Memory of Michael P. Weitzman* (JSOTSupS 333; Sheffield: Sheffield Academic Press, 2001) 77-82; S. Morag, "On Semantic and Lexical Features in the Language of Hosea," *Tarbiz* 53 (1984) 489-511 (in Hebrew); N. Na'aman, "No Anthropomorphic Graven Image. Notes on the Assumed Anthropomorphic Cult Statues in the Temples of YHWH in the Pre-Exilic Period," *UF* 31 (1999) 391-415; J. A. Soggin, "Hosea 11,5 (cf. 10,9b?): Emphatic Lamed?" J. A. Soggin, *Old Testament and Oriental Studies* (BibOr 29; Rome: Pontifical Biblical Institute, 1975) 223; A. Szabó, "Textual Problems in Amos and Hosea," *VT* 25 (1975) 500-524; H. Tadmor, "The Historical Background of Hosea's Prophecies," M. Haran (ed.), *Yehezkel Kaufman Jubilee Volume* (Jerusalem: Magnes Press, 1960) 84-88; M. Tsevat, "Some Biblical Notes," *HUCA* 24 (1952-53) 107-14; E. R. Wendland, *The Discourse Analysis of Hebrew Prophetic Literature* (Lewiston, NY: E. Mellen Press, 1995).

Seventh Didactic Prophetic Reading and Conclusion of the Set: From Being a Boy in Egypt to Future Resettlement in the Land — YHWH's Speech Brings Hope to Postmonarchic Israel, Hos 11:1-11

Structure

I. YHWH's efforts with boy "Israel"	11:1-4
A. Mini-summary of Israel's past (hi)story including YHWH's foundational deeds concerning Israel	11:1-2
B. Another portrayal of YHWH's efforts	11:3-4
II. The nature of the punishment	11:5-7
III. YHWH characterizes the deity as unable to destroy Ephraim/Israel	11:8-9
IV. Glorious future	11:10-11

The unit is a kind of divine and authoritative summary of the (hi)story of Israel. But unlike most (hi)stories it includes events in the future. Although one may refer to it as a description of Israel's trajectory in the axis of time, it is better to understand it as a (hi)story that includes the future, because within the discourses reflected and promoted by the book, the future, from YHWH's perspective, is as certain and as defined as the past. It is exactly this concept that provides so much hope to an Israel that considers itself as existing after a terrifying divine judgment and before the (full) worldly manifestation of YHWH's promises of restoration and hope (see Hos 11:10-11). In fact, the text reflects and shapes a discourse in which past and future seem fixed in a closely linked relationship that is expressed and communicated even at the level of word choice. See the use of verbal forms of הלך "go" in Hos 11:2 and 10, and references to Egypt in 11:1, 5, 11 (see also below), from the perspective of the larger perspective of Hos 4:1–11:11; cf. Hos 7:11 and 11:11 (and cf. also Hos 11:1-2).

In addition, this READING and in particular vv. 8-11 serve as an interpretative key for divine statements such as those in Hos 5:6; 8:13; 9:3, 6, 17; 13:9, 14. It places in perspective the announcements of doom. The intended and primary readership learn that although for rhetorical reasons these divine announcements are crafted in categorical language, they are not to be understood as eternally valid or reflecting by themselves the full extent of YHWH's decisions concerning Israel. In other words, they are supposed to understand the announcements reported in the book not as separate, self-contained units, but as units within the general frame of the book and its interpretative keys, such as Hos 11:8-11. Of course, such an approach is expected in a book to be read and reread, and is consistent with the very existence of a community of readers of the book in postmonarchic Yehud that by itself belies the mentioned categorical claims of doom.

The extent of this unit is set off by several markers of inner coherence (see below), and by its outer limits. The latter are shaped by (a) the concluding, heightening note in 11:11 along with the presence of נאם ה' "YHWH's utterance" in final position (on ה' נאם see Hos 4:1–11:11 STRUCTURE) and along with the beginning of a new thematic unit in Hos 12:1 and by (b) the new opening, namely, כי נער ישראל "when Israel was a boy." Of course, the structural hierarchy of these breaks is open to debate, and some of the mentioned markers may communicate breaks of a lower hierarchical level in the representations of the STRUCTURE of the book of Hosea. For instance, in Hos 2:15 there is a final נאם ה', and, for one thing, the masoretic system of paragraphs marks both instances in the same way. But the נאם ה' in 2:15 is better understood as pointing to the conclusion of a section within a READING than to that of a (partially) self-contained READING, because, among other things, the following verse begins with לכן "therefore" and, accordingly, indicates to the readers that the two textual units are closely interrelated. Nothing like this occurs in 12:1. Moreover, Hos 12:1 begins a new round of constructions of the past that eventually leads to the announcements of hope (cf. Hos 11:7-11 and Hos 14:5-9). In other words, this boundary, which is the boundary of the entire SET OF READINGS in Hos 4:1–11:11 seems quite strongly marked.

The expression כי נער ישראל "when Israel was a boy" in Hos 11:1 is somewhat reminiscent of the opening of 9:10, but again for reasons discussed in Hos 9:1-17 STRUCTURE, it seems reasonable to see there a break within sections within the same READING, at least according to some readings of the text that follow its textually inscribed markers. Yet there is a difference between the break between 10:15 and 11:1 and that between 11:11 and 12:1. Whereas Hos 12:1 does not go back to Hos 11:11, it is possible to read Hos 11:1 as a continuation of Hos 10:15 (see LXX, the Vg, Peshiṭta, cf. Rashi). When this is done, then the כי is likely to be seen as causal and, therefore, meaning "for," instead of, or in addition to, "when." This seems to be another case of a text that allows more than one meaning. As in similar instances, it is reasonable to assume that the text was read in more than one way through the process of continuous reading and rereading for which the book of Hosea is meant. Accordingly, one may consider the two different structures (i.e., the one in which Hos 11:1 represents the beginning of a new READING, and the other according to which Hos 11:1 opens a new section within an existing READING) not only as possible, but as complementary.

In either case, the image of the beginning of the relation between YHWH and Israel in 11:1-4 weaves into the tapestry to which preceding texts such as Hos 9:10, 13 and 10:11 also contribute important threads (also cf. Hos 2:17bβ). Each of them is a partial metaphor or possible way of addressing such a beginning, and all together they convey a better representation of the general construction of that period in the imagination of the authorship and primary readership than any of them separately (see Setting). Hos 11:1-11, whether conceived as a separate READING or as a section in another READING, is still part and parcel of the SET OF READINGS Hos 4:1–11:11, and for that matter constitutes its concluding section. In fact, Hos 11:8-11 not only concludes the SET but represents the heightened point of hope to which the text of this SET moves (cf. with the similar roles of 2:1-3; 2:16-25; and Hos 14:5-9).

Among markers of inner coherence of Hos 11:1-11 as a whole, one may mention the contrastive use of verbal forms of הלך "go" in Hos 11:2 and 10, which to some extent encapsulates the diametrical change in Israel's behavior towards YHWH that takes place in this divinely proclaimed (hi)story of Israel, and which reassures the readers that the ideal future will come to pass. (As mentioned above, the use of similar expressions to construe past and future also connotes a blurring of differences among them that enhances the sense of inevitability of the idyllic future proclaimed by YHWH.) One may also mention the references to Egypt in Hos 11:1, 5, 11, and that to son/sons (or child/children) in vv. 1 and 10. To them one may add the shift in the metaphorical characterization of YHWH from a parent who lovingly takes care of a disappointing child at the beginning of the relationship with Israel (Hos 11:1, 3) and the unit, to that of a roaring lion who leaves little choice to those at whom he roars (Hos 11:10) at the end of the unit. The trajectory of this shifting characterization passes in the middle of the unit through that of a parent who would be legally justified to kill a wayward son/child (as per the discourse of the period; see the potential punishment envisaged in this text and cf. Deut 21:18-20) but cannot do so out of love of the child (Hos 11:7-8). The implied narrative about YHWH, and YHWH's character, is interwoven with that of Israel's (hi)story, as it is shaped and reflected in this unit. The implied narrative about YHWH relates to that conveyed through the shifting images associated with Israel: From a boy who would not tremble before his parents and do as instructed to a trembling bird or dove with not much choice, to a dove/bird that becomes eventually a house dweller. (The basic outline of this [hi]story serves as a central meta-narrative of postmonarchic Israel and appears in different versions across biblical genres; see, for instance, Ps 86:6-17; Ps 106.)

The internal, structural division advanced here is one of several possibilities. A complementary structure of the unit can be easily discerned involving two major units, (I) vv. 1-9 — which by itself is subdivided into (A) 1-4, (B) 5-7 and (C) 8-9 or into (A) 1-7 and (B) 8-9 — and (II) vv. 10-11. (See Simian-Yofre, *Desierto,* 147-49, and Sweeney, *Twelve Prophets,* 112-17, who advocate the first and second subdivision respectively.) Such a structure reinforces the role and message of vv. 10-11 in a way that is consistent with their message in the book.

In addition, it is worth noting that although Eidewall (*Grapes,* 166-67) maintains that there is a "sequential structure" similar to the one advanced here, he also refers to an inclusion structure in which vv. 1-2 and 10-11 serve as the two external rings in an inclusio (v. 1 — out of Egypt; v. 2 walk away from YHWH; v. 10 walk behind YHWH; v. 11 out of Egypt). Even if one does not fully accept all the details of Eidewall's position, there is still a sense of envelope between at least vv. 2 and 10.

For proposals like the one advanced here, see among others Ritschl, "God's Conversion." For other proposals for the structure of Hosea 11 involving the use of chiasmus as the main rhetorical device, see Siebert-Hommes, "With Bands of Love," and De Regt, "Person Shift," 219 n. 18. In addition, numerous other proposals have been advanced. For instance, Wolff (*Hosea,* 193-96) divides the unit into (i) vv. 1-7 and (ii) vv. 8-11; Andersen and Freedman (*Hosea,* 574-76) between (i) vv. 1-4 and (ii) vv. 5-11 — according to them "there are serious structural dislocations in the chapter" which may be "an authentic reflection of the turbulence of indecision, or the byproduct of varieties of textual disarray" (576); Nissinen (*Prophetie*, 235-63) between (i) vv. 1–4; (ii) vv. 5–7; and (iii) vv. 8–11; and Jeremias (*Hosea*, 139-40) between (i) vv. 1-6 and (ii) 7-11. This multiplication of proposed structures is directly related to different interpretations of the text, in some cases to redactional assumptions, and to different understandings of the interplay of the different literary subunits.

This being said, it is worth noting that (textually inscribed) markers of textual coherence are abundant at the level of the microunits, and at times across them as well. Verse 1 is formally bound together by and conveys meaning through the interplay of the pairs נער "boy" and בן "son," Israel — Egypt, and אהבהו "I loved him" and קראתי ל "I called for/summoned [my son]" (on the meanings conveyed by קראתי ל see below). Verse 8a shows a four-fold structure based on double-duty use of איך "how" and the pairs Ephraim-Israel and Admah and Zeboiim, while 8b is based on two niphal verbal forms and the pair לבי "my [YHWH's] heart" and נחומי "my [YHWH's] compassion"; moreover, in the expression in which the niphal form encapsulates the message of the verse, instead of "overturning" the cities/Israel, YHWH's heart "turns around" (the image of YHWH's overturning of Admah and Zeboiim is implied in the text; see Deut 29:22, and below). Similarly, one finds a four-fold repetition of לא "not" in v. 9, and three of these cases involve לא followed by a prefix verbal form in the first person. One may also notice the repetition of יחרדו, often translated as "they shall come trembling," in close textual proximity and linking vv. 10 and 11.

All these markers of coherence serve stylistic and rhetorical purposes. It is worth noting that the same literary devices appear elsewhere in the book. One may compare the repetition of איך in v. 8 with that of אין in Hos 3:4; or the lengthy series of words including the letter א in the same verse with similar repetitions of sounds in Hos 9:6. As in other cases, these literary devices contribute to the rhetorical impact of the text. To illustrate, the repetition of the א in v. 8 brings to the forefront an emphasis on the "I" of YHWH and the affective divine "how" that points at the impossibility of YHWH's complete destruction of Israel, and even links it to the terms Ephraim and Israel. As in other instances, the goal of achieving such repetitions influenced word choice. A good example: it is reasonable to assume that the reference to Admah and Zeboiim, instead of the more common Sodom and Gomorrah, is related to the presence of the א, and even better, an initial א — as is the case in most of the words in this series — in the word Admah.

As mentioned above, there are also strong markers of cohesion across the unit. In addition to the הלך "go" in Hos 11:2 and 10, the references to Egypt and the textual trajectories of the characterizations of YHWH and Israel, one may note, among others, the presence of words from (a) the root שוב "return" in vv. 5 (twice), 7, and 9 — which involve the topics of Israel's return to Egypt, Israel's failure to return to YHWH, and YHWH's turning back from punishment; (b) from the root אכל "eat" in vv. 4 and 6 — which involve YHWH's feeding Israel first, and the sword devouring Israel's/Ephraim's cities later; and (c) from the root קרא "call/summon" in vv. 1 and 7 — contrasting YHWH's calling and Israel's according to one reading of v. 7 (see below).

As expected from a unit that sets in perspective claims advanced in other units (see above), there are a number of textually inscribed signposts linking Hos 11:1-11 to other texts in the book, and vice versa. Cf., among others, 11:2b and 2:15; 11:3b and 5:13; 6:1; 7:1 and also 14:5 (cf. Exod 15:26); and from a different perspective, also 11:3b and 2:10 and see also 5:4; 11:4 and 10:11 (see Setting); 11:5 and 8:13 and also 9:3; 11:9 and 8:5 and 14:5; 11:10 and 5:14, 13:7-8; 11:11 and 7:11, and from another perspective, 11:11 and 12:10. In many of these occasions, the bonds between the two units carry a strong contrastive imagery (e.g., the lion imagery associated with YHWH "the lion" in 11:10 and 5:14; 13:7-8) that conveys the meaning of the text (e.g., YHWH is a terrifying lion who "devoured" Israel — even when it was young, but also one whose roar will lead Israel back to YHWH; see 5:14; 13:7-8 and 11:10).

The text of Hosea 11 implies an awareness of social memories reflected in other books and uses language and metaphors that appear elsewhere in the repertoire of postmonarchic communities. For instance, the reference to Admah and Zeboiim points to a tradition reflected in Deut 29:22 that associates their fate with that of Sodom and Gomorrah, that is, characterizes them as paradigmatic examples of total destruction. The presence of the expression כי אל אנוכי ולא איש "for I am God and not a human person" in v. 9, which can be understood only within the context of vv. 8-9, brings to the forefront the type of issues raised and decided in a very different manner in Num 23:19 and 1 Sam 15:29. (Notice the similarity in language including the use of forms from the root נחם "have compassion" in 1 Sam 15:29 and Hos 11:8.) There are some similarities in both language and structure between Hos 11:1-8 and Jer 31:18-20 (Yee, *Composition,* 219-20). The image of a future roaring lion (YHWH) who is about to bring a fundamental change appears in Hos 11:10, but also elsewhere in prophetic literature (see Jer 25:30; 4:7; and cf. Amos 1:2). More importantly, perhaps, v. 10 raises the image of the return of the exiles from the West, in addition to the South/Egypt and the North/Assyria; cf. Isa 11:11 — for the motif of the return of the exiles from the West see in particular Isa 60:8-9; cf. Joel 4:6-7; Obad 20.

Several expressions and verses demand particular attention. Some of them carry multiple meanings, which all together convey and shape the message of the text. Cases involving vv. 1, 2, and 4 are discussed under Setting, because they shed light on the ideological worldview that is reflected and communicated by the book. There has been a debate about the meaning of the expression in v. 5a, namely, לא ישוב אל ארץ מצרים ואשור הוא מלכו. This debate has influenced the main English translations. For instance, the NRSV reads "they shall return to the land of Egypt, and Assyria shall be their king" (and cf. NAB); whereas the NJB reads, "he will not have to go back to Egypt, Assyria will be his king instead!" It is, however, undeniable that the text as it stands raised among its primary readers a meaning akin to "he will not return to the land of Egypt, but rather it is Assyria who will be his king." This understanding of the expression is grammatically, syntactically, and semantically unproblematic. Moreover, it befits well the role that הוא carries in the second sentence and to which the following description applies "a 'selective-exclusive' force . . . : the subject/focus is singled out and contrasted with other possible or actual alternatives" (citation from Waltke-O'Connor, *Hebrew Syntax*, 297 — although Hos 11:5 is not mentioned, the discussion there applies to this text — see also Macintosh, *Hosea*, 450-51; the contrastive nature of the sentence is also probably hinted at by the choice of a waw-noun opening). The focus of the entire verse is therefore Assyria. The text brings to the forefront the idea that Assyria — instead of YHWH — will be Israel's king because they did not return to YHWH. As the following verse explains, this servitude to Assyria will be accompanied by severe distress (cf. Deut 28:47-48 for a similar idea). Yet the text still leaves the readership with hope, because Israel will not be forced to return to Egypt, which in this context would be tantamount to undoing the link between YHWH and Israel mentioned in v. 1. The text, of course, works within the basic framework of a world in which there are two main earthly powers, Assyria and Egypt (see Hos 7:11; 9:3; 11:11; 12:2); see Setting Hos 5:1–7:2.

The fact that this meaning seems to conflict with texts such as Hos 8:3; 9:3; and 11:11 rhetorically highlights the message, turns the expression into a kind of contextually difficult reading — a fact that may have led to attempts of harmonization with other texts (cf. LXX) — and certainly provides no critical reason to adapt the text to others in the book of Hosea. Yet it raises the question of tension between the statements. This READING clearly relates the statements concerning Egypt in vv. 1, 5 and 11. Israel will come back to its land and houses from Egypt, and, accordingly, Israel would have to have returned to Egypt previously (v. 11), but Israel would not have forfeited YHWH's call (v. 1) and would not return to Egypt in the sense of return to the situation existing before that call (v. 5). Moreover, Israel as a polity would be forced to serve Assyria as their king, but not Pharaoh. If trans-temporal Israel is represented in this READING by northern Israel, then this reading reflects some social memories of the past agreed upon by the literati, namely, that northern Israel was defeated and annexed by Assyria, which in this case is historically accurate.

All this said, it is likely that through the process of reading and rereading of the text, a kind of qere/ketiv situation concerning לֹא "not" and לֹו "to/for him" such as the one attested in Ps 100:3 developed here (cf. LXX Hos 11:4-5 that might reflect the existence of a לֹו reading in the Hebrew tradition). If this is the case, then as the sentence was approached with לֹא the meanings discussed above were advanced; whereas when the sentence was approached with לֹו, the latter was attached to the end of v. 4 ("feed him") and as a result, 5a would be understood as "he will return to the land of Egypt, but rather it is Assyria who will be his king." This message would be consistent with v. 11 and 8:3; 9:3, and provides a kind a system of double reading around this verse, illuminating and setting each other in proportion. Of course, if this is the case, the precise boundaries between vv. 1-4 and 5-7 would fluctuate in a way fully dependent on the manner on which the meaning of לֹו/לֹא is approached by the particular reader.

As in other READINGS in the book, Israel is referred to both in the second and third person (plural or singular). These shifts in grammatical person and number serve rhetorical purposes (see, for instance, vv. 1-2, 7-8) and cannot be used as reliable sources for structural or redactional purposes. It is possible to assign the reference to YHWH in the third person in v. 10 to a human voice that appears nowhere else in Hosea 11, but it is at least as likely that the intended and primary readerships assigned the reference to YHWH, as there is nothing strange in YHWH referring to YHWH in the third person — as demonstrated among others by Judg 2:22; 6:26; 1 Sam 10:19; 2 Sam 12:9; 1 Kgs 17:14; 2 Kgs 20:5; Isa 49:7; Jer 14:10; 17:5; 23:16; 26:2; 27:16; Mic 2:5; 4:7b, 10; 6:5; Zeph 3:12; Mal 1:4. (See also the previous discussion of the reference to Hos 5:4, 6, 7 in Hos 5:1–7:2 STRUCTURE and cf. Revell, *Designation,* §27.3.)

Numerous proposals for textual emendations of the text of Hosea 11 have been advanced (see, for instance, BHS). Some of these proposals are mentioned in this study. For a summary and critique of these and other proposals, see Barthélemy, *Critique Textuelle,* vol. III, 588-96. In addition, claims concerning the secondary character of some subunits or words have been advanced. At times, the result of these claims is the construction of a hypothetical, original text that is substantially different from the one in the book. An obvious example is the relatively common proposal among redactional critical scholars to remove v. 10 as secondary (see Wolff, *Hosea,* 194-95; Mays, *Hosea,* 158; Davies, *Hosea,* 264-65; Jeremias, *Hosea,* 147) and even more so, if both verses 10 and 11 are considered secondary (e.g., Good, "Composition," 48-49). (For an intermediate position, see Simian-Yofre [*Desierto,* 152] who considers secondary v. 10b and 11b.) On verse 10 and its importance see Setting. It is worth noting that within the comprehensive reconstruction of the redactional history of Hosea 11 advanced by Yee, Hosea 11 in its entirety belongs to a postmonarchic redactor (R2). See Yee, *Composition,* 214-29, 316. For another position, see Willi-Plein, *Vorformen,* 276-77.

Genre

Given the fact that Hosea 11 includes speech whose speaker is clearly and unequivocally YHWH, some scholars (e.g., Mays) consider it an oracle, or a set of oracles if they divide the text into separate speeches. Some of these speeches may even be organized thematically. Thus, one may maintain, for instance, that Hos 11:1-7 is a "historico-theological accusation" (see Wolff, *Hosea,* 193). In addition, Bjornard ("Hosea 11:8-9") maintains that the form of vv. 8-9 is "fairly similar to the oracle of doom that we find in 6:4-6" but "instead of the expected conclusion of judgment, there is a total break, with God asserting his love and holy otherness" (16).

The position advanced here, however, is that Hos 11:1-11, as other READINGS in the book of Hosea, neither is an oral work, nor can it be separated from the book of Hosea. It is neither a series of actual individual sayings, nor oracles, though it reports divine speech. Significantly, it does not anchor in any way or form that speech in any typical place, scene, or formal social interaction. The speech is unattached to particular social realia within the framework of the world portrayed in the book. Hos 11:1-11 is a READING within a set of READINGS that exists only as part and parcel of a prophetic book and which is presented to the readers as cotextualized and contextualized but not historicized, even within the world of the book. In other words, it is presented to the intended and primary readers of the book as a text that they should read in a way that is informed by other READINGS within the book, but not by particular historical events, circumstances, social interactions, or typical scenes of life or the like, either within the world portrayed in the book or outside a reconstructed historical world of the eighth century BCE.

Setting

The setting of the writing and primary reading of this, or any portion of the (present) book of Hosea for that matter, is the same as that of the book as a whole. Both writers and readers are among the very few literati of Yehud. This READING is indicative of many aspects of the intellectual and ideological atmosphere within which it was written and which permeates it.

Verses 1 and 2, for instance, carry some multiple-meaning expressions that shed light on the intellectual setting shared by the literati among whom one is to find both the final authorship of the book of Hosea, in its present form, and its target readership. Turning to v. 1, קראתי carries a double meaning. It means "I called/summoned" as the other verbal forms from the root קרא in vv. 2 and 7. As קראתי is so understood, the expression וממצרים קראתי לבני stands for something akin to "out of Egypt I called my son/child." (It bears notice that LXX of this verse reads "his [YHWH's] children," and that the interpretation of the passage in Mt 2:15 clearly reflects the MT rather than the LXX text.) Of course, a reference to "calling my son/child" from Egypt when he was a boy points at the Exodus, and befits both the general tone of the unit with its references to returning to and above all leaving Egypt (esp. see v. 11) and the importance of the Exodus motif in the book of Hosea in general (see discussion in 2:3-25; and, for instance, 12:14; 13:4). קראתי may also be understood as "I called/named/proclaimed." As קראתי is so understood, the expression וממצרים קראתי לבני stands for something akin to "from/since [the days of] Egypt I have adopted (/ called him) my son/child" (i.e., Israel — cf. Exod 4:22-23; Deut 1:31). See Tg; NJPSV; Yee, *Composition,* 217; Nissinen, *Prophetie,* 237-39; Melnyk, "When Israel Was a Child." This reading befits well the image of the parent/child relationship that is so salient in this READING. It is also consistent with the image of the relationship between YHWH and Israel in terms of a family setting, in which YHWH stands for the superordinate and Israel for the subordinate (e.g., parent/child, husband/wife); see Hos 2:17bβ, and cf. 12:10. This reading is strongly reminiscent of the relatively common ancient Near Eastern motif of the kings as the deity's son and chosen one (see 2 Sam 7:14; 1 Chr 17:13; 28:6; Ps 89:4, 26-28; cf. Ps 2:7; and see, among others, Parpola, *Assyrian Prophecies,* xxxvi-xliv, ic; Nissinen, *Prophetie,* 268-98 and bibliography cited there; Levinson, "Reconceptualization," 512-14). Of course, here "Israel" takes the role of the king. The ideological allocation of kingly features to Israel, and the related quasi-royal status assigned to Israel was a relatively common feature of the postmonarchic discourses of Israel (e.g., the deity makes a covenant with Israel rather than with the king). This tendency is sometimes construed as a "democratization" of the royal image, and it functions as such in the sense that it leads to a construction of the office of the king as one of very limited power — an unusual notion in the ancient Near East. The obvious example is the prescriptive "legislation" of Deuteronomy regarding the position, status, and responsibilities of the king (see G. N. Knoppers, "Rethinking," esp. 397-405, and Levinson, "Reconceptualization"). The same tendency can be construed as a "royalization" of Israel, and as such plays an important role as a tool of an underdog's ideological defiance. It is Israel who is the son of the deity, not some mighty foreign king whom Israel serves. (Notice also the parallel approach to remove elements from the earthly king and assign them to YHWH.)

There is also another element of this metaphor. It is obvious that the image of adopting a son, as opposed to birthing one, allows the deity involved in the transaction to remain male. Yet if the son is a baby, he is to be nursed. Thus, usually a goddess enters the picture, either as nurse or as mother, in which case, the image of "adoption" may shift to that of "birth," though nursing may also be associated with adoption. There are clear attestations of this imagery in the ancient Near East, and those in the neo-Assyrian prophetic corpus have been particularly highlighted recently (see Parpola, *Assyrian Prophecies*). Significantly, one finds in v. 4 the following expression, עוֹל עַל לְחֵיהֶם וְאֵהֶיה לָהֶם כִּמְרִימֵי וָאַט אֵלָיו אוֹכִיל. It denotes something akin to "I was for them as those who lift (i.e., remove) the yoke from upon their jaws, that I may offer him food" (cf. Macintosh, *Hosea*, 445-49; Barthélemy, *Critique Textuelle*, vol. III, 594-95; the exchange of plural "them" and singular "him" is only a matter of style). This image directly links to that of Israel as a (trained) heifer in Hos 10:11. Yet at the same time, the precise, and somewhat unusual, textual choices represented in the expression allow it to connote "I was to them like those who lift infants to their cheeks. I bent down to them and fed them" (NRSV, which presents this understanding of the verse as the denoted meaning and reflects an emended text that is favored by scholars as divergent as Schüngel-Straumann, "God as a Mother," 201-4; Mays, *Hosea*, 150, 154-55). This connotation is consonant not only with the image of the deity feeding the baby, but it is somewhat suggestive of the ancient Near Eastern image of the goddess nursing the king (cf. Parpola, *Assyrian Prophecies*, xxxvi-xxxviii and ic n. 165; cf. Isa 49:15; 66:10-13), though it leaves the matter well open, and allows the text to be understood also in terms of a weaned boy (cf. Simian Yofre, *Desierto*, 150). At the same time the text is written in such a way that it allows the motherly image that it partially evokes to receive sustenance from another connoted meaning in the unit. The expression בְּחַבְלֵי אָדָם in v. 4 most likely denotes, "with human ropes," meaning metaphorically "with bonds of friendship" (Macintosh, *Hosea*, 445-46 — following Ibn Janah) or in more concrete terms, "with a light rope," such as those used with children, as opposed to the heavy ropes used for animals, and signifying a paternal, "loving" guidance (cf. Tg, Radak) or most likely a combination of both. At the same time, the expression בְּחַבְלֵי אָדָם is evocative of the image of "birth pangs" cf. Hos 13:13 (cf. Sweeney, *Twelve Prophets*, 114). The result is, of course, a sophisticated network of denoted and evocative meanings with multiple layers of meanings informing each other: in other words, what one would expect from a written text produced to be read, reread, studied, and interpreted by bearers of high literacy. All these meanings are part of the general discourse/s that constitutes the intellectual setting of the book. A few more examples from this READING will suffice. (On images of YHWH's parental love in general, and the adoption metaphor in particular, see also Oestreich, *Metaphors,* 125-49; Nwaoru, *Imagery,* 147-50.)

The word נער "boy" in v. 1 also carries several connotations. It may point to a three-month-old baby (e.g., Exod 2:6). This image certainly fits the paternal metaphor in vv. 1-4. נער also may convey the meaning of servant or representative of a master (e.g., 2 Kgs 4:12, 25). From the perspective of the ancient rereadership, and from that of YHWH in the world of the text, נער on the one hand points at baby Israel at the time of the Exodus and at YHWH's adoption of him, but on the other, also reinforces the sense of failure of the baby (נער) by alluding to the failed expectation that he will grow up to be YHWH's נער (in the secondary sense). Yet, as the primary readership of the book is also Israel, such a reference reinforces their hope and certitude that a day will come in which they will really become YHWH's נער (in the secondary sense). (See vv. 10-11.)

קראו להם at the beginning of v. 2 also carries more than one possible meaning. It is usually translated as "they called them," and the entire expression קראו להם כן הלכו מפניהם is then to be understood as "the more they called, the more they moved away from them," or "as they called them, they moved away from them" (cf. with the structure of the expression in Ps 48:6). Third person and often plural, verbal forms with no antecedent in the text serve to introduce sentences with an indefinite subject. Comparable sentences in English require a formal subject such as an indeterminate "they," "one," "people," and the like. Yet, the literati who were involved in reading and rereading the verse would still wonder who may stand for these indeterminate "they" and "them." For instance, there is a long tradition of interpretation that identifies the "callers" as "the prophets" (see already the Tg and Jerome), and, accordingly, the text was understood in terms of "the more the prophets called them, the more they went away from them," or "as the prophets called them, they went away." This reading of the text is informed by (a) the construction of the prophets as those who called Israel to return, to follow YHWH (see, for instance, in relation to the northern kingdom 2 Kgs 17:13-14; on this aspect of the general construction of the role of prophets of old in Kings and postmonarchic discourse in general, see Ben Zvi, "'The Prophets' — Generic Prophets" and cf. Hos 12:11); and (b) the construction of Moses (and Aaron? Joshua?) as a prophet (see Hos 12:14), since it refers to the first period of Israel after the Exodus. In fact, readings informed by (a) and (b) would see the text as creating a trans-temporal link binding Moses and later prophets on the one hand, and boy Israel of the beginning of the relationship, with the sinful, monarchic Israel, on the other. The latter viewpoint is widely expressed in the book of Hosea (e.g. 9:10; 10:9), and the characterization of Moses as a prophet is part and parcel of the ideological repertoire of the literati of postmonarchic Israel (cf. Deut 18:15; 34:10) and directly expressed in the book of Hosea (Hos 12:14). Yet the obvious fact remains that the impersonal construction, something akin to "*others* called them," allows for complementary interpretations. (These are not alternative interpretations; the point is not "either — or" but "both . . . and." It is a matter of multiple meanings informing each other rather than purging each other.) For instance, a readership that approaches the text in a way strongly informed by Hos 7:11 and the centrality of the motif of Egypt in this reading would tend to understand the text as meaning "they [Israel] called them [Egypt]" (cf. Sweeney, *Twelve Prophets,* 113; Macintosh, *Hosea,* 439-41). Further, one may also notice that קרא ל can be used to convey a meaning of "invite" or even "incite" — see Num 25:2 that deals with the memory of Baal-Peor (cf. Hos 9:10) and with the very beginning of worship of Baal by Israel. This connoted meaning would fit well the context of Hos 11:2 (see Szabó, "Textual Problems," 518; Yee, *Composition,* 217-18). Of course, if the result of their invitation is that Israel worships the baals, and since מפניהם can also be understood as a causative "because of them" (rather than "away from them"; see, for instance, Gen 6:13), then the "others" may be imagined as worshipers of the baals (cf. Holt, *Prophesying,* 58-59) or the baalim themselves. This approach would set Israel's change of attitude after the exodus from Egypt but just before arriving into the land. On these issues see Hos 9:1-17 Setting.

All these complementary meanings of the expression קראו להם כן הלכו מפניהם create a well-interwoven thread. Israel accepted and benefited when YHWH called/led them out of Egypt. But Israel rejected its obligations to fulfill YHWH's call and to become YHWH's boy. Within the discourses of the period, this rejection could be imagined in many complementary ways, namely, as a rejection of the voice of faithful prophets (and by implication of the prophetic books), as trust in foreign powers (e.g., Egypt), as trust and worship of deities other than YHWH, and as a reliance on priests and worshipers of deities other than YHWH and the like. (Some scholars emend these texts and particularly vv. 2 and 4; on v. 4 see above; on v. 2 see, for instance, Buss, *Prophetic Word,* 22; Wolff, *Hosea,* 191-92; Mays, *Hosea,* 150; and cf. LXX.)

The text emphasizes that Israel should return to YHWH (see vv. 5, 7), and as such it is ideologically linked to, and prepares the intended and primary readership for, the calls in 12:7 and 14:2. Significantly, it shares the same viewpoint expressed elsewhere in the book that either Israel fails to return or its return is unsuccessful in the long run (cf. Hos 2:9; 6:1; 12:7). Thus, the text points at the ideological necessity of a divine action to cause Israel to return to its path (cf. 11:10-11 with 2:16-25 and 14:5-9). For an explanation of this viewpoint within the ideological setting of ancient Israel, see Ben Zvi, "Analogical Thinking." Concerning the imagery of Israel coming back from the West, as well as from Egypt and Assyria, verse 10 is crucial to the message of the READING. To be sure, deportation to or even a substantial displacement of Israelite population to countries west of Israel does not necessarily fit the history of the northern kingdom — nor for that matter in a substantive way that of the southern kingdom. Still, it is part and parcel of a general, postmonarchic image of the gathering of the exiles in an ideal future day associated with at the very least a permanent reconciliation between YHWH and Israel (cf. Isa 11:11 and its literary context). It is also possible that in some way references to the return of the exiles from the west may also reflect the actual presence of communities of Israel in these countries (see Isa 60:8-9; Joel 4:6-7; Obad 20).

Hosea 11:1-4 joins other texts in the book, such as Hos 9:10, 13 and 10:11-

13, and revisits the theme of YHWH's early choice of Israel and its eventual rebellion. Each of these texts advances partial metaphors or ways of addressing such a beginning, and all together convey a better representation of the general construction of that period in the imagination of the authorship and primary readership than any of them separately. The representation advanced in this unit within the book of Hosea sets the beginning in Egypt and develops multilayered parent-child imagery. At the same time, it contains allusions to the "heifer" metaphor of 10:11, involves agrarian images, and seems to point to the episode of Baal Peor that marks the beginning of the worship of Baal in Israel within the social memories of the period. On these matters, see above. It is worth stressing, again, that these "social memories" do not have to point to historical events at all, but to facts about the past agreed upon by a particular group.

The text conveys to the readership that the divine speech is to and about Israel as a whole (see vv. 1, 8). Ephraim is considered a particular manifestation of this (trans-temporal) Israel (see v. 8) who began its existence as YHWH's adopted son in Egypt, as per YHWH's initiative, and who will return to the land from the north, south, and west one day, according to YHWH's initiative. The readers and rereaders of the book are, of course, also a manifestation of this trans-temporal Israel. The reference to "their houses" (v. 11) links this transtemporal, ideological Israel with the land, as *their* houses are understood to be in the land, and significantly, remaining *their* houses beyond the limits of time and generations, until the time in which YHWH will roar as a lion and bring the people back to them.

Although it is to state the obvious, one may still mention that the text implies a readership that is aware of certain traditions and of a large body of social memories (see, for instance, the reference to Admah and Zeboiim in v. 8 and see STRUCTURE). This readership shares a social imagination, concepts, and even literary devices. There is no reason to assume that there ever was a particular Hoseanic group of literati who were responsible for the composition of the present book of Hosea and who were socially and discursively separate from other groups of literati in postmonarchic Yehud responsible for, and readers of other authoritative books that eventually were included in, the HB. Such a proposal is also extremely unlikely given that at any time in neo-Babylonian Judah and Persian Yehud there was only a very limited number of people with the literary, linguistic, and cultural-ideological proficiency required for the composition of written works such as the prophetic books. On these matters, see Ben Zvi, "Introduction: Writings, Speeches, and the Prophetic Books — Setting an Agenda"; "A Deuteronomistic Redaction in/among 'The Twelve'"; and bibliography mentioned there.

Many scholars focus on the historical Hosea, as opposed to the character in the book or the book itself, and identify most of the text with Hosea's reaction to, or his stance against, the background of concrete historical events, contemporary with Hosea's words, and within the last decades of the northern kingdom. These scholars would, by necessity, propose corresponding settings for either the entire unit (and remove, accordingly, sections of the text such as v. 10 that cause tensions with their proposed settings; see above) or individual sayings that they presume existed separately and independently from the book of Hosea.

For instance, Bjornard ("Hosea 11:8-9," 16-17) writes concerning vv. 8-9, "it seems logical that we are still before 722 BCE," for "the final disaster, promised continuously throughout Hosea 4–13, has not yet taken place . . . there is even a chance for its gracious prevention." Mays maintains that "the oracle [vv. 1-9+11] could well belong to the middle years of Hoshea's reign when Israel's king had provoked the retribution of Shalmanesser V (727-722) by withholding tribute and appealing to Egypt (II Kings 17:4) and the final end of the nation was all too obvious" (Mays, *Hosea,* 152; cf. Stuart, *Hosea* 177). Macintosh writes:

> The nation's refusal to turn in repentance to Yahweh is decisive and his patience is at an end. 2 Kings 17.4f . . . indicates that Shalmanesser V occupied the majority of the remaining territory of Ephraim, capturing Hoshea but leaving unconquered for the moment the capital Samaria. These observations accord well with the text of this verse [11:6] and suggest that Hosea is speaking of the beginnings (at least) of the terrible process. The verse may reflect a date c. 724 BC. (Macintosh, *Hosea,* 454)

Kaufmann (*Toldot,* 108-9), however, maintains that the date of the text must precede the capture of Hoshea and the beginning of the siege of Samaria. Therefore, he dates the text (and all of Hos 4–14) between 732 and 725 BCE. Clements ("Understanding") suggests, for different reasons, a date for 11:8-9 "shortly after 732 B.C." (422). Other dates have been proposed. For instance, Simian-Yofre assigns the activity of the historical Hosea to the reigns of Zechariah, Shallum, and Menahem, and he sees no reason to assign any (original) text to any time later than the reign of the latter (cf. Simian-Yofre, *Desierto,* 120, 218). As mentioned before, the redactional model advanced by Yee assigns the entirety of Hosea 11 to the postmonarchic period.

This being said, it is worth stressing that Hosea 11 does not require its readers to associate the divine speech with any narrowly defined historical circumstances — e.g., before or after the capture of king Hoshea — or with Shalmanesser's campaign, or with the reign of Menahem. The speech is purposefully devoid of any narrow temporal or historical markers. The divine speech is not presented as intertwined with a particular event in Israelite history. Rather it is presented as reflective and evocative of a larger, mythological construction of Israel's history, that is, one that began with YHWH's initiative that established the deity's relationship to Israel and vice versa (YHWH is the active agent), was followed by Israel's rejection of the obligations that this relationship involved (Israel is now construed as an active agent, but for evil), by YHWH's punishment of Israel for its actions, and then by YHWH's determination to reestablish the relationship on stronger grounds. The intended and primary readerships of Hosea 11, and of the book of Hosea in general, are not asked to historicize the text, to look at historical but "well-hidden" clues, but to set it in the frame of that which is presented as an essentially trans-temporal discourse. This built-in claim of trans-temporal relevance is important for the relevance of the text for communities such as those in which one is to find the authorship and target readership of the (present) book of Hosea. These communities lived centuries later and under very different circumstances than existed in the world in which the character Hosea is set. Of course, claims of trans-temporal relevance are always temporally and socially defined as they are powerful rhetorical tools. Claims of trans-temporal relevance are always advanced by some group at a particular time; in this case, by the small group of literati among whom one is to find the authorship of the present book and its primary target rereadership.

As other readings in the book, Hosea 11 also contributes its share to the characterization of the language of the speaker, here YHWH, as somewhat odd in relation to YHWH's language in other prophetic texts set in the monarchic period (cf. the books of Amos, Micah, and Isaiah and see their superscriptions). One may notice, for instance, (a) the hapax legomenon תרגלתי in v. 3 that is a very unusual tiph'el verbal form (cf. Jer 12:5; 22:25; and see also Ezra 4:7; see Joüon-Muraoka, 59e; cf. GKC 55h), and which is often translated as "I taught to walk," but this meaning is debatable (on the latter, see Yoo, *Israelian Hebrew*, 134-36), and (b) the use of a verbal form of the root מגן "deliver" in v. 8 that appears elsewhere only in the speech of Melchizedek, king of Salem, in Gen 14:20, and in Prov 4:9 (on this form, see Macintosh, *Hosea*, 459, 463).

Intention

The general intention of Hosea 11:1-11 is to communicate and reinforce the positions and the general horizon of thought of the authorship and readership as represented in these texts (see Setting) and to socialize the literati through their shared reading of the material and the larger society through the literati's reading to others of these readings.

Among other things, this READING conveys a strong message of hope in the form of a divine self-disclosure in which YHWH characterizes YHWH not only as a deity unable to completely destroy Israel, no matter the gravity of its deeds, but also as one who will bring Israel back to YHWH and to the land at some point in the future. It communicates and reinforces within the target readership/s images of YHWH as a deity/parent emotionally involved with child Israel and, therefore, as (lovingly and parentally) protective of Israel in a very fundamental sense (cf. Sweeney, *Twelve Prophets*, 115-15; Heschel, *Prophets*, vol. 1, 48-49). The reading stresses that YHWH, because of an essential feature of being the deity, as opposed to any human being, is able not only to control the (justified) divine anger (cf. Radak), but also to turn back from announcements and decisions of punishments: YHWH's heart is one that turns around because of compassion. As such this READING provides an image of YHWH that is similar to one of the images advanced in the book of Jonah (see Ben Zvi, *Signs of Jonah*, passim).

Bibliography

R. B. Bjornard, "Hosea 11:8-9: God's Word or Man's Insight?" *BR* 27 (1982) 16-25; R. E. Clements, "Understanding the Book of Hosea," *RevExp* 72 (1975) 405-23; L. de

Regt, "Person Shift in Prophetic Texts. Its Function and Its Rendering in Ancient and Modern Translations," J. C. de Moor (ed.), *The Elusive Prophet. The Prophet as a Historical Person, Literary Character and Anonymous Artist* (OtSt 45; Leiden: E. J. Brill, 2001) 214-31; C. J. Dempsey, *The Prophets. A Liberation-Critical Reading* (Minneapolis: Fortress, 2000) 157-58; G. S. Glanzman, "Two Notes: Amos 3,15 and Osee 11,8-9," *CBQ* 23 (1967) 227-33; M. D. Goldman, "The Real Interpretation of Os 11,3," *AusBR* 4 (1954-55) 91-92; E. N. Good, "The Composition of Hosea," *SEÅ* 31 (1966) 21-63; A. J. Heschel, *The Prophets* (New York: Harper and Row, 1969); Y. Hoffman, "A North Israelite Typological Myth and a Judaean Historical Tradition: The Exodus in Hosea and Amos," *VT* 39 (1989) 169-82; J. G. Janzen, "Metaphor and Reality in Hosea 11," *Semeia* 24 (1982) 7-44; G. N. Knoppers, "Rethinking the Relationship between Deuteronomy and the Deuteronomistic History: The Case of Kings," *CBQ* 63 (2001) 393-415; C. J. Labuschagne, "The Similes in the Book of Hosea," *OTWSA* 7-8 (1965) 64-76; B. M. Levinson, "The Reconceptualization of Kingship in Deuteronomy and the Deuteronomistic History's Transformation of Torah," *VT* 51 (2001) 511-34; N. Lohfink, "Hos xi 5 als Bezugtext von Dtn. xvii 6," *VT* 31 (1981) 226-28; A. A. Macintosh, "Hosea. The Rabbinic Commentators and the Ancient Versions," A. Rapoport-Albert and G. Greenberg (eds.), *Biblical Hebrew, Biblical Texts. Essays in Memory of Michael P. Weitzman* (JSOTSupS 333; Sheffield: Sheffield Academic Press, 2001) 77-82; J. L. Mays, "Response to Janzen 'Metaphor and Reality in Hosea 11,'" *Semeia* 24 (1982) 45-51; J. L. McKenzie, "Divine Passion in Osee," *CBQ* 17 (1955) 287-89; J. L. E. Melnyk, "When Israel Was a Child: Ancient Near Eastern Adoption Formulas and the Relationship between God and Israel," M. P. Graham, J. Kuan, and W. P. Brown (eds.), *History and Interpretation: Essays in Honor of John H. Hayes* (JSOTSupS 173; Sheffield: JSOT Press, 1993) 245-59; M. Nissinen, *References to Prophecy in Neo-Assyrian Sources* (SAAS 7; Helsinki: The Neo-Assyrian Text Corpus Project, 1998); D. F. O'Kennedy, "Healing as/or Forgiveness? The Use of the Term רפא in the Book of Hosea," *OTE* 14 (2001) 458-74; S. Parpola, *Assyrian Prophecies* (SAA 9; Helsinki: Helsinki Univ. Press, 1997); S. Pisano, "'Egypt' in the Septuagint Text of Hosea," G. J. Norton, S. Pisano, and C. M. Martini (eds.), *Tradition of the Text: Studies Offered to Dominique Barthélemy in Celebration of His 70th Birthday* (OBO 109; Fribourg: Éditions universitaires, 1991) 301-8; Ch. Rabin, "Hebrew *BADDIM* 'Power'," *JSS* 18 (1973) 57-58; E. J. Revell, *The Designation of the Individual. Expressive Usages in Biblical Narrative* (CBET 14; Kampen: Kok Pharos, 1996); D. Ritschl, "God's Conversion. An Exposition of Hosea 11," *Int* 15 (1961) 286-303; E. Schüngel-Straumann, "God as Mother in Hosea 11," A. Brenner (ed.), *A Feminist Companion of the Latter Prophets* (Sheffield: Sheffield Academic Press, 1995) 194-218; J. P. Siebert-Hommes, "'With Bands of Love': Hosea 11 as 'Recapitulation of the Basic Themes of the Book of Hosea,'" J. W. Dyk et al. (eds.), *Unless Some One Guide Me. Festschrift for Karel A. Deurloo* (ACEBT Sup 2; Maastricht: Shaker, 2001) 167-73; J. A. Soggin, "Hosea 11,5 (cf. 10,9b?): Emphatic Lamed?" in J. A. Soggin, *Old Testament and Oriental Studies* (BibOr 29; Rome: Pontifical Biblical Institute, 1975) 223; A. Szabó, "Textual Problems in Amos and Hosea," *VT* 25 (1975) 500-524; M. T. Wacker, "Traces of the Goddess in the Book of Hosea," A. Brenner (ed.), *A Feminist Companion of the Latter Prophets* (Sheffield: Sheffield Academic Press, 1995) 219-41.

Third Set of Readings:
Hope for the Future and Explanation of Past Judgment
by References to Israel's Past, 12:1–14:9

Structure

I. Introduction	12:1-3
II. First Reading	12:1-15
III. Second Reading	13:1–14:1
IV. Third Reading and Conclusion of the SET	14:2-9

This set of readings is marked off by the break between 11:11 and 12:1, which is discussed in Hosea 4:1–11:11, STRUCTURE, and the one between 14:9 and 14:10. The latter is generally agreed upon, given the distinct character of 14:10 and its role as a conclusion reflective of the book as such.

The mainly tripartite division of the body of the book of Hosea, namely, chs. 1–3 (except 1:1); 4–11; and 12–14 (except 14:10), is *one* of the structures that the book suggests, and so is the internal division of 12:1–14:9 advanced here. On the tripartite division see Hos 4:1–11:11 STRUCTURE.

This SET OF READINGS consists of three READINGS and a short section that serves both as an introduction to the entire SET and as an introduction to the first READING, as is the case with the introduction to the first SET OF READINGS. It bears particular note that both introductions contain the only two cases of the expression עם לה׳ ריב "YHWH has a contention/dispute/grievance with/against" in the book of Hosea.

As mentioned earlier, Hos 12:1–14:9 explores further some of the main themes advanced in 4:1–11:11. The SET as a whole shapes a construction of Israel's (hi)story from the early past, through the period of sin and punishment, to its future ideal situation (cf. Hos 11:1-11 STRUCTURE). This trajectory of Israel through time revisits many of the issues addressed in Hos 4:1–11:11 and in particular chapters 8–11.

The first two READINGS deal mainly with the construction of Israel's past. They lead to the high note of the third READING, which serves a double role: (a) as the conclusion of the SET; and (b) as a conclusion typical of prophetic books (e.g., Joel 4:18-21; Amos 9:13-15; Obad 17-21; Mic 7:18-20).

Genre

Each of the texts included in this unit is a PROPHETIC READING. The genre of the unit as a whole is SET OF READINGS. It is to be stressed that these READINGS do not exist independently of each other, that is, by themselves, but as part and parcel of the book of Hosea. As such the meaning conveyed by each one of them to their intended and primary rereaderships is informed by the others. Moreover, at times even word choice and the basic metaphors in one READING are heavily influenced by those appearing elsewhere in the book.

Setting

The setting of the production and the primary reading and rereading of these literary units is the same as that of the book as a whole. It involves a group of (postmonarchic) literati who were aware of ideological constructions of Israel's past, and shared a strong hope for its future. As the different READINGS that constitute this SET OF READINGS are examined in the following chapters of this commentary, central elements of the intellectual world of these literati will be explored.

For a different position concerning the dating of Hosea 12–14 (and its proposed implications for Hosea 4–11 as well) see, for instance:

> As regards the date of composition for the two collections, Hos. 12–14 preserves Hosea's oracles spoken during the course of events initiated by Hoshea ben Elah's overture to Egypt in a hopeless attempt to rid himself of his Assyrian overlord (2 Kgs 17:4). Hosea refers to this event in 12:2(1)b and thereby establishes the setting of the collection as a whole. In the final complex the deportations have apparently begun (14:3[2]) and Samaria, if it has not already fallen, is certainly about to (14:2[1]). The collection may then have been composed shortly after the fall of Samaria in 722, perhaps even during the siege. With respect to Hos. 4–11, the simple fact that they form a collection independent of Hos. 12–14 suggests that the collection was already completed prior to the proclamation of the oracles contained in the latter collection. Otherwise one would expect a single collection encompassing Hosea's entire prophetic activity in the post–Jeroboam II years. A date prior to the overture to Egypt is thus indicated. Hosea's literary efforts at this time may be explained by the assumption of a dormancy in his prophetic appearances (cf. Isa. 8.16-22). Feeling that a period of his prophetic ministry was at a close, he was led to commit to writing the contents of his proclamation. Alternatively, the desire to preserve his words through the impending disaster may have provided the impetus for Hosea's literary activity. In either case a date sometime during the reign of Hoshea ben Elah (731-23) is indicated, in the first case rather the first half, in the latter case rather the second half. . . . The various sources for the book made their way to Judah. . . . Here they were arranged in the current order and provided with a superscript (1:1) sometime around 710, give or take a decade. . . . (Daniels, *Hosea*, 29)

This approach focuses not on the book of Hosea, but on a historical Hosea whose partial biography is reconstructed on the basis of a particular reading of the "various sources for the book," which in turn are possible because of such a characterization of the historical Hosea. For instance, this approach assigns literary activities to the historical prophet and even attempts to read his mind. But it is said nowhere in the book of Hosea that he wrote the book, sections of it, or was involved in written literary activity. Further, it directly and crucially for the dating purposes also unequivocally and exclusively associates the literary (and ideological) motif of sealing a covenant with Assyria but transporting oil to Egypt in Hos 12:2 (see commentary there) with a very specific, one-time political decision. But should one assume that no writer could have written about "sealing a covenant with Assyria but transporting oil to Egypt," and particularly so within the literary context of Hosea 12, except at the very time that Hoshea ben Elah sent messengers to "King So" of Egypt, according to 2 Kgs 17:4? (On the reference to "King So" see Day, "Problem of 'So, King of Egypt'," and bibliography cited there; cf. Na'aman, "Historical Background," 216-17; Becking, *Fall of Samaria,* 50-51, and Goedicke, "End of 'So King of Egypt.'") To be sure, if one assumes that the text must come from a historical prophet/writer who lived during the reign of Hoshea ben Elah and whose proclamation served to a large extent as a commentary on contemporary political events, the answer is likely to be "yes." But these assumptions govern the result of the quest (cf. Ben Zvi, "Studying Prophetic Texts"). Moreover, and to be stressed, this scholarly reconstructed historical prophet/writer Hosea is certainly different from the character Hosea that populates the (present) book of Hosea and through whom the rereaders of the book were supposed to learn about YHWH's word. Significantly, and contrary to the image of the reconstructed historical prophet/writer, the book does not include even one clear reference to a historical event, or to contemporary historical figures. In fact, as this commentary demonstrates, the tendency in the book is *not* to anchor the speeches uttered in the world of the book to any particular, narrow set of circumstances (ct. the book of Jeremiah). Further discussion on these matters is present in the following chapters.

Intention

The main intention of the text is to communicate hope to the readers (that is, Israel). As did the previous SET, this SET reaffirms their hope that it is YHWH's will that they (Israel) will achieve that ideal future at some point. This SET strengthens this hope without advancing any concrete, worldly (or otherworldly) scenario for the process that would narrow the expectations of the intended and primary readers, or allow these expectations to be too closely identified with any historical event. The consistent and highly negative characterization of past Israel serves, in part, as a rhetorical device that conveys the message that YHWH will not abandon Israel, even if confronted with the continuous and extreme wickedness of Israel that characterized Israel's past. Nor will YHWH ever completely destroy Israel. Therefore, the link between YHWH and Israel is construed as one that will withstand any possible action of Israel. Of course, none of this even hinted at the possibility that Israel can avoid YHWH's (just) punishment or can abdicate its obligation to turn to YHWH, even if the ideal and stable future can only be brought by YHWH's actions.

Bibliography

B. Becking, *The Fall of Samaria. An Historical & Archaeological Study* (SHANE 2; Leiden: E. J. Brill, 1992); J. Day, "The Problem of 'So, King of Egypt' in 2 Kings

XVII:4," *VT* 42 (1992) 289-301; H. Goedicke, "The End of "So, King of Egypt," *BASOR* 171 (1963) 64-66; N. Na'aman, "The Historical Background of the Fall of Samaria (720 BC)," *Bib* 71 (1990) 206-25.

First Didactic Prophetic Reading — A Look at Israel's (Hi)Story from a Godly Perspective, Hos 12:1-15

Structure

This READING provides its intended and primary readership with a summary overview of a (hi)story of Israel. This summary overview not only claims to be reflective of the viewpoint of the deity, but is also presented, for the most part, as YHWH's own speech. Thus, this summary is characterized by the book as reliable and authoritative. The summary itself provides a negative evaluation of Israel and leads to the conclusion that YHWH will "repay" Ephraim for his (Ephraim's) mockery of his lord, namely, YHWH — in other words, for the dishonor that Ephraim caused YHWH (see Macintosh, *Hosea*, 513-14; cf. Hos 1:2–2:3 Setting).

This is one of several possible structures of Hosea 12. The extent of this unit is indicated, as usual, by several markers of inner coherence (see below), and by its outer limits. Turning to the latter, there is clear thematic break between 11:11 and 12:1, and some textually inscribed markers point in the same direction (see Hos 11:1-11 STRUCTURE). The break between 12:15 and 13:1 is, however, debatable. The text certainly allows itself to be read with Hos 13:1 as a direct continuation of Hos 12:15. (This position is advocated by, for instance,

Lust, "Freud, Hosea"; and Stuart, *Hosea,* 187; Yee considers Hos 13:1-3 as the postmonarchic redactor's comment on Hos 12:15; see Yee, *Composition,* 249-50.) In fact, although the envelope created by ישיב לו "he will repay him" in vv. 3 and 15 (see below) suggests a demarcation of a unit (12:3-15), a similarly textually inscribed marker leaves matters more open. The envelope shaped by references to Ephraim may be understood as involving vv. 1 and 15 or vv. 1 and 13:1, or probably both in slightly different, but complementary readings of the text.

If 13:1 is considered the end of the READING, then the latter will show a double conclusion (cf., among others, Hos 8:13bβ and 8:14) in which a crescendo movement can be discerned, as the text moves from an announcement about Ephraim's being repaid for its mockery (of its master/patron, namely, YHWH; see v. 12:15) to the statement that Ephraim "died" (13:1). When the text is so read it conveys a clear association between Ephraim's mockery (of YHWH) and its worship of Baal. In other words, the text focuses the attention of the readers on the worship of Baal as a central example of Ephraim's (Israel's) mockery of its master, YHWH. Ephraim insults YHWH by accepting and worshiping another master (cf. Hos 1:2–2:3 and 2:3-25, and see Setting there).

These meanings complement those created by reading Hos 12:15 as the heightened (and only) conclusion of this READING, as suggested by the envelope between vv. 3 and 15. In this case three motifs are particularly worthy of notice: (a) the strong evaluative association between the deeds of Jacob (Israel/Judah/Ephraim) and its mockery and dishonor thrown at its master/patron, YHWH; (b) Ephraim הכעיס "it has provoked"; and (c) the connotations carried by the motif of חרפתו ישיב לו "he (his master/YHWH) will repay him his mockery." The general motif of divine "repayment" associates מעלליו "his deeds" with חרפתו "his mockery" and encapsulates in a general way the message of the entire READING. Significantly, when the text is read in this way, "his deeds" include but do not focus particularly or exclusively on the cult of Baal. The entire (hi)story of Jacob (/Ephraim/Judah/Israel) is its mockery. The motif of provoking (כעס in the hiphil) is a relatively common motif in Deuteronomy (e.g., Deut 4:25), and certainly so in the book of Kings (e.g., 1 Kgs 14:9; it appears more than fifteen times in this book), but it also appears in (hi)storical surveys outside the historical books (see Ps 78:58; 106:29) and in other prophetic books (e.g., Isa 65:3; Jer 11:17; Ezek 16:26). The motif is associated with past actions of Israel that lead to divine punishment (see also Setting). It is worth noting, however, that the precise language used here, כעס in the hiphil without an (explicitly mentioned) object, is very rare: it appears only in 1 Kgs 21:22 and 2 Kgs 21:6, in addition to Hos 12:15. Significantly, the first appears in the context of an announcement of annihilation to the House of Ahab (the paradigmatic sinful House of northern Israel); whereas the second is associated with Manasseh's sins that are reportedly the cause for YHWH's destruction of Jerusalem. Here, the use of כעס in the hiphil and particularly so without an (explicit) object carries the connotation of a terrifying destruction to come upon the one guilty of "provoking." The motif of returning (שוב in the hiphil) חרפה "taunt" upon the one who taunted appears three times more in the HB (Ps

245

79:12; Neh 3:36; Dan 11:18). Its use in Ps 79:12 is relevant here because both cases involve taunting YHWH and suggest a governing assumption that for YHWH's honor to be widely perceived, the taunter is to be punished severely by YHWH (cf. Ps 79:10). In sum, the present READING is better understood as concluding with both 12:15 and 13:1. A reading of the text as one that concludes with Hos 13:1 informs and interacts with one of the text as concluding with Hos 12:15 and vice versa. (Of course, reading Hos 13:1 as attached to 12:1-15 does not preempt it from being read as attached to 13:2–14:1 as well; see 13:1–14:1 STRUCTURE.)

Other proposals for STRUCTURE involving a different understanding of the textual hierarchy of breaks can be advanced. For instance, it is possible and consistent with textually inscribed markers to approach Hos 12:1–14:1 as one READING, within which Hos 12:1-15/13:1 serves as the first main section. If this is the case, then the SET OF READINGS Hos 12:1–14:9 consists of (a) a lengthy READING (Hos 12:1–14:1) that contains three main sections (12:1-15/13:1; 13:1-11; 13:12–14:1) and (b) a concluding READING of hope (Hos 14:2-9). If, or better, when the intended and primary readerships approached the text in this manner, Hos 12:1–14:9 communicated to them YHWH's understanding of the sinful behavior of Israel (/Ephraim) in the past and YHWH's anger about the situation (as well as YHWH's blamelessness), explained to them the consequences of Israel's (/Ephraim's) behavior, but also led them towards the briefer but strongly highlighted CONCLUSION of the SET OF READINGS. It is worth noting that Qyl (*Hosea*, אצ) proposes that the main unit consists of Hos 12:1-13:11; in other words, he brings together the first two sections referred to above, instead of the last two, as is more common. Again, all these proposals advance complementary readings. Each of these readings construes a slightly different understanding of the text, and all of them inform one another and share together in the creation of the tapestry of meanings conveyed by these texts, as these literary units within the Book of Hosea are read and reread again and again, under different circumstances.

In addition, some scholars consider Hos 12:1-2 to be the introduction to Hosea 12–14 rather than an introduction to Hos 12:3-15. It is more likely, however, that it serves both purposes — namely, as an introduction to the entire SET OF READINGS and as an introduction to this READING (cf. the structural role of Hos 4:1-3; see Hos 4:1-19 STRUCTURE).

Different proposals for the internal structure of Hosea 12 have been advanced. For instance, Mays (*Hosea*, 159-71) and the NJPSV propose the following structure: vv. 1-2, 3-7, 8-12, 13-15; whereas Stuart (*Hosea*, 185-86, 188) divides the text into vv. 1-2, 3, 4-7 (further divided into 4-6 and 7), 8-9, 10-11, 12, 13-14, 15 + 13:1; and Qyl (*Hosea*, אצ) divides 12:1-15 into 1-3, 4-7, 8-12, 13-15. The division into vv. 1-2, 3-7, 8-9, 10-12, 13-15 has also been suggested (cf. Wendland, *Discourse Analysis*, 129-30). Sweeney (*Twelve Prophets*, 117-30) divides the verses included in Hosea 12 into (i) 12:1a ("YHWH's Premise: Israel Is Not to Be Trusted"); (ii) 12:1b ("Hosea's Assertion of Israel's Fidelity"); (iii) 12:2 ("YHWH's Premise: Israel Has Made Treaties with Assyria and Egypt"); (iv) 12:3-9 ("Hosea's Use of the Jacob Tradition to Appeal for Israel's Return to YHWH"); (v) 12:10-12 ("YHWH's Reminder to Israel of Divine Fidelity"); and (vi) Hos 12:13–13:3 ("Hosea's Explanation of YHWH's Reminder of Divine Fidelity and Reiteration of Israel's Continued Rejection"). Sweeney's proposal provides an excellent illustration of the already noted interdependence between proposed structures and corresponding understandings of certain themes as central to the message of the text, along with, in the case of Sweeney, a proposed sharp distinction concerning the identity of the speaker (see Sweeney, *Twelve Prophets,* 117-30). A far more drastic approach to the structure of this text than all those mentioned above is taken by those who substantially rearrange it, so as to create what they consider to be the original text. See, for instance, Ginsberg, "Hosea"; Rudolph, *Hosea,* 220-25; and the short survey of rearrangement proposals in Macintosh, *Hosea,* 517.

Turning to the structure advanced in this commentary, which is one of several possible structures, the first main section (12:1-3) introduces this reading and the entire SET OF READINGS (12:1–14:10). This introduction consists of two sections. In the first (vv. 1-2), one may easily recognize the semantic realm evoked by references to מרמה "deceit, treason," כחש "lie," and כזב "lie," the presence of parallel structures that reinforce the conveyed message (e.g., רעה רוח ורודף קדים "he shepherds the wind; he pursues the east wind") and common word pairs (e.g., Assyria — Egypt; notice also דרך — מעלל "way — deed," which appears several times in the book of Jeremiah [e.g., Jer 4:18; 7:3, 5; 17:10; 18:11; 23:22; 25:5; 26:13]; in Ezek 36:31; Zech 1:4, 6; Judg 2:19; and esp. Hos 4:9; and even the — here, splitted — pair מרמה — כזב (vv. 1-2) appears elsewhere in Ps 5:7 and Prov 14:25), and the string composed of "Ephraim — House of Israel — Judah" (cf. Hos 5:5; 6:10-11). The fact that the string is headed by Ephraim here marks the focus of the text (see Hos 12:1, 2, 15), but see below. The main string in the second section (v. 3) is Judah — Jacob. The latter takes the place of Israel (and Ephraim, to some extent) in the former string and is allocated the second slot in the string so as to link directly to v. 4. All these features contribute to the inner textual coherence of the unit. As an introduction, the unit introduces the main themes of the larger unit. It characterizes Ephraim/Israel/Jacob/Judah both as a knave and as a fool (cf. Ginsberg, "Hosea's Ephraim"; Seow, "Hosea 14:10"). In addition, it prepares the target readership for YHWH's judgment. Most significantly, it clearly blurs the conceptual boundaries that the readership could have brought in relation to Ephraim, Israel, Jacob, and Judah. It cannot be overstressed that וריב לה' עם יהודה "YHWH has a grievance against Judah" in v. 3a serves as an interpretative key for the following text as much as ולפקד על יעקב כדרכיו "so [YHWH] will punish Jacob according to his ways." The result is a discursive, necessary, and crucial merging of conceptual horizons. Although the existence of a world of the book (and of social memory) in which there was a northern kingdom, namely, "Ephraim" is clearly expressed, the text strongly subsumes Ephraim under the images of Jacob and Israel, and their associated narratives (e.g., Exodus and significant vignettes of Jacob's life). A similar process is at work concerning the notion of "Judah," which on the one hand points to the southern kingdom, but on the other is also conceptually subsumed under Jacob/Israel. In fact, the point that Judah is conceptually subsumed under Jacob/Israel is strongly advanced in v. 3, and is central to postmonarchic discourses. For in-

stance, there is no reference to the Exodus that would exclude Judah, or to a list
of sons of Jacob in which Judah does not figure. The discursive and ideological
result is, among other things, that a contention against Judah becomes one
against Israel/Jacob, and, conversely, divine complaints against Ephraim become relevant to Israel/Jacob, and therefore to Judah. This discursive and ideological merging of conceptual horizons and images is to be expected in
postmonarchic discourses, for within them the (hi)story of the northern kingdom is not important by itself or if taken as separate from that of trans-temporal
Israel. On the contrary, it becomes significant to the target readership of the
book because it is construed as part and parcel of Israel's (hi)story, and as an
expression of the relationship between YHWH and Israel in the past. This Israel, of course, includes Judah and above all those who considered themselves
as direct descendants of the southern kingdom, namely, the community of
Yehud (cf. Ben Zvi, "Inclusion"), among whom one finds the authorship of the
present book of Hosea and its primary readership. References to Judah are certainly not an afterthought, but a central interpretative key that substantially contributes to the shaping of the significance of the text to its target readership and
is well attuned to the needs of the target readership.

(To be sure, scholars who wish to focus on the [reconstructed] words of
an eighth-century BCE northern Israelite prophet rather than on the present book
of Hosea would tend to emend the text and remove the references to Judah, at
the very least in v. 3; see, for instance, Macintosh, *Hosea,* 473-80; Simian-
Yofre, *Desierto,* 153-54; 260-61.)

Consistent with their role as an introduction to the following text, vv. 1-3
contain a number of terms that directly or indirectly link this subunit to other
verses in the READING. For instance, one may notice the reference to מרמה
"deceit, treason, treachery" in vv. 1 and 8. Moreover, from the perspective of
the rereaders of the text it may be seen as a signpost hinting at the stories about
Jacob to be mentioned later in the READING (cf. Gen 27:35). Similarly, the
same term clearly carries a sense of "treason against one's master" (see 2 Kgs
9:23). This connotation is relevant to v. 2, but serves also to hint at a pattern of
treasonous behavior on the part of Israel against its master/s (cf. v. 15 and
13:1).

As mentioned before, Hos 12:1-3 opens a SET OF READINGS (Hos 12:1–
14:9) that explores further some of the main themes advanced in the previous
SET (Hos 4:1–11:11). It is worth noting that there are some choices of terms in
Hos 12:1-3 likely to evoke in the target rereadership meaningful associations
with other texts in the book. For instance, a readership for whom the image in
12:1 evokes that in 7:2 and vice versa would tend to closely associate the people with their deeds. Similarly, if the reference to the East wind in 12:2 is read
in a way informed by that in 13:15 and vice versa, the result is that the foolishness of Ephraim in 12:2 is exacerbated, and the action of the East wind in 13:15
would be interpreted as one involving some role reversal (cf. 12:2 and 7:13).
The expression ריב לה' עם appears in 4:1 and 12:3. The presence of שד "destruction" or "violence" and כזב "falsehood" in 7:13a and 13b, respectively, at
the beginning of the "Woe to" section was likely to evoke that of כזב ושד
"falsehood and violence" in 12:2. The latter verse, in turn, is also thematically

related to 7:11 — see the central references to foolish alliances with Assyria or Egypt. As mentioned in Hos 7:3-16 STRUCTURE, the pair שׁד and כזב is very uncommon; in fact, it appears only in these two texts within the HB (i.e., Hos 7:13 and 12:2). (On the foolishness of Ephraim and on the reference to Judah in 12:1b see Setting.)

The following main unit construes a (hi)story of Israel from a (reportedly) divine perspective. It begins with a statement of contention (v. 3); cf. Hos 4:1. (There are other elements in Hos 12:1-3 that are reminiscent of Hos 4:4-9; cf. Hos 12:3b with 4:9; see Hos 4:1-19 STRUCTURE.) The reference to יעקב Jacob in v. 3 closely links it to vv. 4-5, which deal with Jacob and his deeds. The pun between יעקב Jacob in v. 3 and עקב "he [Jacob] took the heel/ supplanted/cheated" in v. 4 is obvious. The focus on Jacob's deeds binds together vv. 4-5. The relationship between vv. 6-7 and 4-5 depends to a large extent on the ways in which the intended and primary readerships of the book construed the meaning of v. 5. They could have construed vv. 5-7 as meaning something akin to:

(a) El* — a messenger [of God] — gained ascendancy [and at a connoted, complementary level, "strove"; cf. Hos 12:4] and prevailed [over Jacob]. He [Jacob] cried and he wept and sought his [the messenger's/God's] favor. In Bethel [i.e., the House of El] he [Jacob] found him [the messenger/God], and there he [God/the messenger] spoke with us [Jacob, and by extension, with trans-temporal Israel, including the addressees in the world of the book, and the target readership of the book]: "Truly, YHWH, the Lord of Hosts, YHWH is his remembrance [i.e., the name by which the God is to be remembered; in other words, his name]. As for you (sg.) [Jacob], with the help of your God you shall return [to the land; cf. Gen 28:15, 21].** Keep *hesed*/loyalty and justice and hope/wait expectantly for your God continually [in other words, put your trust in your God at all times, even when this means 'waiting' for God's actions of deliverance]." (Cf. Macintosh, *Hosea*, 483-93; Simian-Yofre, *Desierto,* 153-57; Barthélemy, *Critique Textuelle,* vol. III, 602-4, among others.)

   * The choice of the term El in v. 5 serves multiple purposes. El may be understood as pointing to a god/divine being, immediately identified as "a messenger" [of God], and at least as a connoted meaning it might have carried a meaning of El=God, which would closely associate the image of the messenger and of the sender (cf. the relationship between references to the three men — messengers — and to YHWH in Gen 18:1-16; see in particular, Gen 18:1, 2, 13, 16, and those between a "man" and "Elohim/El" in Gen 32:25 and Gen 32:29, 31). In addition, it creates a substantial pun on the word Israel (see below) in v. 5a and is directly related to the mention of Beth-El (i.e., The House of El) in 5b.

   ** Complementary understanding of the sentence, "As for you (sg.) [Jacob], with the help of your God you shall return to God [i.e., repent]." (This implies a double-duty role for באלהיך תשוב in v. 7; a single-duty role would have resulted in a simple, "As for you (sg.) [Jacob], you shall return to your God [i.e., repent]." In addition, read in this way, באלהיך תשוב creates a significant pun with אושיבך באהלים "I (YHWH) will make you dwell in tents" in v. 10b that connotes a clear message that can be summarized as: since you (i.e., Jacob/Ephraim/Israel) had not returned to your God (אלהיך), YHWH will return you to dwell in tents (אהלים), so you will return to YHWH (the latter is implied in v. 10b, see below).

The mentioned readerships could have also construed v. 5 as meaning:

(b) He [Jacob] strove against El [= God/a divine being] — a messenger [of God] — and he [Jacob] prevailed. He [the text is probably purposefully ambiguous; it points at both the messenger — cf. Gen 32:27 — and Jacob, in different rereadings of the text] wept and sought his [the messenger's or Jacob's depending on the rereading] favor. In Bethel [i.e., House of El] he [ambiguous identity] found him and there he [ambiguous identity] spoke with us [ambiguous identity: either Jacob and by implication trans-temporal Israel, or the messenger of God, God, and the divine realm; cf. Gen 1:26; Isa 6:8].*
   * Morag ("Semantic and Linguistic Features," 491) and others maintain that עמנו in v. 5 should be understood as meaning "with him," in which case, ". . . there he [ambiguous identity] spoke with him [ambiguous identity: either Jacob or the messenger of God]." (Many other scholars emend the text to read עמו with him; e.g., Wolff, *Hosea,* 207; Daniels, *Hosea,* 33, 36-37.)

Or, though less likely, the intended and primary readerships could have also construed v. 5 as meaning:

(c) He [Jacob] strove against El [a divine being] — a messenger [of God] — and he [Jacob] prevailed. He [the text is probably purposefully ambiguous; it points at both the messenger — cf. Gen 32:27 — and Jacob, in different rereadings of the text] wept and sought his [the messenger's or Jacob's depending on the rereading] favor. Bethel [understood as the god/numen of Beth-el] found him and there he [Bethel] spoke with us [Jacob and by implication trans-temporal Israel] (cf. Ginsberg, "Hosea's Ephraim"; Ward, *Hosea,* 207, 210).

If the readers follow (a), then vv. 6-7 are integral to a unit consisting of vv. 4-7. Within this approach, vv. 6-7 convey the divine words and, within the context of the READING and the book of Hosea in general, a strong rebuke to Israel. For the rereaders know too well that Israel will not remain loyal to YHWH, will not keep justice, nor will they "wait" for and trust YHWH. Within this discursive context, the textual reference וישר אל "El prevailed" carries a pun on ישראל Israel and on the meaning given to the name as reflected in the story in Gen 32:29. This pun, however, highlights the theological point: Israel certainly does not prevail over God/YHWH; such a "foolish" idea

250

in fact reflects and expresses that which is wrong with Israel in its relationship with YHWH. Of course, vv. 6-7 represent not only a rebuke of Israel (since its inception in the days of Jacob), but since the words are given to trans-temporal Israel, they also communicate that which is expected of that Israel, including the readership of the book (cf. Hos 10:12, and also with Mic 6:8; Zech 7:9; notice that YHWH will wed Israel in justice and *hesed*/loyalty in 2:21; on the latter, see Hos 2:3-25 Setting).

If the readership proceeds according to option (b) or a closely related variant — because, at least in part, they were influenced by Gen 32:25-32 — then when they consider the speaker in the last sentence of v. 5 to be God/the messenger of God, vv. 6-7 become an integral part of vv. 5-7, just as before. But when they consider that speaker to be Jacob, vv. 6-7 become separate from vv. 4-5 and associated with another speaker. In this case, vv. 6-7 can be seen as an interlude in which a godly voice — probably human — proclaims to both the addressees in the world of the book and above all to the readers of the book — notice the affective use of "you" — that of which they should be aware and mindful. Such short texts serve to socialize the readership around central core tenets and attitudes. When vv. 6-7 are read in this way, they fulfill a structural role similar to that of 6:1-3, according to one of the possible readings of the section (see Hos 5:1–7:2 STRUCTURE). The most substantial change if reading (c) is followed is that vv. 6-7 then carry a restatement of the divine hierarchy: YHWH is the God and "your God," not Bethel. (If one follows Ginsberg ["Hosea's Ephraim"] and his reconstruction of the original text, then the verses would also stress the foolishness of Jacob.)

These considerations demonstrate that the intended and primary readerships of the text would have perceived and constructed the structure of the text in different ways depending on the particular reading they followed. These readings, and particularly (a) and (b) with all their variants, are complementary, inform each other, and all together convey the full meaning of the text as it is construed by the target readership through their continuously reading, rereading, studying, and reading to others of the text.

Verses 8-10 address a different period of Israel's trajectory through time. The readers are asked to jump from Jacob's narratives to the people in the land. According to the social memory agreed upon by the literati in ancient Israel, following the Exodus and the period in the desert, Israel replaced Canaan in the land. Verses 8-9 play with that memory as they inform their target readership that Ephraim is (like) Canaan. One can easily notice that the first slot position assigned to כנען "Canaan" in v. 8 is that usually taken by Ephraim or Israel, or similar terms (see v. 2). Thus, even the choice of the term "Canaan" instead of the expected Ephraim contributes to the message of blurring the difference between the two. Verse 9 continues the trend by portraying Ephraim as the one who reacts to the description of Canaan, which by implication serves to characterize Ephraim as the target of the reference to Canaan. Significantly, the only explicit reference to Canaan in the book of Hosea has nothing to do with "Canaanite rites" (cf. Hos 1:1–2:3 Intention; Hos 4:1-19 Setting; Hos 9:1-17 Setting), but with socio-economic behavior and with Canaan being supplanted by Israel — the latter as per the accepted constructions of the past among the literati. As Ephraim is compared to Canaan, the question that arises within these discourses is whether YHWH will treat Ephraim as YHWH did to the Canaanites (cf. 2 Kgs 21:11-14; Amos 9:7-9). Verse 10 answers this implied question. Ephraim will indeed be cast out of the land, but unlike the Canaanites, it will go through a period of purification akin to that in the desert following the Exodus. The implied result of this process is a return to the land as a purified Israel (cf. Hos 2:16-25 and see Setting there). The reason for YHWH's different approach to Israel and Canaan is clearly expressed: "I am YHWH, *your* (Ephraim's/trans-temporal Israel's) God since (your days) in the land of Egypt" (v. 10). (On this and other aspects of this unit see also Setting.) It is worth noting that the same expression appears in v. 10 and in Hos 13:4. In the latter, the expression is developed in a complementary manner. Certainly, within these discourses, the relationship between YHWH and Israel entails obligations for Israel, which were obviously not fulfilled. Although the expression itself serves different rhetorical roles in Hos 12:10 and 13:4, the verbatim repetition serves to alert the target readership that either one of the usages reflects only a partial aspect of its meaning, and that they should read one occurrence in a way informed by the other. Such a reading creates a tapestry of images that reflects the meaning of the expression more fully than any partial application of it in the narrow context of a particular READING within the book.

An interpretation of this expression in the light of Exod 20:2 and Deut 5:6 (cf. Ps. 81:11) eventually influenced non-masoretic versions of the text and brought it to read "I am YHWH your God who brought you out of the land of Egypt." Such reading shed light on the way in which ancient communities — though later than the one for whom the book of Hosea was written — actually read the text (see Hos 12:10 and 13:4 in the LXX, Peshiṭta, and the Targum, and 13:4 in 4QXIIc; Hos 12:10 is not preserved there). On these issues, see R. E. Fuller, "The Twelve," 241; idem, "Critical Note"; Gelston, *Peshiṭta,* 173; Cathcart, *Targum,* 57, 58; cf. Joosten, "Exegesis," 280 (§4.4).

It bears mention that a number of markers of textual coherence link vv. 8-10 to other units within this READING (cf. the situation with vv. 1-3). First, the unit seems to develop the theme of Jacob/Ephraim as a cheat from birth (see v. 4). Second, one may compare the use of מרמה in vv. 1 and 8, which evokes similarities between Canaan and Israel. Verbal forms from the root מצא "find" (twice in v. 9) clearly evoke a contrast between the image of Ephraim's self-proclaimed (a) "finding of" (in the sense of "happening upon") און "wealth" — but also connoting "might" or "power" — and (b) lack of "finding" עון "iniquity" (notice the pun on און "wealth"). Moreover, both instances of verbal forms of מצא "find" are connected to that in v. 5 in a meaningful way. The text suggests that the divine presence that demanded Jacob to observe loyalty/*hesed* and justice is supplanted by the presence of ill-gotten wealth און that is clearly associated (see also the mentioned pun) with עון "iniquity." In other words, the text constructs a (hi)story of Israel from Jacob to Ephraim's ill-gotten prosperity in the monarchic period, and eventually to punishment and purification. The repetition of אלהיך in vv. 7 and 10 strengthens this message and creates an envelope of YHWH's presence and action surrounding those of Ephraim in vv. 8-9. See also the pun between באלהיך תשוב in v. 7 and אושיבך באהלים in v. 10

(see above). These features not only contribute to textual coherence within the READING but also strongly influence its meanings, and the way in which these meanings are shaped and communicated.

The next unit vv. 11-12 deals with channels of intermediation between YHWH and Israel. In this sense it expands on the matter of communication referred to in v. 5b (and 6-7). In their different ways, both prophetic and cultic activities can be seen as the two basic types of intermediation or interfacing between divine and human realms in ancient Israel. Of course, there is a substantial difference in terms of agency. The initiative in the case of prophetic mediation is YHWH's, but the people are those supposed to take the initiative to worship — in a "proper" way — YHWH in a cultic setting.

The meaning of verse 11 has been debated, and this debate directly impinges on one's understanding of its structural role in the READING, as well as the message/s it conveys. Like other verses in this READING (vv. 3, 7), v. 11 consists of three short subunits. According to one approach, the first subunit, ודברתי על הנביאים most likely denotes something akin to "I [YHWH] have spoken continually to the prophets" (see below). The second subunit, ואנכי חזון הרבתי most likely denotes something akin to "It is I [YHWH] who multiplied revelation" (on חזון see Ben Zvi, *Obadiah*, 11-13). The third subunit וביד הנביאים אדמה most likely denotes "and by means of the prophets I [YHWH] revealed my thoughts/conveyed metaphors/set forth examples/present myself." (The latter option involves a minor repointing of the verbal form; cf. Rudolph, *Hosea*, 221, 223; cf. LXX.) As a result, the entire verse reads "I [YHWH] have spoken continually to the prophets. It is I who multiplied revelation and by means of the prophets revealed my thoughts. . . ." In other words, the text refers to YHWH's continuous efforts to communicate YHWH's words and thoughts to Israel by means of the prophets. YHWH's effort to teach Israel YHWH's ways not only exonerates the deity from any fault, but strongly incriminates those who despite all these divine efforts failed to follow YHWH's ways. When the verse is understood in this manner, it serves a rhetorical function very similar to that of Hos 8:12. In fact, both texts complement each other and together reflect the horizon of thought of the authorship and intended readerships. One focuses on divine communication through YHWH's written teachings (8:12) and the other through the prophets (12:11). The means are interconnected, because divine teachings are carried by prophets (see 2 Kgs 17:13) and, in any case, because the message of the prophets of old reaches the readership of the book in the form of a written text. To be sure, this understanding of the prophets is consistent with features of the general image of the prophets of old that the book of Kings as a whole most likely evoked among its intended and primary readership (see Ben Zvi, "The Prophets"; and see 2 Kgs 17:13-15; cf. also Zech 1:4). When the verse is understood in this way, it points at the failure of YHWH's consistent attempts to communicate YHWH's thoughts/teachings/metaphors/messages to Israel, because they did not listen to the prophets. This understanding is consistent with the structure advanced above.

The verse, however, carries other (secondary) meanings or, at the very least, connotations. These additional meanings lead in different directions. The initial verbal form ודברתי likely denotes here a frequentative or durative sense.

Moreover, the understanding that it points to a future event runs into problems with the second verbal form הרבתי "I multiplied [revelation]." (On these matters, see, among others, Macintosh, *Hosea*, 501-3; de Pury, "Dos Leyendas," 103; Rudolph, *Hosea*, 221, 223; Wolff, *Hosea*, 207, 215.) But it is very likely that the first subunit evoked a secondary meaning in which the reference is made to a future event. In fact, such a reading of the verbal form would be quite intuitive, if the verbal w-qtl form is understood as following the y-qtl verbal form in עד אושיבך באהלים "again I [YHWH] will make you dwell in tents" in v. 10. As the expression is understood as pointing to a future event, it would be rendered by something like, "I will speak to the prophets." In addition, the expression ודברתי על הנביאים can be understood, within this approach, as also meaning "I will speak against the prophets." Once either one of these readings is adopted, several ways of understanding the second verbal form arise. For instance, it may be understood as pointing to a simultaneous action, and the result would be something like Daniels's (*Hosea*, 34) translation of the verse, namely, "I will speak to the prophets. I will multiply vision(s)," or like "I will speak against the prophets, . . . I multiply visions" (understanding "visions" in a negative sense; cf. Jer 14:14; 23:16; Ezek 13:16; Isa 29:7; see Simian-Yofre, *Desierto*, 154, 162-63). Furthermore, the third subunit וביד הנביאים אדמה, at least, evokes the meaning of "by means of the prophets I will destroy/bring destruction (cf. Hos 6:5), even if the key verbal form from the root דמה appears in the piel instead of qal or nifal stems (see Hos 4:5, 6; 10:7, 15). Taking all this into account, the obvious result is that v. 11 is written in such a way that it either denotes or evokes several meanings including those akin to the following:

(a) "I [YHWH] have spoken continually to the prophets. It is I who multiplied revelation and by means of the prophets revealed my thoughts. . . ."

(b) "I [YHWH] have spoken continually to the prophets. It is I who multiplied revelation and by means of the prophets I will destroy [them/Ephraim/Israel]."

(c) "I will speak to the prophets. It is I who will multiply revelation and by means of the prophets I will reveal my thoughts. . . ."

(d) "I will speak against the prophets. It is I who will multiply (false) visions and by means of the prophets I will destroy [them/Ephraim/Israel]."

If, or better, when the target readership followed reading (a) — which is probably the primary meaning — they associated v. 11 with v. 12 and subtly set it apart from v. 10. This perspective is consistent with constructions of the role of the prophets of old in other texts and is consistent with the reported failure of YHWH's continuous attempts to teach Israel (see above).

When the target readership followed reading (c), whether as a main or a secondary or connoted meaning, they closely linked v. 11 to v. 10 and understood it as pointing not at a failure in communication but at a very positive situation that will take place during the future stay (and purification) of Israel in the desert (cf. Hos 2:16-25).

When the target readership followed reading (d), whether as a main or a secondary or connoted meaning, they perceived v. 11 as an announcement of severe punishment that stands by itself and, therefore, would have set it apart from v. 10 with its mainly positive image of hope, as separate from v. 12.

When the target readership followed reading (b), whether as a main or a secondary or connoted meaning, they perceived v. 11 as separate from v. 10, and as standing by itself as a sort of brief encapsulation of the (hi)story of Israel from the perspective of failed prophetic mediation: YHWH has continually in the past attempted to convey YHWH's message through prophets; since the people have continually rejected them, then destruction will follow by means of the (words of) the prophets (cf., among others, 2 Kgs 17:13-15; 21:10-15; 24:2; Zech 1:4; and, of course, Hos 6:5).

Significantly, all these readings are fully consistent with the discourses of the literati of the postmonarchic period and are well supported as either denotations or connotations by the text. It is to be stressed that the question of whether actual authors had in mind all these meanings is not only unanswerable but also immaterial. The target readership did not have access to their minds, but to the text they wrote. It is the text and above all the interaction between the ancient readers and their texts within the general discourses that informed them that became historically significant. All of these considerations point at both the multilayered meanings that the text likely evoked as it was read, reread, and studied by the primary readerships, and the multiple structures that followed them. Verse 11 provides an excellent example in this regard, but it is certainly not the only one in the book of Hosea (see already v. 5 in this READING), nor in the prophetic books, which abound in similar cases, which in the instance of Jonah encompass even the entire book whose basic meanings are conveyed as a tapestry of complementary, partial meanings informing each other (see Ben Zvi, *Signs of Jonah*).

Verse 12 is a brief unit that is held together by a general theme, namely, the worthlessness of improper (past) sacrifices, and by textually inscribed markers of cohesion. They include the repetition of the first two consonants in גלעד "Gilead," גלגל "Gilgal," and גלים "stone-heaps," of the combination of ל and מ in close proximity (see גלים and תלמי "furrows of"), and of the consonantal sounds in זבחו "they sacrificed" and מזבחותם "their altars." The reference to Gilead implicitly links it to Jacob and to the narrative hinted at in v. 13 (cf. Gen 31:25-54 — Jacob and Laban at Gilead). Moreover, the precise wording at the conclusion of the verse, namely, תלמי שדי "furrows of the field," brings to the attention of the readers the only other appearance of the expression in the book of Hosea, and in the Hebrew Bible for that matter, in Hos 10:4. As the target readership of Hos 12:12 approaches it in a way informed by Hos 10:4, the general reference in the latter to "they utter mere words; with empty oaths they make covenants" becomes relevant, and serves to reinterpret the story of the covenant between Jacob and Laban in Gilead reflected in Gen 31:25-54. It is worth noting that word choice even in a brief and closely knitted subunit such as v. 12 may be related to the text of other units in different READINGS or SETS OF READINGS within the book of Hosea, and so is the full range of meanings that it conveyed to the intended and primary readerships.

The final unit before the conclusion and its announcement of punishment (vv. 13-14) offers the reader a paradigmatic contrast between YHWH and Jacob. The two verses are linked by the general theme (e.g., whereas Jacob fled [from the land] to Aram, YHWH brought Israel up [to the land] from Egypt; whereas Jacob put himself voluntarily under servitude, YHWH took Israel out of servitude) and by the two similar but contrastive endings in vv. 13 and 14. The former is ובאשה שמר, usually translated "and for a woman he [Jacob] guarded [sheep]." The latter is ובנביא נשמר "and by a prophet he/it [Israel] was guarded." On these matters, and particularly on the different contrasts and meanings evoked by them, see Setting. The unit is thematically linked to the other references to Jacob and to the Exodus from Egypt in this READING, which in their own ways construe and represent two basic meta-narratives about the beginning of YHWH's relationship with Israel/Jacob.

As mentioned before, the concluding note of punishment in v. 15 creates an envelope with v. 1 (see Ephraim) and with v. 3 through ישיב לו "he will re-pay him." The entire survey of the (hi)story/ies of Ephraim/Israel/Jacob leads thus to the conclusion that their master will repay them their mockery. On v. 15 see above.

A few additional considerations about word choices in this READING are worth noting. The use of ואנכי "but/and I" (vv. 10, 11) is a common stylistic device in the book of Hosea and its distribution within the book is quite even (see Hos 1:9; 2:4; 7:13; 11:3; 12:10, 11; 13:4). It is far less common in other prophetic books, and its distribution is at times uneven (see Isa 49:15; 50:5; 51:15; 54:16; 66:18; nine times in the entire book of Jeremiah but none after Jer 35:14; Ezek 36:28; Amos 2:9-10). In the book of Hosea it clearly serves an em-phatic role.

As mentioned above, the reference to Gilead in v. 12 is consistent with its role in the stories about Jacob that were accepted within the intended and pri-mary readership. It is also likely that the use of the term גלים "stone-heaps" in the verse takes its cue from the role of the stone-heap in the story about Laban and Jacob in Gilead reflected in Gen 31:45-48. The choice of Gilgal as the sec-ond geographic reference in the verse among several alternative locations that could have served similar rhetorical purposes in the verse was most likely due to the repetition of sound created by גלגל (Gilgal) and גל "stone-heap" and the two identical consonants in the terms גלגל (Gilgal) and גלעד (Gilead). This is another example of literary concerns — in this case, achieving proper sound repetition — shaping constructions of the past or the future in prophetic books (cf., among many other instances, Mic 1:10-15; Zeph 2:4-5).

Numerous proposals for emendations of the text of Hosea 12 have been advanced (e.g., עמו "with him" instead of עמנו "with us" in v. 5; see above). For many of these proposals see BHS, and for a summary and critique of some of them, see Barthélemy, *Critique Textuelle*, vol. III, 596-607. As important in this regard are the proposals for a rearrangement of the order of the verses that have been mentioned above.

In addition, claims concerning the secondary character of some subunits or words have been advanced. In most instances, these claims are directly re-lated to assumptions about the Hoseanic (i.e., belonging to the historical prophet Hosea) character of the text of some verses and about its existence in an earlier, oral form that was independent from the book of Hosea. See, for in-

stance, "they [vv. 11-15] give the appearance of being originally separate fragments of Hosea's preaching or, in the case of vv. 13-14 perhaps further reflections by Hosea's disciples on the themes of his original saying" (Davies,
Hosea, 280 — the original reads "vv. 12-13" following the numbering used in
most English translations, but see NAB, NJB, NJPSV; to avoid confusion this
numbering has been "translated" into the one used in this commentary and in
any printed Hebrew Bible). Without denying the likely use of (written) sources
by the authorship of the book, this study shows that the content, message, and
wording of verses are deeply related to their being an integral part of the book
of Hosea.

At times the result of these claims is the construction of a hypothetical,
original text that is substantially different from the one in the book. This may
involve as "little" as the removal of the references to Judah in v. 3 or vv. 1 and
3, and its replacement with, for instance, Israel (see above), or as "much" as the
removal as secondary of some or all of verses 5, 6, 7, 10, 11, 13, 14 (for a summary and critique of some of these proposals see, among others, Daniels, *Hosea,* 39-40). According to Yee, Hos 12:1b, 5-7, 10-12, 12-14 belong to a
postmonarchic redactor (R2). See Yee, *Composition,* 229-48, 298-99, 317; and
cf. her diagram on 317 with Willi-Plein, *Vorformen,* 277. See also, among others, Davies, *Hosea,* 268-69; Neef, *Heilstraditionen Israels,* 22-24; Jeremias,
Hosea, 150; and cf. Lust, "Freud, Hosea," esp. 84-85.

Genre

Hosea 12 is a DIDACTIC PROPHETIC READING, that is, a literary unit within the
prophetic book of Hosea that shows textually inscribed, discursive markers that
were likely to suggest to its intended and primary readerships that they were
supposed to or at least invited to read it as a cohesive unit, within the frame of
the book of Hosea as a whole. It is also part and parcel of a SET OF READINGS
(Hos 12:1–14:9) within that book. This, however, does not mean that the readers are not supposed to approach it in a manner informed by sections of the
book of Hosea outside this SET.

The unit presents its readers with brief closely interwoven speeches that
are either explicitly characterized as YHWH's (see vv. 1a, 10-11) or assigned
by the implied author (and the narrator) to a godly voice that could be construed
as human or divine (e.g., vv. 1b, 2-3 — as mentioned on different occasions in
this commentary, third person references to YHWH/El/God do not imply that
the mentioned readers were supposed to rule YHWH out as a speaker). In fact,
most often words assigned to the voice explicitly characterized as YHWH's and
to the other godly voice are so closely interwoven (e.g., 1a and 1b) that the text
clearly suggests to its intended and primary readership that they should not pay
attention to these potential differences, and certainly should not assign more
authority to one than the other (cf. 1a and 1b). Words are also assigned to
Ephraim, see v. 9, but the citation there is embedded within the speech attributed to the voices mentioned above.

Some expressions and subunits within the READING were likely to evoke within the mentioned readerships some of the expectations associated with particular genres. For instance, vv. 6-7 were likely reminiscent of a liturgical text (cf. Buss, *Prophetic Word*, 74); v. 7 may be considered an exhortation (see Hunter, *Seek the Lord*, 157-66), which in turn may be construed as being embedded in other genres (e.g., cultic, lawsuit). Davies (*Hosea*, 268-69) considers Hos 12:1-2 to be a divine lament over Ephraim; and Hos 12:3-10 a judgment speech (he replaces Judah in v. 3 with Israel and considers v. 6 to be a Babylonian period insertion). It is worth noting that these genre allocations are related to assumptions about clear boundaries separating units, while the book itself suggests multiple possible structures. Moreover, many of these genre allocations are based on assumptions about an oral and independent stage of these units, mainly as brief utterances made by the historical Hosea on separate occasions. Significantly, the intended readership and primary rereadership of the book of Hosea are not asked to approach the book in this manner at all. On the contrary, numerous textually inscribed markers indicate that they should read these texts, in all their denoted and connoted meanings, as an integral part of the book of Hosea and in a way informed by their context in the book (see also Setting).

The reference to the divine contention (ריב) against Judah in v. 3 (cf. Hos 4:1) along with some elements in the text (e.g., the presence of accusations, exhortation, and announcement of judgment at the end, the expression "his blood upon him" in v. 15) could have evoked, to some extent, in the mentioned rereaderships an image of some judicial setting and of a lawsuit. Some scholars go further and have described this unit as a lawsuit, but even they admit that it contains elements that are not fully consistent with this description (see Stuart, *Hosea*, 188 — who maintains that the form of Hos 12:1–13:1 "may generally be described as the 'lawsuit,'" though "there are present elements not usually associated with the lawsuit pattern"). But Hosea 12 is not a report of a lawsuit, nor can its meanings or structure be narrowed to those of some judicial procedure held at a particular time. See STRUCTURE.

Setting

The setting of the writing and primary reading of this, or any portion of the (present) book of Hosea for that matter, is the same as that of the book as a whole. Both writers and readers are among the very few literati of Yehud. This READING is indicative of many aspects of the intellectual and ideological atmosphere within which it was written and which permeates it. For one, Hosea 12 implies an awareness of social memories reflected in other books (see STRUCTURE).

It bears note that questions such as who copied from whom, or, in a far more sophisticated formulation, questions about whether the traditions about Jacob as they appear in the book of Hosea are earlier than and influenced those in the book of Genesis or vice versa are not necessarily productive. For one thing, they involve uncertain matters such as the relative date of the present form of the mentioned books, or the relative date of redactionally reconstructed, hypothetical forerunners of these books, or those of the assumed (written) sources that underlie these forerunners. Moreover, they involve the assumption that when one is confronted with different versions, one must deal with them in straightforward linear temporal terms: one of the versions has to reflect earlier stages of the traditions, and, correspondingly, the other version must reflect later stages. From the perspective of a commentary on the (present) book of Hosea and the ways in which it was understood by its intended and primary readerships, it is much more productive to shift the focus to the set of "facts" about Jacob that were agreed upon within the circles of postmonarchic literati within which one finds the target rereaderships of the book of Hosea. It is this set of "facts" agreed upon that shapes the shared social memory referred to under STRUCTURE. Significantly, within that memory there is much room for malleability beyond a few "core facts" and certainly for multiple representations. Different versions of traditions about Jacob could have easily coexisted, just as different versions of many other traditions and even (hi)storical narratives did among Yehudite literati (see Kings and Chronicles; creation stories — including Prov 8:22-31). On general issues concerning "agreed-upon facts" and degrees of malleability in ancient Israelite historiography, see Ben Zvi, "Malleability," and cf. idem, "Secession," and idem, "Shifting the Gaze."

Several motifs reflected and expressed in this READING shed light on the intellectual setting shared by the literati among whom are to be found both the final authorship of the book of Hosea, in its present form, and its target readership. The motif of Ephraim/Jacob's and in general Israel's foolishness in the past — from the temporal perspective of the readership — so emphatically conveyed in v. 2, but occurring elsewhere — is relatively common in other prophetic texts and within the book of Hosea itself. Isa 1:3 exemplifies well the motif; in this verse Israel is portrayed as unnaturally foolish. As for Israel's foolishness, see also, for instance, Hos 8:7 (see Hos 8:1-14 STRUCTURE and Setting); Hos 3:1 (see Hos 3:1-5 Intention); Hos 13:12; and see also Hos 7:11 and cf. the characterization of foreign alliances there and in Hos 12:2 (see also Hos 10:6). (On the motif of "herding" or chasing the wind, cf. also Qoh 1:17; 2:17, 26; 4:4, 6, 16; 6:9 and cf. 5:15.) This construction of sinful and past Israel as extremely foolish serves to ease the tension between the description of its continuous sin and rejection of YHWH on the one hand and the categorical unreasonability of such actions within the discourses shaped and conveyed by these texts, on the other. In fact, there are very few ideological options open to the literati to alleviate this tension: If Israel behaved in such an implausible manner, it can only be because it was incredibly foolish, or because YHWH made it foolish so as to achieve YHWH's purposes (cf. Isa 6:10).

As mentioned above (see STRUCTURE), as Ephraim (/Israel) is compared to Canaan, the question arises within these discourses whether or not YHWH will treat Ephraim as YHWH treated the Canaanites (cf. 2 Kgs 21:11-14; Amos 9:7-9). The answer given in verse 10 and the different approach to Israel taken by YHWH are grounded in YHWH's selection of Israel in Egypt (cf. Hos 11:1). The stress on the foolishness of Israel in these texts and the comparable emphasis on the characterization of Israel as one who because of its own nature is ready and willing to sin ("a promiscuous woman") in Hosea 1–3 (cf. Hosea 4) are consistent with and reflective of the common construction of YHWH's choice of Israel in postmonarchic discourses as categorically not based on Israel's worth. To be sure, the other side of this construction is that Israel's worthiness is based only on its relationship with YHWH, and on the divine communications and teachings held by Israel (cf. Deut 4:6-8).

Verse 8 also plays with the double meaning associated with כנען/כנעני "Canaan/trader." On the one hand, it is clear from the discussion above that the contrast Israel/Canaan plays a central role in the shaping of the meaning of the verse, but these terms carry another meaning, "trader" (or "land/people of merchants"). It is worth noting that these terms almost always carry negative connotations (see Isa 23:8; Ezek 16:29; 17:4; Zeph 1:11; Zech 14:21). In Hos 12:8, the terms merchant and Canaan are brought together into a shared world of meaning in which "merchant" is associated with being taken out of the land by YHWH, because of iniquity (cf. Zech 14:21). In this verse, the merchant is explicitly associated with מאזני מרמה "deceitful balances" (cf. Amos 8:5; Prov 11:1; 20:23). The negative stereotyping of the trader here reflects a negative attitude towards commerce and commercial economy that is common in many agrarian cultures, and often at least ideologically supported by landed elites, for whom honorable economic activity involves working or making others work their fields. The exception to this rule is Prov 31:24 that perhaps not by chance is associated with a woman's role, and the acquisition of prestige items by rulers and, at times, their commercial enterprises. Of course, these observations reflect an ideological world, and do not mean that postmonarchic (or for that matter, monarchic) elites were not involved in or did not profit from business activities.

As mentioned above, vv. 13-14 offer the target readership a paradigmatic contrast between YHWH and Jacob. The contrastive nature of the relationship between the verses is clear from the outset given that whereas Jacob fled (from the land) to Aram, YHWH brought Israel up (to the land) from Egypt, and that whereas Jacob put himself voluntarily under servitude, YHWH took Israel out of servitude. Moreover, the text characterizes Jacob as one who put himself under servitude for a woman (ויעבד ישראל באשה), and who for a woman watched (sheep) (באשה שמר; on other meanings of this expression see below). These two remarks do not necessarily constitute a positive comment in patriarchal discourses, such as those of the literati of ancient Israel. To be sure, any construction of society in which a man serving for a woman is seen in negative terms is blatantly sexist, but so are patriarchal societies and discourses. Historians who focus on ancient and mainly (if not fully) male readerships in clearly patriarchal societies such as the intended and primary readership of the book of Hosea, and *their* reading of the text, have to take into account sexist positions, even if these stand in strong contradiction to the values that these historians hold dear. Moreover, such historians may often find typical ironies and self-contradictions within these patriarchal/sexist discourses of the past. See below. (On these matters, cf. and ct. Sweeney, *Twelve Prophets*, 127-28.) Of course, YHWH as opposed to Jacob/Israel cannot be imagined as serving for a woman, but more importantly, YHWH is to be served. The target readership of the book knows all too well that this obligation was not met by Israel. Jacob/Israel was willing to serve a woman, but not YHWH.

But there is much more going on in the comparisons advanced by the two verses. The language of the text clearly leads the readership to associate and contrast (a) ובאשה שמר, usually translated "and for a woman he [Jacob] guarded [sheep]" or the like in v. 13b, and (b) ובנביא נשמר "and by a prophet he/it [Israel] was guarded" in 14b. On the surface at least, the text may suggest a comparison between Jacob guarding the flock and Moses guarding Israel (YHWH's flock). But when this approach is taken, an obvious question arises: the woman — a crucial element in v. 13b whose centrality is reflected by and heightened by the repetition of באשה in close proximity — vanishes. If she is to be taken into account, then a new facet of the comparison becomes clear: if Jacob guarded the flock because of a woman, or better because of Jacob's love for a woman, the target readership may consider that Moses (as representative of YHWH) guarded Israel because of YHWH's love for a woman (i.e., Israel), which is a common motif in the book of Hosea (cf. 2:16-25). (Incidentally, this is also a patriarchal image.) It is worth noting that the claim has been advanced that the Heb. root שמר translated above with the sense of "guard" carried the meaning "love," "to be devoted to," "to cling to," in v. 13 (see Morag, "Semantic and Lexical," 502-3; Macintosh, *Hosea,* 508 — Macintosh compares the use here with "to keep thee only unto her" of the marriage service in the Book of Common Prayer). This understanding of the root is consistent with the traditions about Jacob and Rachel (or Leah) reflected in Genesis (see, for instance, Gen 29:20). If there was even a connotation of that meaning of שמר in v. 13, then there is no reason to assume that it disappeared when the readership approached v. 14. The fact that the text clearly relates the two forms makes this even more unlikely. The result would be that an understanding of the text mentioned above would be supported by at least the connotations of the root שמר.

Yet the presence of the pair בנביא — באשה seems to ask the target readership to compare not only YHWH and Jacob, but also "woman" and "prophet" (or Rachel/Leah and Moses). One way of approaching the matter is to suggest that women and prophets represent two different conceptual ways for the continuous existence of Israel. Jacob's way is through progeny, that is, through women. YHWH's way is through a prophet, through the transmission and acceptance of YHWH's word (see de Pury "Dos leyendas," 107-12). Not surprising in a book written by and for (male) literati and which claims to convey YHWH's word, the second conceptual way is evaluated as higher than the first; one is associated with YHWH (and Moses), and the other with Jacob.

It is ironic that a text that reflects and conveys a sense that women and women's contributions to Israel are to be valued less than men and men's contributions, and that contrasts YHWH and YHWH's prophet Moses with Jacob and his woman (women?), makes use of the figure of Moses. According to the memory agreed upon by the literati of Yehud, Moses was hidden by his mother, kept by his sister, saved and raised by Pharaoh's daughter, and later kept and maintained within and by the family of his wife, and eventually saved from death by the same wife, Zipporah. (Very similar points are advanced by de Pury ["Dos leyendas," 109-10, note 33], though he develops them in a slightly different form due to his dating of the relevant texts and due to the emphasis here on readership rather than authorship.)

By providing two contrastive, though complementary stories of Israel's beginning — one through Jacob and one through YHWH's prophet, Moses — Hosea 12 joins other texts in the book (e.g., Hos 9:10, 13 and 10:11-13; Hos 11:1-4) in addressing the theme of YHWH's early choice of Israel and its eventual rebellion. As mentioned on other occasions, all the partial windows on these matters create a rich tapestry that as a whole reflects the universe of discourses/s on these matters that characterized both the authorship and primary target readership of the book.

(Among the many works on the Jacob of Hos 12:13-14, and from a wide range of perspectives, one may mention, Abma, "Jacob"; Ackroyd, "Hosea and Jacob"; Ausín, "La tradición"; Bentzen, "Weeping"; Coote, "Hosea XII"; Daniels, *Hosea,* esp. 50-52; de Pury, "Dos leyendas"; Eslinger, "Hosea 12:5a and Genesis 32:29a"; Fishbane, *Biblical Interpretation,* 376-79; Gese, "Jacob und Mose"; Gertner, "Attempt"; Ginsberg, "Hosea's Ephraim"; Kaufmann, *Toldot,* vol. 3, 134-37; Lust, "Freud, Hosea and the Murder of Moses"; McKay, "Jacob Makes It Across the Jabbok"; McKenzie, "Jacob Tradition"; Neef, *Heilstraditionen Israels,* 15-49; Polliack, "Image"; and Whitt, "Jacob Traditions.")

From the fact that the motif of provoking (כעס in the hiphil) is relatively common in Deuteronomy (e.g., Deut 4:25) and appears numerous times in the book of Kings, and in Jeremiah, it does not follow that the text was written by or for a deuteronomistic circle, as proven by the fact that the motif appears also in Isa 65:3; Ezek 16:26; Ps 78:58; 106:29. It is probably better to refer to a shared repertoire of motifs within the postmonarchic literati. The use of כעס in the hiphil without an (explicitly mentioned) object might have led a readership aware of 1 Kgs 21:22 and 2 Kgs 21:6 to approach Hos 12:15 in a manner informed by the mentioned texts and vice versa, but even if such is the case, this would not mean that the text was written by or for a socially and intellectually separate deuteronomistic circle. On the problematic matter of "deuteronomistic" prophetic books see Ben Zvi, "Deuteronomistic Redaction."

As is the case in other READINGS in the book, the world portrayed in the book is not anchored in any narrow historical setting, or better in any narrow setting associated with the readership's construction of particular events in the past. This is consistent with the general tendency not to historicize the words reported in the READING, but give them as open a background as possible within the general limits shaped in Hos 1:1, and the general focus on the northern kingdom. In accordance with common constructions of the monarchic past, the period is portrayed as one of relative economic prosperity (see Hos 12:9). Perhaps the most interesting note concerning the setting of the world shaped within the book is that to Judah in v. 1, ויהודה עד רד עם אל ועם קדושים נאמן. It is impossible to be certain of the meaning, or meanings of this expression. If it means either (a) "but Judah still roams with God and is faithful with the Holy Ones" (cf. Ps. 89:6, 8; Prov 9:10; 30:3 — or, but less likely, ". . . with sacred objects") or (b) "but Judah still rules with God and is faithful with the Holy Ones," then it would be shaping a temporal quality within the reported divine speech. It would mean that within the world of the book, at the time the expression was uttered, Judah was still different from Ephraim in its relationship to YHWH, but that this difference will disappear. If (b) is followed the difference might have something to do with rule of the Davidic dynasty, though it was about to end too. If these interpretations of the text are correct, then the world of the text may have reflected the memory (and historical reality) that the northern polity was destroyed by the Assyrians, whereas the southern remained till the early Babylonian period. It might also reflect memories and evaluations associated with Hezekiah (see Hos 1:1; and cf. 2 Kings 18–20; Isaiah 36–38; 2 Chronicles 29–32). Yet given the uncertainty about the meaning of v. 1b, much caution is required in this case. For a study of the verse and bibliography see Barthélemy, *Critique Textuelle,* vol. III, 596-600; see also, among others, Macintosh, *Hosea,* 473-77; Simian-Yofre, *Desierto,* 153-54, 260; Pentiuc, *Long-Suffering Love,* 186-87; and Andersen and Freedman, *Hosea,* 593, 601-3. It is worth noting that as the ancient versions show, there was a wide variety of opinions about the meaning/s of verse 1b already in ancient times. The same holds true for medieval commentators and contemporary scholars.

Scholars who focus on the historical Hosea, as opposed to the character in the book or the book itself, who identify most of the text with Hosea's reaction to, or his stance against, the background of concrete historical events that were contemporary with Hosea's words, and who date them within the last decades of the northern kingdom propose corresponding settings for the original versions of the sayings — as abstracted from the text once proposed secondary additions are removed. For instance, Davies (*Hosea,* 269) writes:

> Hos 12:1-2 [original reads "Hos 11:12–12:1" following the numbering used in most English translations] presuppose the vacillation between Assyria and Egypt which seems to have begun only in the reign of Shalmanesser V, and therefore cannot be earlier than 727. 12:3-10 [original reads, "Hos 12:2-9" following the numbering used in most English translations] contain no clear references to contemporary events that can be dated, but the mention of Ephraim's prosperity (v. 9 [original reads, "v. 8"]) fits best the early part of Hosea's ministry, before the Assyrian invasions of 734-33. The sayings in vv. 11-15 [original reads, "vv. 10-14"] are too short to permit even a tentative dating.

Davies is certainly not alone in advancing this type of argument. In fact, he is one of many serious and thoughtful contemporary proponents of an approach that is still very common in research. This being so, it is worthwhile to note briefly some of the assumptions governing this approach: (a) a reading of verses as separate and independent from the book and its literary context, (b) a tendency to historicize the text, and (c) a tendency to assume that the world portrayed in the book must directly and unequivocally be mimetic, and reliably mimetic of that of the historical prophet. Thus, for instance, if the text refers to Ephraim as wealthy, then Hosea must have proclaimed these words when the northern kingdom as a whole was objectively prosperous. On (a) see above. Assumption (b) runs contrary to the tendency in the book *not* to ask its readership to historicize its reported speeches and units. Assumption (c) is extremely problematic the moment the text is taken as literature constructing a past "reality" as any piece of literature does. It also reduces sophisticated, multilayered literature and ideological constructions into no more than a fancy dress for factual historicity. Moreover, even if one were to decontextualize the verses by stripping them of their literary context in the book and assign them verbatim to a particular historical personage, this approach would remain problematic unless one assumes by default that this personage's rhetoric must reliably and objectively describe the external reality of the precise time or period in which the rhetorical piece is proclaimed. The latter can be taken as a matter of faith, but would fall short of the common critical requirements of contemporary historiography. It is to be stressed that these problems impinge directly on the historical reliability of any attempt to reconstruct and historicize a proposed interaction between historical reality and the words that one abstracts from the book and attributes to the historical prophet.

For Sweeney (*Twelve Prophets*, 93-136) Hosea 12 is part of a lengthy discourse, Hos 9:1–14:1. He points at associations between this discourse and the festival of Sukkoth (see, for instance, *Twelve Prophets*, 93-96, 98-99, 103-5, 124-25). The references in 12:10b to dwelling in tents, that is, in this context to the period in the desert, and the expression כימי מועד — on the meaning of the expression see below — have been associated with Sukkoth. Turning to the latter, it is likely that the expression כימי מועד connoted within the primary readership, among other things, some association with Sukkoth, because ימי מועד most likely connoted a sense of "days of the appointed festival" (cf. Hos 9:5) and the latter could have been interpreted as Sukkoth. Notwithstanding the aforementioned remark, it is worth stressing that כימי מועד points at a situation in the past rather than in the present of the speaker (see Macintosh, *Hosea*, 499; Wolff, *Hosea*, 215; Driver ["Linguistic and Textual Problems," 162] translates כימי מועד as "as [in] the days from of old," which is the Targum's understanding of the verse; see NJPSV, NEB). As such, it points to the first time of Israel's stay in the desert, a time in which it dwelled in tents. In a common rhetorical trope, the verse directly relates the faraway past to the future. The future will be like the past; a new beginning will take place. But, of course, as discussed in Hos 2:3-25 Setting, the return to the desert can only be presented as both a return and a novelty (see there), for at the very least, Israel would be aware of the failure that followed its first period in the desert. In addition, the same expression כימי מועד was as likely to evoke within the same readership the image of the priestly אהל מועד "the Tent of Meeting" that stood as the central point of that community of Israel.

References to Israel in the desert may be discursively associated with the festival of Sukkoth. At the same time, it is worth noting that in the book of Hosea they are not restricted to Hos 9:1–14:1 (see Hos 2:16-25). More importantly, they do not have to be directly informed by the actual observation of the festival at the time of the primary readership of the book of Hosea, or at least not any more than references to the Exodus have to be related to the manner in which the Passover festival was observed by the same readership. Should one imagine that the book of Hosea — or relevant portions thereof — was read to the general population during the festival of Sukkoth at some point during the postmonarchic/Persian period, one may reasonably assume that the mentioned connotations would have been strongly activated by the literati performing the reading and among the general population being read to. However, as tempting as such a hypothesis might be, there is no proof that such a reading took place. This being so, the reconstruction of the setting of the first oral performances of the book remains unavailable to us.

Intention

The general intention of Hosea 12:1-15 is to communicate and reinforce the positions and the general horizon of thought of the authorship and readership as represented in these texts (see Setting) and to socialize the literati through their shared reading of the material and the larger society through the literati's reading to others of these readings.

Among other things, this READING conveys a construction of Israel's (hi)story from a divine perspective that points to constant failure, but also hope for a new beginning that is most significantly not associated with Jacob, but with the stay in the desert and with Moses. That is, the prophetic book of Hosea communicates that trans-temporal Israel will be given by YHWH a new beginning in which YHWH's will and knowledge as conveyed to the people by a prophet will stand at the center — worship is also present through the connoted image of the Tent of Meeting. Between failure and hope the READING shapes a period of divine punishment, which from the perspective of the readership has already occurred.

As other prophetic texts and books (e.g., the book of Zephaniah), Hos 12:1-15 shapes an image of Israel's/Ephraim's earthly power and prosperity as deceitful markers. Contrary to expectation, they do not point at divine bliss. To the contrary, they indicate that Ephraim/Israel has not yet been punished for its deeds, and as such it stands farther from the implementation of the time in which the hopeful future will be implemented than does the readership of the book (i.e., postmonarchic Israel). (For a more elaborate discussion of these matters, see Ben Zvi, *Zephaniah*, 337-46, and cf. "Understanding the Message.") As such the text served to lessen the cognitive dissonance between the actual, relatively powerless earthly status of the community of readers during the postmonarchic period and their own construction of the status of powerful but extremely sinful communities of Israel in the monarchic past, and of other nations during their own days.

Bibliography

R. Abma, "Jacob, A Questionable Ancestor? Some Remarks on Hosea 12," J. W. Dyk et al. (eds.), *Unless Some One Guide Me. Festschrift for Karel A. Deurloo* (ACEBT Sup 2; Maastricht: Shaker, 2001) 175-79; P. Ackroyd, "Hosea and Jacob," *VT* 13 (1963) 245-59; S. Ausín, "La tradición de Jacob en Oseas 12," *EstBib* 49 (1991) 5-23; A. Bentzen, "The Weeping of Jacob, Hos. XII 5A," *VT* 1 (1951) 58-59; R. B. Coote, "Hosea XII," *VT* 21 (1971) 389-402; A. de Pury, "Las dos leyendas sobre el origen de Israel (Jacob y Moisés) y la elaboración del Pentateuco," *EstBib* 52 (1994) 95-131; T. B. Dozeman,

"Hosea and the Wilderness Tradition," S. L. McKenzie and T. Römer (eds.; in collaboration with H. H. Schmid), *Rethinking the Foundations: Historiography in the Ancient World and in the Bible: Essays in Honour of John Van Seters* (BZAW 294; Berlin/New York: de Gruyter, 2000) 55-70; G. R. Driver, "Linguistic and Textual Problems: Minor Prophets. I," *JTS* 39 (1938) 155-66; L. M. Eslinger, "Hosea 12:5a and Genesis 32:29a. A Study of Inner Biblical Exegesis," *JSOT* 18 (1980) 91-99; M. Fishbane, *Biblical Interpretation in Ancient Israel* (Oxford: Clarendon Press, 1988); R. Fuller, "A Critical Note on Hosea 12:10 and 13:4," *RB* 98 (1991) 343-57; M. Gertner, "An Attempt at an Interpretation of Hosea xii," *VT* 10 (1960) 272-84; H. Gese, "Jacob und Mose: Hosea 12:3-4 als einheitlicher Text," J. W. Van Henten et al. (eds.), *Tradition and Re-interpretation in Jewish and Early Christian Literature. Essays in Honour of Jürgen C. H. Lebram* (Leiden: E. J. Brill, 1986) 38-47; H. L. Ginsberg, "Hosea's Ephraim, More Fool than Knave. A New Interpretation of Hosea 12:1-14," *JBL* 80 (1961) 339-47; J.-G. Heintz, "Osée XII 2B à la lumière d'un vase d'albâtre de l'époque de Salmanasar III (Djézirêh) et le rituel d'alliance Assyrien: une hypothèse de lecture," *VT* 51 (2001) 466-80; Y. Hoffman, "A North Israelite Typological Myth and a Judaean Historical Tradition: The Exodus in Hosea and Amos," *VT* 39 (1989) 169-82; W. L. Holladay, "Chiasmus, the Key to Hosea XII 3-6," *VT* 16 (1966) 53-64; A. V. Hunter, *Seek the Lord* (Baltimore: St. Mary's Seminary and University, 1982); J. Joosten, "Exegesis in the Septuagint Version of Hosea," J. C. de Moor (ed.), *Intertextuality in Ugarit and Israel* (OtSt 40; Leiden: E. J. Brill, 1998) 62-85; J. R. Linville, "On the Nature of Rethinking Prophetic Literature: Stirring a Neglected Stew (A Response to David L. Petersen)," *Journal of Hebrew Scriptures* 2 (1999), available at http://www.jhsonline.org and http://purl.org/jhs; J. Lust, "Freud, Hosea and the Murder of Moses. Hosea 12," *ETL* 65 (1989) 81-93; D. J. McCarthy, "Hosea XII 2: Covenant by Oil," *VT* 14 (1964) 215-21; H. A. McKay, "Jacob Makes It Across the Jabbok. An Attempt to Solve the Success/Failure Ambivalence in Israel's Self-consciousness," *JSOT* 38 (1987) 3-13; J. L. McKenzie, "Divine Passion in Osee," *CBQ* 17 (1955) 287-89; S. L. McKenzie, "The Jacob Tradition in Hosea XII 4-5," *VT* 36 (1986) 311-22; S. Morag, "On Semantic and Lexical Features in the Language of Hosea," *Tarbiz* 53 (1984) 489-511 (in Hebrew); M. S. Odell, "Who Were the Prophets in Hosea?" *HBT* 18 (1996) 78-95; idem, "The Prophets and the End of Hosea," P. House and J. W. Watts (eds.), *Forming Prophetic Literature: Essays on Isaiah and the Twelve in Honor of John D. W. Watts* (JSOTSupS 235; Sheffield: JSOT Press, 1996) 158-70; S. Pisano, "'Egypt' in the Septuagint Text of Hosea," G. J. Norton, S. Pisano, and C. M. Martini (eds.), *Tradition of the Text: Studies Offered to Dominique Barthélemy in Celebration of His 70th Birthday* (OBO 109; Fribourg: Éditions universitaires, 1991) 301-8; M. Polliack, "On the Image of Jacob in Hosea 12: Typological Approaches in Medieval Exegesis and in Modern Research," *Beit Mikra* 44/156 (1998) 39-54 (in Hebrew); C. L. Seow, "Hosea 14:10 and the Foolish People Motif," *CBQ* 42 (1982) 212-24; S. H. Smith, "'Heel' and 'Thigh': The Concept of Sexuality in the Jacob-Esau Narratives," *VT* 40 (1990) 464-73; R. Syrén, "The Targum as a Bible Reread, or How Does God Communicate with Humans?" *JAB* 2 (2000) 247-64; B. Vawter, "Were the Prophets *nābî's*?" *Bib* 66 (1985) 206-20; E. R. Wendland, *The Discourse Analysis of Hebrew Prophetic Literature* (Lewiston, NY: E. Mellen Press, 1995); W. D. Whitt, "The Jacob Traditions in Hosea and their Relation to Genesis," *ZAW* 103 (1991) 18-43; N. Wyatt, "Of Calves and Kings: The Canaanite Dimension in the Religion of Israel," *SJOT* 6 (1992) 68-91.

Second Didactic Prophetic Reading —
The (Past) Behavior of Israel/Ephraim Leads to
a Future Death, Hos 13:1–14:1

Structure

I. Introduction	13:1
II. First Section	13:1-9
A. Cult	13:1-3
B. Destruction and YHWH's Characterization as Agent of	
Past Blessing, Future Death and Potential Help	13:4-9
1. Emphatic Introduction: I am YHWH . . .	
I Acknowledged You in the Wilderness	4-5
2. Past Behavior and Future Destruction	6-9
III. Second Section	13:9–14:1
A. Kingship	13:9-11
1. Emphatic Introduction	13:9
2. Of Kings	13:10-11
B. Destruction, and YHWH's Characterization	13:12–14:1
IV. Conclusion	14:1

This READING is the last in this SET of READINGS and in the book before the READING of hope that concludes both the SET and the body of the book of Hosea as a whole. This READING brings the stream of images of destruction that exist through the book to a kind of climax that serves as appropriate background and counterfoil to the final message of hope conveyed by Hos 14:2-9 and the book as a whole. The intended and primary readership learned from their rereadings of the book that no matter how much Israel has sinned and how much it deserves to be sentenced to death by YHWH, even after YHWH explicitly proclaimed that sentence, Israel would still remain alive and would eventually return to YHWH. In other words, from the viewpoint of the book as a whole, YHWH, the most reliable and authoritative speaker, is construed as one who communicates within a past world set in late monarchic Israel (i.e., the world of the book) that even if trans-temporal Israel (manifested through Ephraim, Samaria) has chosen a path that leads to death, death will not be their destiny, even if they will be punished. From the perspective of the readership of the book, this is one of the most powerfully comforting messages. It provides an interpretative key for all divine announcements of death to Israel proclaimed by YHWH, but also and mainly it connotes a sense of eternal life for trans-temporal Israel, without diminishing its highs and mostly lows in the past and perhaps the future as well. To be sure, for this rhetorical message to work, a READING such as this one has to carry a strong and clear message of "future death," so as to be countered and reinterpreted by the following READING (Hos 14:2-9).

The structure outlined above is one of several possible structures of Hosea 13. The extent of this unit is marked, as usual, by several markers of inner coherence (see below), and by its outer boundaries. Turning to the latter, there is a clear thematic break between 14:1 and 14:2, and some textually inscribed markers point in the same direction. One may note the imperative opening in 14:2 and the envelope between 13:1 and 14:1. This envelope clearly links ויאשם בבעל "he [Ephraim] became guilty [root אשם] through [ב] Baal" in 13:1 and the similar expression תאשם שמרון כי מרתה באלהיה "she (Samaria) will bear guilt [root אשם] for she has rebelled against [ב] her God" in 14:1. The envelope also links the summary statement of the death of Ephraim (13:1) to images of Samaria's children being dashed in pieces and their pregnant women ripped open (14:1). (On 14:1 see also below.) The presence of a substantial break between 14:1 and 14:2 is widely accepted (e.g., Eidewall, *Grapes*, 193; Davies, *Hosea*, 298). It is textually inscribed in 4QXIIc by an empty line, and its presence is marked also in the masoretic division of the text of Hosea into paragraphs.

The existence of a break between 12:15 and 13:1, however, has been debated. As mentioned above (Hos 12:1-15 STRUCTURE), the previous READING, which begins with Hos 12:1, is better understood as concluding with both 12:15 and 13:1. Yet at the same time and particularly given the close relationship between Hos 13:1 and Hos 14:1, the former serves as the beginning of this READING. (Structural double-duty units are relatively common in the book of Hosea, as demonstrated in this commentary, and they often occur in other prophetic books.)

Other proposals for the inner structure of the READING have been advanced, and for the most part either (a) concern matters of break hierarchy within the unit or minor modifications, or (b) reflect the traditional reluctance to understand verses as fulfilling a structural double-duty role, which is in part related to a focus on the historical prophet's sayings rather than on the book itself. For instance, Mays (*Hosea*, 171-83) and Wolff (*Hosea*, 222-24) divide the text into (i) vv. 1-3, (ii) vv. 4-8, (iii) vv. 9-11, and (iv) vv. 13:12–14:1; Pentiuc (*Long-Suffering Love*, 194-201) into (i) vv. 1-3, (ii) vv. 4-8, (iii) vv. 9-11, (iv) vv. 12-13, and (v) vv. 13:14–14:1; Simian-Yofre (*Desierto*, 166) into (i) vv. 1-3, (ii) vv. 4-9, (iii) vv. 10-11, (iv) vv. 12-14, and (v) vv. 13:15–14:1.

More importantly, there is a substantially divergent understanding of the structure of the READING that is probably as likely as those mentioned above, including the one proposed here, and in fact complements them. The masoretic division into paragraphs marks a substantial break between vv. 11 and 12 — interestingly, it does not mark one between 12:15 and 13:1. Among modern scholars, Buss (*Prophetic Word*, 24-26), unlike those mentioned above, divides the text into two sections (i) 13:1-11 and (ii) 13:12–14:1. The first section he entitles "A Fall from Yahweh, the Only Saviour." He is correct in the sense that a reading of Hos 13:1-11 as a main rhetorical unit emphasizes (and reflects the centrality of) the motif that human leadership and wrongful cult provide no deliverance, but YHWH is the only one able to do so, and as such it serves also to prepare the readership for Hos 14:4. The second main unit, namely, 13:12–14:1, turns into a section that deals mainly with Israel's punishment/destruction and secondarily with reasons that led to it, and YHWH's characterization. (Buss entitles this section "Sheol (No Life from the Womb).") The understanding of the text as structured around these two sections (Hos 13:1-11 and 13:12–14:1) should not be taken as an alternative to the one proposed above, but as complementary to it. Each of them reflects certain emphases in the text and informs the other, and they were likely produced as the book of Hosea was read, reread, and studied by the ancient rereaderships for which it was composed. As demonstrated again and again in this commentary, READINGS in this book (e.g., Hos 12:1-15) tend to allow and even encourage the target readership to approach the text from the perspective of multiple and complementary structures or outlines informing each other.

Before turning to the discussion of the structure mentioned at the beginning of this chapter, it is worth stressing that this READING, as any in this SET of READINGS (Hos 12:1–14:9), explores further some of the main themes advanced in 4:1–11:11 and is closely linked to READINGS in that set by a network of textually inscribed signposts that contribute to the continuous rereading and study of the book within the target readerships. At the same time, it also contains subtle signposts that remind the readers that Hos 13:1–14:1 leads into Hos 14:1-9. A few examples will suffice. Hos 8:4 brings together two main offenses of Israel, the making of kings and of idols (עצבים), which are two main themes in this READING (see v. 2 and 10-11; on עצבים ct. Hos 14:9). Further, חרש עשהו "an artisan made it" in Hos 8:6 finds a counterpart מעשה חרשים "the work of an artisan" in Hos 13:2, and both reflect and communicate a theological mindset in which aniconic worship was seen as a central tenet to such extent that iconic worship of any kind is strongly derided (see Hos 8:1-14 Setting). Explicit references to the "(male) calf/calves" (עגל) appear in Hos 8:5, 6 and 13:2 — also cf. Hos 10:5 and see 10:1-15 STRUCTURE — again linking the two READINGS. There is a difference, however: whereas according to Hosea 8 Israel/Ephraim will be sent into exile and its cities will be destroyed, according to Hos 13:1 Israel/Ephraim dies. Significantly, according to Hos 14:9 Ephraim/Israel will reject the idols (עצבים), and according to Hos 14:4b they will not consider מעשה ידינו "the work of our [Ephraim's/Israel's] hands" (i.e., the calves) to be their gods (cf. and ct. Exod 32:4, 8; 1 Kgs 12:28-29). For a comprehensive list of expressions in Hos 13:1–14:1 that recall the language of Hos 14:2-9 and vice versa see Good, "Composition," 60-61.

The expression כענן בקר וכטל משכים הלך "like a morning mist/cloud or like dew that goes away early" appears in Hos 13:3 and Hos 6:4, but nowhere else in the HB. The expression serves as a signpost suggesting the readers relate one unit in the book to another. Whereas Hos 6:4 informs them that Israel's loyalty *(hesed)* to YHWH is as ephemeral as morning mist or dew and does not last long, Hos 13:3 portrays Israel/Ephraim itself as ephemeral as morning mist or dew, because its does not keep its loyalty to YHWH (see Hos 13:1-2; cf. Hos 14:1). Significantly, in Hos 14:6, it is YHWH who will be like a nourishing dew that does not fail to appear and whose effects are long lasting. It is worth noting that within the world of postmonarchic literati, dew may raise connotations of bringing those who are dead to life (see Isa 26:19); cf. Hos 6:2 (see Hos 5:1–7:2 STRUCTURE) and also 13:14. (On the dew metaphor see Oestreich, *Metaphors*, 157-89.)

The expression ואנכי ה' אלהיך מארץ מצרים "I am YHWH, *your* [Ephraim's/trans-temporal Israel's] God since (your days) in the land Egypt" occurs word for word in Hos 12:10 and 13:4. In the former instance, it serves to explain why Israel will eventually be saved (see Hos 12:1-15 STRUCTURE, Setting); here it serves to emphasize Israel's guilt (see vv. 1-3), while at the same time cannot but evoke in the readers a sense that YHWH will save Israel (see Hos 12:10); cf. also 13:4b with 13:10a and 14:4.

As mentioned above, a central link between Hos 13:1 and 14:1 is shaped by the reference to אשם "being/becoming/bearing" guilt (see above), but one may also cf. Hos 4:15 (and cf. Hos 13:1-2 and Hos 4:14-15); Hos 5:15 (and notice the relationship between Hos 14:2 and Hos 5:15–6:1); and Hos 10:2 (and cf. Hos 13:2). In addition, one may compare Hos 13:5 and 5:3 (ct. Hos 5:4; 8:2); Hos 13:5 and Hos 9:10 (cf. Hos 2:16); Hos 13:7 and 5:14; and Hos 14:1b and 10:14.

The cumulative evidence of the links mentioned above strongly suggests to the target readership of the book that neither this READING nor its wording is independent of other READINGS and word choices elsewhere in the book. The same evidence suggests an authorial voice that interweaves these READINGS.

Turning to the structure advanced here, which, to be stressed, is only one of several possible and overlapping structures, the two main sections (vv. 13:1-9 and vv. 13:9–14:1, respectively) show a similar thematic structure that emphasizes first the sins of the people and then their punishment. Moreover as the text suggests to its primary and intended readership, this structure also characterizes YHWH, through a report of the deity's speech. The first section focuses on cultic offenses, whereas the second focuses on offenses associated with the office of kingship (cf. the structure of Hos 10:1-15). Of course, the two motifs are related, and kings all over the ancient Near East were considered responsible for maintaining proper worship. Moreover, in the book of Hosea trust in a human king is contrasted and considered a sinful alternative to trust in YHWH, on a par with and complementary to trusting in deities other than YHWH, idols, or the like. See Hos 10:1-15 STRUCTURE and Setting (cf. also Hos 14:3-4 and notice also that the metaphorical semantic realm of "lovers" in the book of Hosea includes deities other than YHWH and foreign human kings; for discussions on these matters see Hos 2:3-25 Setting and Hos 8:1-14 STRUCTURE). Significantly, the two sections overlap in v. 9, a pivot verse that refers to both offenses through worship and kingship. Verse 9 denoted or connoted to the target readership a meaning akin to (a) "that caused your destruction, O Israel, your being against me, your help," or (b) "that caused your destruction, O Israel, that in me alone is your help" (but you asked others), or (c) "I caused your destruction, O Israel; it is I, your help" (cf. Barthélemy, *Critique Textuelle,* vol. III, 611-13; Macintosh, *Hosea,* 535-37). These three meanings not only are conveyed by the text but also are closely interwoven and together shape and communicate the meaning of the verse. One may notice that being against YHWH includes and is paradigmatically exemplified in this READING as (a) worship of anything except YHWH (be it Baal or idols, which, of course, cannot help Israel), (b) trust in a human king, in this case, an Israelite king who cannot help Israel either, because YHWH is its help. In other words, meanings (a) and (b) are deeply interwoven (cf. Hos 13:4, 10, each in one of the two main sections). Meaning (c) contributes to this by stating that which would be obvious to the target readership and in any event is explicitly stated in the READING and elsewhere in the book of Hosea, namely, that no one but YHWH brings (or can bring) destruction to Israel, and paradoxically — at least from one possible viewpoint — that this destroyer is also, and always remains, Israel's only (true) help. Notice also the double duty of the "you" and "your" that on one level refer to an implied audience listening to YHWH's words within the world of the book and therefore set in the late monarchic period, but on another refer to the target readerships of the book, for they too are (trans-temporal) Israel.

Turning to the first main section, Eidewall (*Grapes,* 194) is probably correct when he suggests that it "epitomizes the contents of the entire discourse unit." If it serves this role, it can be considered an introduction to the entire READING. Verse 1 is also an integral part and serves to open the first section (vv. 1-9), and in addition, as mentioned above, it serves as a second ending of the previous READING (Hos 12:1-15) and creates a significant envelope with 14:1; see above. Multiple roles often contribute to the textual coherence of a READING. Verse 9 creates an area of overlap between two sections in one READING; v. 1 contributes to the textual coherence of this READING and of the SET of READINGS and the book as a whole. Verse 2 exemplifies that what is encapsulated in v. 1 and v. 3 is clearly and closely linked to both of them by the opening "therefore." (On "Baal" in v. 1 see also Setting.)

The second subunit in this section begins with an adversative "but I am YHWH . . ." in v. 4a that, in sharp contrast to the preceding announcement of future judgment (v. 3), evokes YHWH's deliverance of Israel (see above and cf. Hos 13:10) in the past and sets that example as a self-defining attribute of YHWH. As it does so, it states one of the major issues in this READING, namely, the relationship between YHWH as the savior of Israel and yet also its destroyer (see v. 9; and explanations in vv. 4b-6; 9; 14-15). Verse 4b begins to explain the matter and serves as a signpost to matters discussed in vv. 9-10 and 14:4 — and therefore contributes to the textual cohesion of the READING and the SET of READINGS as a whole.

Verses 4 and 5 are closely bound together by clear repetitions (e.g., the contrastive uses of verbal forms of ידע "know/acknowledge" and ארץ "land," the similar openings אנוכי and אני both "I" [YHWH]). Verse 5 is not only linked to v. 4, but also leads thematically into v. 6. The basic construction of Israel's (hi)storical meta-narrative that the implied author (or narrator) places in YHWH's mouth in vv. 5-6 is consistent with that expressed elsewhere in the book of Hosea (cf. Hos 2:10; 9:10; 10:1-2). First, YHWH "acknowledges" Israel in the desert, in a thirsty land (v. 5; cf. Hos 2:5), that is, YHWH takes Israel under the deity's protection (and control) in the desert (cf. Hos 2:16-17; 9:10; Jer 2:2), where Israel alone would most likely not survive. (On the meaning of ידע as acknowledging in the sense of adopting, taking under protection and control, see Malul, *Knowledge,* 201, 218.) In v. 6a Israel is identified with as well as fed as "sheep" that are kept by YHWH, the shepherd. The area in which this takes place is, of course, not the thirsty land of the desert, but in pastureland, i.e., in the land. (On Israel as YHWH's sheep see Ps 74:1; 79:13; 95:7; 100:3; Ezek 34:31.) But then, when Israel is well fed, it forgets who was feeding it, its shepherd YHWH (cf. Hos 2:10; 10:1-2). Significantly, it is also at the border between the land and the desert that Israel first sins with Baal (see Hos 9:10); see Hos 13:1.

271

In other words, vv. 5-6 evoke, reinforce, and re-present the basic meta-narrative expressed elsewhere in the book in terms appropriate to the literary context in Hos 13:1–14:1 and as part and parcel of this READING.

The basic meta-narrative moves forward in vv. 7-8. Since the sheep (Israel) forget the shepherd (YHWH), the latter undergoes a transformation into various ferocious beasts of prey that will destroy the sheep. The text here expands the imagery present in 5:14. It opens as in 5:14 with the reference to the שחל "lion," but then moves into an image of a swift נמר "leopard" (cf. Hab 1:8; the precise choice of words placed in YHWH's mouth is worth noting, כנמר על דרך אשור "like a leopard I [YHWH] will lurk beside the way"; the word אשור "will lurk" sounds like Assyria; the resulting pun on words conveys a secondary image of YHWH as like Assyria for Israel), then to a דב שכול "a bereaved bear/a she-bear robbed of her cubs" (cf. 2 Sam 17:8; its proverbial image is implied, and hyperbolically punned upon in Prov 17:12), and to a לביא lion or lioness (cf. Isa 5:29; Job 38:39), and ends with the general category of חית השדה "wild beast" (cf. Hos 2:14; Ezek 34:8). The extensive list serves to enhance the rhetorical appeal of the text, focus the readers on the seemingly complete destruction that such a combination of animals will carry out, and, because of the concluding reference to חית השדה, serves at the same time to remind the readers of the text of what is stated in Hos 2:20. In other words, this would not be the end of the road. The destruction will not be total: eventually YHWH will make a covenant with the wild animals, the birds of the air, and the creeping things of the ground and will break the bow, the sword, and war from the land, and as a result Israel will lie down in safety. (On the imagery see Nwaoru, *Imagery*, 150-54; Eidewall, *Grapes*, 195-99; Labuschagne, "Similes," 65-66; on clusters of similes, as in this verse and in v. 3, and its possible ancient near Eastern background see Watson, "Reflexes," 242-43; on Hos 2:20 see Hos 2:3-25 STRUCTURE and Setting.)

On verse 9 see above. Some of the relationships between vv. 1-9 and other texts in the book of Hosea mentioned above are discussed above. Verses 10-11 are kept together by the motif of the king. They revisit and lead to the ideological climax of characterization of kingship. On the approach to kingship reflected and communicated by this READING see Setting.

Verse 12 opens a new subunit (on whose structural hierarchy in different readings of Hos 13:1–14:1 see above). This subunit is united by the theme of Israel's destruction, which is visited and revisited through different images and perspectives. The inner structure of v. 12 is noteworthy. The verse is construed around two word pairs. One of them is common, עון — חטאת "iniquity — sin" (see Hos 4:8; 8:13; 9:9 and many times elsewhere in the HB, e.g., Exod 34:9; Deut 19:15; 1 Sam 20:1; Isa 6:7; 43:24; Jer 50:20; Job 10:6; Ps 32:5; 85:3). The other is based on two qal passive participles beginning with the letter צ, namely, צרור — צפונה "bound up — stored/treasured." Outside these two pairs, and at the center of the structure, stands "Ephraim."

Verse 12 serves as an introduction to the unit (vv. 13:12–14:1) and to a large extent encapsulates and recapitulates in a short memorable saying the sinful situation of Ephraim (/Israel), just before the primary readers are introduced to the last (and final) announcement of judgment against Ephraim (Israel). The emphasis on עָוֹן "iniquity" and חַטָּאת "sin," and the choice of these two terms in particular, are certainly not a matter of chance. The first appears in Hos 4:8; 5:5; 7:1; 8:13; 9:7, 9; 10:10 (Qere); 12:9 and 14:2, 3; and the second either as חַטָּאת or related nominal forms (e.g., חֵטְא) occurs in Hos 4:8; 8:13; 9:9; 10:8; 12:9, and verbal forms appear in 4:7; 8:11; 10:9; 13:2. Cf. Alonso Schökel and Sicre, *Profetas*, 917.

Verse 12 conveys a sense akin to "Ephraim's iniquity is bound up in a bundle" (cf. Isa 8:16; Job 14:17); its sin is stored (cf. Ps 31:20; Prov 2:7; 21:20) (cf. Macintosh, *Hosea*, 542). Whereas Israel may be evanescent (see v. 3), its sin not only is portrayed as well established, well kept, and permanent, but also is possibly preserved as a written document (see Macintosh, *Hosea*, 542; Mays, *Hosea*, 180; Vuillenmier-Bessard, "Osée 13:12"; but ct. with Watson, "Reflexes" 243-46). Within the discourses and literary expectations associated with prophetic literature in general such a statement leads either into an announcement of punishment or some reference to YHWH as forgiving Israel (on the latter, see, among others, Jer 31:34; cf. 2 Chr 6:25, 27). Within the immediate textual context in which v. 12 is situated in the book, it creates an anticipation of divine punishment.

The next verses (Hos 13:13–14:1) bring forward a set of different, though related images that allow the readers to imagine such a punishment, and to envisage its harshness as leading metaphorically to Ephraim's/Israel's death. Verse 13 refers the readers to a general metaphorical realm of human fertility, whereas v. 15 refers to the fertility of the fields. In both cases, the emphasis is on failure and the one who fails (i.e., Ephraim/Israel). Verse 14 links vv. 13 and 15 by means of a theological comment about YHWH and YHWH's relationship with Israel/Ephraim. Verse 14:1 concludes the section with an image of a (foolishly) chosen future of death, expressed through the death of both mothers and children, that is, the future of Israel/Ephraim.

Both vv. 13 and 14 share a stylistic feature: they carry more than one meaning, but these meanings reinforce each other. Thus the multivalence of the text not only draws the attention of the readers, and contributes to the rereadability of the text (see Ben Zvi, *Obadiah*, 4 et passim), but also is placed at the service of the same substantial meaning by a process of converging partial readings informing each other. Verse 13 is written in such a way that it either connotes or denotes the following:

(a) "The pains of a woman giving birth come upon him (cf. Jer 30:6). He, he is an unwise son. When the time comes he will not endure giving birth" (cf. Isa 37:3; cf. Macintosh, *Hosea*, 543-46; Simian-Yofre, *Desierto*, 165).

(b) "The pains of a woman giving birth come for him, but he, he is an unwise son; for the time comes when he shall not present himself where children break forth" (cf. KJV, NAB).

The first meaning asks the readership to imagine male Ephraim/Israel as a woman who painfully dies in the process of giving birth — many women died giving birth in antiquity. In the second case, Ephraim is a son who not only brings pain to his mother at the time of birth, but whose behavior leads to both their deaths. The two meanings belong to the same metaphorical realm. They also provide a sense of completeness by covering the two possible human roles — mother, child being born — involved in giving birth — for obvious reasons, there is no room for the "father" in this metaphorical setting. As the birthing scene leads to the same result (i.e., death), no matter which perspective is taken, the text conveys a sense of completeness through convergence to the portrayal of Ephraim's (/Israel's) death. In other words, a multiplicity of images leads to a kind of univocal message. The latter, in turn, raises within these discourses ideological or theological questions that, significantly, are dealt with in the immediate textual vicinity of the verse. For instance, the readers of the book know about a third personage who from their ideological perspective is involved in the process of giving birth, YHWH (cf., among many others, Isa 66:7-9). Thus, v. 13 carries a discursive thread that calls as it were for a reference to YHWH and YHWH's position about the suffering (and eventual "death") of Ephraim/ Israel in the metaphorical birth scene.

Another important element in the characterization of Ephraim, no matter which partial approach to the verse is taken by the readers in a particular reading of the text, the "son" Ephraim/Israel is portrayed as לא חכם "not wise"; in fact, so unwise as to resist birthing with the obvious consequences that follow. The portrayal of the "son" Ephraim/Israel here recalls and stands in contrast with that of Hos 11:1. On the one hand, one may say that one points to the "son" at the beginning of the relationship with YHWH, and the other to the son towards the end of the monarchic period. Yet both are examples of trans-temporal Israel, and Israel was also conceived at times as liable to sin/foolishness from the beginning (see Hosea chapters 1, 4, 12 and discussions there; on the characterization of Israel as foolish in the book of Hosea see Buss, "Tragedy and Comedy," 73-75).

Moreover, the imagery of birth evokes a potential connotation of a new beginning (cf. Isa 66:7; Ps 22:11; 71:6); the very prospective of a new beginning is nullified here by the foolish character of the son. In this sense, this discourse leads by necessity to matters such as those that are answered in Hos 14:5 (cf. Hos 2:16-25; 11:10 and see commentary there). Furthermore, from the perspective of the rereaders the explicit reference to Israel/Ephraim as לא חכם "not wise" is reminiscent of language present in Hos 14:10. On this matter see Setting.

Turning to v. 14, among the main meanings that this verse likely denoted or connoted to its intended and primary readerships one may mention the following:

(a) Shall I [YHWH] save them from the power of sheol? Shall I redeem them from death? O death, where are your plagues? O sheol [netherworld], where is your pestilence? Pity (or relief) is hidden from my eyes.

(b) I [YHWH] shall save them from the power of sheol. I shall redeem them from death. O death, where are your plagues? O sheol, where is your pestilence? Pity (or relief) is hidden from my eyes.

(c) From the power of sheol I [YHWH] would have saved them; from death I would have redeemed them. O death, where are your plagues? O sheol, where is your pestilence? Pity (or relief) is hidden from my eyes.

(d) From the power of sheol I [YHWH] would have saved them; from death I would have redeemed them. [But] I am your plague, [I will be for you] death. I am your pestilence, [I will be for you] sheol [cf. Isa 5:14]. Pity (or "relief") is hidden from my eyes.

(e) From power of sheol I [YHWH] used to save them [cf. Hos 7:13]; from death I used to redeemed them. [But] I am your plague, [I will be for you] death. I am your pestilence, [I will be for you] sheol [cf. Isa 5:14]. Pity (or "relief") is hidden from my eyes.

(f) Shall I [YHWH] save them from the power of sheol? Shall I redeem them from death? Ah! death, where are your plagues? Ah! sheol where is your pestilence? Pity (or relief) is hidden from my eyes.

(g) From the power of sheol I [YHWH] would have saved them; from death I would have redeemed them. Ah! death, where are your plagues? Ah! sheol, where is your pestilence? Pity (or relief) is hidden from my eyes.

(h) From the power of sheol I [YHWH] used to saved them; from death I used to redeemed them. I am your plague, O death. I am your pestilence, O sheol. Pity (or "relief") is hidden from my eyes.

(i) From the power of sheol I [YHWH] would have saved them; from death I would have redeemed them. I am your plague, O death. I am your pestilence, O sheol. Pity (or "relief") is hidden from my eyes.

(The term "your plague/pestilence" evoked also the meaning "your words.")

It bears particular note that all of these meanings (whether denoted or connoted) converge in one main message, and each contributes from its slightly different perspective a certain background or image supporting the central message: YHWH will punish Israel/Ephraim in the most severe way, even if the deity is surely powerful enough to deliver them. This is an excellent case of extended multivocality used as a rhetorical tool to reinforce an essentially univocal message. In fact, even the most positive possible reading of 14a, and even 14a-ba, can only reinforce the sense of doom over Israel given 14bβ and the clear context in which the verse stands. Scholars who understand the verse as a promise of deliverance — some of whom, but certainly not all, are influenced in part by 1 Cor 15:55 — must decontextualize, that is, remove the verse from its particular place in the book of Hosea. Notice, for instance, the marginal note in the NJPSV, "this verse would read well before 14.5." Of course, the verse does *not* stand before Hos 14:5, nor is there any text of the book of Hosea in which it stood in that position. For further examples and a critique of such positions see Eidewall, *Grapes*, 201-2. Yet, the same blurred, misleading echo of a sound — or seemingly erroneous connotation of a promise — of deliverance within this precise textual READING, becomes a resounding voice from the perspective of the book as a whole (see below).

Verse 15 asks the readers to imagine the matter of YHWH's punishment of Israel/Ephraim through a different metaphorical realm, that of fertility or, better, lack thereof, of the fields. As it serves its rhetorical purpose, it alludes to and reshapes motifs present elsewhere in the book, and thus creates a set of signposts informing each other and shaping communicative messages that encapsulate much of the message concerning the divine judgment against Israel through the process. For instance, in Hos 12:2 Ephraim foolishly pursues קדים "the east wind"; in Hos 13:15 קדים comes to destroy Ephraim. Moreover, in Hos 4:12 and 5:4 רוח זנונים "a spirit"/"wind" of promiscuity/whoredom causes Israel to sin and precludes it from returning to YHWH; in Hos 13:15 it is רוח ה' "YHWH's wind" that brings punishment over Israel/Ephraim (of course, רוח ה' also conveys the sense of "a mighty wind"). Furthermore, in Hos 13:5 YHWH acknowledges Israel/Ephraim in the מדבר "desert/wilderness" at the beginning of their relationship (cf. 2:16-17; 9:10); in Hos 13:15 it is YHWH's wind that rises from the מדבר to punish Ephraim/Israel. One may also notice that according to Hos 10:6, within the context of the failure of the calf worship, ויבוש ישראל "Israel will be ashamed [of its counsel]"; Hos 13:15 contains the expression ויבוש מקורו "its [Ephraim's/Israel's] fountain shall dry up" (for YHWH as Israel's fountain see Jer 2:13; Ps 68:27). The word ויחרב "it will dry up" in 13:5 also carries a pun on the word חרב "sword" in 14:1 (and elsewhere in the book), and together they shape a set of different images (drought, war) each of which from its own perspective points to the same result, namely, destruction for Israel, and all together they provide a sense of completeness (see above). (On 13:15 and 13:13 see below.) Although each of these instances may be due to random chance, three observations are in order. First, from the perspective of the readership it does not matter at all whether the signposts were intentionally created by the actual human author of the book, for they do not interact with such an author nor are privy to his (and less likely, her) inner thoughts. Rather, they read and reread the book of Hosea, and as they did so they construed their implied author or communicator, whose intentions they discerned in the book. Second, it is unlikely that such a heavy concentration of signposts within a single verse is due to random causes. Third, it is unlikely that ancient communities of literati that carefully read, reread, and studied the book would have "missed" the presence of such a concentration. Needless to say, the discussion above carries clear implications concerning Genre and Setting.

As for style, the mentioned tendency towards multiplicity of converging meanings in the preceding verses in this subunit appears also in v. 15. It reads כי הוא בין אחים יפריא (following the MT of the Aleppo Codex, and other codices, pace BHS that reads בן אחים and see below), and, of course, it carries a pun on the word אפרים "Ephraim" (see יפריא). Among the meanings conveyed by this expression, either by denotation or connotation, one may mention:

(a) "since he is the one who behaves willfully among brothers" (see Macintosh, *Hosea*, 550-51);
(b) "though he be really fruitful among his brothers/fellows" (cf. NAB; Barthélemy, *Critique Textuelle*, vol. III, 617-20);
(c) "since he is the one who behaves willfully among the reeds"; and
(d) "though he be really fruitful among the reeds" (cf. NRSV, NJPSV, NASB; Simian-Yofre, *Desierto*, 165-66).

When the text is understood as containing a reference to "reeds" and, therefore, an allusion to Egypt, the text plays with the images of the beginning of Israel, including and informing the social memories referred to by 13:4-5 (and numerous others places in the book of Hosea). (When this approach to the text is taken, the reference to the destructive east wind may be taken as a metaphorical reverse of the east wind in Exod 14:21; cf. Exod 10:13; cf. Sweeney, *Twelve Prophets,* 134-36.) Readings a-b may evoke in the readers social memories associated with Jacob (cf. 12:4), with Ephraim as compared to other tribes, and above all, with monarchic Israel as compared to other kingdoms (i.e., its "fellows"; cf. Barthélemy, *Critique Textuelle,* vol. III, 20).

In addition, there is evidence of a tradition of reading v. 15 that eventually influenced some masoretic mss., according to which the Hebrew text reads הוא בן rather than הוא בין (cf. also the Tg). It seems that this tradition develops further the system of signposts mentioned above by linking this verse to v. 13; see there הוא בן "he, he is a son." The unwise son (הוא בן לא חכם) would thus be compared with "the son of fellows/brothers" (הוא בן אחים), that is, the son of other kingdoms, the one who is subservient to foreigners, who considers them as "fathers" for himself.

The last verse in this subunit and the READING as a whole opens with the expression תאשם שמרון כי מרתה באלהיה "she (Samaria) will bear guilt [root אשם] for [ב] she has rebelled against her God." As mentioned above, it creates an envelope around the entire READING through its use of a word from the root אשם "bear guilt," and the relationship between the summary statement of the death of Ephraim (13:1) and images of Samaria's children being dashed in pieces and their pregnant women ripped open. The image here is reminiscent of that in Hos 10:14, but it is also part of a common thread in the book of Hosea in which images of birth, mothers, and the production of children, or the children themselves, are impaired or destroyed to illustrate the point of the physical destruction of Israel's future (e.g., 4:5; 9:14; 14:1 and cf. 4:10; 9:16 and of course, Hosea 1–3). Such a thread culminates in many ways in Hos 14:1. This climax serves as an appropriate background and counterfoil to the final message of hope conveyed by Hos 14:2-9 and the book as a whole (see Hos 14:7). The latter as such conveys the message that YHWH will indeed redeem Israel from the power of death and sheol (see 13:14), as it were, for Hos 14:2-9 communicates that following YHWH's punishment of Israel/Ephraim, which is to be imagined as death, YHWH will raise the people again (cf. Ezekiel 37). The literary and rhetorical device of alluding to meanings that are obviously incorrect within one setting and reading approach, but that still carry an important ideological truth when seen from a different perspective, is not uncommon in prophetic books; it is substantially used in, for instance, the book of Jonah (see Ben Zvi, *Signs of Jonah, passim*).

Numerous proposals for emendations of the text of Hosea 13 have been advanced. In general these proposals tend to diminish the multiplicity of meanings carried by the text, and, conversely, some are motivated by a sense that the text must communicate a clear and unequivocal sense (e.g., the proposed replacement of the crucial multivalent אֱהִי in v. 14 with either אַיֵּה "where?" — a common proposal — or אָהָהּ "ah!," as proposed by Alonso Schökel and Sicre (*Profetas,* 917). For many of these proposals see BHS (and see also Driver, "Linguistic and Textual Problems," 163-64). For a summary, discussion, and critique of many of these proposals see Barthélemy, *Critique Textuelle,* vol. III,

607-20, and the textual discussions in Macintosh, *Hosea.* It is also worth noting that some ancient versions seem to differ substantially from the MT at some points; see, for instance, the LXX of Hos 13:5, 15. Whether the matter is to be understood in terms of exegetical activity or as pointing to a different Hebrew text is beyond the scope of this commentary.

In addition, claims concerning the secondary character of some subunits or words have been advanced by several redaction-critical scholars. (Of course, these claims assume the existence of a "primary," Hoseanic text.) For instance, Jeremias (*Hosea,* 162-63) considers a portion of v. 2 and the entirety of v. 3 as later Judahite expansions to the text. Davies (*Hosea,* 285) rejects Jeremias's position, but unlike Jeremias, he includes as a possible addition "v. 4, which is an unnecessary and somewhat awkward introduction to vv. 5-8, and consists of phrases paralleled elsewhere, and in some cases only outside Hosea." (He refers here in particular to v. 4b and cf. Isa 45:5, 21.) Davies also maintains that the last line in 14:1 may also be an addition to the text. Emmerson (*Hosea,* 146-51, and esp. 150-51) maintains that Hos 13:2 in its present form reflects the work (and bias) of a Judahite redactor, mainly because of the expression זבחי אדם (on the meanings of the expression, see Setting, below). According to Yee, Hos 13:1-11, 14 belong to a postmonarchic redactor (R2), unlike Hos 12:12-13, 15 and 14:1, which she associates with the earliest Hosean tradition (Yee, *Composition,* 248-59, 317). Good ("Composition," 53) summarizes his understanding of the redactional history of the passage in the following terms: "13:1-8, to which vv. 9-11 had already been joined, was added mainly because of a connection with the preceding poem, 12:3-15, secondarily perhaps by a verbal association with 11:2. To this subcomplex was added an already compiled subcomplex, 13:12–14:1, which came to complete the complex by its thematic relationship to the opening poem, secondarily by some verbal associations with 13:1-8." On the matter of "subcomplexes" existing independently and prior to the book of Hosea, see Genre, below.

Genre

Hosea 13 is a prophetic, didactic READING, that is, it is a literary unit within the prophetic book of Hosea that shows textually inscribed, discursive markers that were likely to suggest to its intended and primary readerships that they were supposed to or at least invited to read it as a cohesive unit, within the frame of the book of Hosea as a whole. It is also part and parcel of a SET of READINGS (Hos 12:1–14:9) within that book, but this does not mean that the readers are not supposed to approach it in a manner informed by sections of the book of Hosea outside this SET.

Most often Hos 13:1-3 is considered an announcement, saying, speech, or oracle of judgment (e.g., Wolff, *Hosea,* 222; for an exception see Franklyn, "Oracular Cursing," for whom, it is a "curse oracle"; see also Franklyn, *Prophetic Cursing,* passim). It is true, of course, that the intended readership of the book is asked to read a report of the words of a speaker (YHWH) who first condemns Ephraim and then announces the results that follow such a behavior (i.e.,

Ephraim's punishment). It is a matter of interpretation, however, whether the readership is supposed to understand the condemnation as an "indictment" and the description of that which causally follows (לכן) Ephraim's actions as a "verdict" (cf. Mays, *Hosea*, 171-72). This kind of terminology assumes that the readership of the book is asked to imagine a "court scene" in which YHWH brings claims against Ephraim (i.e., the deity serves as prosecutor). Then YHWH moves to read the verdict (i.e., the deity serves as the judge), and finally — although not explicitly stated in the text, implicitly assumed by the readership — YHWH moves to execute the verdict against Ephraim (i.e., the deity serves as the executioner). Although it is possible that the text may have evoked such an image, it is at least as likely that the text construes a situation in which the speaker (YHWH) reports about and instructs an implied (and never identified) addressee or addressees of the fate of Ephraim and its reasons. Even from a formal perspective, one may notice that Ephraim is not addressed in the second person; rather, it is always addressed in the third person in vv. 1-3. YHWH, given the deity's power, could be imagined therefore as both a royal figure and a knowledgeable, authoritative teacher. Certainly, it is also possible that the text may have evoked both images in the readership.

At the same time, it is worth stressing two matters: First, the text may, and most likely did, evoke background images within its primary readership, as any piece of literature does, but the text cannot be identified with that which it may evoke in the readership. Even when a literary text is meant to call to mind a court scene, no such text is a court proceeding, and it does not have to be fully consistent with such proceedings. After all, familiarization is as important as defamiliarization for rhetorical purposes, and most often both appear in different ways in descriptions of typical scenes. (On these matters, see Ben Zvi, "Prophetic Book"). In other words, one may argue that Hos 13:1-3 *may evoke* within a particular readership *some image of court proceedings* — even if it defamiliarizes it at the very least. (One may note that the accused is not addressed and is not allowed to state anything; nor is it clear at all that he or she is present during the hearing and that the wronged "person" is the accuser, judge, and executioner. Is the intended readership supposed to construe these features as normal court proceedings?) This, however, would be an argument about the power of the text to recall familiar scenes related to the life of the community of the readership and its defamiliarization. It would not be an argument about the "genre" of Hos 13:1-3.

Second, as the use of the term "Hos 13:1-3" implies, these verses do not exist outside the book of Hosea. They are an integral part of this book. Moreover, and as importantly, the readership is not asked to read Hos 13:1-3 as a decontextualized, independent saying that has no relation to the other texts in the READING or in the book as a whole. The opposite is clearly true. As a result, genre considerations that could have been relevant *had* the text that appears in Hos 13:1-3 been an independent, oral saying are not necessarily relevant to the study of *Hos 13:1-3*.

Of course, genre considerations that apply to the interaction between the readership and the book of Hosea (literary genres exist in the interface between text and reader) do not necessarily apply to oral communications, such as the one proposed by some scholars between their (version of the) historical prophet and his (reconstructed) historical addressees in the course of which the historical speaker pronounced the words that appear in Hos 13:1-3, among other words — one would assume that the prophetic speech would not have been so brief so as to include only about thirty-five words or take only a few seconds.

Similar considerations apply to Hos 13:5-8, which is also generally considered an announcement, saying speech, or oracle of judgment. The main difference is only that Ephraim is now addressed initially in the second person (5a) and then in the third person. The reference to Israel in the second person in 5a serves affective purposes. It contributes to and strongly reinforces the identification of the readership with those whom YHWH "acknowledged" in the desert.

Of course, literary texts may and are likely to use "formulae" common within the discourse/s of the community. They may also appeal to them, but not necessarily reflect them verbatim. For instance, v. 4a (= Hos 12:10a) most likely reminded the intended and primary rereaders of a relatively common "divine self-identification formula" within their discourses (see Exod 20:2; Deut 5:6; Ps 81:11; see also discussion in Hos 12:1-15 STRUCTURE).

Setting

The setting of the writing and primary reading of this, or any portion of the (present) book of Hosea for that matter, is the same as that of the book as a whole. Both writers and readers are among the very few literati of Yehud. This READING is indicative of many aspects of the world of knowledge and discourse within which it was written and which permeates it.

Several motifs reflected and expressed in this READING shed light on the intellectual setting shared by the mentioned literati. Other motifs illustrate the way in which the world portrayed in the book and, therefore, the setting of the speaker's words within the world of the book are described. For instance, the reference to Baal/baal stands at the center of the summary of the cultic offenses as presented in v. 1. As verse 2 develops the matter, the images that are brought to bear, and particularly those of the calves, are clearly reminiscent of images of "improper" Yahwistic worship (for the calf/calves see Exod 32:4, 8, 19, 20, 24, 35; Deut 9:16, 21; 1 Kgs 12:28-29; 2 Kgs 10:29; 17:16; Hos 8:5, 6; 10:5; Ps 106:19; Neh 9:18; for the association between מסכה "molten image" and the calves, see, for instance, Exod 32:4, 8; Deut 9:12, 16; and for the use of molten images for YHWH's cult, see also Judg 17:3-4). This is consistent with the general and generic use of the term "Baal/baal/baals" in the book of Hosea as general code words for "baal-type" deities. It is worth noting that this general and generic use allows not only multiple readings under different circumstances but also multiple identifications of the deity: "foreign" deities as well as the YHWH that the wrongdoers imagine the deity to be and which they do worship within the world portrayed in the book. The crucial ideological and rhetorical matter for the text was that Israel/Ephraim should not have been involved in this type of cult. This being so, the text is not concerned with the precise identity of

THE INDIVIDUAL UNITS

the deity referred to as Baal in v. 1 — whether it was Baal Shamem or YHWH as wrongly conceived and worshiped, or any other "baal" deity. Yet as it does so, the text informs the readership that worshiping YHWH in the wrong way (such as northern Israelites did during the monarchic period, from the perspective of the speaker and the intended readership) is tantamount to worshiping Baal and forsaking YHWH, and that the YHWH that the wrongdoers imagine the deity to be is in fact (or comparable to) a "baal," or a "foreign deity." The aim of the text is, of course, the socialization of the postmonarchic rereadership.

For general considerations on the matter of Baal identities and their influence on the supposed "historicity" of the world portrayed in the book see Hos 2:3-25 Setting. It is worth noting as the book of Hosea rejects "baalistic" worship and "baal," it clearly and emphatically associates the attributes of a fertility deity with YHWH; cf. Boshoff, "Yahweh as God of Nature" and see Hos 2:3-25 Setting.

Given that Baal/baals imagery in the book of Hosea and in the Hebrew Bible focuses on meteorological/fertility attributes, it is also not by chance that the readers are asked to imagine Israel's destruction in terms of mist/clouds and dew, which are, of course, weather phenomena directly associated with the fertility of the field (cf. Hos 14:6; Ezek 1:28; Job 26:8; and also Ps 147:8). Significantly, it also brings the metaphor of מֹץ "chaff," which is construed as the opposite pole of "stability and fruitfulness" — and at times associated with the wicked (see Job 21:17-18; Ps 1:3-4 and cf. Ps 35:4-5).

Finally, and particularly concerning the image of the past that the text projects and against which it sets the speaker's words — within the world of the book — it is worth noting that the description of the wrongful worship concludes "of them, they [impersonal] say: זבחי אדם עגלים ישקון. The Hebrew expression selected here was chosen because of its ability to convey more than one meaning. It probably denotes here either "people who worship/sacrifice, kiss calves" or "people who worship the most, kiss calves," and most likely communicates both meanings. (For a similar construction with אדם see Isa 29:19; see also Ezek 7:24, GKC § 132c; JM § 141d.) In other words, the text first points at those involved in the sacrificial process (priests?) or to superlative worshipers, in the sense of people who make numerous sacrifices to the deity (cf. Job 1:5), and then denigrates them by stating that they kiss, venerate, (the) calves, that is, idols made by human hands. Thus, either the "sacrificers" or the most pious people of the country are associated with idolatry, and their offerings become an insult to YHWH. (Significantly, these "most pious" people can only be construed as wealthy; cf. Job 1:5.) The text, understood this way, is to some extent reminiscent of Exod 32:8 — notice the reference in the latter to the molten image (עצב), to the calf (עגל) to whom sacrifices are offered. Moreover, "kissing" and "bowing down" may serve as related social markers (cf. Exod 18:7) — and are consistent with the general theme of the READING and the usual characterization of cultic wrongdoing that most often includes the topos of wrongful offerings. Understandings of the expression according to these lines are present already in Radak, and among contemporary scholars, see Macintosh, *Hosea*, 522-24. (Notice J. Wesley's note to the verse, "Let all that

281

bring their offerings to these idols, worship and adore, and shew they do so by kissing the calves.") At the same time, the Hebrew expression surely connotes to its readers, at least, a meaning akin to "those who slaughter/sacrifice human beings, kiss calves." On the one hand, the text so understood is ironic and contributes to the foolish characterization of Israel. Rather than slaughter calves (for food) they kiss them; and rather than kiss human beings, they slaughter them. It is a kind of mockery that also creates distance between the speaker in the text and above all the readership of the book that identifies with the speaker on the one hand and the character described in the book on the other (cf. Ibn Ezra according to the "Accepted Commentary"; see Simon, *Abraham Ibn Ezra's Two Commentaries,* 122-23, and cf. the "Alternative Commentary," Simon, *op. cit.,* 290; Buss, "Tragedy and Comedy," 73-75). In addition, although the reference to "slaughtering" human beings does not necessarily demand that they be slaughtered for cultic purposes, the context would support such an interpretation. As a result the text mentioned above communicates, in addition to the meanings mentioned above, a construction of the past in which the worshipers of the calves carry out human sacrifices. This construction of the past is comparable to that in Ps 106:38. Verse 2b shows an excellent case of the use of multiplicity of meanings, denoted and connoted, to portray the worshipers in a strongly negative light, from different perspectives (e.g, "those who offer sacrifices, kiss calves," "those who offer sacrifices the most [or who are truly worshipers] kiss calves," "those slaughter human beings, but kiss calves," "those who offer human sacrifice, kiss calves"). These multiple and partial images contribute threads to the construction of the past in which the world of the book is set. (This multi-valence of the text is not present in the LXX, which shows an imperative formulation, "Sacrifice, men. . . ." The LXX reading is preferred by some scholars; see NRSV, RSV.) (For a summary, and an evaluation of interpretations of the expression, see Barthélemy, *Critique Textuelle,* vol. III, 607-9; cf. Emmerson, *Hosea,* 146-51.)

In verses 10-11 YHWH reportedly repudiates the office of king as one of a false, improper savior (in contrast to YHWH, who is the only real savior). Moreover, YHWH does so from the very outset of kingship in Israel, in a manner that evokes the memory of the events narrated in 1 Sam 8:6-22 (cf. the choice of words in 1 Sam 8:6 and in Hos 13:10, and see also 13:11; cf. Hos 8:4). Further, the text rejects not only the office of the king alone, but also the system of royal high officers that are part and parcel of any monarchic structure of government (see Hos 13:10). It is worth noting that the text does not suggest a worldly alternative but leaves the target readership with a sense that a non-royal leadership that acknowledges and trusts YHWH as their only patron, and socializes Israel to follow YHWH's ways, including proper worship — of course, as both are understood by the implied author of the book that the literati construct through their continuous rereading of the book — would be a worthy leadership. Significantly, all these traits apply to the literati themselves, at least within their own discourses.

Of course, the book of Hosea also includes Hos 3:5. But the text there reflects and communicates a position consistent with an expectation for a future Davide who will not be another king to reign on earth but an elevated, messianic figure whose rule is set in the distant, idyllic future that will be realized one day (see discussion of 3:5; and see also 2:2 — see commentary there). Until these days come, the book suggests that which is required is a leadership such as the one mentioned above.

In the process of continuously rereading the book, the characterization of Ephraim/Israel as לא חכם "not wise" in v. 13 recalls the statement in Hos 14:10. Significantly, the intended readership of the book is construed as diametrically opposite to "son" Israel/Ephraim as portrayed in this READING. This is consistent with the tendency noted above to shape some discursive distance between the readership and the Israel portrayed in the book (see the mocking mentioned above, and see Buss, "Tragedy and Comedy," 73-75). Of course, this is a matter of balance. Both are Israel, that is, manifestations of trans-temporal Israel, but they were not construed nor could have been construed by the readership of the book as entirely similar. The literati for whom the book was written read it and learned from it about YHWH's condemnation of Ephraim/Israel. As they did so, they identified themselves with YHWH and YHWH's positions and as ideologically opposite to the Israel portrayed in the book. The wise literati thus construed themselves not only as "wise" enough to read and understand the book, but also as, and perhaps in part because of that, capable of enduring birth and well positioned for birth, that is, for renewal (cf. Hos 13:13, see STRUCTURE).

Hosea 13 contributes substantially to the characterization of the language of the godly speaker as one that carries multiple meanings, and as one that only those able to ponder its multilayered messages (cf. Hos 14:10) are able to understand fully. As a result, the text hints at a removal of the setting of the communication of meaning between YHWH and the people from (a) a one-time event of divine oral speech aimed at some hearing audience to (b) one of a careful study of YHWH's words.

In addition, as in most READINGS in the book, the verse contributes to the characterization of YHWH's language as somewhat odd in relation to the deity's language in other prophetic texts set in the monarchic period. One may mention, for instance, (a) the hapax legomenon רתת "tremble" in v. 1 (the root is well attested in Mishnaic Hebrew and Aramaic [see Jastrow, *Dictionary*, 1504b] — and once in Qumran [1QHa, col. xii.33], but nowhere else in the Hebrew Bible; this word and v. 1a in general seem to have caused trouble for the translator of the LXX; see Joosten, "Exegesis," 66); (b) the hapax legomenon תלאבות "drought" in v. 5; and (c) the word קטב "destruction" that appears only in Deut 32:24; Isa 28:2; and Ps 91:6. (Yoo [*Israelian Hebrew*, 147-57] considers these and other examples as markers of Israelian Hebrew [cf. Szabó, "Textual Problems," 524]. On these matters see INTRODUCTION.)

As is the case in other READINGS in the book, the world portrayed in this READING is not anchored in any narrow historical setting, or better, in any narrow setting associated with the readership's construction of particular events in the past. No historical events or individuals are mentioned in this READING, nor are any festivals or particular cultic occasions. (Franklyn [*Prophetic Cursing*] associates the verse with "Hosea's cursing at a regionalized festival of the New Moon" [quotation from p. 176]; Sweeney [*Twelve Prophets*, esp. 93-94] associates Hos 9:1–14:1 with Sukkot. See Hos 12:1-15 Setting.)

The literary world shaped in the READING — to be clearly distinguished from the world of intended and primary rereadership of the book of Hosea — is set in a period in which Samaria has not yet been destroyed, and in which there is still a king of Israel, but Israel is already "dead" (cf. 13:1). The fall of the northern polity, the massacre of its children and women, the "disappearance" as it were of Israel are all certain, and they will be manifested soon from the temporal perspective of the speaker in the book.

Scholars who focus on the historical Hosea, as opposed to the character in the book or the book itself, tend to take the sayings they attribute to the prophet out of their *Sitz im Buch* and attempt to date them within the period of time that they assign to the historical prophet. For instance, Davies (*Hosea*, 284-85) acknowledges that vv. 1-3 "could refer to almost any stage of the prophet's ministry" and suggests that vv. 9-11 fit the situation in 724 BCE, but vv. 12-16 fit an earlier period. The reason, according to Davies (*Hosea*, 285), is that "Israel has enjoyed a period of prosperity (v. 15) and needs to be reminded that the evil of the past has not been quietly forgotten (v. 12)." Moreover, according to him (*op. cit.,* 285): ". . . a final catastrophe symbolized by the east wind will soon come, from which Yahweh has no intention of rescuing them (v. 14). This seems to fit the time around Shalmanesser V's accession in 727. . . ."

It is worth stressing that very often the sayings themselves are interwoven into a narrative of late monarchic Israel that is used to date them. The process is therefore circular, namely, the abstracted sayings are dated according to their perceived consistency with a historical narrative that is shaped to a large extent by the sayings themselves, as they are reconstructed and interpreted by the scholar. Wolff provides a good illustration of this type of narrative:

> We have noted that this scene's accusations differ from earlier ones in that they repeatedly allude to previous threats upon Israel's life which did not lead to her renewal: 13:1, 7, 13. In the light of this, it *must* [emphasis added] be concluded that the great danger of 733 lies far in the past and that a phase of relaxed political tension has led to a new increase of transgression (vv. 2, 12) which went hand in hand with political optimism (vv. 14a, 15a). This optimism seems to have been especially strengthened by Israel's dependence upon Egypt after the year 725. However, Hosea [i.e., the historical prophet] already sees the dangerous storm approaching from the East under the leadership of Shalmanesser V (cf. vv. 15b, 3, 8, 9 with 2 Kgs 17:5). Indeed, with its questions and pronouncements in vv. 10 and 11, this scene is correctly understood *only* [emphasis added] if King Hoshea ben Elah had already been imprisoned by the Assyrians. The seldom-mentioned city of Samaria (otherwise only in 7:1; 8:5; 10:5, 7) and the unique announcement of its inhabitants' death points to the same period when the siege on the capital had already begun. Accordingly, the sayings from this scene were very probably proclaimed around the year 724. (Wolff, *Hosea,* 224)

The narrative proposed here is based in part on Wolff's reading of the mentioned sayings, and the same holds true for the similar narrative implied, although not fully developed, in Davies's comments. Moreover, these historical narratives not only are far from the gist of the READING itself, but also run contrary to it. The READING is clearly presented as not anchored in any narrow particular historical period nor associated with a particular event — notice that there is no textual reference to Shalmanesser V, King Hoshea, or his misadventures, or any similar figure or event (and contrast with the book of Jeremiah and references there to historical figures and events), but rather anchored into a literary SET of READINGS and the book as a whole — as demonstrated by numerous markers of textual coherence. The approach represented by Wolff and Davies goes exactly the opposite direction. It separates the READING into individual components, disassociates them from their *Sitz im Buch,* and strongly anchors them in very clear historical events.

Even if one puts aside matters of circular thinking, of the decontextualizing process by which reconstructed oral sayings are created, and of reading against the gist of the book, even within their own discourse, the proposals mentioned above are problematic. First, references to a treasure to be taken from a defeated or to be defeated nation do not have to be contemporaneous with a particular period of prosperity. Second, if one assumes beforehand that the historical prophet proclaimed sayings so critical of society and its leadership, then why *must* a saying like "I give you kings in my wrath and remove them in my fury" (v. 11) be dated to a period slightly after the imprisonment of King Hoshea the son of Elah? Other scholars (e.g., Simian-Yofre; Ginsberg) who also associate the sayings with a historical prophet have proposed different and earlier dates.

Intention

The general intention of Hosea 13:1–14:1 is to communicate and reinforce the positions and the general horizon of thought of the authorship and readership as represented in these texts (see Setting) and to socialize the literati through their shared reading of the material and the larger society through the literati's reading to others of this reading. The process of socialization involves in this case the shaping of shared images through which these literati could metaphorically visualize and construct the fall of Israel/Ephraim and YHWH's role in the process.

This READING serves above all to prepare the readers of the book of Hosea for Hos 14:2-9 and the hopeful conclusion of the book. Paradoxically, the emphatic description of Israel's "death" serves rhetorically not only to convey to the postmonarchic rereadership the magnitude of the future reversal promised in the next READING (14:2-9), but also to reinterpret their very existence as a community of readers of these texts in the most positive terms and as a sign of hope. After all, not only is Israel not dead, though YHWH would have been more than justified in destroying it as the text claims, but it has a great future awaiting it. Yet, the text ideologically construes the readership, i.e., Israel, as a group with an intense tragic consciousness. This is a didactic READING that educates and socializes the readership so as to develop a powerful awareness of a sinful past that could be overcome, but only by YHWH's grace and the most severe punishment and suffering. It promotes a self-identification of the group as one that has lived, sinned, and painfully "died" in the past, and whose present, for which they should be grateful, is a far-diminished version of Israel in worldly terms and stands as a far cry from any image of "restored Israel." In other words, it promotes a self-identification of present Israel as an Israel that still has not healed from, or overcome the deep wounds created by, its sinful past. Yet, at the same time, this present Israel is clearly different from monarchic Israel because of this tragic consciousness, which the latter did not and could not have possessed. It is not surprising therefore that this READING also promotes a balance between the readership's identification with and separation from monarchic Israel. It reinforces the former's self-identification with the wise, as opposed to the latter, and even hints that the main attributes of the primary readership/literati are those necessary for good or even godly leadership, as opposed to those of the failed monarchic elite.

To be sure, this READING is not the only authoritative text in post-monarchic Israel/Yehud that instills a tragic consciousness and a strong awareness of a sinful past. These matters are central to the literati's discourses of the time. Similar lessons were learned from other READINGS within the book of Hosea. The matter is discussed here because this READING is meant to highlight and summarize the sinful past of Israel/Ephraim and its consequences, before the text moves into Hos 14:2-9 — and beyond other books within and beyond the genre of "prophetic book" (cf. Polak, "David's Kingship"). This fact, however, only highlights the importance of this social intention of the READING and contributes to our understanding of why there was so much literary/ideological activity among the few literati who wrote and for whom most of the biblical books in their present form were primarily written (cf. Ben Zvi, "Introduction: Writings, Speeches, and the Prophetic Books"; idem, "Urban Centre").

Incidentally, it is intriguing to compare the substantial convergence on these matters of numerous literary works, each with its own perspective, and on a much smaller scale of convergence, of multiple readings of the same text, each with its own perspective, which is a stylistic device clearly present in this READING.

Bibliography

E. Bons, "La signification de ARKOS APOROUMENH en LXX OSÉE XIII 8," *VT* 51 (2001) 1-8; W. S. Boshoff, "Yahweh as God of Nature. Elements of the Concept of God in the Book of Hosea," *JNSL* 18 (1992) 13-24; M. J. Buss, "Tragedy and Comedy in Hosea," *Semeia* 32 (1984) 71-82; J. Day, "A Case of Inner Biblical Scriptural Interpretation. The Dependence of Isaiah xxvi. 13-xxvii. 11 on Hosea xiii. 4 — xiv 10 (Eng. 9) and Its Relevance to Some Theories of the Redaction of the 'Isaiah Apocalypse,'" *JTS* 31 (1980) 309-19; T. B. Dozeman, "Hosea and the Wilderness Tradition," S. L. McKenzie and T. Römer (eds.; in collaboration with H. H. Schmid), *Rethinking the Foundations: Historiography in the Ancient World and in the Bible: Essays in Honour of John Van Seters* (BZAW 294; Berlin/New York: de Gruyter, 2000) 55-70; G. R. Driver, "Linguistic and Textual Problems: Minor Prophets. I," *JTS* 39 (1938) 155-66; P. N. Franklyn, "Oracular Cursing in Hosea 13," *HAR* 11 (1987) 69-80; R. Fuller, "A Critical Note on Hosea 12:10 and 13:4," *RB* 98 (1991) 343-57; E. M. Good, "The Composition of Hosea," *SEÅ* 31 (1966) 21-63; J. Joosten, "Exegesis in the Septuagint Version of Hosea," J. C. de Moor (ed.), *Intertextuality in Ugarit and Israel* (OtSt 40; Leiden: E. J. Brill, 1998) 62-85; P. A. Kruger, "Prophetic Imagery. On Metaphors and Similes in the Book of Hosea," *JNSL* 14 (1988) 143-51; C. J. Labuschagne, "The Similes in the Book of Hosea," *OTWSA* 7-8 (1965) 64-76; J. Lust, "Freud, Hosea and the Murder of Moses. Hosea 12," *ETL* 65 (1989) 81-93; A. A. Macintosh, "Hosea and the Wisdom Tradition: Dependence and Independence," J. Day, R. P. Gordon, and H. G. M. Williamson (eds.), *Wisdom in Israel. Essays in Honour of J. A. Emerton* (Cambridge: Cambridge Univ. Press, 1995) 124-32; M. Malul, *Knowledge, Control and Sex. Studies in Biblical Thought, Culture and Worldview* (Tel Aviv-Jaffa: Archaeological Center Publication, 2002); J. L. McKenzie, "Divine Passion in Osee," *CBQ* 17 (1955) 287-89; F. H. Polak, "David's Kingship — A Precarious Equilibrium," H. G. Reventlow, Y. Hoffman, and B. Uffenheimer (eds.), *Politics and Theopolitics in the Bible and Postbiblical Literature* (JSOTSupS 171; Sheffield: Sheffield Academic Press, 1994) 119-47; A. Szabó, "Textual Problems in Amos and Hosea," *VT* 25 (1975) 500-524; R. Vuillenmier-Bessard, "Osée 13:12 et les manuscrits," *RevQ* 1 (1958) 281-82; G. E. W. Watson, "Reflexes of Akkadian Incantations in Hosea," *VT* 34 (1984) 242-47.

Third Didactic Prophetic Reading, Conclusion of the Set, and Conclusion of the Body of the Book, Hos 14:2-9

Structure

I. First Section: Concerning a Call to Return to YHWH	14:2-4
A. First (and extended) Imperative Call	14:2
1. Call per se	14:2a
2. Further elaboration: Explanation for the call in terms of Israel's iniquity against YHWH	14:2b
B. Second Imperative Call	14:3aa
C. Third Imperative Call	14:3ab
D. Fourth (and expanded) Imperative Call	
1. Call per se	14:3baa
2. Further elaboration: Direct quotation of the speech that Israel should address to YHWH	14:3bab-4
II. Second Section: Concerning YHWH's Future and Restorative Kindness and Its Effects on Israel	14:5-8
A. YHWH's Future Actions as Protector (and Healer) of Israel	14:5
1. Report of YHWH's future "actions"	14:5a
2. Further elaboration: reason for YHWH's future action	14:5b
B. Metaphorical Report on Israel's Future	14:6-8
1. Characterization of YHWH's future "state" concerning Israel	14:6aa
2. Consequences of YHWH's future "state" and characterization of Israel's future "state"	14:6ab-8
III. Conclusion	14:9

This READING concludes this SET of READINGS and the body of the book of Hosea with an unmistakable message of hope. It reverses images of destruction, punishment, and death and transforms them into messages of hope. As such this READING provides a crucial interpretative clue for the understanding of all the previous messages of judgment. Judgment does not endure forever; rather than bringing death, it carries in itself, through its imagery and very wording, the seed of a new, ideal future (cf. Hos 13:1–14:1 STRUCTURE; cf. with the trajectories interwoven by Hos 1:3, 8; 2:1-3, 24-25; see also Setting below). Moreover, since the text claims nowhere that the setting — within the world of the book — of YHWH's words of hope is different from that of YHWH's words of harsh evaluation of, and judgment against, Israel, this READING magnifies the reported divine message of hope for the future by setting it within a period of intense sinfulness and forthcoming, severe disaster. Moreover, it turns the disaster into a painful but educative experience (see Hos 10:1-15 Intention; and cf. among other passages, Jer 5:17-19).

The unit is set apart from the others in the book by (a) textually inscribed boundary markers and (b) indicators of textual coherence within the unit. Concerning (a), there is a widespread agreement that there is a clear break between 14:1 and 14:2 and between 14:9 and 14:10. For the former see Hos 13:1–14:1 STRUCTURE. The latter is marked by thematic and style changes. In addition, there are two indicators that often point to a new literary unit within the book: (a) the imperative opening in Hos 14:2 (cf. Hos 4:1; 5:1; the vetitive opening in 9:1; and the "functional" imperative in 8:1) and (b) the reference to Israel (cf. 4:1; 5:1; 9:1; 10:1; 11:1). Further, the text shows a crucial envelope Israel-Ephraim that encapsulates the central construction of Ephraim as a manifestation of trans-temporal Israel (v. 9; cf., among others, Hos 7:1; 10:6; 11:8).

Important markers of textual cohesion within the unit which bear much of the meaning conveyed by the READING include the repetition and semantic trajectory of forms from the root שוב "return." The first two (שובה ישראל "Return, O Israel" in v. 2 and ושובו אל ה' "return to YHWH" in v. 3) call for Israel's return to YHWH. The next form appears in the expression משובתם ארפא in v. 5a. The relevant term there is משובתם "their [Israel's] turning away/ waywardness/unfaithfulness." Significantly, the expression points to YHWH's healing (ארפא) of Israel's משובה. (In other words, the latter is treated as a disease that can be cured only by the Supreme Physician [YHWH] — see Setting.) Then שב in v. 5b points to YHWH's anger turning away from Israel; the final form ישבו in v. 8 to Israel's return to life under YHWH's shadow (i.e., protection) in the ideal future. As such, this trajectory epitomizes a central message of the READING. Israel must repent, but YHWH must heal the underlying disease; then YHWH's anger and Israel's corresponding punishment will disappear, leaving Israel to return to the pristine ideal situation of living under the deity's protection, as the latter leaves its role as judgment agent to take on that of healer and patron of Israel.

The first section of this READING is closely connected to the second section and the conclusion of the READING (v. 9) through numerous textual links. As mentioned above, the references to שוב "return" in vv. 2, 3 and to Israel in v. 2 substantially contribute to the textual cohesion of the READING as a whole.

But to them one may add the pun on words created by פרים "young bulls" in v. 3 and פריך "your fruit" in v. 9. The latter in turn puns on the word אפרים "Ephraim," in v. 9, whose first three consonants are most likely not by chance those of the root רפא "heal" (see v. 5; on healing see Setting). See also יפרח "he shall blossom" in v. 6. In addition there is a pun between אשור "Assyria" in v. 4 and אשורנו "I [YHWH, that is, not Assyria] shall watch over him [Ephraim/Israel]," and even between אשור לא יושיענו and אני עניתי ואשורנו in v. 9 "Assyria cannot/shall not save us," and "I shall respond to them and watch them," respectively. The link here stresses the opposition between YHWH and Assyria — present elsewhere in the book; e.g., Hos 5:13-15 — and conveys the idea that YHWH is the only possible patron of Israel. Further, the text carries a case of repetition through semantic correspondence, rather than words or sounds (see מעשה ידינו "the work of our hands" in v. 4 and עצבים "idols" in v. 9 [and cf. Hos 13:2]).

Although the immense majority of scholars agree with the overall demarcation of the unit, numerous other proposals for the internal structure of Hos 14:2-9 have been advanced. A brief survey would suffice. Oestreich (*Metaphors*, 46-55) divides the text into (i) vv. 2-4, (ii) v. 5, (iii) vv. 6-8, and (iv) v. 9. Eidewall (*Grapes*, 208-10) suggests (i) vv. 2-3a ("introductory exhortation"), (ii) 3b-4 ("[proposed] prayer with vows"), (iii) v. 5 ("centre and pivotal point: proclamation of salvation"); (iv) vv. 6-8 ("promises"); and (v) v. 9 ("concluding assurance"). Rudolph (*Hosea*, 249-53) suggests three main divisions, namely, (i) vv. 2-3a, (ii) vv. 3b-4, and (iii) vv. 5-9 (with 6-8 as a subdivision within them). Garret suggests (i) vv. 2-4, (ii) vv. 5-8, and (iii) v. 9. A common division of the text is between (i) "prophetic exhortation to repentance" (vv. 2-4) and "proclamation of salvation" (vv. 5-9); see among others, Davies, *Hosea*, 298-31; Ward, *Hosea*, 226-27; Simian-Yofre, *Desierto*, 170-73. It bears notice that some of these proposals overemphasize the distinction between a godly, seemingly human voice in vv. 2-4 and a godly, seemingly divine voice in vv. 5-9, even if it is not so clear that the speaker in vv. 2-4 is someone other than YHWH (cf. Andersen and Freedman, *Hosea*, 644). In any event, this is a difference that the text tends to blur by means of markers of textual coherence (e.g., the mentioned trajectory of forms from the root שוב). In all fairness, such an emphasis is often due to assumptions concerning the hypothetical activities of the historical prophet and his (reconstructed) proclamation rather than to an analysis of the book of Hosea as a written, sophisticated text to be read and re-read by the literati.

When the focus is on the book itself, it becomes evident that the text allows and even encourages the target readership to approach it from the perspective of multiple and complementary structures or outlines informing each other, as demonstrated again and again in this commentary. In the present case, the structure mentioned above is complemented by, informs, and is informed by structures that set v. 5 apart as either a section or the central section of the READING. The main contribution of these structures is to call the attention of the intended and primary readership to the required role of YHWH as the agent of change and, above all, as the healer of Israel's "disease." Conversely, the structure itself results from a reading of the text that pays close attention to this matter.

A structure like the one advanced here, or for that matter, any structure perceived by the readers that brings together vv. 5-8, calls attention to and reflects readings of the text in which the bliss for Israel that will result from YHWH's future actions is emphasized. Both types of structures (that is, with vv. 5-8 as one unit and with v. 5 as a separate unit) and the meanings that they reflect and convey to the intended and primary readerships are part and parcel of the text.

This READING serves as a conclusion to the body of the book and as such it contains numerous links to other READINGS in the book. Moreover, since its main role is to provide hope and as such to reverse the numerous announcements and descriptions of disaster within this tapestry of connections, those made in this READING would tend to be used to shape a sense opposite to that carried by and associated with the same referent in other READINGS in the book. When this happens, the result is that previous messages of disaster are construed as bearing the seed of future redemption. The same rhetorical, ideological, and literary device is at work, although in a slightly different way, in Hosea 1–3 (see the references there to Jezreel, "She-is-not-pitied" and "Not-my people").

A few examples of the textually inscribed connections between Hos 14:2-9 and other READINGS in the book will suffice at this stage — additional instances will be discussed below. Simian-Yofre (*Desierto,* 173) notices a quite lengthy series of references that connect the language of Hosea 8 and Hos 14:2-9, carry contrastive meanings, and, interestingly, are deployed in opposite sequential order. See (i) לא ממני "not from me [YHWH]" — ממני "from me [YHWH]" in Hos 8:4 and 14:9; (ii) עצבים "idols" in 8:4 and 14:9 — the first points at making them, the latter at rejecting them — (iii) חרה אפי "my [YHWH's] anger burns" — שב אפי "my [YHWH's] anger turns away" in 8:5 and 14:5; (iv) והוא חרש עשהו ולא אלהים הוא "an artisan made it; it is not god" — ולא נאמר עוד אלהינו למעשה ידינו "we will no longer say, 'O Our God' to the work of our hands" in 8:6 and 14:4; (v) המה עלו אשור "they have gone up to Assyria (for help)" — אשור לא יושיענו "Assyria shall not/cannot save us" in 8:9 and 14:4; (vi) התנו אהבים "they [Ephraim/Israel] hired lovers/ celebrated love-affairs [with partners other than YHWH]" — אהבם "I [YHWH] will love them [Israel/Ephraim]" Hos 8:9 and 14:5; (vii) יזכר עונם "he [YHWH] will remember their [Ephraim's/Israel's] iniquity (and therefore punish them)" — כשלת בעונך "you [Israel] have stumbled because of your iniquity (and therefore you shall return to YHWH)"; and (viii) מצרים ישובו "they [Israel/Ephraim] shall return to Egypt" — שובה ישראל עד ה' "return, O Israel, to YHWH" in 8:13 and 14:2. (Simian-Yofre adds to these the thematic contrast concerning "offering" in Hos 14:3 and 8:11.) Although many of the links mentioned above involve common terms and ideas in Hosea, their cumulative weight and the inverted sequential pattern they show were unlikely to be dismissed by the intended readership of the book, and even by its primary rereadership. It is most reasonable to assume that the intended readership of the book is presented here with a consistent system of threads that all together create the tapestry of the text and contribute through their opposition to the meaning of the text. This conclusion is enhanced by the presence of many other connections between the text of Hos 14:2-9 and other READINGS in the book.

Several expressions in Hos 14:2-9 recall and inform those in Hos 13:1–14:1 and vice versa (see Good, "Composition," 60-61). The most obvious of these instances involves the contrastive use of the metaphor of טל "dew" in 13:3 — also in 6:4 — and 14:6. See also the contrastive pattern of use of hiphil verbal forms of ישע "save" in Hos 13:4, 10 that finds its continuation in Hos 14:4, and cf. the latter with the expression in 1:7. The matter is certainly not restricted to connections between expressions in Hos 14:2-9 and Hosea 8 or 13:1–14:1, but spans many other READINGS. One may easily notice that יכשלו בעונם "they stumble because of their iniquity" in Hos 5:5 is reminiscent of כשלת בעונך "you have stumbled because of your iniquity" in 14:2 (cf. Hos 4:5) and vice versa. The same holds true for, among other expressions, נפשו אל עונם ישאו "to their [Israel's] iniquities each one [improper priests] lifts his appetite" in 4:8 and כל תשא עון "lift up/take away all (our) iniquity" in 14:2. The various occurrences of the metaphor of the healer (Hos 5:13; 6:1; 7:1; 11:3), along with the contrast they create between the true and the false healer, inform each other and lead to the heightened conclusion of Hos 14:5, which is a crucial verse that signals the change of attitude of YHWH that is necessary for the reconstitution of the YHWH-Israel true (patronship) relationship.

From the perspective of the readership of the book there are also clear connections between 14:2 and 3:4-5. Because they accept the reliability of the godly speakers in the book, they "know" that the exhortation in 14:2 will be heard eventually, that many years after the loss of temple and monarchic polity (see Hos 3:4) Israel will return to YHWH and a period of bliss will ensue. Similar connections are brought to the attention of the rereaders by the use of crucial verbal forms of ענה "respond" (see Hos 14:9 and cf. Hos 2:23-24; the implicit "return" of Israel at that time is clear from Hos 2:17). To be sure, as in other prophetic books (e.g., Micah, see Mic 2:12-13; 4:1–5:14; 7:11-13/17), the images and descriptions of the ideal future in the book are not identical (see 2:15-25; 3:5; and 14:6-9, and cf. 2:1-2; 11:10-11). Rather, each of them sheds light on some facet of that ideal future that exists in the imagination of the community within which and for which the book was written; as a whole they reflect a horizon of thoughts, dreams, fears, and self-understanding of the community that is unlikely to be univocal.

These considerations show that the text of Hos 14:2-9 was carefully crafted so as not only to maximize textual coherence within the READING itself but also to shape a system of textual signposts connecting this READING to others in the book and vice versa. This system of signposts conveys much of the meaning of the book of Hosea as a whole.

In the structure advanced above, the thematic differentiation between the first and second main sections is clear. The first reports a call to return to YHWH, and the second, a report of YHWH's future actions and their consequences. The difference between the two is also stylistically marked by the shift in openings, from second person imperatives addressed to Israel, to first person (referring to YHWH) yqtl verbal forms pointing at future action.

In addition, numerous markers of inner textual coherence shape the first section (vv. 2-4) as a tight unit. It is structured around four imperative sentences. The first and the last of these are expanded. The first and third open with imperatives of the same verb, namely, שׁוּב "return." The second and the fourth deal with speech. (On the importance of speech and on the ideological significance of the speech in v. 4 see Setting.) Several other markers of inner textual coherence are noticeable. Among them one may mention the repetition of עָוֹן "iniquity" in v. 2 and v. 3 and the (here, contrastive) pair שְׂפָתֵינוּ "our lips" and יָדֵינוּ "our hands" in vv. 3 and 4 (for "lips-hands" cf. Ps 141:2-3; Song 5:13-14). Significantly, "our lips" is associated here with the present of the future speaker, but "our hands" with the past of that future speaker. There is also a clear repetition of sound in אַשּׁוּר לֹא יוֹשִׁיעֵנוּ in v. 4, which continues the repetition of sounds שׁ and שׂ in v. 3. The text in vv. 2-3baa is characterized by the recurring, explicit, and emphatic use of second person references. This emphasis on "you" is marked not only by the four imperatives in the second person within a very brief text but also by one qtl verbal form in the second person כָּשַׁלְתָּ "you [Israel] have stumbled" and by the occurrence of אֱלֹהֶיךָ "your God," עֲוֹנֶךָ "your iniquity," and עִמָּכֶם "with you." Besides these eight second person marked terms, the only significant words that occur in vv. 2-3baa are "YHWH," "Israel," and "words." The relationship between the first two is at the center of the text, and "words" are meant to mend this relationship (see esp. the conclusion of v. 3). The emphatic use of the second person in reference to Israel is intended to carry a strong affective effect on the readership of the book (cf. Deuteronomy, in which a similar rhetorical strategy is widely used). On the one hand, within the world of the book Hos 14:2-4 is presented as a report of a call to monarchic Israel in the past. On the other hand, it is also written so as to resonate with those who identify themselves with transtemporal Israel, and above all, with the target readerships and with those to whom the literati may have read the book of Hosea or portions thereof, because they were unable to read by themselves, that is, the vast majority of postmonarchic Israel.

The leading opening שׁוּבָה יִשְׂרָאֵל עַד ה׳ "return O Israel to YHWH," particularly taking into account its context within the world of the book, is consistent with Deut 4:30; 30:1-2; Lam 3:40 (cf. Joel 2:12; Amos 4:6, 8, 10, 11). (The question is not so much of who copied from whom. Particularly, from the perspective of the ancient literati in Yehud, the issue is one of a shared discursive world that is manifested in several authoritative texts within their repertoire.) The opening is meant to evoke among the target readership a corresponding request and hope שׁוּבָה ה׳ "return, O YHWH" (cf. Ps 6:5; 90:13; 126:4; also cf. Mal 3:7); cf. v. 5b and vv. 5-8 as a whole. (On repentance see Setting).

The text moves from singular "you" in v. 2 to a plural "you" in v. 3 without any change in the actual referent, namely, Israel. As it does so, it prepares the way for Israel's use of the first common plural in the subsequent verses, a "we" that is emphasized through devices similar to those used for the "you" before. One may notice the textual presence of the first common plural cohortatives, and the recurrent ending in שְׂפָתֵינוּ "our lips," יוֹשִׁיעֵנוּ "he shall save us," אֱלֹהֵינוּ "our God," and יָדֵינוּ "our hands" in v. 3bβ and 4. Needless to say, this recurrent "we" carries affective functions similar to those of the emphatic "you." (Of course, the shift from "you" = Israel to "we" = Israel and YHWH = "you" is required by the reported citation of Israel's words to YHWH.)

The expressions נשלמה פרים שפתינו and כל תשא עון וקח טוב in 3b demand particular attention. The former is translated in the NRSV as "take away all guilt; accept that which is good." This expression is shaped around the use of the verbal word pair נשא "lift up, bear" and לקח "take, receive" with one shared subject (see Deut 10:17; 32:11; Isa 57:13; Ezek 3:14; 8:3; 38:13; 2 Chr 16:6). Yet there is a slight defamiliarization of such use, because נשא and לקח are not used in a more or less synonymous way, but carry here a pragmatic, contrastive sense. One of the verbs is meant to carry the meaning of "lift up" in the sense of removing and, therefore, "forgiving" (on this sense of נשא עון see Exod 34:7; Num 14:18; Ps 32:5; 85:3; Mic 7:18), whereas the other "take" has the sense of accepting and surely not that of "forgiving." This contrastive connotation is grounded on the two semantically and ideologically opposite objects, namely, עון "iniquity" and טוב "(that which is) good." Certainly, the choice of these two objects is not haphazard. Not only is נשא עון "take away iniquity" a common expression, but it shapes a textually inscribed link to Hos 14:2 (see above) and to Hos 4:8 (a critique of reportedly sinful cultic establishment). The noun טוב and the people's request from YHWH to accept Israel's טוב play on Israel's previous rejection of YHWH's טוב in Hos 8:3. As such they carry clear messages to the readership: (a) those who rejected YHWH's טוב will end up asking and fervently hoping for YHWH to accept their טוב and (b) YHWH whose טוב was rejected would graciously be willing to accept Israel's טוב. Further, the temporal trajectory of the relationship between divine טוב and Israel conveyed by the book includes also Hos 3:5, which depicts Israel's approach to it in the ideal future.

But what can Israel's טוב be in this context? On the one hand, it refers to that which Israel may be imagined as actually offering within the world of the text in a narrow sense, that is, its words. As such it may refer to פרים שפתינו at the end of the verse (see Barthélemy, Critique Textuelle, vol. III, 620-21; on the meaning of this expression, see below). Moreover, taking into account v. 4, these words can be understood as an implicit confession, a plea for deliverance, and a statement of Israel's pious intentions for the future (cf. Ibn Ezra, "Accepted Commentary"; Andersen and Freedman, Hosea, 645). (It is to be stressed that this interpretation does not hinge on the acceptance of the position that טוב here denotes speech as proposed by Gordis, "Text and Meaning"; cf. Wolff, Hosea, 231.) On the other hand, and from the larger perspective of the target rereadership, טוב may at least evoke that which is pleasant in the sight of YHWH in the form of a set of prescribed behavior (cf. the definition of טוב given in Mic 6:8; cf. Davies, Hosea 302). In any event, the text carries a clearly open term, "(that which is) good." The presence of such an open term by itself serves to draw the attention of the literati, who may interpret it in different though complementary ways as they read, reread, and read to others the text in different contexts and against different circumstances. (On וקח טוב see also Macintosh, Hosea, 561-64; for the position that טוב here and in Hos 8:3 means "covenant" and there וקח טוב denotes "accept the covenant," see Simian-Yofre, Desierto, 168-69.)

The expression ונשלמה פרים שפתינו is governed by a verbal form — that is, ונשלמה — which following the previous imperative forms means something akin to "that we may requite/pay [you]." The following term פרים means "young bulls," and so the text seems to shape a meaning akin to "that we may requite [you] with young bulls." In other words, the text seems to lead the readers towards a reference to the common practice of offering sacrifices as part of a ritual of purification that people who incur and recognize their sin or guilt are required to perform (cf. Lev 4:1–6:23; cf. Sweeney, *Twelve Prophets,* 138). But then with the very last word of the verse, the text alerts the intended and primary readers that it actually points to a slightly different meaning through the inclusion of the word שפתינו "our lips," which stands for "the output of our lips." Since the two nouns, "young bulls" and "our lips," are in apposition, the latter serves to explain the former. Thus, the bulls being offered become identified with "our lips," that is, the words of confession/plea uttered here (cf. Ps 19:15). Therefore, the expression itself may be translated in ways such as "that we may requite [you] with our lips as if they were young bulls," "that our lips be a substitute for young bulls," or "that we devote our lips instead of young bulls" (cf. the Tg; Calvin, *Hosea,* 489, 529; Barthélemy, *Critique Textuelle,* vol. III, 621-23; Macintosh, *Hosea,* 560-65; Mauchline, "Hosea," 719; Kruger, "Yahweh's Generous Love," 29; NJB; NJPSV; Willi-Plein, *Vorformen,* 229-31). This understanding, namely, that the speech — or confession — of the penitent is, at least, equal in value to sacrifices, is very common among medieval Jewish commentators (see, among others, Qara, Rashi, Ibn Ezra, Radak, Tanḥum HaYerushalmi; and cf. b. Yoma 86b). Moreover, from the perspective of the discourses common in the Hebrew Bible, the statement that the words of repentant lips substitute for young bulls is, in fact, simply a variant or particular manifestation of the widespread ideological topos of "the primacy of morality over sacrifices," which is well known not only in the HB (e.g., Mic 6:8; Ps 50:8-23) but also in other ancient Near Eastern texts and discourses. See discussion of Hos 5:1–7:2 STRUCTURE and see Setting below. Notice also that whereas the loss of sacrificial worship is mentioned in Hos 3:4, its future restoration is implicitly included in the more general category of seeking and trembling before the deity in v. 5. The primacy of the latter is clearly communicated by that text.

The Tg., the Vg, and 4QXIIc (see R. E. Fuller, "The Twelve," 242) support the MT concerning פרים שפתינו. But the LXX and the Peshiṭta may be understood as pointing either at a different Hebrew reading or at an exegetical, interpretative approach through which a difficult expression was translated in terms of a more familiar one (for the latter option, see, among others, Barthélemy, *Critique Textuelle,* vol. III, 622). Many scholars have proposed to emend the MT from the present פרים שפתינו "bulls, (the output of) our lips" to פרי שפתינו, "the fruit of our lips." This approach has influenced common English translations such as the NRSV, RSV, NIV, and NASB. Among the scholars who have proposed this emendation one may mention Harper, *Hosea,* 411-12; Wellhausen, *Kleinen Propheten,* 130; Jeremias, *Hosea,* 169, 171; Mays, *Hosea,* 184, 186-87; Alonso Schokel and Sicre Díaz, *Profetas,* II, 918-19; Gordis, "Text and Meaning"; Wolff, *Hosea,* 231; Szabó, "Textual Problems," 524. These proposals are often based on the position that the LXX of Hosea suggests an alternative Hebrew reading, and in some cases they assume that the final מ in פרים is enclitic. The point of departure of these proposals is most often that the scholars proposing them find the MT apposition between "young bulls" and "our lips" harsh, difficult, or the like, which is another way of stating that it contravenes their expectations. In any event, even if one were to accept this emendation, it would not alter the basic meaning of the text, and the more so since "the fruit of our lips" seems to appear as a substitute for an expected reference to the offering after ונשלמה lit. "that we may pay," but in Hos 14:3 actually communicating a meaning of "that we may substitute."

Another, although less likely, possibility is to understand דברים "words" in 3a as referring to "vows" — and perhaps even identifying them with the words in v. 4 — and then interpreting "the fruit of our lips" as a second reference to these "vows." A more drastic but unlikely reconstruction of the meaning of the text involves an emendation that renders the text into "we will pay our vows with the cattle from our pens" (NEB; cf. NAB). Emmerson (*Hosea,* 151-55) claims that this understanding represents historical Hosea's meaning but not that of the present text of the book of Hosea, which reflects concerns of the exilic period (see esp. 155).

The continuation of the statement of the people to YHWH in v. 4 consists of three different but converging negations similarly structured, and a statement of confidence. Each of the negations directly summarizes, reverses, and relates to a major thread in the book. The first concerns the consistent motif of Israel's misplaced trust in Assyria in particular and by implication in mighty foreign kings and nations in general. These are construed as failed saviors unable to save, in sharp contrast to the real savior, YHWH (cf. 5:13-14; 7:11-12; 8:9-10, 13; 11:5-6; 12:2-3 and see relevant discussions in this commentary). The second concerns the motif of trust in military power, which is construed again as standing in opposition to trust in YHWH (e.g., Hos 8:14; 10:13-14 and see relevant discussions in this commentary; and cf. Deut 28:52; Jer 5:17). In addition it likely connotes a reference to reliance on Egypt (see Isa 31:1-3; 36:9).

In any case, both motifs are manifestations of a common construction of the "enemy" in the ancient Near East, and particularly in Assyrian royal inscriptions, as one who foolishly trusts in military power or allies instead of trusting in the deity/ies and, therefore, as one whose defeat is not only certain but justifiable. In Assyrian royal texts, this characterization of the foolish and sinful enemy justifies the Assyrian king's attack against it (see Liverani, "Kitru"; Oded, *War,* passim). In the Hebrew Bible, the same topos is used to justify YHWH's punishment (/attack) on sinful and foolish Israel, or other nations for that matter (see Obad 2b-3 and Ben Zvi, *Obadiah,* 50-60). The text in v. 4 begins to reverse the common characterization of Israel as a foolish and sinful enemy of YHWH. This, in turn, opens the door for "peace" between YHWH and Israel, and for a restoration of the patronship of YHWH over Israel.

It is worth noticing that military power is here placed alongside trusting in Assyria and idolatry. The ideological repudiation of military power conveyed here is consistent with numerous references in the HB (e.g., Isa 31:1; Mic 5:9-10; and in a more positive manner, Ps 20:8; 33:17-18; 44:4-5). This motif leads at times to the construction of images of an ideal, future, peaceful kingdom devoid of all military power, weaponry, and any need for it (see Hos 2:20-21 and discussion there; cf. Isa 2:2-4; Mic 4:1-5). None of the imagined ideal futures in the book of Hosea involves the establishment of a powerful military.

The third negation refers to a topos that exists elsewhere in the HB and is often associated with one of the preceding ones (cf. Hos 14:4 and Isa 2:7-8; see Hos 8:1-14; Mic 5:9-13), but certainly is not part and parcel of a common regional discourse, unlike the others. This topos deals with a rejection of a cult that involves statues or iconic representations in general of the/a deity. Such a cult is portrayed as an expression of idolatry, as the foolish worship and deification of that which people have made. It indicates a theological mindset in which aniconic worship was seen as such a central tenet that iconic worship of any kind is strongly derided (cf. Hos 2:10; 8:4-6; 10:5; 13:2 and see relevant discussions in this commentary; and cf. Deut 4:12-20; Isa 44:9-20; Jer 10:1-16; Hab 2:18; Ps 115:2-8 and see also 1 Kgs 12:28-30; Isa 2:8, 20; 31:7; 42:17; Jer 51:17).

The absence of an explicit reference to B/baal — another thread within the book — within these three negations, or anywhere in Hos 14:2-9, is most likely due to the fact that B/baal is implicitly and polemically associated with the "product of our hands," that is, its godhood is denied and he becomes only an idol (cf. Hos 11:2 and see Jer 2:11; Ps 96:5; 1 Chr 16:26).

Whereas the report about the three negations that Israel should state in its address to YHWH in the future explicates in whom Israel should not place its trust, the conclusion of this section informs the readers in whose hands Israel will place its fate. Given the context, the identity of the latter is never in doubt; it is YHWH. Significantly, however, the choice of words is reminiscent of and creates a link to Hos 1:6-8; 2:3, 25 and plays on the image of YHWH as father of Israel (cf. Hos 1:2-9). On Hos 14:4, and Hos 14:2-4 in general, see also Setting.

The second section consists of two subunits (v. 5 and vv. 6-8). Verses 5 and 6 are connected by their similar openings with yqtl verbal forms in the first person, ארפא and אהיה "I [YHWH] shall heal" and "I [YHWH] shall be." Further, there is a verbal gradation from the fientive, transitive verb "I shall heal" in v. 5aα, to the quasi-fientive verb with a direct object "I shall love them" v. 5aβ, and finally to the stative "I shall be [like dew]." This gradation leads to and shapes a sense of future stability around an ideal state. In addition, one may notice that vv. 5-8 are shaped around a common system of three versets per verse (see Qyl, *Hosea,* 27; cf. Hos 11:1-4) that is not present in v. 4 and v. 9. This also contributes to a sense of particular textual cohesiveness within vv. 5-8.

Verses 6-8 are clearly connected by the thrice repeated ending כלבנון "like [that of] Lebanon," and by vegetation metaphors. Verse 9 is set apart from vv. 5/6-8 by style and theme (see, among others, the paragraph marker in the Leningrad/St. Petersburg Codex). Numerous textually inscribed markers point in this direction, among them: (a) the opening reference to Ephraim, (b) the absence of the ending "like [that of] Lebanon," (c) the speaker's citation of Ephraim's future speech (cf. 3bab-4) — that makes it more reminiscent of the first section of the READING than the second — (d) a new qtl verbal opening in v. 9b that stands apart from those in vv. 5 and 6, and (e) the break in the three versets system mentioned above. Yet at the same time, v. 9 is certainly not completely separate from vv. 6-8, see, for instance, the metaphor of YHWH as a tree. (For other connections between verses 8 and 9 in particular see below.)

Most of the words in v. 5 contribute in one way or another to the textual cohesion of this READING or the shaping of connections of reversal with other READINGS in the book, or both. For instance, משובתם "their [Israel's] turning away/waywardness/unfaithfulness" and שב "turn away/return" participate in the trajectory of forms from the root שוב mentioned above; ארפא "I [YHWH] will heal" contributes to the system of repetition of consonants פ and ר (see above), and its three consonants are part of the name Ephraim. In addition, ארפא is crucial for shaping the connection between Hos 14:5 and 5:13, along with the construction of the opposition between true healer (i.e., YHWH) and false healer (i.e., Assyria). שב אפי "my [YHWH's] anger has turned away" relates in similarly contrastive ways to Hos 8:5 (cf. 13:11). In addition, שב אפי is reminiscent of, and relates a meaning converging with that of 11:9, which, significantly, is a verse that plays a central role in the shift from punishment towards a new ideal future in another message of hope concluding a SET of READINGS (see commentary there). אהבם "I [YHWH] will love them [Israel/Ephraim]" plays a role in the set of connections between Hosea 8 and 14 noticed by Simian-Yofre (see above); note ממנו "from him [Israel]" and ממני "from me [YHWH]" in v. 9. The horizon of thought reflected and communicated by v. 5 is discussed under Setting.

For the reference to טל "dew" in v. 6 see above. The metaphorical description of Israel's ideal future is demarcated by the envelope created by יפרח "he [Israel] shall blossom" in v. 6aβ and ויפרחו "and they [Israel] shall blossom" in v. 8. The expression ויך שרשיו "its [Israel's] roots will strike (root)" in the future portrayed in v. 6 creates a contrastive relation with הכה אפרים שרשם יבש "Ephraim was stricken; its root is dried up" in Hos 9:16. The word pair זית "olive tree" and גפן "vine" (cf. Ps 128:3; Job 15:33) along with דגן "grain" (see below, and cf. 2 Kgs 18:32) point at the entire agrarian system, but the metaphorical emphasis is not on the strength of the economy. In fact, there are several points of contact between the metaphors here and those in Song of Songs 2:1-3; 4:10-16, as usually agreed in contemporary scholarship (see esp. Yee, *Composition*, 138-39; Feuillet, "'S'asseoir à l'ombre" de l'époux"). These include, among others, the comparison with the שושנה "lily" (see Song of Songs 2:1-2; cf. 4:5; 5:13), the reference to "the fragrance of Lebanon" (see Song of Songs 4:11), and the image of sitting under the shade of the husband (see Song of Songs 2:3). The use of the language of love here serves to evoke the text of Hos 2:16-25, another main text of describing the ideal future in the book of Hosea. One may note also that אני עניתי "as for me [YHWH], I will respond" in v. 9 is reminiscent of אענה "I [YHWH] will respond" in 2:23 (cf. 2:24; see commentary there). To these observations, one may add the use of the term דגן "grain" in v. 8 and 2:24 and the reference in the latter to wine and oil (cf. 14:7-8). On ideological trajectories of דגן or "grain" in the book of Hosea see 2:10, 11, 24 and 7:14; 8:7 (the term used there is קמה "standing grain); 9:1; and 14:8.

Unlike the case in 2:16-25, Israel is grammatically referred to as male in vv. 6-8, but gender-related imagery is used here to express hierarchical relations (cf. D. Seeman, "Where Is Sarah Your Wife?"). Thus YHWH is masculinized and Israel feminized; YHWH is the provider and Israel is the one

being provided; YHWH is the upright majestic tree that provides shade and Israel sits under his shade. The language of love is also appropriate here since the
world portrayed in these verses stands in contrast to that of Hos 4:13. The trajectory is clear: While the report about the past portrays Israel involved in improper and sinful worship and sexual intercourse, the report about the future
portrays Israel enjoying a quasi-paradisiacal situation under YHWH's shade,
protection, and love (vv. 5-8).

(Of course, the image in vv. 6-8 is somewhat reminiscent of that of father-
son, but this is so because the latter is a related hierarchical image [note the intertwining of the two in Hosea 1–3; cf. Landy, *Hosea,* 172-74].)

The language of verse 8a has raised considerable debate. יֹשְׁבֵי יֹשְׁבוּ
בְצִלּוֹ יְחַיּוּ דָגָן contains a pun on the words יֹשְׁבוּ יֹשְׁבֵי "those who sit (under his
[YHWH's] shade) shall return" and carries the word דָגָן "grain" (about its importance in the text see above). The expression denotes or connotes to its intended rereadership a number of related and complementary meanings, which
may be reflected in the following renderings: (a) "those who sit in (/under) his
[YHWH's] shade shall return, they will give life to [i.e., raise; cf. Isa 7:21]
grain"; (b) "again, those who sit in his shade shall give life to grain" (cf. Barthélemy, *Critique Textuelle,* vol. III, 623-24); (c) or "those who sit in his shade
shall again revive the growth of grain" (cf. Macintosh, *Hosea,* 573-76);
(d) "those who sit in his shade shall return, they shall revive [like] grain (see
Calvin, "Hosea," 500; KJV); and (e) "they shall return, they shall sit in his
shade, they shall make grain live."

As in Hos 13:13 and 14 (see commentary there), the text carries an expression that bears more than one meaning, but these meanings reinforce each
other. The multi-valence of the text draws the attention of the rereaders and
contributes to the rereadability of the text (see Ben Zvi, *Obadiah,* 4 and passim). Moreover, multi-valence is here at the service of communicating and
emphasizing a large area of converging meanings. These meanings include the
central notion of a future return of an Israel that is characterized as sitting in
YHWH's shade, and of a revived Israel that will dwell again in a fruitful land,
in YHWH's shade. (For a different understanding of the text according to
which there is a level of ambiguity concerning under whose shade the people
will dwell, but not necessarily about other matters, and the text is still understood it as a metaphor referring to the return of deportees, see Eidewall,
Grapes, 216-18.) A number of proposals for, usually, minor textual emendations have been advanced, and they lead to different readings of the text (see,
for instance, Coote, "Hosea 14:8"; and the translations offered in RSV and
NRSV). It is worth stressing, however, that the identification of the referent of
צִלּוֹ "his/its shade" as YHWH does not require any textual emendation (e.g., to
change the expression to צִלִּי "my shade," as proposed by Wolff, *Hosea,* 232,
and others; on this matter, see Andersen and Freedman, *Hosea,* 647; Eidewall,
Grapes, 216-17; cf. Macintosh, *Hosea,* 573, 575; the identification of the referent with Israel [e.g., Rashi, Ibn Ezra, Nogalski, *Literary Precursors,* 67] cannot be sustained unless some character or referent other than "Israel" is artifi-
cially introduced into the text, for "Israel" cannot sit under the shade of
"Israel").

The second part of v. 8 brings to the forefront the image of Israel as a vine (cf. Hos 10:1). Whereas the vine in 10:1 did not withstand the test of time, the renown of ideal future Israel, the vine of Hos 14:8, will last as that of Lebanon (cf. with the ideological trajectory for "grain" described above).

Verse 9 has also been at the center of scholarly debate. The main problem with the verse is how to understand 9a. The question מה לי עוד לעצבים is almost certainly rhetorical — "What more I have to deal with idols?" or "What need have I of any more idols?" — and carries a sense of "I will not deal with idols anymore" or "I have no need of idols anymore." Yet the immediate literary context in which the expression appears, with the opening "Ephraim," turns אפרים מה לי עוד לעצבים into an expression that conveys several complementary meanings. It may be understood as: (a) "[YHWH states:] Ephraim [shall say/will confess, saying] 'What need have I anymore of idols?'" — according to this approach the character YHWH is running (for the sake of the readership of the book) a monologue in which the deity cites that which Ephraim will state in the ideal future (cf. vv. 3baa-4; cf. NJPSV, Tg); (b) "Ephraim [will confess:] 'What need have I any more of idols?'" — according to this approach, the text here represents a dialogue in which the first speaker is Ephraim and the second YHWH (in 9b); Ephraim's words are used here to characterize it, and the verse then carries a meaning akin to "Ephraim's attitude is, what more need have I for idols?" (see Macintosh, *Hosea*, 576-81); (c) [YHWH states:] "Ephraim, what have I to deal with idols anymore?" meaning "Ephraim, I [YHWH] won't deal with idols anymore" (see Andersen and Freedman, *Hosea*, 642, 647); and (d) [YHWH states:] "Ephraim! What have I [YHWH] to do with idols?" which is a rhetorical question that YHWH asks Ephraim. Of course, faced with that question, Ephraim is supposed to respond: YHWH has nothing to do with idols; there is no possible comparison or relationship between YHWH and the idols. In other words, within this reading, Ephraim (/Israel) will recognize its past fault, and return no more to it, and, therefore, the situation portrayed in Hos 4:1 will exist no more (cf. Simian-Yofre, *Desierto*, 169, 172).

All these meanings converge and support each other. In the ideal future, Ephraim/Israel will be transformed, and it will not be joined to the idols anymore. Moreover, it will not confuse its deity/provider with them. Furthermore, YHWH will no longer have to deal with the problem of Ephraim's idolatry. (For proposals of textual emendations rendering the text: "[YHWH states:] What has Ephraim any more to do with idols?" see, among others, Wolff, *Hosea*, 233, 237; cf. the LXX, and among current English translations, NAB, NJB; for a critique of this proposal see Barthélemy, *Critique Textuelle*, vol. III, 624-25; Macintosh, op. cit.; Simian-Yofre, *op. cit.*)

The second half of v. 9 opens with four words that are all marked for "I" (i.e., YHWH). They include two explicit occurrences of אני "I" (the first one, formally pleonastic) and two verbal forms each of which is marked for the first person singular. This emphasis on the speaker and the authority of the speaker is consistent with the role of 9b as a hopeful conclusion and with the self-portrayal of YHWH in relation to Israel. The relational element comes to the forefront towards the end of the verse, "by me [YHWH] your fruit is/will be provided." To be sure, "your" points to the Israel of the future portrayed in the verses 6-9, but the text also allows the readership of the book to identify with that "you." Morag understands אני עניתי ואשורנו, usually interpreted as "It is I who will respond and look after him," as referring to YHWH's treatment of the shoot/Israel and concluding the theme that begins with "I [YHWH] will be like dew . . ." in v. 6. According to him, the expression in v. 9 refers to taking care of the needs of the shoot by preparing the ground, watering it, and watching over it. Given his emphasis on the agricultural element of the flourishing of Israel/shoot, he interprets the emphasis on "I" here, and incidentally v. 9 as well, as part of a discourse the aim of which is to emphasize that it is YHWH, not the idols, who takes care, watches over, and provides for Israel/plant. See Morag, "Semantic and Lexical Features," 496.

As is widely known, Wellhausen proposed to read אני ענתו ואשרתו "I am his Anat and his Ashera" instead of אני עניתי ואשורנו (Wellhausen, *Kleinen Propheten,* 21, 131). Many scholars have strongly rejected his proposal (e.g., Harper, *Hosea,* 415; Wolff, *Hosea,* 233), while others have advanced and elaborated different variants of it (e.g., Margalit, "Meaning," 292-95). A third approach, however, has received substantial support, namely, that the text as it stands carries a pun based on assonance on the names of the goddesses Anat and Ashera (see J. Day, "Ashera," 404-6; Emmerson, *Hosea,* 50; cf. Eidewall, *Grapes,* 218 n. 61; Barthélemy, *Critique Textuelle,* vol. III, 627). For a discussion of these matters see Nissinen, *Prophetie,* 273-75; Gangloff, "'Je suis son 'Anat et son 'Aserâh,'" and note also the extensive bibliography on these matters in Gangloff, "YHWH ou les déesses-arbres?" 48 n. 58). One is take into account, however, that the names of Anat and Ashera are not mentioned anywhere in the book of Hosea, and for that matter that the goddess Anat is not mentioned anywhere in the HB — her name appears only in oblique ways, e.g., as a toponym. In addition, the comprehensive analysis of the tree metaphor by Oestreich (*Metaphors,* 191-225) raises strong objections to an understanding of this metaphor as involving either Ashera or any goddess. Not only is the tree referred in the text *not* a fruit tree, but majestic, coniferous trees can and did stand metaphorically for kings and political powers. Further, the image of living under the shade/protection of the "tree" is used to convey that of living under the protection of a monarch, both in ancient Near Eastern texts in general and in the HB in particular. See also Tånberg, "I Am like an Evergreen Fir." On these matters see Setting below.

Oestreich claims also that the image of the royal tree is associated in Hos 14:5-9 with that of the quasi-paradisiacal trees, providing a sense of "paradise regained." For an additional analysis of the metaphor of the tree in v. 9 see Eidewall, *Grapes,* 219-20. For a substantially different understanding of v. 9 see Wagenaar, "I Will Testify."

Numerous proposals for emendations of the text of Hosea 14:2-9 have been advanced. Several of these proposals have been discussed above. As in other instances, in general these proposals tend to disallow or diminish the multiplicity of meanings that the MT carries. For many of these proposals see Elliger (BHS). For a summary, discussion, and critique of many of these proposals see Barthélemy, *Critique Textuelle,* vol. III, 620-27, and the textual discussions in Macintosh, *Hosea,* 559-81.

Among scholars who advance reconstructions of the redactional history of the text, most tend to consider Hos 14:2-9 as a unit, though they certainly disagree on authorship and date. Some would associate it with the historical Hosea whom they reconstruct (e.g., Davies, Wolff), others with Hoseanic disciples (e.g., Jeremias), and others postmonarchic redactors (e.g., Yee). Still others have advanced claims concerning the secondary character of some minor subunits or words within Hos 14:2-9. For instance, Nogalski considers 14:8a as secondary. He claims, "the theme of the return of the inhabitants denotes a post-exilic perspective, contrary to the remainder of the passage" (Nogalski, *Literary Precursors*, 67-69; quotation from p. 68). The secondary character of this "literary insertion" (i.e., Hos 14:8a) becomes then an important "datum" for Nogalski's proposal for the composition of the "book of the Twelve" (see *op. cit.*, 69-73). Emmerson (*Hosea*, 51-52) maintains that vv. 5-8 and v. 9 originated with the historical Hosea, but vv. 2-4 show no integral relation to vv. 5-9. According to her, vv. 2-4 are editorial, the result of a theological reinterpretation, and of Judahite origin. This redactional conclusion is based mainly on Emmerson's position that "stress on the nation's repentance as a prerequisite to Yahweh's saving action is Judean in origin (51)." Weiser (*Propheten*, 101) and others consider vv. 4b and 5b also as an addition (see also BHS; and cf. Mays, *Hosea*, 187-88). See also the redactional critical proposals advanced by Kruger ("Yahweh's Generous Love").

Genre

Hosea 14:2-9 is a prophetic, didactic READING, that is, it is a literary unit within the prophetic book of Hosea that shows textually inscribed, discursive markers that were likely to suggest to its intended and primary readerships that they were supposed to, or at least were invited to, read it as a cohesive unit, within the frame of the book of Hosea as a whole. It is both an integral component and the conclusion of a SET of READINGS (Hos 12:1–14:9) within that book. At the same time, it is the conclusion of the body of the book of Hosea (Hos 2:1–14:9). The intended readers are asked to approach this READING as both.

Hos 14:2-4 carries a literary representation of a proper call to return to YHWH and evokes the image of such a call within the target readership. The reported call is characterized in the book by its attribution to a godly speaker, a short series of imperatives, and a brief statement of relinquishing sinful attitudes and placing trust in YHWH's mercy. Even if one assumes that there were liturgies that included calls to repent in ancient Israel and that took place either when the community was threatened by disaster and wanted to avoid it, or when the community remembered a past disaster and looked for hope in the future — both, of course, involve processes of socialization and of assigning meaning to events — the text here is surely a literary construction meant to evoke such liturgies rather than a faithful description of them. For one thing, it is extremely unlikely that the entire call to repent, including the statement of the public, would be at the most, only one minute long.

As Hos 14:2-4 contains a literary representation of a proper call to return

301

to YHWH, it also evokes a sense of communal penitence and supplication. When the text is read in a manner strongly informed by that sense, Hos 14:5-9 may be seen as fulfilling the role of the comforting, divine promise that may follow supplications (see Ps 91:14-16 — for an analysis of its Genre and Setting, see Gerstenberger, *Psalms, Part 2,* 166-67; the narrator provides such an affirmation of the divine response to the request of the people in Exod 32:14; cf. Jer 3:21–4:2) or as a portrayal of a full-fledged "lamentation/repentance ritual." (Some scholars have proposed that Hos 14:2-9 follows the model of a penitential liturgy: e.g., Mays, *Hosea,* 185; Tånberg, "I Am like an Evergreen Fir"; cf. Hunter, *Seek the Lord,* 169).

But the text does not say that the addressees of the call within the world of the book, or monarchic Israel or Ephraim as construed by the community of readers, actually followed the summons and repented. In fact, given the knowledge of the past of the intended and primary rereaderships, it is more likely that they understood this to be among the unheeded calls of the past (cf. Zech 1:3-6). If this is the case, then when the text is understood as addressing the readership of the book, it may still be understood — although not exclusively — as following patterns associated with penitential liturgies. But when the text is read as directed to its implied addressees in the world of the book, vv. 5-9 may be understood as a further argument for Israel's return to YHWH. In any event, the text evokes expectations associated with summons to return to YHWH, but also introduces a substantial amount of defamiliarization. This is to be expected since within its literary context its main focus is not on the failed repentance of sinful, monarchic Israel/Ephraim in the past, but on the blessings that YHWH will bestow to future Israel. (See also Setting.)

In addition, contrary to expectations, YHWH does not state that if Israel repents, then the deity will deliver and provide them with a kind of quasi-paradisiacal bliss (ct. Jer 3:21–4:2; Zech 1:3-6). The text is open to more than one reading in this regard (see Setting). This openness defamiliarizes the text further in relation to the expectations that the readership used to associate with models of penitential liturgies.

All this said, it is not difficult to imagine Hos 14:2-9 as being used in liturgy. In fact, Hos 14:2-10 is read as part of the afternoon service for the ninth of Av — the day associated with the destruction of both temples, the expulsion from Spain, and other tragic memories in Jewish traditions — in synagogues that follow the Sephardic or Yemenite tradition, and on Shabbat Shuva, before Yom Kippur, in Sephardic, Yemenite and Ashkenazic traditions (on the intertextual use of Hos 14:2-10 in these settings, see Fishbane, *Haftarot,* 384-85). It is to be stressed, however, that the text of Hos 14:2-10 is not presented to the textually inscribed addressees in the world of the book, or to its intended rereaders, as a liturgy of penitence or as any liturgy. It is possible that already in ancient times the text was abstracted from its literary setting within the book of Hosea and read in particular liturgies in ancient Israel, or that it was reminiscent of similar readings in liturgies of which the target readership was aware, but this cannot be proven. In any case, such a reading of the text of Hos 14:2-10 within a context other than that of the book cannot be identified with the reading of the conclusion of the body of a book or that of a SET of READINGS within a book.

This discussion points at one important aspect of Genre. Genre is not an abstract and absolute category. Genre is an attribute assigned to a work that evolves out of the interaction between a particular readership and text. It concerns textually inscribed markers, but also involves the attribution by the readership of intentions to the implied author of the work. Moreover, within communities of rereaders that approach the text in multiple ways within its context in the book of Hosea — and certainly so if they approach it outside the context of the book — genre considerations that apply to one of these readings may not apply at all or may apply differently to another reading of the same text.

Setting

The setting of the writing and primary reading of this, or any portion of the (present) book of Hosea for that matter, is the same as that of the book as a whole. Both writers and readers are among the very few literati of Yehud. Since the entire body of the book and this SET OF READINGS lead up to the heightened conclusion of Hos 14:2-9, one is to expect that this unit provides a glimpse into important aspects of the intellectual and ideological horizon of the authorship and intended rereadership of the book of Hosea. This expectation is fulfilled.

To begin with, already by means of its emphatic opening, the unit brings the matter of repentance and the question of its necessity or lack thereof to the forefront. Within the general discourse of ancient Israel, true repentance was construed as including not only an admission of past sinful behavior, but also a steadfast avoidance of that behavior and a faithful obedience to YHWH and YHWH's commandments or instructions concerning Israel, as they were conceived by the literati and within the discourses of the period. In the book of Hosea, as in the general discourse of postmonarchic Israel, lack of true repentance is associated with disaster and divine punishment (e.g., Hos 5:4; 7:10), but is true repentance necessary for YHWH's restoration of Israel? In other words, should the literati of postmonarchic Israel not only call for, and be called to, true repentance, but should they not hope for restoration until Israel reaches a state of full and permanent repentance, in response to godly calls to return to YHWH? Moreover, if Israel must fully repent to reach the blissful state, then how can it remain in such a state if it is by nature liable and about to sin again (see commentary on Hos 1:2–2:3)? Do not the lack of repentance and inability to repent lead to disaster and punishment?

The question of how theological discourses later than the book of Hosea, in both Christianity and Judaism, dealt with these matters is not relevant for the purpose of this commentary. (Incidentally, a concept of "grace" or "divine *hesed* for the undeserving" is well attested and prominent in both traditions.) It is central to this commentary that the book of Hosea and its intended and primary readership dealt with these matters and at considerable depth.

Hos 1:2–2:25 in general, and Hos 2:1-2, 16-25 in particular, do not condition YHWH's restoration upon Israel's repentance; in fact, they point to YHWH as the active agent who brings about a new beginning, and in 2:16-25 as the one that eliminates Israel's potential for future sin (see comments under

Setting). Hos 3:5 constructs Israel's (future) repentance as following punishment, and as a first stage in a process towards an ideal, blissful condition. Hos 11:7-11 reflects and communicates — perhaps more emphatically — the same position as Hos 1:2–2:25. Hos 14:2-9, as fitting the concluding text of the body of the book, epitomizes a multi-layered approach that is reflected and communicated by different readings informing each other — in other words, the rich ideological tapestry that results from multiple threads.

Hos 14:2-4 is presented to the rereaders as reflecting true repentance (ct. Hos 2:9; 5:6; 6:1-3). Contrary to, for instance, the summons to repent in Hos 10:12, the one in Hos 14:2-4 is followed by an announcement not of disaster, but of future deliverance. Like the description of repentance in Hos 3:5, it is set to follow a period of disaster (see כי כשלת בעונך "for you have stumbled because of your iniquity"). Thus, the salient position of the summons at the opening of a unit is at the very least likely to suggest to the target readership that the mindset commended in Hos 14:2-4 has some bearing on YHWH's words in Hos 14:5-9, and above all on the fulfillment of the situation and events portrayed there. For instance, it may suggest to them that if they place their trust in YHWH alone — unlike monarchic Israel — they may stand closer to the world of vv. 6-9. The fact that the readership of the book "knows" that monarchic Israel did not heed that call does not detract from the conclusion mentioned above. On the contrary, it explains well why the monarchic polities were destroyed, why "exile" followed, and why the ideal future had not yet been fulfilled. It also suggests to the readers of the book that if they had followed the godly advise of Hos 14:2-4, they would or could have been delivered, and that if Israel eventually follows this advice, the ideal future will be closer to implementation (cf. the ideological horizons of thought reflected and communicated in 2 Kgs 17:13-15; Zech 1:3-6 — see Ben Zvi, "'The Prophets' — Generic Prophets" — and also those in, for instance, Lev 26:3-13).

At the same time, the intended and primary readership of the book of Hosea can easily observe that nowhere does the text state that vv. 5-9 constitute YHWH's reaction to Israel's return to YHWH, even if the latter is construed in the terms conveyed by vv. 2-4. To be sure, the text may be understood that way, particularly if the target readership approaches it with a perspective strongly informed by some liturgical patterns (see Genre, cf. Jer 3:22), but this is only one of several possible readings of the text, and certainly not the most salient one.

Within the world of the book, YHWH's words in vv. 4-9 — along with all the speeches that are reported in the book — are set within the reign of certain kings and, no doubt, in the monarchic period (see Hos 1:1). When the intended and primary readers of the book approach it from this perspective, YHWH's words are not necessarily or even likely an announcement of deliverance meant for the Israel addressed in Hos 14:2, which, of course, is also located in the monarchic period. From this perspective, YHWH's words are, mainly, an announcement about a "paradisiacal" time to come in the distant future, but surely not in the lives and days of the textually inscribed monarchic period Israelites who serve as the implied addressees of the divine speech in the world of the book. On this basis alone, one may conclude that within this type of reading, YHWH's speech is unlikely to have been understood as a possible direct re-

sponse to the summons in vv. 2-4. Further, as one focuses on the target readership of the book of the Hosea, it becomes evident that from their perspective,
monarchic Israel certainly did not heed the summons in vv. 2-4, and therefore
was punished. This being so, it would have been impossible for them to assume
that YHWH's speech in vv. 5-9 was YHWH's response to the people's return to
YHWH, for the latter never happened. This approach does not render vv. 5-9
meaningless. Quite the opposite, it conveys one of the strongest messages of
hope: YHWH proclaims in no uncertain terms that YHWH will bring about
quasi-paradisiacal circumstances for Israel when the latter is not only unrepentant and sinful, but about to be strongly punished. The underlying message is
that no matter how grievous Israel's sins are, they cannot undermine YHWH's
relationship with Israel and the future that YHWH holds for it (cf. Hos 11:1-11;
Hos 12:1–14:9 Intention). Thus, within this ideological, comforting discourse,
Israel should never construe itself as hopeless, no matter the circumstances; on
the contrary, it should always construe itself as full of hope and, in fact, certitude that an ideal future will come to pass. This is a pertinent message to the
community of readers in postmonarchic Israel that experiences a cognitive dissonance between their worldly status and what they thought should manifest
YHWH's will.

Furthermore, the literati, who were supposed to read, reread, and study
the book, would have noted that at the turning point in the text (v. 5), it reports
that YHWH opened the speech with ארפא משובתם "I will heal your turning
away (/unfaithfulness)." In addition to the mentioned networks of meanings to
which this expression contributes (see above; and also cf. Jer 3:22), they would
have noted that the text construes YHWH as healing Israel's "unfaithfulness."
In other words, the latter is treated as a disease that can be cured only by the Supreme Physician (YHWH). Israel cannot heal itself, and without being healed
of "unfaithfulness," no stable idyllic future can be imagined. Thus the text carries also a message similar to that of Hos 2:16-25 and comparable to those of
texts such as Jer 31:31-34; Ezek 36:26-30 (cf. Ben Zvi, "Analogical
Thinking").

In sum, the text conveys to its intended and primary readership a dense
tapestry of meanings that inform and balance each other. The text communicates and reflects an ideological discourse within which Israel should repent
and turn to YHWH, but Israel's repentance is not all. YHWH must and will
transform Israel in a profound way to bring (and maintain) it to a quasi-
paradisiacal situation (cf. Deut 30:1-6 and note explicitly v. 6). Human deeds
cannot disrupt or condition YHWH's long-term will concerning Israel, or the
certitude that it will eventually be manifested, but they do impact the life of human beings, as the case of monarchic Israelites clearly shows. Divine promises
obviate neither punishment nor the obligation of the Israelites to follow
YHWH, but at the same time are not conditioned by either. The text thus explains the past, exhorts the readership to be obedient to YHWH and YHWH's
instructions — as understood by the literati — and at the same time provides
hope for those who could have thought themselves, within a discourse informed
only by worldly circumstances, as hopeless.

One final observation on these matters is necessary. The point made under STRUCTURE that the imagery and the very wording of the announcements of punishment and destruction against Israel/Ephraim/Judah are turned into carriers of hope serves also to construe the godly speaker of punishment, even in the rhetorical fullness of its fury — and there is much of that in Hosea — as one who simultaneously subtly announces the ideal future (cf. Hos 1:3, 8; 2:1-3, 24-25). To be sure, such announcements are not aimed at the implied addressees of the speeches in the world of the book, but at those able to understand these matters, that is, the literati who read and reread the book of Hosea. This construction of the godly speaker is fully consistent with YHWH's characterization in vv. 5-9 as one who states that which will bring about quasi-paradisiacal circumstances for Israel when the latter is not only unrepentant and sinful, but about to be strongly punished.

For other studies on the matters discussed above, see, among others, Wolff, *Hosea,* xxviii-xxix, 237-38; Bright, *Covenant and Promise,* 87-94; Ginsberg, "Hosea," 1022; Buss, *Prophetic Word,* 128-29; and particularly, Oestreich, *Metaphors,* 57-87 and passim; Eidewall, *Grapes,* 208-13; and Unterman, "Repentance and Redemption."

The importance of precise and proper speech in Hos 14:3bab-4 is noteworthy. About half of the textual space allocated to the reported summons to return to YHWH in vv. 2-4 is assigned to the words that Israel should utter. Moreover, whereas two of the imperative forms concern the central ideological concept of return (שובה and שובו, both meaning "return"), the other two imperative forms directly refer to speech (קחו עמכם דברים and אמרו "take with you words" and "say," respectively). The underlying horizon of thought that explains such an emphasis is one in which truthful, proper speech is evaluated highly. A discursive emphasis on proper speech — and conversely a salient rejection of false or improper speech — is relatively common in wisdom literature (e.g., Prov 13:2; 15:26), prophetic literature (e.g., Isa 3:8), and, for instance, Psalm 15. Such discursive emphasis is consistent with educational, instructional, or socializing roles in society.

The expression נשלמה פרים שפתינו in v. 3, which may be understood as conveying a message akin to "that we may requite [you] with our lips as if they were young bulls," "that our lips be a substitute for young bulls" (see above), is consistent with this emphasis on speech and words. The expression in this particular context alongside the other words to be uttered by Israel carries a strong connotation about the proper moral character of the speaker and fully characterizes the latter. Significantly, it is through this connotation that the expression becomes another manifestation of the widespread ideological topos of "the primacy of morality over sacrifices," mentioned above. The stance of the text here neither reflects nor conveys a sense that sacrificial worship is worthless or that it is to be supplanted. Instead, it emphasizes that proper attitude — here expressed in speech — is decisive (cf., among other passages, 1 Sam 15:22 — which is placed in the mouth of a priest; Mic 6:6-8; see also 2 Chr 30:18-20), for without that attitude sacrifices are meaningless (e.g., Hos 5:6). If the supplicant has the proper moral attitude, sacrifices may be obviated. (Patrons in the ancient Near East and in general would certainly consider loyalty and obedience in their clients/subjects a cardinal virtue, but would be unlikely to understand this position as meaning that gifts from loyal and obedient client/subjects are not welcome.)

The salient position of the metaphor of the tree at the end of the body of the book of Hosea calls attention to the metaphor and the likely meanings that it conveyed to the intended and primary readership of the book. It suggests to them that something of major importance is involved in that concluding text. In addition, the text carries a secondary attention-getter. YHWH is compared to a ברוש. Whether the tree is a cypress, as usually understood, or *Juniperus excelsa,* as is more likely (see Oestreich, *Metaphors,* 192-95; cf. Qyl, *Hosea,* קיא), or any other coniferous tree (cf. Tånberg, "I Am like an Evergreen Fir"), the ברוש certainly does not bear fruit. Yet the text states ממני פריך נמצא, which communicates a sense of "from/by/because of me [YHWH/the coniferous tree] your fruit is found." The apparent tension created by a metaphor of a non-fruit-bearing tree providing fruit shapes another attention-getter that leads the readership to focus on the message/s conveyed by the image.

As mentioned above, the image of a majestic tree standing above everything else is used as a royal metaphor, and the associated metaphor of living under the shade of a majestic tree conveys also an image of a kingly protector (e.g., Ezek 17:3-4, 22-24; Lam 4:20; Dan 4:8-9, 17-19; see Parpola, *Letters from Assyrian Scholars,* vol. 2, 108, and ṣillu 5c in CAD). The same image of protection and patronage can be used in relation to deities (see ṣillu 5a in CAD and of temples, see ṣillu 5b in CAD). For comparative purposes, see the text of a neo-Assyrian letter written by Adad-šumu-uṣur in the Sargonid period (possibly in 667 BCE) in which the following is said of the Assyrian king, "a *burašu* is the Lord, my king, who gives life to numerous peoples" (Tånberg, "I Am like an Evergreen Fir," 87; for the relevant text see SLA 318 [i.e., Pfeiffer, *State Letters,* 214-15] = RCAE 657 [i.e., Waterman, *Royal Correspondence,* and note esp. vol. ("Part") IV, *Supplement and Indexes,* pp. 186, 259], but notice also the understanding of the text advanced in LAS 120 [i.e., Parpola, *Letters from Assyrian Scholars,* vol. 1, 88-89; vol. 2, 102-3]). At times, the majestic tree stands for a mighty nation and, indirectly, for its center of power. For instance, Assyria is compared with such a tree in Ezek 31:2-9. Significantly, Assyria is consistently characterized in the book of Hosea as an agent to which foolish Israel/Ephraim looks for assistance rather than turning to YHWH (e.g., Hos 5:13; 7:11-13; 12:1-3). Thus, as it were, Assyria represents a competitor for the structural slot of YHWH, here the majestic tree (cf. Isa 30:2-3 and note the parallel structure, "Pharaoh-Egypt," and the close connection it reflects and shapes between "king" and "kingdom"). Moreover the image of a majestic tree providing shade tends to convey a sense of rootedness, stability, "proper order," and peacefulness (ct. with royal images of the king as a lion or the like; cf. Tånberg, "I Am like an Evergreen Fir"; Oestreich, *Metaphors,* esp. 213-14 and bibliography mentioned in these works).

Thus the body of the book of Hosea concludes with an image that reflects and communicates an image of future, ideal Israel/Ephraim living in prosperity and peace under the protection and kingship of YHWH (compare and contrast with Lam 4:20). Similar ideological horizons are reflected and communicated towards or at the conclusion of other prophetic books (see

Obad 21; Zeph 3:15; Zech 14:9; and cf., among others, Ps 146:10). The image of YHWH as king/tree does not necessarily preclude that of a messianic Davidic king, because the Davidic king may always be construed as a smaller tree, as a vassal of the Great King, YHWH. But the absence of a reference to the Davide at this stage in the book is noteworthy (ct. Amos 9:11; Hos 3:5 at the conclusion of a SET of READING in the book of Hosea; on the latter see commentary on Hos 3:1-5).

Moreover, this absence of reference is balanced, as it were, by the presence of another. The second character in the quasi-paradisiacal word of Hos 14:5-9, Israel/Ephraim, is also metaphorically compared to a tree (vv. 6-7), and kingly attributes are explicitly associated with it. See in particular הודו "its [Israel's] majesty" and cf. Jer 22:18; Ps 45:4. Significantly, הוד is an attribute that can be associated also with the deity (e.g., Hab 3:3; Job 37:22). The conclusion of the book shapes an ideological image not only of a future world in which YHWH will be the King, but also of one in which Israel will be kingly and bear some divine attributes. To be sure, constructions of Israel as fulfilling kingly roles are not unheard of in the HB. The most obvious of them is the idea of a covenant between YHWH and Israel, rather than between YHWH and king. The image of an Israel that receives from YHWH some godly attributes appears already in Hos 2:21. There Israel is betrothed with righteousness, justice, kindness, and mercy. All of which are divine attributes. But all of these images inform vv. 5-9 and are brought together there.

It is worth noting that the Targum seems to recognize the message conveyed by the lack of a reference to a messianic figure in either v. 8 (cf. Lam 4:20) or v. 9. It rephrases v. 8 to state, "they shall be gathered from among their exiles and they shall dwell in the shade of the anointed One," and v. 9 to state, "I, by my Memra, will hear the prayer of Israel and have compassion on them. I, by my Memra, will make them like a beautiful cypress tree" (ET, from Cathcart and Gordon, *Targum of the Minor Prophets*, 61-62). Thus, the Targum recasts these verses so as to explicitly place the messianic king in the text (v. 8), while removing the image of YHWH as the tree in v. 9, and at the same time heightening the trend towards the elevation of Israel in the text by making it the tree of v. 9.

It is worth stressing that although Hos 2:16-25 and 14:5-9 communicate their messages to the intended and primary readerships of the book through very different images, they seem to reflect at a deeper level a similar horizon of ideological discourse. One may notice, for instance, that they both construe an image of a future world in which (a) YHWH is the agent for change — it is YHWH who transforms Israel; (b) YHWH is the provider and Israel the one being provided for; (c) peace, tranquility, and stability are present; (d) Israel gains godly qualities and is transformed forever; (e) there is an element of (metaphorical) marital love — explicit and salient in 2:16-25, connoted in Hos 14:5-9 (cf. the role of the shade of the majestic tree in the "love lyrics of Nabû and Tašmetu"; see Livingstone, *Court Poetry*, § 14, lines 9-11, p. 35); and (f) the future ideal world portrayed includes an image of fecundity restored. Point (f) is particularly important towards the conclusion of the book because it explicitly informs and strongly qualifies other statements about future infertility in the book (e.g., Hos 9:16; 10:1). Significantly, it is not YHWH as bearer of fruit (i.e., a tree bearing fruit) that is seen as a provider, but rather a combination, or combinations, of the images of YHWH as the majestic king who provides shade to Israel, YHWH as the healer (king?) who heals Israel from its inborn unfaithfulness against YHWH, and YHWH as dew that provides fertility for Israel/Ephraim in the future, ideal world. In other words, the text reflects and shapes a construction of YHWH not as a carrier of "fruit" but as a necessary enabler, through whom and because of whom "fruit" is found or obtained.

As for the setting of the speeches in Hos 14:2-9 within the world of the book, as in other instances in Hosea, there is no reference to particular dates, events, social occasions, or the like against which the words of Hos 14:2-9 were proclaimed to the addressees that populate that world. Further, there is no clear reference to the addressees of the text, beyond general references to Ephraim and Israel. The text is quite explicitly not anchored in a particular time or setting within the world of the book, except for the general one set in Hos 1:1. Attempts to do so run contrary to the way in which the book asks its intended readers to approach it. Moreover, given that Hos 14:2-9 is so strongly anchored in the language, images, and themes of the other READINGS in the book, attempts to read these verses or a portion thereof as standing on its own and separate from the other READINGS in the book also run contrary to the way in which the book asks intended readers to approach it.

Of course, if one is interested mainly or even only in reconstructing the (oral) message/s of the historical prophet Hosea to some historical group that presumably existed in the eighth century BCE in the northern kingdom, *instead of* those that the book of Hosea conveyed to its primary rereadership, then one would have to follow a different path. First of all, one would have to attribute some sayings to the prophet (and thus "construct" the historical prophet), remove them from their *Sitz im Buch* and from the networks of meaning that exist on the book of Hosea as a literary work, imagine a possible audience for the historical prophet, and finally look for a possible historical and even social setting within the last decade/s of the northern kingdom that would make sense — in the opinion of the scholar — of the text that she or he abstracted from the book and assigned to the prophet. (This type of approach involves by necessity a number of highly hypothetical assumptions, on which further assumptions are based.) At times this approach leads to the development of a series of biographical vignettes of the reconstructed prophet. For instance, according to Wolff (*Hosea*, 234), "Hosea spoke these words [14:2-9] before the inner circle of the opposition group," and he dates the event to "probably when the end of the Northern Kingdom was in view," even though he concedes that there is "no clear criteria on which to base its date." According to Bright (*Covenant and Promise*, 92-93), "If Hosea ever entertained such a hope [that Israel would repent and so avert judgment] (and he may well have done so), it appears that he abandoned it as the years went by. Hosea saw, or came to see, his people incapable of repentance. . . . So it was that in the farther future, beyond the judgment, Hosea looked for the restoration of Israel in the mercy of God." Similarly, Wolff (*Hosea*, xxix) also claims that at first (the historical) Hosea thought that "after Israel has broken the covenant (1:9), a new beginning of the saving history was not to be expected from a reformation among the people in response to the prophet's warnings. Rather it was to come only as a result of the preconditions which God himself created: in his judgment he would block Israel's path to her idols. . . ." In other words, YHWH's judgment will bring Israel back to the wilderness and to the "saving history." According to Wolff, later in his career, after 733 BCE, Hosea changed his mind for "it . . . became clear that Yahweh's judgment could not bring Israel to obedience." Therefore, Hosea began to understand that Israel will be saved only by YHWH's unconditional love (see discussion on v. 5). It is worth stressing that this approach removes a feature at the heart of the message of the text: The multiplicity of perspectives informing each other and balancing each other about the possible ideological roles assigned to Israel's repentance in the process of redemption that is reflected in and communicated by the book. In its place comes a narrative about a historical prophet who either held one or the other position, but never both at the same time. Significantly, this (hypothetical) narrative serves as an interpretative key for the text, for certain ideas become "proper" at some time in Hosea's life, and others at another time. For instance, if Hos 14:2-9 is assigned to the later period of the prophet, then the text cannot express the theological position that Israel's repentance following the divine punishment plays some substantial role in redemption (cf. Wolff, *Hosea,* 237-38). Conversely, if a text becomes associated with Hosea's early days as a prophet (around 750 BCE) such as Hos 2:4-17, according to Wolff, then the text may convey that "Yahweh's judgment effects Israel's return, rekindling her 'first love' for him" (see Wolff, *Hosea,* 45), despite the fact that 2:15-16 (and 2:16-25 in general) fits much better a claim for an unequivocal and categorical theology that Israel's repentance following disaster plays no role in redemption than does the text in Hos 14:2-9, which although it carries that message, also balances it (see above).

For a critique of explanations of ideological tensions in texts assigned to the historical prophet through the construction of a temporal development in the prophet's ideology based on the presence of unequivocal positions at different times in his life, see Unterman, "Repentance." Unterman, however, also shapes an image of the historical prophet. According to him, these tensions reflect his "inner turmoil" (549). On these matters see also Davies, *Hosea,* 299-301.

At times, attempts to reconstruct the message/s of the historical prophet Hosea to some historical group that presumably existed in the eighth century BCE in the northern kingdom, *instead of* those that the book of Hosea conveyed to its primary readership, lead to a very substantial recasting of the meaning of expressions and propositions. For instance, if one assumes that the historical prophet uttered the text of v. 4 against the background of Israel's possible alliance with Egypt against Assyria during the reign of King Hoshea — something the book does not claim — and if one assumes that the prophet was a preacher (or even a "political activist") very much involved in the foreign affairs of the kingdom, then על סוס לא נרכב "we [Israel] will not ride upon horses" may be understood as carrying a very narrow but timely meaning, namely, opposition to King Hoshea's alliance with Egypt at that time (Egypt is often characterized

310

as a provider of horses; cf. Isa 31:1; and ironically 2 Kgs 18:23-24). See Harper, *Amos and Hosea*, 413; Stuart, *Hosea-Jonah*, 214 (and cf. Ibn Ezra [the Accepted Commentary], Rashi). Conversely, one may assume that when the historical prophet said "we [Israel] will not ride upon horses," he gave voice to his opinion that Israel should repudiate its existing treaty with Assyria and refuse to provide troops to the suzerain king, as vassal kingdoms were obliged to do in times of war. This could be envisaged as happening at the time of the revolt of king Rezin of Aram, of whom king Pekah was a subordinate ally, or at the time of King Hoshea's rebellion. See Sweeney, *The Twelve*, 138 (and cf. Radak).

There is no general agreement among scholars who follow these approaches about which verses to assign to the historical Hosea (see STRUCTURE above), or about the criteria to decide that matter, or about the supposed setting and date of the proclamation of these reconstructed, extremely brief speeches which last for a minute at the very most. Further, if the claim advanced is that the reported speech represents the essence of a larger speech, then one either reconstructs on its basis a larger speech, which brings another level of hypothesis, or one deals with a literary, written phenomenon removed from the setting of the oral speech and therefore raises hypotheses about tradents, the setting of written composition of a text that creates an image of the prophet and the like; all of which also require additional hypotheses, most of which are unverifiable.

In any event, the previously mentioned understanding of verses as independent from other texts in the book, which supposedly record other proclamations involving a variety of times, settings, and audiences and carry an unequivocal message that directly addresses very particular political and foreign affairs matters confronting the monarchic elite of the northern kingdom at very precise moments in its history, is most likely not one of the main ways in which the readership of the book of Hosea in postmonarchic times read the book. It is not by accident that the book consistently avoids any particularities about the dates, places, circumstances, and even the identity of the group addressed by the speaker, within the world of the book. Instead the book of Hosea constantly shows texts that are deeply interwoven with other texts in the book, and that through this interweaving create the tapestry that reflects, reinforces, and communicates the horizon of thought of the community/ies within which and for which the book of Hosea, as a whole, was composed, that is, the intellectual Setting of the book.

Intention

The general intention of Hosea 14:2-9, as with other READINGS in the text, is to communicate and reinforce the positions and the general horizon of thought of the authorship and readership as represented in these texts (see Setting). It serves to socialize the literati through their shared reading of the material, and the larger society through the literati's reading of this material to others. This READING in particular sets in proportion claims advanced in many of the previous READINGS in the book and especially those that involve Israel's punishment.

It reassures the readership that trans-temporal Israel will never be destroyed, no matter how sinful particular manifestations of Israel, such as monarchic Ephraim, may be. Moreover, it unequivocally communicates that a glorious future is in store for Israel/Ephraim.

As mentioned above the text explains the past, and above all both exhorts the intended and primary rereadership to be obedient to YHWH and YHWH's instructions — as understood by the literati — and provides them with hope.

Bibliography

W. S. Boshoff, "Yahweh as God of Nature. Elements of the Concept of God in the Book of Hosea," *JNSL* 18 (1992) 13-24; J. Bright, *Covenant and Promise* (Philadelphia: Westminster, 1976); R. B. Coote, "Hos 14:8: 'They Who Are Filled with Grain Shall Live,'" *JBL* 93 (1974) 161-73; J. Day, "A Case of Inner Biblical Scriptural Interpretation. The Dependence of Isaiah xxvi. 13-xxvii. 11 on Hosea xiii. 4 — xiv 10 (Eng. 9) and Its Relevance to Some Theories of the Redaction of the 'Isaiah Apocalypse,'" *JTS* 31 (1980) 309-19; idem, "Ashera in the Hebrew Bible and Northwest Semitic Literature," *JBL* 105 (1986) 385-408; C. J. Dempsey, *The Prophets. A Liberation-Critical Reading* (Minneapolis: Fortress, 2000) 158-59; G. R. Driver, "Linguistic and Textual Problems: Minor Prophets. I," *JTS* 39 (1938) 155-66; A. Feulliet, "'S'asseoir à l'ombre' de l'époux," *RB* 78 (1971) 391-405; M. Fishbane, *Haftarot* (JPS Bible Commentary; Philadelphia: JPS, 2002); F. Gangloff, "'Je suis son ʿAnat et son ʿAserâh' (Os 14,9)," *ETL* 74 (1998) 373-85; idem, "YHWH ou les déesses-arbres? (Osée XIV 6-8)," *VT* 49 (1999) 34-38; E. M. Good, "The Composition of Hosea," *SEÅ* 31 (1966) 21-63; R. Gordis, "The Text and Meaning of Hosea XIV 3," *VT* 5 (1955) 88-90; A. V. Hunter, *Seek the Lord* (Baltimore: St. Mary's Seminary and University, 1982); P. A. Kruger, "Yahweh's Generous Love: Eschatological Expectations in Hosea 14:2-9," *OTE* 1 (1988) 27-48; C. J. Labuschagne, "The Similes in the Book of Hosea," *OTWSA* 7-8 (1965) 64-76; M. Liverani, "KITRU, KATARU," *Mesopotamia* 17 (1982) 43-66; A. Livingstone, *Court Poetry and Literary Miscellanea* (SAA 3; Helsinki: The Neo-Assyrian Text Corpus Project and the Helsinki University Press, 1989); B. Margalit, "The Meaning and Significance of Ashera," *VT* 40 (1990) 264-97; S. Morag, "On Semantic and Lexical Features in the Language of Hosea," *Tarbiz* 53 (1984) 489-511 (in Hebrew); R. T. O'Callaghan, "Echoes of Canaanite Literature in the Psalms," *VT* 4 (1954) 164-76; B. Oded, *War, Peace and Empire. Justifications for War in Assyrian Royal Inscriptions* (Wiesbaden: Dr. L. Reichert Verlag, 1992); D. F. O'Kennedy, "Healing as/or Forgiveness? The Use of the term רפא in the book of Hosea," *OTE* 14 (2001) 458-74; S. Parpola, *Letters from Assyrian Scholars to the Kings Esarhaddon and Assurbanipal, Part I: Texts* (AOAT 5/1; Neukirchen Vluyn: Verlag Butzon & Bercker Kevelaer, 1970); idem, *Letters from Assyrian Scholars to the Kings Esarhaddon and Assurbanipal, Part II: Commentary and Appendices* (AOAT 5/2; Neukirchen Vluyn: Verlag Butzon & Bercker Kevelaer, 1983); idem, "The Assyrian Tree of Life: Tracing the Origins of Jewish Monotheism and Greek Philosophy," *JNES* 52 (1993) 161-208 (167-68); R. H. Pfeiffer, *State Letters of Assyria* (AOS 6; New Haven: American Oriental Society, 1935); B. N. Porter, *Trees, Kings, and Politics. Studies in Assyrian Iconography* (OBO 197; Fribourg/Göttingen: Academic Press/Vandenhoeck & Ruprecht, 2003); D. Seeman, "'Where Is Sarah Your Wife?' Cultural Poetics of Gender and Nationhood in the Hebrew Bible," *HTR* 91 (1998) 103-25; A. Szabó, "Textual Problems in Amos and Hosea," *VT* 25 (1975) 500-524; K. A. Tånberg, "'I Am like an Evergreen Fir; From Me Comes Your Fruit': Notes on Meaning and Symbolism in Hosea 14,9b (MT)," *SJOT* 2 (1989) 81-93; J. Unterman, "Repentance and Redemption in Hosea," *SBLSP* 21 (1982) 541-50; M.-T. Wacker, "Traces of the Goddess in the Book of Hosea," A. Brenner (ed.), *A Feminist Companion of the Latter Prophets* (Sheffield: Sheffield Academic Press, 1995) 219-41; Jan A. Wagenaar, "'I Will Testify Against Them and Challenge Them': Text and Interpretation of Hosea 14:9," *JNSL* 26 (2000) 127-34; L. Waterman, *Royal Correspondence of the Assyrian Empire* (4 vols.; Ann Arbor: University of Michigan Press, 1930-36).

Conclusion of a Prophetic Book: Hos 14:10

Structure

I. The מי "whoever" section	14:10a
II. The כי "for" section	14:10b

This unit is set apart from the preceding verse by the sharp shift in style and theme. It shows a clear beginning and a tight inner structure. The first section consists of three brief versets, each consisting of two words; the second, of three versets, each consisting of three word-units (see כי-ישרים, "for are right [the ways of YHWH]"). This brief unit shows several common word pairs. One may mention חכם "wise" and נבון "one who discerns" (cf., for instance, Deut 1:13; 4:6; 1 Kgs 3:12; Isa 5:21; 29:14; Prov 1:5; 16:21; 17:28; Qoh 9:11); ישרים "right" and צדקים "righteous" (cf. Isa 26:7; Ps 32:11; 33:1; 112:4; 119:137; 140:14; Prov 21:18; 29:27); verbal qal forms of the roots ידע and בין "know" and "discern," respectively (cf. Isa 44:18; Ps 82:5; 92:7; Prov 29:7; Job 14:21). To these one may add the association between "walking" and "ways" (e.g., 1 Kgs 3:14), the pair created by verbal forms of הלך "walk" and כשל "stumble" (see in Isa 28:13 and cf. Jer 18:15; Prov 4:12), the mental associations between "not knowing" and "stumbling" (cf. Jer 6:15; 8:12; Prov 4:19), and the emphatic repetition of בם "on them" in the second section. All these contribute to the sense of strong textual coherence within the text of Hos 14:10.

As expected in the book of Hosea in general, and Hosea 12–14 in particular, Hos 14:10 is also closely connected to other literary units or subunits within the book. This connection is created by a network of textually inscribed signposts that contribute to the continuous rereading and study of the book within the target readerships. The overall effect is a tapestry of meanings informing each other. To illustrate, the reference to חכם "wise" in Hos 14:10 is reminiscent of, and stands in meaningful contrast to, the occurrence of the same word in 13:13, and to the entire motif of the foolishness of the people that appears in chapters 4, 8, 9, 12, 13 (see Seow, "Hosea 14:10," cf. Ginsberg, "Hosea's Ephraim"). The Israel/Ephraim described in the book displayed foolishness,

but the Israel for whom the book of Hosea is intended is "wise" and understands YHWH's word as communicated to them through their reading and rereading of the book of Hosea. Furthermore, the reference to "know these
[things/matters]," in other words, that which is communicated by the book of
Hosea, plays on the ubiquitous motif of (not) knowing YHWH and YHWH's
deeds on behalf of Israel (cf. 2:10, 22; 5:4; 6:3; 8:2; 11:3; 13:4). One may note
that by knowing "these [things/matters]," that is, this instance of YHWH's
word (Hos 1:1), the intended and primary readerships of the book of Hosea are
encouraged to imagine themselves as reaching, because of their careful reading
of the book, a status a bit like, though certainly far from identical to, that enjoyed by the future, ideal Israel that will "know" YHWH (cf. 2:22).

These readers have, of course, a negative counterpart. Opposite to them
stand the פשעים "transgressors/sinners." Significantly, the word פשעים in
14:10bβ is reminiscent of Hos 7:13 and 8:1. In this case, the text communicates
to the intended and primary readerships of the book of Hosea that those referred to as פשעים in Hos 14:10bβ will fail just as those mentioned in Hos 7:13;
8:1 and because of the same reason, and probably whether they cry to YHWH
or not (see 7:14; 8:2). Their fate is sealed by their status as פשעים. Significantly, the unusual occurrence of פשעים as the opposite term to צדקים "right-
teous," instead of the expected רשעים "wicked" (e.g., Isa 5:23; Ezek 18:20;
21:8; Ps 37:39-40; Prov 10:16; 11:23; 12:5 and tens of times in the HB; note
also the language of Ps 18:22) is most likely due to the link shaped by פשעים
between 14:10 and 7:13; 8:1 (רשע does not appear in Hosea; for the overlap
between the semantic and evocative realms of פשעים and רשעים that allows
this shift, see Ps 37:38).

The reference to כשל "stumble" also points back to other units in the
book of Hosea (see 4:5; 5:5; and 14:2). The reference to דרכי ה' "the ways of
YHWH" plays, through contrast, with those to Israel/Ephraim's ways (cf. 4:9;
9:8; 10:13; 12:3) that led to failure, and divine punishment. Of course, righteous people like those of the intended readership stand in sharp contrast to monarchic Israel/Ephraim, and since unlike the latter they should and will be able
to walk in YHWH's ways, they will not fail. (For studies on the close textual
and thematic relationship between Hos 14:10 and the rest of the book see, for
instance, Seow, "Hosea 14:10"; Sheppard, "Last Words"; and Tooze, *Framing
the Book of the Twelve*, 90-97.)

The "whoever" section is structured in a way closely resembling Ps
107:43, and note also the same opening and similar word choice (see also Setting). Here, as in Judg 7:3 and Jer 9:11, the clause implies a principle of selection. Hos 14:10 communicates that not everyone is able to understand the
meaning/s conveyed in the instance of YHWH's word that the book of Hosea
constitutes. This section characterizes those able to do so as חכם "wise" and
נבון "discerning." The "for" section further identifies them with צדקים "right-
teous people" — a commonplace in wisdom literature — as opposed to the sinners and transgressors, and ascertains the sure success of the former and the
failure of the latter (cf. Ps 1:6; Prov 2:20-22; 3:33; 4:18-19; 10:28; 11:21, 23;
24:16; and passim in Proverbs).

The links mentioned above between Hos 14:10 and the rest of the book serve as a clear textually inscribed marker indicating that the intended readership of the book of Hosea is supposed to read Hos 14:10 as an integral part of the book. Its position and the summary of trends it advances point at its role as a main interpretative key for the book as whole.

Scholars who have focused on either their constructions of the historical prophet or proposed redactional processes have tended to assign Hos 14:10 to a "late," exilic or postexilic redactor strongly influenced by wisdom or dtr. motifs (e.g., Davies, *Hosea*, 309-10; Jeremias, *Hosea*, 174; Mays, *Hosea*, 190; Macintosh, *Hosea*, 582-83; Nogalski, *Literary Precursors*, 68-69; Wolff, *Hosea*, 239; Yee, *Composition*, 140-42; cf. Seow, "Hos 14:10" and ct. Stuart, *Hosea-Jonah*, 219).

Genre

Hosea 14:10 is the CONCLUSION of YHWH's word that was associated with Hosea, i.e., of the book of Hosea. Conclusions of prophetic books provide hope to their rereaders (see Setting). They also set the boundaries of the prophetic book. The actual endings of the prophetic books tend to be highly particular (see, for instance, Isa 66:24; Ezek 48:35; Mic 7:20; Jon 4:11; Mal 3:24). Hos 14:10 is another example. These particular prophetic endings serve as one of the important devices that demarcate the extent of a prophetic book. (On these issues and the larger question of the "book of the Twelve," see Ben Zvi, "Twelve Prophetic Books.")

As mentioned elsewhere (Ben Zvi, *Micah*, 184), contrary to colophons, conclusions are an integral part of the text proper (see the markers of textual coherence mentioned above). Yet like colophons they mark the end of the text. Significantly, contrary to the usual expectations associated with colophons, the conclusions of the prophetic books, including Hos 14:10, contain no information about the actual or fictive author of the book, nor about any scribal aspect of the production of the book such as the name of the scribe making the copy or the purpose of producing the copy (see Leichty, "Colophon"; Pearce, "Statements"; cf. Würthwein, *Text*, 172, 178, 180; on colophons, see, for instance, Lundbom, "Baruch," 89-95; Leichty, "Colophon"; Lambert, "Catalogue"; and idem, "Ancestors"). The preference for "conclusions" over colophons is consistent with the self-effacing character of the compositors of prophetic literature (cf. Ben Zvi, *Zephaniah*, 347-49), their self-effacing present (cf. Ben Zvi, "Urban Center," "What Is New in Yehud?"), and the communal value of the produced copy. It cannot be overstressed that whereas Hos 14:10 does not point to the compositor of the book, it certainly points to and even characterizes the (ideal) readership for which it was intended. The book communicates that although the author is not central, the target readership is, for it is the latter that keeps reading and rereading the book, educating itself through the process, so as to walk in the ways of YHWH. To focus on the identity of the "author" of the text runs contrary to the general thrust of the book, prophetic literature in general, and certainly the interpretative key provided to the readership of the book by Hos 14:10.

It is worth mentioning that Hos 14:10 serves as a kind of second conclusion, as it follows the hopeful, and also unique, conclusion of the body of the book of Hosea (Hos 14:9). Double conclusions, of one sort or another, appear elsewhere in prophetic books; see Isa 66:22 and 23-24; Joel 4:20 and 21; Mal 3:22 and 23-24).

Setting

The setting of the conclusion of the book of Hosea is the same as the setting of the book of Hosea. The conclusion also contributes to our understanding of the world of ideas that characterize that setting and its social location. First, the general thrust of the conclusion is similar to that of Psalm 1, and its close connection to Ps 107:43 has already been mentioned. Significantly, Ps 107:43 serves as the conclusion to the Psalm. Ps 107 is a postmonarchic, educational psalm that shapes a social memory of a past and uses it to understand and celebrate the character of YHWH. This task is not so different from that of the book of Hosea within its intended readership, even if these two works go about it in very different ways, belong to different genres, and follow different conventions. (On Ps 107 see Gerstenberger, *Psalms,* 246-53.) The point is, of course, not to raise matters of "who copied from whom" but to point at the existence of shared horizons of thought among the communities of readers within whom and for whom these texts were composed. Although these horizons of thought are expressed across different genres and each of the latter carries its own conventions, the ideological world of their writers and readers was similar. The same holds true for the numerous connections between Hos 14:10 and wisdom literature (see above), and also for those between Hos 14:10 and dtr. literature (e.g., the motif of "walking in YHWH's ways"). This ideological convergence is to be anticipated because the minimal number of the highly literate in ancient Yehud would not have allowed the existence of multiple *unconnected* social groups developing their own *separate* ideological discourse (cf. Ben Zvi, "Urban Centre"; idem, "Introduction: Writings, Speeches"; idem, "Deuteronomistic Redaction").

Hos 14:10 also conveys a poignant message relevant to matters of theodicy and, above all, hope. Particularly meaningful in a work that describes so much destruction and suffering is the final statement "the ways of YHWH are right." This statement encapsulates the ubiquitous trend in the book to explain and justify YHWH's terrible punishment of monarchic Israel. It serves also as a final proclamation of acceptance of the justice of YHWH's deeds, from the perspective of the readership of the book as it identifies with the speaker in the text. At the same time, it provides hope that if they can qualify as צדקים "the righteous" they will be spared a fate similar to that of sinful monarchic Israel. As such it is a call of hope, and a call for the "proper" socialization and education of the literati themselves first, and through them of all their society at large. The book of Hosea, that is, "YHWH's word" (Hos 1:1), that is, "these matters" (Hos 14:10), becomes a central and promising tool for that purpose.

Texts such as Hos 14:10, and the boundaries they create between (a) those wise and discerning enough to understand the message/s of the book and (b) those who are not, are deeply associated with the general social location of the process of composition, primary reading, rereading, and studying of the book of Hosea, namely, a small circle of literati. These circles saw themselves as the guardian, broker, and interpreter of the knowledge communicated by the divine to Israel in the form of the written texts that they composed, edited, redacted, copied, read, and read to others.

Intention

One of the intentions of the conclusion of the book of Hosea is to mark the end of the book. It serves as an explicit, interpretative key for the entire book, and it characterizes the book as a didactic book, to be read, reread, and interpreted by those who are wise, discerning, and righteous. The conclusion also provides hope to the readers of the book, both by emphasizing the just character of YHWH's ways — including YHWH's punishment of Israel — and the difference between the fate of the "righteous" and the "transgressors/sinners." Furthermore, it suggests a way in which people may bring themselves closer to the former. It also serves to create a sense of an inner group and an outer group, and of boundaries around the literati, and expresses their own understanding about themselves and their role in society. Hos 14:10 clearly encourages education and socialization through the reading and rereading of prophetic books.

Bibliography

J. L. Crenshaw, "Theodicy in the Book of the Twelve," P. L. Redditt and A. Schart (eds.), *Thematic Threads in the Book of the Twelve* (BZAW 325; Berlin: de Gruyter, 2003) 175-91; M. Fishbane, "Biblical Colophons, Textual Criticism and Legal Analogies," *CBQ* 42 (1980) 438-49; E. Gerstenberger, *Psalms, part 2, and Lamentations* (FOTL 15; Grand Rapids, MI: Eerdmans, 2001); H. L. Ginsberg, "Hosea's Ephraim, More Fool than Knave. A New Interpretation of Hosea 12:1-14," *JBL* 80 (1961) 339-47; I. S. Gottlieb, "Sof Davar: Biblical Endings," *Prooftexts* 11 (1991) 214-24; W. G. Lambert, "Ancestors, Authors and Canonicity," *JCS* 11 (1957) 1-14; idem, "A Catalogue of Texts and Authors," *JCS* 16 (1962) 59-77; E. Leichty, "The Colophon," in *Studies Presented to A. Leo Oppenheim* (Chicago: Oriental Institute, 1964) 147-54; J. R. Lundbom, "Baruch, Seraiah, and Expanded Colophons in the Book of Jeremiah," *JSOT* 36 (1986) 89-114; L. E. Pearce, "Statements of Purpose: Why the Scribes Wrote," M. E. Cohen, D. C. Snell, and D. B. Weisberg (eds.), *The Tablet and the Scroll. Near Eastern Studies in Honor of William W. Hallo* (Bethesda, MD: CDL Press, 1993) 185-90; C. L. Seow, "Hosea 14:10 and the Foolish People Motif," *CBQ* 42 (1982) 212-24; G. T. Sheppard, "The Last Words of Hosea," *RevExp* 90 (1993) 191-204; E. Würthwein, *The Text of the Old Testament* (2nd ed.; Grand Rapids, MI: Eerdmans, 1995).

Glossary

ANCIENT ISRAELITE BOOK (Altisraelitisches Buch; hereafter, book) is a self-contained written text that was produced within ancient Israel, and characterized by a clear beginning and conclusion, by a substantial level of textual coherence and textually inscribed distinctiveness vis-à-vis other books, and that, accordingly, led its intended and primary readers (and rereaders) to approach it in a manner that took into account this distinctiveness. The readership of the Hebrew Bible books consisted of those able to read them. The composition of books such as those mentioned above implies a society in which resources are available for the development and maintenance of a group or groups of bearers of high literacy among which one has to identify the writers, direct readers, and rereaders of these books. This definition does not restrict ancient Israelite books to any range of length, principle of composition or redaction, specific language (they may be written in one or two languages, see Daniel and Ezra), particular genre or mode of reading, or single type of literary coherence. Instead it focuses on textually inscribed markers and the most likely way in which the intended and primary (re)readerships approached them. (For a fuller discussion of this and related definitions in this glossary see E. Ben Zvi, "The Prophetic Book: A Key Form of Prophetic Literature," and the chapter "Introduction to the Book of Hosea: A Particular Instance of YHWH'S Word" in this volume.)

AUTHORITATIVE ANCIENT ISRAELITE BOOK (Massgebendes Altisraelitisches Buch) is a subset of ANCIENT ISRAELITE BOOK that consists of books that were deemed as authoritative in ancient Israel, such as the books of Hosea, Genesis, and Deuteronomy.

BODY OF A PROPHETIC BOOK (Hauptteil eines prophetischen Buches) is one of the three main structural components of a PROPHETIC BOOK. It includes the entire book except for the INTRODUCTION and CONCLUSION. The BODY OF A PROPHETIC BOOK consists of (DIDACTIC) PROPHETIC READINGS.

CONCLUSION OF PROPHETIC BOOK (Abschluss eines prophetischen Buches) is the literary unit at the end of the book that not only sets the boundary of the book it concludes, but also tends to convey a sense of uniqueness to the entire work — they tend to be highly particular (see, for instance, Isa 66:24; Ezek 48:35; Mic 7:20; Jon 4:11; Mal 3:24. A CONCLUSION of a PROPHETIC BOOK provides an interpretative key for the book as a whole.

INTRODUCTION TO A PROPHETIC BOOK (Einleitung zu einem prophetischen Buch) is the literary unit at the beginning of such a book that provides a frame of reference, a scheme that not only allows but also strongly informs the subsequent reading of the text. The introduction of the book of Hosea characterizes the book as such, provides a title for the book, identifies it as a separate book, associates it with a particular prophetic figure from the past, and sets the world of the book in a particular time within the construction of their own past held by the intended and primary readers and rereaders. The INTRODUCTION may comprise a SUPERSCRIPTION (as, for instance, in the books of Isaiah, Hosea, Amos, Joel, Micah, Obadiah, Zephaniah), but not necessarily so (see Ezekiel, Jonah, Haggai, Zechariah).

PROPHETIC BOOK, IN FULL: ISRAELITE PROPHETIC BOOK (Prophetisches Buch, voll: Israelitisches prophetisches Buch) is a subset within the genre of AUTHORITATIVE ISRAELITE BOOK that was already recognized in antiquity. This subset consists of books that claim an association with a prophetic personage of the past (e.g., Isaiah, Jeremiah, Hosea, Amos, Micah) and that are presented to the intended and primary readership as YHWH's word. Accordingly, such a book claims to convey legitimate and authoritative knowledge about YHWH. Each prophetic book is associated with a prophetic personage, and *no* prophetic book is associated with more than one prophetic personage. The repertoire of prophetic books reflects and creates a set of accepted prophets of the past with whom authoritative texts may be associated. Those who were competent to read prophetic books, namely, the literati, constituted the primary readership of these books. These literati were the only group in society that had *direct* access to these books and the knowledge about YHWH that they claim to convey. These bearers of high literacy served as brokers of that divine knowledge to those who were unable to read by themselves (i.e., the overwhelming majority of the population). Prophetic books were not intended to be read only once, but to be read, reread, and meditated upon. It is to be stressed that YHWH's word that came to Hosea *signifies* a written book, to be read, reread, and studied.

The basic structure of the prophetic books consists of (a) an INTRODUCTION, (b) the BODY OF THE BOOK that consists of a series of PROPHETIC READINGS, and (c) a CONCLUSION.

PROPHETIC READING OR DIDACTIC PROPHETIC READING (Prophetische Lesung oder Didaktische Prophetische Lesung) is a READING within a PROPHETIC BOOK (e.g., the book of Hosea). As such, PROPHETIC READINGS are texts written so as to be read and reread, and that claim for themselves the legitimacy and authority of a prophetic text, of YHWH's word. These READINGS are, of course, DIDACTIC READINGS. The primary readership was supposed to *learn*, among other things, about YHWH's character, YHWH's relationship with Israel, and the true meaning of Israel's past and its hopes for the future through the continuous reading, rereading, and studying of the book. Others to whom the book or portions thereof were read were also supposed to learn about these matters by listening to particular instances of YHWH's word, that is, prophetic books, as they were read (and interpreted) to them by the literati. The BODY OF THE PROPHETIC BOOK consists of (DIDACTIC) PROPHETIC READINGS. DIDACTIC PROPHETIC READINGS may for rhetorical purposes evoke images associated with other literary genres within the intended and primary readerships.

READINGS (Lesungen) are literary units within a larger text written to be read and reread (BOOK). A book, that is, a written document or product, cannot contain anything but "writings" or, better, "readings," that is, "writings meant to be read." Although the former term (i.e., "writings") brings to the forefront the work of the writer and the material aspect of the "product," the latter conveys a more pragmatic orientation that suits best the type of studies endeavored here. After all, written texts are activated in the imagination of their primary readers by the act of reading, and, in the case of those who do not know how to read, by the act of reading to them. READINGS are literary units that show textually inscribed, discursive markers (such as openings, conclusions, inner textual coherence, thematic focus, and the like) that were likely to suggest to the intended readership of the book that they were supposed, or at least invited, to read and reread these sections of the book as cohesive reading units. The actual, primary readership was probably not too different from the intended readership, and, accordingly, it stands to reason that the text was actually reread by the reading community for which it was composed in a way that resembles, at least in some form, that suggested by the mentioned discursive markers. READINGS are interwoven into the tapestry of the book in such a way that they inform each other, and that their *Sitz im Buch* is neither accidental nor unimportant. Still, these READINGS show a degree of literary unity that sets them apart from their textual environment within the book, although some passages in a book may and do belong to more than one READING. (On the importance of the latter observation see discussions under STRUCTURE and INTRODUCTION.)

SET OF PROPHETIC READINGS (Reihe prophetischer Lesungen) is a set of closely related PROPHETIC READINGS, usually around a certain topic or showing some form of structure. For instance, the body of the book of Hosea consists of three SETS OF PROPHETIC READINGS (1:2–3:5; 4:1–11:11; 12:1–14:9). Each SET begins with references to judgment in the past of the community of readers, and concludes with a note of hope for the same community. Whereas the judgment looks at and interprets the past, the hope looks at the (distant) future of the community of readers.

SUPERSCRIPTION (Überschrift) is the literary unit that stands apart and looks at the following text and above all characterizes it as a unit. Hos 1:1 and similar passages should not be considered the superscription to a PROPHETIC BOOK, but to the body of such a book. Hos 1:1 and similar SUPERSCRIPTIONS (e.g., Joel 1:1;

Amos 1:1; Mic 1:1) are an integral — and most significant — part of their respective books as a whole. In fact, they provided the rereaders of these books with authoritative, interpretative keys that, to a large extent, governed the set of potential interpretations that the texts were allowed to carry. Not only do they not stand apart from the book (a position that is implied in the distinction between superscript and script), but it is misleading to characterize them in such a way. As mentioned above, the INTRODUCTION of a PROPHETIC BOOK may consist of a SUPERSCRIPTION, but not necessarily. (On SUPERSCRIPTIONS see G. M. Tucker, "Prophetic Superscriptions and the Growth of a Canon," B. O. Long and G. W. Coats (eds.), *Canon and Authority: Essays on Old Testament Religion and Theology* [Philadelphia: Fortress, 1977] 56-70.)